ILLUSTRATORS OF CHILDREN'S BOOKS: 1957-1966

A SUPPLEMENT TO

ILLUSTRATORS OF CHILDREN'S BOOKS: 1744-1945

ILLUSTRATORS OF CHILDREN'S BOOKS: 1946-1956

ILLUSTRATORS

of CHILDREN'S BOOKS

1957-1966

COMPILED BY

Lee Kingman

Joanna Foster

Ruth Giles Lontoft

THE HORN BOOK, INC.   BOSTON : 1968

COPYRIGHT © 1968   BY THE HORN BOOK, INC.   BOSTON
Second Printing 1972
GREAT BRITAIN: B. F. STEVENS & BROWN, LTD.   GODALMING

LIBRARY OF CONGRESS CATALOG CARD NUMBER: 47-31264
INTERNATIONAL STANDARD BOOK NUMBER: 0-87675-017-X
PRINTED IN THE UNITED STATES OF AMERICA

GRATEFUL ACKNOWLEDGMENT

is made to the following publishers, authors, and artists for their kind permission to quote and reproduce copyrighted material.

AMERICAN LIBRARY ASSOCIATION, for permission to use quotation from "Creation of a Picture Book" by Edward Ardizzone, *Top of the News*, Vol. XVI, No. 2, Dec. 1959.

ASTOR-HONOR, INC. Illustration by Leo Lionni from *Inch by Inch*, published by Ivan Obolensky, Inc. © 1960 by Leo Lionni. Used by permission of ASTOR-HONOR, INC.

ATHENEUM PUBLISHERS. Illustration by Joseph Low from *Adam's Book of odd Creatures*. Copyright © 1962 by Joseph Low. Used by permission of ATHENEUM PUBLISHERS. • Illustration from *The Happy Owls* by Celestino Piatti. Copyright © 1963 by Artemis Verlag, Zurich, Switzerland. First U.S.A. edition by ATHENEUM. First published in Great Britain, 1965, by ERNEST BENN, LTD. Used by permission of ATHENEUM, ARTEMIS VERLAG, and ERNEST BENN, LTD.

ATLANTIC-LITTLE, BROWN AND COMPANY. Illustration by Ben Shahn from *Ounce Dice Trice* by Alastair Reid. Copyright © 1958 by Alastair Reid and Ben Shahn. By permission of ATLANTIC-LITTLE, BROWN AND COMPANY.

JONATHAN CAPE LTD. Illustration by John Burningham from *Chitty-Chitty-Bang-Bang* by Ian Fleming. © Copyright 1964, by Glidrose Productions Ltd. Illustrations © Copyright 1964, by JONATHAN CAPE LTD. First American edition 1964 by RANDOM HOUSE, INC. Reproduced by permission of JONATHAN CAPE LTD. and RANDOM HOUSE, INC.

CONSTABLE YOUNG BOOKS LIMITED. Illustration by Edward Ardizzone from *Paul The Hero of the Fire*. Copyright © 1962 by Edward Ardizzone. Used by permission of CONSTABLE YOUNG BOOKS LIMITED, London, and HENRY Z. WALCK, INC., New York. • Illustrations by Antony Maitland from *Mrs. Cockle's Cat* by Philippa Pearce. Text copyright © 1961 by Philippa Pearce. Illustrations copyright © 1961 by Antony Maitland. First American edition 1962. Reproduced by permission of CONSTABLE YOUNG BOOKS LIMITED, London, and J. B. LIPPINCOTT COMPANY. • Illustration by William Stobbs from *Jack and the Beanstalk*. © 1965 by William Stobbs. First American edition 1966. Used by permission of CONSTABLE YOUNG BOOKS LIMITED, London, and DELACORTE PRESS, New York. • Illustration by Edward Standon from *The Singing Rhinoceros* by Anna Standon. Copyright © 1963 by Edward C. and Anna Standon. First American edition 1963. Used by permission of CONSTABLE YOUNG BOOKS LIMITED, London, and COWARD-MCCANN, INC., New York. • Illustration by Jenny Williams from *The Silver Wood* by Douglas Kirby. Text © 1966 by Douglas J. Kirby, illustrations © 1966 by Jenny Williams. First American edition 1967. Reproduced by permission of CONSTABLE YOUNG BOOKS LIMITED, London, and FOUR WINDS PRESS, New York.

THOMAS Y. CROWELL COMPANY. Illustration by Barbara Cooney from *A White Heron* by Sarah Orne Jewett. Illustrations copyright © 1963 by Barbara Cooney. First English printing 1964. Used by permission of THOMAS Y. CROWELL COMPANY, New York, and CONSTABLE YOUNG BOOKS LIMITED, London.

DREYERS FORLAG. Illustration by Erik Werenskiold from *Norwegian Folk Tales*. Reproduced by permission of Dreyers Forlag, Oslo.

DOUBLEDAY & COMPANY, INC. Illustration by Ellen Raskin from *Songs of Innocence* by William Blake. Copyright © 1966 by Ellen Raskin. Reprinted by permission of the publisher, DOUBLEDAY & COMPANY, INC.

Growing Point, Northampton, England, for permission to quote from a review by Margery Fisher in *Growing Point*, July, 1964.

HARCOURT, BRACE & WORLD, INC. Illustration by Erik Blegvad from *Mr. Jensen & Cat* by Lenore Blegvad. © 1965 by Erik Blegvad. Reproduced by permission of HARCOURT, BRACE & WORLD, INC. • Illustration by Roger Duvoisin from *Nubber Bear* by William Lipkind. © 1966 by Roger Duvoisin. Reproduced by permission of HARCOURT, BRACE & WORLD, INC. • Illustration from *The Snow and the Sun* by Antonio Frasconi. © 1961 by Antonio Frasconi. Reproduced by permission of HARCOURT, BRACE & WORLD, INC. • Illustration by Imero Gobbato from *The White Stone* by Gunnel Linde, copyright, © 1966 by HARCOURT, BRACE & WORLD, INC., and reproduced with their permission. • Illustration by Felix Hoffmann, © 1959, by H. R. Sauerländer & Company, Aarau. Reproduced from *The Sleeping Beauty* by the Grimm Brothers, by permission of HARCOURT, BRACE & WORLD, INC., and OXFORD UNIVERSITY PRESS, London. • Illustration by Nicolas reproduced from *The Magic Feather Duster* by Will and Nicolas, © 1958, by William Lipkind and Nicolas Mordvinoff, by permission of HARCOURT, BRACE & WORLD, INC. • Illustration by Paul Rand reproduced from *Sparkle and Spin*, © 1957, by Ann and Paul Rand, by permission of HARCOURT, BRACE & WORLD, INC., and WM. COLLINS SONS & CO., LTD., London.

HARPER & ROW, PUBLISHERS. Illustration from *Why So Much Noise?* by Janina Domanska. Copyright © 1965 by Janina Domanska. Reproduced by permission of HARPER & ROW, PUBLISHERS. • Illustration from *Jennie's Hat* by Ezra Jack Keats. Copyright © 1966 by Ezra Jack Keats. Reproduced by

permission of HARPER & ROW, PUBLISHERS.

RUPERT HART-DAVIS, LTD. Illustration by Monique-Alika Watteau from *Le Hibou et la Poussiquette*. French text by Francis Steegmuller. Illustrations copyright © RUPERT HART-DAVIS, LTD., 1961. Reproduced by permission of RUPERT HART-DAVIS, LTD., London.

HOLT, RINEHART AND WINSTON, INC. Illustration from *Sam, Bangs & Moonshine* written and illustrated by Evaline Ness. Copyright © 1966 by Evaline Ness. Reproduced by permission of HOLT, RINEHART AND WINSTON, INC. • Illustration by Maurice Sendak from *The Bee-Man of Orn* by Frank R. Stockton. Copyright © 1964 by Maurice Sendak. Reproduced by permission of HOLT, RINEHART AND WINSTON, INC. • Illustration by Margot Zemach from *The Speckled Hen* adapted by Harve Zemach. Copyright © 1966 by Margot Zemach. Reproduced by permission of HOLT, RINEHART AND WINSTON, INC.

HOUGHTON MIFFLIN COMPANY. Illustration from *Two Little Birds and Three* by Juliet Kepes. Copyright © 1960 by Juliet Kepes. Reproduced by permission of HOUGHTON MIFFLIN COMPANY. • Illustration by Blair Lent from *The Wave* by Margaret Hodges. Copyright © 1964 by Margaret Hodges. Copyright © 1964 by Blair Lent. Reproduced by permission of HOUGHTON MIFFLIN COMPANY and CURTIS BROWN LTD., London. • Illustration by Walter Lorraine from *The Dog Who Thought He Was A Boy* by Cora Annett. Copyright © 1965 by Cora Annett Scott. Copyright © 1965 by Walter H. Lorraine. Reproduced by permission of HOUGHTON MIFFLIN COMPANY. • Illustration from *Lyle, Lyle Crocodile* by Bernard Waber. Copyright © 1965 by Bernard Waber. Reproduced by permission of HOUGHTON MIFFLIN COMPANY. • Illustration by Lynd Ward from *My Friend Mac* by May McNeer and Lynd Ward. Copyright © 1960 by May McNeer and Lynd Ward. Reproduced by permission of HOUGHTON MIFFLIN COMPANY.

ALFRED A. KNOPF, INC. Illustration by Nancy Burkert

from *A Child's Calendar* by John Updike. Copyright © 1965 by John Updike and Nancy Burkert. Reproduced by permission of ALFRED A. KNOPF, INC. • Illustration from *The Witches of Venice* by Beni Montresor. Copyright © 1963, by Beni Montresor. Reproduced by permission of ALFRED A. KNOPF, INC., and ASHLEY-FAMOUS AGENCY, INC.

LITTLE, BROWN AND COMPANY. Illustration by Ivan Chermayeff for *The New Nutcracker Suite and Other Innocent Verses* by Ogden Nash. Text Copyright © 1961, 1962 by Ogden Nash. Illustration Copyright © 1962 by Ivan Chermayeff. By permission of LITTLE, BROWN AND COMPANY and CURTIS BROWN, LTD., New York. • Illustration by Barbara Cooney from *Le Hibou et la Poussiquette* by Francis Steegmuller. Illustrations Copyright © 1961 by Barbara Cooney. French text © by Francis Steegmuller 1959, 1961. By permission of LITTLE, BROWN AND COMPANY. • Illustration by Nonny Hogrogian from *Once There Was and Was Not* by Virginia Tashjian. Text Copyright © 1966 by Virginia A. Tashjian. Illustration Copyright © 1966 by Nonny Hogrogian. By permission of LITTLE, BROWN AND COMPANY.

THE NEW YORK TIMES COMPANY. For some of the material by Rumer Godden which originally appeared in *The New York Times Book Review*, May 8, 1966, in an article "From Beatrix With Love," © 1966 by THE NEW YORK TIMES COMPANY. Reprinted by permission.

OXFORD UNIVERSITY PRESS, INC. Illustration by Victor Ambrus from *The Three Poor Tailors*. © Victor G. Ambrus 1965. First published by OXFORD UNIVERSITY PRESS 1965. First American Edition, 1966, HARCOURT, BRACE & WORLD, INC. Reproduced by permission of OXFORD UNIVERSITY PRESS, London, and HARCOURT, BRACE & WORLD, INC. • Illustration by Clarke Hutton from *A Picture History of Britain*. Copyright © Oxford University Press 1959. © Clarke Hutton 1946, 1958. First published in America in 1946. Reissued in this revised edition 1959 by FRANKLIN WATTS, INC. Used by permission of OXFORD UNIVERSITY PRESS, London, and FRANKLIN WATTS, INC., New York. • Illustration by Brian Wildsmith from *Brian Wildsmith's ABC*. Copyright © 1962 by Brian Wildsmith. First American publication by FRANKLIN WATTS, INC., 1963. Reproduced by permission of OXFORD UNIVERSITY PRESS, London, and FRANKLIN WATTS, INC., New York.

PANTHEON BOOKS, INC. Illustration by Reiner Zimnik from *The Snow Party* by Beatrice Schenk de Regniers. Text © 1959 by Beatrice Schenk de Regniers. Illustrations © 1959 by Reiner Zimnik. Used by permission of RANDOM HOUSE, INC.

PRENTICE-HALL, INC. Illustration by Ed Emberley from *One Wide River to Cross* adapted by Barbara Emberley. © 1966 by Edward R. Emberley and Barbara Emberley. Reproduced by permission of PRENTICE-HALL, INC.

Publishers' Weekly, for permission to quote from an article by Nonny Hogrogian in February 21, 1966 issue of *Publishers' Weekly*.

CHARLES SCRIBNER'S SONS. Illustration by Adrienne Adams from *The Shoemaker and the Elves*. Copyright 1960 Adrienne Adams. Reproduced by special permission of CHARLES SCRIBNER'S SONS. • Illustration from *Backbone of the King* by Marcia Brown. Copyright © 1966 Marcia Brown. Reproduced with the permission of CHARLES SCRIBNER'S SONS. • Illustration by Marcia Brown from *The Wild Swans*. Copyright © 1963 Marcia Brown. Reproduced by special permission of CHARLES SCRIBNER'S SONS.

THE VIKING PRESS, INC. Illustration from *Burt Dow, Deep-Water-Man* by Robert McCloskey. Copyright © 1963 by Robert McCloskey. Reprinted by permission of THE VIKING PRESS, INC. • Illustration by Tomi Ungerer from *Oh, What Nonsense!* edited by William Cole. Illustrations copyright © 1966 by Tomi Ungerer. All rights reserved. Reproduced by permission of THE VIKING PRESS, INC.

to BERTHA MAHONY MILLER

"For my part, I believe it will be the artists, not the scientists, who will show us the way to build a better world for all children."

— *Illustrators of Children's Books: 1946-1956*

CONTENTS

INTRODUCTION .... Lee Kingman   xiii

Part I.   A Decade of Illustration in Children's Books

    1. ONE WONDERS ... . Marcia Brown   2

    2. COLOR SEPARATION .... Adrienne Adams   28

    3. THE ARTIST AND HIS EDITOR ...... Grace Allen Hogarth   36

    4. BEATRIX POTTER: CENTENARY OF
        AN ARTIST-WRITER .... Rumer Godden   54

Part II.   Biographies

BIOGRAPHIES OF ILLUSTRATORS ACTIVE: 1957-1966.........
.... Compiled by Joanna Foster   66

    Brief Biographies   70

Part III.   Bibliographies

A BIBLIOGRAPHY OF THE ILLUSTRATORS AND THEIR
WORKS .... Compiled by Ruth Giles Lontoft   200

    A Bibliography of the Illustrators Active: 1957-1966   206

    A Bibliography of the Authors   249

Part IV.   Appendix

The Kate Greenaway Medal in the United Kingdom   290

Lists of Artists Represented by Illustrations   291

Index   292

INTRODUCTION

This volume arises from what is often called, in the promotional tones of publishing today, The Wonderful World of Children's Books, and we should happily accept the recognition and responsibility implicit in this phrasing.

Surely it is pleasant to think of our field as a wonderful world of creative achievement. But if we admit to being wonderful, we must not create and publish in joyful isolation, working only for our own mutual admiration; for then books lose touch and become too precious. Children's books need a vitality and strength to survive the generations. If we admit to being wonderful, then we must make an extra effort, so that those outside this world better understand the preoccupation of those within it over values and meanings. After all, a child is a child and a book is a book, and one is relieved when in today's competition of media and activities for his time and interest a child sits down with a book. But to those in this field — publishers, editors, writers, artists, librarians, and critics — it is the meaning of the book to the child which is its foundation. What an important, vital, earth-shaking, delightful thing this meaning, this individual communication, sometimes may be! Yet we should not expect every moment with a book to educate, uplift, or stimulate a child; entertainment, enjoyment, escape from reality are as important. But what is forgotten far too often is that it should be good entertainment, pure enjoyment, untainted escape. This is what demands the best of all those taking part in the creation of a book.

Because the eye must alert the mind, the illustration is the initial attraction of the finished product, even though the story may have been written first. So does the illustration compel one to pick up the book, hold it, see more? Does the illustration invite the next step, reading the story? A child is quick to say, "But I don't like the pictures," and then refuse to read the book. The illustration is, then, a compelling element. The excitement found in children's books today is to a large extent in the variety of interesting techniques, styles, and personal expressions with which illustrators can invite the reader.

Illustrators of Children's Books: 1744-1945 dealt largely with the fascinating history and creative development of illustrated books, which eventually culminated in this not too recently recognized field of children's books. The articles stressed the universality of stories, the variety and cultural divergence of their illustration, and the influence of great artists and craftsmen on the illustrator and his work. In writing the book the compilers, Bertha E. Mahony, Louise P. Latimer, and Beulah Folmsbee, intended it for use by the layman as well as librarian and artist. They felt that the purposes of the book were "to show that art in children's books is a part of all art, not an isolated special field. In every period the greatest artists have shared in it. The second purpose is to invite to further reading and study, to wider examination of picture books and illustrated books of the past and present, and to more conscious effort to understand all that is involved in fine bookmaking, for thus is pleasure in books increased; and thus is created a book public discerning in its appreciation, capable of judging pictures and format as well as text; the kind of public that encourages artists to greater heights and advances the bookmaking arts."

This first book stopped coincident with the end of World War II at a crucial point in the social, economic, and cultural life of the modern world. Change in attitudes, in concepts of art, as well as in techniques of fine art and reproduction of fine and commercial art, became a continuing phenomenon. The second volume, *Illustrators of Children's Books:*

1946-1956, compiled by Bertha Mahony Miller, Ruth Hill Viguers, and Marcia Dalphin, recognized the trends of that period — the great expansion of the children's book market, the necessity in view of such rapid change and growth to keep standards high, and the problems of creating truly distinguished art work. In an article "Distinction in Picture Books" which should be read yearly by every children's book publisher, Marcia Brown gave a most constructive analysis, and suggested a list of questions every illustrator and editor could well review as each new book is developed. Also in this book, Lynd Ward discussed the vital areas of the artist's ideas and techniques.

In this third volume, *Illustrators of Children's Books: 1957-1966*, our bibliographer, Ruth Giles Lontoft, says that in the past ten years illustrated children's books have been unsurpassed in both quantity and quality by those of any other period of similar duration. If this indeed be so, our respect and appreciation for the artists who make it possible should be greater than ever. To have some insight into the artist's background, life, philosophy, and techniques enables us to understand and enjoy his work even more. The biographies, compiled by Joanna Foster from facts and statements supplied by the artists themselves, are fascinating reading, and in the articles for this volume we have tried to place an additional emphasis on the artist himself, rather than just on his product — the book. As Charles Keeping says in his biography, "It [illustration] is not so much a job as a way of life."

We would like to emphasize that in this decade 1957-1966, there has been a great restlessness in the field of fine art — attitudes, changes, concepts, new techniques, new media have all exploded with the bang and brilliance of fireworks — and some have faded into the night as rapidly. Others have left an after-image which is constructive and has influence in diverse ways. Our artists are discovering new ways of seeing things as well as of saying things — and this is bound to affect illustration. It is hard to imagine any other relationship than now exists between word,

picture, and printed page, and the shape of books as dictated by press-sheet sizes and capabilities of binding machines. But given the present mood of inventiveness and experimentation, the next decade may well produce valid works which relate illustration and word, but not in our present conventional book form.

While the motion picture is hardly new to this last decade, new applications of its visual techniques are. Joseph Cellini, for example, claims "one of the first things which influenced me as an artist was motion pictures. I was intrigued with camera angles, close-ups, distorted perspective and, of course, the action. I felt this should contribute to illustrating for the young."

Uri Shulevitz also feels he has a visual approach, and sometimes conceives "of a book like a movie, using words only when something cannot be said in pictures. Mostly . . . I try to suggest and evoke rather than state rigidly, in order to encourage the child to participate actively, filling in with his own imagination. This approach is based on the belief that my audience is intelligent and active rather than passive." William Pène du Bois tries to avoid drawing backgrounds, "so that children can place my characters in surroundings of their own."

These are refreshing and reassuring approaches to today's physically active and restless young. If it is at all possible to characterize the books of these last ten years, it might be in the direction of this vitality and freshness of imagination, and the sense of active awareness and participation by the young reader.

The biggest obstacles to reproduction, cost and the limitations of printing techniques, have not yet been overcome. But many new media free the artist and allow the illustrator greater room for expression. Much of the lay public, the interested parent in particular and the well-educated librarian, are more sophisticated in their knowledge of children's books, expect good taste and excellent illustration, and consequently have more appreciation for how an artist works. They are conscious, whether they agree or not with Marshall McLuhan that the medium is the "message" that they live in a visual age. Almost every time the eye moves to record an image — a magazine ad, a TV commercial, a painting, a frame of a movie, a page of a book, — an unconscious judgment is made — does it appeal? does it repel? is it easily understood? does one like it?

Media can be hypnotic and techniques can be too easily facile and meaningless. More than ever the temptations to the artist and publisher are tremendous. More than ever the critical evaluation of a book's success or failure — be it in technique, interpretation, or spirit — is a guide to understanding and maintaining the best in children's books.

If we were to limit McLuhan's statement that the medium is the message to mean that techniques in which books are illustrated and reproduced are the reason for their being, we should only be concerned with how effective paint is as texture, or color is as psychological effect, or drawing is as accurate anatomical rendering. But happily in children's books, the medium is not the message. The artist's creative expression in relation to the child's creative experience is the message — and may it ever be so. In the words of one artist, Madeline Gekiere, "The task of the illustrator just as much as that of the so-called 'fine-artist' is the creation of a new visual world and if possible not a confining visual world, but the kind that gives room to expand in the personal terms of the onlooker."

It might be pointed out that in this last decade, there is much more interchange between 'fine-artist' and 'illustrator'. Earlier, especially in respect to preparation of illustration for commercial reproduction, there was a very sharp line drawn between those in 'fine arts' and those in 'graphics' in many of our best art schools. Since each department can conceivably benefit from the other, it is gratifying that today there is a more mutual respect and understanding of each other's achievements, and that many artists successfully work in both areas. One who pointed out this problem was Janice Holland, who illustrated

more than forty-five children's books before her death in 1962. She wrote, "I always hoped I would illustrate children's books, but I attended a fine arts school where all forms of commercial art were discouraged. For a while I accepted this view and devoted myself to water color paintings of landscapes and figures. . . . Then I went to Pratt Institute with the idea of entering the illustration field. I had come, in the meantime, to feel that the vital arts of this period are in the commercial field. The truth is that most of the great art of the past was in its time commercial, or commissioned work, whether portrait or triptych. I saw that the limitation on the excellence of an illustration was not one imposed by the fact that it was a commissioned work, or even by the exigencies of the reproduction, but the only limitation was the vision of the artist himself."

As our articles in this third volume focus on the artist and his problems in the creation of book illustration, discussion of techniques, some unchanged since quill pens first drew ink lines, some new as acrylic paints and fluorescent paper, becomes important. But what ideas and ideals and motives are behind them? What makes the art in a book succeed in saying something? Or indeed, what does make illustration art?

Much can be gained from artists who have learned and grown in strength with each book. Marcia Brown, whose illustrations have brought her two Caldecott awards and whose experience with a variety of media and texts has given her insight into bookmaking, asks some provocative questions about the last decade of children's book publishing. With the criteria of her article in our second volume firmly in mind, she now analyzes books which succeed or fail, and why. For the most part she has chosen to discuss artists who are willing to experiment, in whose work there is the excitement and fervor which become the continuing creative force the children's book field must have.

This impetus is important because it has become apparent in this as in other creative fields, that artistic and financial success with a particular technique or style can inhibit an artist just as thoroughly as type-casting can strangle an actor. In the long run the artist who gives the best of himself is the one who can innovate new styles and fresh techniques for the varied books he illustrates. Ezra Jack Keats says, "Life is very fickle, and some artists who have been taught to develop styles of their own become stratified and outmoded. I look forward to something new every day." Barbara Cooney, who perfected her techniques in scratchboard through several books until she won the Caldecott Medal for *Chanticleer and the Fox*, writes, "I had always thought: once you succeed, change. So after that I tried pen and ink, pen and ink with wash, casein, collage, watercolor, acrylics — trying to fit the medium and techniques to the spirit of the book." Arnold Lobel, who speaks of children's books as "possibly the only branch of commercial art where one can still have taste and individuality and be valued for it," says, "A good illustrator . . . should have a repertory of styles at his command — like an actor switching from role to role."

In the Biographies, you will find artists discussing fascinating techniques — from sugar-lift Aquatint, through grisaille and reverse glass-painting — to mention only the more exotic — to Zylography. But there is still appreciation for the basic elements of line and texture. Lois Lenski prefers pen-and-ink, claiming, "Simple ink drawings can mean more to a child than a confusion of color," and Marcia Brown feels that "a cut medium, like woodcut, is most beautiful to me in maintaining the graphic unity between illustrations and type." It is reassuring, too, to find old-fashioned time-consuming hard work still recognized as a necessary part of the successful artist's life. For example, Margot Zemach, whose lively illustrations look as if they were spontaneously done, writes, "My art school training was of the sort to build respect for draftsmanship, economy of expression, and the tradition of fine drawing. . . . Frequently I draw the same page 30 or 40 times before getting what seems absolutely right as to movement and expression, freedom and coherence."

When the artist has studied enough to handle his work successfully, then comes his opportunity to create — a book. Here editors, and in larger companies, art directors, have an important role. At best the editor is a catalyst, his rapport with the artist helping to develop the fullest expression in each book. In her article for this volume, Grace Allen Hogarth, children's book editor in the United States and in England for over thirty years, describes this extremely important relationship between artist and editor, particularly in finding new ways to overcome technical problems in preparing art work and printing it.

Between the original art and the finished book are the mechanical processes of plate-making and printing. To some artists, the preparations for the mechanical aspects are necessary obstacles to be overcome in as unobtrusive a way as possible. To others the mechanical processes are a challenge to find the best way to use them well, rather than subdue them.

Making color separations is usually necessary where full color work, separated by a camera, is too expensive. The making of separations is a controversial subject which brings out strong feelings as expressed in the Biographies in this book. See the comments of the d'Aulaires, Leonard Weisgard, and in contrast, those of Roger Duvoisin and Eric von Schmidt.

Since it is the novice illustrator who usually has to cope with separations today, we have included an article by Adrienne Adams on one way of doing them. Miss Adams also has prepared for this book a new illustration for a color-insert so that the comparable steps by artist and printer can be shown in detail.

In her introduction to *Illustrators of Children's Books: 1946-1956*, Bertha Mahony Miller wrote, "There will be more about Beatrix Potter's life and work in the years to come." Fittingly, 1966 saw celebration of the centennial of Beatrix Potter's birth. The essence of Beatrix Potter's books was her integrity: her animals truthfully drawn; her stories honestly derived from human and animal nature; her readers respected; her books created for love of doing them. The lonely childhood and modest artistic training of Beatrix Potter are in such great contrast to the enriched and world-surrounded (on television) lives of most children today, and the abundance of art classes, good and bad, open to all ages, that it is essential to realize what one woman accomplished almost by herself; and how valuable and too often neglected is that clear vision of single-minded purpose — integrity. The ideal of many artists today would doubtless be the same: the wish for unpressured time to devote to study and drawing in such detail as Miss Potter did; the acceptance of a simple honest story, such as hers, in a trade which too often looks for a gimmick as an attention-getter or a sales angle; and the financial freedom to create books for the love of doing them. To recall the ideal of Beatrix Potter, Rumer Godden has contributed an article expanded especially for this volume.

In this edition we did not feel the need for an article on European children's books, since so many of them are appearing in the United States. Books which win the Kate Greenaway Award in England (see Appendix for list) invariably appear also under the imprint of American publishers. For the first time the Hans Christian Andersen award, given formerly only to authors, was also given to an artist, Alois Carigiet, for his illustration of *Anton the Goatherd*. At the end of the next decade, it may be well worth discussing the role of international awards, particularly the newly established (1967) Bienniale of Illustrations Bratislava. But it is a healthy sign that many books other than award winners are being translated for American editions and that European artists quickly become known and are soon approached directly by American publishers.

This international exchange and recognition is encouraging, but let us hope, too, that each country continues to encourage its own artists and writers to maintain their individual and national characteristics as well. It was interesting to hear a Japanese librarian from Osaka, Miss Kyoko Matsuoka, recently say that instead of importing and translating so many American books from now on, Japanese publishers needed to encourage native artists and writers to produce a heritage of their own in children's books for Japanese boys and girls. Let us hope in ten years we will need a section on Japanese picture books.

The illustrations used in this volume have been chosen from suggestions made by our contributors, and by the general editor. Many more illustrations were considered than could possibly be used, and the final selection was based first on illustrations particularly pertinent to the content of the articles, and second, on how effectively an illustration which was originally reproduced in color would be when reproduced in black-and-white and usually also reduced in size. In many cases when there was a choice between an illustration in color and an illustration in black-and-white, the latter was chosen.

In *Illustrators of Children's Books: 1946-1956*, Bertha Mahony Miller wondered what would happen to children in this nuclear age — then just begun. In her vision and faith, she declared, "It will be the artists, not the scientists, who will show us the way to build a better world for all children."

And that is what underlies all these words about and by artists, describing their very different philosophies, motivations, and techniques: the artist's desire to give of himself, to delight the child's imagination, and to develop the most valuable gift human beings have — the ability to communicate with each other: to build that better world, in and beyond the wonderful world of children's books, and to build it with devotion, talent and integrity.

LEE KINGMAN

Part I:
A DECADE OF ILLUSTRATION
IN CHILDREN'S BOOKS

1.   MARCIA BROWN: *Backbone of the King*

ONE wonders if twenty or thirty years from now this middle of the century period of children's book illustration will not seem a spectacular flowering.

The last ten years have seen a dramatic expansion in the publishing of books for children. There have been more children than ever before; more than seventy publishers have juvenile departments publishing close to 3,000 books a year; more and more trade books supplement textbooks in schools; government aid has enabled schools to found libraries or to enlarge existing ones and to buy huge quantities of books for young children.

In order to reap some of the rewards of this market, many publishers formerly not particularly interested in children's books have hastened to form or enlarge juvenile departments. In the consolidated houses made from mergers of two or more companies, several juvenile departments may function under the direction of one managing editor. Much actual editing of manuscripts has to be relegated to associates and assistants. The entry of the communications industry into publishing mergers is bound to have a future effect on publishing in general, and on publishing books for children. The output of books shows almost everywhere the effects of this expansion, and the children and the adolescents and adults they will become will be bound to feel and show it too.

Warehouse storage costs are high, often higher than reprinting costs. Because book ordering is now and will become more and more centralized, teachers, librarians, and parents depend on selected lists, on reviews, on the selection of prize books and their runners-up to guide them in their ordering.

Awards proliferate, and while they act as a stimulus for improving quality, they also have a very great commercial importance. A few books attain a prominence that may be disproportionate to their aesthetic importance and to their value to children. Understandably eager for the publicity and long life assured a prize book, publishers sometimes produce books that appear to be designed to catch the eye of awarding committees, fortunately not always bedazzled by

such blandishments. The fact that often on such committees are some people who use books with children probably means that many choices, if not distinguished, might be books that speak to children. One will always wonder about awards — and the wonderment is probably a good thing. It would be sad if there were not conflicting opinions about outstanding books. That there are so many deserving strong support is a sign of health.

To look over the bulk of picture books and illustrated books for young children published in the past ten years is a stimulating, often exhilarating, chastening, saddening, and eventually numbing experience. Stimulating because there is a tremendous variety of vital and very skillful work being done — and be-

1.
ONE WONDERS...

by Marcia Brown

cause sure, fresh talents like Margot Zemach, Leo Lionni, Janina Domanska, Beni Montresor, Celestino Piatti, Marvin Bileck, Bernarda Bryson, Joseph Low, Tomi Ungerer, Anita Lobel, Edward Sorel, Nicolas Sidjakov, Ann Grifalconi, Nonny Hogrogian, and many others from a variety of countries and backgrounds have brought individuality and fresh points of view to the field. Many illustrators active earlier have constantly renewed themselves and grown. Chastening because among the huge numbers of books published there is slight chance for the individual book to reach children already bombarded with visual stimuli. Saddening because despite the brilliant highlights, the general picture adds up to grayness. Numbing because brighter and brighter, smarter and smarter, they come pouring off the presses. The streams that supply this torrent are hardly deep enough to quench the tremendous thirst for talent.

Attracted perhaps by the financial rewards in a thriving industry, but more probably by a realization that in illustration for children an artist can work honestly, freely, and imaginatively, many artists from other fields of art work have been drawn to children's books. Once past the adults who are barriers or bridges between the book and the child, these artists can draw their personal brand of poetry or nonsense or magic and hope that someone will see it and look at it and understand it. They are fairly sure of having an appreciative audience. But an illustrator for young children would do well to look over that barrier or bridge and consider the child beyond.

Stage design, poster-making, advertising, print-making, painting — all kinds of art work have given a special flavor and reference to the work of artists in picture books. An artist draws on his own experience, his family, his travels, his life other than that connected with books. He needs variety as much as he needs concentration. Between books, many artists return to painting, to printmaking, to entirely different pursuits. Wells don't fill without showers. When one can predict the look of a book, when one knows the subject and the name of the artist and can be reasonably accurate in one's predictions, one can wonder how such an artist looks at his own growth and his obligation to develop himself. The artists who remain freshest and bring a sense of a new experience to what they do seem to be those whose work flows back and forth between books and other activities.

The corps of illustrators for young children in this country is never static. The field is constantly in flux. Some names have dropped out; many others have been added. Some who have made a brilliant contribution, such as Nicolas Mordvinoff, have returned to their own painting or sculpture. Children will miss seeing new, engagingly childlike pictures by Françoise, more dashing cocks and cats of Hans Fischer, or powerfully simple paintings of A. Birnbaum. All these artists are irreplaceable, for they spoke in very individual styles.

Some illustrators seem to have an inexhaustible capacity to renew themselves and maintain through many books a look of freshness. Whether changing direction or style from time to time or continually deepening and intensifying one they had already followed, their work has been of a consistently high level.

Working in black and white line or tinted drawings,

2. NICOLAS: *The Magic Feather Duster*

When the sun made a golden star on the cracked window, Sam knew it was time to expect Thomas.

Thomas lived in the tall grand house on the hill. Thomas had two cows in the barn, twenty-five sheep, a bicycle with a basket, and a jungle-gym on the lawn. But most important of all, Thomas believed every word Sam said.

At the same time every day Thomas rode his bicycle down the hill to Sam's house and begged to see her baby kangaroo.

3. EVALINE NESS: *Sam, Bangs & Moonshine*

Erik Blegvad carries on a tradition we have associated with Ernest Shepard. His decorations and illustrations on a small scale are very accessible to a child and provide the comfort of the known without ever sinking into the mannered or the banal. Edward Ardizzone has demonstrated in many illustrated books and picture books his flair for storytelling, emphasizing now atmosphere, now the heroics a child feels about his own acts. With just enough line to define his characters and hatched tone in a variety of values, he creates a whole atmospheric world. Whether picturing children or animals, Symeon Shimin, by his intensity and dedication, lifts extreme realism to a level of great beauty. William Pène Du Bois creates his own private brand of fantasy, finicky and fascinating. Leonard

Everett Fisher and Anthony Ravielli have lifted technical scientific drawing to a level of beauty as well as accuracy. With delicacy and great charm Adrienne Adams has pictured children's observing of nature and has re-illustrated beloved folk and fairy tales. Evaline Ness's beautiful drawings for *Sam, Bangs & Moonshine* suggest the bleakness of a northern fishing port. The characterizations of Sam and her friend Thomas are delightful. A master of design of space and pattern, she has reached with this book a new depth of feeling.

Perhaps more than any other illustrator, Roger Duvoisin has maintained a fresh point of view in his picture books. Children all over the world have followed the adventures of his beloved Happy Lion, Petunia the goose, or Veronica the hippopotamus.

4. ROGER DUVOISIN: *Nubber Bear*

With wit and affection he draws characters that are true in feeling to both the animals they are and the people they resemble.

Artists from other countries, whether living here or abroad, continue to enlarge our own way of feeling. To our children and to our own artists they often bring a tradition of good graphic design, memories and visions from two worlds. The exchange is always richer, as publishers here and abroad add to their own lists by reprinting books from other countries. Some of our handsomest picture books have first been published abroad, printed to standards we can scarcely meet in this country. Many styles of working have become international as a result of these exchanges.

Fortunately, many styles exist side by side, some exquisitely finished hangovers or harkbacks to an earlier period of luxury editions; some vigorous reflec-

tions of the immediate present, some prognostications of a future climate in children's books, produced more hastily and more carelessly as publishers try to beat labor and production costs.

One doesn't really have to wonder why more publishers have turned to other countries with strong traditions in printing — Holland, Switzerland, Italy, Germany, and now, Japan — for the excellence they require. Printing costs may be lower abroad, but skill is refined and abundant. There is a popular saying that American printers can give better results if they want to — if they could afford the time. After leafing through hundreds of garish and poorly printed books, with muddy color work, blurred registry, pale and blurred type, one wonders. . . . The inferiority of the printing in many of these books is ironic, because the publisher has quite obviously offered the artist freedom to use a variety of graphic processes, of painting techniques.

The old battles of twenty years ago, in which partisans for the new and for openmindedness championed the right of contemporary and even far-out types of illustration to find their way to children, have been won. To see how completely, one has only to look at art work of children themselves, taught in modes derived from the most sophisticated of contemporary art.

Painters have occasionally turned to illustration for children, with varying success. Ben Shahn's drawings for *Ounce Dice Trice* by Alastair Reid are as freshly conceived as the collection of out of the ordinary words and nonsense that make up the text. The line spins and sings, snares the objects in its loops, whizzing around the book with the quick pleasure one feels in the words. Such books are perhaps not for every child, but a very special delight for some children.

Artists with a strong feeling for the possibilities of flat color, like Roger Duvoisin and Nicolas Mordvinoff, have constantly experimented to further their limited means and have come up with results that rival fine prints in graphic interest. They manipulate — scratch, rub, stipple and blot — their plastic separation plates; but their line color remains part of a planographic printing scheme that goes with type. Overprinting of the colors extends the number of colors, but gives an overall harmony difficult to achieve with process colors. The artist relies on his own inventiveness to get the most out of little and make little speak more powerfully. At its best hand-separated flat color has a beauty that suggests that of a stone lithograph.

Laymen show an increasing and often touching interest in the techniques of illustration and bookmaking. A few short workshop sessions can aid one in understanding that illustrators and publishers do have problems. But one wonders at the attempt to absorb in so short a time knowledge of skills acquired over many years by artists constantly experimenting. It is as if "how," once known, will answer "why?" No age is too old for learning to look, but one wonders if a more thoughtful attention to "why?" on the part of laymen might not be more useful to children and their books. One wonders when library schools and colleges of education will add more courses in aesthetics to their curricula and start young teachers and librarians on a course of more perceptive examination of what they are called upon to judge and distribute.

One wonders if the interest in techniques has resulted in better aesthetic judgment. One wonders how much it helps to know if a picture was done in crayon or wash, woodcut or acrylic, if one does not see that the artist woefully missed the point and mood of the story he was illustrating; if hands that are meant to hold, can't; if images crowd the page and distort the focus and meaning of the story and suffocate its message. Much of the attention accorded some types of illustration seems to depend on the isolated picture, often very beautful and fascinating as an object, with almost no regard for whether or not it serves the text well. Judges of illustration can hardly have time to read all the books they are called upon to examine. Their decisions can be enlightening but are most valuable if laymen follow them up by reading and looking at the books and wondering.

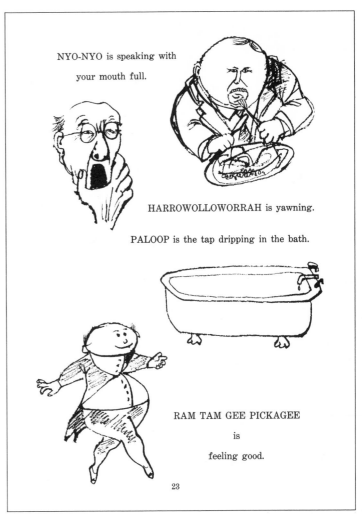

5. BEN SHAHN: *Ounce Dice Trice*

Graphic styles change, of course. It is hard to tell as one looks over the books of the last ten years whether much of the bookmaking one sees is a preview of change in the form of the book as we have known it or is the result of haste in planning or ineptitude on the part of artists and editors in the niceties of bookmaking.

Is it poor planning or greed for space in the average thirty-two-page book that crowds title page and ever-burgeoning copyright information forward right onto the endpapers? The child opens the book as if he turns on a shower faucet. Bang! He's in it. It is hard to tell whether a child is conscious of the beauty or suitability of a title page or if he feels the serenity of enough front matter to ease him into the expectation of pleasure.

With understandable pride publishers seize on any

The Elephant went to look for the molasses at the house of a sugarcane farmer.
The man was so frightened that he ran and hid in the fields.

6. JANINA DOMANSKA: *Why So Much Noise?*

recognition that singles out their books from the crowd. But one wonders about the taste for placing publicity write-ups stressing awards, really hard-sell advertising, in the body of the book instead of on the jacket flap.

Book printing is a small part of the business of offset-printing plants, which get larger and more lucrative contracts from the publishers of glossy magazines and advertising. Picture books have to be fitted into tight printing schedules. More and more attention is being given to cutting time costs. Photographic typesetting can eliminate the casting of the lead slug and provide film for stripping in on the negatives for making the offset plates. Some books have been set with IBM typewriters. One wonders if there will not be a technical changeover in typesetting similar to the change from letterpress to offset about twenty-five years ago.

A book budget may not permit the fine work the reproduction of illustration needs — the color-proving of the whole book before the final run and the proper hand-cleaning of negatives. Color-mixing is often done to formula in a job lot, by the ink manufacturer, and a press is fortunate to have one man who really knows how to mix color and can direct the subtle adjustments that make the difference between banality or beauty in color printing.

With the technical advances made in offset lithography, it does not cost very much more to print a four-color book than it does a two- or three-. After the ink colors are set and approved on the huge four-color presses, the press time is much the same. The cost of additional negatives is less than that of the running time of the presses. From looking at the books, one wonders if some have thought that since a book will cost very little more to print in four colors, why print it in fewer? Why not give it all the color possible? Artists, slightly drunk with the freedom they thought they needed for the full expression of their ideas, have gone overboard with color. Intrigued with all the expressive possibilities of their material, they have explored and exploited every nuance of the story. In a desire to add something of their own to a text, they sometimes have created a counterpoint of design, textures, and details that overwhelm the main theme. One wonders . . . do they find their themes too square? Do they mistrust their simplicity, their obviousness? Or do they just not understand them and their needs?

The time is probably coming when fewer artists will be asked to do color separations. We are seeing more reproductions of elaborate painting techniques as illustration in children's books. Some of these, meticulously finished, hark back to the deluxe and lush editions of an earlier period that were hardly published for the average child.

New standards in bookmaking and new graphic standards will undoubtedly arise as those we traditionally associate with the book break-down. The ex-

hibitions of children's books selected by the American Institute of Graphic Arts have stimulated an interest in book design and bookmaking. The judges have deplored the banal bindings of trade editions, side sewing that sucks in pictures and prevents a book from being held open easily; the mediocrity of illustration in many older children's books; and a general carelessness in manufacturing. Some of their catalogues list all details of production and let the books and their selection speak for themselves. Others admit to a coy confusion of standards among the judges, disparaging their own choices or praising them out of all proportion to their achievement. But the recognition of the need for good design in a young child's book plus the publicity that recognition is now receiving

7. BENI MONTRESOR
The Witches of Venice

are having an effect in raising their quality.

Certain trends, probably developing long before 1956 but much more noticeable now because there are more books, stand out as one looks back over the ten years. One sees fewer books with illustrations inspired by animated cartoons, and, in general, books have a smarter, more "sophisticated" look in color and design. The banal, pastel children of an earlier period have grown up and given way to a new lot of self-conscious little creatures, with chevron mouths up or down, and chevron eyes. Sometimes they are amusing in a wry and satirical way. One wonders what children see in them. Do they see themselves so? One can hardly believe in their gaiety. They look out at us, ever alert to see if we don't find them charming.

The experimentation in the last ten years has moved away from the pop-ups, the "feelies" and obvious tricks to attract attention and is more concerned with ideas. A whole group of books is designed to enter the world of the child as it were at his height. Sometimes they speak to him in his own words; sometimes they lead him out of and beyond his immediate world. Probably because there were very gifted designers to do them, a group of designers' books has appeared. At their best, without quite the order of poetry, these books are beautiful, or instructive, or playful, or provocative, and often all four. While not attempting illustration as we have usually thought of it, these artists have used objects and design elements with great freshness. Occasionally it is impossible to find

three crows flew down from the top of the tree and alighted on the servant's knee.

"We are the three crows whom you once saved from starvation. When we grew up and heard of your search for the sacred apple from the Tree of Life, we traveled over hill and ocean to bring you the apple you seek."

The servant thanked the crows, and with the sacred apple in his hand, started on his way back to the princess.

The princess gazed upon the fruit. "I have no further objection to you as my husband," she said to the youth, whereupon they halved the apple and ate it together. Immediately, the princess's heart was filled with love for the servant.

They were married—and lived happily ever after.

8.   NONNY HOGROGIAN: *Once There Was and Was Not*

Nutcracker Suite Narrative

A little girl marched around her Christmas tree,

And many a marvelous toy had she.

There were cornucopias of sugarplums,

And a mouse with a crown, that sucked its thumbs,

And a fascinating Russian folderol,

Which was a doll inside a doll inside a doll inside a doll,

And a posy as gay as the Christmas lights,

And a picture book of the Arabian nights,

And a painted, silken Chinese fan—

But the one she loved was the nutcracker man.

9.   IVAN CHERMAYEFF: *The New Nutcracker Suite and Other Innocent Verses*

in them any clear demarcation between design and illustration.

Bringing to his books experience in children's theatre and a very sure understanding of children's senses of humor, Remy Charlip has designed some very original and amusing books: with Burton Supree, *Mother Mother I Feel Sick Send for the Doctor Quick Quick Quick; Dress Up; Fortunately.* In them he uses the simplest of visual elements. With his stylized drawings for *Four Fur Feet*, however, he moves into very subtle illustration of the poetic text as the child turns the book to the curve of the mysterious beast's walk around the world.

When a designer-illustrator oversees every detail of the physical book, the results can be very beautiful. Taking her cue from old Armenian manuscripts, Nonny Hogrogian has designed and made simple but

vivid drawings for *Once There Was and Was Not*, a collection of Armenian tales by Virginia Tashjian.

Ellen Raskin has brought a beautiful sense of design to her books illustrated with woodcuts, Dylan Thomas's *A Child's Christmas in Wales*, Ruth Krauss's *Mama, I Wish I Was Snow: Child, You'd Be Very Cold*, and Blake's *Songs of Innocence*.

William Wondriska has linked styles and sizes to objects and the objects that make them.

Ivan Chermayeff's deceptively simple flat-color illustrations for *The Thinking Book* are immediately accessible to a child. In their naive spirit they suggest a child's drawings without copying them. His amusing pictures for Ogden Nash's *The New Nutcracker Suite and Other Innocent Verses* escape the banality of much of the pictured humor that is rather sophisticated for children.

Words can say,
wake up, wake up!
The day is fine,
the sun will shine.

10.   PAUL RAND: *Sparkle and Spin*

11.   BRUNO MUNARI: *Bruno Munari's Zoo*

The lion
does not fear
anyone.

Paul Rand's vivid poster-like images are essences born of enormous skill in distilling a visual point to its most telling simplicity. Although a bit subtle for an average child of picture-book age, his designs developed around the words by Ann Rand are stimulating in idea. *Little 1* is a kind of tour de force in giving personality to the number 1.

There is a constant effort to say old things in new ways to children. One sometimes wonders if the urge to experiment is not a stronger drive than concern with the substance of a book. Picture-book format is obvious for books that are primarily visual. There are some artist-designers who have moved very confidently from the world of adult design to that of children, for perhaps the best of both worlds is interchangeable. But one wonders about the reaction of a little child who picks up some of the books that are clever experiments in typography, in color design, in attempts to enter his private world of imaginative play.

Production costs for some time deterred the publishing of an American edition of Bruno Munari's *nella notte buia*, recently issued by Wittenborn, a publisher of art books. Here very simple elements do not function in the normal continuity of illustrations for a story but serve a poetic idea of some depth. The child is led gently to see and feel that there is more to what he looks at than what he notices at first. At the same time the artist retains the simplicity of his first vision of a natural phenomenon. Caves can tell of the history of the earth, or of man, but a little light in the sky need not be a star to be a delight to the eye.

Artists and editors could well study Munari's picture books. Simple, handsome without being self-conscious, these pictures are informed by a sense of play akin to the child's own, yet respecting his. They are directed by warmth. They prove the absurdity of dogma about what one does for children. They start from a core of affection, with respect for the child's mind and for his own strengths and an awareness of his sense of play, yet are equally aware that the adult who tries to do likewise can fall into the false coyness that exploits that very same playfulness in some of our books.

In recent years we have seen many more books using prints as illustrations. Woodcut is a medium that demands from artists a special fondness for its particular qualities and its harmony with type. The texture of wood, the very force needed to cut it, its tendency to splinter and ruin a line make it a tough vehicle for visual ideas small enough for a book page. But the richness of wood grain, the vigor of a cut line, the variety of tonal effects possible with different kinds of cutting and gouging, the brilliant contrasts between whites and darks, the beautiful colors possible with overprinting one color on another — all these make it a very attractive medium for some types of illustration. Many printmakers have been using it in children's books.

Woodcut is not a medium to be applied to any kind of subject, but occasionally no other would be quite so effective in telling a particular story. Illustrators sometimes misuse it, or do not exploit the very qualities that make it unique when they force it to say what pen and ink or painted flat colors can say. Woodcut prints photographed and printed in halftone lose the graphic harmony between cut line and type and disrupt the optical unity of a page. The mixture of woodcut with other media — with collage, with crayon and pen line — sometimes appears to be a makeshift solution to a problem, though it need not be. Inventiveness sometimes outstrips imagination. One wonders, when one sees an almost identical piece of wood texture serving in book after book as sunrise, sunset, water, clouds — with other printed or drawn images superimposed — was the artist hard up to find another piece of wood?

To Antonio Frasconi woodcut is just as much a natural language as Italian or Spanish or English. It serves him for whatever he has to say. There is no barrier between the artist and the viewer. His woodcuts are internationally known. His books for children, often somber in mood, thoughtful, but always handsome and very expressive, reflect his own belief that

Snow that hurts my feet,
why are you bad?
I am not bad;
the Sun is bad
that melts me.

Nieve que lastimas mis pies,
¿por qué eres mala?
Yo no soy mala;
el Sol es malo
me derrite a mí.

12.   ANTONIO FRASCONI: *The Snow and the Sun*

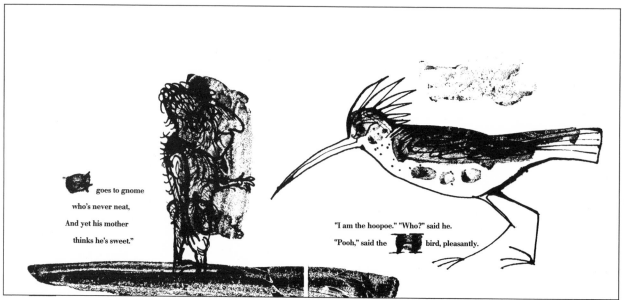

goes to gnome
who's never neat,
And yet his mother
thinks he's sweet."

"I am the hoopoe." "Who?" said he.

"Pooh," said the ▮▮ bird, pleasantly.

13.   JOSEPH LOW: *Adam's Book of odd Creatures*

a child should be helped to move out of himself toward an understanding and perception of the world. Here is artistic responsibility of great depth put at the service of childhood. A feeling artist can put texture and found wood shapes into a poetic context that extends the image it serves and so stimulate an awareness of the unity underlying the similar forces in differing materials.

John and Clare Ross have interpreted the sweep of Whitman, the staccato patterns of city life, in woodcuts for older children. Philip Reed has designed exquisite volumes illustrated with charming wood engravings in color. Leonard Everett Fisher has raised scratch-board technique to the level of fine wood engraving. Blair Lent has used his prints most imaginatively in *The Wave*, filling space with shapes — the gray rolls of thunder, the billowing wave, the tumbling jumble of houses, temples and boats. Here stylization of the forms is a powerful element in their expressiveness. Joseph Low has moved from stylization to an engaging and unhackneyed spontaneity in his drawings and linoleum cuts. The washes of thin color under his prints, a technique commonly used in advertising and in illustrations, always seem fresh and not arbitrary.

Collage has long been known to children's books and has a lively background in cut-paper work. But collage as a medium for illustration, making full use of its capacity for visual metaphor, has flowered in the last ten years.

The urge to invent can easily defeat itself. When the pattern and variety of textures speak too insistently and call attention to themselves as objects instead of subordinating themselves to the picture, collage can be confusing and spotty or overloaded. A child sees a collection of textures more or less resembling the images he looks for. Without some kind of underlying emotional organization and warmth, the artist may have given him strong design, but lace, fabrics and feathers instead of a dignified old man; bits of existence, but not a living creature. A sea can remain chaotic blocks of blue and green paper.

In his two picture books about a little colored boy enjoying a snowy day or learning to whistle, Ezra Jack Keats has used collage very charmingly, using French marbled papers, wallpaper, Japanese silk papers — a

"A tidal wave!" shrieked the people. And then all shrieks and all sounds and all power to hear sounds were ended by a shock heavier than any thunder, as the great wave struck the shore with a weight that sent a shudder through the hills.

14. BLAIR LENT: *The Wave*

"Don't eat me. I am an inchworm. I am useful. I measure things."
"Is that so!" said the robin. "Then measure my tail!"

15. LEO LIONNI: *Inch by Inch*

great variety of textures and colors as background to his simple and childlike stories. The shape of the brown child making an accent against the white or light backgrounds is beautiful. All the visual elements work together to tell the story.

Leo Lionni is one of the most imaginative artists of collage, so skillful that one thinks first of the picture and only later of the means he used. In his *Inch by Inch* there is a scaffold of very lively drawing. The motif of the blades of grass recurs as the inchworm moves along through the book. Each component texture extends the expressiveness of the drawing; the artist confines himself to only those textures and colors needed to carry the inch worm along. In *Swimmy* he stamps, blots, superimposes prints of lace on his blotted watercolor washes. The blotted wet pictures suggest the beautiful, vague, and mysterious world under the sea, where menace and fear are precise if the definitions of that world are not. The technique here always serves the idea.

Simplicity is not always strength, nor does an apparently naive technique reveal simplicity of spirit. At its best, simplicity is a matured richness distilled to its essence, the end of the progress of a creative idea, not the beginning.

With circles and strips of torn paper, the simplest possible means, Lionni made *little blue and little yellow*. It is a profound little book, gay enough to make a child laugh aloud but wise about color mixtures, about judging by appearances, about recognizing the changes brought about by friendship and love. Lionni uses collage with poetic economy.

Little children are reputed to like brilliant colors. Because many easel artists have vivid imaginations and there is money to earn in the lucrative picture book field, some painters who are accustomed to work very freely have turned to the picture book. Occasionally one feels they have become so engrossed in their own picture-making they have forgotten that child on the other side of the bridge and are doing pictures for the bridge itself. A public that buys garish commodities stimulates the publishers to put out more of the same and other artists to go and do likewise. One suspects that some painters enter children's book illustration by mistake. Their misunderstanding of the scale of art work to a book page, their use of heavy painting techniques with thick impasto that overwhelm a simple narrative lead one to wish they had learned more about what a picture book is. One wonders if some artists don't have their editors hypnotized. The axe that should fall on an overwritten text and overcolored, overblown pictures remains suspended, and the overripe offering is sent out.

A host of extremely competent and often gifted illustrators have turned from advertising to children's books. They bring brilliantly stylized techniques, often in hatched pen line, a professional finish to their overall design, and a lively experimentation with shape and format. Many show an endless care in fashioning, in shaping flaccid images into solidity. Styles of draughtsmanship make their own laws, but if one subscribes to traditional conventions in perspective, in the movements possible to human joints, in the space three-dimensional objects occupy, then one must follow through. All the finish in the world cannot disguise the inadequacies of some illustration, the banal color, the failure to respect the facts of the text.

Each period sprouts its own fashions. Clichés multiply when more and more people work hastily and there is little time to digest experience or impressions before giving them forth again. One copies what one has done or what one has seen, often unconsciously.

Night time is coming.

They say good-by.

It has been a lovely day

16. JULIET KEPES: *Two Little Birds and Three*

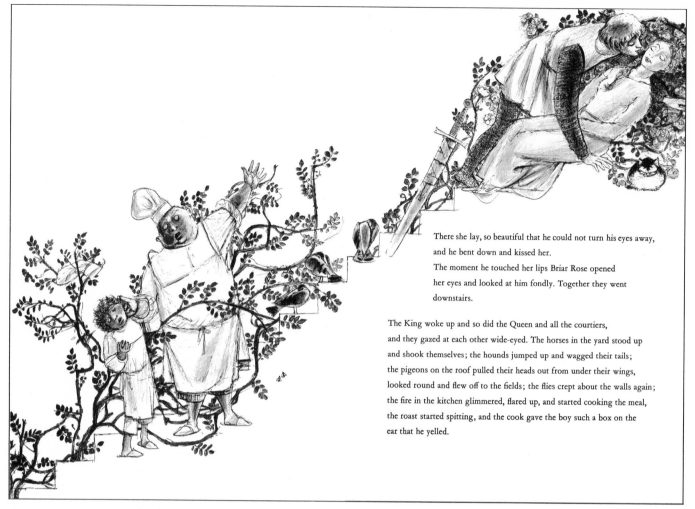

There she lay, so beautiful that he could not turn his eyes away,
and he bent down and kissed her.
The moment he touched her lips Briar Rose opened
her eyes and looked at him fondly. Together they went
downstairs.

The King woke up and so did the Queen and all the courtiers,
and they gazed at each other wide-eyed. The horses in the yard stood up
and shook themselves; the hounds jumped up and wagged their tails;
the pigeons on the roof pulled their heads out from under their wings,
looked round and flew off to the fields; the flies crept about the walls again;
the fire in the kitchen glimmered, flared up, and started cooking the meal,
the roast started spitting, and the cook gave the boy such a box on the
ear that he yelled.

17.   FELIX HOFFMANN: *The Sleeping Beauty*

One can never know whether a child of today, accustomed to supermarket shelves, is startled to find the same repetition of objects lined up in his books. Soldiers, processions — some subjects lend themselves to lineups; some are submerged in repetitive hammering. What starts imaginatively with one image can multiply into a numerical insistence that is as dull and impersonal as those supermarket shelves.

Felix Hoffmann, who has drawn distinguished and beautiful new editions of Grimm, has made of the old verse *A Boy Went Out to Gather Pears* a sturdy and methodical but beautiful little book. Each repetition of the woodcut elements adds something new to the story.

Because in this period many classics published near the turn of the century have passed into public domain, publishers have rushed to reissue them, often in competition with the original, and in editions carelessly or lovingly photographed from the old editions. The arguments about definitive editions go on, not really solving anything, because all that is lacking is the appearance of an artist so capable of entering freshly into the spirit of a book that earlier, loved editions move over to make room for his.

In a recent trade publication a well-known critic wondered out loud about some recent editions of classics. She placed a photograph of a picture from a recent edition publicized as "definitive" next to one from the famous British artist who so clearly had been the more-than-inspiration. In comparing the two, one noticed that on page after page of the new edition only a background would be added to a vulgarized redrawing of the original. Could such similarities in characterization and composition be accidents? Responsible parents and librarians can deplore such practices, but they can only discourage the publication of such ersatz editions by examination, comparison, and choice of the genuine.

It doesn't even take a glance down our glass-and-steel city streets to see why we are in many ways turning back to a cozier age in some of our illustration.

There has been a great spurt of what one could call neo-Victorianism — a harking back to styles of drawing based on the pen and ink techniques, the steel and wood engravings of the last century, and a world apparently fuller of a number of things than ours is. One of the most successful using these techniques, always at the service of his own wit and feeling, is Maurice Sendak. In his illustrations for the tales of Wilhelm Hauff and Frank Stockton, in the exquisite books of Randall Jarrell, he recreates a silvery world, meticulously delineated, in which a child can walk

18. ERIK WERENSKIOLD (1855-1938):
Norwegian Folk Tales

19.   MAURICE SENDAK: *The Bee-Man of Orn*

around; but at the same time he is keeping alive one of
the most vital traditions in children's book illustration
— that of Richard Doyle, Tenniel, and Cruikshank.
Plagiarism is an ugly word and an uglier practice.
While they are strengthening their own illustration
and finding their own ways, young artists understandably imitate the styles they admire and that they relate
to temperamentally. A successful and popular artist
like Sendak has hosts of imitators of the square little
children in some of his picture books. Without the
personal motivation of the originals, they remain
imitations.

One wonders if young artists are sometimes urged to try someone else's style. As in the old tale of the mixed-up feet, is it too difficult for them to find their own when asleep? Watch and wait is all we can do.

With expressive distortions, elongations, compressions, an artist's line follows the impulses of his nerves and feeling, the meanderings of his imagination. The character of a book shows up in the character of the lines in its illustrations — wispy and delicate in the watercolor drawings of Alois Carigiet; blunt and monolithically emphatic in the poster images of Celestino Piatti; crystalline in the crowded details of Marvin Bileck; elegantly simple in the clean lines of Reiner Zimnik. Style in illustration as in writing has a good deal to say about an artist's involvement with his material, his focus, his aims. Why did he do this

particular book? Sometimes how he did it can tell us something about why.

Who presumes to re-illustrate the verses of Edward Lear is up against formidable competition from Mr. Lear himself. Lear has never really been out of fashion with children. Several artists have recently challenged his drawings with their own or have tried to draw humor in a similar vein.

Tomi Ungerer has the keenest sense of the absurd. Beneath an air of innocent gaiety is a very acute wit. His drawings for *Oh, What Nonsense!* a collection of humorous poems edited by William Cole, are delightful in the directness of their line.

With gentle satire and great delicacy Barbara Cooney has recreated the woeful little tragedy of Cock Robin. The satire never bursts out of the minia-

20: CELESTINO PIATTI: *The Happy Owls*

21. REINER ZIMNIK: *The Snow Party*

ture frame of the story. In an unassuming but very skillful way she has been extremely successful in her illustrations for Lear. Her drawings seem extensions of his, so completely has she caught their quality.

Perhaps because of the recognition granted some illustrated fairy tales, but more probably because of the response of children to them in libraries, there has been an enormous number of new editions of old favorites and, once the better known ones were between covers, of those not so well known. Tales, humorous and fanciful, fables, tall tales, hero legends, myths — there is hardly a type of narrative that has not appeared with illustrations. The challenge to an illustrator of such stories is much greater than that

of the books mentioned earlier. A line of intensity must not only be maintained but must build as the story does; characters must be vivid, must occasionally develop inwardly as well as outwardly; compositions of pages must constantly change although dealing with the same basic background. Each element contributes to the power of the telling and helps determine the atmosphere of the story.

Humorous, robust tales have been particularly successful as individual books. One of the strongest new talents to emerge in the last ten years is Margot Zemach. Compare *The Three Sillies, Nail Soup, The Speckled Hen* with any of several treatments of folk tales with the same earthy origins and feel the sureness of her comic vision, the core of warmth in the observation of human foibles and absurdities. The constant invention always remains within the textual framework of the story — witness the stranger in the inn with head down, charging his trousers. Her large-nosed, black-stockinged women look surprised at being caught in ridiculous situations. Here is a very sure touch; the absurd is met head on. This artist gives every promise of growing as she extends the emotional range of her material.

Andersen is one of the most demanding of authors for an illustrator. While some illustrators picture the facts of his stories delightfully, the deeper meanings elude them, glossed over in favor of a pretty charm. The child gets no hint that here is something more than a barnyard fable or an average fairy tale. It is easy to be beguiled by the trappings of a period, to become enmeshed in researches and lose the poetic signifi-

cance of these distillates from several folk origins through the mind and heart of a most unusual man. But what a child remembers is more apt to be the poetic truth of the story than the factual truth of the pictures, if the artist has approached his task with understanding of that truth. Probably not for every illustrator, the stories of Andersen present rare challenges and rare satisfactions for one who is willing to submit himself to them.

Children have been handed all kinds of translations and all kinds of illustrations of Andersen, from the deluxe, to the sweet, to the cozy. Adrienne Adams, Maurice Sendak, Erik Blegvad, Bill Sokol, and Nancy Burkert are some of the artists who have reinterpreted Andersen.

Editors only occasionally have had an active background in sharing books with children in storytelling. Librarians who have that background would do well

Then grandmother cried,
And grandfather sighed,

22. MARGOT ZEMACH: *The Speckled Hen*

to think of the values they subscribe to and their responsibility to the children and to the poet whose words may live in them. If one is courageous enough to tell some of these stories to children, desperate, terror-stricken stories shot with beauty and illuminated by courage and sacrifice, one should choose illustrated versions that face the issues of the stories. To judge from some of the recent editions of folk and fairy tales, one wonders at the emotional and spiritual involvement of the artists who did them. Their books are often brilliant but shallow. They have rushed in where humility, wit and vitality of imagination might have guided them.

Many illustrators have tried to write — with varying success — and occasionally authors have tried to draw — with less. One feels that the desire to do a book may be commendable; but without something to say to children and the means to say it, or even the desire to develop the means, one wonders at the arrogance that expects a child to be interested in half-baked creations, texts or pictures. There is still among laymen a lack of comprehension of the discipline needed to pare a text to a basic line that looks simple. A picture book is as concise as poetry. Text and pictures combine to form an essence that expands in the child's mind.

One wonders why some artists, masters of subjective, poetic stylizations, turn to picture books. Do their editors urge them, or aren't they able to stop them? Their characters are forced into uncomfortable stylizations that strain away most of their feelings.

At the stroke of midnight in came two little men who had no clothes on. They sat down at the shoemaker's table and took all the work that had been laid out for them. With their tiny fingers they began to stitch, sew and hammer so quickly and so nimbly, that the shoemaker was surprised and could not keep his eyes off them. They kept right on until all the work was done and stood ready on the table. Then they darted out of the room.

23. ADRIENNE ADAMS: *The Shoemaker and the Elves*

24 & 25:   ERIK BLEGVAD: *Mr. Jensen & Cat*

Their settings, often exquisite in themselves, presuppose associations a small child could not possibly have. Their distillations can evoke visions for the older, imaginative child, but are often thin fare for the hearty hunger of the picture book age.

On the other hand, the free brush drawings of Juliet Kepes, the fanciful pen drawings of Walter Lorraine, the elegantly evocative line drawings of Madeleine Gekiere, the delicate and crystalline drawings of Bill Sokol, the woodcuts of Helen Siegl, the clean lines of Enrico Arno, have helped to make this a particularly rich period for the illustration of poetry and the design of books that will continue to satisfy a child as he matures.

In the drive to produce more books there is a tendency to take one poem and make a book of it. This is particularly successful with narrative poems and ballads. One wonders whether with the increasing picturing of fantasy, the illustration of subjective poetry will be eventually stultifying or stimulating to the imagination of a child.

As we look ahead to a future of greater technical advances, more urbanization and more centralized control of all our communications, one wonders. . . . The enormous power to create opinion and a whole climate of taste will mean enormous responsibilities. The possibility of a kind of brainwashing and control of attitudes of children through their books will have to be faced by all those working for children.

Already not to be *with* it is to many not to be at all.

The nervous, jittery activity of very competitive city life will have its effect on children. That more young children will have access to books could mean more dedicated and brilliant invention by our artists.

The heritage of the folk tale is one of the most vital possessions we can pass on to children. The renaissance of the folk tale as an individual book for young children is perhaps one of the most valuable trends in the past ten years. The chance for the appearance of many brilliant, original books is always slim. But one wonders if the base of simple, earthy wisdom and the observation of humanity going about its living, trying to scale the mountains of its visions — the chance for the odd one who is usually *not* with it to succeed — may not be our most important gifts to children from this period.

26. TOMI UNGERER: *Oh, What Nonsense!*

27. MARCIA BROWN: *The Wild Swans*

CONFRONTED with a new story, I often have a sinking sensation. Accepting it, months ago, seemed so easy; at that time I was in the middle of another story and was only concerned with finding that I *liked* this one, not with "seeing" the illustrations; or if I could "see" them tentatively, then, I have somehow lost the vision and suddenly, now, it looks formidable. My mind is a blank.

Now I do what experience has taught me and read the story over and over, very slowly, at the pace of reading to a child. At perhaps the fifth reading I begin to "see" it, and I feel better.

With scissors I cut up the galley-proof sheets. I scotch-tape the pieces into the pages of an exact-size dummy. I work with it until everything "fits"; the turning of a page regulates the time and paces it. The picture space gives a chance to enlarge on and augment the story. For some inexplicable reason, I love this part of bookmaking; I have infinite patience with it and do not mind how long the process is.

I am told that it is sometimes a help to a writer, on beginning a story, to put into one sentence what the story is all about, to state its theme in a few words. Similarly, I find it a help, as an illustrator, to turn next to the making of a quick thumbnail sketch of the book — a little four-by-five-inch dummy — in color. It gives me something to depart from, at the least. The editor enjoys seeing the dummy too. At this point there is an easy give-and-take between us; my point of view has not become set. I now have the impetus to plunge in, deeper, and to get at the job I have been fretting over and delaying.

As I return to the full-sized dummy, I must keep in mind the restrictions based on decisions made earlier by the editor and me, technical and economic restrictions, which fence me in. How the book is to be printed, and what the method for preparing the art work for reproduction will be, were decided at the outset. These fences do not bother me, so long as I accept them from the beginning and work within them.

I have used several methods in the making of

books: line drawings, or line plus flat-area illustrations that can be reproduced by means of line engravings; pencil drawings on Dinobase, a sandblasted acetate used in the "direct process," which I will not try to define here; full-color illustrations for offset-lithography reproduction, where the camera is used to separate the colors; and full-color illustration where the artist himself does the separating.

I have decided to discuss the last method because it is the most difficult for me. I use it only when a story seems to push me in that direction, and also because I have a natural inclination toward water-color illustrations.

The hope of the illustrator is that he will be able to retain control of the elements of his design in its

2.
COLOR SEPARATION

by Adrienne Adams

transfer to book page through the hands of the craftsmen who separate it into its parts and put it together again on the printed sheet.

If the separating out of these elements (the four colors, black, red, yellow, and blue) is to be done by the artist, he must, as he does an illustration, keep in mind how he is going to undo it. He must present to the bookmaker not one drawing, but four — one for each color — so that when they are printed, one on top of another (stacked, you might say), the picture is put back together again and resembles the original.

In camera-separated work, this job is done by the camera through the use of filters; it is very costly and not so accurate as you would suppose. When the job is done by the artist, it is painfully tedious. A big risk is that one can become bored and, getting involved in details, lose sight of the whole.

Despite the hazards, I have wanted to work in water colors enough to take a chance when, for instance, I made the little book about a Maine island, *The Light in the Tower*, and again in *Houses from the Sea*. I could not see doing shells and water in pencil on Dinobase with the resulting grainy look, or with line cut and its flat effect. But what method to use? It is easy enough in a book like *What Makes a Shadow?* to make a flat drawing for each color — very much like playing with a simple jigsaw puzzle; and when one has designed for it, the results can be satisfying.

In separating wash paintings for halftone reproduction, I am dealing with overlapping gradations of the four different colors to achieve many other colors. I begin with the shades of black, my most important color, for it tells most of the story. I mentally select out all that is black in my painting and, calling this my key drawing, do it on illustration board. Then — on acetate, so that I can see through to the key drawing — I do a painting of only the red areas. With scotch tape I hinge the red drawing on the left of the key drawing so that I can fold it back out of the way when I do the blue drawing, which I hinge from the top. Then comes the yellow drawing, hinged on the right. One can easily see that it would be cumbersome if all were hinged from the same side, for when working on the top one I would have to view the key drawing through three thicknesses of acetate instead of one.

I take care of the exact fitting of one drawing over another by the use of register marks ⊕, which can be bought, printed on acetate adhesive tape. These help the platemaker too, and they can be removed before the printing stage arrives.

The real stumper, and the part that is difficult to explain without demonstrating, is this: each separated color-painting is done by me in tones of black so that it will photograph better and make a truer plate. Everyone knows that blue photographs weak, red photographs strong. If I do each painting in black, I can keep to truer values. Of course, each plate will be printed in its intended color of ink.

The transfer, in my mind, of (for instance) the yellow areas to black is a difficult problem. For each of the colors it is difficult. As a tool to aid me here I use the Coloron graduated transparencies of printer's inks. The Process colors are my selection. On these Coloron acetate sheets are printed ten bars of a given color, from 10%, 20%, 30% on up to 100% value of that color. Since these are on acetate, I can lay the yellow transparent sheet over the blue sheet, and by moving the yellow sheet around over the varying percentages of blue arrive at the green I have used in the grass area, for instance, of my original painting. It is 30% blue and 90% yellow, I may find. I analyze my whole painting so, lightly writing in the little computations all over the original. When I make the yellow separation, knowing the grass must be 90% yellow, I now paint in 90% black, for at hand I have the Coloron acetate sheet for the gradations of black to guide me.

Such effort does not guarantee precise results. One must consciously design with the hazards in mind. Keep it casual, free. Let the colors overlap carelessly; if a design is very carefully cleancut and a flaw in the registration is made, the error will stand out like a sore thumb. If many areas are loosely put together, one's eye accepts the looseness in its entirety.

I did not follow my own advice when I did *Butterfly Time*. I dared to try to separate butterflies exactly. I will shy away from another challenge like that one; but I did fall in love with the butterflies, and so pushed on, getting terribly involved in the

THE ILLUSTRATION FOR THE FOLLOWING COLOR PAGES, PRINTED BY PRE-SEPARATED ART, WAS PREPARED BY ADRIENNE ADAMS SPECIFICALLY FOR THIS VOLUME TO IL-LUSTRATE HER USE OF SEPARATIONS AND THE CAREFULLY PLANNED USE OF PROCESS COLORS IN CREATING THESE SEPARATIONS.

Key drawing of black areas, done on white illustration board with pencil line, grey wash, and strong blacks and whites.

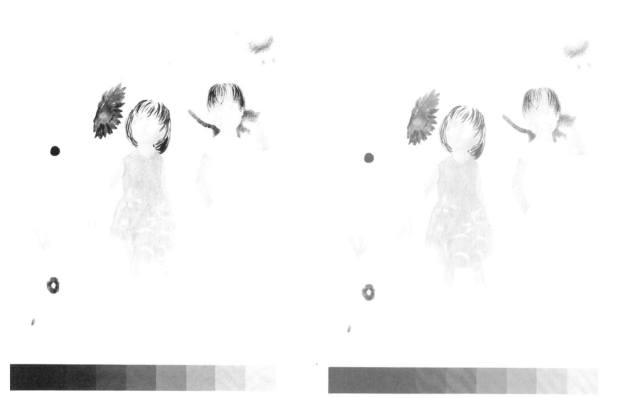

Artist's separation in black for red areas.

The plate printed in magenta.

Artist's separation in black for yellow areas.

The plate printed in yellow.

Artist's separation in black for blue areas.

The plate printed in blue.

Progressive proofs are made to see if any correction in color is needed.

minutest details. Have you ever observed the marbleized underside of the wings of a Painted Lady? Or a Red Admiral? Attempting to separate the elements into overlapping color areas was madness. I was able to find and buy specimens of these beautiful but elusive creatures so that I could hold and turn and study them. When I got home and discovered the tiny labels on the pins supporting them, I was filled with doubt; the Great Spangled Fritillary had been caught in 1937! How true could its colors be — had they faded greatly? Almost immediately I saw two Fritillaries in our yard. I followed them and knew that mine was just as rich in color as the living ones. And then I saw a Red Admiral; I could have caught it had I not one, just as brilliant, on a pin, captured eighteen years before.

It is far more reasonable, and simpler, to separate the colors for a fable or fairy tale. Any color I have used is arbitrarily chosen. It need register as perfectly as possible and be pleasing to the eye. That is all.

Most of what I have said here has had to do with the real *chore* part of bookmaking. I thought it might be the least well-known part and not uninteresting. Every kind of work we do has its tougher, trying moments. To balance, here, I could mention a higher moment. It does not come, as you might think, when I hold the finished book in my hand and find my effort was all so very worth while. I never feel so. I have regrets, then, that I cannot do the book over.

Rather, the moment is that one of optimistic new hope I feel as I begin the next one — hope that now, given another chance, I will do a *better* book.

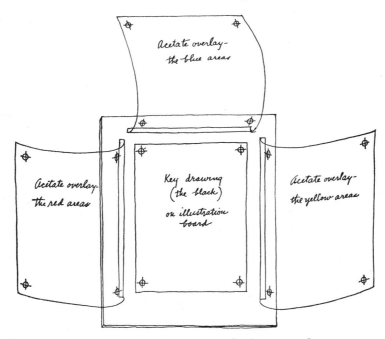

DIAGRAM OF ASSEMBLING OF ARTIST'S ACETATE SEPARATIONS

Hinging the acetates (see text) is merely for the convenience of the illustrator; the bookmaker must take the arrangement apart for photographing.

DURING the decade since the publication of *Illustrators of Children's Books: 1946-1956* there has been a widespread and spectacular proliferation of the picture book. This has been due partly to the desire of the artist for the fuller expression of his art that color and wide pages give him. It is due also to a rapid acceleration in the development of printing techniques. Indeed it is difficult to determine which is cause and which effect.

Distinction in writing for children was first recognized with the Newbery Award in the United States in 1922 and with the Carnegie Award in Great Britain in 1936. Distinction in illustration, however, was not recognized in the United States until the Caldecott Award was first given in 1938, while the Kate Greenaway Medal was established in 1955 for British illustration.

This is interesting when one considers that from the earliest times illustration has been considered essential for children. As far back as 1658 Comenius remarked that "pictures are the most intelligible books that children can look upon." The picture attracts the eyes, the child asks a question and is led to the reading of the text.

The first printed books were often crude but very gay. Small editions were printed, and it was possible to color by hand, using regiments of children: one with a blue brush putting in all the blues; the next with red, the next with yellow, and so forth. Later hand-engraved wood blocks or metal plates by craftsmen like Edmund Evans made printed illustrations in color possible, beautiful, and relatively inexpensive. Nearly all of the books with colored pictures by Walter Crane, Randolph Caldecott and Kate Greenaway were produced by this gifted color-printer. Then, alas, the age of the machine put the printed word into large editions, but only the simplest black-and-white line drawings could be reproduced because of the expense of printing in color. Only in very recent years, with the development of lithographic techniques, has the machine at last become the servant of the painter and the picture book

has again, as in the time of Caldecott and Greenaway, become his chosen medium.

Brian Wildsmith, one of England's outstanding artists, has said that he is frustrated by the restrictions of the printed page, the author's demands, and the technical limitations of ordinary illustrating. It is interesting to study his work in the light of these remarks and to see how, from the black-and-white illustration of stories by various and varied authors, he has moved slowly and certainly to his own picture books in which he can reach, in blazing color, his fullest creative expression. In this he has been helped and encouraged by his editor, Mabel George of the Oxford University Press in London, and by his

3.
THE ARTIST
and HIS EDITOR

Grace Allen Hogarth

American editor, Helen Hoke Watts of Franklin Watts in New York.

Robert McCloskey, an American artist, also started his career with drawings in black-and-white and jackets in limited color. An early example of this, *Yankee Doodle's Cousins* by Anne Malcolmson, was first published in 1941, and is still in print. He, too, with the help of his editor, May Massee of the Viking Press, moved forward to his own picture books. At first, in *Make Way for Ducklings*, which won the Caldecott Medal in 1942, he used sepia and white without color. But eventually he was able to use full color, a notable example being *Time of Wonder*, which won his second Caldecott Award in 1957.

These two artists, both of whom have been acclaimed with medals, are now spending most of their time on full-color picture books which they have written themselves or planned from traditional material. Brian Wildsmith is more brilliantly original in his color work; Robert McCloskey more traditional in color and possibly the better of the two in line.

Edward Ardizzone, the best known and most loved of all English artists, says in an article, "Creation of a Picture Book":

Writing the text for a picture book also has its particular difficulties, the main one being that the tale has to be told in so few words, yet must read aloud easily and sound well when read. Another difficulty

28. EDWARD ARDIZZONE: *Paul, The Hero of the Fire*

is that, at the turn of each page, and one rarely has more than one hundred and twenty words between the turns, the text must end with a natural break, a note of interrogation or suspense. With rare exceptions, the professional writer who is no artist finds this extremely difficult, if not impossible, to do. Not being visually minded, he cannot leave out enough; he must elaborate; he cannot visualize how the picture will tell the story. And this, I think, is why the best picture books have been created by artists who have written their own texts. It is a one-man job. . . .

I have in the course of years, illustrated many books by various authors, and many of these books have been for children. Illustrating other people's books is never quite so easy or so pleasant as illustrating one's own. If one has no feeling for a book, neither for its language nor imagery, then the task can be a difficult and weary one. As a professional, to get a book like this is all in the day's work and no excuse for making bad drawings, though I fear that it sometimes leads to indifferent ones.[1]

Most artists, whether professional or not, chafe at the restraints and restrictions of an author's text, especially in picture books. Many of them, as Edward Ardizzone says, are happiest when they can write their own stories, which give thém space and a text to order or, as in Wildsmith's *The Lion and the Rat*, a traditional story which they can edit to suit their pens and brushes.

This urge to self-expression is understandable. But is an *illustrator*, whose work may be defined as the interpretation and illumination of an author's text, less a creative artist because of the restrictions placed upon him? History denies this. Cruikshank and Phizz illustrated Dickens; Caldecott did not need to alter any text; Rackham made Grimm terrifyingly real to a generation of children; and Ardizzone, in the same article, goes on to say:

On the other hand when it comes to illustrating a fine and poetic writer, then it is a different matter.

[1]Edward Ardizzone, "Creation of a Picture Book," *Top of the News*, Vol. XVI No. 2, December 1959, and *Junior Bookshelf*, December 1961.

To illustrate Walter de la Mare's *Peacock Pie* was sheer delight, and sheer delight it was, too, to illustrate the poems and prose of such writers as James Reeves and Eleanor Farjeon. . . . Before I finish I would like to mention one book which is not strictly a children's book and which is by the author of some of the greatest prose ever written in the English language. The book is *The Pilgrim's Progress* and I cannot resist including a short passage from the opening page: "I dreamed, and behold I saw a man clothed in rags, standing in a certain place, with his face from his own house, a book in his hand, and a great burden on his back. I looked and saw him open the book, and read therein; and as he read, he wept and trembled; and not being able longer to contain, he brake out with a lamentable cry, saying, 'What shall I do?'"

This is noble language, but to me the genius of Bunyan is shown in the phrase "with his face from his own house." This phrase instantly visualizes the scene for us. Christian has his back to his house. The house is obviously visible but must be some way off on the edge of a distant town, and the town itself must be surrounded by a flat, sad and somewhat open landscape.

I illustrated the wonderful book about fifteen years ago. But for twenty years before then, it had been my ambition to do so.[2]

There are illustrators who respond to the challenge of a difficult text. Ardizzone is, perhaps, happiest and most relaxed in his own picture books, but he can meet and accept the demands of *The Pilgrim's Progress* or *Peacock Pie*. Antony Maitland, a young English illustrator who won the Kate Greenaway Medal for his pictures in *Mrs. Cockle's Cat* by Philippa Pearce, told the librarians in a talk following the presentation of the award how much he enjoyed this delightful story. He said, however, that when Mrs. Cockle's balloons carried her skyward, the author's description of this exciting event went on for over a thousand words. She first described the ascent in the damp foggy mist; then the pleasant warmth on Mrs. Cockle's knuckles as she approached the sun; she wrote at length of the sky above, the rain

[2]*Ibid.*

29. ANTONY MAITLAND:
Mrs. Cockle's Cat

cloud below, the joy of running and jumping from cloud to cloud, the appearance of sun and air and cloud forms, and the changes in all this which happened over a whole morning and part of an afternoon. Moreover, the author was fascinated by Mrs. Cockle's thoughts, memories and feelings during her sky adventure. It was obviously fun for the author to think of this lovable old woman up in the clouds and fun, too, for the children; but what can an illustrator do with a minimum of eight pages to fill with virtually the same picture? Antony Maitland succeeded because he had the necessary imagination, humor, and skill. There is Mrs. Cockle's anxious face, quite close through the mist, a full-length figure dangling in the sunlight, two pages of the intrepid old woman leaping over clouds, a beautiful full-color spread of Mrs. Cockle floating over the "silently flowing" Thames and its green shores, and finally two pages which show her tumbling helter-skelter down to the water below.

When a picture book artist is struggling with an author's unmanageable manuscript, the editor who is responsible for the end product is often tempted to ask the author to cut his text or rewrite it with pictures in mind. This is, however, dangerous ground. All reviewers have a deep reverence for the written word.

When Barbara Cooney cut the text of *A White Heron* so that it could become a picture book, she made a work of art that I am certain Sarah Orne Jewett would have loved. But the book was received with a storm of protest in the United States. Even in England, where the author was not widely known, Margery Fisher wrote in *Growing Point*:

> The text has been cut and edited, for the most part discreetly. I hope I shan't seem pernickety if I say I wish more of the author's beautifully shaped sentences had been left untouched. . . . The more leisurely style of the last century is valuable in its own right and a joy to anyone reading aloud. I believe children who delight in words will respond to this finely wrought but very human story. There is no doubt that this edition will attract them for its open print and fine layout and for the incomparable colored illustrations.[3]

[3]Margery Fisher, *Growing Point*, July 1964.

30. ANTONY MAITLAND:
     Mrs. Cockle's Cat

31. BARBARA COONEY:
A White Heron

To this the editor can only say that if the long senten- ces had been left there would not have been room for any "incomparable colored illustrations." The editor's decision is, perhaps, a larger one. Is the material wrong, or right, for a picture book? In the case of *A White Heron* I feel that the editor, Elizabeth Riley of Thomas Y. Crowell, made a decision which has increased the author's audience and given her a new stature.

32. BARBARA COONEY: *Le Hibou et la Poussiquette*

An artist's interpretation and the power of his brush or pen must inevitably mark the author's work with the imprint of another mind and another personality. There is a striking example of this in the American and British illustrations for *Le Hibou et la Poussiquette*, Francis Steegmuller's translation into French of *The Owl and the Pussycat* by Edward Lear. In the American edition, Barbara Cooney made the rhyme into a light-hearted picture book in a squarish shape that would delight young children as well as adults and make them laugh. She used color — turquoise for sea, yellow that is true *citron*, and shades of green from grass to olive. Monique-Alika Watteau, who decorated the English edition, chose a tall thin book and made sophisticated black-and-white designs rather than realistic illustrations. Her book is more serious and more adult. By studying these two editions of the same translation of Lear, one can see how easily the visual image as described by the author can be interpreted altogether differently by different artists. The editor who chooses the illustrator has, then, a responsibility as serious as that of accepting the manuscript for publication.

33. MONIQUE-ALIKA WATTEAU: *Le Hibou et la Poussiquette*

Some years ago I tried my hand at illustrating and have had a deeper affection for artists ever since. When *St. Nicholas Magazine* was revived by May Lamberton Becker in the thirties, Laura E. Richards contributed a series of poems which were later published in the book called *Tirra Lirra*. One of these verses, "The Mameluke and Hospodar," was given to me to illustrate for *St. Nicholas*. It began, "A Mesopotamian Mameluke was pricking it over the plain. . . ." When I drew him with spiked football boots, the author wrote to Mrs. Becker:

This is a most delightful picture, clever, spirited, very funny. I congratulate you and Miss Allen heartily. *Qua* picture, it leaves nothing to be desired: *Qua* illustration of my ballad, it is — shall I say — inaccurate?

"Pricking it over the plain"; the Mameluke was on horseback, cf. Century Dictionary: "Prick: to spur on, to ride rapidly." cf. also Spenser, The Fairy Queen: "A gentle knight was pricking o'er the plain."

Miss Allen (apparently) connects "pricking" with football boots!

When I confessed that I hadn't read any Spenser for some years, I was forgiven and I did not have to change my odd interpretation.

Not all authors are so kind. David Fletcher writes in *The Horn Book:*

> . . . what horrors one has to endure. Scratchy illustrations in which a phony impressionistic technique conceals not only the lack of drawing but most of the objects depicted as well. Drawings of figures without any background at all; very, very widespread these are, yet every child I have ever asked disapproves of these creatures that apparently float in space or spend their lives amid the snowy wastes of the Pole. Drawings that cover the most trivial happenings while neglecting the important or exciting events of the book. Three drawings on consecutive pages and then nothing for fifty. Fair little girls ruthlessly dyed brunette and raven-tressed beauties bleached into corn-hued blondes; tough little tykes turned into simpering sissies; a jacket discarded in favor of a tartan shirt and — oh! a thousand and one mistakes of this nature, all of which a child spots at once and pounces upon.[4]

The editor, caught between author and illustrator, often keeps them firmly apart. It is not difficult to understand this after reading the above. On the other side, the artist can also be firm. When one of them was asked to design a jacket for a book about the war-time escapades of some children evacuated from Guernsey to northern England, he wrote that he was sorry to have to return the book, but under the circumstances he could not undertake to do a wrapper for it. He went on to say that he thought it was no book for children and that he spoke as the father of a large family, as an officer of many years' experience and as an artist dedicated to the production of books for children. It was not, he said, a book for children, but a hand-book for potential delinquents.

It is true that the marriage of author and illustrator is not often made in heaven, but I have come to believe that the editor must try to make this marriage work. The best books are not always those in which a rarely gifted writer draws his own pictures, but those in which an illustrator, working in harmony with an author, enriches the written word and adds a new and valid dimension. A successful collaboration is worth many failures, and the give and take can be mutually rewarding.

William Stobbs, another winner of the Kate Greenaway Medal, has many times worked successfully with his authors. If he makes a hilly background when it should have been flat, he cheerfully levels it down. Nevertheless, when he once appeared on a platform as part of a Brains Trust team that included an author who confessed that she had several times altered her text to suit a slightly inaccurate illustration, he was seen to leap to his feet, crying, "Let me embrace you!"

Nonny Hogrogian, who won the Caldecott Award in 1966, is an artist who has worked in a publishing house and can say:

> The manuscript does come first and from this everything grows. The story sets the pace, calls for a particular kind of art work, type face, format, paper and binding. It was when I began to realize how important all of these things are to a beautiful and well-integrated book that the excitement set in.[5]

In the gentler world of 1865 when *Alice's Adventures in Wonderland* first made its appearance, the author was able to express his views on the "defective" printing, a matter in which he was most scrupulous. At his insistence the majority of the first issue was withdrawn. It is unthinkable today that an author or artist could achieve the rejection of a printing job. Fortunately, however, an editor can, and sometimes does; but he is hampered by the sad fact that his public is largely uncritical and will often accept without comment books that should be rejected. A reviewer may possibly spot defective printing, but a good story, even with unreadable type and poor illustrations, will sell. Without the support of his customers, the editor's case is weakened and unless the printing is bad enough to scream aloud, author and illustrator must suffer.

[4]David Fletcher, "Pictures on Paper," *The Horn Book Magazine,* February 1961.

[5]Nonny Hogrogian, *Publishers' Weekly,* February 21, 1966.

The beanstalk grew quite close to Jack's window, so all he had to do was to step out into the branches. At once he began to climb and he climbed and he climbed and he climbed and he climbed: higher and higher, till his arms and legs ached. Clouds rolled below him, but still the beanstalk went higher. Far, far below, he could see his mother and their little cottage.

34. WILLIAM STOBBS: *Jack and the Beanstalk*

It is interesting today to consider the printing techniques that directly affect the artist; to compare them with those of 1865, or those of 1936, and decide whether the artist should be the servant of the machine, or the machine the servant of the artist.

In 1936 Leslie Brooke was established in England and the United States as an outstanding illustrator of children's books in the tradition of Caldecott and Walter Crane. When proudly, as editor, I sent him a copy of *Little Tim and the Brave Sea Captain* by Edward Ardizzone, he wrote:

I think Little Tim is an excellent hero of a most alive book and I congratulate you and the Press [Oxford University Press] on having brought it out without losing the vitality of the first drawings, without an over-insistence on the duties of book-making that would inevitably have tamed them down. It carries out fully the effect that it suggests

— of a home-made picture book put together by a father for his son. (Quite likely it's nothing of the sort — but the work of a middle-aged daughter of an inland vicarage — one never can tell.) Whatever it be, the results are authentic — the work of somebody who knows the sea, and sailor folk and seaside houses and smoky chimn — but I can't spell the plural.

You will have to expound the method of it all to me some day: it is described as lithographed — yet I seem to find traces of a half-tone screen everywhere: but that will wait, and my enjoyment of it all is immediate. . . .

Leslie Brooke was generous in his praise of other artists, and it was inevitable that he would appreciate the work of Edward Ardizzone, who shared his affection for and understanding of children. The question about lithography is also of interest because, as an artist, Leslie Brooke stood in the period of transition from stone to metal, which was to revolutionize color printing. To him "lithographed" implied hand work and usually a large stone, on which the artist etched out his design mirror-backwards for printing by lithography. Leslie Brooke himself may have done some of his own work in this way, but it is more likely that, like Beatrix Potter, he painted his pictures (the colored ones) as he wanted them in the finished book. The camera, which had by now taken the place of the hand of craftsmen like Edmund Evans, then photographed out the three primary colors — red, blue, yellow — plus black, from which four photographs for four separate plates were made, with a screen to cut down the strength where more delicate shading required it. But these color pictures were printed by letterpress — that is, from a raised printing surface. It was necessary always to print them on coated shiny paper because on a matt paper the delicate raised surface of the screening would clog with ink. Leslie Brooke did not realize when he wrote to me that experiments in photolithography were proving successfully that this letterpress technique could be used and the separate plates with their fine screens could be printed on ordinary matt-surface paper.

The principle of lithography, discovered by Senefelder at the beginning of the nineteenth century, is the basic one that oil and water do not mix. There is, therefore, no raised printing surface, but a stone or a metal plate treated in such a way that the printer's ink adheres to the required sticky areas and does not adhere elsewhere. So delicate is the touch of the lithographic plate on the paper that even the finest screens do not clog with ink. When artists worked on stone, they achieved a soft effect by drawing lightly, a solid effect by drawing heavily, but there was, of course, no screening. When, however, the camera and the metal plate came to be used by the lithographic printer, a whole new field of color reproduction became available to the artist.

It is interesting that one of the first picture books printed by photolithography was the one about which Leslie Brooke wrote: *Little Tim and the Brave Sea Captain*. The four basic color plates were on metal thin enough to wrap around cylinders which, one at a time, as they turned, printed each color onto a rubber cylinder which, in its turn, printed the image onto the paper. This gave an even softer effect than if printed directly onto the paper and allowed the image to be front-to on the plate since it was reversed on the rubber and printed right way round on the paper. In America this process is called "offset lithography" because the colors are *offset* from metal or rubber to paper. In England, although the process is the same, the work of the camera is more often honored than the work of the rubber cylinder, i.e., "photolithography," or, abbreviated, "photolitho."

The first edition of *Little Tim* was printed in New York in the summer of 1935 and had the rough passage of all pioneers. In particular, the ink failed to dry because it was very hot and very damp; the paper expanded and then contracted, making the register of one color on the next uncertain, and there were all kinds of minor technical hitches. The final result was a large sixty-four-page book, carrying the color on thirty-two of these pages with blanks in between. This was not intended, but was the result of the drying problem. It was, nevertheless, a most beautiful book and, as Leslie Brooke said, "printed without losing the vitality of the first drawings."

A milestone had been passed and a discovery made about the printing of picture books. Why then did they not at once pour forth in a stream from the new presses? The answer is a simple one: cost. The hours spent by the camera man, and even more by the technician who had to retouch and correct the camera's work, made photo-offset lithography possible only for *Fortune* and other high-priced magazines or gift books. Moreover, picture books could not be printed in very large editions (which would have helped the cost per copy) and it was difficult to persuade buyers to pay very much when the product went to sticky hands and tearing fingers.

In the United States the clever editors persuaded

their illustrators to do the work of camera and retoucher by making their own separations for each
color. Sometimes an artist was paid an additional fee
for making his own color separations, but often a
royalty covered both the work of separating out the
colors and the original art work. This labor of the artist greatly cut production costs. Indeed color might
not have been possible at all if the artist hadn't
learned to cooperate in this way. The result was quite
like the old lithography from stone and, since the work
was done by hand, shading was obtained by softening
the line, often by crayon strokes, and not, at first, by
a mechanical screen. The development of this craft of
color separation by American artists from the mid-

thirties to the present day is a fascinating chapter in
printing and publishing history. As the artist's skill
developed, the printer's skill also improved until it
was possible to produce an almost flawless result
in, for example, *A White Heron* with Barbara
Cooney's illustrations. Her earlier color separations
had, for the most part, been simply line drawings with
areas of solid color, as in *Chanticleer and the Fox*
and *The Little Juggler*. Her separations for *A White
Heron*, however, were given a wash effect which she
obtained by tying chamois leather over her brush.
The printer faithfully reproduced each delicately
shaded separation by using a screen in the making
of his plates.

35. EDWARD STANDON: *The Singing Rhinoceros*

practised and practised AND PRACTISED.

For various reasons, such as free education, better wages and shorter working hours, there became less difference between upper and lower classes, rich and poor. Ordinary men and women claimed the right to their say in the government of the country, and in the parks on Sundays all kinds of ideas were freely expressed, though some speakers got into trouble with the police.

Free libraries were opened where people could borrow books to read if they could not or did not want to buy them.

New universities were opened in different towns, and clever men who could not afford the fees could often go to them without paying.

47

36.   CLARKE HUTTON:
A Picture History of Britain

Barbara Cooney is a master in this craft, but one thinks also of Lynd Ward, Marcia Brown, Maurice Sendak, H. A. Rey, and many other American artists. Since their work made it possible to produce picture books at reasonable prices, the market in the United States has been flooded with them. There are now all degrees of skill; all manner of sizes and shapes.

In England, on the other hand, where the picture book had had its early start with Caldecott, Greenaway, Crane and their followers in the early years of the twentieth century, later English artists either found the work of color separation unattractive or lacked the necessary skill and training. It is possible also that editors found it easier to import American and Continental picture books. For whatever reason, from the thirties to the fifties, the picture book in England can, perhaps, be said to have languished.

Edward Ardizzone learned to do color separations, so also did V. H. Drummond and William Stobbs, while Clarke Hutton was a true lithographer, either on metal or on stone; but the artist in England never really became the craftsman plate-maker that he did in America, except in the case of the non-fiction Puffin picture books.

As I have said, color printing in most countries continued to improve during this period. Certain artists whose work could command a sufficiently large printing to bring the price per copy down, were produced by photolithography, which had reached a very high standard. Air-conditioning, better cameras, and precision presses printing two or even four colors at once, made the first production of *Little Tim* in 1936 seem very primitive. This development in printing was most noticeable on the Continent. But the work,

37. LYND WARD:
   My Friend Mac

63

for example, of Virginia Lee Burton in *The Little House* and Bemelmans in the *Madeline* books, which were printed in the United States, as well as the later *Tim* books of Ardizzone in England, were most successfully printed by photo-offset lithography. The improved machine made beautiful color possible, but for most picture books the cost still remained prohibitive.

Recently the machine has become increasingly accurate so that expensive correction has been largely eliminated, and electronics — the Vario-Klischograph (or scanner) — may in time replace the work of the camera altogether. With this relatively new machine another revolution in lithographic printing may well emerge, a revolution as important to the artist as the move from stone to metal thirty years ago. It is interesting to observe that England and the Continent,

where the artist has not become skilled in separation work, have been readier to experiment with the Vario-Klischograph for picture books than the United States, where the habit of Man rather than Machine has now become deeply rooted. As yet the electronic scanner cannot reproduce all kinds of painting and drawing successfully, and it is limited by restrictions in size. But if it fulfills its promise, the artist will be better served than ever before and will be free to use a full palette without restraint.

An experiment in color reproduction with the Vario-Klischograph will be seen in Pauline Baynes's full-color illustrations for A *Dictionary of Chivalry* by Grant Uden, to be published early in 1968, by Constable Young Books, Ltd., in England and Thomas Y. Crowell in America. At the time of writing, work is in progress with the printer in Eng-

land, W. S. Cowell. This will reveal the potential of
the Vario-Klischograph since artist and printer together studied the idiosyncracies of the machine before any painting was done. In the early development
of any new printing technique, this collaboration of
artist and printer is wise, and to this end the services
of the publisher's editor can be invaluable. As the
machine is perfected, its weaknesses may well be
eliminated until every test and problem supplied by
the artist will be met and solved. Another recent
book for which the same printer made use of the
Vario-Klischograph was *The Silver Wood* by Douglas J. Kirby with pictures by Jenny Williams, which
Four Winds Press will publish in America in 1967.

As the printing machine and the printing craft
have developed, the expansion of the market for children's books has also helped with the problem of cost.
It has always been true of lithography that once the

plates have been made and corrected, the printing of
a large edition can substantially reduce the cost per
copy. Publishers have therefore endeavored to print
as many copies as possible in one run, or printing. At
the Frankfurt Book Fair, at the Children's Book Fair
in Bologna, at editors' desks in the United States,
Great Britain and on the Continent, cooperative
plans are made, and as a result many picture books
have been printed inexpensively by expensive photolithography. This is true of most of the books of Brian
Wildsmith, Anna and Edward Standon, John Burningham, and *The Three Poor Tailors*, illustrated by
Victor Ambrus, winner of the Kate Greenaway
Medal for 1965. With very careful pre-planning
American and English editions as well as those in
foreign languages (with a change in the black plate)
can bring the printing to thirty or forty thousand
copies and the published price to a reasonable figure.

38. JENNY WILLIAMS: jacket for *The Silver Wood*

39. JOHN BURNINGHAM: *Chitty-Chitty-Bang-Bang*

40. VICTOR AMBRUS: *The Three Poor Tailors*

But the sun was hot and the tailors grew very thirsty,
so they decided to go to the inn to rest and eat.

Cooperation between countries, however, can be as difficult as that between author and artist. There is more of what one can label "moral" editing in the United States than in England. A picture book in which, for example, a hiccupping hippo is cured by laughter when he meets a beautiful girl hippo who suffers from the same complaint is considered by the American editor to be "suggestive" and the girl must become, alas, a friend of unspecified sex. Also in America today it is impossible to marry a black bunny to a white one, or to allow golliwogs in picture books. With a world-wide edition, moreover, difficulties of negotation can lead to disaster, and while a first printing may be achieved successfully, the reprint can prove impossible. Sweden, Switzerland and the United States may sell the book quickly and need an early reprint, while England and Germany may be slower off the mark. Since the whole operation is geared to a large printing and a low per-copy price, plans can break down and even end by forcing the book out of print.

Many American publishers do not now need foreign cooperation for a large printing of a picture book. Sales of books by Maurice Sendak, Barbara Cooney, Ezra Jack Keats, Evaline Ness, Nonny Hogrogian, Marcia Brown, Robert McCloskey and many others are sufficient to justify a large printing which is designed only for the American market.

Electronics and modern printing presses are today giving the artist and his editor a new freedom to be creative. It is to be hoped that in the years leading to the next volume of *Illustrators of Children's Books* there will be an even wider and more spectacular proliferation of the picture book.

And birds came!
All sorts of birds,
fluttering
and twittering
and cooing.
They all knew Jennie.
Some ate out of her hand.
Others hopped happily on her head.
Soon every last crumb was gone,
and away they flew!
For a while Jennie forgot about her new hat.

41. EZRA JACK KEATS: *Jennie's Hat*

WHALE OF A TAIL!...
    Or 'twas t'other-way-round —
the tail of a whale had pulled up
Burt!
    Burt grabbed the pump handle
and hung on while he swung around,
this-a-way, that-a-way. The giggling
gull teetered on the tip of the tiller
and laughed fit to split.
    Burt finally slacked up on the
line, or 'twas t'other-way-round —
finally the *tail* slacked up on the line.
But then the tail began to thrash
about, this-a-way, that-a-way, in
such a manner as to call Burt's attention to the fact that there was a

42. ROBERT MC CLOSKEY: *Burt Dow, Deep-Water-Man*

43. BRIAN WILDSMITH: *Brian Wildsmith's A B C*

54

BEATRIX POTTER is unique. Studying her life again, in the light of all the centenary year has brought us — the drawings never before shown; her letters; above all, the *Journal*, one begins to understand a little of why she is unique, and what are the qualities that make up the quality that is Beatrix Potter.

In the world of children's books there have been a few of those most fortunate of people: authors who are also artists and so can illustrate their work, or artists who can write their own text. Most authors — and artists — have to search for this 'other self', and this invariably ends in a compromise because no matter how sympathetic the personalities, two visions can never be exactly the same. As a writer I have to admit to a feeling of shock when I first see how the creatures of my imagination appear in the illustrator's imagination, though I do not think any author could have been better served than I, with Adrienne Adams, William Pène du Bois, Jean Primrose — especially Jean Primrose and Carol Barker — all talented and sensitive artists. To be free of this 'shock', to have the double talent of being able to write *and* draw and paint must be supreme satisfaction. Yet in most cases it does not attain to this, because when the two talents are possessed by one person, the satisfaction is usually marred — one side or the other is stronger; either the illustrations are good but the text is weak, or the story is strong, the illustrations sketchy; very rarely do they balance. But never, I think, has there been a double gift of such calibre as Beatrix Potter's, certainly not in books for small children.

1966 saw her centenary. A hundred years had passed since their first child, a daughter, Helen Beatrix, was born to Mr. and Mrs. Rupert Potter, an upper middle class couple living in a large house: Number Two, Bolton Gardens, in Kensington, London. The Potters were rich, with fortunes on both sides from Lancashire cotton mills; but in their nursery extreme plainness was the ruling, with strictness, quietness and discouragement of all personal vanity. Sir John Everett Millais, a friend of the family, offered to paint the rosy little dumpling of a girl — she was to be a dumpling

all her life — but the Potters refused in case it would make her self-consequential. Beatrix Potter kept to these plain precepts all her life and she would have been astounded, perhaps in her odd way not best pleased, if she could have known what this July of 1966 called forth. Not even the people most concerned with her — her publishers, Frederick Warne and Company; her biographer, Margaret Lane; and that most patient and devoted of her adherents, Mr. Leslie Linder who edited *The Art of Beatrix Potter* and deciphered the code of her journal — had any idea that the public response would be so overwhelming.

The Journal of Beatrix Potter from 1881 to 1897 that has taught us so much about her was published for the centenary. Experienced publishers though

4.

BEATRIX POTTER: centenary of an ARTIST-WRITER

by Rumer Godden

they were, Frederick Warne originally planned to bring it out in a limited and expensive edition, thinking there would be little demand for it. Mr. Linder persuaded them otherwise; he had had the manuscript six years before he found the key to its code and even then the deciphering was a feat of love and patience because it was written in miniscule handwriting. But he knew the value of what he had 'opened'; he convinced Frederick Warne of its worth, and the *Journal* was published in the ordinary way. It became a best seller.

Essays and articles on Beatrix Potter appeared, too, in magazines and newspapers on both sides of the Atlantic, while the Beatrix Potter Exhibition at the National Book League in London broke all records.

The League had never had such crowds, crowds of all ages, two or younger to ninety-two or older; young couples brought their children and one had the refreshing sight of still another generation taking to Beatrix Potter — little children, thank God, do not change — and there were delighted cries as Tom Kitten or Mrs. Tiggy-Winkle or Peter Rabbit were recognized in the show cases. At the same time there were serious critics of art, art students and fellow artists, all looking and learning as they studied the drawings.

Very interesting, too, was it for Mr. Linder, the editors of Frederick Warne's, myself and other devotees of Beatrix Potter to watch the palpable puzzlement of some publishers and children's editors as they tried to understand what caused all this enthusiasm. Perhaps they had been schooled in the belief so prevalent nowadays that books for small children must be comical, facile, innocuous as to drama — and large in size. The Beatrix Potter books are none of these things; they are small, extremely dramatic, not blinking the facts of life and birth and death; they are not easy, often having long rhythmical words that make no concessions to baby talk, and they have a staid solemnity about them, much like the solemnity on a small child's face when he is intent on something. Of course children love to laugh, and Beatrix Potter has humour of — as Margaret Lane[1] calls it — a very ironical and loving kind; but she knew that small children are essentially serious, even grave, a fact that such editors do not seem able to grasp. To make children laugh is not necessarily to capture their hearts.

To such eyes and tastes, Beatrix Potter's soft greens, greys, sepias and pastel colours, her careful detail seem what they would call old fashioned. One guesses they would have much the same reaction to a Constable or a Samuel Palmer, artists with whom Beatrix Potter has been compared, though she said it was absolute bosh and utter nonsense when told this. Beatrix Potter cannot be 'old fashioned' because she has never been 'fashionable' — only, and steadily, loved with an increasing love. Her sales are counted now not in thousands but in millions, and are rising every year.

There is undoubtedly a charm about her books, charm not meaning 'charming,' but the noun charm in the sense of a spell; 'charm' not 'magic' because magic suggests whimsy which is far removed from Beatrix Potter's work. The books have a quality, something extra beyond the writing and painting, a quality that makes her books, as perceptive critics have said, in fact the *only* real and outstanding classics for small children. This may seem an astonishing claim. There must, one thinks, be others. The Winnie the Pooh series? But A. A. Milne does not qualify for both art and literature; besides, for me, he always wrote

with one eye on the grown-ups. Some of the other animal series? By comparison they all seem overdone. The claim is true: no one else has succeeded in equalling Beatrix Potter.

She was always an unusual person; unlike most of us, she was never 'alloyed' — perhaps because she was strangely solitary. The Victorian upper classes had the custom of immuring their children away in nursery and schoolroom under the strict supervision of a nurse or governess, and seeing little of them. Beatrix's brother, Bertram, was not born until she was six years old and, as soon as he was old enough, was sent away to school — something not considered necessary for young Beatrix. Nor, it seemed, did she have any friends but worked and lived a lone child.

Solitude and dullness can be rich soil for a child who often relieves it by building up an intense inner life, a life of imagination; even in those days Beatrix — and sometimes Bertram — stitched odd bits of paper together into little drawing books, and filled them. Beatrix's were — as Margaret Lane writes in *The Tale of Beatrix Potter* — 'as careful of detail as a child naturalist of ten years old can be; but here and there on the grubby pages fantasy breaks through — mufflers appear round the necks of newts, rabbits walk upright, skate on ice, carry umbrellas, walk out in bonnets and mantles like Mrs. Potter's.'[2]

Beatrix Potter has had so many imitators that it is difficult for us to realise how original was this fantasy. She created a whole new province of the animal world, one that if it were not for herself, intelligent people would deplore because it has become, not a world of animals but animal humans doing human things with human thoughts. She alone has succeeded in keeping the balance, which is why the originality remains; no one else has been able to capture it. Miss Potter seems to have been aware of this and once wrote: 'Thank goodness, my education was neglected. . . . The reason I am glad I did not go to school — it would have rubbed off some of the originality (if I had not died of shyness. . . .')[3] The shyness was certainly a factor in keeping the young Beatrix to her-

[1]*The Tale of Beatrix Potter.* A Biography by Margaret Lane. Frederick Warne & Co., Ltd.: London and New York.

[2]Ibid.
[3]Ibid.

self; but there was also an obstinacy — obstinacy or the instinctive integrity of the true artist? The Potters were not, as they have often been accused of being, quite blind to their daughter's talent, though it was called 'a taste for drawing'; the first governess they gave her, Miss Hammond, encouraged it, as the remarkable early drawings of flowers and interior details show; and — probably through Miss Hammond's in-

stigation — from the age of twelve until she was seventeen, Beatrix had drawing lessons from a Miss Cameron and even gained an Art student's certificate from the Science and Art Department of the Committee of Council on Education — to give it its sonorous title. Was it, one wonders, a forerunner of the Royal Drawing Society whose examinations became widely known? The fifteen year old Beatrix's certificate testi-

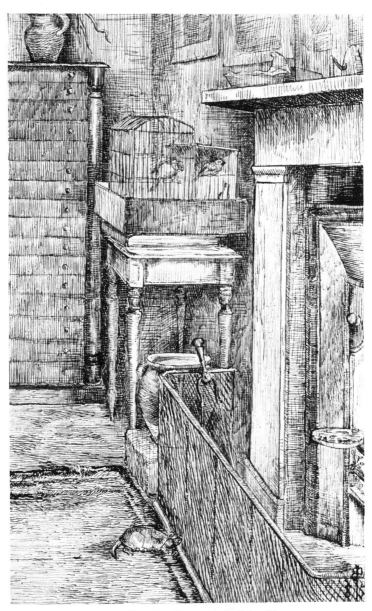

44. BEATRIX POTTER: *Drawing, Corner of the School Room*
2 Bolton Gardens, Nov. 26th, 1885

fies that 'in freehand drawing, practical geometry, linear perspective and model drawing' she was of Second Grade. It was the only certificate of education she ever gained and is in a drawer of the room at Hill Top, Sawrey, in Westmoreland where her pictures and books are shown. 'I have great reason to be grateful to her [Miss Cameron],' she wrote in the *Journal* of 1883, 'though we were not on particularly good terms for the last good while. I have learnt from her free-hand, model, geometry, perspective and a little watercolour flower painting.'[4] It is interesting here to note that Beatrix Potter's later flowers do not compare with her berries, leaves, ferns and animals.

[4]*The Journal of Beatrix Potter from 1881 to 1897.* Transcribed from her code writing by Leslie Linder, Frederick Warne & Co., Ltd.: London and New York.

Unless otherwise noted, all the direct quotes from Beatrix Potter are found in this source.

'Not on particularly good terms.' In 1884, through Millais, Beatrix Potter went to a Mrs. A. for twelve lessons. 'Can have no more as Mrs. A.'s charge is high,' she writes, but adds in characteristic fashion: 'Of course, I shall paint just as I like when not with her.' After the second lesson doubt, even worse doubt than she had had with Miss Cameron, set in. 'Believe, though I would not tell any one on any account, that I don't like it. . . . Wish it did not cost so much. . . .' Later it got worse — and worrying. 'Had a model for the first time at Mrs. A., a nice little old lady . . . who will come out a ghastly object with Mrs. A.'s tones and lights.' '. . . my temper has been boiling like a kettle.

45. BEATRIX POTTER: *Drawing, Woodland Sketch*

. . . I do wish these drawing lessons were over so that I could have some peace and sleep of nights!' ' . . . I can't bear those horrid paints and, they've put me out for using my own'; and of Mrs. A.'s style: '. . . shall I catch it? I think and hope my self-will which got me into so many scrapes will guard me here. . . .' One wants to say thank God for the self-will! Mrs. A.'s methods seem to have been meretricious in the extreme — but Beatrix was troubled, not only for that; she was probably fighting the opinions of her father and mother as well. 'I hope it is not pride that makes me so stiff against teaching,' she wrote when she was eighteen. 'It [painting] cannot be taught, nothing after perspective, anatomy and the mixing of paints with medium. . . .'

There is much emphasis nowadays on being trained, being taught. Quite an elderly teenager will say, 'Oh, we haven't done that' as an excuse for not knowing a book or a poem as if, outside school, there were no ears or eyes, no minds that could explore for themselves. Young people cannot start to work unless they are 'trained' for it — and the training is often looked on as a kind of abracadabra able to bestow 'instant talent' where perhaps there was none before; talent itself gets overlaid with facility, instead of developing, growing stronger and individual as it would if it used its own muscles — its own power — instead of someone else's. These were things that Beatrix Potter instinctively knew, but for a girl of eighteen to set her opinion up against the Olympian adults of 1884, perhaps even such an impressive adult as Millais, took much courage. Yet Beatrix steadily went her own way.

I have on my desk as I write one of her small home-made portfolios, its boards covered stoutly in holland and lined with white linen, with linen flaps to guard the sketches; it is shabby, its edges worn to grubbiness, worn because all through what have been called those 'hidden decades', Beatrix Potter's twenties and thirties, it went with her on countless visits to the National History Museum, to other museums, to different interiors, and exteriors of streets, a door-step,

gables, windows. Perhaps it was the heavy ornateness of Bolton Gardens that made Beatrix Potter love simple things so much: flagged floors, scrubbed tables, a polished oven door, rag rugs; with her artist's eye for detail, she delighted in the shape of a saucepan or a flat iron: a pattern of sprigged calico, the colour of a pink and white pie dish. 'It is all the same, drawing, painting, modelling . . .' she wrote '. . . the irresistible desire to copy any beautiful object which strikes the eye. Why cannot one be content to look at it? I cannot rest, I must draw . . .' The 'queerest things,' as she said herself, struck her with beauty. 'I caught myself in the backyard making a careful and admiring copy of the swill bucket, and the laugh it gave me brought me round.'

There were no more lessons except, when her cousin Alice came to stay, the two of them thought they would learn a kind of printing called Platinotype and they had a couple of 'excessively expensive lessons' at the Polytechnic. They were going to have a number, but the lessons were a guinea each! This awe of what seems a fairly reasonable price, even taking the difference in the buying power of money today, does throw a dislikeable light on Mr. and Mrs. Potter; very little money, beyond that for her absolute necessities, was spent on Beatrix yet the Potters were extravagant over themselves. At one time they went to fancy dress balls and for each occasion costumes were especially made by the theatrical *costumiers* Simmons; if wigs were necessary they, too, were made, but at Willy Clarkson's. Mr. Potter, for instance, had a complete Elizabethan costume, perfect in every detail even to the handsewn boots; a court dress — but it may have been used for going to court — had buttons of real diamonds. He spent lavishly on his photography, yet a guinea for a lesson for the talented Beatrix was deemed exorbitant. It is not strange that at times she felt bitter. 'It was a singular thing,' she writes in a footnote to the *Journal*, 'when I had always shown a taste for drawing, that I should have reached the age of seventeen [*and lived in London. R. G.*] without being taken to see any collection of pictures other

46. BEATRIX POTTER: *Drawing, Cinderella's Carriage*

than . . .' The footnote breaks off so that we shall never know what it was she did see.

She made up for this later. 'I have been to no less than four picture galleries this afternoon.' The *Journal* is full of notes made on these visits, all of them careful analysis of the paintings; her own impressions and summings ups were sometimes exceedingly frank! '1882 . . . Went to the Academy. . . . Think it rather bad. Few striking pictures, many simply shocking,' and often in these notes the unmistakeable frustration shows. Bertram by now had left home and was an established artist and, 'That picture by Angelica Kauffman is something,' Beatrix Potter wrote in the *Journal*, 'it shows what a woman has done.' Or, 'Went on

to the National Gallery. . . . Swarms of young ladies painting, frightfully for the most part, O dear, if I was a boy and had courage!'

Millais helped her by showing her how to mix her paints: he was kind but one wonders if he ever dreamed that, for sheer fame, his 'little friend' would one day outshine him, rich and fashionable academician as he was? Perhaps he had an inkling of her worth; he knew that Beatrix looked at things with her own eyes and had a clear vision, remarkable in so young a girl. '. . . Plenty of people can *draw*,' he said once to her, 'but you . . . have observation.'

She had indeed and grew into a fine naturalist. A 'packing list' of this time shows the unique mixture of talents and interests that were beginning to emerge; after a few necessary clothes the list runs:

> Spirit bottles
> Virgil
> 2 Bird skeletons
> Paint stoat's eyes
> Dress scraps [*for making patchwork or to study for animal clothes? R. G.*]
> Knitting

This — one could call it professional — interest in nature may seem odd in a city-bred woman but the Potters had always left London twice a year; in the spring for the West country, in summer for Scotland, and later, the Lakes where Beatrix Potter discovered her lasting love for the Westmoreland fells, its villages and people. This love gives her books an element not often found in books for little children, the deeply felt beauty of the countryside, the authentic 'dewy freshness' so often spoken of. Mr. and Mrs. Potter, strict and possessive though they were, made this love possible, perhaps unwittingly, and it seems they did not stand in their daughter's way when the success of the books allowed her to buy Hill Top Farm and

47. BEATRIX POTTER: *Drawing, The Rabbit's Dream*

Castle Cottage — though until she married she could only 'visit,' not live, in them. It is marvellous to think that from the money made by such little books she was eventually able to buy not only these loved homes, but thousands of acres of fell and farmland which she gave to the National Trust.

As children those country months had been what she and Bertram lived for, and they did not only play in them; Margaret Lane gives an account of their finding a dead fox, skinning it and boiling it and finally, with their small hands articulating the skeleton. Back in stuffy Bolton Gardens, Beatrix lived those months over again in her mind, fostering what grew to be a quiet passion for small wild animals and remarking their minutest details in pages and pages drawn and painted with skeletons, beaks, claws, fur and feathers. She carried her observations to a minuteness of which most of us do not dream. In the *Journal* she wrote of the deaths by sad accident of a family of snails she had kept, some of them for a year, all of them distinct and named. 'I am very much put out . . .' she wrote, '. . . they have such a surprising difference of character!'

Her parents let her keep the strange assortment of creatures she brought back to Bolton Gardens: newts, snails, lizards, a hedgehog, rabbits, mice. When she was seventeen, she visited Portsmouth. 'In the High Street was a charming bird-shop where they had a most incredible number of dormice. . . . Am considering how it would be possible to convey some home.' Through all the visits to the Fleet, the historic *Victory* with its memories of Nelson, the trips across the water, she was obsessed by those mice. 'Again looked upon those dormice. Would they carry in a biscuit canister? They are grievously afflicted with tickles.' She does not say if she bought them, but we know she had a dormouse, Xarifa, who died in her hand. 'I wonder if ever another doormouse had so many acquaintances . . .' she wrote in grief. '. . . Mr. Bright, Mr. T. Millais, and Mr. Leigh Smith had admired and stroked her.' There was Benjamin Bouncer, the rabbit who travelled on a leather strap and ate peppermints. There

was the real hedgehog who sat for Mrs. Tiggy-Winkle and did not care over much for posing. 'So long as she can go to sleep on my knee she is delighted, but if she is propped up on end for half an hour, she first begins to yawn pathetically and then she *does* bite!'[5] There were mice, particularly Hunca Munca and Tom Thumb, in the glass doll's house. Hunca Munca met her end by falling off the chandelier.

As the books were published, the animals were necessary because, whilst brilliantly inventive in writing, Beatrix Potter could never draw nor paint anything from imagination — which is why, on a visit to Sawrey, so much springs to life: in Hill Top is the very cooking range of the Roly Poly puddings; the garden of Tom Kitten is there; the farmyard of Jemima Puddleduck. Countless corners of the village are in the books, and the village store is the shop in *Ginger and Pickles*.

It was the same with the details: if there were a cup, like the Spode in *The Tailor of Gloucester*, she had to find the right cup. In clearing up Castle Cottage after her death, her heirs found the handkerchief worn as a shawl by Jemima Puddleduck. Nor could Beatrix Potter draw humans; Mr. McGregor for example is always in the far distance and, if one examines the originals of Mrs. Tiggy-Winkle, in one painting the figure of Lucie is stuck on, because Miss Potter tried over and over again to 'get her' — and never did. One suspects that she did not look at humans as deeply as she looked at animals; indeed it seems she saw people as animals rather than animals as people, a subtle distinction. 'How amusing Aunt Harriet is . . .' she writes in her *Journal*, 'she is more like a weasel than ever. . . .'

Probably Beatrix Potter, as a perfectionist, was the first artist-writer to treat children's books with the respect due to literature and art: to visit museums for them, research, study, consult, no detail being too small, no source too far; but her drawings needed her own text to bring out their full strength. The illustrations that, before she came to her own books, she did for Bre'r Fox and Bre'r Rabbit in the Uncle Remus

[5] *The Tale of Beatrix Potter*. A Biography by Margaret Lane. Frederick Warne & Co., Ltd.: London and New York.

tales are curiously wrong, quite out of keeping, as are the few she did for *Alice in Wonderland* and I have always thought the paintings that match *Appley Dapply's Nursery Rhymes* and *Cecily Parsleys's Nursery Rhymes* feeble in comparison with the rest of her work.

The best of all the Beatrix Potter books is *The Tailor of Gloucester*. Its spell is complete, a spell compounded of the old tailor's fever dream, the ancient city with its gables and cobbles and the moonlit Christmas Eve into which the legend of the animals' talking at midnight comes like a peal of bells; the words are so skillfully chosen that the whole book has a rhythm of rustling and scampering, of tapping and little voices laughing, all as light as mouse feet, maddening Simpkin the cat but coming to the old tailor's rescue. This is perhaps the most subtle children's book ever written, yet it is crystal clear and seizes a child's imagination with its pitiful refrain, 'No more twist. No more twist.' It is as exquisitely worked as the rare embroideries that Beatrix Potter studied in the Victoria and Albert Museum and painted into the Lord Mayor's waistcoat; the original water colours for *The Tailor of Gloucester* are so fine that their full beauty cannot be seen without a magnifying glass.

Beatrix Potter's work was done in full colour from water-colour originals, with none of the fuss over separations or fancy camera and plate work which are such obstacles today between the artist's original and the reproduction. How closely Frederick Warne & Company reproduced her subtle shades could be seen at the Exhibition by comparing the originals with the printed pages; the fidelity is amazing — yet Peter Rabbit was published in 1902 when, one supposes, printing was not technically as good as it is now.

Printing, perhaps, was not; but when I asked Mr. Linder why colour separations are so much used nowadays, he answered sadly that the greater control was needed now because the standard of skill of the personnel is not as great as in Miss Potter's days when the work was done by *artists* and *craftsmen*. Mr.

Evans, who did all her colour work, was a pioneer of three-colour printing and his system had just been introduced when her books were written.

Another factor, said Mr. Linder, that made this three-colour process so effective in her case was that her work was virtually perfect and needed no corrections when making the plates.

Costs have risen fantastically, we all know that; but perhaps we should seek to swing back from modern elaborateness to the Potter and Warne simplicity; that and their modesty, for Beatrix Potter said her books were made small to fit children's hands, not to impress grown ups. Her wise publishers have kept this modesty, making none of the so-called improvements that many editors think necessary nowadays; the format of the Beatrix Potter books has not varied one iota since *The Tale of Peter Rabbit* was first published.

Few of us can hope to be a Beatrix Potter with her double gift — she was *sui generis*; but we can use her as a touchstone when temptation comes on us to work faster, to be slick, produce cheaply, consent to limit our words, aim for money instead of worth, sacrifice truth for effect. Yes, how many of us insist on truth?

The truth of Beatrix Potter's animals always comes through their clothes and occupations; they are exact, never sentimentalized. Baby rabbits, for instance, do look exactly like the illustrations of Peter Rabbit or Benjamin Bunny, soft and endearing until picked up when they show the surprising life and kick that are in these characters. Under the prettiness of kittens and rabbits, of ducks and mice, is this reality that doesn't mince matters; Beatrix Potter knew that humans prey on animals, animals prey on one another and through all the books runs the toughness of real life. It is this that gives the best books their drama: Peter Rabbit's tenseness and uneasiness in Mr. McGregor's garden pervades *The Tale of Benjamin Bunny*; the cat in *The Tale of Johnny Town Mouse* stalks all through the book; and is there a more sinister character in literature than the foxy Mr. Tod?

This sounds horrifying, yet Beatrix Potter is abso-

48.   BEATRIX POTTER: *Illustration, The Tale of Two Bad Mice*

lutely to be trusted. Another outstanding quality is her balance; she always knew when to stop and knew, too, that most children like to be harrowed so long as the story turns out well in the end as hers invariably do: though Jemima Puddleduck — that silly goose — falls into Mr. Tod's clutches, the children know that Kep the collie dog is on his way to save her: the baby rabbits are restored to Flopsy; the cat is dodged by the mice. This balance is unfailing, and she can convey it by implication: the stillness of the dolls in *The Tale of Two Bad Mice* has the whole of dollness in it and sets off the liveliness and badness of the mice, Tom Thumb and Hunca Munca. Yet bad as they were they, too, keep the Potter balance: Tom Thumb puts the crooked sixpence in the dolls' Christmas stocking; Hunca Munca comes to sweep the dolls' house every day — with the stolen broom and dustpan — and the children's sense of fair play is satisfied. The

illustrations too help to keep this reassuring balance: the text may be filled with suspense — and even though it is a thimbleful it is real dramatic suspense — but the accompanying picture is tender with that reassuring atmosphere of home.

Simplicity, modesty, truth, balance: these are the qualities to be found in Beatrix Potter and, over-riding all of them, love. How many of us paint or write for love, as she did? For love of the work itself which has nothing to do with being paid for it, or with self-expression or fame? Beatrix Potter's whole heart and soul and mind went into her books: she could not do them with anything less and when, at forty-six she married the lakeland solicitor who had helped her with the buying of Hill Top, there were no more books of the old calibre.

She became Mrs. Heelis, a notable sheep-farmer.

Part II:
BIOGRAPHIES

49. ELLEN RASKIN: *Songs of Innocence*

FOREWORD

THE 452 men and women included in this second supplement to *Illustrators of Children's Books: 1744-1945* live in all parts of the world and are of all ages. Of this number, 59 illustrators have appeared in all three volumes. For some of these, such as Ludwig Bemelmans, Françoise, and Le Grand, this ten-year period has seen the end of a long and fruitful career. But many others, such as Leonard Weisgard, Barbara Cooney and Edward Ardizzone are still actively contributing to the field of children's books. The entries for these people and the additional 127 who first appeared in the second volume have been revised and updated, in most cases by the illustrators themselves. A star appears beside the names of those people who have been in the earlier volumes. In this volume 266 people appear for the first time. Many of these have been illustrating children's books for most of this ten-year period. A few have just begun in the last year or so, but the work they have done leads us to believe that they will continue to be active in the years to come.

In each of the entries there is biographical data and in most cases information on the illustrator's background and training. In a number of entries, there is an expression of the illustrator's philosophy or approach to illustrating children's books. I have tried, when possible, to use the illustrator's own words, so that, despite the brevity of the entries, one can get a sense of the person.

One of the most evident changes in the last ten years is the growing variety of techniques and materials that are being used in the preparation of illustrations, particularly those that are to be printed in color. Several things have contributed to this. There are new materials available, such as acrylic paints. There is the desire on the part of a number of illustrators, both young and old, to experiment with different textures and combinations of materials. And there is the increasing willingness on the part of the publishers to go along with new techniques and approaches to illustration. One of the results of this growing variety is a new awareness and interest on

the part of those who use children's books in how the pictures were made. Therefore, in preparing for this volume, I asked all of the illustrators to indicate what techniques and materials they have used in various books. They were also asked about their style and if they felt that it had changed over the last ten years. "Looser and freer" — again and again these two words were used by the illustrators to describe how they felt their style had changed. Joseph Low used them and went on to say that he felt the change was "partly because of personal development, partly because editorial attitudes have allowed it, partly because reproduction techniques have improved."

How art work is to be reproduced radically affects its preparation, again most particularly in the case of

BIOGRAPHIES of illustrators active: 1957-1966

COMPILED BY **Joanna Foster**

color illustrations. In all printing, the primary or basic colors must be printed separately, using a separate plate for each color. To prepare these printing plates, either the colors in a painting can be separated photographically by the printer, or the original art work can be prepared by the illustrator in such a way that each color is on a separate sheet. In the entries, this is referred to as making separations or, in some cases, as doing the color on overlays. To have the illustrator prepare the art work as separations is far less costly than to have it done photographically. The last ten years have seen an increase in the number of books illustrated in color and this has gone hand in hand with an increase in the number of illustrators who prepare their art work as separations. They often do this on request from the publisher rather than by their own choice, and in some entries there are expressions of the distaste that many illustrators have for doing separations. This attitude is well known. Far more interesting is to discover that there is also a group of illustrators who are enthusiastic about this method of working. "At first I couldn't abide separations," writes Eric Von Schmidt, who has since become very excited about "the effects and possibilities we have now that the old boys didn't." Roger Duvoisin is another who feels that acetate separations offer endless possibilities, commenting "it is the closest thing to old stone lithography. Since no camera is involved in separating the colors, the artist gets exactly what he puts in."

50.   IMERO GOBBATO: *The White Stone*

Throughout, I have pointed out artists who work only in full color or only in black-and-white, as well as those who work with limited color. There are several people now working only in black-and-white who look forward to an opportunity to do a book in color. There are others who find working in black-and-white particularly challenging and satisfying, and several

who would agree with Imero Gobbato that "I have not found yet a new medium which surpasses the old pen and ink in capacity for detail, chiaroscural richness or affinity for photographic reproduction." At the beginning of this ten-year period, concern with black-and-white illustration seemed somewhat eclipsed by the exciting developments in color, but as this period drew to a close, it appeared that more critical attention was beginning to be focused on it.

It is interesting to note the number of people who, after illustrating several children's books, have begun to write as well as illustrate them. This is particularly true in the area of picture books. I have tried to point out in the entries where the illustrator is also the designer of the book. This means that he is responsible for the layout of the pages, the choice and placement of the type, the design of the jacket and the binding. Though it vitally affects the illustrations, the design of the book is not automatically the illustrator's responsibility, nor are they all skilled in this. However, particularly in the case of picture books, illustrators may become involved with the design.

A growing number of illustrators, it appears, have been able to make a full-time career of illustrating children's books. Over half of the 502 artists in this volume devote the major part of their time to book illustration. Another 23 are teaching art as well as illustrating, 43 are primarily painters or printmakers, and 5 are theatrical designers. Of the 100 or so people who do commercial art as well as book illustration, 28 are graphic designers. Among those illustrating for magazines and advertising as well as books, it is interesting to find a number of them commenting on the greater satisfactions of book illustration as compared to the more lucrative commercial work. "What impressed me most about children's books," Bernard Waber writes, "was the unlimited, unrestricted opportunity for creativity and originality. An illustrator could rise to the top of his talent or quickly come to grips with his own limitations."

Illustrators of Children's Books: 1957-1966 deals with illustrators whose work is familiar to children in the United States and England. As I was compiling the entries, artists' letters had to be translated from Polish, Czech, French, German and Italian. There were letters from Japan, Greece, Mexico, Denmark, Sweden, and Finland. The number of people in this volume who live and work in countries other than the United States and England serves to highlight the universality of the illustrators' own special language — the language of lines and planes and color.

I am grateful to all those who have helped me in the preparation of these biographies, in particular, Joan C. Cole, Amy Kellman and Ruth Shire, the staffs of the New York Public Library and the public libraries of Weston and Westport, Connecticut.

Lyle was always one for sharing.

17

51. BERNARD WABER: *Lyle, Lyle Crocodile*

BIOGRAPHIES OF ILLUSTRATORS ACTIVE
FROM 1957 THROUGH 1966

*Asterisk following name of artist indicates an entry for this artist in either or both of the previous volumes, *Illustrators of Children's Books: 1744-1945*, and *Illustrators of Children's Books: 1946-1956*. Entries have been made under names by which each artist's work is best known, with cross references from real names to pseudonyms. In the case of an artist working under his actual name as well as his pseudonym, the entry is under the actual name, with a cross reference from the pseudonym. For books published from 1957 through 1966, illustrated by these artists, please see Bibliographies, starting on page 206.

ABRAHAMS, HILARY RUTH

Born April 18, 1938 in London, England where her childhood was spent. Attended St. Martin's School of Art, Royal College of Art, London.

"I illustrate because it comes naturally to me — I enjoy painting but I am not a painter — I like graphic representational details. I love the pen and black ink and have no need to use color; if I do, I prefer full color or nothing at all. But I always feel a good illustration in black-and-white should show color by itself — indeed it is part of the richness of a drawing," writes Hilary Abrahams. As a child she went to boarding schools where she was encouraged to paint and then went on to St. Martin's School where she took the National Diploma in Design. She considers herself lucky to have met Edward Ardizzone as a teacher at the Royal College of Art. After graduating in 1962, she began free-lancing. A year later, she married a Dutch typographer, Jan van de Watering, who is designer to the Cambridge University Press. They have a young daughter and make their home in Cambridge, England.

ADAMS, ADRIENNE*

Born in Fort Smith, Arkansas. Childhood spent in Okmulgee, Oklahoma. Attended Stephens College, Columbia, Missouri; University of Missouri; American School of Design, New York.

After graduating from the University of Missouri, Adrienne Adams returned to Oklahoma to teach in a rural school for three years. The urge to become a commercial artist took her then to New York where three months of art school was all she could afford. She began free-lance work immediately, doing displays, murals, decorative textiles, and illustrating books. Adrienne Adams speaks of this as being the " 'golden age for designers,' for there is always work for them." She is married to John Lonzo Anderson, a writer, whose *Bag of Smoke*, a story about the Montgolfiers, the first balloon ascensionists, was one of the first books for which she made the illustrations. Most recently she has illustrated *Ponies of Mykillengi*, also written

by her husband. A trip to Denmark and Iceland inspired her pictures for this book as well as for *The Ugly Duckling*. The Andersons now live "on twenty-seven acres of white birch in Hunterdon County, New Jersey." Adrienne Adams works primarily in full color, most often using either tempera, gouache, watercolor or crayon. In an article in the November 1965 issue of *American Artist*, she said "I enjoy color work more than black-and-white, but I think it is good for an artist now and then to have to depend solely on monochrome. It is certainly possible, without color, to get great variety — contrasts between plain and patterned areas; between soft and sharp edges; between strong movement and static quietness." When she does her own color separations, she uses transparent colors to show the work more nearly as it will appear in reproduction. A number of her books have been separated photographically enabling her to make her original paintings with opaque colors. Two of her books have been runners-up for the Caldecott Medal: *Houses from the Sea* in 1960 and *The Day We Saw the Sun Come Up* in 1962. She received the Alumnae Achievement Award from Stephens College in 1964. Her article on Color Separation, which appeared in the April 1965 issue of *Horn Book*, has been reprinted in this volume.

ADAMSON, GEORGE WORSLEY*

Born February 7, 1913, in New York City, and childhood was spent there and in Wigan, Lancashire, England. Attended Mining and Technical College, Wigan; Wigan School of Art; Liverpool University, Education Department; Liverpool City School of Art.

Born in New York City of Scots and Lancashire parents, George W. Adamson lived there only seven years; then Wigan, Lancashire, England, became his home. After studying art there and at the Liverpool City School of Art, where he did many experiments in aquatint, dry point and the etching processes, he exhibited in the Walker Art Gallery in Liverpool and at the Royal Academy. Then he taught, traveled and made drawings. In 1939, his work first began to appear in *Punch* and since then he has done cartoons, illustrations and many covers for that magazine. In 1940 he joined the R. A. F., had sojourns in Iceland, Texas, and Canada, flew the Atlantic as navigator, and, in July 1942, joined the Squadron in Coastal Command, flying the Catalinas. He saw the sea from Archangel to Gibraltar, visited the Bahamas and traveled through Spain. After operational flying he served as official war artist to R. A. F. Coastal Command. In 1944 he was married to Peggy Diamond. For seven years after the war he lectured in illustration and engraving at Exeter College of Art; then began free-lancing as illustrator, humorist and book designer and was elected a member of the Society of Industrial Artists. Mr. Adamson has devised and written several books in the past few years and has illustrated some fifty others. "There are adult books, educational stories, poetry and picture books for children, in full color, water color, in oils, in pen, in black-and-white with mechanical tint — serious and comic — an everchanging pattern that I enjoy. I often do the design of complete books, especially if there is only a little text or if the text is handlettered or is part of the pictures. More now than ever, I am very keen to draw with economy — to get character and a sense of realism and ease." The Adamsons have two sons and live in Exeter, Devon, England.

AKINO, FUKU

Born July 25, 1908 in Futamata, Tenryu City, Japan where her childhood was spent. Attended Sizuoka Normal School.

"Our house was isolated on a hill and I had no friends in my childhood. Passing so much time alone, I became very interested in painting and drawing. Afterwards I became a teacher in a primary school, but I thought my character did not suit with teaching." Miss Akino then went to Tokyo and was "apprenticed to a private teacher of Japanese painting." After his death she went to another teacher, this time in Kyoto. She entered the various exhibitions sponsored by the Ministry of Education and won several prizes. In this way she became well-known as an artist. In 1948 she helped to form the Sinseisaku Association and continues to be one of the chief members. The first children's book that she illustrated was *Urihime*, a folk story published by Fukuikan Children's Books of Tokyo. She has received a number of honors, among them the Mainichi Prize given by the Mainichi Newspaper and the Uemura Shoen Prize, the highest award for a woman artist. At present, she is Assistant Professor at the Kyoto Municipal Art Academy. For *The Cock and the Ghost Cat*, she used "glue, water and stone color, gold and silver leaf, and gold and silver powder. I paint often with spatula and fingers instead of a brush." Her home is now in Kyoto and she is the mother of six children.

ALAIN, pseud. (Daniel Brustlein)

Born in Alsace, France.

Though born in France and often spending a good deal of time in his Paris home, Alain is an American citizen and also has a home in New Jersey. He paints and exhibits in both countries but most of his work in graphics is done in the United States. He frequently contributes cartoons to the *New Yorker* magazine and a book of these, *Alain's Steeplechase*, was published in 1957 by Simon and Schuster. He has illustrated several children's books, including some he has also written, such as *One Two Three Going to Sea*.

ALBION, LEE SMITH

Born in Rochester, New York. Childhood was spent in Rochester and Bronxville, New York. Attended Radcliffe College; Teachers College of Columbia University; Art Students League, New York City; The Art Center, Los Angeles.

Because her father wanted her to be a children's book illustrator, Lee Albion was given art equipment as soon as she could hold a crayon and sent to art school at age ten. "Consequently I hated to draw and paint." Not until she attended the old Grand Central Art School during her last year at high school did she begin to see what she had missed. After college, under Frank Reilly's influence at the Art Students League she wanted to do magazine illustration, but found the competition was "horrendous." She began doing black-and-white spots for the *Saturday Review* and *Gourmet* along with story illustrations for *Scholastic* and *Jack and Jill*. "I married in 1965 and moved to Miami where my husband is an attorney. We have a boy born in July 1966 and I now share my studio with a baby crib. I do illustrations for books because I don't seem able to stop. I read a manuscript and I can visualize the whole thing. I ache to set it down on paper. I think, too, of the child who is to read the book and I want him to love each page and feel the atmosphere of the story." For *Cato, the Kiwi Bird* Mrs. Albion used glass printing. For other books she has used water color, pen and ink, and chalk.

ALCORN, JOHN

Born 1935 in Corona, Long Island, New York. Childhood spent on Long Island. Attended Cooper Union, New York, and studied there with Philip Grushkin, George Salter and Jerome Kuhl.

Since 1959, John Alcorn has been a free-lance artist completely, first in New York City and then from his home in Ossining, New York where he lives with wife, Phyllis, and their four boys. Before this he had worked for several months in the art department of *Esquire* and then in the CBS art department under Louis Dorfsman, whom he credits with developing his interest in typography. An article on Mr. Alcorn in the June 1, 1964 issue of *Publishers' Weekly* comments on the quite remarkable use of Victorian type faces in *Books*, which was selected by the American Institute of Graphic Arts as one of "The Fifty Books of the Year," and quotes him as saying, "The use of type is important. Most faces can be good — it depends on how they are used." John Alcorn's distinctive commercial work is well-known and has been represented in a number of major shows as well as in such magazines as *Horizon*, *McCalls*, and *Playboy*. He has also done a number of book jackets, as well as books. His first children's book was *Where in the World Do You Live?* in 1962. The *Publishers' Weekly* article noted, "Interestingly, John prefers book work to the more remunerative commercial commissions. There's more enjoyment for him, fewer limitations, and deadlines are far less tight. He averages around six months for book illustration."

ALIKI, pseud. (Aliki Liacouras Brandenberg)

Born September 3, 1929. Childhood spent in Philadelphia and its surroundings. Graduated from the Philadelphia Museum College of Art in 1951.

"Family portraits — Peter Rabbit's and my own — were my first two paintings exhibited," says Aliki. This was when she was in kindergarten. "I drew constantly, attended Saturday classes in art; studied piano and became aware of music." After art school, she spent a summer in Barbados, B. W. I. and then worked for a year in the display department of a New York store. Returning to Philadelphia, she free-lanced in advertising, display, mural painting and greeting cards. In 1956 she traveled in Germany, Italy, Greece and Switzerland where she met her husband. After her marriage in 1957, she lived in Berne and Zurich and wrote and illustrated her first children's book, *The Story of William Tell*. Since the Brandenbergs' move to New York City in 1960, Aliki has been mainly involved in illustration though she has also been working in clay, collage, silver, ceramics, enamel, papier-mâché, needle and thread. She loves to make dolls and has made a tapestry from remnants. The Brandenbergs have two small children. About her style of illustrating, Aliki writes, "Some books strike me as needing a 'modern' design, simple shapes, bright colors, contemporary type, etc. Others definitely need an 'old-fashioned' approach. I work in gouache (*A Weed is a Flower*) pen and ink, dyes and water color. *The Story of William Penn* was ink line and water color. I use illustration board, textured paper, vellum or whatever other paper fits the subject and format." She has worked in black-and-white, full and limited color. With limited color, she does her own separations on acetate or heavy tracing paper.

AMBRUS, VICTOR

Born August 19, 1935 in Budapest, Hungary where his childhood was spent. Attended the Hungarian Academy of Fine Art, Budapest; Royal College of Art, London.

"I was very interested in drawing from about the age of six, when with my grandfather's guidance I started drawing horses and historical subjects like knights in armor, Hungarian Hussars, etc." He continued drawing through grammar school and at eighteen entered art school where he studied graphic design, etching and lithography for three years. "In October 1956, the Hungarian uprising broke out, and students of the Academy became involved in the Revolution. After weeks of hopeless, tragic struggle five students of the Academy lay dead and Soviet troops took control of the city. I left the country by escaping to Austria." In 1957, he entered the Royal College of Art in London and received his diploma three years later. He began illustrating for publishers in his second year at the college and later became a free-lance illustrator and lecturer in illustration at a local art college. "In the last five years, I've illustrated about sixty-five books, mainly for children. I am now a British subject, married to an English girl who is also a painter and we have one small son. I hope to go on illustrating full color picture books and novels of historical subjects. My favorite hobby is collecting antiques, mainly old weapons and costumes, and reading books on 18th and 19th century history." Mr. Ambrus works in both black-and-white and full color. He characterizes his work as realistic, decorative and strongly influenced by etching. "I prefer to work without separations, in full color, mixing the various techniques — colored ink, water color, oil pastel, etc." In 1959 he received the award of Royal Scholar from the Royal College of Art. He is Associate of the Royal College and also of the Royal Society of Engravers. He was twice runner-up for the Kate Greenaway Medal before receiving it in 1966 for *The Three Poor Tailors*. An article on Mr. Ambrus appears in the March 1964 issue of *Junior Bookshelf* (England).

AMES, LEE JUDAH*

Born in New York City where his childhood was spent. Attended Straubenmuller Textile High School and Columbia University.

Lee J. Ames, who has been largely self-taught, showed unusual artistic promise in early childhood. In Public School 12 in the borough of Queens where he received his elementary education, the art teacher had the students work with oils and the mural which the boys did there is still in the main lobby of the school. Mr. Ames' experience has included doing animated films for the Walt Disney Studios, magazine comic strips, and advertising. He has recently been devoting his major effort to book illustration, has illustrated prolifically for many different publishers, and was artist in residence at Doubleday and Company. He still likes to do oils when time permits. He writes that his chief interest is his family which includes his wife, Jocelyn, and their children Alison Sally and Jonathan David. They live in Deer Park, New York.

ANDERSON, CLARENCE WILLIAM*

Born April 12, 1891 in Wahoo, Nebraska. Attended Wahoo High School and the School of the Art Institute of Chicago.

After art school, C. W. Anderson moved to New York and early in his career developed an interest in horses, an interest which soon absorbed him completely and eventually dominated his work. Beginning with drawings and etchings of horses, which the artist made largely for his own instruction and pleasure, he became a specialist in this field. In 1936 he wrote and illustrated *Billy and Blaze*, his first of many books about horses. Those that have followed have included books for young children, older boys and girls, and also such studies of thoroughbred horses as *Deep Through the Heart* and *A Touch of Greatness* for all ages. His most recent book is *Another Man O' War* published in the fall of 1966. A perfectionist where reproduction of his drawings is concerned, Mr. Anderson experimented with several media before he finally began working in lithography. Most of his book illustrations are made directly on the stone. Although better known, perhaps, for his illustrations, Mr. Anderson has always painted in color, his special interest being landscape. It is his conviction that the landscape in a horse subject should have the character and individuality of the place where the horses are found. Another point he makes is that the horse, from a purely artistic standpoint, possesses such perfect rhythmic proportion that it is entirely unnecessary to resort to either exaggeration or distortion to achieve good design and composition; that if an artist is capable enough he should, in the same painting, satisfy both the horseman who knows nothing of art, and the art critic who knows nothing about horses — and, further, that he should be able to accomplish this without sacrificing any part of his own artistic integrity. Mr. Anderson's prints have been displayed in most important galleries and museums throughout the country. To date there have been forty-eight books and portfolios published. Mr. Anderson makes his home in Mason, New Hampshire.

ANGELO, VALENTI*

Born June 23, 1897 in Massarosa, Tuscany, Italy. His childhood was spent there and in California.

Writing of his early life in Tuscany, Valenti Angelo says, "I first became interested in drawing when Jacobo, the village wood-carver, found me making ducks of mud beside a puddle. From that time on I was allowed to go to his shop and might stay as long as I desired. 'Do it over again and again,' he would say. 'Do it until there is nothing more to do with it. And always do your best.'" When he was eight years old Valenti came to America and lived for a while on New York's Bleecker Street. His vivid impressions of that brief stay in Little Italy were given substance forty-odd years later in his book *The Bells of Bleecker Street*. In California he went to school for two years, then he had to go to work in the fields. Later he worked as a laborer in paper mills, chemical factories, in steel and glass works. Finding that evening art classes could not give him what he wanted, he trained himself, pursuing his own study through libraries and museums, "and learned a great deal that my few school years had failed to provide." In 1926 he made his first illustrations for a book for the Grabhorn Press. Since then he has devoted most of his time to decorating books, among them the folio edition of *Leaves of Grass* and the *Song of Songs Which is Solomon's* for which he illuminated not less than 180,000 initials. In the past thirty-five years he has illustrated two hundred and twenty-five books, thirty-seven of which have been included in the Fifty Books of the Year exhibits of the American Institute of Graphic Arts. In 1937 Ruth Sawyer won the Newbery Medal for *Roller Skates* which Valenti Angelo had illustrated. In that same year he turned his hand to writing and has now published fifteen books which he has both written and illustrated. The first of these, *Nino*, is the "offspring of my memories of the little village in the Tuscan Hills." *Golden Gate* recaptures his early days in America. All of the books are peopled with farmers, fishermen and laborers, the ordinary everyday men, women and children of many backgrounds, who epitomize for him the dignity of human life and the ideals of brotherhood and democracy. In 1923 Valenti Angelo married Maxine Grimm. They have two children and make their home in Bronxville, New York.

ANGLUND, JOAN WALSH

Born January 3, 1926 in Hinsdale, Illinois where she spent her childhood. Attended the Art Institute of Chicago and the American Academy of Art, Chicago.

"My happiest memories of childhood were the hours I spent tucked away in our great dark dusty attic surrounded by mountains of books," writes Mrs. Anglund. "Both my mother and father were artists and our lives were filled with drawings and paintings — in our house we didn't write a letter or message, we drew it. I think it was this combination of solitude and the habit of expressing every idea visually that led to my doing books. Another impetus was the delight — the strong sense of life and joy — I found in my own children." Mrs. Anglund, her husband Robert and two children, Todd and Joy, live in a pre-Revolutionary house in Westport, Conn. "Many of the backgrounds for my illustrations come from our own house. The little girl on the first page of *A Friend is Someone Who Likes You* is Joy as she was, at seven, when the book was begun. *The Brave Cowboy*, of course, is Todd." The kitchen of her house was an old blacksmith's forge and above it "reached by a hidden staircase," is the room she uses as a studio. "I work slowly, or rather steadily and quietly like a spider spinning, sometimes re-doing a drawing four to eight times. It takes about five months to do one book. My illustrations always serve my idea — the words — to me the thought of a book is first." Some of Joan Anglund's books, such as *A Friend is Someone*

Who Likes You, have been done in pen and ink line drawings with two color overlays done on frosted acetate "to achieve soft half-tones"; others were done with full water color. "For these, I do the pen and ink line drawing first which is printed in blue and then I color it with water color." Mrs. Anglund's poems and drawings have been featured in *Ladies Home Journal* (December 1966) and in *Woman's Day*. *A Friend is Someone Who Likes You* was selected one of the "Ten Best Illustrated Books" by the *New York Times* in 1958 and *The Brave Cowboy* received the Society of Illustrators Award in 1959.

ARDIZZONE, EDWARD JEFFREY IRVING*

Born October 16, 1900 in Haiphong, Vietnam. Childhood from the age of five years was spent in England. Attended Clayesmore School.

"I have always loved drawing," Edward Ardizzone writes, "and in childhood ill-spent much of my time scribbling over my lesson books. The first big influence in my life was a present, given to me at school, of a pocket edition of *Pilgrim's Progress*, with many thumbnail illustrations by an artist unnamed. These illustrations fascinated me and I used to copy them. After leaving school I worked in an office in the city of London and it was not till I was twenty-six, seven years later, that I was able to leave and become, what I had always wanted to be, a full-time professional artist and primarily a painter of pictures." His first two children's books, *Little Tim and the Brave Sea Captain* and *Lucy Brown and Mr. Grimes*, were written and illustrated in 1935. "These were made up without any thought of publication but just to amuse my two eldest children, then six and four years old." Mr. Ardizzone's third child was born in the first year of the war. During the war he served in the army, first as a gunner, and then as an official war artist in France, Italy, Sicily, Libya, Normandy and Germany. Since the war he has written and illustrated thirteen new children's books (he now has nine grandchildren to tell stories to), and has illustrated more than 120 books by other authors, one of which, *The Little Book Room* (1955) by Eleanor Farjeon, was awarded both the Carnegie Medal in England, and the International Hans Christian Andersen Medal. "The medals of course go to the author but it has been an honor to be associated with it." Edward Ardizzone's own book, *Tim All Alone*, published in England in 1956, was the first winner of England's Kate Greenaway Medal. Mr. Ardizzone has taught a UNESCO Seminar in India and also been a tutor at the School of Engraving, Royal College of Art in London. The Ardizzones live in London, but have a country cottage also. Autolithography is his favorite technique — although he has used all the usual ones — since he is a lithographer as well as a painter and illustrator. Mr. Ardizzone has used balloons with hand-lettering as part of the illustrations, and in some cases has designed as well as illustrated his books. About his work, he has written "The

illustrator draws to some extent like a child. He does not copy from life, but makes it up. He has a 'think' and puts a line around his 'think'. If he is a good illustrator, he has a great deal of knowledge. He knows what many different things look like, so when he has a 'think' it is an informed one." Mr. Ardizzone is an Honorary Associate of the Royal College of Art and a Fellow of the Society of Industrial Artists. An article about his work appeared in the December 1959 *Top of the News*.

ARNO, ENRICO*

Born July 16, 1913 in Mannheim, Germany. Childhood was spent in Berlin. Attended Helmholtz Realgymnasium, Berlin, and Vereinigte Staatsschulen für freie und angewandte Kunst, Berlin.

Enrico Arno studied to became a painter at the State Academy in Berlin, Germany. In 1935 he changed from fine art to applied art, studying lettering and calligraphy for one year. He worked from Berlin through a British agent for several publishers in London and, at the beginning of World War II, went to Italy. There he was active in the book field, doing illustrations and jacket designs. In 1947 he emigrated to the United States and has been working since then in New York City. His field widened and included everything from a postage stamp (Fort Ticonderoga) to a seventeen foot mural for the Church Street office of the Alco Company in New York. He taught Lettering at Pratt Institute and Painting at Columbia University and has done illustrations for almost every major magazine, record covers, book jackets and books. His aim has been not to be confined to any specialty. Therefore he has used a wide variety of media, from silverpoint to oils, from paper sculpture to ceramics. He works primarily in black-and-white and two colors. In making separations he uses Strathmore paper for the key drawing, frosted acetate for overlays in flat colors and prepared acetate for washes. His hobby is puppetry. Enrico Arno lives in Sea Cliff, Long Island, New York.

AUERBACH, MARJORIE

Born December 10, 1932 in Astoria, New York. Childhood was spent in Flushing, New York. Attended University of Wisconsin, Madison; Art Students League, Cooper Union, New York City.

"I received much encouragement for my early art work from my father who was an enthusiastic collector of old prints, etchings and books," writes Marjorie Auerbach. The family's membership in the Heritage and Limited Editions book clubs during her childhood introduced her to the work of Fritz Kredel, Fritz Eichenberg and Boardman Robinson. "In elementary school, I dressed up my written assignments and reports with a cover design, illustrations, and decorations in the margins." After attending the High School of Music and Art in New York City, she went to the University of Wisconsin and studied silk screen, etching and lithography. A traveling exhibit of Antonio Frasconi's work inspired her to try woodcuts. Later she worked in commercial art by day, while attending Cooper Union at night. Book jackets were among her early assignments and she soon realized "that a good book jacket requires the artist to distill the essence of a whole book into a single image. I wrote my first story when I had some pictures in mind and my editor said, 'Well, write something!' I did and the book was *Seven Uncles Come to Dinner*. I have done most of my work in wood-cut and linoleum cut because they are media that are simple and direct and I enjoy the physical business of cutting into woodgrain, the inking and rice paper, etc. A woodcut can be easily printed in my crowded New York studio which I some-times share with my husband who is an art director." Marjorie Auerbach usually works in three colors and characterizes her work as representational and expressionistic.

AVERILL, ESTHER HOLDEN*

Born July 24, 1902 in Bridgeport, Connecticut where her childhood was spent and where she went to public school. Attended Vassar College; Wellfleet Art School, Cape Cod, Massachusetts; Art Students League, New York; Brooklyn Museum Art School, New York.

Esther Averill writes, "My only art instruction for several decades was the conventional sort scantily administered in many public grammar schools of the early 1900's. It never occurred to me to pursue my studies outside of school. But from memory or photographs I drew many caricatures of people—monotonous caricatures, since I had no techniques with which to develop and nothing in particular to say. Later, in Paris, where I lived from 1925 to 1935, my love of the graphic arts found satisfaction in collaborating with gifted illustrators in designing the Domino Press books for children. In 1944 I illustrated my first juvenile, *The Cat Club*. In this little book I tried to express my affection for the four-foots who had brought me so much happiness. When it came to such a complicated matter as drawing cat's legs in rapid motion, I lifted humbly from Steinlen's *Des Chats*. But in my subsequent cat illustrations, all in the Jenny Linsky series, I have followed my own instinct. Two factors have undoubtedly — if sometimes subconsciously — influenced me: the old folk prints (*images d'Epinal*) which I loved in France, and a search for a clear, simple style in my writing for children." In 1954, *Jenny's Birthday Book* was selected one of the "Ten Best Illustrated Children's Books" of that year by the *New York Times*. Esther Averill makes her home in Brooklyn, New York.

AYER, JACQUELINE BRANDFORD

Born May 2, 1930 in New York City where her childhood was spent. Attended Syracuse University; Art Students League, New York City; Beaux Arts and Ecole Paul Calin, Paris.

Born of Jamaican parents, Jacqueline Ayer drew at an early age and has always been interested in decorative and patterned art. In her early years her father was an artist, later turning to ad-vertising. She has lived in the East, Bangkok and Hong Kong for ten years. According to Mrs. Ayer her work is "decorative in effect, but representational in fact." Although she primarily uses four colors as in *A Wish for Little Sister*, she used black-and-white for *Humpy*. She designs the books she illustrates and has written three of the five that she has done. Concerning separa-tions, she says, "I consider the chore of separations a good tonic — like knitting or carpentry — and would not be sorry to do without it." Jacqueline Ayer, who has received the Society of Illustrators Gold Medal, divides her time between her work as a fabric and dress designer for Design-Thai and illustrating and writing children's books. She and her two daughters, Margot and Elizabeth, make their winter home in London and spend summers in Bangkok.

BACON, PEGGY (Margaret Frances)*

Born May 2, 1895, in Ridgefield, Connecticut. Attended Kent Place School, Summit, New Jersey; Art Students League; and New York School of Fine and Applied Art.

Peggy Bacon is the daughter of two well-known artists, Charles Roswell and Elizabeth (Chase) Bacon. As a child she be-gan to draw pictures before she could talk. She studied under such famous artists as Jonas Lie, John Sloan, George Bellows, Kenneth Hayes Miller, and Andrew Dasburg. She married Alexander Brook, artist (they were divorced in 1939), and has a son and daughter. Peggy Bacon taught drawing and com-position at the Fieldston Ethical Culture School from 1933 to 1938. She has also taught at the Art Students League, Corcoran Gallery of Art, Stella Elkins Tyler College of Fine Arts, Hunter College, New School for Social Research, summer schools and private workshops. Her drawings have, over the years, appeared frequently in the *New Yorker* and other magazines and she has illustrated sixty books. Sixteen of these — eight of them for children — she wrote as well as illustrated. The first of her own children's books, *Lion Hearted Kitten*, was published in 1927. Her illustrations for Tom Robinson's *Buttons* appeared in 1938. Peggy Bacon's pastels, drawings, drypoints and etchings are owned by the Metropolitan and the Whitney Museums, New York City; Brooklyn Museum, Chicago Art Institute, Los Angeles Museum, Carnegie Institute of Pittsburgh, the San Diego Fine Arts Gallery, and many other museums and private collectors. She has had twenty-one one-man shows in New York City and many in other cities, and has exhibited in group ex-hibitions here and abroad. In 1956 she was elected to the National Institute of Arts and Letters. She was recipient of an award from the National Academy of Arts and Letters and a

Guggenheim Fellowship. Peggy Bacon, who considers her work as naturalistic and satirical, works primarily in black-and-white. Her home is in New York City.

BALTZER, HANS

Born in 1900 in Berlin.

Mr. Baltzer's father was a carpenter and he was the youngest of five children. He had no one to teach him but somehow he knew that drawing was what he must do. In 1924 he took the plunge into commercial art and during the early years there were many difficult times. He has since then illustrated a number of books and won a silver medal at the International Book Art Exhibition in Leipzig. Hans Baltzer particularly enjoys working on children's books. His home is in East Germany.

BANNON, LAURA*

Childhood was spent in the country near Traverse City, Michigan. Was graduated from State Normal School, Kalamazoo, Michigan, and the School of the Art Institute of Chicago. Died in December 1963.

Laura Bannon's background of training and experience were those of a painter. As a member of the Chicago Society of Artists she exhibited at the Art Institute in Chicago and at other galleries. Painting was supplemented by teaching at the School of the Chicago Art Institute, as well as supervising the Junior Department of the school, where she pioneered in the field of progressive education for children. Traveling experiences in Mexico, Peru, Japan and Hawaii resulted in an occasional book for children, among which were *Manuela's Birthday*, 1939, and *Gregorio and the White Llama*, 1944, which received an award from the Chicago Society of Typographical Arts, and she ultimately resigned to devote her time to writing and illustrating books for children. She illustrated a number of books for other authors, but wrote as well as illustrated many more, including one book for adults, *Mind Your Child's Art*, 1952. All her regional books were a result of living at the spot with sketch book in hand. Her home was in Evanston, Illinois. In 1962, Miss Bannon was honored with the Children's Reading Round Table Award for her contribution to children's books.

BARKER, CAROL MINTURN

Born February 16, 1938 in London, England. Childhood spent partially in the United States, mainly in England. Attended College of Art, Bournemouth, Hampshire; School of Art, Chelsea, London; Central School of Arts and Crafts, London.

"My father was a painter and designer and worked at home, so there was a very creative atmosphere throughout my childhood. I began drawing and painting early and started my first sketch book at the age of ten in Paris," writes Carol Barker. For a year she worked under her father on graphic design and attended the School of Art in Chelsea for painting. "This meant I was able to attain a solid training in abstract design and typography and have the freedom of self expression in painting as well." Later at the Central School she experimented in as many media as possible. She feels that her father's help and inspiration has been most influential in her work, more so than her art school training. In 1958, she began to free-lance and has illustrated a number of children's books, primarily in black-and-white. Her first full color picture book was the result of a trip to Greece in 1960. H. E. Bates wrote the story of *Achilles the Donkey* around Carol Barker's pictures. It was translated into several different languages and has also appeared on Australian television. Her second picture book, *Achilles and the Twins*, was done in a combination of media. The jacket design is mainly collage. The illustrations are designs using wax as a basic texture with ink and water color providing the color. She planned the whole book, using type and handlettering so that she could see the integrated whole. Mrs. Barker lives in England with her husband and two sons.

BARRY, KATHARINA MARIA

Born March 15, 1936 in Berlin, Germany. Childhood spent in Europe. Attended Kunstgewerbeschule, Zurich, Switzerland.

With the exception of one year in grade school in Mt. Kisco, New York, Katharina Barry was educated in Europe. While studying scientific drawing, lettering and typography at the Kunstgewerbeschule in Zurich, Switzerland, she met Robert Barry, her future husband, an American graphic artist and children's book author-illustrator. For a year after their marriage, the Barrys lived in San Juan, Puerto Rico, where they discovered some old wooden type in a small printing shop. From this stemmed Mrs. Barry's idea for her first book, *A is for Anything* in which many of the old wooden letter forms are used in combination with pen and ink. The Barrys and their two sons now live in a restored carriage house, "Driftwood," in Newport, Rhode Island — ideal for Mrs. Barry's hobbies which include books, old houses, antique toys, the sea and sea shells.

BARRY, ROBERT EVERETT

Born October 7, 1931 in Newport, Rhode Island. Attended the Rhode Island School of Design; Academy of Fine Art, Munich, Germany; Kunstgewerbeschule, Zurich, Switzerland.

Mr. Barry writes, "A number of my relatives, at least as far back as I have been able to trace, were craftsmen of one sort or another. This respect for doing things well with one's hands seems to have carried through to me. My writing and illustrating I consider a contemporary craft, one I enjoy and find completely satisfying." His work which is generally in black-and-white or two colors is done with dry brush or pen and ink and wash. The Barrys have traveled considerably and lived in Switzerland, Germany, Puerto Rico and various spots in the United States. They have often "had to set up a temporary working corner to fit the needs of the moment." In September 1967, Mr. Barry will be teaching in the art department at Averett College in Danville, Virginia "and I am looking forward to this experience as an extension of my craft."

BARSS, WILLIAM

Born July 1, 1916 in Syracuse, New York. Childhood spent in Ohio. Attended Columbus (Ohio) Art School; Child-Walker School of Design, Boston, Massachusetts.

William Barss' interest in painting was encouraged by his parents during his early childhood. In art school, he majored in fine arts. During World War II, however, he became an illustrator in the Office of War Information spending two years in India and China. After the war he stayed in China as Cultural Relations Officer for the U.S. Information Service. In the late 1940's he began doing book jackets and since then has illustrated adult and children's books. He writes, "I prefer children's books because the illustrations can be more imaginative and there is much more opportunity for the use of color and decorative design. Having five children of my own, ranging in age from twenty-five to five, I feel I know something of the way a child thinks and am fascinated by their imagination." Mr. Barss works primarily in full color. For *Hilili and Dilili* he used casein. Commenting on this medium, he says, "I have found that casein is most suitable for me, combining wash with impasto, getting textures by the use of brush, painting knife and other tools." Although he personally prefers decorative illustration, he uses a meticulous, representational approach for the "Beginning Science" books, thus fitting his style to the subject. Mr. Barss, his wife, Currie, and three of their children live in a saltbox house built in 1820 in Boston, Massachusetts. "I work at home in a converted barn studio. We own an island off the coast of Nova Scotia where we spend part of our summer painting, sailing, fishing and loafing."

BARTSCH, JOCHEN

Born December 30, 1906 in Striegau, Silesia, Germany where he spent his childhood. Attended School for Applied Art, Breslau; Academy for Applied Art, Munich; Reimannschule, Berlin.

Jochen Bartsch's first professional training was at the School of Ceramics in Bunzlau which came after he had worked in the manufacturing of china. His first love, however, was drawing and he finally left ceramics for graphic arts and studied with Paul Hampil at the School for Applied Art in Breslau. In Munich he studied under professors Ehmcke and Teutsch and then began as a free-lance illustrator. In 1940 he was drafted into the German Army and when taken prisoner in France in 1945 spent his time painting on the barrack walls. After the war, he began as a press-illustrator and then branched out into book illustration where his special love is children's books. In 1957 and 1962, *Gebrauchsgraphik* published articles on Mr. Bartsch's work. In the earlier article, Carl Heussner characterizes Bartsch's work with these words: "It is just this in part somewhat baroque and individual humor which lends to his work its quite original and thoroughly personal note and manifests itself on paper as the quite natural expression of an affectionate way of looking at the world." His work which ranges from the playful and fanciful to the earnest and dramatic has largely been in black-and-white in those books that have been translated into English and for these he uses pen and ink. For his color work he uses etching, zylography, collage, water color, and tempera, often combining pen and ink with the latter two. Two books he has illustrated have won special honors: *My Greatgrandfather and I*, the 1959 Jugendbuchpreis in Germany; and *Der Nette König Mandolin* was on the Honor List of the 1965 Austrian prizes. Three others have been on the "Best Books of the Year" lists in Germany for the past three years. Mr. Bartsch was married in 1953 and has one son. He and his family live in Gauting, Germany.

BAYNES, PAULINE DIANA*

Born September 9, 1922 in Brighton, England. Childhood was spent in India for the first five years, then in southern England. Attended Hillside Convent, Farnborough, Hampshire; Beaufront School, Camberley; Farnham School of Art; and Slade School of Fine Art, London.

Owing to the fact that her father was working in India, Pauline Baynes' childhood was spent entirely in hotels and guest houses, — a different place for every school holiday. Miss Baynes refers to her scholastic career as "undistinguished" though she was elected, at the age of sixteen, to membership in the Women's International Art Club, from which she later resigned, and she returned to teach art at her main school — Beaufront. "During the war," she says, "I worked at the Camouflage Development and Training Centre under the Army, but in a civilian capacity. And then I went to draw charts at the Admiralty Hydrographic Department, meeting a lot of interesting people in both establishments." For ten years after that she kept house for her parents, doing all her art work at night, between 8 p.m. and 5 a.m. She believes her work has been entirely influenced by mediaeval and Persian painting, and, having made a study of costume, she enjoys specializing in historical books. When working in black-and-white, she generally uses a pen with a very fine nib and ink. "For my full color work, I practically always work in gouache and use a dry brush technique — mainly to cover up the somewhat messy pencil work (as I never do roughs) underneath." *Tom Bombadil* was a case in which she designed as well as illustrated the book. In 1961, she married Fritz Otto Gasch and "now my working hours are more civilized. We live in the smallest cottage ever built, near Farnham in Surrey, and have four dogs." Miss Baynes is a member of the Society of Industrial Artists.

BEATTY, HETTY BURLINGAME*

Born October 8, 1906 in New Canaan, Connecticut. Childhood was spent there and in central New York State: Syracuse in the winters and Cazenovia in the summers. Attended Goodyear-Burlingame School, Syracuse; School of the Museum of Fine Arts, Boston; George Demetrios School of Drawing, Gloucester, Massachusetts; and Summer School of the Pennsylvania Academy of the Fine Arts, Chester Springs, Pennsylvania.

During her four years at the Boston Museum School, Hetty Burlingame Beatty was awarded two annual scholarships. She studied sculpture under Charles Grafly and drawing under George Demetrios. In 1929 she went to Europe, spending a winter in Florence and one in Rome working in both sculpture and drawing. Returning to the United States to spend her winters in New York and her summers on Cape Ann, she continued to work in sculpture, exhibiting in most of the national exhibitions. She had a one-man show at the Macbeth Galleries in New York and, later, at the Worcester Art Museum. "During these years," she writes, "I found that my love of horses in particular and all animals in general, created a happy bond of interest with all the children I knew, and led to constant requests to draw them pictures and tell them stories. In 1939 I spent a year on a beef ranch in Colorado, which added much subject matter of mutual interest. In 1945 I decided to go into writing and illustrating children's books professionally." To date she has published thirteen books, eleven of which she illustrated. In 1959 she married Lewis Whitney, sculptor, metal craftsman and founder of the Pewter Shop in Rockport, Massachusetts. Now they live in Bermuda for eight months of the year, in a house designed by Hetty Beatty, and the remainder of the year in Connecticut. Miss Beatty works primarily in black-and-white or full color. For black-and-white, she uses scratchboard with an Exacto blade and various ground-down dental tools to get a woodcut effect. This technique was used in *Bucking Horse* and *Bryn*. She finds tempera the most effective medium for color work and used this in *Moorland Pony* and *Droopy*. Concerning her style, she writes, "My work is something of a cross between representational and decorative, leaning steadily toward bold simplicity."

BEER, RICHARD

Born in London, England. Attended Ardengly College, Sussex; Slade School, and University College, London; Atelier 17, Paris.

Along with his painting, printmaking and illustrating, Mr. Beers travels extensively and also is Lecturer in Print Making at the Chelsea School of Art in London. In 1955 he was stage designer for the Royal Ballet's "Lady and the Fool." He has had several one-man shows of his paintings and his prints are in the collections of the Victoria and Albert Museum, London, The Metropolitan Museum of Art in New York and several other museums of note.

BEHN, HARRY*

Born September 24, 1898 near Prescott, Arizona. Childhood was spent in Arizona. Attended Harvard University.

Harry Behn was born in a mining camp near mountainous Prescott, Arizona, and grew up there and in desert Phoenix. In the *Horn Book* for June 1952 he has written of the serene and happy childhood he had even in a frontier community, where he took for granted the "stir of danger about me," and of the books which meant the most to him: Andersen's *Fairy Tales*, *Gulliver's Travels*, *Uncle Remus*, *The Wind in the Willows*, *The Wizard of Oz*. After high school he traveled as an assistant travelogue cameraman through all the National Parks, and became a member of the Blackfoot tribe. At Harvard, Mr. Behn was a member of Professor Baker's drama workshop, and organized the Phoenix Little Theater after graduation. Later he went to Sweden as an American-Scandinavian Fellow. Over the years he wrote movie scenarios in Hollywood, taught at the University of Arizona, started the *Arizona Quarterly* and a radio station in Tucson. Since 1949 he has written and illustrated books for children. Mr. Behn speaks of his art training as being "a slow accretion of trial and error, begun when I submitted drawings to *St. Nicholas Magazine* in 1904 . . . a matter of fragments between doing anything else." However, he did have art courses in school and college, he does paint and he had a successful one-man show. "Still," he writes, "I feel that my illustrations are not so much art as something I visualize as a lino or woodcut to go with a poem already written and headed for a book that I also visualize very clearly. . . . What I am trying to say, is that I see the whole book, and the pictures are only a part of it." Concerning his later work he says, "In the past ten years, I have written for two granddaughters now in their teens two archaeological novels and have adorned them with emblems which might be called illustrations, and have decorated a book of poems with pen drawings. I have had two exhibitions of paintings and am preparing another." A speech by Mr. Behn appears in *Elementary English*, April 1965, and an article about him in the November 1960 issue of *Elementary*

English. Harry Behn and his wife, Alice, live in "a Japanese house in a Japanese garden on a rocky mossy hill jutting into a lake" in Greenwich, Connecticut. They have three children and seven grandchildren.

BELL, CORYDON*

Born July 16, 1894 in Tiffin, Ohio. Childhood spent there and in Sandusky, Ohio. Attended University of Michigan and Western Reserve University, Cleveland, Ohio.

Among Corydon Bell's earliest recollections was an ability to express himself through drawing. Prone on his stomach for hours at a time he recorded a small world in pictures. At six he was building theater models complete with scenic backdrops. From pre-medical study at the University of Michigan he changed to an English major at Western Reserve University, with the intent of going on to Harvard for drama, but World War I put an end to study. After a tour of duty in bacteriology, and incidental conducting of the camp theater orchestra, he found himself faced with three possible and humorously diverse choices: publicist for a new major symphony orchestra; research fellow in bacteriology; pianist for a traveling vaudeville act. He chose art. Optimistically he opened a small studio, and with a brochure of untutored work, solicited commissions. It was a case of "learning as you go." It was also the beginning of twenty years of commercial art, which gradually became mixed with book design and illustration. His early pictorial interest in how people live and what they use and make, plus a tenacious photographic memory for detail, have proved invaluable in the visualizing of drawings for children's books. Mr. Bell's wife is the writer, Thelma Harrington Bell; they have three children and eight grandchildren. The Bells live two and a half miles from the village of Cashiers, North Carolina, on a 4,000 foot mountain in the Blue Ridge. Mr. Bell works largely in black-and-white as in *The Riddle of Time* which he co-authored with his wife. Two colors, with separations done on dinobase using crayon, were used for *String, Straightedge and Shadow*. Describing his work as representational with overtones of the decorative, Mr. Bell goes on to say, "Actually I have experienced four or five very noticeable changes of style in my career. My present style probably began to crystalize with the drawings for *Mountain Boy* in 1947." With few exceptions, he has designed all the children's books he has illustrated (five of these he has also written). "It is fortunate, I believe, when an artist has the ability and experience to control the type and lettering that must become an integral part of his book. In the case of jacket and binding designs, as well as title pages, I accurately indicate on the sketches the handlettering I intend to do and also the type face and sizes to be employed."

BELTRAN, ALBERTO

Born March 22, 1923 in Mexico City where he spent his childhood. Attended Escuela Libre de Arte y Publicidad, Mexico.

"My father wanted me to be a tailor," recalls Alberto Beltrán. After much insisting on his part he "finally received permission to attend the Free School of Art and Publicity when I was fifteen. I worked for some time as an assistant to a comic-strip illustrator, but I was much more interested in engraving — wood and linoleum cuts — and finally decided to try my hand at it." In 1958, he received the National Engraving Award and took first place in the engraving section of the First Interamerican Painting and Engraving Biennial in 1960, both of which took place in Mexico City. "I have always been interested in illustrating children's books, but they are rarely published here in Mexico. However, I have illustrated readers to be published in Indian languages." His black-and-white illustrations for *Maya, Land of the Turkey and the Deer* were done in pen and brush and ink. For another book *Todo Empezo El Domingo* he used charcoal along with these.

BEMELMANS, LUDWIG*

Born April 27, 1898 at Meram, Tirol, Austria. Attended Konigliche Realschule at Regensburg and Rothenburg, Bavaria. Died October 1, 1962.

In a conversation with his daughter Barbara in *Father Dear Father* (1953), Ludwig Bemelmans says, "I was born in a hotel and brought up in three countries — when I was six years old I couldn't speak a word of German, because it was fashionable in Europe to bring up children who spoke nothing but French. And then I lived in other hotels, which was a very lonesome life for a child, and the only people you met were old ones, below stairs and upstairs. In my youth the upstairs was a collection of Russian grand dukes and French countesses, English lords and American millionaires. Backstairs there were French cooks, Roumanian hairdressers, Chinese manicurists, Italian bootblacks, Swiss managers, English valets. All these people I got to know very well." He speaks of running away from the hotel to play with the children of Tirolean and Bavarian woodchoppers, teamsters, boatmen and peasants. In 1914 he came to this country and four years later became a United States citizen. He has recorded in the Foreword to his book *My War with the United States* (1937) that on sailing for America from the port of Rotterdam, he bought two pistols and much ammunition to protect himself against Indians for, from his reading of the books by James Fenimore Cooper and others, he expected to find many Indians on the outskirts of New York City. He enlisted with the United States Army for the First World War but did not go overseas. His first books were for children: *Hansi* (1934) and *The Golden Basket* (1936). In 1939 came *Madeline*, of all his children's books probably the most widely known. It was for a sequel to this book, *Madeline's Rescue*, suggested to him by Phyllis McGinley's small daughters, that he was awarded the Caldecott Medal in 1954. Concerning his work, Mr. Bemelmans said in his Caldecott Award acceptance speech, "I wanted to paint purely what gave me pleasure, scenes that interested me; and one day I found that the audience for that kind of painting was a vast reservoir of impressionists who did very good work themselves, who were very clear-eyed and capable of enthusiasm. I addressed myself to children." According to an article in the October 1966 issue of *Elementary English*, Ludwig Bemelmans worked hard planning each book but cared little for the technical aspects. "For example, he would not do the labor necessary to separate his work into the four colors needed for printing *Hansi*. This was done for him by his good friend Kurt Wiese." Other articles about Ludwig Bemelmans and his work appear in the August 1954 *Horn Book* and the January 1957 *Elementary English*.

BENDICK, JEANNE*

Born February 25, 1919 in New York City where her childhood was spent. Attended High School of Music and Arts; Parsons School of Design, New York; and New York School of Fine and Applied Art.

Jeanne Bendick's New York City childhood "which was fun," she writes, was "punctuated by yearly vacations at the shore or in Maine. A great many people in my family drew, and from the earliest time I can remember, I was writing stories and illustrating them, any time I had a few minutes and a nice white piece of paper. I always wanted to be an illustrator, and I love working with children — they have so many fresh, new ways of looking at things!" Mrs. Bendick has written about half of the hundred or so books that she has illustrated. She and her husband, Robert Bendick, a television and film producer-director, live in Rye, New York. Their two children, Bob Jr. and Karen, are in college. In 1965 Karen wrote and illustrated a book which was published. Working primarily in black-and-white and two colors, Jeanne Bendick describes her style as "relaxed representational." She generally uses pen or brush and ink for black-and-white as in *A Fresh Look at Night*. For color she uses prismacolor pencil on vellum as in *Who Lives at the Seashore?* She designs her own books and always works with separations in doing her illustrations.

BENNETT, RAINEY

Born July 26, 1907 Marion, Indiana. Childhood spent in Oak Park, Illinois. Attended University of Chicago; American Academy of Art, Chicago; Art Institute of Chicago; George Grosz-Maurice Stern School, New York.

Rainey Bennett's active interest in painting began during his years at the University of Chicago. A commission to do a mural for the People's Gas Company exhibit of the 1933 Century of Progress led to work with the Federal Art Project. Through project exhibits he was associated with the Downtown Gallery

from 1936 to 1952. His reputation as a watercolorist brought several traveling commissions including two trips to South America. His pictures are owned by a dozen museums. Institutional Christmas advertising for Marshall Field and Company led to his career in book illustration, first in textbooks and then in children's books. Working mainly in full color, Mr. Bennett uses several media. For *Little Chameleon* by Sylvia Cassedy, he used black line and gray, red, yellow and blue half-tone separations. For *What Do You Think?*, he made separations for black and two flat colors. Mr. Bennett received the *New York Herald Tribune* Spring Children's Book Festival Prize for *The Secret Hiding Place* in 1960. *After the Sun Goes Down* was selected for the Children's Book Show, 1961-62 of the American Institute of Graphic Arts. He lives in Chicago and his wife Anne. They have three children.

BERG, JOAN, see Victor, Joan Berg

BERRILL, JACQUELYN

Born November 5, 1905 in South Carrollton, Kentucky where childhood was spent. Attended University of Toledo; New York University.

Jacquelyn Berrill writes that she wrote and illustrated her first book to answer her three children's questions about the Maine seashore where they lived during the summers. Illustrated on scratchboard, these books were "simple and direct." Concerning the scratchboard technique she says, "I like the dramatic effect of the technique and believe it is perfect for illustrating animals with fur." She uses this technique for all of her books which are done in black-and-white. Mrs. Berrill's husband is a zoologist. For a number of years he was a professor of Zoology at McGill University, Montreal, Canada, and their three children, Peggy, Elsilyn and Michael, who are now grown, were reared in Montreal. The Berrills now live in Swarthmore, Pennsylvania.

BERRY, WILLIAM DAVID

Born May 20, 1926 in San Mateo, California. Childhood spent in Los Angeles County, California and Phoenix, Arizona. Attended Art Center School, Los Angeles; The School of Applied Arts, Glendale, California.

"I didn't really 'become' an artist; looking back along the picture-littered trail it seems that my present occupation began almost as soon as I was able to maneuver pencil or scissors. Even the subject matter has changed but little. When I was three years old I was cutting recognizable freehand silhouettes of various animals and birds, and by the time I was five I had produced my first book, a unique natural history transcribed by a doting grandmother and illustrated with pencil drawings. The art might be attributed to precocity, but the interest in animal life was simply the way my mind worked; animals were the symbols with which I dealt with the world. Subjectively, at least, I was like Mowgli growing up in his jungle, and animals seemed to me more real than human beings," writes Mr. Berry. He recalls storing up "every scrap of information" on animals, anticipating trips to the natural history museum and zoo, and owning a miniature menagerie. He fluctuated between illustration and science noting that, "If the artist won over the scientist, the scientific attitude left me with a great respect for objective honesty; I'm a stickler for accuracy even in a cartoon." An Eskimo hunter once told him that his pictures "told the truth" and he has valued this judgment. Concerning his work William Berry says, "I'm a free-lance artist-illustrator-writer, dealing chiefly with wildlife subjects; my wife and I work together on silk-screen prints (serigraphs)." He has designed the two books that he has written and the one he and his wife wrote together. Although he has worked with color separations as in *Deneki*, he feels that the process is time-consuming and frustrating for the artist when realism is desired. He prefers painting. William Berry, his wife and two sons spent five years at Deneki Lakes near Mount McKinley National Park. They now live in Fairbanks, Alaska.

BERSON, HAROLD

Born November 28, 1926 in Los Angeles, California. Attended University of California at Los Angeles (B.A. in Sociology); Grande Chaumiere Academy, Paris.

Harold Berson writes, "I have been drawing since I was a little kid. I've always read a good deal and was always trying to draw pictures of scenes from the books I read. I never wanted to become an artist, seriously, until I had a chance to use the G.I. Bill in Paris." After working for the Bureau of Public Assistance in Los Angeles following graduation, he decided to pursue an art career. Gloria Surmac, former art director of *Humpty Dumpty* magazine, gave him his first commission in New York, and he still draws for that magazine. He also credits his wife, Paula, an artist herself, for giving him a great deal of advice and encouragement. He usually works in brush or pen and ink; if color is called for, he uses acetate overlays or Bourges sheets. *Raminagrobis and the Mice* was done in brush and ink. Although he is primarily an illustrator, for *Raminagrobis and the Mice* he selected an old folk tale and rewrote it. He and his wife enjoy traveling, music and ballet. They make their home in New York City.

BETTINA, pseud. (Bettina Ehrlich)*

Born March 19, 1903 in Vienna, Austria. Her childhood was spent in Vienna and in Grado. Attended Wiener Frauenerwerb-Verein, and Kunstgewerbeschule, Vienna.

Bettina was the second of two daughters of a mining engineer father. Influenced by an artistic mother, she was always painting and drawing, and as early as five years of age wrote and illus-

trated a little story. The many months spent in the house built by her father on Grado, an island near the Adriatic Sea, have been the inspiration for all her work. She first painted in oils, then took up lithography, and then printing on a hand press, and in 1936 began hand-printing textiles. She received a silver medal for textiles at the Exposition Internationale des Arts in Paris in 1937. One of her hand-printed books has been acquired by Albertina, Vienna's famous print room. In 1930, she was married to the sculptor, Georg Ehrlich, and in 1938 when the Nazis came to power, the Ehrlichs settled in London. It was during the blitz that she wrote and illustrated her first children's book, *Poo-Tsee, The Water Tortoise*, which was published in 1942. She has published many other books since then in both England and the United States. She became a British citizen in 1947 and spent the next two years visiting the United States. Although Bettina lives in London she makes frequent visits to Vienna and to Italy. In all her books, Bettina uses pen and ink for the black-and-white drawings and water color for the full color pictures. "I strongly dislike separations and do not do them any more," she writes. "My aim in illustration is that the picture should express precisely what the text tells you; that the pictures should be lively and the objects represented as well drawn as is within my capacity." Concerning her approach to the books she also writes, "When the idea of a story has taken shape in my mind, I write it down on the same sheet of paper on which I sketch the illustration so that unity is born at once. The text is usually rewritten two or three times until I like it. The final illustrations are done after galleys of text are received and pasted into position." She plans the book especially carefully when black-and-white pages must alternate with full color, avoiding, for instance, mention of color in the text on pages to be illustrated in black-and-white.

BILECK, MARVIN*

Born March 2, 1920 in Passaic, New Jersey where his childhood was spent. Attended Cooper Union, New York, and London School of Architecture, London, England.

Marvin Bileck has written, "Childhood, as I look back on it, was an enjoyment of stories, sports, and scouting. While the comics interested me in drawing funny pictures, gradually I found that anything I drew gave me a thrill. I liked to invent characters and loved to see people 'come alive.' Scouting introduced me to nature which inspired a basic sense of growth. Artistically speaking, 'I was born' when I came to Cooper Union. Here I learned the substance of pictures. Architecture — my major — gave me the concept of structure. I try to make and build everything in the picture. Design introduced me to the flat plane, taught me to organize the elements and taught me of rhythm in drawing. Graphics brought me closer to the 'book,' and here within the fragrance of printer's ink, I saw the evolution of reproduced work and knew that engraving, etching and book illustration were of meaning to me." In World

War II Mr. Bileck served for four years in North Africa, Europe, and England. After the war he studied Gothic architecture in England, and, returning to America, he finished his work at Cooper Union and entered book illustration. Whenever possible, "I try to relate the autographic and photomechanical processes," he writes. "A *Walker in the City* was an instance where the glass was lacquered, and the illustrations needled in as in etching, the copper plate resulting from this drawn negative. This made for more direct finer line." For *Nobody's Birthday* and *Sugarplum* he used pencil on acetates. Pencil and water colors were used for *Penny* and *Rain Makes Applesauce*. Concerning changes in his style in the last ten years, he says, "Abstract and aesthetic considerations are more intimately connected to the naturalistic and humanistic. I believe in the people and want them to be more 'real' and to exist in their imagery, while ten years ago abstract participation was so blinding that I was decorating pages, and my people were artificial and had no depth." Marvin Bileck usually designs the books he illustrates. "I consider a body of type as dynamic and functional a shape-form as any part of the illustration" and has made use of hand-lettering and calligraphy within the illustrations. About *Rain Makes Applesauce* he says, "I was delighted by the imagery and excited by the thought of my pictures giving rise to such fantasies and how as they grew they implicated more and varied ramifications of these imaginings. In *Penny*, I was intrigued by the scale — that by getting way down to this low level one could see landscapes across a tablecloth and one could feel the arched-strength in wispish things such as blades of grass which almost feel like high trees." Four books illustrated by Mr. Bileck were honored at the American Institute of Graphic Arts Children's Book Shows. In 1965, *Rain Makes Applesauce* was selected one of the "Ten Best Illustrated Children's Books" by the *New York Times* and was also a runner-up for the Caldecott Medal. He is presently an Assistant Professor at the Philadelphia College of Art, teaching drawing, book design and calligraphy.

BIRO, VAL (B. S.)*

Born October 6, 1921 in Budapest, Hungary where his childhood was spent. Attended Jaschnick School of Art, Budapest; Central School of Art and Crafts, London.

Mr. Biro writes, "I think that the Hungarian background helped to form my style, a rather irreverent approach to life, the peculiar un-savage humor of the Hungarians, imbued with the decorative nature of Hungarian folk-art. I came to England in 1939 and set out in my studies to become what we now call a graphic designer, acknowledging my early and abiding fondness for books and print of all sorts. An eight year spell in book publishing followed, not only to earn some money (of which I had none) but also to get an insight into the methods and techniques of book-making. This became invaluable and served me well in my free-lancing which began in 1953. I am not a

children's illustrator primarily; much of my work is in the adult field and for magazines. But I get a lot of commissions for children's books and enjoy them immensely. What I enjoy above all is a *variety* of subjects and moods. In the past ten years my style has gotten bolder, simpler, less detailed or niggly, perhaps heavier in line and looser in color." He works in a number of media, such as gouache, water color, auto-lithography, etching, photography. "Scraperboard is a big favorite of mine. Fluorography, a new American technique for full-color reproduction, has served me well lately. Here I separate all four colors on acetate, in special inks — interesting chances for technical experiments." Mr. Biro lives in England.

BJORKLUND, LORENCE F.*

Born in St. Paul, Minnesota. His childhood was spent there and in surrounding states. Attended Pratt Institute, Brooklyn, New York.

"I was brought up in a family of Swedish background in a typical midwestern Swedish community in the city of St. Paul," Lorence F. Bjorklund has written. "When I was seventeen a friend and I took a rowboat from St. Paul (the headwaters of navigation on the Mississippi River) to New Orleans, a trip of some eighteen hundred miles, which we rowed in two months and eight days. This trip gave me the impetus to take many more like it (but mostly by land) and it has followed that my interests in illustration have usually been on some geographic or historical subject, well spiced with things seen or learned on my travels. I won a scholarship to Pratt Institute and came to the East Coast to study and eventually to build a studio and home. My hobbies are various, from working with precision machine tools to fishing off the coast of Maine where I have a summer studio." Mr. Bjorklund has done magazine and advertising illustration, but his greater pleasure is in illustrating books about America, particularly adventure stories. He continues to enjoy travel, and, with his wife, Katherine, and daughter, Karna, has taken many trips, particularly in the West and Canada. The Bjorklunds live in Croton Falls, New York. Mr. Bjorklund works primarily in black-and-white for which he uses charcoal, graphite and Wolff pencil. He has illustrated over 100 books in a style which he describes as realistic.

BLAKE, QUENTIN

Born December 16, 1932 in Sidcup, Kent, England where childhood was spent. Attended Downing College, Cambridge; London University Institute of Education.

Although Quentin Blake was not trained as an artist, he began drawing for *Punch* in 1949. He attended life classes at the Chelsea School of Art after he left college and London University, and began free-lancing in 1957, illustrating his first children's book in 1960. He has taught English at the French

Lycee in London and now teaches illustration in the School of Graphic Design of the Royal College of Art. For his black and white drawings Mr. Blake uses a pen with an extra fine point. Recently he has also used fibre-tipped pens. He uses a brush and pastel or oil pastel for two color work. Full color work is generally done in "mixed technique" — oil pastels with water-color, designers' colors, and colored inks. Describing his style as decorative he says, "I don't especially adapt my way of drawing for children. It's more a question of having an imaginative sympathy with the kind of incidents you're depicting and then you hope they like it." There is an article in the December 15, 1965 issue of *Punch* concerning Mr. Blake who now lives in South Kensington, London.

BLEGVAD, ERIK*

Born March 3, 1923 in Copenhagen, Denmark, where his childhood was spent. Attended Østersøgades Gymnasium, Øregaards Gymnasium, and Københavns Kunsthaandvärker-skole (Copenhagen School of Arts and Crafts) 1941-1944.

Erik Blegvad spent the years of the German occupation at art school and as an artist in a Copenhagen advertising agency. Early in his career he illustrated a Danish translation of Mme. Prunier's *Fish Cook Book*, and various works on fishing written by his father, Dr. Harald Blegvad, a famous biologist and deep sea investigator. After the liberation he spent a few years in the Royal Danish Air Force, and was attached as interpreter to British forces at the Military Government in Germany. He traveled in Belgium, Holland, and France, and, finding that he could not establish any business in Paris, he went to London and worked for a year as a free-lance artist. Returning to Paris in 1948, he worked for *France Soir, Elle, Femina*, and illustrated a book for Editions Odé called *Les Pays Nordique*. In 1950 he was married to an American painter, Lenore Hochman, and they came to the United States the following year. Since then, he has illustrated articles and stories for various periodicals, including *Esquire, Saturday Evening Post, McCall's* and *Woman's Day*, for which he does the annual Calendar. Among the many books he has illustrated are two of Andersen's stories which he translated. He writes, "To date I have had my greatest pleasures in book illustration with two books: my wife's first book, *Mr. Jensen and the Cat*, and *The Margaret Rudkin Pepperidge Farm Cook Book* which contains many hundreds of my favorite drawings." For his work in black-and-white, Erik Blegvad uses pen and India ink. A transparent water color wash, or a mixture of water color and poster colors are used for full color work. To avoid separating with overlays, Mr. Blegvad uses a method long practiced in Copenhagen for Sunday supplements. He puts the colors on the reverse of the original black key drawing. For this process he uses a one ply paper and a light table.

BOBRI, V.,* pseud. (Vladimir Bobritsky)

Born May 13, 1898 in Kharkov, Ukraine, where he attended the Kharkov Imperial Art School.

As a young man Bobri worked in the theater as scene designer for drama and ballet, — at seventeen designing sets for the Great Dramatic Theater at Kharkov. During the Revolution he fled as a refugee, eventually reaching Constantinople. In the Crimea he met up with a band of gypsies and earned his way as a guitar player in their chorus; he worked with archeologists in the Crimea and Turkey, and painted icons in a Greek monastery on the island of Halki, and through all his wanderings he always carried a paint brush and drawing pad. He made decorations and costumes for the Ballet Russe of Constantinople to earn his passage money to come to America, arriving in the United States in 1921. Here he opened his own textile establishment, painted murals for night clubs, and, in the thirties, began to do advertising art and book illustration. He has won the Art Directors Award for Distinctive Merit and has become well known in the field of commercial design. Bobri is almost as well known in musical circles as he is among artists. He is editor and art director of the *Guitar Review*, a magazine which has won two awards from the American Institute of Graphic Arts; he is a composer and his *Danza En La* was performed in New York Town Hall in 1936; he has been President of the Society of the Classical Guitar since 1945, and he has directed radio broadcasts of chamber music. He is an authority on Gypsy music and folk lore of all countries.

BOBRITSKY, VLADIMIR, see Bobri, V., pseud.

BOCK, VERA*

Born in St. Petersburg, Russia. Childhood was spent in Europe and the United States. Attended schools and art schools in Europe.

Vera Bock's Russian mother was a concert pianist; her American father was an international banker. During her early childhood in Russia the emphasis of education was on languages. She learned Russian, French, German, and English, reading books in all four. She was still a child when, at the onset of the Revolution, her family left Russia and came to the United States. There her education was continued under private instruction. Art has been the constant in her life, for the older she grew the more it attracted her. On subsequent trips to Europe she studied drawing and painting under European artists. Spending a year in England she devoted herself to the study of wood engraving, illuminating, and heraldry, developing at the same time an interest in printing and photoengraving. Vera Bock's career as an illustrator began in 1929 with Bonsel's *Adventures of Maya the Bee*, and Ella Young's *Tangle-coated Horse*. She now has a great many books to her credit, all of which she has designed as well as illustrated, including *A Critical History of Children's Literature*, 1953. She also does work for magazines and book jackets. In 1946 her work was shown at the Morgan Library in the "International Exhibition of Illustrated Books" and in May 1945 an article about her appeared in *American Artist*. Vera Bock lives in New York City.

BODECKER, NILS MOGENS*

Born 1922 in Copenhagen, Denmark. Attended boarding school, Birkeroed Kostskole, from the age of about ten to eighteen. Studied economics and architecture, and then received his art training at the School of Applied Arts (Kunsthaandvaerkerskolen) in Copenhagen.

At the age of six N. M. Bodecker began in oils with an easel he himself had made, though his mother soon gave him a real one. His father was an enthusiastic collector of pictures, mostly contemporary paintings, and filled the house with them, and this doubtless gave added stimulation to the boy's interest in drawing and painting. His father, however, knowing how little artists receive for their work, wanted his son to be a lawyer rather than a painter. The art teacher at his boarding school was an inspiration to the children and gave them a free hand to try various methods of expression, teaching them pottery making, mural painting, and other things. The headmaster too thought it important that the children be occupied with something they liked to do. He did not worry about grades and, if a child had talent for painting, he saw no reason for teaching him too much spelling. N. M. Bodecker, however, gave up painting in oils when he was about twenty, and became more interested in writing. He finished his studies in 1944 and, through a former classmate who was the editor, he began working as editorial assistant on what was at that time the leading art magazine in Scandinavia. At the age of twenty-one he had published a volume of poetry, and three years later a second one, both of which he says were "very unsuccessful." Later he worked for a jazz magazine, where he did his first drawings for publication, and on newspapers. Along with magazine assignments he began doing cartoons and a weekly cartoon strip on topical — sometimes political — events, for *Politiken*, the largest newspaper in Copenhagen. He still works for it occasionally. Mr. Bodecker came to the United States in 1952 and has been doing free-lance work ever since, chiefly magazine and, what he prefers — book illustration. He still writes poetry but finds it difficult to do in English. Mr. Bodecker and his American wife have three sons.

BOLOGNESE, DONALD ALAN

Born January 6, 1934 in New York City where childhood was spent. Attended Cooper Union Art School, New York City.

Since his graduation from Cooper Union in 1954, Donald Bolognese has worked as a free-lance illustrator. His drawings have appeared in the magazine and book sections of the *Herald Tribune* and other New York publications. He has illustrated over fifty children's books including *The Sleepy Watchdog*, written and illustrated by his wife and himself. In 1964 Mr. Bolognese was commissioned to execute a series of woodcuts and calligraphic texts entitled "The Miracles of Christ" for the Vatican Pavilion of the New York World's Fair. He also published a book of the same title containing reproductions of the woodcuts and texts. Donald Bolognese uses "just about every medium from pen and ink to woodcut including water color and collage." Concerning the character of his work, he tries to be guided by the subject matter. He says, "Although I have done many decorative subjects I believe *More Beautiful than Flowers* by Joan Lexau is closest to me." *Plays and How to Put Them On* was included in the American Institute of Graphic Arts Children's Book Show in 1962. Mr. Bolognese, who is also a calligrapher, has written an article on Chancery cursive for *Jubilee* magazine that has been extensively reprinted for use in teaching. He and his family live in New York where he has been teaching lettering and calligraphy at Pratt Institute since 1960.

BONSALL, CROSBY BARBARA

Born January 2, 1921 in New York City where her childhood was spent. Attended American School of Design and New York University School of Architecture, New York City.

Crosby Bonsall's entry into the children's book field was the result of a doodle. A doll manufacturer, visiting the small advertising agency in which she was a partner, bought the rights to manufacture the doll doodled on her drawing board. She created a family of dolls and used them as characters in her first book. Since then Mrs. Bonsall has written and illustrated six books; has written six other books (two under the name of Crosby Newell); and illustrated three books for other authors. Working primarily in black-and-white and two colors, Crosby Bonsall characterizes her work as representational. She is married and lives in Hillsgrove, Pennsylvania.

BOOTH, GRAHAM CHARLES

Born July 24, 1935 in London, England. Childhood spent in England and Canada. Attended East Los Angeles College; University of California at Los Angeles; University of Southern California.

"I always knew I would be an artist of some sort or another. I can remember drawing all over everything including my lesson books. I would doodle away the time and pay for my habit by writing 'I must not draw on my English notebook' one thousand times." After working for a short time in a plywood mill in Canada, Graham Booth attended art school. His main interest was design and after his training he was with Canadian advertising agencies for five years before beginning to free-lance and teach at the Vancouver School of Art in 1963. He went to California to get his Master's Degree in order to teach at the university level and *Henry the Explorer* grew out of his thesis. He had long had the ambition to illustrate and design a book for children, and for his thesis he made a complete study of the problems surrounding the development of such a book. For this book, he used colored inks and designer's colors in combination. He explains, "I could flood them on and mix them wet letting the ink itself take on new dimensions. Other times I would let one color dry, then glaze over the top of it with another. And other times I would bleach back the ink to lighten it or remove it altogether. I used designer's gouache (tempera) to bring out the texture in areas that interested me." Mr. Booth is now using colligraphs. "This consists of mounting various textures on a board and designing them and finally inking up the board and printing it like a wood block." Graham Booth lives in Placentia, California with his wife and young son and teaches art at Fullerton Junior College.

BORTEN, HELEN

Born June 20, 1930 in Philadelphia, Pennsylvania where her childhood was spent. Attended the Philadelphia College of Art.

After attending the Philadelphia College of Art on a four-year scholarship, Helen Borten became a free-lance artist and has illustrated book jackets, record album covers, greeting cards, as well as numerous books. She is constantly experimenting with different media. For *Do You See What I See?* she used monotype. She used water color for *Do You Move As I Do?* and collage and mixed media for *A Picture Has a Special Look.* She designs as well as illustrates her books. *Do You See What I See?* was the first of several books she has written as well as illustrated and it was chosen both as one of the "Ten Best Illustrated Children's Books" in 1959 by the *New York Times* and for the Children's Book Show of the American Institute of Graphic Arts. She lives in Lafayette Hills, Pennsylvania with her husband and two sons, Peter and Laurence.

BOSWELL, JAMES

Born in England.

James Boswell is a well-known British painter of portraits and abstracts as well as an illustrator of such books as *Little Cat Lost* by Sir Compton MacKenzie. Among the various exhibits of his work was one composed of his drawings of cats.

BRANDENBERG, ALIKI LIACOURAS, see Aliki, pseud.

BRIGGS, RAYMOND REDVERS

Born January 18, 1934 in London, England. Childhood was spent in Wimbledon, London. Attended Wimbledon School of Art; Slade School of Fine Art.

Raymond Briggs writes that he wanted to be a cartoonist and went to art school at fifteen. At the Slade School of Fine Art, he discovered he was not a painter and started doing illustration jobs while still in school. For book illustrations, which he prefers to advertising and magazine work, he uses pen and ink for black-and-white illustrations and gouache for color. He considers his work to be representational and hopes that over the past few years it has become "less soft-romantic and more tough-comical." He has designed as well as illustrated many of the books he has done and has also written three of them. *The Mother Goose Treasury* received the 1966 Kate Greenaway Medal; *Fee Fi Fo Fum* was a runner-up for this award in 1964. Raymond Briggs lives forty miles from London with his wife, who is a painter.

BRIGHT, ROBERT*

Born August 5, 1902 in Sandwich, Massachusetts. Childhood was spent in Goettingen, Germany, until twelve, then in Sandwich. Attended Browne & Nichols, Cambridge, Massachusetts; Phillips Academy, Andover, Massachusetts; Princeton University.

Robert Bright writes, "Although I was born on Cape Cod I was brought up from the age of one until I was twelve in the Hanoverian University town of Goettingen, celebrated for mathematics, physics, and legend. The Brothers Grimm, the etymologists, gathered their fairy tales there; Hamelin, the Pied Piper's town, was not far away. I suspect that the roots of my work as illustrator and author of children's books lie right there. My specialty is picture books and I generally use acetate in two and three color separations, although I have done at least one book in four colors. I write all my own texts and generally do the layouts. I use no models and draw, not what I see, but what I feel I see. People who have watched me at work tell me that I smile as I draw. It is an indication of the pleasure and satisfaction I get from what I am doing." In 1959 a film of *Georgie*, made from the original drawings, was selected to be shown at the Brussels World's Fair. Mr. Bright's home is in La Jolla, California.

BROOMFIELD, ROBERT

Born July 21, 1930 in Brighton, Sussex where his childhood was spent. Attended Brighton School of Art and Crafts.

Robert Broomfield recalls spending most of his boyhood on a sizeable farm on the South Downs near Brighton. After a year of studying for an engineering degree, he decided to study art.

In 1955, he joined an advertising agency and two years later began to free-lance. About his work, Mr. Broomfield says, "Most of my work now is illustrative and is equally divided between drawings for 'Blue Peter,' a BBC television program for children, and for children's books." He works primarily in color, "generally with pen and colored ink wash as used in *Mrs. Mopple's Washing Line.*" He regards his work as "freely decorative" and designs as well as illustrates his books. Mr. Broomfield lives in England with his wife, Megan, and young son.

BROWN, JUDITH GWYN

Born October 15, 1933 in New York City where her childhood was spent. Attended Cooper Union, Parsons School of Design, New York University, New York City.

As long as she can remember, Judith Brown has always wanted to draw. She attended the High School of Art and Music, and Cooper Union before going on to New York University and earning an undergraduate degree in Art History and English. She feels that this background gave her a "good historical framework" for illustration. She learned the technical part of book design and offset printing when she worked for a printer doing paste-ups and book jackets. In 1962, she illustrated her first book, *Mr. De Luca's Horse.* Since then she has illustrated twelve books and has written and illustrated two others. Concerning her techniques, she says, "Until recently I have worked with pen and ink using a flexible Pelikan fountain pen and ink on Strathmore board. The overlays which supply the color in the picture books are wash on prepared acetate done with a sable brush. Recently I have begun to use crayon as a medium both for black-and-white illustrations and for full color jackets. I continue to be delighted at the subtlety one can get by mixing these colors on paper." Judith Brown lives in New York City with her husband who is an atomic physicist.

BROWN, MARCIA*

Born July 13, 1918 in Rochester, New York. Childhood was spent in various small towns in New York State. Attended New York State College for Teachers, Albany; Columbia University, Graduate School of Philosophy; Woodstock School of Painting, studying under Judson Smith; New School for Social Research, New York, studying under Yasuo Kuniyoshi, Stuart Davis, and Louis Schanker; Art Students League, studying under Julian Levi.

Marcia Brown writes, "My interest in making picture books comes in an almost unbroken line from the constant reading and drawing of my childhood. Pictures popped into my head as I read, and I read voraciously, — my favorite books being the fairy tales of Andersen, Grimm, Perrault, and the *Arabian Nights.* While in college I started to paint summers in Wood-

stock. After three years of teaching, I continued under Kuniyoshi and Stuart Davis in New York. My first four books were finished while I was working in the New York Public Library where I had a chance to meet and work with interesting people and books, from this country and abroad. Travel, storytelling of folk and fairy tales to children, puppetry, and a constant interest in painting, all have influenced my work. I like making books for young children whose imaginations are vivid and whose associations are few." In the summer of 1953 Marcia Brown taught puppetry in the University College of the West Indies and traveled into the country districts of Jamaica to give puppet shows. Her home is in Manhattan where she has a studio overlooking the rooftops of the city to the George Washington Bridge. Since 1956 Marcia Brown has divided her time between New York, Europe and Hawaii. Italy, Sicily and Venice provided the inspiration for *Tamarindo!* and *Felice.* Her trips to Hawaii gave her background in Hawaiiana for *Backbone of the King,* which was illustrated in one color linoleum prints. Concerning her technique she writes, "What experimentation I have done with different techniques has been to find the best way to express what I felt about the book at hand. A cut medium, like woodcut, is most beautiful to me in maintaining the graphic unity between illustrations and type." The recipient of many prizes and awards, Marcia Brown was twice winner of the Caldecott Medal, in 1955 for *Cinderella* and in 1962 for *Once a Mouse.* The American Institute of Graphic Arts Show for 1958-1960 honored *Felice, Peter Piper's Alphabet* and *Tamarindo! Once a Mouse* was thus honored for the 1961-62 AIGA show, and also received a Citation of Merit from the Society of Illustrators. *Felice* was also honored by the Society in 1959. Marcia Brown was cited for the Hans Christian Andersen Honors list in 1964. She was a United States nominee for the Hans Christian Andersen award in 1966.

BROWN, PALMER*

Born May 10, 1919 in Chicago, Illinois. Childhood was spent in rural Pennsylvania, and in Evanston, Illinois. Attended Swarthmore College (B.A.) and University of Pennsylvania (M.A.)

"Aside from four years' service with the Air Force during World War II, there is little to add to the data above," writes Palmer Brown. "For the past ten years I have lived in an old stone farm-house, with some garden and many weeds. I shouldn't need to say that as an illustrator I am untaught. Perspective and anatomy defeat me. I first took pen in hand in 1953, to illustrate *Beyond the Pawpaw Trees,* to the purpose that picture and text might be more closely in harmony; and to the degree that what is crotchety and crabbed in the story is equally askew in the pictures I may have succeeded. Attention to minute detail and fanciful over-elaboration of it probably reflect at the same time a sympathy with wood-engraving and a constitutional inability to think of a tree except in terms of all its leaves." Palmer Brown's drawings have appeared in various magazines both for adults and children, including *Gourmet, Woman's Day, Story Parade* and *Jack and Jill*. He lives on a one acre farm in Bareville, Pennsylvania.

BRUNHOFF, LAURENT DE*

Born August 30, 1925 in Paris where his childhood was spent. Attended Lycée Pasteur; Académie de la Grande Chaumière.

Laurent de Brunhoff was twelve years old at the death of his father, the creator of *Babar*. At that time he was already deeply interested in painting and he used to sketch Babar for his own amusement. He finished his studies during the War and in 1945 he began to devote himself entirely to painting and working in an art academy in Montparnasse. At the same time he began his first book of *Babar* which he undertook both out of pleasure and to carry on a tradition. *Babar et Ce Coquin d'Arthur* appeared in 1946. Laurent de Brunhoff continued painting, his work being exhibited with that of a group of young painters in the Galerie Maeght and also in the Salon de Mai. Three more *Babar* books appeared, all of them translated into English and published in the United States. The characters in his fifth book in the series, *Babar et le Professeur Grifaton*, were in-inspired by his two children, Anne and Antoine. This story made its first appearance in the magazine *Elle*. In addition to his other activities, Laurent de Brunhoff is much interested in engraving and satirical drawing. His home in in Paris. Mr. Brunhoff works primarily in color, full color for the Babar books and four colors for *Serafina the Giraffe*. For *Serafina*, he did separations on acetate. He states that his style for the Babar books will never change, but that the style of his other books has become freer. He is responsible for the design as well as the illustrations of his books. An article on him appeared in a December 1965 issue of *Life*.

BRUSTLEIN, DANIEL, see Alain, pseud.

BRYSON, BERNARDA

Born March 7, 1903 in Athens, Ohio. Childhood spent in Athens, Ohio and traveling with her parents. Attended Ohio University; Ohio State University; Cleveland School of Art; New School for Social Research, New York.

With grandparents and great-grandparents who were teachers, preachers and college professors, a mother who was a Latin professor at Ohio University and a father who was a newspaper editor, it is not surprising that Bernarda Bryson grew up with an orientation toward mythology and classical literature. She writes that she "began to draw very badly, very early and also to write. Always illustrated the fly-leaves of my mother's music sheets, the fly-leaves of books, and all other available white spaces." Though Bernarda Bryson took art courses in whatever

school she attended, she majored in philosophy at college and had intended to pursue it in some sort of professional way. She first worked on several small newspapers, then taught etching and lithography for a year and then worked at commercial art — all the time continuing to paint, draw and write. She married Ben Shahn, the well-known artist, and "devoted four or so years exclusively to offspring." When she resumed illustrating, it was for such magazines as *Harper's, Scientific American* and *Fortune*. One of the first books that she illustrated she also wrote, *The Twenty Miracles of Saint Nicolas*. "This was a rewarding experience in every way. Since then I have illustrated numerous children's books, enjoying most of them enormously." Recently she has written and illustrated *The Zoo of Zeus* which she calls "my first jocular essay into the classical material which I really love intensely. I expect to continue in this direction." *Wuthering Heights* in the Macmillan Classics is an example of several books she has done "in a complicated fine line in black-and-white." Others, like *The Return of the Twelve*, were done in a more open line. "I've done several books in pencil, a way of working I greatly enjoy, such as *The Sun is a Golden Earring*." Others she has done with washes in color. Bernarda Bryson lives with her family in Roosevelt, New Jersey. An article on her work appeared in *Print*, September, 1955.

BUEHR, WALTER FRANKLIN*

Born May 14, 1897 in Chicago, Illinois. Childhood was spent in Illinois and Michigan. Attended Detroit School of Design; Philadelphia Museum School of Industrial Art; Art Students League, New York.

Walter Franklin Buehr enlisted at the age of nineteen in the first Camouflage Section of the United States Engineers and was sent to France in 1917 where he spent several months with the French Army. Back again with the United States Army, he saw action in the battles of Saint-Mihiel and the Argonne. After the war he married and lived for several years in California, then returned to New York where he has lived and worked ever since. Always interested in the sea, Mr. Buehr has been sailing boats ever since 1940. His interest in the sea led him to write his first book, *Ships and Life Afloat* and it was a natural step from that to working in the field of children's books. Mr. Buehr lives part of the year in his house on Elbow Key in the Bahamas where he races his dinghy. Working primarily in two colors, he uses ink and wax pencil on a transparent acetate plastic, with a separate drawing for each color. He also writes and designs books, which number forty-seven. He has been given the Art Directors Club of New York's Gold Medal.

BUFF, CONRAD*

Born 1886 in Switzerland where his childhood was spent. Studied in Switzerland, and at Art School in Munich.

Conrad Buff, who came to this country when he was nineteen, lives with his wife in Pasadena, California. He says that he is more truly a Westerner than many a native son. Born the son of an Alpine farmer, and the descendant of a long line of Alpine people, he left milking cows when his artistic aptitudes earned him an entrance to a government school to learn the designing of lace. The work was arduous, limited, too exacting, and at eighteen, with some hard-earned francs in his pocket, he took off to study art in Munich. Shortly thereafter an understanding mother supplied the wherewithal and Buff landed in America. He went west directly, stepping off the train at a cow station near the Dakota-Wyoming line, and found there exactly what he had dreamed about when, as a boy, he had read James Fenimore Cooper. Despite the obstacle of a strange tongue and the economic question of existence, he felt that he was home. He worked as a ranch hand, sheepherder and house painter. Every spare hour he spent in painting pictures. He has received numerous awards and is represented by paintings and lithographs in many museums. As a mural painter, his murals in the Edison Company building in Los Angeles and the First National Bank in Phoenix are the most representative. While he works in many media — oil painting, tempera, lithography, screen printing and serigraphs — murals are the things he loves best to do, for his style adapts itself to large architectural spaces. He feels the style of his illustrations has become more direct and simpler over the past ten years. For a number of these he has used pencil; in the case of *Elf Owl* and *Trix and Vix* he used pencil on a plastic sheet.

BURCHARD, PETER*

Born March 1, 1921 in Washington, D. C. Childhood was spent in New Jersey and Connecticut. Attended The Avon School, Avon, Connecticut; graduated from Philadelphia College of Art.

During his school years Peter Burchard was especially interested in literature and in writing, and he was an enthusiastic athlete. His father, a lawyer and an amateur artist, encouraged his early interest in the graphic arts. At the age of eighteen he decided to become an illustrator but his professional training was interrupted by World War II. In the Army he served the Signal Corps as a radio operator on a troop transport, and during the War his drawings appeared in *Yank* and *Mademoiselle* magazines. After finishing his professional training in 1947 he became a free-lance illustrator. He has done magazine illustration and has illustrated close to 100 books, most of them for children. In the late 1950's he started writing and is the author of two picture books, a short history of ballooning, several historical novels for young adults and one biography for adults. A Guggenheim Fellowship beginning in the summer of 1966 was used to complete another biography. His home and studio are in New York. He is the father of three and his elder daughter is studying art at the same school he attended. Peter

Burchard, who describes his work as representational, usually does full color book jackets with black-and-white half tone drawings inside. He often mixes media, using wash and casein paints or designer's colors. Charcoal drawings were used for *Jed*, while wash and casein were used for *Roosevelt Grady* and *Pirate Chase*.

BURGER, CARL VICTOR

Born June 18, 1888 in Maryville, Tennessee where childhood was spent. Attended Maryville College; Stanford University; Cornell University; School of the Museum of Fine Arts, Boston.

"My great interest in animals has dictated my choice of subjects and almost all my professional practice has dealt with the depiction of birds, mammals and fishes," writes Carl Burger who was born and reared in the mountainous country of eastern Tennessee on the edge of the present Great Smokies National Park. He compromised on his college career and studied architecture at Cornell because his father, a small town bank president "literally shuddered" at the idea of his studying art. He continues, "My most treasured college experience was a close association with a great naturalist-artist, the late Louis Agassiz Fuertes, painter of birds. From him I learned much and first got the idea of turning my interest in nature to practical use by becoming an animal painter." After college Mr. Burger worked with the novelist Kenneth L. Roberts on the *Boston Sunday Post* for four years. Since the early 1930's he has worked free-lance, doing along with illustrating a set of murals for the Bronx Zoo, and large paintings for the New York Zoological Society and the New York Aquarium. Working primarily in either black-and-white or full color, Carl Burger describes his work as "highly representational but with great attention to decoration." He uses oil, water color, charcoal and Wolff carbon pencil. *All About Dogs* was done mainly in Wolff pencil. Mr. Burger and his wife Margaret live in Pleasantville, New York. They have a grown son, Knox, who is an editor for a publishing company.

BURKERT, NANCY EKHOLM

Born February 16, 1933 in Sterling, Colorado. Childhood spent in Michigan, Missouri, Illinois, Wisconsin. Attended University of Wisconsin (B.S. and M.A. in Applied Art).

"I illustrate books because I enjoy 'visualizing' a literary work; illustration is like staging a play — designing the sets, the costumes, the lighting, 'casting' the characters," writes Nancy Burkert. She describes her work as representational with emphasis on draughtsmanship and particularization, explaining, "I am trying to restore the individualized face — I have used models for most of my people and would hope the reader might recognize my characters were he to meet them on the street.

I think there is great pleasure in differentiating the infinite variety of forms in nature. I try to have a locale even if a specific one is not indicated in the story. I always have in mind what time of year it is. I try never to *generalize!*" For the black-and-white drawings in *Jean-Claude's Island*, she used conté pencil and crayon. The full color pictures for Andersen's *The Nightingale* were done with brush and colored India inks. This book was an Honor Book in the *New York Herald Tribune's* Spring Book Festival in 1965 and was given the Gold Medal by the Society of Illustrators in 1966. Nancy Burkert also paints in water color and has had her works exhibited in Chicago and New York. She lives in Milwaukee, Wisconsin with her husband, Robert, who is Associate Professor of Art at the University of Wisconsin, and their two children, Claire and Rand.

BURN, DORIS

Born April 24, 1923 in Portland, Oregon. Childhood spent there and in Waldron Island and Bellingham, Washington. Attended Oregon State; University of Hawaii; University of Washington (B.A., 1947).

"Drawing has always been play," writes Mrs. Burn. "To be drawing and still have everyone credit me with working seems almost too good to be true. When I was little I used to buy those little bundles of pastel colored pads at the dime store and fill them with the adventures of three little stick men named Fred, Herbert and Junior. I've lived all my life in the Pacific Northwest except for brief sojourns to New York and Hawaii. But there isn't much point in mentioning any place other than the little island in the San Juan group of Puget Sound. This is home. It was my father's land. My children were born there, and someday it will be theirs. Life is still relatively primitive. We use kerosene lights, draw water from a well and heat our houses with wood from the forests. I have four children: Robin, Mark, Cameron and Lisa. They have all gone to the delightful one room school on the island." *Andrew Henry's Meadow* (1965) is Mrs. Burn's first book, with another one in the making. This was done in black-and-white with a crow quill pen, a sable brush and ink on bristol paper. "Lacking a light table, I used to tape my drawings to the window in order to trace them." About illustrating she writes, "An illustrator is really a sensitive accompanist, intensely aware of atmosphere, mood and the human gesture and of the visual elements which express these. To me this interpretive ability takes precedence."

BURNINGHAM, JOHN MACKINTOSH

Born April 27, 1936 in England where he spent his childhood. Attended Central School of Arts, Holborn, London.

It wasn't until he was twenty that John Burningham decided to become an artist and began his studies at the Central School

of Arts, since he does not recall any desire from an early age to paint. "I started writing and illustrating my own books," he writes, "as a means of getting my work published." His first book, *Borka, The Adventures of a Goose Without Feathers*, got his career in illustrating off to a flying start by winning the Kate Greenaway Medal in 1963. This, like the books that followed, are largely done in full color using "an enormous selection of materials: printer's ink, crayons, gouache, cellulose, montage, charcoal, india ink, pastel, photostats, etc." He has commented that, "an artist is crippled in this country by the reproduction of his work, so I put a lot into my drawings, knowing I'll be left with something." Mr. Burningham, who is married and lives in London, also designs murals, posters, and does magazine illustrations. About illustrating for children, he writes, "One must not be patronizing, a beautiful picture is not enough — a mixture of action, detail and atmosphere is important."

BURTON, VIRGINIA LEE*

Born August 30, 1909 in Newton Center, Massachusetts. Childhood was spent there and in Carmel, California. Attended California School of Fine Arts, and Demetrios School of Drawing and Sculpture, Boston.

Virginia Lee Burton's father was the first Dean of Massachusetts Institute of Technology. Her husband, George Demetrios, is a well-known sculptor and teacher. She has two sons, Aristides and Michael, and it was for them she wrote her books. She writes, "My characters and locale (with one exception, *Calico*) I have chosen from what I have found about me. An engine on the Gloucester Branch of the Boston and Maine is the heroine of *Choo Choo*. 'Mary Ann', Mike Mulligan's steam shovel, I found digging the cellar of the new Gloucester High School. *The Little House* [for which she received the Caldecott Medal in 1943] was inspired by the moving of our own house 'into the middle of a field with apple trees growing around,' and *Katy* is the pride and joy of the Gloucester Highway Department. Each new book is an incentive to the artist to spread his roots — to reach out and add to the store of subject material from which he can draw." About *Song of Robin Hood* she writes, "I studied up on Twelfth Century England, when the monks scribed and illuminated their beautiful manuscripts and it was never how long it took to make a book, but how well you could do it. Not wanting to imitate their work but wanting to keep the spirit of those times I worked for two years developing a medium and technique suitable for the ballads of Robin Hood. I deduced that the monks had drawn their inspiration from the 'flora and fauna' around them, so, with a little research, I found plants which probably grew in the twelfth century in England but also could be found growing here in my own back yard. Then with the whole family taking up archery, Folly Cove became Sherwood Forest and I could draw my subjects from life. As a designer and illustrator, I was grateful to have had the opportunity of doing this book with no dead-line, perfect reproduction, and the complete liberty of doing it just the way I wanted. *Life Story*, which was published in 1962, took me eight years to complete. The research for it was an education in itself. My publishers are still waiting for me to finish my book on design which I have been teaching and also practicing with the Folly Cove Designers for the last twenty-five years." The Demetrios' home is at Folly Cove, Gloucester, Massachusetts. Their two sons now live in San Francisco and have children of their own.

BUSONI, RAFAELLO*

Born February 1, 1900 in Berlin, Germany. Childhood was spent and schools attended in Germany, Switzerland and the United States. Died in March 1962.

Rafaello Busoni was the son of a renowned Italian pianist, and so, as a child, he came to take travel as a matter of course. From the time of his first one-man show in Zurich when he was seventeen, his oils and water colors were widely exhibited. "Always I wanted to become a painter," he wrote. "I remember struggling with the problem of how to draw a nose 'as it looks' from full face when I was six, and I had my first oil paint set when I was eleven. During the First World War we lived in Switzerland where drawing is considered the very elemental base for any of the fine arts. I tried every technique of the graphic arts: lithography, etching, woodcut, and every means of direct drawing. Although I spent most of my time painting, I cannot remember any period in which I did not make illustrations for my own pleasure. I chose my topics from among plays and operas and wrote the text myself to make the books complete. I have made more than twenty such handwritten books. When my son, Mario, was old enough to enjoy books, I got interested in children's books. Quite naturally, out of little talks with my child, evolved my first geographical books which I both wrote and illustrated." Between the years 1948 and 1952 Mr. Busoni worked for Audio-Video Filmstrips making close to two thousand drawings. Mr. Busoni illustrated both trade and text books, including several for the Limited Editions Club and the Heritage Press, and worked on the development of a full color reproduction method which reduces the cost of linecuts. For several years Mr. Busoni dedicated much of his free time to drawing individual dancers and ballets. His last work was a biography of Cervantes, *The Man Who Was Don Quixote*, which he wrote and illustrated.

CAMERON, POLLY

Born October 14, 1928 in Walnut Creek, California. Childhood spent in California and Arizona. Attended Phoenix College; University of California at Santa Barbara.

Although Polly Cameron has had no formal art training, she has worked in all areas of graphic design during the past fifteen years. During that time she toured Europe and North Africa for three years. She is the author and illustrator of seven books for children, in addition to her work as sculptor and graphic designer. Polly Cameron works in a variety of media, although she confines herself generally to two color illustration. For *I Can't Said the Ant*, she used line drawings executed with a fine brush water color on a slightly waxy surfaced tracing paper. She explains, "The waxy surface makes the line slightly erratic, giving it a freer look than ink on paper, i.e., all the lines do not adhere to the surface and the accidental element can be nicely effective. A simplified 'woodcut' without all the work was used for *A Child's Book of Nonsense*. The effect was accomplished by scraping away unwanted color areas on colored acetate, leaving the desired lines rough and free. My last book, *The 2-Ton Canary*, was executed in the strangest way yet — it was all 'stamped.' Very difficult to explain, but it is a book of riddles, so did not have to have the needed continuity of a story, yet I wanted the drawings to have a related feeling. By 'stamped' I mean that the texture that I wished to duplicate was transferred from object to paper via a stamp pad. No drawn lines were used. This includes most of the lettering which I stamped from a child's toy." Polly Cameron has also used pen and ink, paint and crayon. She attributes this variety in technique to the fact that "I am more a designer than an illustrator." Miss Cameron designs her books often using type as an intricate part of the pictures. Among her varied interests are "art and design of all kinds, my classic Morgan sports car, my French sheep dog and my home, a 150-year-old Victorian Gothic house overlooking the Hudson River in Sneden's Landing, New York."

CARIGIET, ALOIS*

Born in 1902 in Truns (Grisons), Switzerland, and there his childhood was spent.

Alois Carigiet was the seventh of eleven children of a mountain-farmer family. After going to school for ten years he served an apprenticeship in a painting shop, working afterwards as a commercial artist, with posters and theatrical scenery his specialties. Since 1939 Mr. Carigiet has worked as a painter and advertising artist. His is especially known for his murals. He speaks of his children's books as being "an expression of the longing for the lost paradise of his youth." Mr. Carigiet's illustrations were first seen in the United States in *A Bell for Ursli*. In 1966, *Anton, the Goatherd*, which was the first book he both wrote and illustrated, was published in this country. For his contribution to international children's literature, he was awarded a Hans Christian Andersen International Children's Book Medal for 1966. Alois Carigiet lives in Zurich, Switzerland.

CARLONI, GIANCARLO

Born in Italy.

Mr. Carloni, who lives in Milan, has illustrated a number of children's books in Italy in partnership with Giulio Cingoli. The first of these to be published in the United States was *Gaetano the Pheasant*. In 1964, they won the Prize Venezia and are now devoting most of their time to designing cartoons.

CARROLL, RUTH ROBINSON*

Born September 24, 1899 in Lancaster, New York. Childhood was spent in New York City and, in summer, in the Pocono Mountains of Pennsylvania. Attended St. Agatha Episcopal School, New York; Vassar College; Art Students League, New York City and Woodstock, New York; Cecelia Beaux' Portrait Class, New York; Hugh Breckenridge's School, Gloucester, Massachusetts.

Ruth Carroll has written that her interest in drawing began with murals "which extended three feet above the floor — since, at the time, the artist was only two and one half feet tall." While in school she wrote and illustrated stories about her pets for the school magazine. Every summer she attended nature study classes for children. At Vassar College she majored in Art. While she was a junior, one of her landscapes in oils was exhibited by the Pennsylvania Academy, and, after graduating, with honors, some of her landscapes were bought by the Newark Museum. She had many commissions for murals and portraits, and, whenever children posed for her, she told them stories and "found out what kept them from wriggling." Her first book, *What Whiskers Did*, was a story told entirely in pictures. In 1928 she married Latrobe Carroll, a writer-editor. She asked him for a little help here and there until gradually he found he was a collaborator. *Where's the Bunny?*, which was the result of her studying the needs of very young deaf children, is used in many schools for the deaf. Mrs. Carroll loves illustrating for children "because it focuses into one medium all her main interests: art, books, nature, and children themselves." Working in both black-and-white and full color, Ruth Carroll says, "I am a painter, not a draftsman, so the techniques I like are those that give me the most freedom. I like charcoal-pencil and pastel crayons best of all. A single pen and ink line is not much fun for me." The black-and-white illustrations for *The Picnic Bear* were done in charcoal pencil, fine pen and Venus pencil. *Danny and the Poi Pup* was done in full color using pastel pencils. Describing her style as representational, she says, "My drawings are never done in quite the same way for each successive book." Mrs. Carroll is the recipient of an award given by the American Association of University Women (North Carolina Division) for *Peanut* and *Digby the Only Dog*. The September-October 1950 *Horn Book* contains an article written by Ruth Carroll. She is the subject of an article published in the November 13, 1955 issue of the *News and Observer* of Raleigh, North Carolina. The Carrolls, who lived for a number of years in North Carolina, now make their home in New York City.

CELLINI, JOSEPH

Born June 13, 1924 in Budapest, Hungary where his childhood was spent. Attended the Academy of Fine Arts, Budapest.

"I still recall the excitement of my first experience with books," writes Joseph Cellini. "The most fascinating part of it was the pictures. So in the natural course of events, I decided to become a painter. My grandfather most enthusiastically encouraged this. He was an eminent sculptor who had come to Pest from Italy to design and execute the statuary for one of the largest churches there. My father, a physician, looked a little askance upon this endeavor, but my grandfather won out." While studying to become a painter, Joseph Cellini continued to be interested in illustrating books. "I wanted to put on paper what would have excited me as a young person. I thought that illustrating books for children could and should influence them, for the artist can teach them how to look at things. One of the first things which influenced me as an artist was motion pictures. I was intrigued with camera angles, close-ups, distorted perspectives and, of course, the action. I felt this should contribute to illustrating for the young." In 1956, Mr. Cellini and his wife, who is also an artist, came to the United States from war-torn Hungary. "We both work in a large, light studio, Eva at one end of the room and I at the other. We are fortunate that we have been accepted here as people and as artists. We are citizens and we are grateful that we could and do stay here in the U.S.A." Mr. Cellini uses all of the modern techniques for reproduction. "We work on board, paper, hot and cold press, paints, dyes, acrylics, dinobase as well as other acetates. For black-and-white I use scratchboard, pencil, wash, tempera, etc. Since this is a country in which one can find new media and try new methods, I avail myself of this whenever possible, mainly trying to get the best reproduction possible for my work."

CHALMERS, MARY EILEEN*

Born 1927 in Camden, New Jersey. Childhood was spent in southern New Jersey. Graduated from the Philadelphia Museum School of Art in 1948, and attended the Barnes Foundation, Merion, Pennsylvania.

Mary Chalmers is primarily a painter. Her work is represented in various private collections, and one of her lithographs is owned by the Barnes Foundation. She writes, "I grew up in various towns in southern New Jersey, and there were also two years in an airport (we lived in the living quarters attached to a hangar) when I was around the ages of three and four. My parents consider those two years rather a wasteful adventure, but I look back on them as a profitable, pleasant time. For myself. I have a sister two years older who is also an artist." After graduating from art school Mary Chalmers spent several years doing commercial art work, but her interest was in book illustration, particularly children's picture books, and in 1955 she did her first children's book for Harper and Brothers, *Come for a Walk with Me*. Since then she has written and illustrated eleven books as well as illustrated books for other authors. "In the past ten years, I've learned to stay with a drawing longer," she writes. "In the earlier books, such as *The Cat Who Liked to Pretend*, it is a naively drawn cat, not because that was the way I thought it ought to be done, but because that was the best I could do! *The Three to Get Ready* cats, while far from perfect (perfect to my mind is a Beatrix Potter cat) are more literally drawn." She generally works in black and one or two colors. For *Three to Get Ready*, she used pencil with color overlays. "For the past several years I've been using Kemart board which is treated to fluoresce under purple light. This fluorescence in the paper permits the use of erasing and scratch techniques. The use of this special paper makes for much truer reproduction of pencil." Miss Chalmers, who lived for several years in Pennsylvania, has recently moved to Haddon Heights, New Jersey.

CHAMBERLAIN, CHRISTOPHER

Born 1918 in Worthing, England. Attended Clapham School of Art and Royal College of Art.

Mr. Chamberlain's training at the Royal College of Art was interrupted by six years in the Army during World War II. He is primarily a painter whose work has been exhibited in England and Australia and is owned by a number of museums. He is married to Heather Copley and in at least two books their drawings have appeared together, *London's River* and *Heroes of Greece and Troy*. In the book *Artists of a Certain Line* he is quoted as saying, "Good drawing results from a conflict between competence and sensibility. Blended in some mysterious way a true marriage of these qualities is rare."

CHAPPELL, WARREN*

Born July 9, 1904 in Richmond, Virginia where childhood was spent. Attended University of Richmond (B.A. 1926); Art Students League, New York; Offenbacher Werkstatt, Offenbach-am-Main, Germany; and Colorado Springs Fine Arts Center.

Warren Chappell writes that when he was eleven years old Boardman Robinson's war drawings, made in Russia in 1915, were the earliest influence in bringing him to illustration. "After graduating from the University of Richmond I went back to the Art Students League where I had first begun to study. From 1928 to 1931 I worked as art director of the promotion department of a national magazine, then to Offenbach-am-Main where I learned punch-cutting and type-making in the studio of the late Rudolf Koch and at the Klingspor Type Foundry. When I returned to the United States, in 1932, I began work

in my own studio and for the next three years was occupied largely with lettering, decoration, and typographic design. During this time I was an instructor at the League in wood-cut and wood engraving and published *The Anatomy of Lettering* which was written in memory of Rudolf Koch. In 1935 I went to Colorado Springs to work as an instructor and to study with Boardman Robinson. Since then I have returned to New York where I have done the body of my illustrated work and the great share of my book typography. During this time I designed the 'Lydian' type family for American Typefounders, and 'Trajanus' for D. Stempel in Frankfurt. My work has its roots in the classic approach to drawing as it was developed by the Italian and Dutch painters. I despise technique and search for method only. In this the lucidity of Michelangelo's pen drawings, the shorthand of Rembrandt's sketches and the professional and yet humble attitude of Daumier toward illustration, have served as a constant reminder of what can be done. My own ideal for my music series (books such as *The Nutcracker*, *The Sleeping Beauty*, *Coppelia*) would be drawings by Poussin with colors laid in by Hokusai's wood-cutters." Mr. Chappell points out that his approach to preparing art work for offset printing takes into consideration his earlier letterpress experience. In making separations, he generally uses retoucher's warm greys which give him control of the values and allow for good photographing quality. Mr. Chappell lives in a pre-Revolutionary house in Silvermine, Norwalk, Connecticut.

CHARLIP, REMY*

Born January 10, 1929 in the Brownsville section of Brooklyn, New York, where his childhood was spent. Attended Cooper Union, New York; Black Mountain College, Black Mountain, North Carolina; Merce Cunningham School, New York.

Remy Charlip's work has grown out of the influence of the avant-garde theatre dance. A graduate of the Fine Arts Department of Cooper Union, he decided upon a theatrical career and was given a scholarship in Dance at Reed College in return for designing sets and costumes and teaching crafts and painting to children. He continued his dance training in New York and, at the same time, taught design, did choreography for The Living Theater, illustrated for magazines and wrote articles for dance magazines. His first book, *Dress Up and Let's Have a Party*, was published while he was on a dance tour with Merce Cunningham. Mr. Charlip's home is in New York City where he has been active for a number of years in The Paper Bag Players, a group offering creative theatre for children, which he helped found in 1958. Four of his more recent books show the influence of this activity, since three are plays, *The Tree Angel*, *Jumping Beans*, and *Mother Mother I Feel Sick Send for the Doctor Quick, Quick, Quick*; a fourth book, *Fortunately*, grew out of an improvisation. He has also choreographed a poem-play by Ruth Krauss and is now teaching courses in book illustration at the School of Visual Arts and in children's theatre at

Sarah Lawrence College. His book, *It Looks Like Snow,* has been made into a movie. In 1965 the Greenville (Delaware) Elementary School named its library for Remy Charlip and set aside a small room to house a collection of his original drawings, book dummies, letters and photographs. "I like to interpret the text in what I think is a suitable style, therefore paper collage worked well for *What Is the World?,* water color for *The Dead Bird,* line for *Where Is Everybody?,* and silhouette with four colors in *Mother Mother I Feel Sick Send for the Doctor Quick, Quick, Quick.*" An article on Mr. Charlip's books appeared in the June 1966 issue of *Print* magazine.

CHARLOT, JEAN*

Born in 1898 in Paris where his childhood was spent.

An American citizen born in France, Jean Charlot is nevertheless known to critics as "that great Mexican artist" because of his murals at the University of Mexico, frescoes at the Ministry of Education in Mexico City, and various writings on Mexican art and archeology. Of Mexican descent on his mother's side, he did not, however, go to Mexico until he was twenty-two. His career as an artist began in Mexico in 1921. He has been associated as an artist with Dr. Silvanus Morley, director of Carnegie excavations at Chichen Itza in Yucatan; and he has been instructor of art in the Art Students League, Chouinard Art Institute, and Florence Cane School, New York. In addition to his mural work, canvas painting, and teaching, his time is filled with writing, lecturing, archeological research, book illustration and the perfecting of a new process of lithograph printing. Jean Charlot has done forty murals for churches, banks, universities, hospitals, schools and public buildings throughout the United States, Mexico and in the Fiji Islands. His easel paintings are in collections in many countries, and he has illustrated over seventy books and portfolios. His early book illustrations for children include those done for Melchor G. Ferrer's *Tito's Hats,* 1940, Anita Brenner's *Boy Who Could Do Anything,* 1942, and Margaret Wise Brown's *Child's Goodnight Book,* 1943. Books which won the Newbery Medal in two successive years were illustrated by Mr. Charlot: *Secret of the Andes* by Ann Nolan Clark in 1953, and *And Now Miguel* by Joseph Krumgold in 1954. He has received two honorary degrees: D.F.A. from Grinnell College, Iowa in 1946 and LL.D. from St. Mary's College, Indiana in 1956. He is now Emeritus Senior Professor at the University of Hawaii and Senior Specialist at the East West Center in Honolulu where he lives. He is also writing an art column for the *Honolulu Star-Bulletin.* Jean Charlot who works mainly in two colors, characterizes his style as architectural. He usually employs direct brush or pen drawing on acetate, making his own color separations. He designed *The Timid Ghost* by Anita Brenner and *Kittens, Cubs, and Babies* by Miriam Schlein. In the spring of 1966, Jean Charlot was honored by the Honolulu

Academy of Arts with an exhibition entitled, "Jean Charlot Retrospective — Fifty Years 1916-1966."

CHERMAYEFF, IVAN

Born June 6, 1932 in London, England where childhood was spent. Attended Harvard University; Institute of Design, Chicago; Illinois Institute of Technology; Yale University School of Design.

A well-known graphic artist, Ivan Chermayeff is a partner in the firm Chermayeff and Geismar Associates and has recently been President of the American Institute of Graphic Arts for three terms. Though his brother followed his father in becoming an architect, Mr. Chermayeff aimed his studies at graphic design. He received four Moholy-Nagy scholarships for study at the Institute of Design and with another fellowship took a B.F.A. degree from Yale University. Before free-lancing, he was assistant to Alvin Lustig and an Assistant Art Director at Columbia Records. He has illustrated six children's books to date, the first being *The Thinking Book.* For these books he has generally used "pen, pencil, brush and cut paper." Mr. Chermayeff, his wife and their two small daughters, make their home in New York City. An article about his work, which has won a number of awards, appeared in *Print,* September 1959.

CHWAST, JACQUELINE

Born January 1, 1932 in Newark, New Jersey where childhood was spent. Attended Newark School of Fine and Industrial Art; Art Students League, New York.

"I'm an illustrator because drawing has always been one of the things I've liked best. I have an older cousin, an artist who entertained me as a child with caricatures of myself and others we knew. And now I find it very satisfying to have such a world to order to my tastes. I'd like my drawings to act out for the child some of his own feelings, especially the inappropriate ones," writes Jacqueline Chwast. Her book *When the Babysitter Didn't Come* is about her own two small daughters. She is married to Seymour Chwast, an artist and designer, and their home is in New York City. Her work, to date, has been done in pen and ink.

CINGOLI, GIULIO

Born in Italy.

Mr. Cingoli who works in partnership with Giancarlo Carloni has illustrated a number of children's books published in Italy. His work has become known in the United States through the picture book *Gaetano the Pheasant.* Mr. Cingoli and Mr. Carloni, who live in Milan, are now devoting themselves to designing cartoons. In 1964, they won the Prize Venezia for Cartoons.

COBER, ALAN E.

Born May 18, 1935 in New York City where his childhood was spent. Attended University of Vermont; School of Visual Arts, New School for Social Research and Pratt Graphic Center in New York.

Alan Cober had an artist uncle who discouraged him from going to art school, telling him he had no talent. But at college, where he intended to study law like his father, he was encouraged by an art instructor and so left and went to art school. Since then his black-and-white illustrations have appeared in such magazines as *Sports Illustrated, Redbook,* and *Seventeen* as well as in several children's books. "I have always liked illustration because I have always enjoyed seeing my work printed in the thousands." He describes his work as "graphic with powerful design." In 1965, Mr. Cober was chosen Artist of the Year by the Artists Guild of New York. Articles about Mr. Cober and his work have appeared in *Art Director,* March 1966; *Idea* (Tokyo), June 1965; *Print,* November 1963; *Gebrausgrafik* (Germany) September 1965. He lives with his wife and two children in Ossining, New York.

CONNOLLY, JEROME PATRICK

Born January 14, 1931 in Minneapolis, Minnesota where his childhood was spent. Attended University of Minnesota.

"Rather early in life I developed a liking for wildlife, especially birds," Jerome Connolly writes. "When I was about twelve, I met a wildlife artist, Francis Lee Jaques, and spent many hours watching him paint diorama backgrounds at a natural history museum." Mr. Connolly is now one of only about twenty-five diorama painters in the United States and his work is to be seen in natural history museums all over the country. His first assignment after college was at the Illinois State Museum, where he met and married his wife, who is an editor. The Connollys and their small daughters make their home in Stamford, Connecticut. Though most of his time is spent in his museum work and in painting wildlife, Mr. Connolly has also illustrated five books, the first of which was *Study of Fishes Made Simple* published in 1962. He does most of his non-museum work in a small study in his home. For books like *Travels of Monarch X,* he uses three or four colors, making separations on sheets of thin, frosted plastic which has a tooth surface, He works on this with pencil, brush, pen and sometimes an air brush or inked sponge.

COOMBS, PATRICIA

Born July 23, 1926 in Los Angeles, California. Childhood spent in St. Louis, Missouri. Attended De Pauw University, Indiana; Michigan State; University of Washington.

Patricia Coombs was born in Los Angeles, the daughter of an engineer whose work took him to many parts of the country. After graduating from high school in Florida, she studied art at De Pauw University and Michigan State before going to the University of Washington and taking first a B.A. and then an M.A. in English literature. While working toward her doctorate, she met and married James Fox and they moved first to New York, then Minneapolis and more recently to Waterford, Connecticut where they live now with their two daughters. She writes, "Recently I have been doing volunteer work in the library of our new grade school, and have found it immensely interesting and stimulating. The children are so enthusiastic and their delight is so contagious, you want to rush home and write more and more books. I don't think there is any experience quite comparable to holding a copy of a book you've written that is dog-eared, tattered, and smudged from use." Miss Coombs writes as well as illustrates her own books. She works primarily in black-and-white or two colors and for the books about Dorrie the witch she uses pen and ink with color separations made on acetate.

COONEY, BARBARA*

Born August 6, 1917 in Brooklyn, New York. Childhood was spent on Long Island where she attended Great Neck Preparatory School. Also attended Briarcliff School; Smith College; Art Students League, New York.

"My father was a stockbroker, my mother painted pictures for fun; so her children did too, and that's how it all began," writes Barbara Cooney. "We lived in a suburb of New York and went to school there. Summers were spent in Maine. After boarding school and college I trudged around New York City with my portfolio. Then I began to write books for myself so I could draw the sort of pictures I wanted. At the Art Students League I learned etching and lithography." In 1940 appeared Bertie Malmberg's *Åke and His World* with Miss Cooney's illustrations, and in 1941 the first of her own books, *King of Wreck Island.* "In the summer of 1942 I joined the WAC, and later in that year married Guy Murchie, Jr., war correspondent and author." For a while the Murchies with their small daughter lived in Belchertown, Massachusetts, on a co-operative farming venture. Later they bought a farm in Pepperell, Massachusetts, where they ran a children's camp in the summers. In 1947, after divorcing Guy Murchie, Jr., Barbara Cooney went with her daughter and son to live in Waldoboro, Maine, and later in Acton, Massachusetts. In July, 1949, she married Dr. Charles Talbot Porter and returned to live in Pepperell where her husband has a general practice. She now has another son and daughter: Charles and Phoebe Ann. The Porters live in a rambling sixteen-room house built in 1818, surrounded by broad lawns, tall trees, and lovely gardens, one of Barbara Cooney's special interests. A number of the plants pictured in *Chanticleer and the Fox,* for which she received the 1958

Caldecott Medal, are in her garden. She also housed chickens, while working on this book, to act as models. In 1963, she and her family spent a summer in France, where she gathered the visual impressions that resulted in the illustrations for *Mother Goose in French* and a French version of "Wynken, Blynken, and Nod" called *Papillot, Clignot et Dodo*. She describes her work on these books as well as earlier ones in the film, "The Lively Art of Picture Books." Scratchboard was the medium that she used most frequently before *Chanticleer and the Fox* and she wrote an article about it in the April 1964 *Horn Book*. "I had always thought: once you succeed, change. So after that I tried pen and ink, pen and ink with wash, casein, collage, watercolor, acrylics — trying to fit the medium and techniques to the spirit of the book." To date she has illustrated over sixty books. Articles about Barbara Cooney appeared in the *Horn Book*, August 1959 and *Library Journal*, April 1959.

COPLEY, HEATHER (Diana Heather)

Born December 13, 1920 in Brewood, Staffordshire, England. Spent childhood there, in Filey, Yorkshire, and London. Attended Clapham School of Art and Royal College of Art, London.

Heather Copley says that she refused to attend school after the age of thirteen. "Had always wanted to be an artist anyway." She began her studies at the Royal College in 1939 and in 1940 married the artist, Christopher Chamberlain. Their daughter Sarkia is now grown and is a dress designer. After serving in the Civil Defense in World War II, she finished her studies at the Royal College. "I like drawing but I prefer to be thought of as a painter who draws rather than an illustrator. "She exhibits her paintings regularly at the Royal Academy and is also a part-time lecturer at St. Martin's School of Art in London.

CORCOS, LUCILLE*

Born September 21, 1908 in New York City where her childhood was spent. Attended Art Students League, New York.

Lucille Corcos writes, "I began painting professionally in 1929 in Brooklyn Heights, New York, engaging simultaneously in both fine and commercial art. My commercial career began with the creation of illustrations for children's books that I tried unsuccessfully to have published. At that time the editorial consensus was that they were not suitable for children. So, to go to the other extreme, I took them to the Condé Nast Publications where the late Frank Crowninshield ordered a cover for *Vanity Fair* on the spot. Since then, I have illustrated many books, both for children and adults." She married an artist, Edgar Levy (who is presently on the faculty of Pratt Institute) in 1928. They have two sons, David and Joel, live in Rockland County, New York and have a summer home on Fire Island.

She illustrated a four volume complete edition of *Grimms' Fairy Tales* which was published by the Limited Editions Club in 1962. Her son Joel was the inspiration for three books that she wrote as well as illustrated. These and *From Ungskah to Oyaylee* for which she also wrote the text were illustrated "by making color overlays, although I work primarily in full color." Her paintings have been shown in museums all over the United States as well as in South America and Europe, and are in the permanent collections of such museums as the Whitney Museum in New York and the Museum of Tel Aviv.

CORWIN, JUNE ATKIN

Born June 1, 1935 in New York City. Childhood spent in Fieldston, Riverdale, New York. Attended Sarah Lawrence; Yale University, School of Design (B.F.A.).

"My interest in drawing and painting started early in my childhood, and was encouraged by my mother, who is a painter, and by my father, who is a psychoanalyst with an interest in art and in the artist," writes June Corwin. She was influenced by the drawings of Aubrey Beardsley noting, "There is the sinuous and satirical line and witty and surprising use of black and white. I found more fascination in them than I did in the fine collection of children's books provided for me by my parents." At the Yale School of Design she studied with Josef Albers. While a student she met and married Arthur Corwin, a graduate of Cooper Union and a student in sculpture at Yale. He is also an architect and is now in private practice as well as teaching at Cooper Union. They have two children, Matthew and Susannah. Mrs. Corwin writes, "It is to them that I attribute the direction that my work has taken, both fitting into and evolving out of family life. The method of my painting and drawing is stream of consciousness, in which I allow thoughts, feelings and fantasies to materialize in the work, one thing suggesting another, sequentially, rather than executing a painting or drawing that has been preconceived in theme and detail," explains Mrs. Corwin. Working only in black-and-white she describes her work as neither wholly decorative nor representational. She hopes that "my drawings evoke a particular and rather subjective way of seeing objects and situations." Commenting on her style she says, "My style has not changed, so much as evolved over the past ten years. It is a direction I took in my earliest work, and am still working to bring to realization." For *Serendipity Tales* she used pen and ink. Mrs. Corwin and her family live in Rowayton, Connecticut.

COSGRAVE, JOHN O'HARA II*

Born October 10, 1908 in San Francisco where his childhood was spent. Attended Marin Junior College, University of California, California School of Fine Arts, and the studio of André Lhote, Paris.

As a boy John O'Hara Cosgrave II haunted the San Francisco docks where the ships come in. "I had my first boat, a re-modeled Navy twenty-eight-foot whaleboat, at fourteen," he writes. "At eighteen I re-built another whaleboat and sailed it until I left San Francisco in 1930 to go to Paris. I spent two years there, painting at Lhote's in the morning, and in the afternoon drawing the old houses of Paris. In the summer I went to seaports on the coast of France and painted ships. I also took a tour of France, Switzerland, Germany, Austria, Hungary, Holland and Belgium, drawing ships wherever they were to be found." Upon his return to this country, Mr. Cosgrave began a career which has included Christmas cards for the American Artists Group, book jackets and book illustration, and illustration and covers for such magazines as *Motor Boating, Yachting, Life* and *Fortune*. In 1938 he illustrated *Log of Christopher Columbus' First Voyage to America*, and in 1943 a selection of Robert Frost's poems, *Come In, and Other Poems*, and Clara Ingram Judson's *Donald McKay, Designer of Clipper Ships*. Soon after his marriage to Mary Silva, a children's book editor, he built a very modern house on Patuisset Island in Pocasset, Massachusetts, "called the Crows Nest by the Cape Codders because it sits up on columns in order to get the view of Red Brook Harbor and Hen Cove." In 1962 the Cosgraves made this their year round home, after having divided their time between Cape Cod and Brooklyn for a number of years. It was in that year, also, that his maritime history, *America Sails the Seas*, was published. An expert on ships, as well as an ardent sailor, he is particularly concerned that "in ship drawings the rigging must be absolutely correct. To check I have a reference library of over two hundred books." In 1963 he wrote and illustrated *Clipper Ship*. For the past few years, besides illustrating and painting, he has been doing silk screen prints of ships for the Woods Hole Art Gallery.

COSGROVE, MARGARET LEOTA

Born June 3, 1926 in Sylvania, Ohio. Childhood spent in Ohio, Illinois, Vermont and New Jersey. Attended Chicago Art Institute; University of Chicago.

"I had a double childhood in a way: the opportunities of growing up both in a small town — in days when small towns were content to be small towns — and of spending several years in cities, for a change of pace and outlook . . . Art was to me at that time mostly a matter of storing up impressions and ideas rather than of execution and expression," Margaret Cosgrove writes. She began her career doing medical and surgical illustrations for adult publications. "This is a narrow and highly specialized field, and I made every effort to broaden out from it into more of the biological sciences. In my own pursuit of these related subjects, and with much working with children, I have felt the great need for an approach that is neither over-popularizing and exploiting the natural sciences in general, nor the presentation of a textbook." She has written as well as illus-

trated her books for children. Working primarily in black-and-white and two colors, she describes her work as representational and works in several media. For *Eggs* and *The Strange World of Animal Senses* she used dinobase and lithograph pencil. *Strange Worlds Under a Microscope* was done in wash, and pen and ink was used for *Wonders of Your Senses*. Margaret Cosgrove lives in New York City.

CRICHLOW, ERNEST T.

Born June 19, 1914 in Brooklyn, New York where childhood was spent. Attended Commercial Illustration School of Art; Art Students League, New York.

"I would like to consider myself an artist-illustrator because I divide my time between painting, illustrating and teaching. I devote a large portion of my painting to the expression of the urban Negro. As a Negro, I feel a special responsibility to deal with the material as honestly as I can in my book illustrations," writes Ernest Crichlow. His paintings have been shown throughout the country. His first one-man show in September 1953 consisted of a series of paintings reflecting the reality of the child in his environment. At the time of the show, he noted, "I have observed how children come into the world free of prejudice, how their play in the early years is free and whole-some, with an honest acceptance of their fellow-children re-gardless of superficial differences. Most of my paintings deal with the children I know best, Negro children, in whose faces and bodies I try to show their hopes and aspirations." His illustrations, to date, have been primarily in black-and-white. The Crichlows and their son live in Brooklyn, New York, where Mr. Crichlow teaches painting at Brighton Art Center.

DANSKA, HERBERT*

Born October 16, 1927 in New York City. His childhood was spent in The Bronx, New York. Attended New York public schools, graduating from the High School of Music and Art; Art Students League, New York; Pratt Institute, Brooklyn; Académie Julian, Paris.

Herbert Danska's professional career as an artist and illustrator began after his discharge from the United States Air Corps in 1947. He has worked in most phases of applied art and has done magazine illustrations in addition to book illustration. His interest in folklore, film and cinema, and his family have had a significant influence on his work. At present, Mr. Danska has a second and parallel career as a film maker. He has been pro-ducer-director and cameraman on several commissioned social documentaries. "I have just completed my first theatrical full feature. It's a dramatic film which I directed and co-authored, entitled "Sweet Love, Bitter." In 1962 his short film, "The Gift" received a Golden Eagle and also awards in the Venice and Vancouver Film Festivals. His illustrations, he describes as "expressive-graphic," with strong drawing as a basic element, no matter what the medium. Water color is his most used medium and it is combined with pen and ink, wax and occasionally "limited collage." Over the past ten years, he feels that his style has changed "from the softer and lyric to simpler, more direct, and much greater economy of means."

DARLING, LOIS MAC INTYRE

Born August 15, 1917 in New York City. Childhood spent in Riverside, Connecticut. Attended Grand Central School of Art and Columbia University, New York City.

Lois Darling writes, "As a child I spent a ridiculously large part of my life living on and 'messing about in' boats. Almost as much time was spent in drawing and sculpting." World War II started shortly after she finished art school and she took a job making ship models for the Navy, followed by two years in the WAVES. In 1946 she married Louis Darling whom she had met in art school. While doing illustration work for *Yachting* and *Rudder*, she also studied zoology for the next four years at Columbia University. Two years later, after a job as staff artist at the American Museum of Natural History, she began to work with her husband in writing and illustrating the books they have done together. "As for technique," she writes, "I use lamp black and a brush for line drawings. This resembles pen and ink, but only rarely do I use a pen."

DARLING, LOUIS*

Born April 26, 1916 in Stamford, Connecticut. Childhood was spent there and in Farmington, Connecticut. Attended Grand Central School of Art, New York, and studied privately with Frank V. DuMond and Frank Reilly.

Louis Darling gives this account of himself: "I have always lived either in the country or in smallish towns and have been, since a very early age, devoted to the woods, the fields, and the water. Between the ages of nine and twelve I became, under the influence of Ernest Thompson Seton, an Indian. As the years passed this interest went through the hunting and fishing stage and grew into my lifelong devotion to, and interest in, the biological sciences. When the time came to choose a career, the other abiding interest of my life won out and I went to art school. After three and a half years in the Air Force, spent mostly in England as a photographer with the 8th, I went to work at commercial art. I also married Lois MacIntyre, a zoologist and an artist, whose help has meant everything. A job illustrating an adult book on trout fishing led to a jacket of a juvenile fishing book which led to illustrations for over fifty children's books of various kinds. One of the earliest books I illustrated was Beverly Cleary's *Henry Huggins*. In 1954 I caught up with the biological interest and have written and illustrated six books of my own on natural history and seven

more in collaboration with my wife, Lois, all on biological subjects." The Darlings make their home in Old Lyme, Connecticut. In 1966 the John Burroughs Medal was given to Mr. Darling for *The Gull's Way* and also in recognition of the author's prior works. This Medal is given annually for the year's outstanding book of natural history. Mr. Darling does his art work in either black-and-white or full color. For *Penguins*, pencil was used; for *Coral Reefs*, tempera. *The Gull's Way* was illustrated with pencil drawings and photographs. "As I made the photographs myself, I consider them the same as my drawings. I expect to use more in the future." About illustration, he writes, "When I was a child the pictures of Pyle, Wyeth and Rackham were the ones that were magic for me. This has given me an unshakable belief that children like work that is craftsmanlike, beautiful and real."

DAUGHERTY, JAMES HENRY*

Born June 1, 1889 in Asheville, North Carolina. Childhood was spent in Indiana, Ohio, and Washington, D.C. Attended Corcoran School of Art, Washington, D.C.; Pennsylvania Academy of the Fine Arts; and studied with Frank Brangwyn in London.

"My earliest impressions," James Daugherty writes, "are of the life and people on the farms in small towns of the Ohio Valley. My grandfather told stories of Daniel Boone and his buckskin men as he had heard them told. My mother, full of fun, sang the Negro songs and told the stories she had learned in Virginia. My father read aloud splendidly, and during long hours, and even days of my boyhood, read me the fine books of England and America from Chaucer to Mark Twain while I drew pictures. It was he who directed me to the Library of Congress and to the Art School in the basement of the Corcoran Art Gallery. After a year at the Pennsylvania Academy I spent two wonderful years in London where my father was agent for the Department of Agriculture, and also had some travel in France and Italy. It was in London I first read Walt Whitman and became fired with his vision of America and its possibilities. During the First World War I worked in shipyards in Baltimore and Newport News camouflaging ships for the Navy, and it was while doing this work that I became friends with the distinguished illustrator Henry Reuterdahl. Later I painted murals for Loew movie houses in New York City. My first book-illustrating commission was given me by May Massee, to make pictures for Stewart Edward White's *Daniel Boone*." Mr. Daugherty's own *Daniel Boone* won the Newbery Medal in 1940. His first picture book was *Andy and the Lion*, 1938. Since then James Daugherty has written and illustrated more than fifty books. He has had many one-man shows of his paintings and is represented in a number of collections. His wife, Sonia, is an author for whose books he is "official illustrator." They live in Weston, Connecticut and have one grown son, Charles Daugherty, who is also an author-artist. Concerning his work, Mr. Daugherty says, "It has been my practice in illustrating books (after long meditation and prayer) to seize a thin stick of charcoal and draw on a sheet of tracing paper the image before my inner eye. Happily this is sometimes a right and flowing design or again the first of a series that build up to the final harmony. This drawing I place down on a sheet of paper and rub off a light grey transfer. This I rapidly ink in without alteration, happy if some of the freshness and vitality of the first drawing remains. Line and design are all and the first of all the commandments is simplify."

D'AULAIRE, EDGAR PARIN*

Born September 30, 1898 in Campo Blenio, Ticino, Switzerland. Childhood was spent in Paris, Florence, and Munich. Studied at Art Academy and Hoffman School, Munich; in Paris, with André Lhote and Galani.

Edgar d'Aulaire comes from an old Huguenot family; his mother was an American, his father an eminent society painter in Italy. His first artistic influence came from his father and from book collectors. After giving up architectural studies in Munich, he began the serious study of art at the Art Academy there, concentrating on the pure study of nature. He then went to the Hoffman School, Munich. At Lhote's in Paris, he studied the principles of abstract composition and later, at Galani's, the graphic arts. In Florence he studied fresco painting, and always maintained a close contact with modern French book illustrators and mural painters. He illustrated fifteen books published in Germany, two published in Paris. In 1925 he married Ingri Mortenson, and in 1929 they came to New York where they continued to live until 1941, making yearly journeys to France and Norway. In 1931 *The Magic Rug* was published, and the next year *Ola*, forerunner of many children's books written and illustrated in collaboration by Ingri and Edgar Parin d'Aulaire. Beginning with *Abraham Lincoln* which received the Caldecott Medal in 1940, they have turned to the history of their adopted country for a number of their books. The d'Aulaires now divide their time between their farm in Wilton, Connecticut and Upper-Lee Farm near Woodstock, Vermont. Mr. d'Aulaire writes, "During the last ten years we have only finished two new books, *The Magic Meadow* and *Greek Myths*, which took years and years of research. Besides we had to completely redraw the Lincoln book. We tried to keep the drawings as close as possible to the originals, though we made a point of making at least one small change in each picture, which brightened the tediousness of the mechanical work. Instead of stone-lithography we had to use acetates for the new Lincoln. With a heavy heart we had to give up our beloved stones, not because our backs broke but because the offset printers hate to handle them. We try to work the acetates just like the stones, but you cannot get as much life out of the dead material."

D'AULAIRE, INGRI MORTENSON PARIN*

Born December 27, 1904 in Kongsberg, Norway, where childhood was spent and schools through Junior College were attended. Also studied at Institute of Arts and Crafts, Oslo; Hoffman School, Munich; and Académies Lhote, Gauguin, and Scandinave, Paris.

Ingri Parin d'Aulaire's artistic background came from her father's brother, best known through his poems put into music by Grieg and Sinding and for his translations of the Icelandic Edda from Old Norse into modern Norwegian. "At sixteen, because my mother insisted on college training before artistic development, I took matters into my own hands and laid my paintings before Harriet Backer, Norway's most eminent woman painter, who gave me her full support," writes Ingri Parin d'Aulaire. "I studied art at Oslo for a year, then spent a year at the Hoffman School in Munich, later going to Paris. In 1925 I married Edgar Parin d'Aulaire, but continued at art school until 1929. After traveling all over Europe and North Africa we came to America to live. After our son, Per Ola, was born in 1939, we moved to Lia Farm, in Wilton, Connecticut where our second son, Nils Maarten, was born in 1948." Per Ola is now married and Nils began college in the fall of 1966.

DAVIS, DIMITRIS

Born 1905 in Chanea, Crete, Greece where childhood was spent. Attended Royal Academy of Fine Arts, Munich, Germany.

Dimitris Davis, who is a native of Crete, began his studies there and continued at the Royal Academy in Munich. Usually working in black and white, he describes his work as "free style, naturalistic." He writes, "My ink and water color technique, as in *An Island for a Pelican*, is probably characteristic of my work." Davis, who is primarily a painter, now lives in Athens, Greece.

DE ANGELI, MARGUERITE LOFFT*

Born March 14, 1889, in Lapeer, Michigan. There and in Philadelphia, Pennsylvania, childhood was spent.

Marguerite de Angeli says that she grew up in a family where the father was a born teller of tales with a gift for drawing and the mother was quiet and efficient, saying to her children, "You can do *anything* you *really* want to do." Drawing, painting, writing and singing were chief interests during her childhood. However, it was not until after her marriage and her children were partly grown that opportunity came for her to study illustration with the help of an artist neighbor, Maurice L. Bower. According to Mrs. de Angeli most of her work was carried on while rearing five children. Usually she worked in the center of family activity as opposed to people who must have cloistered quiet for creative work. Almost any place served as a studio — a corner of the kitchen, a room upstairs, the dining room near the window where the light was good. For over thirty years, Mrs. de Angeli has been writing and illustrating children's books. *Ted and Nina Go to the Grocery Store* appeared in 1935, followed in 1936 by her well-known *Henner's Lydia*. In 1950, *The Door in the Wall* won the Newbery Medal and in 1961 it was given the Lewis Carroll Award. Mrs. de Angeli works in both black-and-white and full color, often using Wolff pencil and water color. "The first several books were done on glass and I made the separations." For her more recent books she has not done the separations. Philadelphia is her home. She has received a number of honors: in 1958, she was made a Distinguished Daughter of Pennsylvania; in 1963, she received the Lit Brothers' Good Neighbor Award and was also honored by the Graduate Library School of Drexel Institute; in 1965 she was one of ten authors honored by the Governor and his wife. The de Angelis have thirteen grandchildren and one great-grandchild, many of whom now serve as models for their grandmother's illustrations.

DE MISKEY, JULIAN

Born December 21, 1908 in Hungary. Childhood was spent in Europe and the United States. Attended art schools in Cleveland and New York; University of Paris.

"Pictures and the love of pictures influenced my childhood and I recall collecting and treasuring my battered picture books years after they were given me. Each of them opened a new door to a marvelous little playhouse where the characters came alive especially for me to act out their fascinating comedies or dramas. It was like TV watching today, without the screen. Later my picture fever became so acute that I covered the margins and all avaliable white space in my school books with my own primitive drawings. In high school I became the official artist of the school paper and won the fantastic amount of $25 in an essay concerning a traveling show of paintings that visited our small town. At present the illustrating of books is in the nature of returning to childhood the pleasures I received from it. In between my sophisticated paintings, *New Yorker* covers, and magazine illustrations the work on a book is a welcome change of pace. My wife, Shari Frisch, is also a painter and book designer, so that the appreciation of the well designed, well illustrated book is very sincere in our family," writes Julian de Miskey. He works in either black-and-white or full color. His favorite black-and-white technique, which was used for *Chucaro*, is pen and ink line with crayon shading. The de Miskeys live in New York City.

DENNIS, WESLEY*

Born May 16, 1903 in Boston, Massachusetts. Childhood was spent at Falmouth on Cape Cod. Attended New School of Art, Boston. Died 1966.

Wesley Dennis worked in the art departments of several Boston newspapers, as did his brother, Morgan Dennis. He did fashions for Jordan Marsh, then went to Filene's, doing mostly Christmas cards, and later, portraits. "I didn't like any of these jobs," he said, "so decided to concentrate on painting horses, as I liked to be around them. I hung around race tracks all over the country, camping out in a beach wagon and selling pictures of horses to their owners." For a while Wesley Dennis lived on a farm in Montgomery, New York, carrying on his art work and raising sheep and pigs on the side. Later, he lived in Warrenton, Virginia, the heart of the fox hunting country. Children came out by the bus-loads to see his pets. These included horses, dogs, peacocks, bantam chickens, emus from Australia, ducks that liked their backs scratched, black snakes, a pet fox and a tame crow. Since *Flip*, 1941, Mr. Dennis had illustrated over seventy-five books, including *King of the Wind* for which Marguerite Henry received the Newbery Medal in 1949. *Tumble*, which he wrote as well as illustrated, was finished a few weeks before his sudden death in the fall of 1966.

DE PAOLA, TOMIE

Born in Meriden, Connecticut where his childhood was spent. Attended Pratt Institute, Brooklyn, New York.

Since his graduation from Pratt in the 1950's, Mr. de Paola has done a good deal of painting, including a number of murals, has taught art at the Newton College of the Sacred Heart in Massachusetts, and has done scenic design and also some acting at Colby Junior College in New Hampshire. He has been particularly interested in liturgical art and many of his murals have been for churches, such as those in the Weston Priory in Vermont. The first children's books that he illustrated were *Sounds* and *Wheels* published in 1965. These were done with color separations on acetate. He illustrated two books in 1966, one of which he also wrote, *The Wonderful Dragon of Timlin*. He has been living in New York and Meriden, Connecticut, but in late 1967 he plans to be in San Francisco, teaching and studying.

DIMSON, THEO AENEAS

Born April 8, 1930 in London, Ontario, Canada where childhood was spent. Attended Ontario College of Art; Danforth Technical School.

Theo Dimson claims that he became an artist because he was unsuccessful in the restaurant business. Beginning his career as a commercial artist in 1950, he has been involved in many aspects of graphic design. He works primarily in black-and-white but uses a number of different media. For *The Sunken City*, he used brush and ink. Pen and Magic Marker ink was used for *The Double Knights*. Over the past ten years his style has changed from loose brush line to controlled pen line, with more use of complex decorative detail. In 1961, he received a Senior Arts Fellowship from the Canada Council to visit designers in Japan. Articles about him have appeared in two magazines published in Japan, *Idea* in 1959 and *Graphic Design* in 1961. His work has received a number of awards including those of the Toronto and Montreal Art Directors Shows and the Graphica '65 Show. His work has appeared in the American Institute of Graphic Arts Packaging Show and its Children's Book Show of 1964. Mr. Dimson is married and has three children.

DINES, GLEN*

Born November 19, 1925 in Casper, Wyoming. Childhood was spent in Central Washington. Attended University of Washington, Seattle, Sacramento State College, Sacramento, California; Art Center School, Los Angeles.

Glen Dines, the youngest of a family of three, received his schooling through high school in Yakima, Washington. He has lived and traveled extensively in Wyoming, Idaho, Montana, Oregon, and Washington. He received both A.B. and M.A. degrees from Sacramento State College. His professional art background includes magazine illustration and murals, and, in commercial art, layout and advertising. During his Army service he was Staff Artist for the Pacific edition of *Stars and Stripes*, General Headquarters, Tokyo, Japan, and he was Art Director for the Ernie Pyle Theater, Eighth Army Special Service, Tokyo, from 1945 to 1946. For the past few years he has been general editor of Macmillan's *Frontier West Series* and has written or illustrated many of the titles in it. One of these, *Bull Wagon*, is an example of his work using alternate two-color and four-color illustrations, for which he did each color, including the black, on a separate sheet of acetate using pencil, ink and conté crayon. The book jacket was done in full color using watercolor and opaque tempera and, unlike the interior, was camera-separated. "I use small sketches, scaled to page size on a visual board to plan the layout and illustrations in order to provide continuity throughout the book," he writes concerning the designing of the books.

DOBRIN, ARNOLD JACK

Born June 6, 1928 in Omaha, Nebraska. Childhood spent in Los Angeles, California. Attended Chouinard Art Institute, Los Angeles; Academie de la Grand Chaumiere, Paris; New York University.

"In the writing and illustrating of children's books," Arnold Dobrin explains, "there is in some way a recreation of that early time of childhood. The creator is able to live it through, to live it out. I feel, as do so many other artists, that there is very little choice in the matter of working or not working. The impulse to work is almost compulsive." He works primarily in three-color preseparated art using a variety of media on acetate overlays. For *Taro and the Sea Turtles*, printed in black and brown, he used black watercolor India ink, black chalks, oil chalk and "a large variety of watercolor and oil brushes." Concerning his work he writes, "I work also for the joy of the work itself, for the experience of using a particular kind of ink or paint, of knowing the character of a brush or a piece of paper. I work in order to know that incomparable pleasure in the sequence of beginning, middle, end, that is, the process of bringing to full completion the passing wisp of an idea." The February 1967 *Horn Book* has an article written by Arnold Dobrin. The Dobrins and their two young sons live in Westport, Connecticut.

DOMANSKA, JANINA

Born in Warsaw, Poland where her childhood was spent. Attended Academy of Fine Arts, Warsaw.

As a small child, drawing got Janina Domanska in trouble, since she drew caricatures of her teachers to amuse her classmates. She was asked to change schools but her mother made peace. During World War II drawing, almost miraculously, got her out of trouble. After the destruction of Warsaw, she was shipped to a concentration camp in Germany. Several days after her arrival, she was sketching near the barb wire fence and was noticed by a prominent man in town. He arranged to have her released to him in exchange for portraits she painted of his family. After the war she spent five years in Italy studying and painting. Her paintings have been exhibited there and in Warsaw. When she arrived in this country, she could speak four languages, but not English. She took a job as a textile designer and, as her English improved, she began to spend her lunch hours going to the various publishers with her drawings. She has now illustrated more than twenty-five books. For one of these she did the text, *Why So Much Noise?* and for another, *Master of the Royal Cats*, her husband, Jerzy Laskowski, a journalist and bookseller, did the text. *The Coconut Thieves* was the recipient of several awards including the picture book prize in the 1964 *New York Herald Tribune* Spring Book Festival. Using primarily pen and ink, water color and pencil, Miss Domanska has illustrated a number of books in black-and-white such as *More Tales of Faraway Folks* and a new edition of *The Trumpeter of Krakow* as well as picture books in four colors, doing hand separations. Miss Domanska now makes her home in New Fairfield, Connecticut.

DRISCOLL, BARRY

Born in England.

Barry Driscoll is an English illustrator who has illustrated such books as *Digging For Dinosaurs*, *Apes and Monkeys*, and *Mountain with a Secret*.

DRUMMOND, VIOLET H.*

*Born July 30, 1911 in London, England. Her childhood
was spent in London and Sussex. Attended The Links, Eastbourne; Le Chateau Vitry-Sur-Seine, Paris; St. Martin's
School of Art, London.*

As a child, Violet Drummond lived with her mother and two
sisters in London and used to go for walks in nearby Hyde Park.
It was probably these walks that gave her many of the ideas
which she afterwards turned into her stories for children illustrated by herself. She went to a school at Eastbourne, but says
that she did not take full advantage of the general education
given, as she was usually drawing imaginary characters in her
exercise books. Later she went to a finishing school in Paris
where the drawing master tried to persuade her to stay in Paris
to study painting. She returned to England, however, and was
presented at Court to the late Queen Mary. Soon afterwards she
went to India to stay with friends and when she came back
she attended St. Martin's School of Art for a short period.
During the Second World War she did some war work in the
First Aid Nursing Yeomanry, and looked after her son, Julian.
It was for this son, who now has a small boy of his own, that she
wrote and illustrated her first children's story in 1939, *Phewtus,
the Squirrel.* This first book and several of the ten that followed have been reissued in the 1960's in a larger format with
new illustrations. In 1957, her book *Mrs. Easter and the Storks*
won the Kate Greenaway Award in England. Along with her
illustrating, which she does both for her own books and for
those of other authors, she has recently made a series of
eighteen ten-minute cartoon films for the BBC Children's
Programme, based on the *Little Laura* books. She writes, "the
animation was simple — cut out figures on a moving background. I wrote the stories, designed and cut out the figures and
painted the backgrounds." Violet Drummond is married to
Anthony Swentenham, a member of the London Stock Exchange, and their home is in St. John's Wood, London. An
article about Miss Drummond appeared in the October 1949
issue of *Junior Book Shelf* magazine.

DU BOIS, WILLIAM PÈNE*

*Born May 9, 1916 in Nutley, New Jersey. Childhood was
spent mostly in France.*

"At the age of eight, I went to France with my parents and
sister," writes Mr. du Bois. "My life there was spent mostly
between three places: boarding school in Versailles, weekends
in Paris which inevitably included a trip to the Cirque d'Hiver,
and Villerville, a small resort town in Normandy. I must have
gone to the circus more than the average child; I believe
thirty times a year was my usual quota. My best friend in school
was a young Russian whose mother was a lion tamer and whose
father walked tightrope above the lion cage. All of this love of
the formal excitement of circus life must have somewhat influ-

enced my life and choice of a career. But, on the other hand,
my father is an artist, my mother a designer of children's clothes.
One of my grandfathers wrote extensively on book designing; the
other was an appraiser of art objects. I seem to have taken the
line of least resistance." Mr. du Bois's first book, published when
he was nineteen, was *Elizabeth the Cow Ghost.* A new edition
of this was published in 1964. *Three Policemen* and *The Great
Geppy* followed, and in 1948 he received the Newbery Medal
for *Twenty-one Balloons.* In his speech of acceptance of the
medal in the *Horn Book* for July of that year he spoke of the
years of discipline at the Lycée Hoche and that the "sense of
order and careful planning gained therefrom, has been to me of
infinite use and influence." His sister speaks of her brother's
three great loves: France, the circus, and Jules Verne. From
Jules Verne grew his intense interest in all mechanized inventions. About his own books he writes, "There is very little
description in my stories. I try to make them jump from
chapter to chapter like a program of vaudeville acts, full of
rather unusual action." He has illustrated not only his own
books but also those of other authors. "In illustrating, I try to
contribute elements not mentioned in the text in order to
fatten the fare. I try to avoid drawing backgrounds so that
children can place my characters in surroundings of their own.
I found it hard to read as a child, so I try to entice and drag
a child's wandering mind through the text, from drawing to
drawing, as one dangles a carrot in front of a stubborn donkey's
nose." Though he travels a good deal, Mr. du Bois makes his
home in New York City.

DUCHESNE, JANET

*Born May 11, 1930 in London, England. Attended Bromley
College of Art and Royal Academy Schools, London.*

Janet Duchesne writes, "I drew a great deal as a child, encouraged
by my mother who herself had an art school training. But,
until at the age of eighteen I gave up my idea of being a
zoologist, I had not planned to be a professional artist." While
studying art she won several awards for landscape and portrait
painting. "Until my marriage and the arrival of my daughter
in 1965, I still painted and had an occasional portrait commission; but now I can only find time to continue with a little
illustration work. I think my training as a painter was a good
foundation for illustrating books." Miss Duchesne works primarily in black-and-white using pen and ink. When she has
used color it is done with overlays on a black-and-white drawing.

DUVOISIN, ROGER ANTOINE*

*Born August 28, 1904 in Geneva, Switzerland. Childhood
was spent in Switzerland and France. Attended the College
Moderne, Geneva; Ecole des Arts Decoratifs and Ecole des
Beaux Arts, Paris.*

Roger Duvoisin's education was influenced by his father, who was an architect, and other friends and relatives who were in artistic professions. He drew and painted throughout his boyhood. He also began to study music at the age of seven. After attending the *Ecole des Arts Decoratifs*, where he studied mural painting and stage scenery, he went to work at the Geneva Opera Atelier des Decors. He also designed scenery for other productions, painted murals, did posters, illustration and worked in ceramic. Eventually, he was offered the job of managing an old pottery plant which Voltaire had founded in the little town of Ferney-Voltaire. He considered settling there when the old manager began to make trouble for him, broke pieces at night, mixed up orders, and even threatened to cut Roger Duvoisin's throat one dark night. He decided to move to Lyon where he became foreman of a large textile designing studio. This is what led him to America. The art director of a large American textile firm offered him a contract to go to New York, with the condition that he must stay at least four years. He signed the contract and sailed to America with his new bride. The textile firm went bankrupt during the depression, but at about the same time, he had his first book published. It was *A Little Boy Was Drawing*, one of two books he had done for his son, thus realizing an old dream to write and illustrate children's stories. Other books followed, some of which he just illustrated; others he wrote as well. He also did magazine illustrations and various commissions, including a few mural paintings. In 1948, he received the Caldecott Medal for *White Snow, Bright Snow* by Alvin Tresselt. In 1956 he won the first prize for children's books awarded by West Germany for his illustrations for *The Happy Lion*, written by his wife. In 1938 he became an American citizen and designed and partly built his own home in Gladstone, New Jersey. The Duvoisins have two grown sons and every two or three years travel abroad for long periods of time. In writing about his work, Mr. Duvoisin says that he considers the fewer the colors, the better the challenge. *Hide and Seek Fog* was in full color gouache, while the illustrations for such books as *Veronica* and *Red Bantam* were the result of separations done by hand with the help of tints printed on acetate and worked with knife, sandpaper and eraser. For *Petunia Beware*, he did separations on acetate in pen, brush, and ink. He feels that acetate separations offer endless possibilities because it is the closest thing to old stone lithography. Since no camera is involved in separating the colors, the artist gets exactly what he puts in. "When text permits, I am now trying to do pages where the very flat solid inks, characteristic of lithographic printing, will dominate. *The Rain Puddle* is an attempt to do this."

EARLE, OLIVE LYDIA*

Born in London, England. Childhood was spent mostly in Horton Kirby, Kent, England. Attended National Academy School of Fine Arts and Parsons School of Design, New York.

As a child in England, Olive Earle showed evidences of becoming a naturalist. At the age of eight she was making pictures of the parts of flowers, hunting for birds' nests and reporting her discoveries to her big brother who was an amateur ornithologist. The children had all kinds of pets from the usual dogs and horses to white rats and even a young eagle. When she grew up she continued to pursue her interest in natural history, as a worker in the field and an observer at the Biological Station for Research in Bermuda, and at an aquarium in Florida. As an artist she has been largely self-taught, though at the private school she attended she received good instruction from a visiting professor, and in this country she has attended art school for short periods. "Probably," Olive Earle writes, "I absorbed a sense of design from the paintings that were all around at home; my father was a collector of fine art but did not think a mere female could aspire. Secretly, he was a bit proud of my work before he died — but he never told me so. It just 'wasn't done' in our family!" Her work has been exhibited in the American Museum of Natural History, the Brooklyn Museum, the Los Angeles Museum, and others. She has painted murals and has made illustrations for many science books and several encyclopedias, and is the author and illustrator of articles for magazines, including *Natural History*. Olive Earle is the widow of the artist Harry R. Daugherty and lives on Staten Island, New York. She has written and illustrated eighteen books for children, with most of her drawings done in pencil.

EASTMAN, P. D. (Philip Dey)

Born November 25, 1909 in Amherst, Massachusetts where his childhood was spent. Attended Amherst College; Art School of the National Academy, New York.

P. D. Eastman writes, "I have always considered myself primarily a writer, the picture maker in me being a secondary asset — I am comparatively new to the children's book field, having worked previously in the animated motion picture field. In Hollywood I was associated with UPA Pictures, in their story department for seven years. I have illustrated books of other authors, and I am the author of a book illustrated by Roy McKie, but I feel I am most successful in the dual role of author and illustrator." Mr. Eastman worked for the Disney Studios and for Warner Brothers Cartoons before World War II. In the Army Signal Corps during the war he was assigned to a unit, under the direction of Frank Capra, which produced Army orientation films. His immediate commanding officer was Theodor Geisel. While at UPA he was one of the creators of the "Gerald McBoing Boing" film, the first non-Disney animated motion picture to win an Academy Award. He began free-lancing in the 1950's creating educational and commercial animated films in New York. *Sam and the Firefly* was his first book. Mr. Eastman has two grown sons. His wife, Mary, is a photographer and they live in Westport, Connecticut. Describing his style as "representational and cartoonish," he generally uses black and two or three colors, making separations with sets of non-photographic "blues" of his black key drawing.

EHLERT, LOIS JANE

Born November 9, 1934 in Beaver Dam, Wisconsin where childhood was spent. Attended Layton School of Art, Milwaukee; University of Wisconsin, Milwaukee.

A free-lance illustrator, Lois Ehlert has been involved in a variety of aspects of design and illustration. She was a four year scholarship student at the Layton School graduating in 1957. While a student at the University of Wisconsin, she did layout and production work at the John Higgs Studio. From 1959-1964 she did layout and design illustration at the Jacobs-Keelan Studio and for four years she taught children in the Junior School affiliated with Layton School of Art. Her work for children includes designing toys and games, a series of basic art books, and sets for the Moppet Players, a children's theater in Minneapolis, Minnesota. In her books, Lois Ehlert uses a variety of media. *I Like Orange* was done in collage; *Limericks by Lear*, printed in six colors, was done in mono-print and collage; *What Is That Sound?* was in "pen and ink etching line." She describes her work as "design illustration" and either designs the book herself or makes suggestions as to the layouts. In 1964, she was represented in the Creativity on Paper Show and has also received many merit awards from the Art Directors Club in Milwaukee, Wisconsin where she lives.

EHRLICH, BETTINA, see Bettina, pseud.

EICHENBERG, FRITZ*

Born October 24, 1901 in Cologne, Germany where childhood was spent. Attended State Academy of Graphic Arts, Leipzig, working under Hugo Steiner-Prag.

After study at the Academy in Leipzig, Fritz Eichenberg became a roving artist-reporter for various newspapers and magazines. As a social and political cartoonist-commentator, he foresaw the rise of Hitler's regime which he had caricatured publicly. He left the country early in 1933 as an accredited artist-reporter. Traveling and working his way through Central America and the United States, he decided to make New York his home. He returned to Nazi Germany long enough to bring his wife and daughter to New York. Returning at the height of the depression, he worked on the WPA Art Project, did cartoons for the *Nation*, and taught at the New School for Social Research. Books had always been his great love, and even in his student days, he had illustrated editions of three classics. Helen Gentry of Holiday House was the first to make use of his engravings in a small edition of *Puss in Boots* which was in-

cluded in the American Institute of Graphic Arts Fifty Books of the Year 1937. In the next few years he illustrated *Padre Porko*, and *Heroes of the Kalevala*. In 1937 he began a series of books for the Limited Editions Club including *Gulliver's Travels*. He has interpreted some of the most powerful figures in literature — Poe, the Brontës, Swift, Dostoevsky, Tolstoy, Pushkin, Turgenev, Shakespeare and Goethe. He has written and illustrated two picture books, *Ape in A Cape* and *Dancing in the Moon*. He has contributed many articles to art publications, and a Pendle Hill Pamphlet, "Art and Faith." He is an active printmaker, with work in many important print collections. Since 1947 he has taught at Pratt Institute in Brooklyn and for seven years was chairman of its Department of Graphic Arts where he started the Pratt "Adlib" Press. He is the founder and director of the Pratt Graphic Art Center in Manhattan and editor of a journal of printmaking, *Artist's Proof*. Mr. Eichenberg now lives in New York City and is working on a comprehensive book on creative printmaking. He works primarily in black-and-white using various media. Wood engravings were used for *Puss in Boots*; acetate separations for *Ape in A Cape* and *Dancing in the Moon*. Water color and scratchboard were used in other books. Articles about Mr. Eichenberg's work appeared in *American Artist*, November 1950 and *Graphis*, No. 43, 1952.

EINZIG, SUSAN

Born 1922 in Berlin, Germany. Studied painting in Berlin and then at Central School of Art, London.

As a young person, Susan Einzig's main interests were in mathematics and physics though she had also drawn and painted from an early age. At sixteen she began studying painting in Berlin. By spring of the next year, 1939, she was in London and two years later, because of the war, she was working in a factory. After the war she taught for several years at St. Martin's School of Art. As a source of income, she turned to illustrating. In the book *Artists of a Certain Line* she is said to feel that "most books are better off without illustrations but [she] states emphatically that painters make the best illustrators." She works mainly in black-and-white as in *Tom's Midnight Garden*.

ELGIN, KATHLEEN*

Born January 13, 1923 in Trenton, New Jersey. Childhood was spent in Columbus and Dayton, Ohio. Attended Dayton Art Institute and Columbia University.

After graduating from high school in Xenia, Ohio, Kathleen Elgin attended the Dayton Art Institute for two years, studying in Decorative Arts, her interest developing in stained glass. Later she worked in a glass studio for two years on the commission of a History of Medicine window for the Mayo Clinic. During the Second World War she executed technical manuals for the Air Force. She came to New York in 1945 and began free-lancing in advertising, turning after six years to the field of book illustration. Since then, she has written as well as illustrated several books. Miss Elgin, who works primarily in black-and-white, describes her work as representational and decorative. She notes that in the last ten years her style has changed from pure line to half tone, and that she has perfected her dry brush technique. In 1962, she had a one-man show of her dry brush drawings. Miss Elgin lives on Fire Island, New York.

EMBERLEY, ED (Edward Randolph)

Born in 1930 in Malden, Massachusetts. Childhood was spent in Cambridge, Massachusetts. Attended Massachusetts College of Art (M.F.A.); Rhode Island School of Design.

When he was working for an advertising firm, Ed Emberley "had no thought of going into children's book work." At the firm he did cartooning, worked with type and pasteups. On the strength of his outside greeting card work, he began free-lancing. He hired space in an art group in Boston and in the first week he started on *The Wing on a Flea* which was published in 1961. For the past five years he has spent half his time illustrating and writing children's books, and the other half illustrating textbooks and magazines. Mr. Emberley has three small handpresses for experimenting with type and woodcuts. He has just acquired an offset press "on which I intend to further my education." He writes, "I am interested in all phases of bookmaking, paper, illustrations, text, type, design, concept, history." His wife, Barbara, has written stories for him to illustrate. Their barn loft houses their Bird in the Bush Press, for which they are collecting old wooden type. Bird in the Bush Press books are tiny, two by two inches and from eight to sixteen pages long. The Emberleys and their two children, Rebecca and Michael, live in a seventeenth century saltbox house on the Ipswich River in Ipswich, Massachusetts. Their favorite pastime is sailing up and down the Northeastern sea coast, in their boat called "Dulcinea." Ed Emberley works in several media, generally using full color or two colors and doing separations with various materials. *Rosebud* was done in four colors. *Yankee Doodle* was done in woodcuts in red, white and blue. Woodcuts were also used for *Paul Bunyan*. He designs as well as illustrates and set his own type for *Yankee Doodle*. He notes that his style changes constantly. There is an article about Ed Emberley in the October 15, 1963 issue of *School Library Journal* and one by him, "The Crow-Quill Pen," in the October 1966 *Horn Book*.

ERDOES, RICHARD

Born July 7, 1912 in Vienna, Austria where his childhood was spent. Between 1933 and 1938 studied art in Vienna, Berlin and Paris.

"My father was a Hungarian and I come of a family of actors and opera singers," says Richard Erdoes. "In school I covered my lesson books with drawings to the horror of my teachers." While studying art, like other European art students, he would take yearly summer trips to Florence and Rome. He also hiked through Yugoslavia and much of Central Europe. Hitler was the cause for a more serious kind of travel. "As he moved in one side of a country, I moved out the other side — one frontier at a time, until in 1940, I faced the Atlantic Ocean." Mr. Erdoes came to the United States and after two months with *Stage* magazine, he began free-lancing. His commissions included not only magazine illustration and advertising, but also animated films and mural painting. Among his murals are those in the Museum of Fine Arts in Richmond, Virginia, and on the ship, "Santa Maria," of the Grace Line. But he feels book illustration is far more satisfying than advertising or magazine work. Among his first books were the *Time Reader's Cook Book*, and a picture book, *The Cat and the Devil*. He has a great interest in history and has been working on a picture history of Rome. Another strong interest in American Indians has taken Mr. Erdoes and his wife and three children on numerous camping trips to the various reservations. On one occasion, he was engaged to guide a BBC television crew on a trip through the western states and the reservations. From this interest has grown the plan for a series of twelve books on American Indians which he is doing for older children. Mr. Erdoes, who has done his book illustration primarily with tempera and pen and ink, designs as well as illustrates his books. He considers himself particularly fortunate that his wife is also a designer and helps him extensively.

ERHARD, WALTER

Born June 14, 1920 in Mount Vernon, New York, where his childhood was spent. Attended Pratt Institute and Art Students League, New York; University of Maryland.

Walter Erhard's earliest memories are of going off by himself and drawing. When he started art school it was with the idea of becoming an art teacher. At Pratt Institute he studied illustration under Bridgeman. Then came World War II, during which he served as an interrogator with the Army in Germany. Later at the Art Students League he studied painting and graphics and began to do a good deal of textile designing. Since about 1956 he himself has published a line of greeting cards under the name of the Imp Press. He illustrated his first children's book, *My Time of Year*, in 1961 and since then has done four others. "They have all been in limited — two or three — color," he says. "My approach is as a painter. I think in spots and masses of color and then accentuate with the line." The first book was done in waxy chalk. For others he has used pen and ink or wash. Mr. Erhard makes his home in White Plains, New York.

ETS, MARIE HALL*

Born in Wisconsin where childhood was spent. Attended New York School of Fine and Applied Art; University of Chicago (Ph.B.); School of the Art Institute of Chicago; University of Chicago and Columbia University (graduate work); and studied under Frederick V. Poole.

"Of my early childhood, I remember my brother's teasing and summers in the great north woods," Marie Hall Ets writes. "I was the fourth of six children in a minister's family. When I was seven years old an art supervisor became interested in my drawing and gave me instruction, so I decided to be an artist. After entering college I left to study art and in one year had a diploma in interior decorating and a job in San Francisco. As my fiancé was going to war, we married. After his death friends persuaded me to enter social work, and while finishing the university I lived at Chicago Commons Settlement House. Much of my social work was with and for children, including a year in Czechoslovakia in Child Health. In child psychology at Columbia I became interested in children's interpretation of drawings and *Mister Penny* followed. My marriage to Harold Ets linked me to the field of medical science from which came *The Story of a Baby*. During his fatal illness, *In the Forest* was made in the woods of Ravinia. The necessity to live only in the present gave us a feeling of oneness with nature which no physical death could destroy and we delighted in pet creatures of the woods and in the children who wandered in and out leaving fingerprints on my drawings." Mrs. Ets has written and illustrated seventeen books since her first in 1935. "In search of material, I have spent some weeks or months in such places as The Little Children's Home, an orphanage in Oklahoma, La Jolla, California, Tijuana, Mexico and Cairo, Egypt. Her home is now in New York City. "In illustrating for little children," she writes, "I have tried to keep my eye and mind on the child — not on art critics. Of course I have had to do acetate separations in recent years, but I still return now and then to my black-and-white paper batik. All adults insist that children like bright colors in their books, but I find they like black-and-white as well if the figures stand out enough and have action and life." About *Nine Days to Christmas*, winner of the Caldecott Medal in 1960 and written in collaboration with a Mexican friend, Aurora Labastida, she notes that they wanted to make it a story of a Mexican city child, for seventy per cent of all Mexicans live in cities. Mrs. Ets explains, "To avoid possible criticism of bias and unfairness in picturing the Mexican people, I used actual characters throughout, except for the little girl (the real Ceci was too large and too blonde)." Marie Hall Ets has had several runners up for the Caldecott Medal — *Mr. T. W. Anthony Woo*, 1952, *Play With Me*, 1956, *Mr. Penny's Race Horse*, 1957 and *Just Me*, 1966. Two books have been Honor books at the *New York Herald Tribune* Spring Book Festival — *Oley: The Sea Monster*, 1946, *Gilberto and the Wind*, 1963. *Play With Me* was also chosen an Honor Book for the Hans Christian Andersen Medal.

EVANS, KATHERINE FLOYD

Born January 2, 1899 in Sedalia, Missouri. Childhood spent in Kirkwood, Missouri. Attended Chicago School of Design; School of the Chicago Art Institute; Grand Chaumiere, Paris. Died August 1964.

Katherine Evans lived a large part of her life in Evanston, Illinois where she was active in art circles and helped to found the Artists' Market which later grew into the Evanston Art Center. It was after the death of her husband in 1948 that she began to illustrate children's books. Her daughter writes that "although she wrote as well as illustrated many of her books, she much preferred illustrating." Many of her books were based on her own travels to Mexico, Ethiopia, Morocco and Europe. *Nemo Meets the Emperor* resulted from her own opportunity to meet Haile Selassie while in Ethiopia. Seven of her books during the past ten years were retellings of old fables such as *The Boy Who Cried Wolf* and *The Man, the Boy, and the Donkey*. In all she illustrated close to seventy books before her death in 1964 at her summer home on Washington Island, Wisconsin.

FALCONER, PEARL

Born in Dundee, Scotland. Childhood was spent in Scotland and London. Attended St. Martins and Central School, London.

After studying art in London, Miss Falconer began her career doing fashion drawing. From this she widened out to portraits, murals, and then story illustration for magazines. For many years she has done covers and illustrations for *Harper's Bazaar*. She has also done dress designing for films and "then became interested in children's books." She enjoys book illustration and now devotes most of her time to it. She is a Fellow of the Society of Industrial Arts.

FAVA, RITA, see Fegiz, Rita Fava

FEASER, DANIEL DAVID

Born May 28, 1920 in Dauphin, Pennsylvania. Childhood spent in Eastern Pennsylvania. Attended Philadelphia Museum School of Art; Westminster Choir College, Princeton, New Jersey.

After World War II, Daniel Feaser began a career in commercial art with the encouragement of a friend. He worked for department stores and advertising agencies in Philadelphia and Miami, Florida. He called his early efforts "learn while you earn." In 1957 he joined the National Park Service. He writes, "There in the Branch of Museums I had the wonderful opportunity of painting diorama backgrounds, wildlife habitat settings and about every phase of exhibit work including designing complete 'visitor centers'. It was here that I met Harold Peterson, historian and arms expert. He is the author of the three books I've illustrated. I make my home in Fairfax County, Virginia. Recently added a studio to the house. There in the evenings, after work, I pursue my first love, wildlife illustration. I'm busy at the present time trying to master the new acrylic paints which almost demand a more direct statement in that they dry so quickly." His black-and-white book illustrations have been done in pencil.

FEGIZ, RITA FAVA*

Born June 2, 1932 in Rome, Italy. Childhood spent in Italy and in Philadelphia, Pennsylvania. Attended Philadelphia Museum School of Art.

Rita Fegiz writes of her background, "I came to the United States, my mother's country, when I was thirteen and continued my high school education, and then went on to art school for four years. As well as illustrating, I do children's portraits and keep on with painting for myself as much as I can. No doubt the roots out of which my work has grown can be traced to my childhood in Europe. There a child has art all around him: at home, in schools, in churches and even in the parks where he plays. He is given drawing lessons by his governess even before he can write. All my European friends drew, and drew extremely well; they stopped as they grew older. I went on." She lived and worked in the United States for a while and then returned to Rome, where in 1962 she married Carlo Fegiz, an Italian architect. They have two little girls, Marta and Cristina. "It is now ten years that I have been illustrating and hope always to continue. It just seems that children are my favorites to draw and to draw for." She works primarily in black-and-white and designs the books she illustrates. *The Long Nosed Princess* was a prize book in the 1959 New York *Herald Tribune* Spring Children's Book Festival.

FENNER, CAROL ELIZABETH

Born September 30, 1929 in Hornell, New York. Childhood spent in Almond and Brooklyn, New York and Shelton, Connecticut. Attended Herbert Berghof's School of Dramatic Arts; New Dance Group School; Irving Burton's Dance School; Curt Conway's Theatre Arts School.

Carol Fenner recalls that her earliest inspiration was a fellow first grader who drew perfect circles. "I thought it would feel wonderful to be able to do it too. I practiced everywhere. In the process I began to draw other things." Later she practiced sketching baseball players in motion. "One of my aims at that time was to be able to sketch the pitcher in his wind-up before he threw the ball. (I never did.)" Her strongest influence was her aunt, the author and librarian, Phyllis Fenner. "My aunt Phyllis, who told magical stories, gave us wonderful books and

loved us all. She smelled good and everything she did held wonder and warmth and tasted delicious." Carol Fenner's illustrations for two picture books, which she also wrote, are in black-and-white and two colors, done in line with the colors on dinobase overlays. "While I am writing a book, certain of the pictures are already shaped in my mind. Others develop as I am laying out the dummy. Some come as a surprise. I spend a long time on my characters' faces and bodies before they are the right people. Sometimes it happens right away and sometimes it takes several weeks. But, once my character is *there*, I have little trouble making him appear page after page." Carol Fenner is married to an Air Force officer, Jiles B. Williams, and at present they are living in the Philippines, which is the setting for the book she is working on at this time.

FERNS, RONALD GEORGE

Born October 14, 1925 in London, England where childhood was spent. Attended St. Martin's School of Art, London.

"Although illustrating children's books is a comparatively recent venture, I first started illustrating a children's feature in English *Good Housekeeping* somewhere around 1946, and continued without a break until quite recently," writes Ronald Ferns. He entered art school at age fourteen and after three years began work in the art department of a small publishing firm. Soon after, he designed and painted scenery at a vaudeville theatre. Six months later he began free-lancing. One of his first assignments was for English *Vogue*. Most of his work has been in illustration for magazines and advertising. He has also designed a mural for the Festival of Britain 1951 Exhibition; carpets for the Time-Life building in London; costumes and decor for the ballet, "Fate's Revenge." Since his marriage in 1962, Ronald Ferns has lived by the sea in Cornwall. Mr. Ferns works primarily in black-and-white and occasionally in full color. He describes his work as decorative-whimsical. Pen and ink line was used for *Fireworks for Semolina Silkpaws* by Gladys Williams.

FETZ, INGRID

Born March 8, 1915 in New York City. Childhood spent in New York, New England, Ohio and Michigan. Attended School of Special Studies, Columbia University; Workshop School of Advertising and Editorial Art, New York City.

"Almost as far back as I can remember I have been drawing and making things, reading and loving books, and then working with and relating to children. Therefore, illustrating children's books seemed the most natural occupation to embark upon. I was already thinking along these lines while still in high school, but it took a long time and many detours, working at a variety of jobs, before I was able to begin realizing my ambition. My father, an engineer and photographer, born and educated in Switzerland, always managed to maintain a workshop of some sort, where he spent long hours inventing and making things and processing his photographs. The printing of photographs has never lost the quality of magic for me. My mother, a children's librarian, was a graduate of Pratt Institute in Brooklyn. While studying there she came under the influence of Anne Carroll Moore. She read aloud very well and, thus, introduced me to the wealth of children's books available at the time. My grandfather, a printer's devil at thirteen, was closely associated with the publishing field, in one capacity or another, throughout his life. It was he who first made me aware of the cosmos of a book, that all of its parts must be in harmony for it to be visually and tactually successful. Today, I am still concerned with the book as a whole and, therefore, like to be involved in the design as well as the illustration." While at the Workshop School, Ingrid Fetz studied with Eugene Karlin and Ezra Jack Keats. Besides teaching art to children for a number of years, she was also the Director of the Cambridge, Massachusetts Art Center for Children. Concerning her work, Ingrid Fetz notes, "At present my work is primarily executed in black-and-white, line and half-tone, with color separation on acetate. As the subject of a book and its literary style can influence the choice of medium, style, and form, I continue to be interested in exploring new media, and new ways with the old. For an illustration to be meaningful and alive it must bring a new dimension to the text while at the same time, being consistent with it. For me, this involves more than familiarizing myself superficially with the manuscript. I must structure its world and people extensively, and know what lies between the lines; only then can I have the hope of conveying a conviction of veracity and credibility, and by so doing, to invite the viewer to enter and explore. The years spent teaching art to children and those spent watching my own daughter grow, plus vivid memories of my own childhood, provide a wonderful store of feelings and visual impressions that are constantly influencing what and how I draw." Miss Fetz lives outside Ossining, New York with her daughter, mother, guests and pets ranging from white mice to monkeys.

FIAMMENGHI, GIOIA*

Born September 29, 1929 in New York City, and there her childhood was spent. Attended St. Joseph's Academy and Cathedral High School, New York; Parsons School of Design, and Art Students League, New York.

"My home atmosphere was very European and very Italian," Gioia Fiammenghi writes, "since my mother is of Italian origin and my father was born in Milano, Italy. As a child I was always interested in the arts and studied ballet and piano. I liked to sew and made complete wardrobes for my dolls even going so far as to cut a piece off my mother's fur scarf to make a fur coat for my doll. I started drawing when I was eleven and began attending life classes at fifteen. I majored in art in high school and won a scholarship for Parsons for three years. I went with Parsons to Europe where we travelled extensively throughout France and Italy for six months drawing and painting. Upon my return to the United States I worked for an advertising agency but after a year and a half left to do freelance work. I have spent two summers in Colombia, South America, where my father is a banker, doing quite a bit of drawing and painting there. Besides books, I do magazine illustration and advertising. I feel my work has been greatly influenced by my European background and fine arts background at the Art Students League." In 1959 Gioia Fiammenghi married an Italian, Guido Caputo. They live in Monte Carlo, Monaco with their three young sons. She says, "My husband is my critic and I show my drawings to my children to get their reactions." About her recent work she adds, "Last year I had some paintings on exhibit in the American Consulate in Nice. Besides illustrating I hope to do more painting and drawing outdoors. When I need models I mobilize everyone in the household, husband and children included. Wherever we go, my sketchbook goes with me." Working primarily in black-and-white and two colors, Miss Fiammenghi starts with black-and-white thumbnail sketches. For *Noisy Nancy Norris* she used colored inks for the book jacket, and crayon, pen and ink, and flat, opaque gouache for the illustrations. She feels that her style has gotten looser over the past ten years and notes that she has done more experimenting with media. She designs about half the books she illustrates and sometimes uses handlettering. She uses acetate separations for washes or flat painting and vellum separations for crayon effects.

FISCHER, HANS ERICH*

Born January 6, 1909 in Berne, Switzerland, where childhood was spent. Attended Gymnasium, Berne; Kunstgewerbeschule, Zurich; Ecole des Beaux Arts et Arts Decoratifs, Geneva, where he studied under Paul Klee. Died April 19, 1958.

Hans Fischer was the oldest of five sons of Kaspar Fischer and Emma Chevalier Fischer, both school teachers. As a boy he was a great observer of nature. While very young he used to make sketches not only of plants and animals but also caricatures of people around him. In 1933 he married Bianca Wassmuth who was also a student at the academy in Zurich, and a hand-weaver. They were commissioned to decorate weekly the windows of a well-known sports shop in Berne. At the same time Hans Fischer made many illustrations for the Swiss humorous magazine *Nebelspalter* as well as assisting with the commercial films of Pinchever. In 1937 he and his wife moved to Zurich, and while he continued drawing for magazines and working in the field of advertising, he painted all the scenery for Cornichon, a group of young comedians and musicians who presented satiric sketches of national and foreign events and politics. It was for his eldest daughter, Ursula, that Hans

Fischer illustrated his first children's book, *The Traveling Musicians*, which was published in Switzerland ten years later, and the *Good-for-Nothings* was done for his son, Casper. The inspiration for his later books also came from his own children. His youngest daughter, Barbara, in particular, begged her father to tell her stories and to draw them. For adults he illustrated the fables of La Fontaine and Aesop. Hans Fischer had numerous exhibitions of lithographs and drawings not only in Switzerland but in Paris, and at the Biennale in Venice in 1951, and in Sao Paulo in 1955. His children's books are now published in Switzerland, the United States, Germany, Yugoslavia, Poland and Japan. His main occupation was painting, especially in Swiss public schools where the children gathered around as he worked. His largest mural, however, is at Kloten, the international airport in Zurich.

FISHER, LEONARD EVERETT*

Born June 24, 1924 in New York City. Childhood was spent in Sea Gate, Brooklyn, New York. Attended Brooklyn College; Yale School of Fine Arts (B.F.A., 1949; M.F.A., 1950); Art Students League, New York; Studio of Moses Soyer; Yale-Norfolk Summer Art School; Hecksher Foundation.

Leonard Everett Fisher completed his formal training at the Yale Art School where he received, in addition to two degrees, the Weir Prize, the Winchester Fellowship and an appointment as Assistant in Design Theory. In 1950 he was awarded the Pulitzer Art Fellowship, using it for travel in Europe to "look at art, meet people and come away with some artistic experience." He became Dean of the Whitney Art School in New Haven, Connecticut in 1951. A veteran of World War II, he served at home and overseas as a topographic specialist with the U.S. Army Corps of Engineers. As a painter, Mr. Fisher has had his paintings exhibited regularly over the years. His dual career as an illustrator began in 1954. Since then he has illustrated over 125 children's books and educational materials. Several of these have appeared in the American Institute of Graphic Arts Children's Book Shows and in 1964 the New York Times selected his *Casey At the Bat* as one of the year's "Ten Best Illustrated Children's Books." In 1963 three of his works, originally done for children's books, were incorporated into a mural for the Washington Monument. In his illustration, whose style he describes as "disciplined and masculine," Leonard Fisher uses a variety of media including scratchboard, gouache and egg tempera, pen and ink and wash, both on paper and on dinobase. Over the past ten years, he notes that his picture book illustrations have "moved toward two-dimensional decoration, while the black-and-white work (principally scratchboard) has moved in the opposite direction toward form or three-dimensional solids." Scratchboard is the medium he is using for the books in the "Colonial American Craftsmen" series, which he also writes. Of the conception of this series he says, "I have always been interested in all forms of visual ex-

pression and related crafts. Painting is the craft in which I was trained. I prefer the term 'craft' to that of 'art.' Craft implies a high order of specific knowledge, training and manual skill. Too much of our creative produce is poorly crafted . . . I felt that I had to convey the idea that artistic freedom is not necessarily individuality void of obligation, but the expression of independent intellect molded by conscience and made communicable by disciplined manual skill." Mr. Fisher, his wife Margery and their three children live in Westport, Connecticut, where his studio is in one wing of the house.

FLEISHMAN, SEYMOUR*

Born January 29, 1918 in Chicago, Illinois, where his childhood was spent. Attended School of the Art Institute of Chicago.

Seymour Fleishman writes, "Almost all my life has been spent in or near Chicago, with the exception of four years during World War II. Three years of that period I was in Australia and New Guinea. Although I do a great deal of advertising art, my deepest interest is in book illustration. I believe that good illustration must first of all be true to the spirit of the writing. If, in addition, it succeeds in creating a harmonious enrichment of the type and format of the book, and is also a personal creative expression of the artist, the result is a most rewarding and successful achievement. This is rare but worth working for." About his family, he writes, "I live in an old Victorian house in a near-central section of Chicago with my wife and two daughters. We enjoy family camping in the summer and this interest led to the writing and illustrating of a book, *Four Cheers for Camping*, published by Albert Whitman." This is one of two books he has written as well as illustrated. Working primarily in two colors, he has illustrated a great many books for other authors.

FLOETHE, RICHARD*

Born September 2, 1901 in Essen, Germany. Childhood was spent in Germany. Attended Realschule, Pyrmont; Pedagogium Oberrealschule, Giessen; studied art in Munich, Dortmund, and Weimar.

Richard Floethe early showed his artistic propensities by drawing caricatures of his teachers in his school books. "I find it difficult to identify the roots out of which my work has grown," he writes. "All I know is that from earliest memory a pencil presented itself as something to draw with and I have been using one ever since. After leaving art school, where I specialized in the graphic arts, I was commissioned to execute a large mural at the International Exposition in Cologne in 1928. Shortly after its completion I sailed for America where I have since resided. In 1950 I moved with my family to Sarasota, Florida, where I am an instructor at the Ringling School of Art. My wife is a writer, and together we have done seventeen books." The Floethes have two grown sons. Besides many illustrations for both children's and adults' books, Richard Floethe has executed jacket designs, displays, posters, advertising and other forms of commercial art. In the field of fine arts he is known for his water colors and prints, some of which are in the collections of the Metropolitan Museum, St. Louis and Philadelphia Museums, and the Spencer Collection of the New York Public Library. Mr. Floethe has been twice winner of the Limited Editions International Competition for Book Illustration in 1934 and 1936, and many of his books have been selected by the American Institute of Graphic Arts for its Fifty Books of the Year shows. The March-April 1946 issue of the *Horn Book* has an article by Richard Floethe about illustrating.

FLORA, JAMES*

Born January 25, 1914 in Bellefontaine, Ohio where childhood was spent. Attended Urbana University, Urbana, Ohio, for two years; Art Academy of Cincinnati for five years; Atelier 17, New York, where he studied with Stanley William Hayter.

James Flora is of Franco-Italian ancestry, and grew up in a small mid-western town. He writes of having had a "very good mid-west boyhood." While at art school he worked as assistant to mural painter Carl Zimmerman. In 1938 he met the writer Robert Lowry and together they formed The Little Man Press, publishing books and pamphlets until early 1942. They did their own press work, typesetting and much wood engraving. In 1942 Mr. Flora went to Columbia Records where he worked for eight years as the Art Director and Sales Promotion Manager. The next two years he spent traveling and painting in Mexico. His first book for children, *The Fabulous Firework Family*, evolved out of this Mexican experience and his own children's demand for stories and pictures. "My preference for all primitive arts plus the hard creative work and wood engraving done during the days we published The Little Man have been most influential in forming whatever style and individuality there is in my work. Two years study at Atelier 17 with Stanley William Hayter have helped polish and perfect what had already been formed." Working primarily in full color, James Flora describes his work as stylized and decorative. "I use all sorts of media: pen and ink, transparent and opaque water color, pencil on dinobase, and in my last book, I used fluorographic tempera. I choose the medium which seems to best fit the feeling of the illustrations I am making." He used gouache for *The Day the Cow Sneezed* and pen and ink for *The Talking Dog* (the one book he did not also write). *My Friend Charlie* was done in pencil. He designs as well as illustrates his books and on occasion uses handlettering and type to "heighten the excitement of a pictured situation." James Flora lives with his wife and five children — and his boat — on Long Island Sound in Rowayton, Connecticut.

FORBERG, ATI

Born December 19, 1925 in Germany, where her childhood was spent. Attended Black Mountain College.

Mrs. Forberg is the daughter of Walter Gropius, the German architect who headed the famous Bauhaus from 1919 to 1928. "My husband, Charles Forberg, is also an architect. We have worked together frequently in the past on exhibitions and graphics of various kinds. Before concentrating primarily on children's books, I used to free-lance much more in advertising, display, graphics and book jackets. My husband and I lived in Chicago for many years and were closely connected with the Institute of Design (he as a teacher and I as a student), which influences much of our approach to design. Black Mountain College, under J. Albers, was, of course, the primary and most important factor in both of our educations. Albers was a phenomenal teacher, whose inspiration is inexhaustible. We now live in a remodeled brownstone in Brooklyn Heights, which includes an office for both of us. We have two daughters and I am working on children's books almost exclusively, more out of default than real intention. I would really like to do more graphic work for adults and am interested in making movies." For her work, which has been either in black-and-white or full color, she has used a wide variety of media.

FORTNUM, PEGGY*

Born December 23, 1919. Childhood spent in Harrow, Middlesex, England; Equien, France; and Crowborough, Sussex, England. Attended Tunbridge Wells School of Arts and Crafts, and the Central School of Arts and Crafts, London.

"As a child," writes Peggy Fortnum, "I loved painting and ballad-writing and dressing up like the characters I invented. I owe a great deal to one of my sisters, a born story-teller who was also a keen artist, to the encouragement I had from Heath Robinson who was shown some of my childish sketches, and Sir Frank Brangwyn who awarded me a prize at a Young Artists exhibition of painting. I became a book illustrator by accident rather than design. After receiving injuries in the Auxiliary Territorial Service I was discharged with a pension and given a war grant which enabled me to live in London and study at the Central School of Arts and Crafts. During my first year there I met John Farleigh who was then the Art Director of The Sylvan Press who was looking for an artist to illustrate a children's book. He asked me to do a few drawings which he submitted to the publisher who engaged me at once. This was followed by more illustrative work which included books by Eleanor Farjeon and Patricia Lynch, among others. After training in London I was also engaged in textile designing and teaching arts and crafts at various schools." Her most recent creations include an endearing monster of a Reluctant Dragon, and the famous bear called Paddington. Of Paddington Miss Fortnum writes: "After reading the story I draw directly with pen and ink, often producing many versions and sometimes choosing the first. I work from imagination, memory and references more than direct studies. Drawing from life is often essential but the main source of nourishment is my own story of experience and imagery." In 1958, Peggy Fortnum married Ralph Nuttall-Smith and they live in Swinview, West Mersea, Essex, England.

FOSTER, GENEVIEVE*

Born in 1893 in Oswego, New York. Childhood was spent in Whitewater, Wisconsin. Attended University of Wisconsin and Chicago Academy of Fine Arts.

Drawing was one of Genevieve Foster's favorite pastimes as a child. On the top floor of her grandfather's big house, in a room filled with paintings, wax fruits, and plaster models made by numerous uncles, aunts and cousins, she and her friends formed an art studio one summer, and took turns doing portraits of one another. They also designed costumes, inspired by fashions in copies of an old magazine, *Godey's Lady's Book*, which they found stacked in a corner. Years later it was Genevieve's plan to become a fashion designer, when, after graduating from the University of Wisconsin she went to Chicago to attend the Academy of Fine Arts. Her first job as an artist, however, found her making huge designs for stained glass windows. This was followed by other kinds of drawings for newspapers, magazines and booklets. After her marriage, Mrs. Foster worked and lived in a studio apartment in Chicago, which she and her engineer husband designed and built, and later in their home in Evanston. As her two children, Orrington, Jr., and Joanna, were growing up their interests became hers. Illustrations which she did for *Child Life* magazine led to illustrating children's books. This, in turn, led her to writing the books as well as illustrating them. Her first book *George Washington's World*, told what was happening all over the world during Washington's lifetime. All the things that could best be told in drawings were sketched in, as the words were being written. The book was carefully laid out, page by page, and then text and illustrations were finished. This first book, published in 1941, was followed by eleven others. Mrs. Foster, who is now working on *The World of William Penn*, has, for the past few years, had a studio-apartment in the shadow of New York City's Empire State Building. Her black-and-white drawings for books such as *The World of Christopher Columbus and Sons* were done with pen and ink. The two-color illustrations in such books as *Abraham Lincoln* and *Birthdays of Freedom*, were done with opaque water color. Articles on Mrs. Foster and her work appeared in the *Horn Book*, June 1952.

FOSTER, MARIAN CURTIS, see Mariana, pseud.

FRAME, PAUL

Born May 4, 1913 in Riderwood, Maryland. Attended National Academy of Design and Columbia University, New York City.

Paul Frame started his career as a staff artist at Lord and Taylor. Just before World War II, he decided to concentrate on doing free-lance art work and has illustrated many books since then. He is married and has two daughters. He and his family make their home in New York City.

FRANCÉS, ESTEBAN

Born 1915 in Port Bou, Spain. Attended University of Barcelona.

Esteban Francés, a Catalonian by birth, took a law degree at the University of Barcelona to please his family. Instead of going into practice, however, he turned to painting. At the defeat of the Republicans during the Spanish Civil War, he went to Argentina and then to Mexico where he lived from 1940 to 1945. In 1946, Lincoln Kirstein urged him to come to New York City and design the sets and costumes for the New York City Ballet's *Renard*. This was the first of more than twenty productions that he designed for them in the following years. His paintings have been exhibited in Paris, London, Barcelona and in the United States. While in this country he illustrated two picture books, *A Handful of Surprises* and *The Thread Soldier*. At present he is living in Majorca.

FRANÇOIS, ANDRÉ*

Born November 9, 1915 in Rumania. Childhood spent there, in Hungary and in France. Attended Ecole des Beaux-Arts, Paris, and Cassandre's School of Fine Arts and Poster Design.

André François is French, though he was born in Rumania where he spent most of his childhood. Mr. François works in various art fields. As a painter he has had several one-man shows and for the theatre he has designed sets and costumes for both plays and the ballet. His well-known work in the graphic arts, which he feels was perhaps most influenced by the work of George Grosz, has won him various awards including a Gold Medal from the Art Directors' Club of New York. He has illustrated for such magazines as *Vogue*, *Femina*, and *Holiday*, has done a number of covers for the *New Yorker* and his drawings of a humorous or satirical nature have appeared in *Punch*. The first of his children's books to be published in this country was *Little Boy Brown* in 1949. Among his more recent books are *Tom and Tabby*, illustrated in gouache, and *Grodge Cat*, illustrated in pen and ink and pencil. Articles about André François, who lives in Grisy-les-Platres, Seine et Oise, France, have appeared in *Graphis*, March 1958 and November 1959.

FRANÇOISE,* pseud. (Françoise Seignobosc)

Born 1900 in Lodeve, Herault, France. Attended College Sevigne, Paris. Died August 1961.

Although Françoise began to draw at the age of eight, she studied art only after college. Some of the little books she did for Tolmer, the Paris publisher, found their way to the United States. "So I myself went over there one day," she wrote, "and I did not regret it. Doing books for American children is the pleasure of my life. Sometimes I get letters from young admirers and I feel very happy when I do, especially because I am not satisfied with my work, most of the time. I am always afraid to be 'too French' for American children, but Miss Dalgliesh gives me courage, and says that I am not too French!" Françoise had a winter studio in Paris and in summer lived on a farm in southern France where, like Colette, she had "many, many animals." Animals and children loved Françoise for she was gay and friendly and knew the things they liked. Children followed her and begged her to draw pictures for them and to tell them stories. Among her first books to be published in the United States were *Gay Mother Goose* and *Gay A B C*, both published in 1938. The naive style in which she illustrated her books is the result of seeing things as children see them and would draw them if they had her technical ability. Before her death on August 15, 1961, Françoise came to New York almost every year, for a long visit.

FRANKENBERG, ROBERT CLINTON*

Born March 19, 1911 in Mount Vernon, New York, where his childhood was spent. Attended Art Students League, New York.

Robert Clinton Frankenberg writes, "I remember as a young boy receiving a treasured copy of Ernest Thompson Seton's *Two Little Savages.* Although I read it with great enjoyment many times for its vivid description of the outdoors, I did not realize until years later its true attraction for me was its complete credibility. When I began to study, art schools listed their subjects as drawing, composition, and painting — period. With these rather general accomplishments, I began my career. As I grew older and more experienced in my work, I realized that other things are as important to the illustrator as the more obvious tools of his trade: rich background in reading, an understanding of the period and location in which the story is set, an interest in the subject matter, careful and intelligent research, honesty of presentation. I am Chairman of the Department of Drawing at the School of Visual Arts in New York City, where I have been on the faculty since 1947. I am married and have my home and studio in New York City, and although I have lost count of exactly how many books I have illustrated, it is well over a hundred." *Glooscap and His Magic* and *Jambo, Sungura* are examples of his black-and-white work done on dinobase which he finds "gives a rich strong feeling to a drawing similar to a lithograph."

FRASCONI, ANTONIO*

Born April 29, 1919 in Montevideo, Uruguay, of Italian parents. Attended Circulo de Bellas Artes, Montevideo; Art Students League, New York, to which he received a scholarship in 1945 to study with Kuniyoshi; New School for Social Research, New York, to which he received a scholarship in 1947 to study mural painting with Camilo Egas.

From the time Antonio Frasconi was a small boy he was interested in drawing and during his teens he was a political cartoonist on a newspaper, studying and working on his own time in woodcuts and painting. At twenty he had his first one-man show of drawings. Later a scholarship brought him to the United States where he has continued to live, first in New York City and then in South Norwalk, Connecticut. In 1946, he had his first one-man show in this country at the Brooklyn Museum of Art, followed by over sixty others both in North and South America and in Europe. Along with his shows have gone many honors, including such varied ones as the Guggenheim Foundation's Inter-American Fellowship in graphic arts to illustrate Walt Whitman and Garcia Lorca (1952); a Grand Prix in the 1960 Venice Film Festival for a film that incorporated 100 of his woodcuts; the commission based on competition for the design of a postage stamp commemorating the anniversary of the National Academy of Science. Perhaps the most significant honor is the recognition that, as Charles Parkhurst said at the opening of the Baltimore Museum of Art Show in 1963, "Frasconi has been in part personally responsible for setting the standards of quality and character of a current woodcut revival." Besides his reputation in the field of fine art, his woodcuts have also been commissioned for advertising, magazine illustration, record covers, and Christmas cards. His first children's book was *See and Say*, which reflected his own multilingual experience. All of his books, both for children and adults, are ones he has designed as well as illustrated with woodcuts, sometimes using handlettering, which he prefers to type. He usually works in color and prints all of his woodcuts by hand, rubbing a spoon over a paper laid on an inked block. This method allows him to get "variations of tone which could not be obtained by the more even pressure of the handpress." Mr. Frasconi is married to Leona Pierce, also a print maker and they have two boys, Pablo and Miguel. Articles about Mr. Frasconi include those in *Graphis* No. 77 and No. 100, *Print*, Vol. IX No. 6, *Time*, December 20, 1963, and *Art in America* No. 4, 1961.

FRASER, BETTY (Elizabeth M.)

Born February 25, 1928 in Massachusetts, where childhood was spent in Newton, Wellesley and Marshfield Hills. Attended Rhode Island School of Design.

Betty Fraser's career may have begun at the age of seven when she reports that she won $2.00 in an Easter egg coloring contest. "I went to art school because it was easier than college. Drawing an electric light bulb on top of books on top of a table was the exam and fortunately in high school I had an old-fashioned teacher who stressed proportion, perspective, etc. After art school I worked twelve years in advertising. The loveliest thing that ever happened to me was to settle down on my own and to be rewarded (paid) for what I do. So since 1962 I have been a full-time illustrator. I like pen and ink the best and find I am going from intricate line to very intricate. Because of working in line so much I do a lot of color separation which is tedious but the reproduction is better." Miss Fraser lives in New York City.

FREEMAN, DON*

Born August 11, 1908 in San Diego, California, where his childhood was spent. Attended Principia, St. Louis, Missouri, and Art Students League, New York.

"I always wanted to draw and paint," writes Don Freeman, "so it was no wonder that I headed for New York immediately after finishing high school. I earned my living by playing a trumpet in dance orchestras while studying art under John Sloan and Harry Wickey. I began drawing impressions of actors and plays on Broadway, and the New York *Herald Tribune* and the New York *Times* used my work for years. All this enabled me to keep my loves all rolling along together — Art, the Theater, Music, Life and Lydia. Lydia is my wife. We are now happily at work writing and illustrating children's books, thanks to our boy Roy." In addition to writing and illustrating books of his own, Mr. Freeman does theater drawings and cartoons, and has illustrated stories by many other writers. In 1962, *Come Again, Pelican* was given an award by the Southern California Council on Children's Literature. Almost all of Don Freeman's books have been illustrated in full color. For *A Rainboy of My Own* he made the separations in water color on acetate. Since 1960, Mr. Freeman has been combining his love for drawing and the theater in still another way. "I've taken to giving chalk-talk lectures in all parts of the country, for colleges, schools, clubs, television and in theaters. I draw to music and use special effects such as fluorescent chalks in order to give the effect of city lights at night, etc. I enjoy creating and performing these shows, especially for children." The Freemans make their home in Santa Barbara, California.

FRY, ROSALIE KINGSMILL*

Born April 22, 1911 on Vancouver Island, British Columbia. Childhood was spent there, in Hertfordshire, England, and in South Wales. Attended St. Margaret's School, Swansea; Central School of Arts and Crafts, London.

"I have always lived in beautiful surroundings, first in Vancouver Island where I was born and lived until I was four, when my parents returned to Britain. We spent some years in an aunt's lovely old timbered Paper Mill in Hertfordshire, and my younger sister and I have spent blissful hours in the old barns and garden, surrounded by the river which streamed under the ancient waterwheel in a fall that could be heard throughout the house. From here we moved to South Wales and once again found ourselves with a wonderful garden full of trees to climb and streams and woods in which to play. I was eighteen when we moved to our present home, by the sea this time, on a lovely unspoilt coast. Here my room overlooks the bay and I hear the waves on the beach as I work. I spent five years at a London Art School concentrating mainly on book illustrating. Since then I have spent most of my time writing and illustrating children's books, except for the six war years when I served as a Coder and Cypher Officer in the Women's Royal Naval Service. There have been painters on both sides of the family, but I feel sure it is from two miniature painters on my Mother's side, James Dowling and his sister Mary, that I inherit my love of painting tiny things — the heroine of my first book was a bumblebee!" Rosalie K. Fry has written the above from her home in Swansea, South Wales.

FUJIKAWA, GYO

Born in Berkeley, California. Childhood spent in southern California. Attended Chouinard Art Institute, Los Angeles, California.

Miss Fujikawa was born and grew up in California, her father having migrated to the United States from Japan at the age of sixteen. She had always liked to draw, but it was her high school art teacher who set her on her way by helping her get a scholarship to art school. In 1939 she joined the Walt Disney Studios, going from there to the New York offices of the Fox Film Company and then becoming art director for a pharmaceutical advertising agency where she stayed for eight years. Since then she has free-lanced. "My main work is in the field of advertising, packaging and magazine illustrations," writes Miss Fujikawa, who also has to her credit the design of two United States postage stamps. "Children's books are fun projects for me." The first of these, *Babies*, a hardpage book for very young children picturing white, Asian and Negro babies doing everyday things, appeared in 1963 and was one of two for which she did the simple text. Since then she has illustrated editions of *The Night Before Christmas* and *A Child's Garden of Verses*. Gyo Fujikawa lives in New York City.

FUNAI, MAMORU R.

Born June 7, 1932 in Kauai, Hawaii where childhood was spent. Attended Honolulu Academy of Arts; Pittsburgh Institute of Art; Cleveland Institute of Art.

"After my training at the various art schools, I worked four years as a greeting card designer. Then for a year I worked in advertising as a designer. In 1962, I came to New York City and began my career as a free-lance illustrator." Among this artist's books are *Burning Rice Fields* which was done in pastels, *The Big Fight* done in ink on ricepaper, and *Baby Elephant*, done in designers' gouache.

GALDONE, PAUL*

Born in Budapest, Hungary. Childhood spent in Hungary. Attended Art Students League, New York, studying with George Grosz, Louis Bouché, Guy Pène du Bois.

Paul Galdone came to the United States at the age of fourteen, and worked at any job he could find, as errand boy, electrician's helper, etc., studying evenings at the Art Students League. For three years he worked in the Art Department of Doubleday and Company. During World War II he served with the United States Army Engineers, and after leaving the service he began to free-lance, working for many publishers, doing book jackets and illustrating prolifically both adult and children's books. Paul Galdone characterizes his work as representational and humorous. He usually works in pen and ink and wash, often making separations, and designs his picture books which are almost all based on well-known poems or folktales. Mr. Galdone is a painter of landscapes and portraits as well as an illustrator, and he is much interested in gardening and forestry. He is married, has two children, Joanna and Paul Ferencz, and their home, which he and Mrs. Galdone designed, is in New City, Rockland County, New York.

GALSTER, ROBERT MILLER

Born July 19, 1928 in Dollville, Illinois. Childhood spent in Illinois and Mansville, Ohio. Attended Parsons School of Design, New York City.

"The isolation of farm life in childhood may have been responsible for my early interest in drawing, and, being the eldest of eight children, I also had an eager audience for my first work. After three years in the U. S. Army where I was assigned to a job of creating posters for the camouflage engineers, I migrated to New York City. I began my professional career designing record album covers, progressed to book jackets and then logically to book illustration." Robert Galster works primarily in two colors, preferring to use transparent vellum for separations. "My technique is essentially linear. I use brush and India ink, employing a line broken by the use of frisket applied in various ways, as in *North, South, East and West.*" He also designs posters for Broadway plays and has done ones for such hits as "Barefoot in the Park," "Bus Stop," and "The Odd Couple." He has a great interest in collecting maps and in photography, which he considers his hobby. He has traveled in Mexico and Europe but considers New York his home.

GEER, CHARLES*

Born August 25, 1922 on Long Island, New York and his childhood was spent there and in New Jersey. Attended Dartmouth College, Hanover, New Hampshire, studying with Paul Sample, artist in residence; and Pratt Institute, New York.

World War II interrupted Charles Geer's college education. Two and a half years at Dartmouth were followed by three years in the Navy where he served as a torpedoman on a destroyer. After the war he studied for a year and a half at Pratt Institute and since then has been a free-lance illustrator, chiefly in the book publishing field. "Most of my work," he writes, "is in books for children eight to twelve-years-old and jackets for teenage books. I use pen or brush and ink for the illustrations with charcoal or wash when the job permits a halftone. For full color jackets I use water color or gouache but many are done with overlays." He, his wife and four children live in a log cabin he built himself, near Lebanon, New Jersey. From 1960 to 1964 he was a member and then President of the Readington Township Board of Education and recalls it as "a highly rewarding experience." His other interests include hiking, camping, sailing, canoeing and painting pictures.

GEISEL, THEODOR SEUSS, see Seuss, Dr., pseud.

GEKIERE, MADELEINE*

Born May 15, 1919 in Zurich, Switzerland where her childhood was spent. Attended Gymnasium, Zurich; Sorbonne, Paris; Art Students League, New York.

"Growing up in Switzerland," writes Madeleine Gekiere, "I was able to travel a good deal in the art centers of the world — Italy and France. While I did not decide on being an artist until I came to this country in 1940, I was always keenly interested in painting. At present I devote most of my time to Fine Art but very much enjoy doing book illustrations. I am married and live in New York City, a very stimulating place for a painter." She has had several one-man shows of her paintings and drawings in New York City and since 1958 has been an instructor of drawing and painting at New York University. Her illustrations are done in black-and-white, as in *John J. Plenty and Fiddler Dan*, where she used charcoal and grease crayon. Five of the books she has illustrated have been chosen by the *New York Times* for their annual list of the "Ten Best Illustrated Children's Books." About illustrating she writes, "The task of the illustrator just as much as that of the so called 'fine artist' is the creation of a new visual world and if possible not a confining visual world, but the kind that gives room to expand in the personal terms of the onlooker."

GENIA, pseud. (Genia Katherine Wennerstrom)

Born August 9, 1930 in New York City where her childhood was spent. Attended Pratt Institute, New York University, and New School for Social Research, New York City.

"I was born into a family of artists and from childhood have always thought of being one," writes Genia. In high school she won several art awards and then went on to Pratt where she met her husband who is also an artist-designer, and with whom she has collaborated on several free-lance assignments. Since leaving Pratt, she has illustrated approximately 100 books, and although primarily an illustrator, she has also done projects ranging from magazine design and illustration, fashion, greeting cards to a 90-foot sign that sits atop a mountain in New Jersey. Over the last ten years she feels that her style of line has changed from a light one to being bold "and a trip to Mexico strengthened my color sense. I love working in bold colors." Genia and her husband have three sons, the youngest born in 1966. They live in Forest Hills where she shares a studio made out of a greenhouse on their penthouse terrace "with two alley cats who drink tinted water from my watercolor jar."

GILL, MARGERY JEAN

Born April 5, 1925 in Coatbridge, Scotland. Childhood spent in Harrow-on-the-Hill, Middlesex, England. Attended Harrow School of Art; Royal College of Art, England.

"I have been drawing for as long as I can remember and was pretty set in my ways by the time I was four years old," writes Margery Gill. At the Royal College of Art she studied etching and engraving, and while still in college was married in 1946. Her first daughter was born in 1948, the year that she graduated, and a second was born in 1951. "They make me feel like Grandma Moses only less successful. The need to earn, yet remain at home, turned me to illustration. I did one or two books between 1947 and 1952, but I didn't really get going until about 1954. So far as materials and techniques are concerned, I've done more black-and-white drawing for reproduction in line than anything else. I have done a certain amount of full color work, but hope to do a great deal more in the next year or so." Her home is now in England.

GLANZMAN, LOUIS S.

Born February 8, 1922 in Baltimore, Maryland. Childhood spent in Virginia.

"As a country boy raised in Virginia, I was very much impressed with Norman Rockwell's covers for the *Saturday Evening Post*," writes Louis Glanzman. "I have now done covers for the *Post* and know Norman Rockwell personally." Besides liking to draw as a child, he was an avid reader and, since he had no formal training, credits most of his artistic knowledge to books. As part of his self-training he copied paintings of the old masters on a small simple scale so that he had the basic pattern. At sixteen, he got a job creating strips for comic books. Later he enlisted in the Air Force and worked with the *Air Force Magazine* in New York. Since then magazine illustration has been his specialty. A number of cover portraits of which he is particularly proud have appeared on *Time* magazine, and a portrait of Abraham Lincoln is in the Ford Theatre Museum. He was married in 1945 and has four daughters. To entertain them he often makes humorous drawings in pen and ink line similar to the ones he did for the three *Pippi Longstocking* books. The Glanzmans live in Sayville, Long Island, New York. An article on Mr. Glanzman and his work appeared in *American Artist*, January 1963.

GLASER, MILTON

Born June 26, 1929 in New York City. Childhood was spent in the Bronx, New York City. Attended High School of Music and Art; Cooper Union; Academy of Fine Arts, Bologna, Italy.

Milton Glaser, who always had his family's encouragement in pursuing art, says that a long illness at the age of ten "probably had more to do with my becoming an artist than anything else." After graduating from Cooper Union in 1951, he received a Fulbright grant and studied in Italy. "It was crucial to my development. I studied etching with Giorgio Morandi and stayed two years." In 1958, Milton Glaser and his wife Shirley spent another year in Rome where he did a series of lithographs. Meanwhile, in 1954 he and Seymour Chwast formed the Push Pin Studios which has gained an excellent reputation in the field of graphic design, has won a number of awards, and now employs nine other people. Along with doing a great deal of illustration, design for advertising, and book jackets as well as books, he also teaches a course at the School of Visual Arts in New York City. The relationship of design and illustration is an important one to Milton Glaser, as is explained in an article in *Graphis*, No. 92, 1960. Other articles about him and his work have appeared in *Gebrauchsgraphik*, May 1964, *American Artist*, September 1958, *CA*, July 1962 and *Idea* (Japanese), October 1964. His work has brought him a number of honors including the Gold Medal of the Society of Illustrators and that of the Art Directors Club.

GNOLI, DOMENICO

Born May 3, 1933 in Rome, Italy.

At the age of eighteen, Mr. Gnoli began his professional career as a painter and graphic artist with an exhibition in Brussels. Since that time his work has been shown regularly in Rome, Paris, Geneva, London, New York and other cities. His work is represented in the collections of the Museum of Modern Art and the National Gallery of Art. He has designed sets for "As You Like It" at the Old Vic and "The Merchant of Venice" at Schauspielhaus in Zurich. The first book with his illustrations to be published in this country was *Orestes or the Art of Smiling* in 1962. The first children's book was *Alberic the Wise and Other Journeys*. Mr. Gnoli and his wife live in Rome.

GOBBATO, IMERO

Born December 28, 1923 in Milan, Italy. Childhood spent in Italy. Attended Liceo Artistico, Milan; Institute of Fine Arts, Venice; Academy of Fine Arts in Milan and Venice.

"I inherited my inclination for drawing and painting from my maternal grandfather. He died the year I was born but very early in life I became acquainted with his studies in pen and ink and water color. I was also given some of his materials to play with when still a small child. Pen and ink became soon my favorite medium and, in many ways, still is. My father chose for me a classical education, but when I reached sixteen, he became convinced of the strength of my vocation and consented to send me to an art school." Mr. Gobbato explains that after his schooling he began to illustrate for books and magazines in Italy, but that he has often interrupted this work with other activities. "For years I worked as a professional naval architect. I also built boats myself and for two years lived with my wife aboard a houseboat which I designed and built at the edge of the Everglades in Florida. I have worked as a set designer for the movie industry in Los Angeles and as an art restorer in New York. And I travelled rather extensively for twelve and more years across Europe, Latin America and the United States. I am now living in Maine, alternating between a house on the mainland and a small fisherman's cottage on one of the outer islands. Maine and its people are still vastly uncontaminated by the soul-destroying cult of the superfluous that almost everywhere else undermines man's sense of value." About his work as an illustrator, he writes, "I am a narrative artist, a teller of stories by means of images. I illustrate children's books because I love illustrated books. Of the new media, the colored acetate sheets by Bourges seem to be the most valuable. They allow perfectly controlled color separations giving a final effect half-way between color woodcuts and multilayered graffitos. I have not found yet a new medium which surpasses the old pen and ink in capacity for detail, chiaroscural richness or affinity for photographic reproduction."

GORDON, MARGARET ANNA

Born May 19, 1939 in London, England where her childhood was spent. Attended St. Martin's School of Art, Chamberwell School of Arts and Crafts; Central School of Arts and Crafts, London, England.

"My father was a violinist and my mother a pianist, so I had artistic leanings and a prejudice against a musical career," explains Margaret Gordon. "I have always found drawing one of the most intensely pleasurable ways to spend time and one day, whilst cleaning my teeth, I made the daring decision to try and earn my living at it. Art school training taught me to draw with the emphasis on realism. My husband taught me that having learnt how to do this I should forget it, and try to develop a more personal style. My husband is a publisher, whom I met while trying to get free-lance work, and it is entirely thanks to him that my drawing developed and that I met people who liked it and were willing to publish it. I left art school in 1960 and taught art part-time for five years. Only very recently have I had the opportunity to work in full color in children's books." For her color work she uses ink and gouache with the paint sometimes applied over candle-wax. In *Noah's Journey* she made special use of handlettering for labeling the animals and for decoration.

GOREY, EDWARD ST. JOHN

Born February 22, 1925 in Chicago, Illinois where he spent his childhood. Attended Harvard University.

Edward Gorey graduated from Harvard University with a B.A. in 1950. He has illustrated books by a number of different writers, but is perhaps best known for the books he has written and illustrated. The first of these was *The Doubtful Guest* published in 1957. All of his work is in black-and-white and is done with a Gillott Tit Quill pen and Pelikan ink on a matt finish paper. The books he has written himself are handlettered. An article on his early work by Edmund Wilson appeared in the *New Yorker* and was reprinted in Mr. Wilson's book *The Bit Between My Teeth*.

GORSLINE, DOUGLAS WARNER*

Born May 24, 1913 in Rochester, New York where his childhood was spent. Attended Yale School of Fine Arts; and Art Students League, New York.

Douglas Gorsline has been interested in art from childhood. After studying at the Art Students League he started out in fine arts, in the Reginald Marsh tradition. About 1944 he included in his area commercial art and illustrating, working for many different publishers. He has written as well as illustrated two books: *What People Wore*, a history of costume, and *Farm Boy*. He is still working in the fine arts field as well as continuing in advertising and book illustration. He describes his work thus, "Though my painting is partially abstract and contemporary as to material, my commercial work seems usually to be in the historical vein. I consider my painting entirely American in origins and point of view, but my commercial style derives from the Hogarthian, English line tradition." His illustrations have appeared frequently in *American Heritage* and *Horizon* magazines. Mr. Gorsline's fine art has won numerous awards and is represented in various collections such as those of the Library of Congress, Corcoran Art Gallery, Chicago Art Institute and the Whitney Museum of American Art.

GRABIANSKI, JANUSZ

Born July 24, 1929 in Szamotuly, Poland. Childhood spent in Poznan, Poland. Attended Academy of Art, Cracow and Warsaw.

Mr. Grabianski was introduced to painting by an uncle and was already well known as an artist during his student days. His talent for painting animals is something he attributes to long hours spent observing and sketching in the zoo. He has a fondness for animals, children, flowers, fast cars, his new home in Warsaw, and travel. His travels have taken him to Australia, Switzerland, Italy, Greece and in 1966 to the United States for several weeks. The Mediterranean countries inspire him especially and he is much influenced by the French Impressionists, particularly Raoul Dufy. He has won a number of international awards including the Gold Medal of the 1960 Milan Triennale. Two series of stamps which he designed have been issued in Poland. Mr. Grabianski has two daughters, Kascha and Ditta. Kasha, who attends Warsaw's School of Music, paints and has done a butterfly picture that her father included in one of his books. In all of his work he uses water color, tempera and also chalks.

GRABOFF, ABNER

Born June 28, 1919 in New York City. Childhood spent in East Orange, New Jersey. Attended Brooklyn Museum Art School, New York City.

Abner Graboff is active as a designer and illustrator in the field of commercial art as well as in the field of children's books. He had been doing commercial art for several years before he was commissioned to illustrate his first children's book, *The Sun Looks Down*, published by Abelard Schuman. Since then he has done several books by other authors as well as some he has written himself, most recently, *Mrs. McGarrity's Peppermint Sweater*. This book was illustrated with collage. "As I continue to work in the field of children's books," he writes, "I find I gravitate to the utilization of objects to represent themselves, or, because of their form and texture to stand by themselves." Mr. Graboff lives just outside New York City.

GRAHAM, MARGARET BLOY*

Born in Toronto, Canada. Childhood spent in Ontario, Canada. Attended University of Toronto (B.A.); Institute of Fine Arts, New York University, and the New School for Social Research, New York City.

Margaret Bloy Graham writes, "I was born and educated in Canada but used to spend summers in England and the United States. As a child, being read to meant more to me than drawing, and when I grew older, reading became my favorite pastime. When I was ten, I attended the Saturday morning classes of the Art Gallery of Toronto. The classes were excellent: we were never told *how* to draw, but encouraged to do many different things. I went on to study art history at the University and one summer worked in the display department of a store, doing big oil paintings for window backgrounds. The art director encouraged me and I began to think of a career as an artist. One of the paintings inspired my first book, *All Falling Down*. In 1943 I came to New York City and began with various jobs — in a printing company, as a ship draftsman during the war, and on a fashion magazine. I did illustrations for the Condé Nast publications and eventually worked into doing mostly children's books." Miss Graham, who says she loves doing children's books, has to date illustrated twenty, of which thirteen have been written by her husband, Gene Zion. These include the popular picture books about *Harry the Dirty Dog* and *Dear Garbage Man*, on the 1957 *New York Times* list of "Ten Best Illustrated Children's Books." *All Falling Down* and *The Storm Book* were runners-up for the Caldecott Medal and *The Meanest Squirrel I Ever Met* was in the Children's Book Show of the American Institute of Graphic Arts. She usually works in three colors, doing the basic black drawings in pencil and wash and the color separations on paper in wash over a light table. At present she is living in Cambridge, Massachusetts.

GRAMATKY, HARDIE*

Born April 12, 1907, in Dallas, Texas. Childhood was spent in Los Angeles, California. Attended Stanford University, Palo Alto, and Chouinard Art School, Los Angeles.

Hardie Gramatky writes, "After leaving high school I got a job in a bank, then I 'ghosted' for a comic strip artist and later turned to animating Mickey Mouse. However, I always managed to find time to develop my talent as an artist. Jobs helped me through University and Art School, but I kept time for sketching. When I moved to New York I had a studio in a loft overlooking the East River. The boats fascinated me so that I did nothing but make drawings of them all day long. Each one took on a definite personality and soon a story had developed around them, which became *Little Toot*. In 1946, the Gramatky family moved to Westport, Connecticut, where I have divided my time between magazine illustration and writing for children — my great love. My first book in Connecticut, *Creeper's Jeep*, was influenced no doubt by the little red jeeps running around town and by the big farm that was across the way then." Trips around the United States, to South America, Europe and particularly Greece have all inspired picture books. His other work has included writing and illustrating for most of the national magazines and a commission in 1966 to go to Viet Nam and do some on the spot paintings. He works primarily in full color with water color the medium for all his books. He does separations by painting in black using a full range of values in a separate picture for each color. *Little Toot* was made into a motion picture by Walt Disney and *Hercules* was done as an iconographic motion picture by Weston Woods Studios. His water color paintings have won a number of awards and are in the permanent collections of a number of museums. The Gramatkys have one daughter, who was recently married. Articles about his work have appeared in *Elementary English*, October 1960, May 1965 and *American Artist*, May 1962.

GREENWALD, SHEILA ELLEN

Born May 26, 1934 in New York City where her childhood was spent. Attended Sarah Lawrence College, Bronxville, New York.

At New York City's High School of Music and Art, Sheila Greenwald was an art major, and says of those years, "The school gave an excellent groundwork for drawing and painting, and I'm deeply indebted to it. At Sarah Lawrence, finding the painting course unsatisfactory, I was a Literature major and doodled in the margins. After graduation in 1956 I put a bunch of doodles together and took them around to the book editors. I've done to date some thirty-eight books, half of which are for adults. Most of the books have been done in black-and-white using India ink and a crow quill pen. Sometimes there have been two or more colors for which I have done separations." In 1960, she married George Green, a surgeon, and they have two small boys, Samuel and Benjamin. Their home is in New York City.

GRIFALCONI, ANN

Born September 22, 1929 in New York City. Childhood spent in New York City, Westchester County, New York and Indiana. Attended Cooper Union, Hunter College, and New York University, School of Education (B.S.), New York City; University of Cincinnati, Ohio.

Miss Grifalconi majored in art both in high school and college, and after graduating from Cooper Union went into advertising art. She left this for a two-year sojourn in Ohio and then returned to New York to go into teaching art and free-lancing in display design and illustration for magazines and books. After ten years of teaching, she has given it up to work full time at illustrating. In 1963 she co-authored and illustrated *Camping Through Europe by Car*. "I then wrote and illustrated a picture book, *City Rhythms*, for young children. It is about life in the city which I love. This book was done mostly in three-color separations and full color aniline dye. Textured crayon was sometimes added and also a loose line. I have also illustrated

many books by other authors covering subject areas from jingles and steamboats to the American West and a time span from fourteenth century Italian poetry to the present. I particularly enjoy doing historical work and Indian and Negro subject matter, for no reason I can think." Miss Grifalconi makes her home in New York City.

GROSSMAN, NANCY S.

Born April 28, 1940 in New York City. Childhood was spent in Oneonta, New York. Attended University of Arizona and Pratt Institute (B.F.A., 1962).

"No one paid much attention to my drawing when I was little, except that they always saved the paper from the spaghetti boxes for me to draw on." Nancy Grossman was the oldest of five children and when she was six years old her family moved to a farm in Oneonta which they shared with two other families. "There were sixteen children altogether. The farm left a deep impression on me. I especially like drawing animals." In 1949 the family moved to Puerto Rico for about a year. After high school in Oneonta, Miss Grossman went to Pratt and studied graphic art and illustration. Her main interest and work while in Pratt and in the years since has been in the area of the fine arts. She has received from Pratt both a foreign travel scholarship and their Contemporary Achievement Award in the Fine Arts. "At first I was doing expressionistic, figurative painting primarily in oils. Then I started adding things to the paint and also doing wooden collages." In 1965 Miss Grossman received a Guggenheim Fellowship and in early 1967 she is going to have her fourth one-man show of collages, constructions and welded-steel sculpture. She illustrated her first book, *Life and Death of the Sun* in 1963 and her first children's book, *Far Out the Long Canal* in 1964. "That first children's book was very significant to me. In the last year I have become really committed to illustrating. When I walked in to see Ursula Nordstrom about possibly illustrating a book, I was lugging a huge portfolio which must have looked like it weighed 500 pounds. I suppose it must have been kind of scary to an editor, but she is very special and she did give me that first children's book. To date, I've worked in black-and-white mostly — pen and ink or pencil — but I hope to do more in color."

GUGGENHEIM, HANS

Born 1924 in Berlin, Germany. Childhood spent in Germany, England and Guatemala. Attended Art Students League; New York University.

Hans Guggenheim, who makes his home in Cambridge, Massachusetts, pursues parallel careers in art and anthropology. Besides illustrating books, such *The Elephant's Bathtub* which he did in pen and ink, he has done illustrations for such magazines as *Natural History* and *MD*. He writes, "Because of extensive traveling around the world for *Life* magazine in 1957 and subsequently as an anthropologist, I have been primarily interested in illustrating books about countries that I have visited and often work from my own sketches. In my work I am opposed to producing a homogenized view of the world in which all differences become submerged. My drawings try therefore to cope with people as they are, not as we think they should be. Some of my non-ethnographic work tends to be more stylized and humorous. Some of it has a rather oriental flavor." Mr. Guggenheim is married and besides finishing up his Ph.D. in Anthropology at New York University, he is also working as an anthropologist and curriculum designer at Educational Services, Inc. His work with this company leads him to be especially interested in illustrations for fifth and sixth grade level "with the amount of humor or lack of it that seems most appropriate at that level."

GROVES-RAINES, ANTONY (Ralph Gore Antony)

Born in County Down, Ireland. Childhood spent in Ireland, England, Scotland, France, Germany, Spain, Italy and Switzerland. Attended Tonbridge School, Kent, England; Christ's College, Cambridge, England and studied in France and Germany.

"Both my father's and my mother's family were accustomed to draw and paint for pleasure, and my paternal grandfather wrote numerous books for boys. My mother studied under Whistler. I believe she is the last of his students who still survives. Almost all our family, children and adults, took sketch books on picnics and tours abroad. We spent a lot of time in Europe and were always in and out of picture galleries, cathedrals, castles and palaces." As a small boy Mr. Groves-Raines remembers getting lost in the Louvre through "lingering too long over the 'Relief of the Bastille' by Delacroix. My family were annoyed, however, when I took up painting professionally, as I was studying to go into the diplomatic service. They felt, rightly, that it was wiser to paint for pleasure and earn one's living from more reliable sources. I do illustrations for money, but I try to do them as well as I can. I don't think I would illustrate for pleasure but *would* probably continue to paint in oils even if I could afford not to." Besides illustrating books for other authors, Mr. Groves-Raines has written and illustrated one of his own, *The Tidy Hen.* As to his method of working he writes, "I normally make a waterproof neutral tone painting and then color it with transparent liquid waterproof colors or water color. Sometimes I do separations, mostly for book jackets. In black-and-white, I prefer a line and wash drawing." Mr. Groves-Raines lives Killinchy, County Down, North Ireland.

HAAS, IRENE*

Born June 5, 1929 in New York City where childhood was spent. Attended Black Mountain College, North Carolina; Pratt Institute, Brooklyn; Art Students League, New York.

"After overcoming a burning ambition to be a scenic designer," writes Irene Haas, "I went to designing patterns for china and wallpaper. My compensation at this time was in etching and lithography. Then, very slowly, with the help of an artist's agent, I went into the field of magazine and advertising illustration. This agent was also responsible for my very happy meeting in 1954 with Margaret McElderry at Harcourt, Brace and my finding the work I love best. I believe that my style, taste, even provocation, stems from what I liked as a child. I loved pictures I could 'live' in, literally for hours. I find illustrating such a satisfying thing because I like to get involved in 'setting a stage' and in drawing the characters — casting the right types. I often spend days on one character." Before *Tatsinda*, which was done in full color with pencil, ink and water color, Miss Haas worked entirely in black-and-white with a fine point pen and ink. Many of the books she has illustrated have appeared in the American Institute of Graphic Arts shows and have been honored in the *Herald Tribune* Children's Spring Book Festival and in the *New York Times* annual lists of the best illustrated children's books. "My output of books for the last few years has been considerably lessened by the joyful distractions of marriage and a baby boy, but I hope I will never have a day go by without a book to work on."

HADER, BERTA HOERNER*

Born in San Pedro, Mexico. Childhood was spent in Mexico, Texas and the city of New York. Attended University of Washington, Seattle, and California School of Design.

Berta Hader's parents were Americans living in Mexico because of her father's business. When she was a small child her mother spent much time making water color sketches of Mexican houses and courtyards. The family moved to Texas, then to New York where Berta had most of her schooling. In 1919 she came back to New York from the West Coast and began to specialize in children's feature pages for magazines. In that same year she married Elmer Hader, and a few years later began collaborating with him on the illustration of books for children. Their first book together was a Macmillan "Happy Hour" edition of *The Ugly Duckling* in 1927.

HADER, ELMER STANLEY*

Born 1889 in Pajaro, California. Childhood was spent in San Francisco. Attended California School of Design; Académie, Julian, Paris.

Elmer Hader's high school studies were interrupted by the earthquake and fire of 1906. He then worked as silversmith's apprentice, surveyor's assistant, and locomotive fireman before taking up the study of painting at the California School of Design. Vaudeville was his stepping stone to the three years in Paris where he worked under the direction of François

Flameng, Albert Deschenaud, and others. There followed a summer in Brittany and a sketching trip to England. In the First World War he served in the Camouflage Corps of the A.E.F. After the war he opened a studio in New York City, and in 1919 he married Berta Hoerner and moved to Nyack, New York. Shortly after, they started building their present home on Willow Hill, which they continued building for many years. "It is a lifetime task. *The Little Stone House* (1944) gives the pleasanter side of our experiment. The heavy snow that blanketed this region the winter of 1946-47 not only gave us plenty of exercise with shovels, it provided the motif of *The Big Snow*, for which the American Library Association was kind enough to award us the Caldecott Medal in 1949. In the following years, the little animals and birds that share our hillside provided work, amusement and ideas for stories." In the last ten years, the Haders have added nine books to their long list. All of these, with the exception of *Two Is Company, Three's a Crowd*, have been done in black-and-white, usually pencil drawings, and full color painted in water color.

HALE, KATHLEEN*

Born May 24, 1898 in Scotland. Childhood was spent in Scotland, Yorkshire, and Manchester. Attended Manchester High School for Girls; Manchester School of Art; Reading University; Central School of Arts and Crafts, London.

Miss Hale writes that when her father died she was five years old, young enough to be affected by the unhappiness that followed, and she became something of a "problem child." She learned little at school and "spent most of the nine years there sitting outside the class room in disgrace. The headmistress was a remarkable woman, and decided, since I had a talent for drawing, writing original essays, and French, that I should be allowed to spend my time at these lessons and let the rest go by. She even arranged for me to attend Life classes at the Manchester School of Art which, at my age then, was unheard of." Kathleen Hale won a scholarship for art at Reading University for two years, then set off for London, having sold her bicycle in order to pay the fare to get there. This was in 1917. She got a job in the Ministry of Food and was drafted to a market gardener's nursery. After the war she minded babies, mended, collected bad debts for a window cleaner, and worked for an interior decorator; but small jobs in her own line came her way — designing book jackets, posters ("I did a poster that became famous all over London.") and illustrating children's stories. Whenever she could, she studied at London art schools. She married, went to live in the country and had two sons, for whom the Orlando books were written. Miss Hale, who is a Fellow of the Society of Industrial Arts, lives in Oxford, England.

HALL, DOUGLAS

Born July 23, 1931 in Doncaster, Yorkshire, England, where his childhood was spent. Attended Doncaster School of Art; Leeds College of Art; Royal College of Art.

For Douglas Hall, drawing came easier than anything else and so he went to art school. He began his career as a book illustrator and has done not only children's books but also adult fiction, textbooks and book jackets. He observes that, "I think the reason I do illustrating is because books fascinate me and I enjoy playing a part in them. I share the studio at our home (in Tunbridge Wells, Kent, England) with my wife Dorothy who helps design some books, but whose main interest is in textile design. We have two small boys, Jonathan and Alexander." Except for jackets which he has done in full color, most of his work has been in black-and-white or two colors. "*The Sea for Breakfast*," he says, "a humorous and semi-documentary adult book, was one of the most interesting for me because I went 'on location' to the highlands of Scotland for material and discovered, as it were, a new world. Much of the information I acquired was later used for illustrating *Storm from the West*. A new book, *How Edward Saved St. George*, was originally designed by Dorothy and myself in full color but the pressure of economy forced it to be published in two colors. Although the drawings are all mine, the layout and color balance was shared."

HALL, NATALIE WATSON

Born August 21, 1923 in Pittsburgh, Pennsylvania. Childhood was spent in New York City. Attended Ogontz School, Rydal, Pennsylvania; Yale School of Fine Arts; Art Students League, New York City.

Mrs. Hall writes, "I came from a family of high academic achievement and from an early age, I took another route, floundering in prep school and only finding myself when I began art school." After college and additional art studies, she was for a time Commercial Art Assistant at a workshop in the Virgin Islands. Her heart, however, has always belonged to New York City where she now lives. *The World in a City Block*, which she wrote and illustrated in full color using prisma pencils on dinobase, reflects this interest. About her work she writes, "Writing and illustrating are to me a means to be heard. My books 'freeze' for me certain points of view I feel should be stated." Mrs. Hall is the mother of four teenage children.

HAMBERGER, JOHN F.

Born August 17, 1934 in Jamaica, Long Island, New York. Childhood spent there and in Yonkers. Attended the School of Visual Arts, New York City.

"I have always loved animals and nature and consider them my specialty," says John Hamberger. "When I wasn't drawing them, I was playing with them. At fourteen, I tried to get a job at the zoo on Saturdays, but they had no opening." Mr. Hamberger does a good deal of painting now, but received most of his training in graphic design. The first book that he illustrated was *The Fox Friend*. He has also illustrated several of the Golden books and articles for *Boy's Life* magazine. *The Day the Sun Disappeared* was the first book that he both wrote and illustrated. He has worked in pen and ink and also in full color, for which he has made separations. Mr. Hamberger is married and makes his home in New York City.

HENDERSON, LE GRAND, see Le Grand, pseud.

HIM, GEORGE

Born in 1900 in Lodz, Poland. Childhood spent in Warsaw. Attended the University of Bonn in Germany; State Academy for Graphic Arts, Leipzig, Germany.

George Him began his college education in Moscow, where he studied law at the State University for a year, sketching in his spare time. He was also greatly interested at that time in mythology and ancient history. It was at the University of Bonn that he completed his education and received a Ph.D. This was followed by four years of studying art. He returned to Poland, and was planning to take a walking trip around the world when he met Jan Lewitt with whom he formed the famous designing team of Lewitt-Him in 1933. One of the first books they illustrated was *Lokomotywa* (Locomotive). After they went to England in 1937, they did another well-known train story, *The Little Red Engine Gets a Name*. They stayed together as a team until 1954. George Him is ranked as one of England's most successful graphic and exhibition designers. He also works with animated films and in the past few years has illustrated an increasing number of children's books. Most of these have been done in full color. One or two have been done in limited color with separations but he dislikes the process. Two articles on George Him have appeared in *Graphis*, No. 94 (March, 1961) and, earlier, in No. 74.

HOBAN, LILLIAN

Born May 18, 1925 in Philadelphia, Pennsylvania where her childhood was spent. Attended the Museum School in Philadelphia and Hanya Holm School of Dance.

Mrs. Hoban writes, "As a child I wanted to illustrate children's books and started classes at the Graphic Sketch Club in Philadelphia at the age of fourteen. I won a scholarship to art school where I majored in illustration — and met my husband Russell Hoban. After our marriage we moved to New York, and I gave up illustration to study dance professionally. I

taught dance until the birth of our third child, and then became part of a team with my husband, when I illustrated *Herman the Loser* (1961). He was in the process of changing his career from illustrator to writer, and I have been illustrating his books along with those of other writers since that time. I work in a large north-light studio in our home in Wilton, Connecticut. We now have four children, plus a Newfoundland dog and a Maine Coon cat. When I sit down in the studio to work on a book, I have exactly the same feeling of concentration and complete engagement that I had as a child when I first started to paint and draw. Being involved in making children's books is my idea of the good life." Mrs. Hoban works in black-and-white or two colors. For many of her books such as *Bread and Jam for Frances* she has used pencil. More recently she has begun to use pen and ink and wash.

HODGES, C. WALTER*

Born March 18, 1909, in Beckenham, Kent, England. Attended Dulwich College and Goldsmith's College School of Art, London.

In art school C. Walter Hodges studied book illustration under Edmund J. Sullivan. At the same time he developed an enthusiasm for the theater, and he left art school with the ambition of becoming a stage-designer. He worked for a time at an art theater in Hampstead, London; but working in art theaters in those days (1928-30) was not any way to earn a living; eventually he was obliged to take a job in the art department of an advertising agency. Neither he nor the agency enjoyed the few months of this adventure, and he left to become a free-lance illustrator. After a few lean months the work started to come in, and from that time onward he says he began seriously to learn his craft. "It did not come easily, and does not come easily even today." After a period illustrating books and magazines in England, he spent a year in New York in 1936-37, and there began to write a children's book, partly in order to provide himself with a congenial subject for illustration. This book, *Columbus Sails*, was published in the fall of 1939, just in time for World War II to interrupt the beginning of his career as a writer. He spent five years in the Army, and saw service as a Camouflage Officer in Normandy, Holland and Germany. After the war he resumed his career as an illustrator, but to this he now added writing, mural painting and exhibition and stage design. He also specialized in an abstruse problem of Theater History, the reconstruction of Elizabethan playhouses, and wrote books and articles on this subject. This led to an association with London's Mermaid Theater, which he helped to design, and for which he has designed settings and costumes for Shakespearean productions. His exhibition designs include the reconstruction of Lloyd's original 17th century Coffee House, for Lloyd's of London, and a complete commemorative exhibition for another London insurance company, the United Kingdom Provident Institution. For them also he has painted a large mural. Another of his murals is in the London Chartered Insurance Institute. He has illustrated well over seventy books, eight of which he has written himself. His book *Shakespeare's Theatre* won the Kate Greenaway medal for the best British children's book illustration for 1964; and his story *The Namesake* was runner-up for the Carnegie Medal, and was given the British place on the Honor List of the Hans Christian Andersen Award for 1966. Mr. Hodges lives in Bishopstone, Sussex, England. An article on him appears in the October 1957 issue of *American Artist*.

HOFF, SYD

Born 1912 in New York City where he spent his childhood. Attended National Academy of Design.

"Early gods of mine were all the comic strip artists, such as Tad, Hershfield, and Opper," writes Syd Hoff. "I couldn't wait to get into the field, and when, at age eighteen, I sold a drawing to *The New Yorker*, I gave up the 'fine art' I was taking at art school." Mr. Hoff has contributed to all the national magazines and has had a daily comic strip with King Features Syndicate. In 1958, he switched to a one-panel, daily cartoon called "Laugh It Off" which he still does. His first children's book was *Muscles and Brains* in 1944. "But my first real big hit was *Danny and the Dinosaur* in 1958 which was followed by a dozen others." He has illustrated two books by Allan Sherman and two others by Joan Lexau. The others he has written himself. He does his illustrations with line and wash on pebbleboard, using dinobase for separations. Mr. Hoff and his wife, who have two grown daughters, live in Miami Beach, Florida.

HOFFMANN, FELIX*

Born 1911 in Aarau, Switzerland. Attended the state art schools of Karlsruhe and Berlin, Germany.

Felix Hoffmann, the son of a musician, was born in Aarau, Switzerland where he still lives and has a studio on a mountainside with a view of meadows and forest on three sides. In the smaller of the two studio rooms he does lithographs, etchings, woodcuts and drawings. In the larger room, he works on his designs for murals and the beautiful stained glass windows that are commissioned for schools, churches, and other public buildings. In 1932 he illustrated his first book, for a Swiss publisher. Since 1957, he has done a number of picture books of such Grimm fairy tales as *The Wolf and the Seven Kids*, *The Sleeping Beauty* and *Rapunzel*. These, he explains, were originally done for his own four children but have since spread around the world, having been published in such distant places as London, New York and Tokyo. These books were done in five-color lithography, directly on the stone, as were the 100 black-and-white drawings for the *Picture Bible*. For *Told in Poland* he drew the color separations for the three-color pictures on acetate.

Mr. Hoffmann, who designs his books as well, has also illustrated a number of special editions of adult books. In 1957 he was given the Swiss Children's Book Award. From 1960 through 1964 he has regularly been on the Honor List of the Hans Christian Andersen Award, and in 1963, *The Seven Ravens* received the Picture Book Award in the New York *Herald Tribune* Children's Spring Book Festival. An article on Mr. Hoffmann's work appears in the Spring 1962 *Texas Quarterly* (Texas University).

HOGNER, NILS*

Born July 22, 1893 in Whitinsville, Massachusetts. Childhood was spent on a farm and in Boston, Massachusetts. Studied under Iver Nyeberg at the Royal Academy of Arts in Stockholm, Sweden; at the Rhodes Academy, Copenhagen, Denmark; under Arthur M. Hazard at the Boston School of Painting; and later attended School of the Museum of Fine Arts, Boston.

Nils Hogner's father, a doctor, wanted him to follow a medical career, but Nils showed such an interest in drawing and was so firm about his desire to become a painter that his father sent him abroad to study art. During World War I he served with the A. E. F. in France. In 1930 he joined the faculty of the University of New Mexico as an art instructor, returning to New York in 1932. Since that time he has devoted himself to book illustration and mural painting. Many of his children's books are written by his wife, Dorothy Childs Hogner. Among their early books are *Navajo Winter Nights*, 1935, and *Animal Book*, 1942, and in this period Nils Hogner also illustrated Glenn Balch's *Indian Paint*, 1942. Mr. and Mrs. Hogner find much of the material for their animal and nature study books on their farm in Litchfield, Connecticut, and in the surrounding woods, fields, rivers and ponds of the Berkshire Hills. As their hobby is raising herbs, they have written several books on herbs and cooking, and have won one of the top silver trophy awards for a kitchen herb garden at the International Flower Show in New York. Mr. Hogner has also written and illustrated several picture books on his own, and has done a number of murals in banks, schools and private homes.

HOGROGIAN, NONNY

Born May 7, 1932 in New York City where her childhood was spent. Attended Hunter College; studied with Antonio Frasconi at New School for Social Research, New York City.

In an article about Nonny Hogrogian in the *Horn Book*, August 1966, John Paul Itta explains that she comes of a family that would be sympathetic to a child with an artistic leaning. "Her mother dabbled in painting . . . her sister was an interior decorator before she married. Her father to this day copies Renoir, Homer, Monet and others." After college there was a brief period of showing her portfolio with no particular success and then the offer of a job as a production assistant and designer in the children's book department of Thomas Y. Crowell. Of this she writes, "The excitement of the work did not come right away. It wasn't until I was saturated with Elizabeth Riley's well-used expression 'the word comes first' that I learned the meaning of bookmaking. The manuscript does come first and from that everything grows." She was given the chance to illustrate her first book, *King of the Kerry Fair*, in 1960 and did it with woodblocks. She also used this medium for *Poems of Stephen Crane* and *Hand in Hand We'll Go*. For *Always Room for One More* she says, "I decided on pen and ink and a bit of wash and chalk to get the heathery quality I wanted." For this book she received the Caldecott Medal in 1966. Since beginning to illustrate books, Miss Hogrogian has divided her time between doing this on a free-lance basis and also serving as designer for the children's books of Holt, Rinehart and Winston and then Charles Scribner's Sons. Her illustrating is done in a studio in her New York apartment. An article by Miss Hogrogian appeared in *Publishers' Weekly*, February 21, 1966 and articles about her work appeared in *School Library Journal*, March 1966 and in the *Horn Book*, August 1966.

HOLLAND, JANICE*

Born May 23, 1913 in Washington, D. C. where her childhood was spent. Attended Corcoran School of Art, Washington, D. C.; Pratt Institute, School of Illustration, Brooklyn, New York. Received water color training under Eliot O'Hara. Died in 1962.

"From the time I can remember," wrote Janice Holland, "I aspired to be an artist — probably because my mother had such ambitions and sacrificed them for marriage. I always hoped I would illustrate children's books, but I attended a fine arts school where all forms of commercial art were discouraged. For a while I accepted this view and devoted myself to water color paintings of landscapes and figures. However, the pursuit of a fine arts career ceased to attract me when I found my ideals were very different from those of the leading fashions in the fine arts. It was then I went for a few months to Pratt Institute with the idea of entering the illustration field. I had come, in the meantime, to feel that the vital arts of this period are in the commercial field. The truth is that most of the great art of the past was in its time commercial, or commissioned work, whether portrait or triptych. I saw that the limitation on the excellence of an illustration was not one imposed by the fact that it was a commissioned work, or even by the exigencies of reproduction, but the only limitation was the vision of the artist himself. At the time I did my first illustrations for children I knew very little about children or children's books, my background being wholly artistic. However, after many years in the field, I have learned that to work for a child audience is the greatest of opportunities. Children are more interested and single-minded in giving themselves to what they read. I'm also convinced that children seek truth instinctively, and I'm dedicated to the old adage that 'Beauty is truth, truth, beauty.' Insofar as I am able, I try to give them these two things." Until her death in 1962, Janice Holland lived in Washington, D. C. She had illustrated more than forty-five children's books.

HOLLING, HOLLING CLANCY*

Born August 2, 1900 at Holling Corners, Jackson County, Michigan. His childhood winters were spent in Au Sable and West Branch, Michigan, and summers in Jackson County. Graduated from School of the Art Institute of Chicago.

Holling Clancy Holling was born Holling Allison Clancy, the first name honoring his maternal grandfather who was the last male in his branch of the Holling line. As a young artist, he sometimes signed his drawings with a simple "Holling." After the death of his father, in 1918, the "Holling" was often appended beneath "Holling Clancy." Thus evolved the signature under which his books have been written. To avoid confusion, before his marriage in 1925 the professional signature became his legal name. As a child he was interested in nature, especially wild creatures, an interest which he had the opportunity to follow in the woods of northern Michigan and during summers on his grandfather's farm. His mother developed his love of music and poetry. His father, a superintendent of schools, was a wise teacher who was seldom too busy to answer questions or show him where to look for answers. "At age eleven," he writes, "I decided that when I grew up I would write books and illustrate them so that other children could understand about things which interested them." From then on he filled many notebooks with his sketches of things he saw or imagined. Research findings and bits of story ideas were jotted down as well as his notes on first-hand experiments and experiences. On a scholarship to the Chicago Art Institute, he studied draftsmanship and the graphic art processes. It was during a year at the Taos Art Colony in New Mexico that he first became keenly aware of color. After graduating from art school, he produced his first publication, *Sun and Smoke*, and began a job with the Zoology Department of the Chicago Museum of Natural History. Three years later, Mr. Holling was engaged to teach art on the 1926-27 globe-circling cruise of the first "University Afloat." His wife, Lucille Webster Holling, went with him. On their return to Chicago, they worked together in advertising art and in writing and illustrating their first books. In 1937 the Hollings spent a year traveling in a studio-trailer gathering data for future books. They settled in Pasadena and devoted all of their time to the series on Americana. They are presently working on a series of books dealing with the American Indians. An educational film entitled "The Story of a Book," produced by Churchill Films, shows how the Hollings produced the book *Pagoo*. Holling and Lucille Holling were the joint recipients of the 1961 Award given by the Southern California Council on Literature for Children "for a body of work of lasting value."

HOLLING, LUCILLE WEBSTER*

Born December 8, 1900 in Valparaiso, Indiana. Her childhood was spent in various towns and cities of Indiana and Illinois. Attended the School of the Art Institute of Chicago.

Lucille Webster Holling's father was a Canada-born portrait photographer, her mother a school teacher of pioneer Vermont stock. An older sister, Mildred, who became an artist, influenced Lucille's early artistic efforts. Graduating from high school in 1918, she attended Chicago's Art Institute where she met her future husband. Meanwhile, as her sister's after-school apprentice, she learned drawing for reproduction. After a time in Taos, New Mexico, she returned to Chicago to design theatrical scenery and costumes, draw for fashion publications, and, in 1925, to marry Holling Clancy Holling. For eight months in 1926 and 1927 the Hollings traveled on the first University World Cruise, with Holling teaching Art and Lucille designing for the Drama Department. World travel influenced their work for the following decade. Maintaining the Holling Studio until 1937, they produced national advertising art and foreign travel brochures; Lucille illustrated a number of books; and, working together they illustrated books for textbook publishers, did fifty-two full-page syndicated features, "World Museum Dioramas," and painted murals. Among their best known books of this period were *Book of Indians*, 1935, and *Book of Cowboys*, 1936. In 1938 they set forth to collect Americana on a 90,000 mile studio-trailer trip which lasted a year. In California, Holling began his career as writer-illustrator, with Lucille working with him in all his work. In 1942 she took time to study ceramics, and taught Red Cross "Arts and Skills." In 1951 she designed and oversaw the construction of their studio residence in Pasadena, on four acres of San Gabriel foothills.

HOUSER, ALLAN C.*

Born June 30, 1914 in Apache, Oklahoma. Childhood spent on a nearby farm. Attended Santa Fe Indian School, Utah State Extension Courses.

Allan Houser writes, "My interest in art began when I was very young. I sketched with a pencil as far back as I can remember. It was through my father's storytelling of his experiences travelling with Chief Geronimo and later acting as the Chief's interpreter, that I built up a beautiful and deep love for my cultural background. It gave me a feeling of pride and through the years, I have tried to show this constantly in my paintings and sculpture and also my book illustrating. My father would

tell me that whatever you attempt, do it the best you can. As I have matured and become more critical I hold to this very strongly. In the last ten years I have been doing a lot of experimenting with new media and new approaches to give my work a more contemporary and fresh look."

HOUSTON, JAMES ARCHIBALD

Born June 12, 1921 in Toronto, Canada. Childhood spent in Ontario. Attended Ontario College of Art, Toronto; Ecole Grand Chaumiere, Paris; Hanga Un-ichi Hiratsuka, Tokyo, Japan; Atelier 17 William Hayter, Paris.

At the age of nine, James Houston's aunt gave him a story to illustrate because he had always done so much drawing. When a little later he got a check for $3.00 from a magazine for these illustrations he decided to make his living at art. A second parallel ambition came into his life when at the age of twelve Dr. Arthur Lismer, just returned from Africa, played African music for his art class and danced among them with his face covered by a great carved mask. "It shook me to the core, and I was hooked forever on the art and lives of primitive people." He visited the Canadian Arctic for the first time in 1948, later served nine years as the first Civil Administrator of West Baffin Island, and deserves the credit for introducing Eskimo carvings into the art world. He still serves on the Canadian Eskimo Art Commission and regularly visits his friends among the Eskimos. *Tikta'liktak*, an Eskimo legend that he frequently heard while he was with them, was named 1965 Book of the Year for Children by the Canadian Library Association. It is illustrated in wax pencil on acetate. His travels have taken him to Mexico, Iceland, Alaska, Russia, most of Europe, and Japan where he studied printmaking. His paintings and lithographs are in the collections of several Canadian museums and private collections. Since 1962, he has lived in New York where he is Associate Director of Design for Steuben Glass. About his illustrating he writes, "I am fond of pencil renderings, pen and ink, woodcut engraving and dry point. I also sometimes like to use a loose wash as background for these precise mediums."

HOWARD, ALAN*

Born December 1, 1922 in England. Childhood spent in Nottingham. Attended Nottingham High School; Caius College, Cambridge; School of Oriental and African Studies, London; Nottingham College of Art and Crafts.

Alan Howard intended originally to have an academic career. He read classics and history at Cambridge, receiving an M.A. degree in 1952. Then he decided that Art was what he really wanted. He especially likes, and feels that he is probably influenced by, Henri Rousseau, Breughel, Botticelli, and the work of children and primitive people. Of his own work he likes best *The Crocodile* illustrated in pen and ink, *The Bus that Went to Church* illustrated in gouache, and *The Faber Storybook*. Mr. Howard is married, has three children and lives in Preston, England.

HUGHES, SHIRLEY

Born July 16, 1929 in Hoylake near Liverpool, England where her childhood was spent. Attended Liverpool Art School and Ruskin School of Drawing and Fine Art, Oxford, England.

Shirley Hughes, whose married name is Vulliamy, recalls that as a child she enjoyed writing stories and illustrating them. "We had many picture books which made a vivid impression on me. Some were late Victorian, others were illustrated by Arthur Rackham, Heath Robinson, Edmund Dulac, Ernest Shepard — I loved all of these. At the Liverpool Art School I studied costume design with the idea of becoming a dress or stage designer. At the Ruskin School we did a highly academic art course. We were also taught lithography, grinding our own stones, working on them in ink and chalk and rolling out our own prints. I started to be interested in illustration in my last year and after I left school came to London to find work as a free-lance illustrator." She is married to an architect and they have two boys and a little girl. "I very rarely use them as models because they won't stay still long enough, but seeing them grow up, I find it easy to produce drawings of children of all ages out of my head. Reading to my children has been a tremendous help in comprehending how children want pictures to interpret their stories and the vital importance of detail. My husband is a very good draftsman himself and an unfailingly helpful critic." Shirley Hughes works mostly in black-and-white using a fine, very springy nib and drawing ink on cartridge paper, sometimes combined with a limited amount of brush work. In her full color work, she uses designers' gouache overlaid with pen and ink.

HURD, CLEMENT*

Born 1908 in New York City. Childhood was spent there and in Locust, New Jersey. Attended St. Paul's School, Yale College, and Yale Architectural School. Also studied painting in Paris for two years, chiefly in Leger's studio.

After his studies at Yale and then in Paris, Clement Hurd worked in New York as a free-lance designer. In 1938, William R. Scott asked him to illustrate his first children's book. He recalls that "there was a wonderful sense of cooperation and enthusiasm among all of us working to create fresh and good children's books for a younger age level. My illustrations for Margaret Wise Brown's *Bumblebugs and Elephants* were done in flat bright colors, showing simple objects." Since then he has devoted most of his time to illustrating children's books.

In 1939 he married the author, Edith Thacher, and they have since done over thirty-five books together and nearly as many individually or in collaboration with others. In about 1958, he began experimenting with weathered wood and old boards lying on the beach outside of his San Francisco Bay studio. "The grain and textures in these woods made very interesting effects when printed on rice paper. I used them very timidly in *The Diggers*. It also seemed right, especially with the paper quite wet for the underwater setting of *Wingfin and Topple*. Although it is a technique which will not suit all stories, in the right place it offers a richness that would look overworked and fussy if painted by hand." Two of his favorites among the earlier books he illustrated are *The Runaway Bunny* and *Goodnight Moon*. The Hurds and their son live in Mill Valley, California and spend their summers in Starkboro, Vermont. An article about Mr. Hurd and his work appears in the February 7, 1966 issue of *Publishers' Weekly*.

HUTCHINSON, WILLIAM M.

Born June 22, 1916 in Norfolk, Virginia. Childhood spent in Virginia and West Virginia. Attended Cleveland Art Institute.

"My happiest recollections," recalls William Hutchinson, "are of childhood summers in the mountains of Virginia. Probably as a result of those summers, I've always particularly enjoyed outdoor life and natural history. My family always loved to read and there were always books present, so it seems perfectly natural that I should want to illustrate the books I have loved all my life. I can't ever remember having 'nothing to do' as a child because I was always content to be left alone with pencils and paper to draw. A truly dedicated high school art teacher provided needed instruction, encouragement and direction. My professional life has always revolved around illustration whether in advertising or the book field." Illustrating books began as a side line for him when he returned from four years in the Pacific during World War II. Gradually he became occupied full time with children's books, both trade and textbooks. "Most of the books have been for children eight and older. My work has been done largely for black-and-white reproduction, although I have enjoyed doing several books in four-color process. I find myself using two different techniques for black-and-white line, one running to fine line and the other to the use of mass and a heavier pattern, depending upon the subject matter, and not, of course, using both in the same book. At present I live and work at home in Westport, Connecticut."

HUTTON, CLARKE*

Born 1898 in London, England, and his childhood was spent there and in Gravesend, Kent. Attended Central School of Arts and Crafts, London.

Clarke Hutton became, at the age of seventeen, assistant to William Pitcher (known by the assumed name, "Carl Wilhelm") designer of the long line of ballets, at London's old Empire Theater. He worked with "Wilhelm" for ten years and then, in 1926, a visit to Italy completely changed his interests. Painting and the graphic arts absorbed his attention. Returning to London he studied at the Central School of Arts and Crafts under A. S. Hartrick, R.W.S., who encouraged him to do lithography. Founding his early work in this medium on Daumier and other classic lithographers, he saw the possibilities of it as a medium for book illustration. On the retirement of Hartrick from the Central School of 1930, Clarke Hutton became Instructor in Lithography in his place — which post he holds at the present time. Among his earliest children's books were *A Country ABC*, 1940, and *I, The Autobiography of a Cat*, 1941. He is illustrator and part author of the "Picture History" Series for the Oxford University Press which he considers a most important part of his work. These he illustrates in four-color autolithography and also designs. In recent years, he has also illustrated such books as the Limited Editions Club's *The Prince and the Pauper* and *Kenilworth* and *Almayer's Folly* for the Folio Society. His home is in London.

HYMAN, TRINA SCHART

Born April 8, 1939 in Philadelphia, Pennsylvania. Childhood was spent in that city and its suburbs. Attended Philadelphia College of Art; Boston Museum School; Konstfackskolan, Stockholm, Sweden.

Mrs. Hyman writes that she grew up surrounded by woods and fields in a family that celebrated lovely German Christmases. "I illustrated my first book, self-written, at four and there was never any doubt in my mind that I would illustrate books when I grew up. My idols were, and still are, Howard Pyle, N. C. Wyeth and Arthur Rackham." In art school she studied under Henry Pitz and shortly after her marriage to Harris Hyman in 1959 she began studying graphics under Ture Bengst in Boston. "In 1960 my husband, who is a mathematician and engineer, and I left for Sweden where we lived for a year and a half." While there she illustrated her first book *Toffe Och Den Lilla Bilen* for Raben & Sjogren. After a tour on a tandem bicycle of England and Scandinavia, the Hymans returned to Boston where they lived for four years and Trina Hyman began illustrating in earnest. "In the spring of 1965 we moved to New York, where I now live with my husband, three-year-old daughter, Katrin, a Swedish friend, four belligerent cats, and 123 (last count) house plants. I am a frustrated farmer. I work mainly in pen and ink and water color, although occasionally I draw with a brush." Her work to date has been primarily in black-and-white or two colors.

IPCAR, DAHLOV*

Born November 12, 1917 in Windsor, Vermont. Childhood winters were spent in New York City, summers in Maine. Attended City and Country School, Walden School and Lincoln School, New York; Oberlin College, Oberlin, Ohio.

From her home, Robinhood Farm, Robinhood, Maine, Dahlov Ipcar writes, "I have been painting since earliest childhood. My parents, William and Marguerite Zorach, are both artists. From the beginning I was surrounded by creative activity — painting, sculpting, batiking and embroidering — so that art came naturally to me. I remember our walls were painted with the garden of Eden, and at the age of seven I started a frieze that traveled around my room, full of large and fanciful animals, bright colored horses and ostriches and dinosaurs. My parents never tried to direct me or give me instruction in art. They both felt that academic training had hampered and misdirected their art, and they wanted mine to develop as naturally as possible. I never attended art school. The schools I attended were all 'progressive.' Perhaps through all this I have managed to keep a little of the child's 'natural' approach to painting and fresh view point. At least, I like to think so. I was married at eighteen, and since then my husband and I have been living on our farm in Maine the year round. He was an accountant who didn't like the business world. For the past thirty years he has run our small dairy farm, and I have helped with the farm work, painted pictures, illustrated and written books, kept house, and raised two sons. We have always enjoyed our life on the farm, even though it has been hard physical work. As an artist I am happy to be surrounded by the beauty of field and forest and animal life. All these things are part of my life and my pictures." Mrs. Ipcar has had seven one-man shows in New York City, her work is represented in a number of museums, including the Whitney and the Metropolitan, and she has done several murals. Since 1950, she has written the text of the books she has illustrated. Her picture books are in two to four colors, for which she does the separations. Two articles by Mrs. Ipcar have appeared in the *Horn Book* magazine, October 1961 and February 1966.

JACQUES, ROBIN

Born March 27, 1920 in London, England. Childhood spent there and in Hertfordshire.

Robin Jacques writes that during his childhood his family had several homes and "seemed always on the move, a pattern that has persisted until now. My first job, at fifteen, was in an advertising agency which I found profoundly uncongenial but was obliged to persevere with, my family being without the means to send me to art school. The war in 1939 broke this pattern and I was mustered into the army and soldiered until 1945. I then began to illustrate books on a free-lance basis, and with the exception of a short phase as art director of two magazines, I have continued ever since. The main advantage of this way of work is that my wife and I have been free to live and work in the countries of our choice." To date these have included Mexico, the United States, the south of France and a year in Africa. Mr. Jacques, who is a Fellow of the Society of Industrial Artists, is also the author of a book on illustrations, *Illustrators at Work*, published by Studio-Vista. His most usual medium for all books is ink-drawing, sometimes with a full color frontispiece. His color work is done with a black ink drawing and either color overlays or color washes.

JANSSON, TOVE

Born August 8, 1914 in Helsinki, Finland. Childhood spent in Helsingfors. Attended Art schools in Helsinki, Stockholm, Sweden and Ecole des Beaux Arts, Paris.

"My mother is a designer and my father was a sculptor," writes Miss Jansson. "To get peace for their work they gave me a pencil to handle as soon as I was old enough to hold it. We lived in Finland, Helsingfors, during the summer in the archipelago farthest out into the sea — as we do now. When I was small we went for summer journeys to Sweden and also to the islands. If something has influenced my books it may be these summer islands and, of course, the sea." Besides being the author-illustrator of ten children's books, she has also illustrated Swedish editions of such books as *Alice in Wonderland*, *The Hobbit* and *The Hunting of the Snark*, did a strip cartoon of "Moomin" for a London paper (now written and drawn by her brother Lars), and paints murals and in oils. She began her illustrating at the age of fifteen, "first in comic papers and then in other kinds of publications. In 1939, I wrote (in Swedish) my first children's book. When I illustrate my stories I never get this feeling I have when I write, of walking in a strange world that was my own long ago. I don't draw for myself, but for those who shall read the stories, and I draw to clarify, to emphasize or to alleviate. The illustrations are simply an attempt at explaining what I have perhaps failed to express in words, a kind of footnotes. Also they are there out of consideration. What is too frightening can be alleviated in an illustration, what is only hinted at can be intensified, a happy moment can be lengthened. What the self-absorbed writer has skipped because it jarred his style, the illustrator can portray in minute detail to amuse the reading child. And the illustrator can simply omit those pictures that would only impede the child's own fantasies." Tove Jansson has won numerous awards for both her writing and illustrating in the Scandinavian countries. Her books have been on the Honor List of the Hans Christian Andersen Medal four times and in 1966, she received the Medal itself.

JAUSS, ANNE MARIE*

Born February 3, 1907 in Munich, Germany. Childhood was spent in Munich and in Austria. Studied at the State Art School in Munich.

Anne Marie Jauss is the daughter of the German landscape painter George Jauss. After studying at Munich State Art School she lived for a few years in Berlin, then traveled in Spain, Morocco, Austria, and Paris. In 1932, she left Germany and lived in Lisbon, Portugal, where she had several one-man shows, exhibited with modern Portuguese painters, and worked as an illustrator, designer and decorator. She has lived in the United States since 1946 and has had several one-man shows of her paintings here. Some of her dry points, as well as paintings, are in various collections. Her travels have taken her to New England, Florida, California, and Puerto Rico, with her home being first in New York City and then, since 1962, in northern New Jersey. Miss Jauss has written and illustrated several children's books, as well as illustrating a number by other authors. About her work she writes, "I always wanted to illustrate children's books. This was finally realized when I came to this country. It gives me as much satisfaction as painting. For me personally there is only one approach to illustration: to do something sincere and essentially very simple. My inspiration never comes from contemporary art but from the past and especially from folk art."

JOHNSON, CROCKETT, pseud.*
(David Johnson Leisk)

Born October 6, 1906 in New York City. Childhood was spent on Long Island, New York. Attended Cooper Union, New York and New York University.

Crockett Johnson grew up on Long Island, learned some art at New York University and Cooper Union, worked in an ice plant, in Macy's advertising department, and played professional football. He art-edited several magazines and contributed to others. For three years he drew a weekly cartoon feature known as "The Little Man With the Eyes" for *Colliers*. His comic strip "Barnaby," ran daily for ten years in most American and a dozen foreign newspapers and appeared in book form. *Barnaby* has been adapted for television and is still appearing in translation in an Italian publication. He has written and illustrated fourteen children's books, including *Harold and the Purple Crayon* and its six sequels. He has in the past also illustrated several books by other authors including three by his wife, Ruth Krauss. He characterizes his illustrations as "simplified, almost diagramatic, for clear storytelling, avoiding all arbitrary decoration." He generally does a black drawing in line or wash and then makes color overlays, often using several Ben Day screens. He is responsible for the design as well as illustration of his books. The Johnsons make their home in Rowayton, Connecticut.

JOHNSON, EUGENE HARPER*

Born in Birmingham, Alabama, where his childhood was spent. Attended Académie Julian, Paris; American Academy of Art, Chicago; School of the Art Institute of Chicago; National Academy School of Fine Arts, New York; Pratt Institute, Brooklyn, New York.

As a child Harper Johnson showed ability in a number of different fields, including painting, singing, playing the violin and writing poetry. Before he was twelve his work attracted the attention of a student of Gene Paul Lawrence, Professor D'launey, who was impressed with the boy's various abilities and later arranged for the young artist to go to France to work for several years in his studio. During this time Harper applied himself diligently to both art and music for even greater than his interest in art was his ambition to become a violinist. He had a successful but short musical career, touring Europe and Africa playing the violin, which ended when he broke his left wrist with a fall from a horse and was never again able to finger the violin. From then on he turned all his attention to painting, studying at the Académie Julian before returning home to continue his studies in American art schools. Until he had made a name for himself in the field of art he earned his living at a variety of uncongenial jobs — from dish washing to newspaper reporting and steel working — in none of which did he show any competence. After about three years of struggle, his career as an illustrator was at last successfully launched. His illustrations have appeared in national magazines, he is established as a muralist and portrait painter, and his paintings hang in many art galleries and private collections. During the War he served for a year as a private in the Special Services Division. In 1949 he entered the field of book illustration and now has a great many books to his credit under the imprint of a number of different publishers. Impressions made by a tour of North and East Africa in 1955 found expression in his book *Kenny*. Mr. Johnson met his wife, Anita, when they were both students at Pratt Institute in 1945. They have three children, Eileen, Iona, and Eugene Harper, Junior. In 1966, Harper Johnson left on an extended trip to Africa.

JOHNSON, JOHN E.

Born May 14, 1929 in Worcester, Massachusetts. Childhood spent in Berks County, Pennsylvania. Attended Philadelphia College of Art.

Though Mr. Johnson's parents were Swedish, they had a farm in a part of Pennsylvania that was almost entirely German Dutch. He can remember that the other children who came to the one-room school often could not speak English in the early grades. "Being the youngest and only child at home, with few toys because of the Depression, I entertained myself by playing with the dog and drawing." After art school, he spent two years in the Army and then went to New York to work with a small

greeting card company. The next seven years saw the company grow and his job became more and more administrative. "I thoroughly enjoyed working with the young artists coming up, but I myself was hardly drawing at all." In 1961 he decided for drawing and jumped into free-lancing without any fixed idea which direction he would take. "I had taken illustrating from Henry Pitz in school so it was natural to consider books." Since then he has illustrated twenty-four books, and has done some advertising illustration and work for a number of magazines including *McCalls* and *Woman's Day*. One of his first books was *Just Around the Corner* which he particularly enjoyed because of the problems of organizing it visually and developing the proper format. To date most of his work is in pen line, in some cases with wash or color overlays. His early work with greeting cards gave him considerable experience with the problems and processes of printing which he feels has been of help to him in illustrating. Mr. Johnson's wife, who was a fellow art student, often helps him in preparing various jobs. They have two children and make their home in New York City.

JOHNSON, MILTON

Born August 16, 1932 in Milwaukee, Wisconsin where his childhood was spent. Attended Art Institute in Milwaukee; Museum School of Fine Arts, Boston; studied with George Demetrios, Folly Cove, Massachusetts.

Mr. Johnson remembers an early interest in drawing people and also receiving a great deal of encouragement from his family and friends. From his early teens he studied art formally and informally and after art school in 1960 was given a Travelling Fellowship from the Museum School of Fine Arts in Boston. Four years in Japan gave him the opportunity to employ Eastern concepts as well as those he learned from George Demetrios, whom he credits as being very important in his development in design and drawing. He says his great love of drawing comes from "its being so personal and immediate." He illustrates in pen and ink, as in *Andrew Jackson* by Margaret Coit, though his other work includes painting and prints which have brought him several awards.

JONES, CAROL ANN

Born August 17, 1942 in Birmingham, England. Childhood was spent in Bournville, Birmingham, England. Attended Moseley Secondary Art School and Birmingham College of Art and Crafts.

"At the age of thirteen, I passed an examination that took me to Moseley Secondary Art School," writes Carol Jones, "and I guess this was the starting point." At sixteen, she began a five-year course at the Birmingham College of Art and Crafts and took the National Design Diploma specializing in children's book illustration. She took a postgraduate year in illustration and then moved to London, where she taught two and a half days a week "illustrating the rest of the week and on school holidays." In 1966 she went to Canada with plans to stay about a year. "I use many ways of obtaining an effect — stippling, resists, cut and torn paper. I've just finished a book of Eskimo tales where I used a soap ground, black painted on top and worked into with an old pen nib, using a second color overlay. I enjoy using full color best, but one has to do more black-and-white work."

JONES, HAROLD*

> Born February 22, 1904 in London, England, where child-hood was spent. Attended St. Dunstan's College, and Royal College of Art, London.

"When I was about seventeen," Harold Jones writes, "I spent a year in the country where I worked as a farm student. The beauty of the countryside in Warwickshire made a great impression on my mind — especially as I had always lived in a town. Later in life, when I was doing Lavender's Blue, I relied on these vivid memories to form the background to my pictures." The following year he attended art school at Goldsmith's College in London, and had as one of his teachers Edmund Sullivan, who had been the teacher of Arthur Rackham some years past. "As students we did all we could to get Sullivan to draw on the side of our paper and these superb little drawings we would treasure for years." Several years later, in 1924, he gained a scholarship to the Royal College of Art, "where Sir William Rothenstein, the principal, inspired us to draw and compose in the best academic traditions. Following my art training, I taught for a number of years in a boys' school in London, but the urge within me to create was too strong for me to continue full-time teaching for long. I gave up my employment as a teacher and started life as a professional artist. My first illustrations appeared in 1937. Walter de la Mare and I collaborated to produce This Year, Next Year, a series of poems and pictures depicting the four seasons. It has been my pleasure to illustrate many children's books since then. Undoubted pleasure it surely is, for to work for children is an inspiration in itself. I have two daughters and I have written and illustrated a book for each." These are A Visit to the Farm and The Enchanted Night. For his first book, This Year, Next Year, Harold Jones used auto-lithography. For Lavender's Blue, he used water color and pen and line in full color that was separated photographically. "I felt that I wanted to get nearer to a truer facsimile than this achieved. I was introduced to Astrofoil, a transparency which could be laid over one's key drawing." He used this method of hand-separating the colors for several books including The Pied Piper of Hamelin. Mr. Jones is always responsible for the design as well as illustration of his books. Lavender's Blue has received several honors, including honorable mention for the Hans Christian Andersen Medal. Harold Jones' home is in Putney, England.

KAHL, VIRGINIA CAROLINE*

> Born 1919 in Milwaukee, Wisconsin where her childhood was spent. Attended Milwaukee-Downer College (B.A. in Art); University of Wisconsin (M.S. in Library Science).

"Because I am a full time librarian, I feel reluctant to call myself an artist," writes Miss Kahl, who lives in Milwaukee, Wisconsin. "Yet I enjoy doing the illustrations for my picture books more than I do writing the stories." She did not think of trying to produce a picture book of her own until she went to Austria as an Army librarian. "Interest in art of the medieval period, as well as the experience of living in a country where the past is very much alive and the examples of folk art and medieval art are abundant, helped to develop the simple decorative style that I seem to have." Her seven years in Europe gave her the impetus she needed to attempt children's book illustrating. Miss Kahl's stylized and decorative work is done usually in two or four flat colors using designers' colors. For these she makes separations on acetate. An article by her concerning Austrian children's books appeared in the February 1955 Horn Book.

KANE, HENRY BUGBEE*

> Born January 8, 1902 in Cambridge, Massachusetts. Child-hood was spent there and in the State of Maine. Attended Phillips-Exeter Academy, and Massachusetts Institute of Technology.

"I can hardly remember the time when I was not drawing. Photography entered my life in 1912 at the advanced age of ten, and the two have occupied equally important places in my affections," writes Henry Kane. "Although I have written and illustrated several books of my own and illustrated many more written by others, both for children and adults, it has been done heretofore as an avocation. In 1966 it became my major occupation upon retiring from M.I.T. where, for 26 years, I had been Director of the Alumni Fund. My illustrations have been both photographs and drawings, primarily but not entirely in black-and-white, using such things as pen and ink and scratchboard, and almost wholly in the field of nature. Mrs. Kane and I have three children and, as of the moment, a like number of grandchildren. Our home is in Lincoln, Massachusetts."

KARLIN, EUGENE

> Born December 15, 1918 in Kenosha, Wisconsin. Childhood spent in Kenosha and Chicago, Illinois. Attended Art Institute, Chicago; Art Students League, New York City; Colorado Springs Arts Center.

At age five Eugene Karlin was attending free art courses at Jane Addams' famed Hull House in Chicago. According to an article in the March 1966 issue of American Artist, his mother did her marketing in the open stalls on Maxwell Street, while he attended art class. In later years he had to fight off neighborhood bullies who tried to steal his three cents carfare. All his art education was the result of scholarships. In 1943, he became the first and only staff artist for *Fortune* magazine. Along with his free-lance work, Mr. Karlin has also taught at Cooper Union Art School, 1949-1957, Parsons School of Design, 1948, Workshop School of Advertising and Editorial Art, 1949. At present he teaches at Pratt Institute and the School of Visual Arts. His work has been exhibited at many group shows including the Metropolitan Museum, New York, Art Institute, Chicago, and Corcoran Gallery, Washington. In addition Mr. Karlin has done extensive work in advertising art and magazine illustration. Working in black-and-white or full color, he uses pen and ink mainly. For the Marianne Moore version of *Puss in Boots* he used pen and ink with pastel overlay. Mr. Karlin characterizes his work as romantic, and, over the years, feels that his style has changed from expressionistic to lyrical. Mr. Karlin works on a smooth-surfaced printing paper which provides a slick surface for his swift pen. For the drawing he uses an old-fashioned pen holder with a Spencerian steel nib no longer manufactured. In order to develop virtuosity in drawing he has purposely narrowed his field to this area. Mr. Karlin, his wife and two teenage daughters live in Sunnyside, New York.

KAUFMANN, JOHN

Born 1931 in New York City where most of his childhood was spent. Attended Pennsylvania Academy of Fine Arts, Philadelphia; Art Students League, New York; and Instituto Statale D'Arte, Florence, Italy.

Mr. Kaufmann remembers that his favorite subject for drawing as a child was war planes. "Each was drawn in profile with its guns bristling and a fierce pilot in every cockpit." His love of flight included some drawings of birds and he still enjoys painting them. It also caused him to take the Aeronautical Course at Brooklyn Technical High School, after which he went to work in an aircraft factory. "I crossed back into the visual arts by a strange side door," he writes. "A friend, noticing my talent for painting Santa Clauses on the office doors suggested I try technical illustration. I did. After a number of years of doing isometric and perspective drawings of Cold War hardware, I got married and left for Florence with my wife Alicia." There he studied mural and fresco. They traveled through most of Europe before returning to New York. His wife was working in the children's book department of Knopf and when, at one point, they were desperate for an illustrator for a book on Oceanography, she suggested her husband. Equally important was the chance to illustrate *Killer of Death*. Since this beginning he has been working steadily in the field. About his work he says, "Because I have encountered in my technical illustrating people who have rationalized away the social consequences of

their life activities, I now value my work more. To me, good books for children are diametrically opposed to the engineering of missiles and the manipulation of public opinion." To date, Mr. Kaufmann has worked mostly in black-and-white. "I use India ink for my black which allows me to work back over an area without picking up what has already been put down underneath. Often I wet my paper first and paint quickly into the moist areas before they dry." He feels that something well done in line has a directness and candor that no more complex technique can match. The Kaufmanns have two small sons and live in Fresh Meadows, New York.

KEATS, EZRA JACK*

Born March 11, 1916 in Brooklyn, New York where childhood was spent.

Born and brought up in Brooklyn, Mr. Keats began to draw before he was ten years old. He was encouraged by his mother, less openly by his father, and by a man across the street who asked him to letter his candy store sign. Although the winner of several prizes and scholarships, he has always preferred to teach himself. "Life is very fickle, and some artists who have been taught to develop styles of their own become stratified and outmoded. I look forward to something new every day." He studied and traveled abroad for a year, spending most of his time in Paris. Before entering the children's book field, he had painted murals, done magazine illustration, posters and taught painting. "In about 1956," he writes, "while exhibiting my paintings at the Associated American Artists Gallery, I was asked to do a jacket for a novel by V. Sackville West. Elizabeth Riley of Crowell saw the book and asked me to do a jacket for a juvenile novel. She liked what I did and suggested that I illustrate a children's book. And so I suddenly found my field — one which fuses my feelings for children, storytelling and painting." Mr. Keats first used collage in *The Snowy Day* which won the 1963 Caldecott Medal. According to an article in *Publishers' Weekly*, April 4, 1966, he says, "My use of collage in *The Snowy Day* occurred so naturally I hardly realized it at the time. I had planned to use just a bit of patterned paper here or there as I worked on the book. But then one thing called for another. When the book was finished, I was somewhat startled to discover that my way of working had been transformed. For *Jennie's Hat* such things as dried leaves, strips of fabrics, and old Valentines were used in addition to the painting." In addition to this article in *Publishers' Weekly*, there are articles about Mr. Keats and his work in the August 1963 and June 1964 issues of *Horn Book*, and the November 9, 1963 *Saturday Review*. Ezra Jack Keats makes his home in Brooklyn.

KEEPING, CHARLES WILLIAM JAMES

Born September 22, 1924 at Lambeth, London, England. Childhood spent there. Attended School of Art, The Polytechnic, London.

"I was born just off Lambeth Walk, the famous street market. My paternal grandparents were costermongers (street traders), my maternal grandparents were seafaring people. My father was a professional boxer. We lived next to a stablery so the carthorse was a great symbol to me as a boy. I never drew trees or landscape because I never saw any. Mostly men and horses, women with children, prams, carts and barrows and all the things in a city market place of the 1930's. Such things produce a simple image, a figure against a wall, a caged bird against a lace curtain. From this I think developed whatever style I have today. I don't like my drawings to illustrate a particular incident, but more to set a mood throughout the whole book," writes Charles Keeping. During World War II, he was a wireless operator in the Royal Navy. "After the war I attended art college part time while working as a rent collector in Paddington — marvellous for a potential illustrator, it's a crumby, seedy part of London with a wealth of stories and characters." Later on a full-time study grant he worked in drawing, lithography, etching and engraving. His lithographs have been exhibited in London, the United States, Australia and Italy. The Victoria and Albert Museum in London is one of the many galleries and museums owning Mr. Keeping's works. Since 1956 he has illustrated about eighty books and has also done work for the BBC. He taught lithography and illustration at the Polytechnic until it closed and is presently a lecturer in drawing at Croydon College of Art. In 1952, he married Renate Meyer, a painter and printmaker. With their own three children and one adopted West Indian boy, they live in a huge rambling Victorian house in Bromley, South London and keep many animals including a cart horse. About his materials he writes, "In black-and-white I mainly use India ink with steel nib or bamboo pen that I cut myself. Sometimes I use a Chinese brush. I draw from imagination, although if I was drawing a story about a cat, I would like one in the studio. In color I use a mixture of gouache, tempera, water colors, ink and sometimes printer's inks. As a lithographer, I like to work on plastics and often suggest it to publishers. Illustration to me is a vehicle for expression of one's ideas. It is not so much a job as a way of life."

KENNEDY, PAUL EDWARD

Born October 7, 1929 in Indiana. Childhood spent there and in Chicago, Illinois. Attended Skowhegan (Maine) School of Painting and Sculpture; Indiana University (M.F.A. 1953).

"My father was a trumpet player with a talent for drawing. Some of my earliest memories are of sitting on his lap while he drew pictures for me, inventing stories as he drew," writes Mr. Kennedy. "I went to a small high school in Indiana that had no art instruction. So I began painting independently in water colors and oils. During my senior year while I was struggling between a career as a concert pianist and one as a painter,

I entered the Scholastic Magazines Art Contest and won a gold key in the regional show." At Indiana University, after two weeks as a piano major, he switched to art and earned a Master of Fine Arts degree. After service in the Air Force, he came to New York and in 1955 married Emily Price. When she enrolled in a course in writing for children, he tried his hand at illustrating one of her stories. It was published as *Otto the Growly Boy* and Mr. Kennedy has been illustrating ever since, with twenty-four books to his credit. He works primarily in black-and-white, although *The Skeleton in Armor* is in color. The Kennedys, who have a six-year-old daughter, live in New York City.

KENNEDY, RICHARD*

Born September 4, 1910 in England. Childhood was spent in the south of England and in London. Educated at Marlborough. Attended Central School of Arts and Crafts, London.

"When I was sixteen," writes Richard Kennedy, "I entered a publishing firm and later worked as a reporter on a newspaper. When I was twenty-two I attended art school for the first time but left after a year to take a job in an advertising agency. I continued to attend an art school in the evening. I became a book illustrator by chance, owing to a letter to a friend illustrated with a sketch of two airmen playing chess. The friend showed it to a publisher who gave me a commission, and my first book was illustrated while serving in the ground force of the R. A. F. The sculptor, Gaudier-Brzeska, has been the greatest inspiration of my artistic life." Mr. Kennedy, who lives in Maidenhead, Berkshire, England, generally works in pen and ink as in the Penguin edition of *Peter Pan* and in *Finn the Wolfhound.*

KEPES, JULIET*

Born June 29, 1919 in London, England. Attended Askes Hatcham School, London; Brighton School of Art, Brighton, England; School of Design, Chicago.

Juliet Kepes has written, "As far back as I can remember I was always drawing, and as far back as I can remember I was always fascinated by living, moving and acting things. Growing up in a big metropolis did not allow much opportunity for seeing any other creatures but cart horses, dogs, cats and birds. These I looked at for hours on end and then drew from memory. Coming to this country in 1937 I went to the School of Design in Chicago and graduated from there." The Art Institute of Chicago, the Baltimore Museum, Worcester Museum, De Cordova and Dana Museum in Lincoln, Massachusetts, Gropper Gallery in Cambridge have exhibited her work. "Children's books have always fascinated me and in 1944 I began work on *The Five Little Monkeys.*" Since then she has written and illustrated five of her own picture books and illustrated six books by other authors. "I do prefer to do it all myself," she writes. "I have worked in black-and-white as well as color, and made all the separations for all of my books, usually done with acetates. I also design the layout, end paper, jacket, title page, and choose the type. My materials mainly consist of water color paper, Japanese, Strathmore, charcoal, drawing and tracing papers as well as illustration boards on which I do the black and white drawings, and acetates for the overlays. My tools are pencils, pens, quills and brushes of all types; inks, water color, casein and gouache paints." Several of her books have received honors: *Two Little Birds and Three*, *Five Little Monkeys* and *Beasts from a Brush* have been chosen among the Ten Best Books by the *New York Times*. *Lady Bird, Quickly* was chosen as Honor Book by the *New York Herald Tribune*. *Give a Guess* received a Certificate of Excellence from the American Institute of Graphic Arts and *Frogs Merry*, a Citation of Merit from the Society of Illustrators. She is married to Gyorgy Kepes, with whom she has collaborated on several architectural murals and the design for a children's room which was published in *Interiors* and later carried out in *Life* magazine. They have two children, a son, Imre, and a daughter Judy, and make their home in Cambridge, Massachusetts.

KESSLER, LEONARD P.*

Born October 28, 1921 in Ohio. Childhood spent in Pittsburgh, Pennsylvania. Attended Carnegie Institute of Technology, Pittsburgh, graduating with a B.F.A. in Painting and Design.

Leonard Kessler became interested in art at the age of seven when he attended classes, of a very informal and creative nature, at the local neighborhood center. Mr. Kessler says, "I believe now that much of my feeling for art, and present philosophy of graphic communication can be directly traced to those classes at the Irene Kaufmann Settlement art school. However, I dropped out of the school at the age of ten and became interested in music. It was not until graduation from high school that I again became interested in art." In World War II Leonard Kessler entered the United States Army and spent three years with the United States Infantry Division, as Staff Sergeant. Upon release from the service he entered Carnegie Institute. After graduation he moved to New York City, and has been illustrating and designing children's books since 1951. His work is primarily in black-and-white or two colors, using line for the key drawings and putting the second or third colors on overlays, as in *The Sad Tale of the Careless Klunks*. Although he feels his style has not changed basically in the past ten years, there is "more emphasis on the over all design of the book as a complete unit — moving from page to page as a movie goes from frame to frame." Three of Mr. Kessler's books have been selected for the *New York Times'* Ten Best Illustrated Books:

Fast Is Not a Ladybug in 1954, *Heavy Is a Hippopotamus* in 1955 and *Big Red Bus* in 1957. Mr. Kessler, his wife Ethel, and their two children, Paul and Kim, live in Rockland County, New York.

KETTELKAMP, LARRY DALE

Born April 25, 1933 in Harvey, Illinois. Childhood spent in Urbana, Illinois. Attended University of Illinois, Pratt Institute.

"I have drawn ever since I can remember and have had a parallel interest in music," says Larry Kettelkamp who still pursues both these interests. He illustrated for the high school newspaper and yearbook and sang Gilbert and Sullivan roles. While in college he also worked up a magic show, which he used to earn money. "At the time I was in school, Herbert Zim was at the University and had already written a number of children's books. Although I had majored in painting my stronger interest was illustration. I submitted some samples of art to one of Zim's publishers and they gave me the job of illustrating one of his books, *The Sun*." Larry Kettelkamp was nineteen when he illustrated this first book. Later, at Pratt Institute, he took all of the undergraduate illustration courses at once and, while there, wrote and illustrated *Magic Made Easy*. After his discharge from the Army in 1956, he worked for several years with Herbert Zim on *The Wonderful World* encyclopedia, and then as art director for Garrard Press. Since 1962, he, his wife Florence, and their three children have lived in Honesdale, Pennsylvania where he spends three days a week as staff artist for *Highlights for Children* magazine. About his materials, he writes, "I have used pen and ink, wash, charcoal, Wolff pencil, chalk, sponge, gesso with ink on top, scratched Bourges paper and zippitone cut with a razor; also photographs and flat halftone screens; and have prepared almost all of my books in either two or three color separation." Mr. Kettelkamp, whose interest in music is reflected in his books, plays the piano, classical guitar and recorder. He has several of his own poems set to music for his wife to sing to his guitar accompaniment. About his books he writes, "*Spirals* is one of three books (the other two being *Shadows* and *Puzzle Patterns*) that I have done which most clearly express a point of view very important to me. I would call this point of view, or principle, dynamic symmetry — the combination of opposites which were before unrelated."

KIDDELL-MONROE, JOAN*

Born August 9, 1908 in England. Childhood spent in Essex, Cheshire and London. Attended Willesden and Chelsea School of Art.

Joan Kiddell-Monroe is half-Scottish, half-Welsh. Her love of sketching animals as a child led to art school, and the necessity to earn a living kept her working in an advertising studio for many years. Eventually, she tells us, she "shook off the shackles and embarked on a precarious free-lancing career." In 1939 she married the well-known Canadian portrait painter, Webster Murray. She believes that the turning point in her career came when the baby giant panda arrived at the London Zoo and she was inspired to write and illustrate her first book, *In His Little Black Waistcoat*. This was the first of eight books that she has both written and illustrated. "In 1944 I gave up my war work to produce, for a change, a son, James Euan. When in 1951 my husband died, we toured Africa and now live in Mallorca, where I continue illustrating — but writing for children, no more." Miss Kiddell-Monroe has illustrated over two hundred books and although she works in whatever manner is requested of her, she prefers black and one color or flat halftones, as she uses in the "Myths and Legends" series. She has also used a fine pen line combined with a flat colored ink not confined to the pen outline. Other media that she has used include scratchboard, broad chalk, dry brush and ink wash. In commenting on her style over the past ten years, she writes, "My several styles have not changed, but I have added to them, and now that I have more time from illustrating, paint portraits, landscapes and what not in oils."

KIMBALL, YEFFE

Born March 30, 1914 in Mountain Park, Oklahoma. Attended Art Students League and studied in France and Italy with Leger, Corbino and others.

Yeffe Kimball, a painter of American Indian ancestry whose work is in the permanent collections of many museums, has had fifty-five one-man shows since her first in 1946. Born in Oklahoma, Miss Kimball is an authority on American Indian art and culture, and is a consultant on native arts for the Portland Art Museum and the Chrysler Museum. She is the illustrator and co-author of *The Art of American Indian Cooking* as well as the illustrator of several other books, including *The Story of the Totem Pole* in 1951 and *The World of Manaboza* in 1965. She makes her home in New York City.

KIRN, ANN MINETTE

Born April 4, 1910 in Montgomery City, Missouri where childhood was spent. Attended William Woods College; Chicago Academy of Fine Arts; St. Louis School of Fine Arts; Columbia University.

"I have always loved books, and even when quite young I made books about any and everything," writes Ann Kirn. After college and art school, she worked as a fashion illustrator. "Not liking city life, I decided to return home and collaborate on a story, *Pinky Marie*, with a friend. It was published, and we had a contract for our second book, when the war and the

paper shortage interrupted. There was a shortage of teachers, too, so I taught second grade. Then in 1958, wanting to illustrate again, and not having anyone to write for me, I decided to try writing. An old cover of *Vogue* inspired my first story, *Leopard on a String*. I saw it and thought — leopard on a leash, that is fun — leopard on a string, that is more fun! Children love color, so I always work with two or three, sometimes four colors. Generally, I use black in halftone and the other colors are flat. I do all of the separating as I find that by experimenting with the acetate you can get many exciting textures. *Leopard on a String* is a very active story so I painted with casein on a textured paper, Japanese mulberry paper, then scraped some of the paint off, giving a fractured dynamic texture. *Full of Wonder* has the soft textures created by rubbing over the objects with a crayon. I used ink-resist for the discolored-with-age look of the illustrations for *Nine in a Line*, since I was trying to give a feeling of old Arabic illuminated manuscripts. While researching for *Bamboo*, I found the Japanese calligraphy most beautiful, and my illustrations lost much by not having it. So I conceived the idea of using captions with each illustration and having the end papers give the translation." *Full of Wonder* was selected by the *New York Times* as one of the Ten Best Illustrated Children's Books in 1959. Miss Kirn, who is Associate Professor of Art at Florida State University, lives in Tallahassee, Florida with her mother.

KNIGHT, HILARY

Born November 1, 1926 in Hempstead, Long Island, New York. Childhood spent on Long Island and in New York City. Attended Art Students League, New York.

Hilary Knight writes, "I attribute any abilities I possess to the fact that both my parents are artists and writers. My father, Clayton Knight, is well-known for his aviation paintings and books. My mother, Katharine Sturges, has done fashion drawings, fabric designs as well as many children's books." His own career began when several of his humorous drawings were published in *House and Garden* and *Mademoiselle*. His famous illustrations for *Eloise* by Kay Thompson came out in 1955 followed by three sequels. One of his first books he designed and illustrated for children was *Hilary Knight's Mother Goose*, for which he selected the text. He also wrote *Where's Wallace?* and *The Christmas Nutshell Library*. He comments, "I like to work in different mediums and have done books in a variety of styles. Very often the type of book suggests a medium. Charles Dickens' *Captain Boldheart* and *The Magic Fishbone* was done in pen and ink with color washes somewhat in the manner of Thomas Rowlandson. *Beauty and the Beast* — one of the few non-humorous books I've done — was purely decorative illustration, done in flat color with a bold pencil outline. I've done pen and ink, as in *Eloise*, and several books in a hard wax pencil on both a cold press board and on dinobase. I avoid doing separations whenever possible, finding it a very limiting way of working." Mr. Knight who has his studio in midtown New York spent most of 1966 traveling in Europe. An article about him appears in the March 1963 issue of *American Artist*.

KOCSIS, J. C., pseud. (James Paul)

Born April 27, 1936 in Buffalo, New York. Childhood spent in Bethlehem, Pennsylvania. Attended Fleisher Art Memorial School and Philadelphia College of Art, Philadelphia.

As a child of twelve, James Kocsis received a small set of oil paints for Christmas and he remembers painting his first two pictures that New Year's Eve as his parents were preparing to leave for a party. "The result of this was training by two professional artists and dozens of commissions and a mural assignment. At the age of fourteen, I had my first one-man show and knew that the rest of my life would be devoted to painting and illustration." He received a four-year scholarship to the Philadelphia College of Art where he studied under Jacob Landau and where he himself has been teaching since 1965. After graduation from art school, Mr. Kocsis was inducted into the Army where his work included designing murals and typography. He was sent to Germany and while in Europe was able to do some traveling on his own. After his discharge, he wrote and illustrated a series of magazine articles for children and has continued to illustrate for both magazines and books. His interest in working for children has been influenced by his ten years of leadership experience, starting in 1949, with the American Camping Association and the YMCA, specializing in American Indian lore. Mr. Kocsis, who works primarily in black-and-white, "devised a new technique which is essentially scratchboard" for *Trouble on Heron's Neck*, and continues to develop other special techniques for his illustrations. He and his wife live in Philadelphia, Pennsylvania.

KOMODA, KIYO (Kiyoaki)

Born March 3, 1937 in Yokoguro, Saijo-shi, Japan. Attended Los Angeles City College and Chouinard Art Institute, Los Angeles.

Kiyo Komoda was the sixth child of a Japanese farmer and he attributes his early start at drawing to the fact that "there was a war going on and my parents could not afford any children's books. Also most of the time the rest of the family were very busy farming. My childhood solution was to make pictures and occupy myself in the world of imagination." He used chopsticks and tea to draw his first pictures which were similar to pen and ink drawings. He recalls, "it was sad to see pictures dried out" on the table. When his elder sister married and came to the United States, Mr. Komoda was encouraged to join them. While a student at Los Angeles City College he worked

as a houseboy, gardener, gas station attendant, truck driver and night club waiter. "I would have made a very good truck driver or a farmer — which I wouldn't have minded being if I couldn't make it as an illustrator. I tried very hard to succeed." Now, as well as illustrating and doing book jackets, Mr. Komoda is also art director for two technical magazines. He and his wife, Beverly, an illustrator, have a small son and since 1963 have made their home in Ridgefield, New Jersey.

KRAUS, ROBERT

Born June 21, 1925 in Milwaukee, Wisconsin where childhood was spent. Attended Layton Art School, Milwaukee; Art Students League, New York City.

Mr. Kraus' first cartoon appeared on the children's page of the *Milwaukee Journal* when he was eleven. He continued with this early bent and has done cartoons for all the major magazines, particularly *The New Yorker*, where his work has appeared regularly for fifteen years. He is also the creator of a series of animated cartoons for television and movies. "Up to now," writes Robert Kraus, "my cartoons have been big and bold and my books gentle and delicate. I like happy endings." He has written and illustrated fourteen children's books and illustrated three others. Mr. Kraus now works primarily in color when doing his books. He describes his style as "personal realism." "When I did *Miranda's Beautiful Dream*, I was influenced by Beardsley and used a dotted line which I have also used in *Penguin's Pal* and *The Bunny Nutshell Library*." He is also responsible for the design of his books and tries to relate the type to the illustrations in a quiet way. "I find writing and illustrating a great challenge as well as an experience in which I let things happen and let my unconscious take over — it is hard to write about the process." Mr. Kraus, his wife and two children live in Ridgefield, Connecticut.

KREDEL, FRITZ*

Born February 8, 1900 in Michelstadt, Odenwald, Germany. There and in Darmstadt his childhood was spent and schools through the Real Gymnasium were attended. Studied art at Kunstgewerbeschule, Offenbach-am-Main.

Fritz Kredel writes, "After the Real Gymnasium I went to war as *Fahnenjunker* to become an army officer. After the war I was first apprenticed in a pharmacy, and later worked with horses on a farm in Pomerania. Always fond of making drawings and water colors, I finally went to the art school in Offenbach-am-Main and became a student of Professor Rudolf Koch. In 1924 I went to Italy with Professor Victor Hammer from Vienna. Returning to Offenbach in 1925, I taught art under Koch. Left school in 1934 after Koch's death and went to Frankfort-am-Main to continue with other students the *Werkstatt Rudolf Koch*. In 1936 I went to Austria to join my friend Professor Hammer again. Came to the United States in 1938, have become an American citizen, and feel just fine over here." While still living in Germany Fritz Kredel was a recognized artist and had illustrated several books. Since coming to the United States he has illustrated a great many more, both for adults and children, including a *Decameron*, 1940, for the Limited Editions Club, Andersen's *Fairy Tales*, 1942, Dickens' *Christmas Carol*, 1943, and *Robinson Crusoe*, 1945. Mr. Kredel taught at Cooper Union Art School from 1940 to 1942. He married Anna Epstein in 1926, their children are Stephen and Judith Charlotte, and their home is in New York. Mr. Kredel has worked in various media, most recently using woodcuts for *The Golden Journey*. An article about his work appeared in *Motif No. 4* (England). Among the honors he has received are the Golden Medal for Book Illustration, Paris 1938; the Silver Jubilee Citation of the Limited Editions Club, 1954; The Goethe Plaquette, Germany 1960.

KRUSH, BETH*

Born March 31, 1918 in Washington, D. C., where her childhood was spent. Attended Philadelphia Museum School of Art.

"Washington, D. C., where I lived," writes Beth Krush, "was a wonderful place for a child — parades, band concerts, a fine zoo, national shrines to see again and again with every visiting relative, and my favorite, the Smithsonian, where my grandmother would place herself on a bench facing a mammoth painting of the Grand Canyon and let me roam for hours among the dinosaur bones and wax Indians. I always loved to draw, my parents kept me supplied with paper and pencils and my 'home town' supplied me with subject material. Joe and I met at the Philadelphia Museum School of Art. Art school was a joy after years of being sent to the office for drawing in study hall. I won the illustration prize for the girls and Joe won the illustration prize for the boys. We also won an assortment of other prizes for water color, graphics and drawing. We were married during World War II, and since the War we have worked at the business of making pictures together and separately. When we work together we usually pick the incidents and talk over the staging together, then Joe does the first composition and perspective sketch. Then I rework that, adding my ideas and looking up costumes, interiors, plants, animals and people. Most often Joe does the final rendering in his own decorative line. But we have our individual pride and each likes to do work that is all his or hers." Though the Krushes work primarily in black-and-white as in *The Borrowers*, they have also used full color and limited color. It is usually flat color done as overlays of acetate. At present, Mrs. Krush teaches two days a week in the Illustration Department of the Moore College of Art. Beth and Joe Krush live near Valley Forge with their red-haired son who draws, plays the piano and tuba, and builds model airplanes.

KRUSH, JOE*

Born May 18, 1918 in Camden, New Jersey where his childhood was spent. Attended the Philadelphia Museum School of Art.

"Joe and I both grew up in typical row house neighborhoods of the twenties," writes Mrs. Krush, "Joe in Camden, New Jersey, where the busy Delaware River and the local airport (which had a real Ford Tri-Motor!) were major attractions. Though Joe denies any childhood ambition to be an artist, he filled notebooks with drawings of boats and won prizes for his model planes and boats. During the War Joe was with the Office of Strategic Services and attended the original meeting of the United Nations as a graphic designer, and the war guilt trials in Nuremberg, Germany." She speaks of her husband "building" his drawings with a love for how things work. "He likes to tackle anything in the art line and has done a great variety of work in many media — posters, album covers, advertising and magazine illustrations, story books and text books. He teaches illustration one day a week at the Philadelphia Museum School." At present Joe Krush is absorbed in building radio controlled model airplanes, which are flown from a "high field" at Valley Forge. The Krushes are also learning to play tennis, adding another activity to their many interests. The Krush home in Wayne, Pennsylvania, is a Victorian summer house which they're still "re-doing."

KUSKIN, KARLA SEIDMAN

Born July 17, 1932 in New York City where childhood was spent. Attended Antioch College and Yale University School of Fine Arts (B.F.A. 1955).

Karla Kuskin writes, "I began to write verse at the age of four or five and I have always enjoyed painting and drawing so that putting the two together seemed to happen rather naturally." Concerning her first book she says, "At Yale I printed my first book for children. I set the type, made linoleum cuts for the illustrations, was pressman and also bound a few of the forty copies myself. The book was done to accompany a paper I wrote at that time on the history and design of children's books. The book was called *Roar and More*. It was for children who could not yet read, or those who were just beginning to recognize letters. I picked the type so that each word would look like the animal sound it represented. So that a child could tell if it were loud, soft, tiny by seeing (without reading) it." The book was published in a slightly different form with two colors being used instead of many colors. Since then, Mrs. Kuskin has written and illustrated fifteen books and illustrated others. For *Jane Anne June Spoon and Her Very Adventurous Search for the Moon* which is in four colors, she used a Japanese pen with a soft bamboo tip which produced a heavier black line than she usually gets with a croquill pen. The overlays were done on a heavy Strathmore paper since washes need a lot of texture. She describes her work as decorative and somewhat naive, trying to keep the design simple, yet giving attention to small details and decorative patterns and textures. Designing the book is very important to her and in some cases she has used type as an integral part of the illustration as in *All Sizes of Noises*. Three of her books have been chosen for the shows of the American Institute of Graphic Arts, and articles about her work have appeared in *Book Production Magazine*, November 1956 and in *Young Readers Review*, March 1965. She is married to Charles Kuskin, an oboist, and with their two small children they live in an old red brick house in Brooklyn Heights, New York. On the top floor with a view of surrounding tree tops is Mrs. Kuskin's studio.

LAITE, GORDON

Born July 11, 1925 in New York City. Childhood in New York, Yonkers, Mt. Vernon, and on a farm 9 miles north of Utica, N. Y., North Gage Corners. Attended Beloit College in Beloit, Wisconsin and the Art Institute of Chicago.

Gordon Laite's parents were Polish immigrants, his father dying before he was born. Because his young mother was destitute, he was taken and "raised by Blanche Fisher Laite as her own." Under the name of Blanche Fisher Wright she had illustrated *The Real Mother Goose* in 1916. His foster father, Charles Laite, was a featured actor on the Broadway stage in the 20's. "I have drawn, colored and painted since the age of six. The work of Howard Pyle, the illustrations for *Wind in the Willows*, even Pogany and Maxwell Parrish all affected my early impressions. A course in Art History made the progress of man's artistic endeavor vivid and so alive. From this dates my inability to pin myself to one style." Mr. Laite married in 1948, and in 1955 he and his wife "embraced the teachings of the Baha'i faith. Out of this has grown a supreme delight in doing illustrations depicting natural inter-racial association as well as showing people of other lands." The Laites and their three children live in Gallup, New Mexico where "we have discovered the beauty and integrity of the American Indian. Their painting and weaving have had their influence, too." He works with ink in line, line and wash, or line in several colors with color laid over. He also uses at times watercolor, gouache, and casein.

LAMB, LYNTON*

Born April 15, 1907 in India. Childhood was spent in London and Somersetshire. Attended Kingswood School, Bath, Somerset; Central School of Arts and Crafts, London.

Lynton Lamb has written, "At my boarding school in the country outside the ancient city of Bath, I learned Latin and Greek and left with the ambition of either writing or painting. (I have since done both.) After two years in a business office I went to the London Central School of Arts and Crafts,

where besides drawing, painting, engraving and lithography, I also studied printing and bookbinding. (I was later to design the binding of the Bible used at the Coronation of Queen Elizabeth II.) As a painter I am a member of The London Group and an occasional exhibitor at the Royal Academy. I have served on the Arts Council of Great Britain and am a visiting teacher at the Slade School of Fine Art. I am author of the textbooks *Preparation for Painting: The Methods and Materials of the Artist* and *Drawing for Illustration*." The first children's book which he both wrote and illustrated was *Cat's Tales*. Besides working as author and artist for many book publishers, Lynton Lamb is production advisor to Oxford University Press, has served on the British Council of Industrial Design and is past president of the Society of Industrial Artists. He has designed many British postage stamps. During World War II Mr. Lamb served for five years in the Royal Engineers. He is married, has two sons and two grandsons, and lives "in the country where I work on books, paint landscapes, play cricket, interest myself in village affairs, and visit London as seldom as possible, since all my creative work is done at home." His home is at Sandon, near Chelmsford, Essex, England.

LANDAU, JACOB*

Born December 17, 1917 in Philadelphia, Pennsylvania and there his childhood was spent. Attended the Philadelphia Museum School of Art for four years; the New School for Social Research, New York, for two years; and the Académie de la Grande Chaumière, Paris, for two years.

Jacob Landau began to draw quite early and became known as an "artist" while still in elementary school. By the time he had graduated from art school he had begun a successful career as an illustrator of books and magazines, had won a number of prizes and had exhibited frequently. A move to New York meant the beginning of a second career. There he worked first as an office boy and later in an advertising art studio, returning gradually to book illustration along with advertising and editorial illustrating. During World War II he spent two years in Italy in the Special Services, Engineer Command. There his graphic ability led him into photographic work, layout and poster design, and the editing and illustrating of the publication *At Ease*. Following the war he returned to illustration and advertising design doing work for such leading firms as Container Corporation, IBM, and Steuben Glass. He has taught at the Philadelphia Museum School and since 1957 at Pratt Institute where he is now Chairman of the Department of Graphic Art and Design. Mr. Landau, who is equally at home in water color, drawing or printmaking, has had a number of one-man shows in Paris, New York and other cities, as well as being represented in the collections of ten of the leading museums and libraries. The most recent of the awards he has received is a National Arts Endowment Grant for the year 1967. Jacob Landau is married, has two sons, and makes his home in

Roosevelt, New Jersey. For *Man and Magic*, he used wash and line (Sumi ink) drawings on rice paper. Over the past ten years he feels his work has become "less overtly narrative, more symbolic, expressive." Articles on Mr. Landau have appeared in *Gebraudisgraphik #11* in 1962, *American Artist* in October 1956, and in *Current Biography* in December 1965, and an article by him entitled "Yes-No, Art-Technology" appeared in the Wilson Library Bulletin, September 1966.

LANGNER, NOLA

Born September 24, 1930 in New York City, where she spent her childhood. Attended Music and Art High School, Bennington College, Art School affiliated with Yale School of Fine Arts (summer course).

"I was an only child and always enjoyed being indoors," writes Nola Langner. "Even as a child I wanted to illustrate children's books. I spoke German as my first language and had many German picture books. Those very graphic books of the 1930's with their pale colors and dependence on line and their many details of small animals and insects in every picture were my first and strongest influences in art." After college, she started out doing paste-ups for a magazine. "Having become intimate with rubber cement, I went on to a TV art studio. This was my only "training" in commercial art. I learned everything else about books by actually doing them and making mistakes from which I learned. I married a sociologist and to make up for my quiet childhood, I now have five children, two Siamese cats, one white rabbit, eight mice and — recent additions — three ravenous turtles. The children all draw and paint and also are *too good* as critics. They have a nasty way of picking out the very things I know I should do over." Mrs. Langner lives in New York City and "works in a little room behind our kitchen. My husband is an excellent photographer and I often use his photographs as research material for books." She works primarily in black-and-white or limited color and says about her style, "I use color sparingly. I've also found that pencil is my medium right now. I like its softness and I can go from roughs to finishes without losing the original freedom of the sketches. My work has gotten less flat and decorative and as I've become more interested in people and how they look, more realistic in a way and more tonal."

LARSEN, SUZANNE KESTELOO

Born October 30, 1930 in Richmond, Virginia where her childhood was spent. Attended Richmond Professional Institute of the College of William and Mary; Ringling School of Art, Sarasota, Florida.

Mrs. Larsen writes, "Though I never planned to be an illustrator, I have no doubt that my pleasant childhood is tied up with my enjoyment in doing children's books. I studied to be a fashion designer and illustrator. It was not until I married an artist, Robert Larsen, and had had two of our three children that I had the good fortune to collaborate with a neighbor and we sold our first children's book." Besides illustrating other children's books, she has taught art and nursery for two years at a private school and had a part-time job designing for Frank Colson, a well-known potter in Sarasota, Florida where she lives. "We live," she writes, "in an open air type house on a sandy road with much tropical growth all around us. My husband paints in the center of the house where all activity goes on around him. I have a small corner for my art work but the table is usually piled with the children's tennis shoes and comic books." She has worked primarily in black-and-white. "I enjoy doing drawings of a decorative nature and lean heavily on an ornate line."

LASELL, FEN H.

Born May 15, 1929 in Berlin, Germany. Childhood spent in Europe, Massachusetts and Vermont. Attended Bennington College and Boston University.

"I was fortunate in my childhood to be exposed to some very beautiful books, the illustrations of which I cherished with a kind of reverence. I always wanted to perpetuate the kind of pleasure I got from these pictures and to point out to others the beautiful aspects of the things I saw around me. I first turned my artistic ability to the theatre, designing sets and costumes. It wasn't until I was married, with three children that I realized I was socially ill-suited to the artificial life of the theatre. I then started a new kind of life, studying with George Demetrios who, in teaching me to draw, was able to impart a dignity to art which I had not hitherto comprehended. Working with what materials I had at hand, namely a pencil and paper, I wrote and illustrated my first book, *Michael Grows a Wish*. My materials and techniques are not exciting, often just a fine ball-point pen with wash. My first quick sketches are probably my best work — often only a few inches high — but I'd never be satisfied to have these printed, so end up working slowly and deliberately. I do my own separations, usually without any color sketch, once my color scheme is determined." Fen Lasell and her family live in Ipswich, Mass.

LASKER, JOE (Joseph Leon)

Born in 1919 in Brooklyn, N. Y. where he spent his childhood. Attended Cooper Union Art School, N. Y. and painted in Rome on a fellowship.

"Painting is my first love. But I like to vary it with making woodcuts and illustrating children's books. Also, being a 'fine artist' doesn't support me and my family, so I teach and do illustrations." Mr. Lasker has received several fellowships for painting: Edwin Austin Abbey Memorial Fellowship, Prix de

Rome, and a Guggenheim Fellowship, and he is represented in the Whitney Museum, the Philadelphia Museum and the Joseph Hirshhorn Collection. He has taught at City College in New York City, at the University of Illinois and is now teaching at the Famous Artists School near South Norwalk, Conn. where he and his wife and three children live. Mr. Lasker's style has changed from "semi-decorative to outright realistic" as in *When Grandpa Wore Knickers*, done with a combination of ink, water color and crayon. *Snowtime* received a Certificate of Award at the 14th Annual Exhibit of the Chicago Book Clinic. There is an article on his painting in *Parade Magazine*, September 1963.

LATHROP, DOROTHY PULIS*

Born April 16, 1891, in Albany, New York, where her childhood was spent. Studied at Teachers College, Columbia University; Pennsylvania Academy of the Fine Arts; Art Students League, New York.

"It was undoubtedly being in my mother's studio, watching her at work, encouraged by her to experiment with brushes and paints for myself, and receiving from her much training which gave me my first interest in art," Dorothy Lathrop has written. "Talk of art and artists was part of my daily life from earliest childhood. Perhaps my interest in books came to me from my paternal grandfather who had a bookstore in Bridgeport, Connecticut. In fact during the early years, I wrote more than I drew." At Teachers College, Miss Lathrop studied drawing with Arthur Dow. From there she received a diploma in Teaching and taught for two years, beginning to illustrate in 1918 while still teaching. At the Pennsylvania Academy she studied under Henry McCarter, and at the Art Students League with F. Luis Mora. In 1931, encouraged by Louise Seaman of the Macmillan Company, she wrote and illustrated her first book, *The Fairy Circus*. Since then she has written and illustrated many books for children — most of them about animals. She works in oil, watercolor, pen and ink and lithographic pencil and insists on live models, so the Lathrop household always includes many animal friends. In 1930 the Newbery Medal was awarded to Rachel Field's *Hitty* which Dorothy Lathrop illustrated. The first award of the Caldecott Medal was made to Miss Lathrop's *Animals of the Bible* in 1938. She received the Eyre Medal of the Pennsylvania Academy of Fine Arts in 1941, and a Library of Congress prize in 1946 and her work is represented in the permanent collections of the Library of Congress, and the Albany Institute of History and Arts. Dorothy Lathrop and her sister Gertrude Lathrop, a distinguished sculptor, lived for many years in Albany, New York and then moved to Falls Village, Connecticut.

LATTIMORE, ELEANOR FRANCES*

Born June 30, 1904 in Shanghai, China. Childhood was spent in China, with a year in Europe, and without formal educa-

tion. Attended California School of Arts and Crafts, Oakland; Art Students League, and Grand Central School of Art, New York.

"I was the fourth child of David and Margaret Lattimore," Eleanor Lattimore writes. "When I was a year old my family moved to North China and it was there — in Paotingfu, Peking and Tientsin — that I grew up. My father was a teacher in Chinese government universities, and in between his classes he taught all five of his own children. When we came to the United States we lived first in California, then in New Hampshire where my father was a professor at Dartmouth College for many years. After art school in New York I free-lanced as an artist. My first book, *Little Pear*, was written in 1930. Since then I have done little drawing except for making pictures for my own books. In my work I have drawn on the various backgrounds of my life." Her husband, Robert Armstrong Andrews, also a writer, died in 1963, and she now lives in Durham, N. C. near one of her two sons. Eleanor Lattimore works primarily in black-and-white, using brush and ink, as in *Little Pear*. She describes her work as "representational, to match my stories which are the 'true-to-life' kind."

LAZARE, GERALD JOHN

Born September 25, 1927 in Toronto, Ontario, Canada, where his childhood was spent. Attended Oakwood Collegiate, Toronto and took Famous Artists Course.

As an artist, Gerald Lazare is self-taught and writes that "the only training I received was at the age of twenty-one when I enrolled in the Famous Artists Course. I began professionally by illustrating comic strips during World War II when I was sixteen. The greatest impetus to my work came when I studied on my own for a year in Paris and London at the age of twenty-five." Since 1955 he has free-lanced, working in advertising, magazine illustration and books. "A good book to illustrate is the most satisfying. The feeling of permanence that a book has is very rewarding. I spend most of my time working in my studio on the third floor of our house in Toronto. I like jazz, especially Duke Ellington, whose music I often play while working; and looking at any painting by Edgar Degas is my particular kind of heaven." He has a nine-year-old son "who is just now becoming interested in art." Illustration in black-and-white, such as *Queenie Peavy*, was done in pen and ink. But he does most of his work in full color, often using gouache. He feels that in recent years his style has changed from "a rather tight realism to a looser more imaginative approach."

LE GRAND,* pseud. (Le Grand Henderson)

Born May 24, 1901 in Torrington, Connecticut where his childhood was spent. Graduated from Yale School of Fine Arts in 1925. Died January 25, 1964.

"There is little to report about my art work," Le Grand wrote, "until the night I found myself gazing at the shadowy bulk of a yak in the Central Park Zoo. 'Why is a yak?' I asked myself, and found no available information on the subject. I decided to write an illustrated book about it. A juvenile book seemed the proper medium, as children's minds, being uncluttered with the trivia of years, would approach the subject without strain. I enjoyed doing the book so I wrote and illustrated others. The Mississippi River also seemed a source of material, so I built a shanty boat in which I drifted down to the Gulf of Mexico. My experiences on this trip led to the Augustus books. When he heard I was leaving the river, an old riverman told me, 'You've squashed the mud of the Mississippi a'tween your toes, and you'll come back. You'll be a'settin' up there in New York some day and then all of a sudden you'll see just as clear the river a'shinin' and a'sparklin', and a shanty boat bobbin' up and down, and you'll smell the river an' the mud — an' you'll come back.' " In spite of the call of the Mississippi, Le Grand and his wife spent a year in the British West Indies and then sailed their twenty-four-foot sloop, "White Wings" in and around this Caribbean paradise tracing the routes of bygone pirates and then up to Maine. He wrote and illustrated thirty-three books for children, all characterized by a great deal of humor, and also was the author of an adult novel, Home Is Upriver. Though most of his books were done with lithograph crayon on coquille board using an acetate overlay, several were in watercolor or in pen, brush and ink. He loved color and all his life was a painter of landscapes working in oils and pastels, but because of printing costs, his illustrating was confined to one color and black-and-white. Le Grand died at Charleston, South Carolina, aboard the "White Wings" on his way to Florida and hurrying to meet a deadline on a new book.

LEIGHTON, CLARE VERONICA HOPE*

Born 1901 in England. Attended the Slade School of Fine Art, University of London; studied wood engraving at London County Council Central School of Art and Crafts.

Miss Leighton's parents were both writers and in 1947 she wrote a biography of her mother, who wrote thrillers for the London Mail, called Tempestuous Petticoat: Story of an Invincible Edwardian. She illustrated her first book when she was seventeen and when she was twenty-seven she was elected a member of the Society of Wood Engravers. In 1930 she won first prize at the International Engravers Exhibition at the Art Institute of Chicago, and nine years later came to the United States to live, becoming a citizen in 1945. After lecturing at Duke University for two years, she came to New England and built a contemporary house in Woodbury, Connecticut which is still her home. When she first came East, she did a set of twelve engravings about New England industries for use on Wedgwood plates. Along with her engraving which

has won her many honors, including an Honorary Doctorate of Fine Arts from Colby College, Miss Leighton has also designed for Steuben Glass, has done several commissions for stained glass windows, including thirty-seven windows for St. Paul's Cathedral in Worcester, Massachusetts, and is currently working on a hugh mosaic for the apse of a chapel in Monroe, Connecticut. In the field of book illustrations, her black-and-white wood engravings are in over twenty books by such authors as Thomas Hardy, Emily Brontë, Thornton Wilder and H. M. Tomlinson. More recently she has illustrated three anthologies of poetry for young people compiled by Helen Plotz, the first of which was Imagination's Other Place. She has written and illustrated twelve books, two of which were for children: The Musical Box and The Wood that Came Back.

LEISK, DAVID JOHNSON, see Johnson, Crockett

LEMKE, HORST

Born June 30, 1922 in Berlin, Germany. Childhood spent in Berlin. Attended Staatliche Hocheschule für Bildende Künste in Berlin.

"From the age of twelve, I wished to become a painter and was designing and painting all the time. My older brother procured for me reproductions of the French Impressionists which I copied. And to call forth new ideas, he provided me with books by writers such as Hoffmann, Poe, Dickens and Twain for the purpose of illustrating them. In September 1939, as war was declared and just half a year before my leaving examination, I was compelled to leave school because of a cartoon of mine representing the then Propaganda Minister Goebbels. Moreover, no further school was allowed to accept me. But, I had luck again and the High School of Plastic Arts admitted me. My teacher was Gerhard Ulrich to whom I owe very much. From 1941 to the end of the war I was a soldier. After the war I went to Heidelberg." Mr. Lemke says in describing his present home, "In 1955, I bought a 400 year old farm house which looks over Lake Maggiore in the south of Switzerland and reconstructed it. I live in that little paradise where I can work undisturbed and in a wonderful quietness." He characterizes his illustrations as "entertaining, with good and sly humor," and his preference is for "cheerful, dreamy and scurrilous books like Mark Twain, Dickens or the fairy tales of Grimm. For the black-and-white illustrations I am working with pen, brush and colored pencil. But for picture books I use tempera, water color, collage, pen, colored pencil and crayon. In the course of years, my stroke has become lighter and looser. I write my illustrations just as I would write a letter."

LENSKI, LOIS*

Born October 14, 1893 in Springfield, Ohio. There and in Anna, Ohio, her childhood was spent. Attended Ohio State

University (B.S. 1915); Art Students League, New York; Westminster School of Art, London.

"My paternal grandfather was Polish, and my grandmother Russian," Lois Lenski writes. "It is possible I may have inherited artistic gifts from them. All my conscious influences, however, have grown out of my American environment. My father was a Lutheran minister. When I was six we moved to Anna, Ohio, where I learned to know and love small-town and country life. During my four years at art school in New York, I worked part time at all kinds of odd jobs to pay my expenses. In 1920 I went to Europe on slender savings, and spent some months in Italy. It was while studying with Walter Bayes at the Westminster School in London that I did my first illustrating of children's books — *The Golden Age* and *Dream Days* by Kenneth Grahame, and Vera Birch's *Green-Faced Frog*. In 1927 I began writing and illustrating my own books. *Skipping Village* and *A Little Girl of 1900* grew directly out of my own childhood in Ohio. *The Little Auto* and other early picture books were largely inspired by the interest and needs of my small son. In 1929 we moved to Connecticut and I began to absorb some of the richness of historical background. *Phebe Fairchild Her Book*, 1936, was the first of a group of books for older children growing out of life in a New England environment. With *Bayou Suzette* in 1943, I began my series of American regional books, gathering material for pictures and stories at first hand in the regions. The second of these, *Strawberry Girl*, a story of the Florida Crackers was awarded the Newbery Medal. In 1952, I began a series of *Roundabout America* books for younger children. Together with the Regionals, they tell how children live, work and play in various sections of our country. They aim to create and foster in American children a friendlier understanding of the many communities and people which make up the total picture of America today." *Strawberry Girl* was given the Newbery Medal in 1946; *Bayou Suzette* the Ohioana Medal in 1944; and *Judy's Journey* the Child Study Association Award in 1947. Miss Lenski, who now makes her home in Florida, works primarily in black-and-white and two colors. Her regional books are largely illustrated with pencil drawings, while the historical and Roundabout America books are done with ink drawings, and the picture books are illustrated with ink and one flat color. Her work is characterized by its great simplicity because of her feeling that "simple ink drawings can mean more to a child than a confusion of color." Miss Lenski designs her books and does the lettering for the jackets and title pages.

LENT, BLAIR

Born January 22, 1930 in Boston, Massachusetts where his childhood was spent. Graduated with honors from Boston Museum School in 1953. Studied in Europe in 1954.

"My childhood is still very real to me; it was a solitary one and books were my greatest pleasure," writes Blair Lent. "My imagi-

nation was full of the tales I read and I would write my own little stories and draw pictures to illustrate them. My first picture book was about a chocolate rabbit; it wasn't published. It was an Easter gift for my mother and father about thirty years ago. When I wasn't reading, I was dreaming." His dreams about traveling were fulfilled by the Amos Cummings Memorial Traveling Scholarship that took him to Europe in 1954. On his return he again and again submitted his stories to publishers without any luck. "So I designed tin can labels and advertisements for bank loans until Emilie McLeod of Atlantic Monthly Press encouraged me, and with her help *Pistachio* became my first published book." At the same time he was asked to illustrate *The Wave* by Margaret Hodges, which subsequently was a runner-up for the 1965 Caldecott Medal, was included in the American Institute of Graphic Arts Children's Book Show and annual Fifty Books Show, and received a Silver Medal for book illustration at the Sao Paulo Bienal in Brazil. All of Mr. Lent's books have been illustrated with cardboard cuts and color overlays, a technique which he describes in the August 1965 issue of the *Horn Book*. He is very often responsible for the design as well as the illustration of his books. Blair Lent, who lives in Cambridge, Massachusetts, says about his work, "I have very strong feelings about children's literature. Books were important to me as a child and it is for that little boy that I am working. I can never know other children's innermost thoughts as well as I can remember my own."

LEVINE, DAVID

Born 1926 in Brooklyn, New York. Attended Tyler School of Fine Arts, Philadelphia; Hans Hofmann School, New York City.

David Levine's black-and-white drawings, many of them highly satirical, are featured in every issue of *The New York Review of Books*. They also appear in *Horizon*, *Esquire* and *McCall's*. His work has won him several prizes including the Tiffany Foundation Award and Maynard Prize and the National Academy of Design's Thomas B. Clarke Prize. He has had six one-man shows in New York and has been exhibited at many museums across the country. In 1964, he illustrated *The Fables of Aesop*, which was commended in the annual show of the Society of Illustrators. Another children's book with his illustrations, *The Heart of Stone*, was also included in that show as well as in the Children's Book Exhibit, 1963-64, of the American Institute of Graphic Arts.

LEWIS, RICHARD WILLIAM

Born July 11, 1933 in Avondale, Pennsylvania where his childhood was spent. Attended Philadelphia Museum School of Art. Died August 16, 1966.

Richard Lewis was the oldest of five children. His home was near the small village of Avondale, Pa., with woods, orchards and open fields surrounding it. His early interest in natural history and the urge to draw everything extended into his profession of illustrating. After his graduation from the Philadelphia Museum School of Art in 1955, he served in the Army from 1956 to 1958. In 1964, after living five years in New York City, the Lewis family consisting of his wife Mary and their two small sons moved to 70 acres in the northwestern corner of Sullivan County, N. Y. "to a house in dire need of entire repair and dilapidated barn but with the most beautiful hemlock woods, laurel fields and trout stream in the world." Mr. Lewis worked primarily in black-and-white, using an ink wash as in A Summer Adventure.

LIONNI, LEO

Born May 5, 1910 in Amsterdam, Netherlands. Childhood spent in Holland, Belgium and United States. Ph.D. in Economics from the University of Genoa, Italy.

"In Amsterdam, where I spent the first 12 years, I lived within two city blocks of two of the best museums in Europe. I spent most of my time there — and quite naturally assumed that one day I would be a painter. I started to draw and paint then and have done it ever since. It was by chance that I made my first children's book 'Little Blue and Little Yellow.' I improvised a story for my grandchildren while riding on a train and decided to make it into a book." Mr. Lionni came to the United States in 1939, and was for some years art director of N. W. Ayer & Son, the large Philadelphia advertising agency. In 1950, he became art director of *Fortune* and also served as a design director for the Olivetti Corporation of America. From 1949 to 1957, he was Chairman of the Graphic Design Department of the Parsons School of Design and also President of the American Institute of Graphic Arts. For several years, he was Managing Editor of *Panorama* (a Time-Life publication in Italy) and is now a graphic arts consultant to various publications. He lives in a house of his own design overlooking the Bay of Genoa, making two or more trips to the United States each year. Of the six picture books written, designed and illustrated by him, Mr. Lionni writes, "I like to invent a technique for each story. I have used drawing, gouache painting, collage, crayon. And since technique and style are naturally related my style too varies from book to book. What remains constant and personal is a way of telling a story." *Inch by Inch*, which was a Caldecott Medal runner-up in 1960 and received the Children's Book Prize in Germany in 1963, is done in rice paper collage. Pencil point drawings illustrate *On My Beach Are Many Pebbles*. In *Swimmy*, which was chosen as the Best Picture Book in Germany in 1965 and was selected as one of the "Ten Best Illustrated Books" in 1963 by the *New York Times*, Mr. Lionni used water colors, rubber stamping and pencil.

LIPINSKY DE ORLOV, LINO SIGISMONDO

Born January 14, 1908 in Rome, Italy. Childhood spent in Rome and Munich. Attended the British Academy of Arts and Royal Academy of Arts in Rome.

A distinguished painter, etcher, scenic designer and muralist, Mr. Lipinsky de Orlov came to the United States in 1940 and was naturalized in 1945. He is represented in the permanent collections of the Metropolitan Museum of Art, the Library of Congress, the New York Public Library and many others; he has received such honors as the Diplome d'Honneur, silver medal, of the Exposition de Budapest, 1963, and the Joseph Pennell Prize of the Library of Congress. He, his wife and two children, have a home in New York where he is the Head of Exhibits Design for the Museum of the City of New York and Art Consultant to the Italian Embassy. They also have a home in Rome, Italy.

LIPPMAN, PETER J.

Born May 19, 1936 in Flushing, New York. Childhood was spent in New York City. Graduated from Columbia College in 1957 (B.A.) and Columbia School of Architecture in 1960 (B. Arch.). Attended Art Students League, New York.

"As a child, I drew and painted intermittently," writes Mr. Lippman. "In college, I took courses in the School of Painting and Sculpture at Columbia University and also spent a considerable part of my time working on the college literary magazine, *The Columbia Review*, as its art editor. After a tour of duty in the Army, I worked very briefly for an architect and decided that I preferred graphics. I turned to children's books as I considered it one of the most promising areas in which to do artistically worthwhile commercial work." In 1965, Mr. Lippman spent the year abroad "mostly in Spain and Portugal where I divided my time between children's books, magazine satire, and sculpting in bronze. My hobby is collecting 19th century illustrated books and children's books." Mr. Lippman's work to date has been in black-and-white or limited color. His illustrations for *Oscar Lobster's Fair Exchange* were done in pen and ink. For *Plunkety Plunk*, he used linoleum blocks in three colors. *Plunkety Plunk* was picked as "One of the Ten Best Illustrated Children's Books" by the *N. Y. Times* in 1963.

LOBEL, ANITA

Born June 3, 1934 in Cracow, Poland. Childhood spent in Poland and Sweden. Attended Pratt Institute, New York.

"I feel very strongly that an artist working in the field of children's book illustration should by no means compromise on the graphic design quality of his work. Our senses are bombarded by so much ugliness from our earliest days that it is to be hoped that picture books do open a child's eyes and start at least a germ for a future esthetic sense. I have always loved to draw flowers and I love needlework and tapestries as well as embroidery. During my years as an art student, I spent most of my time drawing and painting monumental figures. When I had to make a living I became a textile designer. Picture books have opened to me an opportunity to bring back some of my old fat friends and put them in landscapes filled with floral designs!" Mrs. Lobel, whose decorative work is usually in black-and-white or two colors, explains, "I usually plan a book as a play. The pictures become 'scenes' with 'principals' and 'chorus' grouped and regrouped according to what is then happening in the story." She and her husband, Arnold, make their home in Brooklyn, N. Y.

LOBEL, ARNOLD STARK

Born May 22, 1933 in Los Angeles, California. Childhood spent in Schenectady, New York. Graduated from Pratt Institute, New York (B.F.A.).

"I don't know why I became an artist — it never really occurred to me ever to be anything else. Fate was kind though, to place me in children's books — possibly the only branch of commercial art where one can still have taste and individuality and be valued for it. I try to write and illustrate one book and just illustrate two or three others in the course of one year." Mr. Lobel describes his work as "decorative, representational, humorous. A good illustrator, I think, should have a repertory of styles at his command — like an actor switching from role to role. I have only been illustrating since 1960 so I feel, at the moment, that I am just finishing kindergarten with respect to the development of my work. It gives me joy to say that I really loathe most of my work after it has aged about two years." His work is primarily in black-and-white or three colors, using pen and ink or pencil. He does separations with wash and pencil on thin opaque white paper on top of a light table for transparency, and usually is responsible for the design as well as the illustration of his books. Mr. Lobel and his wife, Anita, make their home in Brooklyn, N. Y. *A Holiday for Mister Muster* was selected "One of the Ten Best Illustrated Children's Books" by the *New York Times* in 1963.

LONETTE, REISIE DOMINEE

Born February 13, 1924 in New York. Childhood spent in New York and on Long Island. Graduated from Pratt Institute, Brooklyn, and studied at Art Students League, The New School for Social Research, and School of Interior Design, New York.

"I have always wanted to draw or paint or try to create something. There has never been anything else for me. It is my way to exist. I am happy to be able to work with books." For eight years, Reisie Lonette was a staff artist for Doubleday. In 1952, she married Vincent Nocera who was also an artist — "we had fun together." Mr. Nocera died in 1964 at the age of 37. "I have two children, Marc and Marisa. When she was not yet five, my daughter wrote a little book of poems, *One Day Means a Lot*. I did the drawings and designed the book and it was published by Bobbs Merrill." Except for book jackets, Miss Lonette works in black-and-white and two colors, using pencil and wash, and characterizes her work as "representational with some whimsy." In designing a jacket "I usually do hand-lettering. It seems to integrate more with the illustration."

LORRAINE, WALTER HENRY*

Born February 3, 1929 in Worcester, Massachusetts where his childhood was spent. Attended Classical High School, Worcester; and Rhode Island School of Design, Providence.

Walter Lorraine has written this account of his life, "Throughout my childhood I could always be found doing drawings of one kind or another (the settings for these creative efforts were usually my mathematics and English classrooms). I took no formal art training until I attended Rhode Island School of Design after two years in the Navy. From the last years in elementary school through high school I had a very clear goal for a life's work. I planned to become either a mechanical or aeronautical engineer. In this respect my years in the Navy were the most decisive in my life. My duties introduced me closely to what I proclaimed my chosen profession. I found the work much too cold and impersonal for my taste. On leaving the Navy, I fell back on what I had always considered an avocation, and applied and was accepted at Rhode Island School of Design. The school was a revelation pointing up within a few short months that art or its application was the only way of life for me. Anything happening after this seems anticlimactical. I graduated from school and obtained a position as book designer and production manager of juvenile books at Houghton Mifflin Co. My work as a book illustrator stems partially from a natural love of books and art and partially from a learned love of books and good design through this association. The work I do with books has led me to instruct a general book design course at the Museum of Fine Arts School day school, and a typography course under the graphic arts executive training program at Boston University evening school. I am married and have four children, a boy and three girls. My wife, Anita, is a former student of the art school I attended and currently teaches dance to children in Newton, Massachusetts where we live." Mr. Lorraine's work is generally characterized by a humorous stylization but he writes, "I do not like to think of myself as employing any particular style or approach to my illustrations, though I realize inevitably a personal flavor comes through. I prefer to let the text word dictate the approach. My concern is with expression and content first and foremost rather than technique of execution, although I am most comfortable using some form of pen line." *I Will Tell You of a Town* in 1956 and *Dear Rat* in 1961 were included among the "Ten Best Illustrated Children's Books" of the *New York Times*. An article by Mr. Lorraine appears in the December 1963 *Horn Book*.

LOW, JOSEPH*

Born August 11, 1911 in Coraopolis, Pennsylvania. Early childhood was spent there, and later in Oak Park, Illinois. Attended University of Illinois, 1930-32, and in 1935 studied for six months at Art Students League, New York.

Studying art at the University of Illinois Joseph Low discovered that the medieval woodcut had special meaning for him, and, in the words of Henry C. Pitz, he "followed the trail through book stores, libraries, print rooms, through Chinese calligraphy, 18th century chap-books, early Renaissance engraving, German wood-blocks, and the folk arts of all countries." He acquired a press and type and studied typography and wood engraving alone. At the Art Students League he studied drawing with George Grosz and later with Vaclav Vytlacil, continued to spend much time in museums and libraries, and by 1941 was doing some free-lance work in New York. Beginning in 1942 he taught design and graphic art at Indiana University for three years, and while there set up printing equipment under the auspices of the University and designed and executed a number of pieces under the imprint of the Corydon Press. In 1946, he moved to Morristown, New Jersey and later to New-town, Connecticut. He has divided his time between art and design work for such magazines as *Look, Holiday, Fortune;* the operation of his Eden Hill Press for publication of his own material; and the illustration of books and book jackets. He writes of his book illustrations that they have generally been in three color "but this seems to be changing; the last two have been full color." His style has also changed somewhat in the last ten years. It is "looser and freer, partly because of personal development, partly because editorial attitudes have allowed it, partly because reproduction techniques have improved." For his two and three color work he most commonly uses a reed pen with brush tones and does separations "always on paper overlays. I hate acetate." Mr. Low's work in the graphic arts has been exhibited in a number of cities in the United States as well as in Europe and South America. He has received awards from such groups as the American Institute of Graphic Arts, Society of Illustrators and the Art Directors Club. Mr. Low, who is married and has two daughters, now lives in South Norwalk, Connecticut. An article on Mr. Low appeared in *American Artist*, October 1951.

LUBELL, WINIFRED MILIUS*

Born June 14, 1914 in New York City and her childhood was spent there, with summers in Maine. Attended Ethical Culture School, New York; Art Students League, New York; Duncan Phillips Museum School, Washington, D. C.

"My approach to art is simple," writes Mrs. Lubell. "I want to communicate. I feel the only way an artist can grow and enrich her work is by direct contact with people and nature. Because of this deep rooted conviction, I have chosen to concentrate on illustration and the graphic media — lithography, etching, and the woodcut. The woodcut is my favorite medium, because I enjoy the whole process, from cutting the block through the printing." Her woodcuts have been in exhibits in Philadelphia, Boston, Dallas and New York City, where she has also had a one-man show of prints and drawings. A former teacher of art, Mrs. Lubell has for the last few years been working with children as a volunteer in play therapy at Grasslands Hospital in Valhalla, N. Y. and finds her work "the most rewarding thing I've ever done. I am one of those incredibly lucky people. I have done what I like to do in life. And my work has naturally sprouted out of what I like doing — raising children, living in the country, and drawing. And what's even more idyllic, I have a husband who aids and abets me in all this, and children who too have helped." Mrs. Lubell and her husband Cecil, editor of *American Fabrics Magazine*, have lived in Croton-on-Hudson, New York, in the same house for over twenty years. Their two sons are now grown. The Lubells have created a number of children's books together. "I have done much of the research and preliminary writing on books with my husband. But he then writes them." Her illustrations are in both black-and-white and four-color, for which she always does separations, usually on a mylar acetate. In every case she designs the book as well as illustrates it.

LUZZATI, EMANUELE

Born June 3, 1921 in Genoa, Italy. Childhood in Italy and Switzerland. Attended Ecole des Beaux Arts in Lausanne, Switzerland.

During World War II, Emanuele Luzzati was living and studying in Switzerland. After returning to Italy in 1945 he did stage settings, illustration and pottery. His first book, *Chichibio and the Crane*, was illustrated in color pencil and gouache. The other three, drawn from the animated films that Mr. Luzzati had first made of the same stories, were done in oil pastel and watercolor. As a film one of these, *The Thieving Magpie*, has received thirteen international awards and was nominated for the Oscar award in the United States. Leo Lionni writes of him in *Graphis* (No. 108, 1963): "Lele deals with his work the way he deals with people. He tackles it easily, generously and without pretensions. . . . He works with the quick deftness of a Japanese calligrapher. His signs are disconnected and seemingly unreal, like the letters of an exotic alphabet. But in the end everything falls into place and spells out a charming, gentle and joyful art."

MAC KENZIE, GARRY*

Born September 7, 1921 in Portage La Prairie, Manitoba, Canada. Childhood was spent in England and California. Attended Chouinard Art Institute, Los Angeles.

"I was born in Manitoba," writes Garry MacKenzie, "but spent the first years of my life in the south of England. When I was five my parents returned to America — this time to Hollywood, California, which remained my home until I came to New York City in 1945 to pursue a career as an illustrator of children's books. This had been my plan from childhood. I received my formal training in art from the Chouinard Art Institute in Los Angeles, to which I was granted an art scholarship in 1941. From 1949 to 1952 I lived in Cambridge, England, where I continued my work, and devoted as much time as I could to the study of the English landscape painters. My chief admirations in art, and those which I feel have principally influenced my work in the past, and will probably continue to do so increasingly in the future, are Samuel Palmer, the French illustrator Grandeville, and Chinese and Japanese painting of the classical period." Garry MacKenzie lives in St. George, Staten Island, New York. His work has been primarily in black-and-white. He has used pen and ink with pencil in such books as *Here Come the Cottontails.* Concerning some change in his style he writes, "I have been painting in oils for the last four years and certain abstract elements have entered into my illustrations."

MC CLOSKEY, ROBERT*

Born September 15, 1914 in Hamilton, Ohio where his childhood was spent. Attended Vesper George School, Boston, and National Academy of Design, New York.

As a child, Robert McCloskey drew, painted, enjoyed making things, and later won a scholarship to the Vesper George School where he studied for three years. In 1934 he went to New York, studying for two years at the National Academy, and spending his summers working in Provincetown under Jerry Farnsworth. His first commission was the bas-relief on the City Building of his home town. After an interlude of odd jobs, he returned to New York with the idea of his first book, *Lentil,* 1940, and at the same time got a job assisting Francis Scott Bradford on a mural in Boston. It was while he was at art school in Boston that he had first noticed the family of mallards in the Public Gardens. Returning to Boston to work four years later he witnessed the traffic problem created by the passage of the mallard family, and from there developed *Make Way for Ducklings* which was awarded the Caldecott Medal in 1942. In 1941 also appeared Anne Malcolmson's *Yankee Doodle's Cousins* for which he made the illustrations, and in 1943 his own *Homer Price.* Painting and illustrating in New York were interrupted by induction into the Army in 1943 and assignment to Fort McClellan, Alabama. In 1948-49 he

went to Rome as a Fellow of the American Academy there. He writes that he did very little painting but learned mosaic technique — both in glass and marble. He has made several trips to Mexico to paint, but Maine has been the main source of inspiration for his books. Mr. McCloskey is married to Margaret Durand, the daughter of the author Ruth Sawyer, and they have two daughters. Some years ago they bought an island in Penobscot Bay, Maine, near Deer Isle, and there they spend their summers. At other times their home is in New York. In 1958, he was awarded a second Caldecott Medal, for *Time of Wonder.* This book and several others have been made into iconographic films by Weston Woods Studios, and there is a film, "Robert McCloskey," in which the artist talks about the way in which he works. In 1964, Miami University awarded him an honorary degree of Doctor of Literature.

MC CLUNG, ROBERT MARSHALL

Born September 10, 1916 in Butler, Pennsylvania where his childhood was spent. Attended Princeton University (A.B.); Cornell University (M.S.); New York University (writing courses).

"I enjoyed a very active boyhood and was constantly exploring the woods and fields about my home, collecting frogs, snakes, turtles, insects and cocoons. Several months each summer were usually spent on my grandfather's farm where I became an enthusiastic collector of moths and butterflies." Robert McClung says that all these years he was making pictures but never took any formal art training. At Princeton, he majored in biology but then went into writing for advertising before serving five years of active duty in the Navy during World War II. In 1948, he received his master's degree in Zoology from Cornell and also began writing and illustrating books for children, the first of which was *Sphinx, The Story of a Caterpillar.* He continued to do one book a year for seven years and at the same time was on the staff of the New York Zoological Park, eventually becoming Curator of Mammals and Birds. In 1956, he decided to devote full time to writing and illustrating, adding since then fifteen more books to his list. The most recent of these is *Moths and Butterflies and How They Live* which was illustrated with a mixture of wash, pencil and ink. For his life-cycle stories, such as *Ladybug,* he uses acetate overlays for the additional colors. Mr. McClung's wife, Gale, is editor of the *Mount Holyoke Alumnae Quarterly* and "we both have studies on the second floor of our big old house in Amherst, Massachusetts. Our family includes two boys, Bill and Tom, a fifteen-year-old dog, Jerry, a kitten, Fred, and sundry smaller pets."

MC CREA, JAMES

Born September 12, 1920 in Peoria, Illinois. Childhood spent in Florida and Indiana. Attended University of the South,

Sewanee, Tennessee; Ringling School of Art, Sarasota, Florida; Pratt Institute; special classes at Brooklyn Museum and New York University.

In 1945, following three years of service in the merchant marine, James McCrea worked for a year in a ceramics studio and then became an apprentice in the private studio of the wood engraver Bernard Brussel-Smith for a year. For ten years he taught typography at Cooper Union and has also done book design and typography for Random House and Basic Books. He and his wife, Ruth, met in art school and, except for the war years, have been working together ever since. The McCreas who live and work in an old house in Bayport, Long Island, New York, write that, "In our cellar is a small sixty-year-old hand press. We have used it for printing block prints, broadsides, and a series of small Christmas booklets which have been issued annually since 1949 under our imprint which is The Little Press. The press has played a part in the production of our children's books. We design them and set the type by hand. The press is used to pull reproduction proofs, and these proofs of the type are then pasted up with the art work. In this way we are able to handle the type areas as an integral part of the page." An article on The Little Press appeared in the December 1962 issue of *American Artist.*

MC CREA, RUTH

Born May 28, 1921 in Jersey City, New Jersey. Graduated from the Ringling School of Art, Sarasota, Florida; attended classes in book design and drawing at Brooklyn Museum and New York University and in writing at Columbia University, New York City.

Like her husband, James, Ruth McCrea grew up with an interest in books and did some writing and drawing as a child. The McCreas were married in 1943 and have three children, James, Ruth and Claire. Besides the work that they have done together, Ruth McCrea has illustrated more than thirty books for Peter Pauper Press, including Dickens' *A Christmas Carol, The Story of the Other Wise Man,* and *Japanese Fairy Tales.* In 1949, she wrote and illustrated a children's book, *A Present for Molly.* The McCreas are best known for the picture books that they have written and illustrated together. There are four to date, the first of which was *The King's Procession* in 1963. This was chosen for the Fifty Books Show of the American Institute of Graphic Arts that year. About these books they write, "We try to visualize the book as a whole, and our aim is to make not a story, not a picture, not a page, but a book. The techniques which we use tend to be more 'printerly' than 'painterly'! The black drawing may be done with pen, or brush, or linoleum cuts, but usually for line reproduction rather than halftone. There are most often two or three additional colors, and they are done in black ink on Herculene overlays. Often, for these, we cut stencils and use a brayer and printing ink — sometimes overprinting to create additional colors."

MC CULLY, EMILY ARNOLD

Born July 1, 1939 in Galesburg, Illinois. Childhood spent in Illinois, New York City, Garden City, Long Island. Attended Brown University (B.A. Pembroke College), Rhode Island; Columbia University (M.A. in Art History).

"I have always liked to draw but did not decide to become an artist until after I had graduated from college. I worked at menial commercial jobs before making a portfolio designed to appeal to magazine advertising and trade book art directors. Over a period of two years jobs began to come in. I was assigned my first children's book, published in 1966, because an editor at Harpers saw a poster of mine and boldly suggested that I might be able to enter this field. I enjoy the relative freedom and scope of the work. I have worked with pen and ink line drawings in my first two books and am now working on a three-color separated picture book. My style tends to change to meet my conception of whatever story I'm doing. I think I would be bored working the same way all of the time." Mrs. McCully and her husband live in Swarthmore, Pennsylvania. Her husband teaches at Swarthmore College.

MC GAW, JESSIE BREWER

Born October 17, 1913 in Clarksville, Tennessee and her childhood was spent in that state. Attended Duke University; Peabody University; Columbia University; University of Houston; American Academy in Rome; Memphis Art Academy; Ohio Wesleyan University.

Mrs. McGaw's father was a classical scholar and she herself is a professor of Latin and English at the University of Houston. She has two children and when her son was young she found that while he liked Indians, he didn't like to read. "I decided to do a book he would like," she writes. Knowing of the Plains Indians who used pictures for words through her studies in the origins of language, she did extensive research so she could "write" a book with this word-sign language. This resulted in *How Medicine Man Cured Paleface Woman* in 1956. She has published two others since then. At the back of the second, *Painted Pony Runs Away,* she included a chart showing the similar pictures drawn by Egyptians, Chinese and the Plains Indians. She has illustrated her books in black and red, using a primitive style with little perspective. Most recently she has been working on a fourth book in which "I am trying to reproduce pictures of the gestures made by Chief Red Horse as he related his part in the Battle of Little Big Horn. A written description of these gestures is on file at the Smithsonian."

MC MULLAN, JAMES

Born June 14, 1934 in Tsingtao, North China. Childhood spent in China, India and Canada. Attended Pratt Institute, New York.

Mr. McMullan's grandparents were Anglican missionaries and his father was a business man who, in 1941, joined the British Army in Shanghai. For the next five years the family moved about from Canada to India to China and back to Canada again. He came to the United States in 1951, studied art in Seattle and then after a stint in the Army attended Pratt Institute for three years. In 1959, he became an American citizen and made his home in New York City. His paintings and drawings have been commissioned for book jackets, advertising, book and magazine illustrations, and have received recognition from the Society of Illustrators, the American Institute of Graphic Arts and in the March-April 1965 issue of *Print* magazine. He is now associated with Push Pin Studios, having joined them in 1964. One of the first children's books he has illustrated is *Kangaroo, Kangaroo*, for which he used collage.

MAITLAND, ANTONY JASPER

Born June 17, 1935 in Andover, England. Childhood spent mostly in England with some time in the Far East and Germany. Attended West of England College of Art, Bristol.

"As one of six brothers," Antony Maitland recalls, "I found that privacy was only possible by withdrawing into a world of imagination; it may be that I draw for children who feel the same way. I certainly draw on the memory of my own childhood when selecting what part of a story to illustrate and I frequently use a child's eye level when composing a drawing." As an art student, he says he was without any real ambition until a Leverhulme Research Award made a year of travel and study in Europe possible, "and I began to see and draw with real enthusiasm. For several years I made a living from illustrating and designing jackets only. *Mrs. Cockle's Cat* was almost my first illustrating work." It won for him the 1961 Kate Greenaway Award. Besides illustrating he now paints, designs, creates murals, and does graphic work for exhibitions and feels that "none of these things is more or less important than the other. This variety ensures that each job is approached as a fresh and individual problem. The changes of scale are exciting too — from designing a name plate for books to remodeling the facade of a building (Madame Tussaud's Wax Works). This is for me the only way to stay alive artistically." Antony Maitland works either in black-and-white or full color. Both are used in *James and the Roman Silver* which he also wrote, taking the setting, various details and even the plot from childhood memories of Somerset. His illustrations are generally a combination of line and wash and he takes a special interest in the lettering for a jacket or title page since it can convey a feeling of period and mood. Mr. Maitland makes his home in London.

MARIANA, pseud. (Marian Foster)*

Born in Atlanta, Georgia, and childhood was spent in Georgia. Attended Sophie Newcomb Art School, New Orleans, Louisiana; Art Students League, New York; Académie de la Grande Chaumière, Paris.

Mariana writes, "I grew up in Georgia in what had begun as a suburb of Atlanta but had been allowed to lapse back into the country. There were pine woods around and fields of broomstraw. We rode our bikes along red-clay roads, quite unbothered by traffic, except for an occasional mule-drawn wagon. We picked blackberries in the summer and on frosty days hunted for persimmons fallen in the grass. But the real center of interest was a doll house which belonged to a young friend. It was a real little house which stood in the yard and was big enough for a child to walk around in. Here, my sister and I were constant visitors. Two cats shared our world and a St. Bernard, Dolly, who wrought havoc in the doll house and took our combined efforts to evict. I always liked to draw and I found a fellow spirit who shared my interest. Together we pooled our resources and sent off for a book on anatomy, which was a good idea in as much as our art class at school consisted of drawing the plaster heads of Julius Caesar and Dante or copying the covers of the *Ladies Home Journal*. Later on I studied art and got most of my training at the Art Students League. For a number of years after art school, I made drawings for fashion and advertising, until I ventured into the children's book field which I'd always longed to do. I live in New York, but as soon as I can in the summer, I get off to a quiet spot on Long Island where I have a little house, not much bigger than that doll house of years ago. There I still ride a bike but along very different roads." Her work is mostly in watercolor and gouache, with the black-and-white put in using Chinese ink stick. Many of her original drawings are now housed in the Mariana Room of the Hockessin Elementary School Library in Wilmington, Delaware. In September 1952, *Life* magazine ran an article about Mariana and *Miss Flora McFlimsey*. *The Journey of Bangwell Putt* was selected for the 1966 "Fifty Books Show" of the American Institute of Graphic Arts.

MARINO, DOROTHY BRONSON*

Born November 12, 1912 in Oakland, Oregon. Childhood was spent in Oregon, Missouri, and Kansas. Attended University of Kansas, Lawrence, where she studied drawing and painting under Albert Bloch; Art Students League, New York, studying with William McNulty, Yasuo Kuniyoshi, Robert Johnson and others.

Dorothy Marino was fifth in a family of six children. She writes, "When I was about six years old we moved to Missouri because my mother was homesick. The family of eight descended upon the big old farm house near Sedalia, Missouri, where our grandfather had settled at the time of the Civil War.

We spent a happy summer with uncles and aunts and cousins while our father found a teaching job in Missouri. From then on the farm was known as 'The Old Home Place' to the six children who never had a home of long duration throughout their childhood. The earliest school years were in Maitland and Amity, Missouri — two small country towns. Then my father gave up teaching and bought a book store in Lawrence, Kansas, where the children could attend the University." After graduation, Dorothy Marino went to New York City where she earned a living at various jobs while studying art. Becoming interested in the illustration of books, she wrote and illustrated *Little Angela and Her Puppy* to bring her work to the attention of publishers. This won the Helen Dean Fish Award. Mrs. Marino lives in Brooklyn, New York with her husband, John Marino, and their daughter, Nina, who was born in 1949. Her work is generally in two colors, as in the Buzzy Bear books, for which she prepares separations on acetate.

MAROKVIA, ARTUR*

Born July 21, 1909 in Stuttgart, Germany. Childhood was spent in Germany. Studied painting at Akademie, Stuttgart, Germany; in Italy; and at Académie de la Grande Chaumière, Paris.

Before coming to the United States in 1949, Artur Marokvia painted in Greece, Yugoslavia, Finland, Russia, Spain and Austria. He was also a student of music and a pianist in Germany, worked as an engineer without a diploma while studying music, and later studied ballet in Paris. He has had numerous exhibitions of his paintings in Paris where he lived for more than fifteen years. His home is now New York City, but he spent the years of 1964-1966 in Mexico drawing and painting. Mr. Marokvia works in both black-and-white and color. For black-and-white he has used lithographic crayon together with pen on etching paper in order to obtain the effect he wants.

MARRIOTT, PAT (Patricia)

Born May 16, 1920 in Cheshire, England. Childhood spent in London. Attended Westminster School of Art and the Chelsea School of Art.

Pat Marriott explains that she has always loved to draw and so quite naturally went on to art school. She is now a free-lance illustrator doing all of her work in black-and-white. She uses India ink, stipple and textured materials, as in *The Cat's Tale*. Of the many books that she has done, she likes best *Rinkin of Dragon's Wood* by Thora Colson. She lives near Stowmarket, Suffolk in England.

MARS, WITOLD T.*

Born September 1, 1908 in Poland where his childhood was spent. Attended secondary school in Cracow, Poland; Academies of Fine Arts, Cracow and Warsaw, Poland.

The son of a writer of children's books, Witold T. Mars has been interested in illustration since early childhood. At the ages of nine, eleven and fourteen he illustrated his mother's books published in Poland. After graduation from the Academy of Fine Arts in Warsaw in 1932 he began his career as painter and illustrator. He traveled widely in Europe completing his artistic studies, his work during this period being shown in leading exhibitions in Poland as well as abroad. During the Second World War he served with the Polish Forces in Great Britain and participated in the campaigns of the British Liberation Army on the continent of Europe from 1944 to 1946. After the war he resumed his artistic work in London, painting and exhibiting his pictures in several galleries in London, Edinburgh, Glasgow, Sheffield, Bristol, and others. At the same time he continued as an illustrator for several English publishers. In 1951 he settled in the United States and has illustrated books for various American publishers. His work has also appeared in *Harper's Magazine* and other periodicals. He lives in Forest Hills, Long Island, and in 1965 was elected a member of the Polish Institute of Art and Science in New York.

MARTIN, STEFAN

Born January 10, 1936 in Elgin, Illinois. Childhood spent in New York City and Roosevelt, New Jersey. Attended Art Institute of Chicago.

"As a child I lived and drew pictures in the environment of an artistic family. I am the son of David Stone Martin, a well-known illustrator and graphic artist. . . . Art was a day to day thing, as much a part of life as breathing and eating. While attending the Chicago Art Institute I worked as an apprentice at the Sander Wood Engraving Company. It was at this shop I learned every aspect of wood engraving. I think that unless I had gone through this rigid work discipline I could not have mastered the techniques of wood engraving, the knowledge of how to hold the tools, the hand becoming almost the mind." Mr. Martin, who is married and has four children, has his home and studio in Roosevelt, New Jersey. In nearby Summit and Princeton, New Jersey, he teaches printmaking at local art centers and in 1964 and 1965 was asked to demonstrate wood engraving at the New Jersey Pavilion of the New York World's Fair. His work in various media has been shown widely and has already been purchased for several collections. One of the first children's books that he illustrated was *Ronnie and the Chief's Son* in 1962. For *The Sparrow Bush* he did wood engravings and about this work he writes, "I draw directly on the wood with an idea in mind, interpret what I drew with engraving tools and finally print the block."

MASON, GEORGE FREDERICK*

Born October 18, 1904 in Princeton, Massachusetts where his childhood was spent. Attended Worcester Art Museum School and Clark University, Worcester, Massachusetts.

"My chief interest is Nature," writes George Frederick Mason. "My youth was spent on a farm where I had to work long hours at hard labor. I did not learn to appreciate the interests of nature until long after I had left the country and spent many years in the world's largest city where I worked in a natural history museum. While associated with this museum I began to realize that I was fortunate to have been brought up on a farm where there was so much association with out-door life and living plants and animals. My life has been influenced by both of these environments, and I believe each to be of equal importance in developing my career." Mr. Mason uses pen and ink or, as in the case of *Ranch in the Rockies*, dry-brush for his black-and-white drawings. For his color work he generally uses pastel and he also designs and writes the text for his books. Mr. Mason and his wife, Caroline, make their home in Princeton, Massachusetts.

MASSIE, DIANE REDFIELD

Born July 27, 1930 in Los Angeles, California where her childhood was spent. Attended Los Angeles City College; Occidental College; Los Angeles County Art Institute.

"I have loved to draw since early childhood, and drew all the time during those early years . . . my father was an artist. I was trained as an oboist and became a professional musician. I have been first oboist with the Honolulu Symphony for five seasons and with the Pasadena Symphony." While in Honolulu, she wrote and produced four plays as well as getting married. After she and her husband, David, moved to the east coast and their first child was born in 1957, she became interested again in drawing and writing. "I started by writing down some of the bedtime stories I told my daughter Caitlin, such as *The Baby Beebee Bird* (1963). Her husband is at the Courante Institute and teaches mathematics at New York University and they make their home in Califon, New Jersey. Mrs. Massie's *A Turtle and a Loon and Other Fables* was an honor book in the 1965 *New York Herald Tribune* Children's Spring Book Festival. It, like the others, was done with inks and black pencil in a style she characterizes as "more fanciful than pure representational."

MATHIESEN, EGON*

Born November 25, 1907 in Esbjerg, Denmark. Childhood spent in Vejle, Denmark. No art school — self-taught.

Egon Mathiesen writes, "All my childhood I was painting and designing. My father was a tailor, and I got pasteboard from him, but no colors. So I made them myself, and painted snow with toothpaste and made red color with brick dust and blue with powder from my father's marking chalk, and so on." About children's books he says, "To express oneself for children one must find a rhythm in pictures and words which children will feel and understand," and, "If the story is not a reality for the one who tells it, it will not be a reality for the child. Nobody is so sensitive as a child." Mr. Mathiesen has written, designed, and illustrated a number of books for children, and a book of essays on painting in his native Denmark, and has received the Danish government prize for books for young children. *The Blue-Eyed Pussy* was the first of his books to be published in the United States. Another picture book, *A Jungle in the Wheatfield*, received the prize in the 1960 *New York Herald Tribune* Children's Spring Book Festival. Mr. Mathiesen calls himself an "abstract painter working with the reality of color and nature." He has executed murals for the Tivoli Concert Hall in Copenhagen, and for the City Hall of Varde. For the abstract painting "Children Play," he received the Eckersberg Medal from the Royal Academy of Denmark. He is married to Else Fischer-Hansen, also a painter, and they have one daughter, Mariane. Their home is in Copenhagen. An article about Egon Mathiesen's work appeared in the February 1966 issue of the *Horn Book*.

MAXEY, DALE

Born March 7, 1927 in Anderson, Indiana; childhood spent in Lexington, Kentucky.

"I work mainly for children," Mr. Maxey writes. "First of all, because I like children, but also because it gives me a chance to live in the fantasy world of the child. I left school at a very early age to work on race horse farms and my love of animals stems from that early period. My animals or people are never realistic, but rather impressionistic. This also carried over into my sculpture, which is a combination of abstraction and fantasy. I have no children of my own, but many young friends, enabling me to see both sides of the life of a child. I find them to be just people on a smaller scale, without the sophistications and inhibitions of an adult. Out of a desire to appeal directly to children, I have studied their drawings in an attempt to capture, as they do, pure imagination and a natural sophistication." Mr. Maxey and his wife Betty, who is also an artist, were living in Highland Park, Illinois in 1961, when they visited England on a holiday. They were so taken with London that they decided to stay on permanently. He had illustrated children's books for several publishers including Random House and when the Maxeys moved to London, they put him in touch with Milton Shulman, who wrote *Preep, the Little Pigeon of Trafalgar Square*. Mr. Maxey works in full color, using a Japanese crayon to achieve brilliance of color. He designs as well as illustrates his books, and in some cases has also written the text as in *Seeing London*. All of his drawings are done on a semi-transparent onion-skin paper, in order to draw on both sides, giving the effect of underpainting.

MAYS, LEWIS VICTOR, JR.*

Born July 2, 1927 in New York City. Childhood spent in Bronxville, New York. Attended Yale University.

Following naval service in World War II, Victor Mays received a B.A. from Yale University where he took an honors dual major in history and art. "I illustrated every paper I turned in throughout school and college," he writes. "It seems natural to continue this as a career." He entered the publishing field by writing and illustrating a whaling story for boys, *Fast Iron*. Following service as a naval officer during the Korean War, Mr. Mays wrote a second book, *Action Starboard*, and began to illustrate for a variety of book and magazine publishers. "Maritime and military history are my favorite subjects, but I enjoy researching and drawing any period, recent or ancient. I believe history is where my representational approach to graphics best fits in. I work in line or tone, depending on the book and its mood, and also employ several methods of color separation, although I prefer the freedom of painting directly." Fond of sailing and salt water, Lieutenant Commander Mays is an active reserve officer and lives with his wife and three children in a Federal period house near the shore in Clinton, Connecticut.

MILHOUS, KATHERINE*

Born November 27, 1894 in Philadelphia and grew up there and in Pitman, New Jersey. Attended Philadelphia Museum School of Industrial Art, and Pennsylvania Academy of the Fine Arts.

"I was born in the old part of Philadelphia," Katherine Milhous writes, "on the wrong side of Market Street. But my father, a printer, kept shop on both sides of the street — once down by the docks, another time only a block away from where Benjamin Franklin once opened his 'New Printing Office in High Street near the Market,' and again just a stone's throw from Independence Hall. My studio was for thirty years in the heart of Philadelphia, and day and night I could hear the rumble of printing presses (not my father's) on the floor below. My background is Quaker and Irish, Methodist and Catholic, with a dash of Pennsylvania Dutch from the Palatinate. That is where the love of design comes in. I began to draw as soon as I could hold a pencil. The family moved to New Jersey and in the camp-meeting town where my school days were spent, I never saw a good painting or piece of sculpture, or heard fine music. Returning to Philadelphia to go to art school, I made up for lost time. I worked for scholarships, did newspaper drawings at night, saved money to travel and to paint in foreign countries. But it was on camping trips through Pennsylvania in an old

Dearborn wagon drawn by a plow horse that I learned to know the folk art of my own people. I have tried my hand at sculpture and murals, water colors and oils. All that I learned in these media, and all the background I gained by traveling at home and abroad, stands me in good stead in the writing and illustrating of children's books. Nor is this enough: there must be that indefinable something that the young reader will recognize." Katherine Milhous' first children's book illustrations were done for books by Alice Dalgliesh. Then in 1940 appeared her own first book, *Lovina*. Also drawn from her Pennsylvania Dutch background was *Herodia, the Lovely Puppet* published in 1942 and *The Egg Tree*, for which she received the Caldecott Medal in 1951. Miss Milhous designs her own books and during World War II was designer for other books as well. *Through These Arches* was the work of many years and grew out of her life-long affection for Philadelphia and its history. It was undoubtedly born during one of the "long walks about the early city" that she has enjoyed over the years.

MILLER, EDNA ANITA

Born March 8, 1920 in Weehawken, New Jersey. Childhood spent in New York City. Attended Traphagen School of Fashion, New York City.

As a child, Edna Miller lived with her parents and older sister in an apartment overlooking Central Park, in New York City, next to the American Museum of Natural History. She recalls, "I developed a great love of animals mainly because, as an apartment-dweller, I was not permitted to have what I wanted most — a dog. There were substitutes, however: two turtles, a white mouse, a rabbit and a small alligator. At the zoo in Central Park I made childish sketches of my favorite animals. The Museum of Natural History was my second home." After her training at the Traphagen School of Fashion and Design she worked as a designer of sport clothes. During this period she married Ted Miller, an architect and cartographer. They traveled extensively in Europe, North Africa, Mexico and the United States. After the birth of her son Ted in 1950, she turned to illustrating as a second career. Mrs. Miller tells us: "I have learned that nature writes its own stories . . . there need only be an interested observer." She illustrates in full color; brush and ink illustrations appear in *The Buffalo Are Running* and pencil technique was used for *Wildlife Teams*. Of her style she writes, "I feel each page is a design in itself and must have balance, coordination and simplicity. I worked only in black-and-white before I wrote and illustrated *Mousekin's Golden House*. It was my first experience in using full color. After illustrating many juvenile books it became apparent to me that the writer could only tell part of the story unless the artist was creative and extremely perceptive. I have concluded that the ideal juvenile book should come entirely from one source — both words and drawings." The Miller family lives in the Ramapo Hills, near Warwick, New York.

MILLER, MARILYN JEAN

Born November 12, 1925 in San Francisco, California where her childhood was spent. Attended California School of Fine Arts, San Francisco; Art Students League, New York City.

"When I was about ten, I started attending Saturday classes at the San Francisco Art Museum which led to a scholarship at fourteen for Saturday classes at the California School of Fine Arts. After high school, I attended as a full time student for six years, under one scholarship or another. I studied every phase of art, but concentrated on lithography and won several prizes in museum shows. A scholarship to the Art Students League brought me to New York." She began free-lancing while still studying, with a wide range of illustration jobs. Her first major account was *The Reporter* magazine which used a great deal of her work for six or eight years. For most of these black-and-white drawings she used a bamboo pen on water color paper, giving a rough broken line. She also used this for her first children's book, *Curious Missie*, published in 1953. While she was living in New York, she did a great deal of illustrating for all the national magazines as well as *This Week, The New York Times Magazine,* and various industrial accounts. She also did a number of book jackets and it was through that work "almost accidentally, I began handling children's books." Marilyn Miller is the wife of Al Hormel, a commercial artist, and when the oldest of their three children was three, they moved to Weston, Connecticut. "Since moving out of Manhattan, I have tended to concentrate more on textbooks and children's books." She has used a number of materials, including a good deal of pencil in recent years. For her color work she generally makes separations on acetate. About her work she writes, "My drawings are pretty straightforward without too much distortion for the sake of design — anatomically correct but done with an interesting line quality. I usually draw directly in ink (or whatever I'm using) without preliminary work such as rough sketches. I find that sitting down and simply doing a finish gives a fresh look to the result. If changes are required, I generally do another new drawing from scratch." An article on Marilyn Miller appeared in the December 1954 issue of *American Artist*.

MILLER, SHANE

Born January 25, 1907 in Reading, Pennsylvania; childhood was spent in Philadelphia, Pennsylvania. Attended the School of Industrial Art, Philadelphia; Art Students League, New York City; New School for Social Research (creative writing) in New York City.

"I began to draw at the age of six when I received a blackboard and colored chalks for Christmas. After art school in Philadelphia, I went into business, establishing and running an art service. After five years of this I went to New York and free-lanced as an artist, and also did some magazine writing." Be-

ginning in 1938, he spent several years doing animated cartoons, becoming involved in both the writing and the drawing of them. After returning to New York, he started illustrating children's books. One of these which he both wrote and illustrated, *Peter Stuyvesant's Drummer* (1959) he has since made into a color film. Other books that he has written and illustrated include *The Romans* in the "Life Long Ago" series and *The Hammer of Gaul: The Story of Charles Martel*. In 1959, he made a sketching trip to the Dominican Republic and in 1966 he traveled to Israel in connection with preparing a biography of General Yadin. When not traveling, he makes his home in New York City.

MILLS, YAROSLAVA SURMACH, see Yaroslava, pseud.

MINALE, MARCELLO

Born December 15, 1938 in Tripoli, Libya where his childhood was spent. Attended Instituto Tecnico G. B. della Porta, Naples, Italy.

After studying art in Italy, Marcello Minale first worked in Milan for an architectural magazine and then in Rome where he was in charge of interior and graphic design for a Scandinavian company. From there he went to Finland where he spent two years and in 1962 he went to London as an Art Director for the advertising agency, Young and Rubicam. There he met Brian Tattersfield, and in 1964 they formed Minale, Tattersfield, Ltd. with the intention of producing work with a high artistic and commercial level in the areas of advertising, television, packaging, exhibition, industrial and furniture design as well as book and magazine design. Mr. Minale started illustrating children's books after submitting some animal drawings which he had done for fun to a London publisher. The result was *Creatures Great and Small*. His interest in children's books takes the form of a hobby ("there is no money in it"). His illustrations have been done in two colors using various media: for *Creatures Great and Small*, he used color applied to board and scratched; for *The Black Pencil*, photographs and drawings; for *The Proud Scimitar*, cut pages and elementary drawing. Mr. Minale lives in London with his wife and step-daughter.

MITSUI, EIICHI

Born in Japan.

Mr. Mitsui belongs to a group of Japanese painters whose work has been greatly influenced by Western art. For many of the books he has illustrated, however, he has used the traditional Japanese brush and black ink. One of his first books published in this country was *Joji and the Dragon* by Betty Jean Lifton in

1957. He has since then illustrated several books by Mrs. Lifton who had become acquainted with his work when she lived in Japan in the early 1950's.

MIZUMURA, KAZUE

Born in Kamakura, Japan where her childhood was spent. Attended Women's Art Institute, Tokyo; Pratt Institute, Brooklyn, New York.

"I always liked to draw and that was the only thing I could do really well among all the things I had to learn during my school years. Thus it was natural for me to enter the Art Institute, though I did not particularly want to be an artist. I guess I always wanted to be just an ordinary happy wife. So, for a short time, until World War II ended my dreams, I was a wife and mother. After I lost my husband and daughter, I taught traditional Japanese sumi-e painting and worked in the field of commercial art in postwar Japan. I came to the United States in 1955 on a scholarship to Pratt Institute. After Pratt, I worked as a textile designer for four years. In 1959, I was asked to illustrate The Cheerful Heart and since then I have gradually established myself as an illustrator. For the first few years I was commissioned for strictly Japanese themes. In doing the illustrations for Japanese stories, there was little I could do beyond the authentic representational illustrations that were expected. Luckily, Elizabeth Riley of Crowell understood my problem and encouraged me to write my own text. The result was I See the Wind." Miss Mizumura lives and works in a house overlooking Long Island Sound in Stamford, Connecticut.

MONTGOMERIE, NORAH MARY*

Born April 6, 1913 in London, England and childhood was spent there at West Dulwich and in Richmond, Surrey. Attended Putney School of Art, London.

After leaving art school, Norah Montgomerie free-lanced in London before going to Scotland to join a publisher's staff as an illustrator. There she met William Montgomerie, a poet, teacher and authority on Scottish ballads and folksong, whom she married. Studies of their two children led to commissioned portraits of children, nursery murals, and children's book illustrations. Because of the children, they took a house facing the beach at Broughty Ferry near Dundee, where they still live. For their children, they collected traditional rhymes, games and tales. Encouraged by Walter de la Mare, they edited Scottish Nursery Rhymes published in 1946. This and a second collection Sandy Candy were republished in 1964 under the title The Hogarth Book of Scottish Nursery Rhymes. In 1949-1950, the Scottish Educational Journal published a series of her illustrated street and singing games. Among her other books, there have been two picture books which she wrote herself. For these she also did the color separations. At present Norah

Montgomerie is working with her husband's help on a comprehensive collection of Scottish Highland legends and tales. Apart from work, her great passion is visiting her two young grandchildren, and Italy.

MONTRESOR, BENI

Born March 30, 1926 in Verona, Italy. Childhood spent in Verona and Venice. Attended Verona Art School; Academy of Fine Arts, Venice; Centro Sperimentale di Cinematographia, Rome.

It was in 1950 that Beni Montresor, competing with some 200 candidates, won a two-year scholarship to study cinema at the Centro Sperimentale in Rome. For seven years after his graduation he was a set and costume designer working all over Europe with such directors as Rossellini. He has worked on over twenty-five films, as well as many stage plays and operas. Among the operas whose designs have brought him acclaim are the 1961 production of "Vanessa" in Spoleto, the 1962 production of "Pelleas et Melisande" at the Glyndebourne Festival, the 1965 production of "Cenerentola" by the Metropolitan Opera of New York. This last was the basis of the illustrations for his version of Cinderella published the same year as a children's book. His sketches for "The Last Savage" by Menotti were published in book form by the New York Graphic Society on the occasion of the American premiere of that opera. His deep love of the opera is also apparent in the children's book which he illustrated, giving the story of The Magic Flute. By the time he was twenty, Mr. Montresor had already had five plays and a group of fables for children produced on the Italian and Swiss Radio. After coming to the United States in 1959, he not only illustrated a number of children's books but also wrote and illustrated three of his own. The first was House of Flowers, House of Stars. Three of his books were chosen for the 1961-62 Children's Book Show of the American Institute of Graphic Arts. In 1965, he received the Caldecott Medal for May I Bring A Friend? by Beatrice de Regniers. Word of this award first reached him at the Schubert Theater in New Haven where he was involved in the out-of-town opening of the musical "Do I Hear a Waltz?" for which he had created the sets and costumes. May I Bring a Friend? was done in three colors. There was a basic line drawing in black and then five overlays for a screen of the black, and a screen and solid of each of the other two colors. "I find it more exciting to use three colors than four. There is more challenge," Mr. Montresor has said. He now lives in New York, traveling to Europe frequently. Articles on him have appeared in Opera News, February 8, 1964, Show, March 1962, Horn Book, August 1965, School Library Journal, March 1965.

MORDVINOFF, NICOLAS, see Nicolas, pseud.

MOY, SEONG

Born April 20, 1921 in Canton, China. Childhood spent in China and St. Paul, Minnesota. Attended St. Paul School of Art; Art Students League and Hans Hofmann Art School, New York.

Mr. Seong Moy, who has illustrated three children's books and a Limited Edition version of *Uncle Remus*, is best known as an artist and teacher. He has taught art at Columbia University, Vassar and Smith Colleges, University of Minnesota, as well as at Cooper Union Art School and the Pratt Graphic Art Center. His work which has won a number of awards is represented in many museums, including Museum of Modern Art, Metropolitan Museum, Whitney Museum, Tel-Aviv Museum and London's Victoria and Albert Museum. *Print* magazine for June-July 1954 has an article on Mr. Moy who, with his wife and their two daughters, now makes his home in New York City.

MOZLEY, CHARLES

Born May 29, 1914 in Sheffield, England where his childhood was spent. Attended Sheffield School of Art; Royal College of Art, London.

Charles Mozley writes, "Soon after completing my training at the Royal College of Art, I was called up into the Army in World War II for six years. After the war I did posters for different theatre and film companies and soon after that began doing book jackets and illustrations." Mr. Mozley's work has been exhibited in several galleries and his pictures are in a number of collections including that of the Imperial War Museum. At the Festival of Britain, there were several large murals he had been commissioned to do. Mr. Mozley lives in London with his wife and five children.

MUNARI, BRUNO*

Born October 24, 1907 in Milan, Italy. His childhood was spent in Badia Polesine (Rovigo), Venice. Attended Technical Institute of Naples; no formal art training.

Bruno Munari is a painter, sculptor, photographer, illustrator and designer of books, toys and mobiles. He made his debut as a member of the Italian Futurist Movement. Later he become interested in making mobiles which he calls *macchine inutili*. He is well-known as an original designer and illustrator of unconventional picture books for children and for his *libri illeggibili*, books without words, for adults. His children's books were designed for his son, Alberto, when he was small. For all of these he has used tempera. He considers himself a painter first and then a designer, and has received among other awards a Golden Medal of the Triennale of Milan, and several Golden

Compasses for industrial design. Articles about his work appear in *Graphic Design* (Japan) No. 1, 1959 and No. 13, 1963. Bruno Munari's home is in Milan.

NESBITT, ESTA

Born November 19, 1918 in New York City where her childhood was spent. Attended Traphagen School, New School for Social Research, Columbia University, China Institute, Art Students League, Workshop of the Pratt Graphic Art Center, New York City.

"I knew I was an artist when I was six years of age. It was a fact; I announced it as so. I've never disputed it; it is one of life's problems. I cannot know what contributed to that awareness, I accept it," writes Esta Nesbitt. She also remembers that she "loved the Saturday long hikes to the library and rainy days sitting on the window sill reading." In her early career as a fashion, advertising and magazine illustrator, she was awarded several citations for her work. In 1960 while she devoted herself to further study in painting and print-making, she was asked to illustrate *The Town Across the Water*. This she did with a "series of sugar-lift aquatints, a difficult medium to control but extremely rewarding." The technique used for *Jon the Unlucky* grew out of her studies of Oriental painting and calligraphy with Chiang Lee. *The Stars Are Silver Reindeer* was a combination of "metal printing" and line drawings printed on English watercolor paper. "I work with separations on whatever I feel gives the character I need. I do a lot of experimental preparation exploring various techniques. I also concern myself with hand-made papers, as they are the 'support' of the art." Two books she has designed as well as illustrated. A number of prints and drawings made for books have also been exhibited in various national print shows. Mrs. Nesbitt is married to a sculptor and industrial designer, Saul Nesbitt, and they have three daughters. "We live in New York City in a brownstone house we bought years ago when the children needed all the space the studio had occupied. Now I have one studio for bookmaking, one for painting and printmaking and still another in our beach house on Long Island." Besides working in all these studios, she also is an instructor at Parson's School of Design.

NESS, EVALINE

Born April 24, 1911 in Union City, Ohio. Childhood spent in Pontiac, Michigan. Attended Ball State Teachers' College, Muncie, Indiana; Art Institute of Chicago; Art Students League, New York City; Academia de Belles Artes, Rome, Italy.

"I didn't start studying art until I was out of college," writes Evaline Ness. She went to the Art Institute with the idea of becoming a fashion artist and at the same time supported her-self by doing fashion modeling. Her first marriage to Elliot Ness took her to Washington, D. C. where along with her social activities as the wife of a high federal administrator, she also studied at the Corcoran Art School. In 1946, she came to New York and began illustrating for *Seventeen*. This led to fashion drawing for Saks Fifth Avenue from 1947 to 1951. For three years she traveled and studied mostly in Europe before returning to New York and fashion work. In 1960, she was asked to illustrate *The Bridge* by Charlton Osborn which began an active period doing a great many book jackets as well as a growing number of picture books. *Josefina February* was the first book she wrote and illustrated. It grew out of a year's stay in Haiti and on publication was selected as a Notable Book by the American Library Association and an Honor Book by the *New York Herald Tribune*. More and more of Evaline Ness's time has been devoted to doing her own picture books, the most recent of which, *Sam, Bangs and Moonshine*, was awarded the 1967 Caldecott Medal. Evaline Ness has used a wide variety of media — collage for some, wood block cutting for *Tom Tit Tot*, and a line and wash technique for *Sam, Bangs and Moonshine*. An interesting account of the conception of that book is given by Ann Durell in the March 1967 *School Library Journal*. Other articles about her appear in the October 1964 and August 1967 *Horn Book* and in *American Artist*, 1956. Evaline Ness who lives in New York works at a studio in her home with "a cat who sits on all my artwork and eats my kneaded erasers."

NETHERWOOD, ANNE

Born September 27, 1940 in Bacup, Lancashire, England, where her childhood was spent. Attended Rochdale College of Art; Manchester College of Art; University of London Institute of Education.

"I have drawn and painted as long as I can remember," writes Anne Netherwood. "This was encouraged by my family and at Grammar School from where I went to Art College. My painting developed from the usual academic representationalism to semi-abstract expressionism, particularly influenced by early twentieth century art. I was interested in trying to combine the arts of poetry and painting, often using a poem as the subject for a painting or drawing. In my last year at Manchester I won a travel scholarship to Italy. I then went to London to do a year at the Institute of Education. At the end of that year, 1962, I married Gerald Wilkinson, who is also a painter and designs and illustrates books for the University of London Press. I now have two small daughters and it is since I have been tied to the house with a young family that I have started to illustrate books. Both books have been poetry and I am not interested in illus-trating any other sort of book." Her drawings which are in black-and-white were done with pen and ink.

NICKLESS, WILL

Born 1902 in Essex, England.

Will Nickless writes, "I started work at fourteen and was making drawings at eighteen for an advertising agency. In 1920, I joined a paper, *The Motor*, and made technical drawings of motor cars and later general figure work for both editorial and advertising. I left to go free-lancing which I have been doing ever since." Until 1958, he lived in London and then moved to his present home in Rotherfield, Sussex, England. "In 1964, I had two feet of snow in the garage-way, and no work. I tossed up whether I should paint or write a book. I wrote a book, *Owlglass*, and illustrated it. Since then have written *The Nite-hood* and *Molepie*." Before writing *Owlglass*, he had illustrated a number of books including *Most of Rider-Haggard* and a Penguin edition of *The Ugly Duckling*. Besides writing and illustrating, he has "a private press on which I occasionally print my own poems. I illustrate, bind and so on and issue them in limited editions. I paint pictures and when I get enough I hold an exhibition. The last was in 1964. I also etch and a series of antiwar etchings were reproduced in *The New Leader* in 1939 — they had no effect on the war. I have made four violins and two violas, a six-inch astronomical telescope and several locomotive models, all these for fun, of course."

NICOLAS,* pseud. (Nicolas Mordvinoff)

Born September 27, 1911 in Leningrad, Russia. Childhood was spent in Russia, and in Paris where he attended Lycée Jeanson de Sailly and Ecole des Roches. Also attended the University of Paris receiving a degree in Latin, Philosophy and Languages; later painted under Fernand Leger and Amédée Ozenfant.

At the age of seven, Nicolas Mordvinoff, who was the grandson of Admiral Alexandre Mordvinoff, escaped with his parents from the Russian Revolution to Finland and then to Paris. While still at school he contributed cartoons and illustrations to French newspapers and magazines. In 1934, he left Paris for Tahiti and lived in the South Pacific for thirteen years, devoting his time to painting, experimenting in etching, wood engraving and monotype printing — a technique which he later used to illustrate *The Ship of Flame* and Kipling's *Just So Stories*. While he was there he met William S. Stone, an American writer, who persuaded Nicolas to illustrate his *Thunder Island* (1942). After this they collaborated on two other children's books: *Pepe Was the Saddest Bird* and *The Ship of Flame*. In 1946 Nicolas came to the United States, becoming a citizen five years later. In 1949, he had a one-man show of his paintings in New York City. The following year he began his collabora-tion with William Lipkind in *The Two Reds*, the first of several picture books by "Will and Nicolas." Their second book,

Finders Keepers, received the Caldecott Medal in 1952. Nicolas Mordvinoff has illustrated for other authors as well and in 1954 he shared with Natalie Savage Carlson the *New York Herald Tribune* Children's Spring Book Festival Prize for *Alphonse That Bearded One*. He has in almost every case designed the books that he has illustrated. "Most of my illustrations in color were done with separations on various kinds of acetate either in pen and ink or crayon or brush or a combination of all three. *The Boy and the Forest*, done in woodblocks was my last book. Since then, 1964, I have taken up sculpture and painting again on a full time schedule." Mr. Mordvinoff makes his home in New Jersey. An article on him appeared in the August 1952 issue of the *Horn Book*.

NONNAST, MARIE*

Born July 4, 1924 in Jenkintown, Pennsylvania, where her childhood was spent. Attended Moore Institute of Art, Philadelphia.

Marie Nonnast writes, "I have been drawing as long as I can remember. In Abington High School I won a four year scholarship to the Moore Institute of Art where I studied Advertising Art and Illustration. After graduation I immediately began freelancing, and did some work for the *Saturday Evening Post* and *Country Gentleman*. I did quite a lot of work for *Holiday Magazine*, mostly illustrations for animal stories or articles, and in the last few years I have been illustrating books. A few years ago I illustrated Edwin Way Teale's 'Birds of America' for *Woman's Day* magazine which involved 300 bird paintings in full color. I am married to a consulting engineer and am now living in New Hope, Pennsylvania. My son is at Tyler School of Fine Art." An article on Miss Nonnast appeared in *American Artist*, May 1957.

NORDENSKJÖLD, BIRGITTA

Born January 2, 1919 in Linköping, Sweden where she spent her childhood. Graduated from Konstfacksskolan in Stockholm.

Birgitta Nordenskjöld took a five year course at Konstfacksskolan, which is the industrial design school of Sweden. Following her graduation, she became a teacher of drawing in the same school. She now has three children and explains that she began to illustrate books to please them. She has illustrated many books in the last ten years, particularly for the Swedish publisher, Rabèn & Sjögren.

NUSSBAUMER, PAUL EDMUND

Born May 2, 1934 in Lucerne, Switzerland. Childhood spent in Meiringen in Canton Bern. Attended secondary school and Art School in Lucerne.

"When I was five," writes Mr. Nussbaumer, "I started drawing and drew mostly trains as my father was a railway technician." He was not encouraged by his family, but went nevertheless to art school for five years and then spent half a year in Rome painting. Afterwards he made his living doing advertising and designing for a big textile firm. "When I had earned enough money I went to live in the Ticino, the Italian part of Switzerland, married and started anew to paint and also to make picture books for children." He has done three books, the first of which, *Away in a Manger*, was written by his wife, Mares. They have one child, a small boy named Nicholas.

OBLIGADO, LILIAN ISABEL

Born April 12, 1931 in Buenos Aires, Argentina. Childhood spent there and in United States. Studied painting with several people in Argentina including Vincent Puig.

"My father's ancestors settled in Buenos Aires about 250 years ago; they came from Seville, Spain on one side, from Germany on the other. My grandfather, Rafael Obligado, was one of the major classic poets of Argentina. After reading Walter Scott novels most of his youth he decided to build a castle on the hills overlooking the Parana river, and he did. It is now standing there, improved by every generation who has lived there since. It is a very odd sight in the middle of the pampas. But we all love it, and the surrounding land, the river, the islands, the many kinds of birds . . . that is why I love nature so much, and animals. I would go around with a pencil and pad sketching continually. I loved to write and draw long involved stories which I would send to my grandmother. Illustrating books has always appealed to me and I tried a bit of it in Buenos Aires, but soon went back to New York in 1958 and began getting commissions almost immediately." Since then she has illustrated over fifty children's books including, recently, four books in the McKee series of readers. Her full color work is done in water color and designers' colors. Her black-and-white drawings, largely in books for older children such as *A Dog Named Scholar* "were rendered in prismacolor pencil, on dinobase. I am best at free sketching, and with dinobase — it being so transparent and having a thick grain — one can just trace off from the original sketch without losing much of the light quick touch." She has also used dry brush and gouache with a touch of pen and ink. Miss Obligado, whose husband Dr. Pedro Simonetti died in 1960, lives in New York City but makes frequent trips to her family home in Argentina.

OECHSLI, KELLY

Born February 23, 1918 in Butte, Montana. Childhood spent in Seattle, Washington. Attended Cornish School of Art, Seattle.

"I grew up in a houseful of books — those of Pyle and Wyeth and Frederic Remington being the most worn and clearly recalled. I live with my wife and four children and work at home. The younger children are interested in what I do; the older children couldn't care less. Perhaps this helps me to keep things in some sort of perspective," writes Mr. Oechsli, whose home is in Hawthorne, New York. He works in both black-and-white and color, often doing separations for his color work. Over the past few years, he feels his style has changed from the purely decorative toward being more traditionally representational.

OHLSSON, IB

Born August 9, 1935 in Copenhagen, Denmark, where his childhood was spent. Attended Randersgade Skole; the School of Decorative and Applied Arts, Copenhagen.

Mr. Ohlsson remembers being taught art in public school. " 'Shadows,' said our art teacher, 'come in three shades, shadow 1, the light one, shadow 2, the somewhat darker and shadow 3, the deep shadow.' It was made very clear to us in school that art was nothing to fool around with or take lightly or have fun with! I think I started to draw because I saw my older brother draw. When exactly I decided to make a career of what I liked to do best, I cannot recall, but despite the 'shadow-theory' and its creator I went right on drawing." While in art school he became an apprentice to a graphic designer and worked in the studio during the day and attended school at night. "The work in the studio consisted mostly of lettering, package designs and layouts with some advertising design thrown in from time to time. Tooth paste, detergent and sun tan lotion are fine things to be involved with when it comes to making money — but they are difficult things to live with day in, day out on a professional basis if one intends to stay reasonably sane. I had started free-lancing after four years with the studio and little by little I was able to do book illustrations full time. In 1960, I decided to try working in New York. I had spent the summer of 1950 in an international boys' camp in Pennsylvania and had been eager to return." In New York he worked for a year with a designer while he took his portfolio around to the publishers. He lives with his wife and young son in Kew Gardens, New York City, where he also has his studio. "I prefer working at night, ten or eleven in the evening to four or five in the morning being, in my opinion, the best time for penning lines and dots on paper."

OLDS, ELIZABETH*

Born December 10, 1897 in Minneapolis, Minnesota where her childhood was spent. Attended University of Minnesota; Minneapolis School of Art; Art Students League, New York.

Elizabeth Olds has worked as a painter with oil, water color, and casein, and as a printmaker, with lithography, silkscreen and woodblocks. "Occasionally," she writes, "finding in some painting or print I have done, the idea for a book, I branch off into writing and illustrating a picture book for children. This is my 'doublelife,' though in actuality it is a continuation, in another field, of my work as a painter or printmaker." Children showed so much interest in a silkscreen print, "The Fire," that she recognized the nucleus of a book, and out of the print grew *The Big Fire*. Out of an experience by the sea on Long Island, watching and painting sea and water-birds, grew her *Feather Mountain*. Elizabeth Olds has traveled widely in the United States, Mexico and Guatemala and has lived not only in various parts of this country but also in France and Italy. She now lives in New Hampshire and New York, where she has maintained a studio for many years. She was the first woman to receive a Guggenheim Fellowship in the field of painting. She has had a number of one-man exhibits of her paintings in New York and has been represented in print exhibitions in numerous museums. Her first children's book, *The Big Fire*, was illustrated by making key drawings on lithographic stone which were then transferred to zinc plates. Miss Olds made the additional color plates by drawing with lithographic crayon directly on other zinc plates. For *Plop Plop Ploppie* and *Little Una*, she worked with woodblocks "using the textures of different woods, mahogany, sugar pine, weathered house-siding, birch, textured pressed wood along with pencil line. A jig-saw was used for cut-outs and a mechanical electric tool freely used for cutting instead of a knife."

OLSEN, IB SPANG

Born June 11, 1921 in Copenhagen, Denmark where his childhood was spent. Attended college and took examination as a teacher; Royal Academy of Arts, Copenhagen.

Over the years, Mr. Olsen, who makes his home in Denmark, has done a great deal of illustrating, first for magazines and then later primarily for books. He also does book jackets, posters, and is a printmaker working in lithography and zincography. Several years ago he began to write as well as illustrate children's books, doing such books as *The Boy in the Moon* and *The Marsh Crone's Brew*. His own four children, as well as the other children he comes in contact with, encourage him in his writing and illustrating. "I have done a lot of children's portraits," he writes, "and have published two collections of them. I also have made a number of TV productions for children." His books have won several prizes, including two from the Danish Ministry of Culture, one in 1965 from the Danish association called Friends of Books, and a Diploma of Merit signifying that in 1966 his work was represented on the Honor List of the International Board of Books for Youth.

OSBORN, ROBERT C. (Chesley)

Born October 26, 1904 in Oshkosh, Wisconsin. Attended Yale University; British Academy, Rome, Italy; Académie Scandinav, Paris, France.

Robert Osborn is well-known for his satirical drawings which have appeared in four adult books, including *The Vulgarians* (1961), and in numerous magazines such as *Look*, *Harpers*, *Fortune*, *Life* and *Punch*. He writes of his work, "It seems to me that my best work draws on impressions felt before I was six." For the first children's book that he illustrated, *The Song of Paul Bunyan & Tony Beaver* in 1964, he may well have drawn on his childhood memories. "My father was a lumberman. He had three saw mills and surrounding timber in Northern Wisconsin and Upper Michigan." All of Robert Osborn's work is in black-and-white and for his adult books, he writes, designs and also letters the text. Mr. Osborn, who is married and has two children, makes his home in Salisbury, Connecticut. Articles about his work have appeared recently in *Graphis*, July 1961, *Art in America*, April 1963 and December 1964, and in *Horizon*, May 1962.

PALAZZO, TONY*

Born April 7, 1905 in New York City where his childhood was spent. Attended High School of Commerce, Columbia University and New York University, New York City.

From 1941 to 1958, Tony Palazzo was art director of *Esquire*, *Coronet*, and *Collier's* magazines and for the advertising agency, Laurence Fertig and Company. He has had several one-man shows in New York and Chicago, and his work has been exhibited in various museums, including the Museum of Modern Art, New York, the Pennsylvania Academy of the Fine Arts, and the Art Institute of Chicago. He entered the children's book field with his illustrations for Al Graham's *Timothy Turtle*, first published in 1946. He has since written as well as illustrated twenty-two books, beginning with *Susie the Cat and Charlie the Horse*, has edited and illustrated eight more, and has illustrated eight books by other authors. He works in black-and-white pen and ink as in *Timothy Turtle*, full color tempera as in *The Lord Is My Shepherd* and three colors, preseparated on acetate, as in *Thai, Kao and Tone*.

PAPAS, WILLIAM

Born July 15, 1927 in Ermelo, Transvaal, South Africa. Attended art schools in South Africa and Kent.

William Papas was born of a Greek father and German mother in South Africa where the impact of his political cartoons has been such that he has been banned from the country since 1965. His hobby was always drawing. He hitch-hiked around Europe for two years, during which time he sketched, became

a dish-washer in Sweden, walked the streets of Hamburg in a bill-board advertisement, became an excellent baby-minder and in England became a riveter's mate. He returned to South Africa in 1951 and joined the *Cape Times* as staff artist. He held yearly exhibitions of his drawings. He arrived in London in 1959 with a very large portfolio, a wife and three very small children. He joined the *Guardian* in the same year to do feature drawings and later did a cartoon strip and political cartoons for the *Sunday Times* in London. In the last few years Papas has found time to write and illustrate a number of children's books. "I prefer writing and illustrating children's books," he says, "especially on social and political themes. It is a form of elongated cartooning." His ambition is to devote his time to painting and continuing his "elongated cartoons" on a little island in Greece.

PARKER, EDGAR

Born 1925 in Meridian, Mississippi where his childhood was spent. Attended University of Alabama; studied painting with Amedee Ozenfant and at Brooklyn Museum School, New York.

After finishing high school, Edgar Parker went first to the Junior College in Meridian, Mississippi and then on to the University of Alabama where he studied art. Along with painting he also studied etching and engraving, when he came to New York City. His first book which he wrote and illustrated was *The Duke of Sycamore* published in 1959. About the style of his illustrations he writes, "The grisaille employed in the illustrations was developed as an antithesis to my line work which is as capricious and distorted as the former is disciplined and literal. If, for example, my subject is an ordinary-man-in-a-business-suit, I treat him in line; whereas a mouse in a plumed hat is a marvel well worth evoking 'in the flesh.'" His grey and black monochromes are prepared first as a wash, then abraded with a typewriter eraser, built up again with light brush strokes, rubbed with a softer eraser, built up again, repeating this process until the desired effect is achieved. Often the last rubbings are done with his thumb. Along with his books, Mr. Parker has also painted murals and designed such things as record album covers and book jackets.

PARNALL, PETER

Born May 23, 1936 in Syracuse, New York. Childhood spent in Southern California and Connecticut. Attended Cornell University; Pratt Institute School of Art.

As a child, Peter Parnall always lived in the country and his interest in animals made him so sure he wanted to be a veterinarian that he went to Cornell University to study for it. Finding he was more interested in drawing specimens and creatures of all sorts, he left school and worked on a horse farm, managing also to sell a few drawings. At Pratt Institute he studied advertising for two years and then left to become art director of a small magazine. For about five years he was an art director for an advertising agency and, he writes, "managed to sell more drawings for ads and magazines as I went along. Now I am art directing on a free-lance basis, all the while trying to sell books. I only started to see book publishers in earnest one year ago. I started by doing only wildlife illustrations in pen and ink, branched out into tempera, then combined black-and-white with color washes and found the sky was the limit when dealing in inks." Working at home on a farm beside the Delaware River, he says he is able to enjoy his wife and small son more than most people can. "Frequent talks with neighboring farmers are pleasant breaks in the day and hasten my education at a far faster pace than did those with my advertising co-workers. I set a lot of stock in my walks, at least twice a week for two or three hours, watching deer and various other creatures. It is during these walks that I make the most progress, both in creating new projects and learning a little something about myself." He illustrated his first book *The Cheechakoes* in 1962 and is presently working toward writing and illustrating his own books.

PASCAL, DAVID

Born August 16, 1918 in New York City, where his childhood was spent.

"I was born and raised in the slums and ghettos of New York. Libraries and books became my refuge. Next to paintings and drawings I revere books as man's greatest achievement — an expression of his profounder nature. I can still remember loving the magnificent illustrations of fairy tales in contradistinction to the violent hates and frustrations which closed in my childhood environment. I guess I sensed that another world existed, lovelier than the ugly one I was born into and forced to inhabit. The other visual influences were comics, cartoons and movies. I loved drawing and it was logical to start by selling my cartoons. They have appeared in every major American magazine as well as in many abroad. I found that illustrating a book with many drawings on one theme was a great challenge. It demands more from the artist. I use the simplest of materials, pen and ink on paper, or a simple wash, as in *Fifteen Fables of Krylov*. I treat my children's books as total creations. Children are young living adults, not idiots to be pandered to. My two latest books while set in time a few hundred years ago, are as modern as today's newspaper and serious as Camus in what they try to say, while being funny." David Pascal's work is expressionistic. He uses the emotional quality of the narrative as a base for the rendering, rather than thinking of decorative effects.

PATON, JANE ELIZABETH

Born May 16, 1934 in London, England. Childhood spent in London, Wales and Southern England. Attended St. Martin's School of Art and Royal College of Art, London.

Miss Paton writes, "Art had always been my favorite subject at school, so at the age of sixteen, I decided that art was to be my career and that I should like to specialize in children's book illustration. The first four years of my art training were spent at St. Martin's School of Art. After that came three years in the School of Graphic Design of the Royal College under the tutorship of Edward Ardizzone. In 1957, my final year, I was commissioned to illustrate my first children's book, *The Twins in Ceylon* by Harry Williams, and I decided to launch out as free-lance artist. I now live in a large Victorian family house with my sister who is an established dress designer, her husband and three children. The children are indeed very valuable little models for my drawings. They are the main characters in my book, *Mr. Crankle's Taxi*. At the top of the house, I have a large studio with a splendid view of the Surrey countryside. My parents have retired to Provence in Southern France, so I am fortunate enough to be able to say that I have two homes." Jane Paton works in both black-and-white and full color.

PAYNE, JOAN BALFOUR*

Born December 2, 1923 in Natchez, Mississippi. Childhood was spent mainly in Minneapolis, Minnesota. Attended Northrop Collegiate School for Girls, Minneapolis, through the ninth form; after that had private studies under a tutor while studying art with Gustav Krollman of the Minneapolis Art Institute.

Joan Balfour Payne grew up in a large residential hotel in Minneapolis, of which her father was the manager. She writes, "I have liked to draw and paint ever since I can remember, and began very early to illustrate stories which my mother, Josephine Balfour Payne, made up for my amusement. My first published work was in collaboration with my mother. We did several books together, she as author, I as illustrator. We left Minnesota in 1941, returning to Mississippi to live on an old family plantation at Church Hill, a few miles above Natchez. I spent the autumn of 1950 abroad and in August of 1952 I married a cousin, John Barber Dicks, Jr., of Natchez, and we went immediately to Nashville to live where he was completing his doctorate in physics at Vanderbilt University. I wrote my first book for children that winter and illustrated it. We are now living in Sewanee, Tennessee, where my husband is a professor of physics at the University of Tennessee Space Institute. We have four children, two boys and two girls." Since 1957, she has illustrated six books for other authors as well as five she has written herself. For her most recent book, *Pangur*

Ban, she used crayon, pencil and pen on dinobase. In this book, which she also designed herself, she attempted some approximations of early Irish art forms and script. An article about Miss Payne appeared in the October 1966 issue of *The Delta Review*.

PEET, BILL (William Bartlett)

Born January 29, 1915 in Grandview, Indiana. Childhood spent in Indianapolis. Attended John Herron Art Institute, Indianapolis, Ind.

Mr. Peet writes, "Until I was 12, we lived no more than a half hour hike from the open countryside. On Saturdays and all during the summer my two brothers and I would organize safaris to explore the region. One of my most memorable experiences was a trip to my grandfather's farm. It was the first train trip for me and since I was so very fond of the farm country it was a great pleasure to see it all pass by in rapid review. Animals have always been of special interest to me and drawing had been my main hobby from the time I was old enough to wield a crayon. I drew just about anything that came to mind, all sorts of animals, trains, fire engines, battles, football games, or what have you. During high school it occurred to me that drawing was the one thing I liked to do that could be turned into a profession, and later I was awarded a scholarship to the John Herron Art Institute." Bill Peet, who began as a sketch artist in the movie industry in California, later also became a screenwriter. His custom of storytelling at bedtime to his two sons started him writing children's books. Mr. Peet's nine picture books have been done in four colors with separations made on acetate. "In getting started on a story I make many rough preliminary sketches of the main characters. This way I become well acquainted with them before going into the finished writing." In 1958, he received a special citation from the John Herron Art Institute for being one of the outstanding students in the history of the school.

PERL, SUSAN

Born September 1922 in Vienna, Austria where her childhood was spent.

"From art school I was expelled for lack of talent," Miss Perl writes, "yet at twelve, I was illustrating for the children's section of a great Viennese newspaper, *Der Tag*. I could never adjust to what teachers wanted." She says she started drawing while still in the perambulator. "I was a very withdrawn child and just sat with my pad and drew but not from Nature, only from 'inside' so to speak, fairy tales etc." Before coming to North America, her travels took her to Switzerland, Italy and Egypt. She arrived in California and worked her way eastward, finally settling permanently in New York City, where for seven years she was on the staff of *Vogue*. Besides illustrating children's books, she is a regular contributor to such publications as the *New York Times*, *Saturday Review*, *Good Housekeeping* and has designed stage settings and costumes for ballets in Germany and Switzerland and for the Metropolitan Opera in New York City. Her work has been exhibited in Europe and in 1965 she was awarded the Palma D'Oro Award as one of the best cartoonists in the International Cartoonist Exhibition in Italy. In her book work, she has illustrated for a number of authors, usually working in pen and ink and water color, as in *The Barber of Seville*. "I hate to make rough sketches — I like to read the manuscript and draw at the very moment of emotional impact. I work best early in the morning, after a good night's rest. During the time I am illustrating a book, I have to live a very quiet life to keep the inspiration flowing. People tell me I make funny faces when I draw. I live the characters I am drawing like an actress." Miss Perl says she has been a student of psychology and metaphysics for many years and loves classical music, travel, children and animals. "My family are five alley cats who live with me."

PETERSHAM, MAUD FULLER*

Born August 5, 1889 in Kingston, New York. Childhood was spent in New York State, South Dakota and Pennsylvania. Attended Vassar College and New York School of Fine and Applied Art.

Maud Petersham's father was a Baptist minister and she was one of a family of four girls. Growing up in a parsonage, she loved to hear the tales told by the visiting missionaries. In the summertime, she visited her Quaker grandfather and listening to his stories gave her great awe and respect for what had gone into the making of America. She graduated from Vassar and then studied art in New York City. Her first job was at the International Art Service, and it was there that she met a rising young commercial artist, Miska Petersham, who had come to this country in 1912. It was not until Maud and Miska Petersham were married and began working together that they found the work that they liked best — making books for children. After illustrating a number of books for various authors, the Petershams began writing as well as illustrating. The first of their own books was *Miki*, published in 1929, which pictured the life in Hungary that Miska had known as a boy. Several years before this, in 1923, their son Miki had been born and they had built the home and studio in Woodstock, New York where they lived for many years. One of their best known books, *The Christ Child*, was inspired by a three-month trip to Palestine. In 1941 *An American ABC* was published, the first of many books that reflected their deep interest in the development of the United States. A companion volume, *The Rooster Crows*, was awarded the Caldecott Medal in 1946. This partnership, one of the best known and most productive in the children's book field, ended with Miska Petersham's death on

May 15, 1960. Continuing in the spirit of their work, Maud Petersham illustrated *The Shepherd's Psalm* which was published in 1962.

PETERSON, BETTY FERGUSON

Born November 9, 1917 in London, England. Childhood spent in British Columbia, Canada. Attended Art Students League, New York; art courses given by the Extension Division, University of California.

"From the days of my childhood in British Columbia, I have loved nature. Farm life abounded in baby chickens, pet rabbits and even a pet pig. As a child I loved drawing the animals. I developed drawing technique by attending the Art Students League, where I discovered painting. Then followed a period of marriage and child rearing. I continued to paint and study but have found much more time since the marriage of my daughter in 1958 to pursue what I now consider my career." Mrs. Peterson works in two colors primarily, using brush and ink on rice paper as in *The Bunny Who Found Easter*. She describes her work as impressionistic — "I try to apply painting feelings to illustrating." Her home is in San Francisco, California.

PETERSON, RUSSELL FRANCIS

Born in Montclair, New Jersey. Attended Harvard University and College of Charleston, Charleston, South Carolina.

After World War II, in which Mr. Peterson served in a ski regiment of the 10th Mountain Division, he studied at the College of Charleston and began his career in the field of children's museums. Later he became interested in research and spent some years on the staff of the Mammal Department of the American Museum of Natural History. As a mammalogist, he accompanied two museum expeditions to New Guinea, explored the outback of North Central Australia and traveled both in the South Seas and in the Arctic. He is particularly interested in writing and illustrating books on natural history. He makes his home in Locust, New Jersey with his wife, who is also a writer, and their four children.

PETRIDES, HEIDRUN

Born March 8, 1944 in Posen, Poland. Childhood spent in Munich and Hamburg, Germany. Attended art school in Munich.

"At the age of six," Miss Petrides writes, "I went to a children's painting school where I learned to paint with thick brushes and much color. At fifteen, I wrote and illustrated *Hans and Peter* for my little brother. The wax chalks I used for the pictures let me compose in great forms. In the following years I began

to draw a great deal and to paint in water colors. As subject matter I took the streets and houses of Hamburg, all the things in my room and the model in a life drawing course at the art school." In college Miss Petrides has been studying science and education. She has recently illustrated a book of funny animal poems written by a friend which is to be published and is now planning to do more illustrating of children's books. Her home is now in Hamburg, Germany.

PIATTI, CELESTINO

Born January 5, 1922. Attended School for Applied Arts, Zurich, Switzerland.

Before the publication of his two picture books, *The Happy Owls* in 1963 and the *A B C* in 1965, Celestino Piatti was already widely known as one of Switzerland's outstanding graphic designers. Before opening his own studio in 1948, he had been a commercial art teacher during the years 1938-1942, did his military service, and for four years was a commercial artist in the studio of Fritz Bühler in Zurich. Having won various competitions with his graphic work, he quite readily received commissions in all areas of commercial art: advertising, designing exhibitions, illustration, packaging and posters. His posters, which are particularly well-known, have been exhibited and received awards on all five continents. In 1964 a film called "Piatti-Eulen" was produced for television by H. Stricker. Articles on Mr. Piatti appeared in *Graphis* #66 in 1956 and *Graphis* #115 in 1964. In 1962 his book *Reisen mit Pinsel Stift und Feder* (*Travels with Brush, Crayon and Pen*) was published in Basel, Switzerland by Werner und Bischoff Verlag.

PINKNEY, JERRY

Born December 22, 1939 in Philadelphia, Pennsylvania where he spent his childhood. Attended the Philadelphia Museum College of Art.

In 1960 Jerry Pinkney moved from Philadelphia to Boston and after a year and a half as a designer-illustrator with one of Boston's leading design studios, he and two other illustrators started Kaleidoscope Studio. "I now have my own studio working as an illustrator and designer. Besides this Boston studio, I also have one at home." At his home in Sharon, Massachusetts, Mr. Pinkney is surrounded by three sons and one daughter. Mr. Pinkney, who characterizes his work as decorative — but recently becoming less decorative and more realistic — does his illustrations primarily in full color, making separations for them.

PITZ, HENRY CLARENCE*

Born June 16, 1895 in Philadelphia where childhood was Spent. Attended Philadelphia Museum School of Art and Spring Garden Institute, Philadelphia, Pennsylvania.

Since Henry Pitz grew up in an atmosphere of books and music, he developed an early enthusiasm for Howard Pyle, Edwin Abbey and the British book illustrators. He is a painter, print maker and muralist and works in the fields of book, magazine and advertising illustration. He has illustrated over 160 books, the majority in the field of children's books. Among his early books are *Micah Clarke* (1922) by Conan Doyle, *Prester John* (1928) by John Buchan and *Voyages of Columbus* (1931) by Washington Irving. In 1963 he illustrated James Fenimore Cooper's *The Spy* for the Limited Editions Club. About this he comments, "I was able to bring to this all the knowledge accumulated in writing and researching our two books on American costume." These two books of which he was co-author are *Early American Costume* and *Early American Dress* and are still another indication of Henry Pitz's strong bent for history. He is the author-illustrator of seven books on technical aspects of drawing and painting as well as numerous magazine articles. He has also written extensively on book illustration with articles in such magazines as *American Artist, Horn Book, Print Quarterly, American Heritage* and *Design Magazine* and two books, *Treasury of American Book Illustration* and *Illustrating Children's Books* (Watson-Guptill, 1963). Mr. Pitz has over the years won many awards for drawings and water colors and is represented in the permanent collections of numerous museums. He has taught at the Pennsylvania Academy of the Fine Arts, is Professor Emeritus of the Philadelphia College of Art where for twenty-five years he was Director of the Department of Illustration and Decoration, and has been a visiting lecturer or critic at the University of Pennsylvania, Cleveland Institute of Art and the Newark School of Art. At present he is on the faculty of the Pennsylvania Institute of Art and Culture. His home is in Plymouth Meeting, Pennsylvania, and he has been recently working on a documentary film about N. C. Wyeth which is being sponsored by the Pennsylvania State Museum.

POLITI, LEO*

Born November 21, 1908 in Fresno, California, where early childhood was spent; later in Milan, Italy. Attended Art Institute, Royal Palace of Monza, near Milan.

"When I was seven," Leo Politi writes, "my family took me to Italy where I lived for seventeen years. I started to draw even before we went to Italy, and before we left America my mother bought me a colorful Indian Chief costume and when I wore it to school in Italy the boys and girls watched me with wonder and followed me to and from school; in fact I became so great a center of attention that my teacher had to ask my mother not to let me wear it to school. One of the books I liked best in Italy was *Pinocchio*, illustrated by Attilio Mussino. At the age of fifteen I was awarded a scholarship to study at the Art Institute at the Royal Palace of Monza near Milan, for-

merly the residence of King Umberto the First of Italy — a beautiful building surrounded by a great park with lovely old trees and a lake. Here, too, were gardens and a zoo where we drew flowers and animals. It was from this school that I was graduated as a teacher of art. The deepest impressions of my travels in Italy were the works of art in churches and museums, the lovely northern lakes and the beautiful hillside country of central Italy. We also lived in London one year where I went to school. I remember one street where I used to go to watch artists draw on the sidewalk. On my return voyage to America, on the way to California we sailed through the Panama Canal and I was fascinated by the warm beauty of the Central American countries. This, and a later journey to Mexico, made me wish to study and learn more of Latin America and its people, their customs and their great civilization. When I first saw Olvera Street, the colorful Mexican street in Los Angeles, I thought it would be just right for work and for studying. So I settled there where I have sold pictures ever since. More than anything else, I love to draw pictures of small children." He is married and has two children. Mr. Politi has illustrated many books by other authors, including Ruth Sawyer's *The Least One*, 1941, and Helen Garrett's *Angelo the Naughty One*, 1944, and has done a great deal of illustrating for children's magazines. In addition he has written as well as illustrated a number of children's books, among them *Song of the Swallows* which was awarded the Caldecott Medal in 1950. In 1960, he was given the Regina Medal by the Catholic Library Association "for his contribution to children's literature." Leo Politi has worked almost entirely in full color, using water colors "but sometimes I mix them with white and the colors become chalky, a tempera-like process. For my earlier books, I did the illustrations in four-color overlays but since *A Boat for Peppe*, I have made all the illustrations without having to use overlays."

POLLACK, REGINALD M. (Murray)

Born September 29, 1924 in Middle Village, Long Island, New York. Childhood spent in New York City. Attended Académie de la Grande Chaumière, Paris.

Reginald Pollack, who spends the largest part of his time painting, writes in regard to his interests as a child, "I always drew pictures, because words seemed to leave something out. I liked best the books that gave me a lot to look at, especially *The Brownies* and the pre-Disney *Pinnochio*. Later I realized that to tell my own story with pictures, I had to model myself after the greatest artists so that I would be able to draw anything that came to mind. This has taken a long time — by now, I can draw a lot of things that begin to show the outlines of my story." Mr. Pollack uses pencil or, as in the case of *The Quest of the Gole*, pen and India ink since he believes "that the simplest of materials are still the best and most useful."

PORTAL, COLETTE

Born March 9, 1936 in Paris, France. Attended Ecole de Dessin Academique et Classique, Paris.

Colette Portal says that she has always drawn, that at school she filled her notebooks with colored drawings and as a consequence was poor at almost every subject — especially spelling — except drawing. After four years at art school she did some work for greeting cards. The first of her books, *The Life of a Queen*, was one that she also wrote. It is illustrated in full color with Chinese inks. She is married to a well-known designer, Jean Michel Folon, and they have a small son.

POWERS, RICHARD M.*

Born February 24, 1921 in Chicago, Illinois and here his childhood was spent. Attended Loyola University, Chicago; Chicago Art Institute; University of Illinois, Art School; New School for Social Research, New York.

Richard M. Powers writes, "I have trained myself to do a variety of work; writing and illustrating for children being among the more interesting varieties. While I should certainly not care to do children's books only, I should be equally reluctant to eliminate them altogether. In a good deal of the 'adult' work I do there is little or no opportunity to do anything fresh; in the children's field freshness is the essential quality of the best work. I have been doing more writing recently, *The Cavedwellers* for example, with a view to that ideal situation of doing the whole book, art, design and text. I entered the Army in Chicago and was stationed at the Signal Corps Photo Center in Long Island City for the last three years of the war. When I was discharged I stayed on in New York and have lived in the East ever since. Besides New York City, I have lived on Monhegan Island, Maine; in Dorset, Vermont; Croton Falls, New York; and I now live in Ridgefield, Connecticut." Mr. Powers has also illustrated under the pseudonym "Terry Gorman." He is a painter and has had nine one-man shows in the past ten years as well as having his work exhibited in a number of museum exhibitions. An article on Mr. Powers appears in the January 1960 issue of *American Artist*.

PRICE, CHRISTINE*

Born April 15, 1928 in London, England. Childhood was spent in Gerrards Cross, Buckinghamshire, England, and in Irvington-on-Hudson, New York. Attended Vassar College; Art Students League, New York; Central School of Arts and Crafts, London.

"My childhood in the English countryside gave me a love of history, nature and the out-of-doors, and from these roots my work has sprung," Christine Price writes. "In 1946 I made my first pictures for children's books and was busy illustrating until 1949, when I returned to England for two years of art study. While there I finished writing and illustrating a book for children, *Three Golden Nobles*, and started another, *The Dragon and the Book*. Since my return to the States, I have lived at Castleton, Vermont, with occasional travels here and there, generally with a book in mind — a journey to Spain and the Near East in 1963 to do research for *The Story of Moslem Art*, a visit to Greece in 1965 and a field trip to Florida for the illustrations for *Cypress Country*. Natural history, especially the study of birds, continues to be my chief hobby. During the last ten years, I have spent most of my time in writing and illustrating my own books. I have tried to vary my technique and the mood of my drawings according to the book, whether or not I had written the text. I feel that an illustrator should be self-effacing, forgetting his own personality and mannerisms and immersing himself in the author's story, trying to see the characters and scenes through the author's eyes. These years have seen the fulfillment of two dreams for me: the opportunity to work on picture books and the chance to enter wholeheartedly into book design. It is the greatest joy to me to plan the complete book. The designing of picture books is sheer fun; planning a book of the length of *Made in the Middle Ages* presents more of a challenge but enthusiasm drives one through the difficulties. For the careful drawings needed in this book and *Made in the Renaissance*, I had to evolve a new technique. There were two flat colors to be used, and in doing the separations I made the black drawing in ink on the acetate overlay and scratched into the dark areas with a razor blade, as though I were using scratchboard. This helped me in delineating and modelling the rather complicated objects in the illustrations. I have found working on each book a fresh experience, and above all, a way of sharing delight."

PRICE, GARRETT

Born: November 21, 1896 in Bucyrus, Kansas. Childhood spent in Saratoga, Wyoming. Attended University of Wyoming and Art Institute of Chicago.

As a child, Garrett Price says he devoured the cartoons and illustrations in the many magazines and newspapers that came into his home. Later, he illustrated the University of Wyoming Annual for three years and then after a year at the Chicago Art Institute, he took a job as an illustrator on the *Chicago Tribune*. During World War I, he was editorial and sports cartoonist on the *Great Lakes Navy Bulletin*. Since 1925 he has been on the staff of the *New Yorker* and is best known for his cartoons and the more than 100 covers he has done for that and other national magazines. Garrett Price describes his book illustrations as representational vignettes. They are usually done as ink outline with half-tone washes. Mr. Price and his wife live in Westport, Connecticut.

PRIMROSE, JEAN LOGAN

Born June 16, 1917 in Glasgow, Scotland. Her childhood was spent there and in London, England. Attended Hammersmith Art School, City and Guilds of London Art School, Faculty of Arts, London.

Miss Primrose was born into a musical family. Her brother is the well-known viola player, William Primrose. "I started in music," she writes, "but when the constant music practice proved to be too much for the neighbors, I gave up my piano, since it was a hobby for me as against the professional status of the rest of the family. I feel all this lay dormant and emerged some years later in the form of Art. My portrait painting has been exhibited in the Royal Academy, the Royal Society of Portrait Painters and elsewhere." Miss Primrose's portraits include many of children. Through Rumer Godden's sister, her children's portraiture came to the attention of Miss Godden, who was at the time looking for an illustrator for her children's books. This resulted in Jean Primrose illustrating all of Rumer Godden's children's books. The first one, *Miss Happiness and Miss Flower*, was a runner-up for the 1961 Kate Greenaway Medal in England. Because of the combined doll and human elements in this book and *Little Plum*, Miss Primrose combined a representational and a decorative treatment. "For the decorative part concerning the two Japanese dolls, I attempted to stamp on all of the colors, using various materials leaving a texture — net, leaves, flowers cut out on the ends of cork, grasses, linens and so forth." Though she considers London her headquarters, she spends most of each year painting in America, Jamaica and Canada — and, in between, continues to illustrate books.

PROVENSEN, ALICE*

Born August 14, 1918. Childhood was spent in Chicago. Attended the School of the Art Institute of Chicago; University of California at Los Angeles; and Art Students League, New York.

Alice Provensen is the wife of Martin Provensen, also an artist and illustrator. As children both Alice and Martin loved books and the illustrations of Rackham, Dulac, Pyle and the other great illustrators of children's books. Although they both lived in Chicago and attended the same art schools and the University of California, they did not meet until they were quite grown. The ambition of both was to make beautiful books themselves, so when they met it was very natural that they should pool their talents. They have a daughter, Karen, and their home is on a farm near Staatsburg, New York, in Dutchess County; surrounded by their favorite models: geese, goats, cats, chickens, ducks, sheep and lambs.

PROVENSEN, MARTIN*

Born July 10, 1916. Childhood spent in Chicago, New York, Boston, Washington, D. C. and California. Attended University of California at Los Angeles.

Martin Provensen is married to Alice Provensen, who collaborates with him on children's book illustrations. Their friend Gustav Tenngren introduced them to a New York publisher, and this contract resulted in their first book, *The Fireside Book of Folk Songs*, which was followed by many others. They wrote as well as illustrated *The Animal Fair*. Their illustrations have been exhibited and have received a number of awards. Their books have been included in the American Institute of Graphic Arts Shows and appeared on several of the annual listings by the *New York Times* of the "Ten Best Illustrated Children's Books." The Provensens write, "Our style is constantly changing, as we have never felt we have been successful in solving all the problems illustration involves, but we do not indulge in random experimentation, working rather toward the goal of directness and simplicity, the ultimate objective being the authentic statement." The Provensens work in full color gouache, design as well as illustrate their books, and in some cases make special use of lettering as part of their compositions. Articles about them have appeared in *American Artist*, 1959 and *Famous Artists Magazine*, 1961.

PURDY, SUSAN GOLD

Born May 17, 1939 in New York City. Childhood spent in Dayton, Ohio and Wilton, Connecticut. Attended Vassar College; Sorbonne and Ecole des Beaux Arts, Paris; New York University.

"Because my mother is an artist," writes Mrs. Purdy, "I have been surrounded by paintings and other forms of art since childhood. I was always encouraged to experiment with different art materials, and at first worked primarily with various craft techniques. After graduating from college, where I majored in Fine Arts (painting) and English, I worked for two years as a textile designer in New York City. After my marriage in 1963 to Geoffrey Purdy, we moved to a farmhouse in Wilton, Connecticut. While still in high school, I had taught arts and crafts in several summer camps. In the summers of 1964 and 1965, I co-directed the Wilton Music and Art Day Camp for girls six to twelve years old. The camp was a valuable testing ground and source of ideas for future books. Now however, the camp has been temporarily discontinued because of the pressure of work on these books." Mrs. Purdy has prepared separations, either on acetate or bristol blues, for all of her books, three of which have been in full color.

QUACKENBUSH, ROBERT MEAD

Born July 23, 1929 in California. Childhood spent in Phoenix, Arizona. Graduated in 1956 from Art Center School, Los Angeles.

As a child, Robert Quackenbush spent a great deal of time reading, drawing and building things. In high school his art teacher, Frances Kanpanke, encouraged him. After military service and graduating from art school where he studied advertising design, he went home to Phoenix and a job with an advertising agency. A year later he went to New York City and continued in advertising but felt restless. He took a course at The New School for Social Research from Clare Romano which introduced him to woodcuts, now one of his favorite and most used media. In 1961, he got his first illustration commission from *Sports Illustrated* and shortly afterward began free-lancing. Since then he has done illustrations for magazines, advertising and books — his first was *The Steadfast Tin Soldier* in 1964 — and has had his work exhibited in a number of shows. In his illustrating of children's books he has used not only woodcuts but also water colors as in *The Selfish Giant* and crayon and wash as in *A Long Long Time*. He has designed as well as illustrated his books and with the exception of his water colors, works entirely with separations either on acetate or with wash on rice paper. His magazine assignments have taken him to such places as Greece, Italy, England and the Scandinavian countries, but his studio-home is in New York City, where he stores his hundreds of woodblocks by hanging them in rows on his wall. An article on Mr. Quackenbush appears in the April 1965 issue of *American Artist*.

RAIBLE, ALTON ROBERT

Born November 14, 1918 in Modesto, California. Childhood was spent in the central valley of California. Attended California College of Arts and Crafts in Oakland.

Alton Raible describes his art career as beginning when his parents provided him with pencil and paper to keep him quiet while they ran their lunch counter. "I received my first art lesson at five and a half," he continues, "when my Mother pointed out that only one end of a house is visible at a time. Words of encouragement from my high school teacher increased my enthusiasm for an art career, but the goal was achieved rather slowly since after graduation I worked six years in a bank and one year in a shipyard, before going to an art college." Alton Raible now teaches art at the College of Marin which "has provided opportunity and conserved enough energy to permit me to paint and make serigraphs. I became involved with children's books through Zilpha Keatley Snyder when Atheneum accepted her fantasy, *Season for Ponies*. The editor, Jean Karl, liked the samples Mrs. Snyder persuaded me to send in and gave me the commission — and has since given

me four more. It has been a surprising development and a very satisfying one." Mr. Raible characterizes his work as representational and works primarily in black-and-white or two colors using acrylic polymer applied with painting knives for a base texture over which ink washes, pencil, sandpaper, and pen and ink may be used — or any other material that provides black or white. *Rolling the Cheese*, 1966, was in two colors plus black using overlay separations on acetate with ink washes. His wife and a partner run the Pacific Day School, an ungraded primary school. "If the children at the school don't react favorably to a picture," Mr. Raible comments, "it's worth reconsidering before sending it off." The Raibles and their two children live in San Anselmo, California.

RAND, PAUL*

Born August 15, 1914 in Brooklyn, New York where he spent his childhood. Attended Pratt Institute and Brooklyn Institute of Arts and Sciences. Also studied at Parsons School of Design, and under George Grosz at Art Students League, New York.

Paul Rand is a designer, author, painter, teacher, and illustrator. He was apprenticed to George Switzer Studios for two years, and at the age of twenty-three was art director of *Esquire* and *Apparel Arts* magazines. He writes, "Illustrating and designing children's books is strictly not business with me. It is done solely for pleasure and fun. And, incidentally, helps my so-called serious work — which is often not so much fun. Book jackets and book designing also are a pleasant hobby (and a form of expiation) having devoted most of my life to doing advertising art." Mr. Rand's books have been selected for the American Institute of Graphic Arts Exhibits. He has won the Art Directors Club Medal, and has received numerous awards from the Society of Typographic Arts, and many other associations, and he is a Fellow of the British Royal Society of Arts. Both *I Know a Lot of Things* (1956) and *Sparkle and Spin* (1957) were selected for "The Ten Best Illustrated Children's Books" by the *New York Times*. Mr. Rand, who has taught at Cooper Union and Pratt Institute is an honorary Professor of Tama University, Tokyo. In addition, he is the author of *Thoughts on Design*, Wittenborn, 1946, *The Trademarks of Paul Rand*, Wittenborn, 1960, and numerous articles published both here and in England. A book entitled *Paul Rand* by Yusaku Kamekura was published by Knopf, 1960. Mr. Rand, who lives in Weston, Connecticut, is presently teaching at Yale University and is consultant to IBM, Westinghouse, and other corporations.

RASKIN, ELLEN

Born March 13, 1928 in Milwaukee, Wisconsin where she spent her childhood. Attended the University of Wisconsin.

"My first love was music — the piano," writes Miss Raskin. "I didn't consider studying art until my third year at the University of Wisconsin. I have been a successful illustrator and designer in New York City for the past ten years. I combined both ambitions for the first time in *Songs of Innocence* for which I illustrated Blake's poems, and set them to music. In this book I reverted to my original style — woodcuts. Over the past few years I have developed a great many techniques — *Nothing Ever Happens on My Block*, fine line cartoon with color overlays; *Edgar Allan Poe*, pen and ink pointillish; *The Jewish Sabbath*, heavy line decorative with flat color overlays." Miss Raskin works primarily in four colors and characterizes her work as decorative illustration. She always designs and does the necessary mechanical preparation for the books, and in some cases also writes the text. She has used type and lettering in special ways, particularly in *Nothing Ever Happens on My Block*. A large part of her work has been book jackets and book covers, having made over a thousand since she started free-lancing. She has also done magazine, pharmaceutical and advertising illustrations. Ellen Raskin has received awards from the American Institute of Graphic Arts, Society of Illustrators, Art Directors Clubs of New York and Detroit, Type Directors Club, and the *World Journal Tribune's Book Week* which chose *Nothing Ever Happens on My Block* as a Prize Book in the 1966 Spring Children's Book Festival. She now lives in New York City with her teenage daughter, Susan.

RAVIELLI, ANTHONY*

Born July 1, 1916 in New York City where he spent his childhood. Attended Cooper Union and Art Students League, New York.

"I learned to draw before I learned to walk and my first artistic works were rendered, literally, on the sidewalks of New York long before I was old enough to attend school. Crowds collected to watch in amused amazement as a five-year-old artist, wielding sticks of colored chalk, covered the streets with fiery dragons and daring knights in mortal combat. After attending Textile High School, I continued my art studies and then began my formal career as a portrait painter and later went on to illustrating and a long association with advertising agencies. Even World War II failed to interrupt my career, for during three years of service I painted instructional murals and designed visual training aids. When I returned to civilian life, I broadened into medical illustration, a subject that has always fascinated me. It was during this restless period that I decided to experiment in technique and try other media. Having worked in oil, tempera and water color, I tried etching and wood-engraving. These led to the development of my present scratch-board technique. In 1954, I used this technique for *Wonders of the Human Body*, the first of five books in the area of science that I have written. For *The World Is Round*, I used colored inks on scratchboard. I work with separations on two-color illustrations only. I prefer to render full color illustrations for process reproduction." Mr. Ravielli designs as well as illustrates his own books. "Strangely, my book illustrations led me into still another specialty. *Wonders of the Human Body* brought me to the attention of *Sports Illustrated* in 1955. The editor was attracted to my technique and my facility in drawing the human body in action. My long association with that magazine has established me in the field of sports illustration. I live in Stamford, Connecticut in a rather large house with a studio attached. I have a very patient wife and three impatient children. I prefer to work at night when the children are asleep and the phone stops ringing, so my work day usually begins at 9:00 P.M. and ends about 8:00 A.M.

REED, PHILIP

Born January 17, 1908 in Park Ridge, Illinois, where his childhood was spent. Attended Art Institute of Chicago.

Mr. Reed writes, "My father was a very bookish man. He ran a private press for some years during my boyhood and I served as printer's devil. I suppose that is where I became interested in the physical appearance of books and printing. I do not remember a time when I was *not* interested in illustration. I illustrated most of my school books in the margins to the disgust of my teachers. My first woodcut was cut when I was nine or ten. It was a crow and not a bad one. I have cut a lot worse since! I opened a printing shop, Broadside Press, when I left art school and have either had one, or been associated with one ever since — hence my interest in fine typography. It was my good fortune to study at the Art Institute of Chicago when the late Ernst Detterer was head of the department of typography and illustration. He was one of the finest teachers of graphic art and was a tremendous influence. At that time, I devoted much time to studying the work of Pyle, Caldecott, Lovat, Fraser, etc. — all of whose work, I think, had an influence on the work I have done since. Almost all of my work has been engraved, and, of course, printed letterpress. I use a great deal of color — almost always five or six colors, frequently seven." Philip Reed does the design as well as the illustrations of his books and sometimes does the text. In addition, he does the typography, sometimes hand-setting the type. For his outstanding woodcuts, Mr. Reed has received countless awards and his work can be seen at the Library of Congress, Art Institute of Chicago, Victoria and Albert Museum in London and throughout the world. Articles discussing his work appeared in *American Artist*, May 1948 and September 1949. Married and the father of three children, he is now living in St. Joseph, Michigan where he is associated with the A. and W. Roe Company.

REY, H. A. (Hans Augusto)*

Born 1898 in Hamburg, Germany. Childhood was spent in Germany.

H. A. Rey's first children's books were published in France and England while the Reys were living in Paris in 1937. Together with his wife, Margaret Rey, he was working on some new books, when Hitler's armies overran Europe in 1940. The Reys managed to leave Paris on bicycles the day before the Nazis entered the city. They finally reached Lisbon and from there went to Rio de Janeiro, Brazil, a place quite familiar to them, for Mr. Rey had lived there earlier for twelve years and they had been married there in 1935. Their goal was the United States and they arrived in New York in October 1940 with four new manuscripts, one of them *Curious George* which was published by Houghton Mifflin in 1941. In 1946 the Reys became American citizens. They now live during the winter in Cambridge, Massachusetts and during the summer in Waterville, New Hampshire. Mr. Rey begins each book by making a dummy in pencil on onion skin paper and colors these rough sketches on the back of the paper. "From those roughs," Mr. Rey explains, "I do complete color separations — the black key drawings in wash, india ink, and black crayon on drawing paper. The overlay I do in black and gray crayon, gray gouache, and flat Bourges grays on acetate. As a rule, I make *no* full color original drawings." Mr. Rey designs and illustrates his books, and collaborates with his wife on the texts. He letters the story right on the dummy so the printer can follow the layout closely. "This way," he writes, "text and illustrations are all of one piece." In addition to the *Curious George* books, H. A. Rey has written two books on astronomy, *The Stars — A New Way to See Them* and *Find the Constellations*, both using a new method of star identification he has invented.

RIBBONS, IAN*

Born August 20, 1924 in London, England, where his childhood was spent. Attended Beckenham School of Art, Kent, and The Royal College of Art, London.

Ian Ribbons speaks of his urban outlook, his preoccupation with people, affairs and the minutiae of daily life resulting naturally in his interest in illustration as against decoration. "War service in India and Burma, travel in Italy, Sicily, Yugoslavia and Austria, and a perpetual liking for exploring new corners of London all confirm a belief in human happenings as the basis of any art that concerns me." He has an ambition "to combine the spontaneity of illustration with the permanence and color of painting." After teaching art for a while he gave it up to become a free-lance illustrator and painter. Mr. Ribbons, who works primarily in pen and ink, brush, and splatterwork, feels that over the past ten years his style has "become simpler with more emphasis on figures as against background."

RIPPER, CHARLES L.*

Born October 28, 1929 in Pittsburgh, Pennsylvania. Childhood spent in Evans City, Pennsylvania. Attended Art Institute of Pittsburgh.

"My earliest memories of childhood," writes Charles L. Ripper, "are of the weekend walks with my father as he searched for scenes to paint. As soon as his easel was set up I would entertain myself catching insects, watching birds and turning over every stone in sight. My mother was the art teacher in the local school and I always had all the paper I needed for drawing. I drew constantly from first grade on, and by the time I was twelve I knew I wanted to be an artist by profession. My love for nature grew also; I spent every free hour in the woods. While in art school I illustrated an article for *Nature Magazine* and through it was asked to illustrate my first book. I finished the sixty drawings for this book just before my twentieth birthday. My first full-time job was with Carnegie Museum, as staff illustrator. I spent the next two years in the army as a map draftsman." Charles L. Ripper was artist and layout man for Standard Printing and Publishing Company from 1953 to 1965. He is now a free-lance illustrator and lives with his wife and three daughters in Huntington, West Virginia. Mr. Ripper, who works primarily in black-and-white, has used various media such as pencil and charcoal, wash, and scratchboard. He did two books with pencil on grained acetate. He works out the page breaks for his books and does the dummy, design and art for the jackets. With the exception of *Song of the Seasons* Mr. Ripper also wrote the text for his books. In addition to his books, Charles Ripper has done twenty full-color paintings for the National Wildlife Federation in Washington, D. C. to be used on their conservation stamps.

RISWOLD, GILBERT

Born in Chicago, Illinois. Childhood was spent in Oak Park, Illinois and Salt Lake City, Utah.

Mr. Riswold writes that "through the years I have found myself involved with various fields of art work — first through an artist in the family and early association with books and the performing arts; then an introduction to motion pictures and special effects work in Air Corps Training Films; then in poster, advertising, editorial art, and portraits in California and New York. The adventure into illustrating children's books is comparatively recent and certainly most engaging. It would appear that all these varied experiences have been useful in solving the problems and approach each book presents. I do employ a variety of media in illustration for several reasons — it sometimes helps develop the desired mood or atmosphere of the story; for the change of pace it affords; for personal experimentation." For example, Gilbert Riswold has worked in oil, *Goodnight Mr. Beetle*; ink line, *Schoolbell in the Valley*; and pastel, *Lucy Gray*. He has worked primarily in full color. For separations, when he does them, he prefers vellum. His style, which he characterizes as realistic, "has moved from being rather representational to a more interpretive realism." Gilbert Riswold has won awards from the Art Directors Club of Chicago for his posters and from the Society of Illustrators for

Poems for Weather Watching and *Goodnight, Mr. Beetle.* He and his wife live in Newtown, Connecticut where he also has his studio.

RIVOLI, MARIO

Born January 31, 1943 in New York City where he spent his childhood. Attended School of Industrial Art, School of Visual Art, and the Art Students League, New York.

"I'm lucky," says Mr. Rivoli, "I have always wanted to be an artist. In English class I'd draw people. I worked one year in a real estate firm drawing floor plans which killed me. I decided then never to go back to a nine-to-five position. I love art nouveau — its freedom. Many of my art nouveau illustrations are decorative. I play with this style and have a good time. My other work, line drawings in pencil, is an expression of me and of the present." Mario Rivoli's first book, *A Song for Clowns,* was in black-and-white. In *Do Tigers Ever Bite Kings,* he used linoleum blocks (four colors and tints of those colors). "Each block was cut, then printed with oil base ink and finally positioned as original art. Color separations for each color and each tint were registered." In 1965, Mr. Rivoli won the Society of Illustrators Award. He lives in New York City and owns a shop called "The Tunnel of Love."

ROBBINS, RUTH

Born December 29, 1918 in Newark, New Jersey. Childhood was spent in New Jersey. Attended Pratt Institute, Brooklyn and the School of Design in Chicago.

"Since school I have always worked in some field of graphic art," writes Miss Robbins. "In 1957 my husband, Herman Schein, and I started Parnassus Press, a children's book publishing house. Since then I have concentrated fully on books for children, as designer, illustrator, author, and production manager. When my son was a little boy I learned that children respond in many surprising and uninhibited ways to art and drawings in books, giving the artist great freedom and an opportunity to think creatively. I design as well as illustrate each book, and therefore, find every book I do a complete experience in creating a visual expression — absorbing the story, exploring materials and techniques, selecting the type, and developing a concept for the book as a whole. Every manuscript is different and requires a new 'seeing' or visual expression. My materials and techniques are varied, responding to the requirements of the story. I have worked in pencil on vellum, dry brush, wet wash on rice paper, and ink line on wet rice paper." *A Penny and a Periwinkle,* for instance, was done with wash and pen line on wet rice paper in three colors, color separated. Miss Robbins finds it important to discuss the illustrations and the mechanical requirements with the printer before the finished art is made to achieve the best results in printing. Miss Robbins and her family make their home in California.

ROBERTS, DOREEN

Born 1922 in London, England where she spent her childhood. Attended S. W. Essex Technical College School of Art; Slade School of Fine Art, London University; London University Institute of Education.

"From an early age I enjoyed drawing more than anything else," says Miss Roberts. "Unable to afford training, I worked as an office clerk for two years. During World War II I joined the Women's Land Army and after demobilization in 1945, I secured an ex-service grant for training." Since 1952, Doreen Roberts, who makes her home in London, has been head of the art department of a girls' grammar school. She writes, "I simply love drawing, so children's books are the obvious answer. If I had to choose, I would work in black-and-white. I use the conventional materials such as gouache, ink, oil crayons, brushes, pen, and an occasional help with a fingernail. I am trying to get as much out of them as possible and use them freshly. Since I am interested in ancient and medieval history, western and oriental, my favorite subjects are knights, Moors, battles, etc. — anything romantic and vigorous. I find films a source of excitement and inspiration. The specimens which were instrumental in getting me the commission to do *Saul* were inspired by the film 'El Cid' which I found very beautiful visually." Doreen Roberts won an award in 1963 from the Worshipful Company of Goldsmiths giving her a term's leave which she spent in Canada making drawings and studying the work of the National Film Board.

ROCKER, FERMIN

Born December 22, 1907 in London, England. Childhood was spent in England until he was eleven, when he moved to Germany. Attended County Council School in London, Realschule in Berlin, Municipal School of Arts and Crafts, Berlin.

"I have come to most things rather late in life," writes Mr. Rocker, "and book illustration is one of them. The first book I illustrated, *A Pet for the Orphelines,* was published by Harper in 1962. I actually manifested an early interest in drawing and painting but it was not until I reached my thirties that I devoted all my time to those pursuits. After finishing school in Germany I worked for five years as a commercial lithographer, serving a full apprenticeship in that trade. Later when I came to the United States, I drifted into the animated cartoon field. From about 1938 on I devoted all my time to painting, etching, and lithography. I tried my hand — not too successfully — at commercial work. I finally discovered that of all the commercial applications of art, book illustration, while not the most remunerative, was the most satisfying one. An added factor may have been my inability to come to terms with art and music that need to be 'explained' before they can be enjoyed. Children, before they receive their cultural brainwashing at least, seem to share my sentiments in this regard. I have not found working with a simple, uncompromising ink line too easy, yet with the exception of *The Piper*, which used wash drawings, this is the technique I have used in almost all my books. On most of my jackets the key drawing was done in ink and the added colors with pencil or crayon on acetate or dinobase." Mr. Rocker's work has been shown at the Library of Congress, Metropolitan Museum of Art, and Brooklyn Museum, among others. It has won awards at the Philadelphia Print Club and the Brooklyn Museum. Mr. Rocker has a ten-year-old son who, in addition to other interests, likes to draw. His wife, Ruth, is a free-lance copy editor and they live in New York City.

ROJANKOVSKY, FEODOR STEPANOVICH*

Born December 21, 1891 in Mitava, Russia. Childhood was spent in Reval (now Tallinn) and St. Petersburg (now Leningrad). Attended Reval High School and Academy of Fine Arts, Moscow.

"Two great events determined the course of my childhood," says Feodor Rojankovsky. "I was taken to the zoo and saw the most marvelous creatures on earth . . . and while my admiration was running high, I was given a set of crayons. My father was a school director, my two elder brothers had a talent for painting, and my love for art was born in our family. After the death of my father, when I was five, the family passed through hard times but we never parted from Father's valuable Library, until a revolution destroyed it. There were big books in this library and I sat for hours admiring them. I remember so vividly Milton's *Paradise Lost* and *Don Quixote* and the *Bible* with the magnificent illustrations by Doré. The whole environment in which I was brought up pushed me toward artistic expression. I was eight or nine when I started, together with my sister, to draw illustrations for *Robinson Crusoe*, one of my favorite books. . . . Later, when I went to school in Reval Tallinn . . . my love for art was enhanced and strengthened by a passion for nature . . . all these early contacts with nature played a decisive role in my development as an artist. In 1912 I entered the Moscow Fine Arts Academy but two years later I was serving as an officer in the 1914-17 campaign. My regiment traveled through Poland, Prussia, Austria and Rumania. My war sketches were reproduced by art magazines. During the Revolution I started to make children's book illustrations for the young Ukrainian Republic. In 1919 I was mobilized by the 'Volunteer Army' (White Army), and soon my military career was finished behind barbed wire in Poland. Since then I have seen many countries and had many occupations." In Paris Mr. Rojankovsky did work for several publishers, but his first children's book to be published there (and also in America) was *Daniel Boone*, Domino Press, 1931. Illustrations for many children's books followed, including several by Esther Averill, and a series devised by Père Castor to be printed in quantity and sold cheaply. In 1941, after the German occupation of

Paris, Mr. Rojankovsky came to the United States. His *Tall Book of Mother Goose* appeared the next year, and from then on he has illustrated nearly 100 books. Mr. Rojankovsky has worked in various media, largely in black-and-white or full color, but occasionally in two or three colors, for which he has done separations on acetate. For his full color work he has used lithography, water colors and gouache. In 1956 his illustrations for John Langstaff's *Frog Went A-Courtin'* received the Caldecott Medal. Mr. Rojankovsky has also received the Art Directors Club Gold Medal for color illustration in advertising, and, in 1953, the Silver Medal of the Silver Jubilee of the Limited Editions Club. He lives with his wife and their daughter Tanya, born in 1948, in Bronxville, New York. Articles about the artist have appeared in *Library Journal*, March 15, 1956; *Horn Book*, August 1956; *American Artist*, January 1957.

ROSE, GERALD

Born July 27, 1935 in Hong Kong where he spent his childhood. Attended the Royal Academy, London.

Trained as an artist and a working painter, Mr. Rose writes, "I started illustrating children's books when I met my wife who was then teaching in a primary school. At that time she was frustrated by the lack of reasonable picture books so we were stimulated into producing something ourselves. *How St. Francis Tamed the Wolf* was the first." Although Mr. Rose works primarily in full color, he has also done a lot of work in black-and-white. "When using full color," Mr. Rose continues, "I work mainly with gouache but might also incorporate colored inks, wax, oil crayons or any other variety of materials which might be in the studio." Even though he often works with acetate color separation, Gerald Rose prefers to produce a straight painting. He designs the complete book some of the time and helps shape the text when working with his wife. Gerald Rose was winner of the Kate Greenaway Medal in 1960 for *Old Winkle and the Sea Gulls*. He is currently teaching in the Graphic Design School of the Maidstone College of Art.

ROSS, CLARE ROMANO

Born August 24, 1922 in Palisade, New Jersey. Childhood was spent in New Jersey. Attended Cooper Union School of Art; Ecole des Beaux Arts, Fontainebleau, France; Istituto Statale d'Arte, Florence, Italy.

See entry for Ross, John.

ROSS, JOHN

Born September 25, 1921 in New York City where he spent his childhood. Attended Cooper Union School of Art; Ecole des Beaux Arts, Fontainebleau, France; Istituto Statale d'Arte, Florence, Italy.

John Ross and his wife, Clare Romano Ross, are an artistic team whose personal and professional lives are closely allied. "We collaborate on our books," writes Mrs. Ross, "doing separate illustrations by each of us, yet establishing a direction immediately, so that there is a cohesive, unifying quality in the work. Because we are each fine artists on our own, working in print and painting with separate identities, we feel we can collaborate on books and submerge identities more easily. Since we are printmakers, our relation to the book is very close. We both feel very strongly about a commitment the artist can have to the interpretation of literature." The Rosses were awarded Louis Comfort Tiffany Grants for printmaking and lived in Italy for a year, while Mrs. Ross had a Fulbright grant. In 1965-66, they were artists in residence with the U.S.I.A. exhibition "Graphic Arts, U.S.A." in Romania and Yugoslavia. In addition to working on their own prints, they traveled throughout both countries giving lectures and demonstrations. John Ross writes that they "love to work in woodcuts, but have done many books making color separations on acetate, mainly, and also in line. *Leaves of Grass* was done with woodcuts and *Labor Day* in collage." Both Clare and John Ross have won a number of awards for their work and are represented in many permanent collections. John Ross, who received the prize award in the Second International Color Print Exhibit in Switzerland in 1961, served as President of the Society of American Graphic Artists from 1961 to 1965. The Rosses, who live in Englewood, New Jersey, teach at Pratt Institute, Manhattanville College and the New School for Social Research in New York City. Articles about the couple have appeared in *Art in America*, Fall 1960 and April 1965; *Artist's Proof*, Vol. 5, 1963; and *At Cooper Union*, Summer 1964.

ROSSELLI, COLETTE

Born May 25, 1916 in Losanna, Switzerland. Childhood was spent in Florence, Italy. Attended Ecole di Perfectionnement Langues Etrangeres, Lausanne, Switzerland and Italian High School.

Colette Rosselli is an artist and writer who has published many books in Italy for which she has done the text, illustration and design. Her talents extend to reporting for various Italian magazines and newspapers. In addition, her work has appeared in *Vogue* in 1952 and 1953 and *Mademoiselle*. Mrs. Rosselli writes, "Since I was a small girl, six or seven years old, I always have been drawing or painting. I have never been to painting school." She describes her work as representational and decorative. She has worked in black-and-white and color using pencil, pen, and water color, and makes special use of type and handlettering. She adds, "Presently I am dedicated to oil painting (I am painting fantastic animals) and my technique is extremely precise and minute." Mrs. Rosselli lives in Rome.

ROUNDS, GLEN H.*

Born April 4, 1906 at North Wall, South Dakota. Childhood spent on ranches in South Dakota and Montana. Attended Art Institute, Kansas City, Missouri; Art Students League, New York.

"The horse ranch I grew up on," Glen Rounds writes, "was forty miles from the railroad, but the country was well-stocked with cowboys, sheepherders, bronco busters, wolf trappers, and an occasional sheriff, outlaw, or broken-down buffalo hunter —accomplished yarn spinners, many of them. After high school, wandering from place to place, I picked up skills. I became a right good baker, for one thing. Sign painting proved to be still better, and lightning portraits an improvement on that." He began to experiment with etching and engraving and to paint and draw a good deal. "In 1935, I accidentally started writing stories to go with my drawings, which I have continued to do." Among his early books are *Ol' Paul, the Mighty Logger* (1936) and *Blind Colt* (1941). Since World War II, when he served three years in the Army, he has drawn his son as he has grown up and "instead of cowboys and horses I draw animals and insects from the nearby swamps much of the time." Mr. Rounds works mostly in black-and-white. "From book to book I've used a wide variety of tools — pen, pointed sable brush, large frayed and frowsy bristle brushes, and lately homemade ones of a few bristles from a house painter's brush glued into the end of a reed and trimmed to suit my humor of the moment. This is more the result of improving printing processes than a matter of style. Even ten years ago the drawings for *Trail Drive* (1965), done as they were with a ragged three-bristle brush on charcoal paper, would have probably come out badly. But then, as now, I am more concerned with the movement and characteristic gesture of people and animals than with literal representation. All I try to do is show how the man or creature moved and his stance in the space he occupies." Mr. Rounds and his family make their home in Southern Pines, North Carolina.

RUBIN, EVA JOHANNA

Born 1926 in Berlin, Germany, where she spent her childhood. Attended Hochschule für bildende Künste, Berlin studying with Professor Kaus and Professor Stabenau from 1946 to 1951.

Miss Rubin, who lists her materials as "pen, ink, and patience," characterizes her work as decorative. She generally designs as well as illustrates her books, and does her own color separations. She has illustrated ten books and has been cited for several awards in Germany. *Three by Three*, written by James Kruss, was named one of the fifty most beautiful books published in Germany in 1963. The International Youth Library in Munich selected *Der Bose Bar*, also illustrated by Miss Rubin (to be published by Macmillan in 1967) as one of the best books published in Germany in 1964. She took first prize at the 1964 competition of the Berliner Porzellanmanufaktur and was awarded medals at the 1965 Internationale Buckunstausstellung in Leipzig. Eva Rubin is married to an architect, Rainer König, and lives in Berlin.

RUSSON, MARY GEORGINA

Born May 14, 1937 in Birmingham, England where she spent her childhood. Graduated from Birmingham College of Art and Crafts (National Diploma in Design and Illustration).

Mary Russon was the second eldest of five children. After graduation from grammar school at sixteen and "several unexciting jobs at home, I began nursing training in order to live in London. After four unhappy years, I qualified as a State Registered Nurse and went home as lost as ever. Shortly afterwards, at twenty-three, my parents allowed me to go full-time to the College of Art where I had been taking evening classes. My first love was the theatre and I intended to study theatrical design, but eventually it became obvious that book illustration would be more suitable to my work." After college, she returned to London "where work soon came in thick and fast" and where she now lives with her young daughter. "Most of the work is in black-and-white using simply a pen and india ink. I do lots of jackets, mostly in three-color line; it is a joy occasionally to have a full color one. I hope to do more full color work as time goes by. I love to illustrate 'profuse' subjects, e. g. supermarkets, architecture, crowds, streets, churchyards, rubbish heaps or anything with lots and lots of pattern and detail, when working in black-and-white. Everyday subjects are preferable, unless there is enough historical or geographical reference material to allow one to become completely immersed in the subject."

SANDBERG, LASSE E. M.

Born February 17, 1924 in Stockholm, Sweden where he spent his childhood. Attended Anders Beckman's Art School.

Mr. Sandberg writes, "Nothing special in my childhood influenced me to be an artist. After several years as a press photographer I started making cartoons for magazines and daily papers. In 1950 I married Inger and moved from Stockholm to the countryside (Värmland) and lived in an old farmhouse, where we nowadays spend our holidays. Inger finished her education as an infant school teacher, and in this connection we both studied a great deal of child psychology and read a lot of children's books, so that we became interested in this special subject. In 1953 we made our first picture book together (*Faret Ulrik Far Medalj*)." Mr. Sandberg, who does the illustrations and designs all his wife's text, works primarily in full color and two colors. He has done a lot of work with collage although he finds it sometimes difficult to reproduce satisfactorily. He

characterizes his style as humorous and naive. About working with children's books, he writes, "This is what has given me the most satisfaction of all the different types of illustrations I have been doing. I find that appealing to children's fantasy is enormously stimulating, and according to my opinion it is a very important cultural task to create children's books because these are the child's first meeting with literature." Mr. Sandberg won the 1965 Elsa Beskow Plaque for the best children's book illustrations for *Lilla Spoket Laban* and in 1966, he was given an Honorable Mention by the International Board on Books for Young People in connection with awarding the Hans Christian Andersen Medal. The Sandbergs live in Karlstad, Sweden with their three children, Lena, Niklas, and Mathias. Mr. Sandberg adds, "I work at home, since I like to have the children around me, while Inger writes in a small studio house, five minutes from home."

SARGENT, ROBERT EDWARD

Born March 26, 1933 in Northfield, Vermont where his childhood was spent. Attended Vermont Junior College.

Mr. Sargent recalls that "one of the significant things in my childhood that later directed my interest to animals in fairy tales was the fact that my father was a very skillful hunter and in the shed where I went for wood there was always a rabbit, a fish, or a deer hanging from the roof beams. The sight of the blood and the smell of death frightened me. It seemed so terribly unfair to be a rabbit for example without horns, claws or fangs to fight back. I have always drawn and painted. Paper wasn't sold in very large sizes in our area so I found that by turning rolls of left-over wallpaper on the back, I could find plenty of room to express myself. I had a place in the forest to go, where it was quiet. There, on a great flat rock, I could spend the whole day. I went so often there, that after awhile, it seems like the animals expected me." Mr. Sargent has worked in a number of related fields, coming to writing and illustrating books for children in 1965. Before this he spent nine years in Europe where he wrote and illustrated for children's television in seven countries. He produced documentary film for children in Scandinavia, designed book jackets and has had his lithographs exhibited in Europe as well as various cities in this country. His home at present is in New York City.

SASEK, MIROSLAV

Born November 18, 1916 in Prague. Studied architecture and painting in Prague; Beaux-Arts School, Paris.

For almost twenty years, Mr. Sasek has thrived on a nomadic life. From 1947 to 1951, he traveled and studied in England, Holland, Belgium, Italy, Spain and North Africa. In 1951, he made Munich his home base, but has continued to spend much of his time on painting trips around the world. He first conceived of a series of guide books for children while on a three-week vacation in Paris. He observed many families of tourists with Baedekers, but noticed that no one told the children anything. His first book, *This is Paris*, was published in 1959. Since then he has written and illustrated thirteen of this now famous series.

SAVIOZZI, ADRIANA

Born April 8, 1928 in Florence, Italy where her childhood was spent. Attended Academy of Belle Arts, Florence.

Miss Saviozzi writes that she grew up "surrounded by the beautiful artistic environments of Florence, Italy." After completing her studies, she became interested in children's books as a writer and illustrator. Many of her books published in Italy are used in the schools. She works in black-and-white and color and does separations in several different ways. *The Orphelines in the Enchanted Castle* by Natalie Carlson is an example of her work in black-and-white. She is married to Alfio Mazza, who is also an artist, and has a son, Paul Peter. She came to the United States in 1956 and lives with her family in New York City.

SCARRY, RICHARD MC CLURE

Born June 5, 1919 in Boston, Massachusetts where he spent his childhood. Attended Boston Museum School; Archipenko Art School, Woodstock, New York; Eliot O'Hara Watercolor School, Gooserocks Beach, Maine.

Richard Scarry has been a writer and illustrator of children's books since 1946. His work is what he calls "anthropomorphic, almost always using animals acting and speaking like people. I feel that in the youngest age group this is the best way to teach them." Mr. Scarry works primarily in full color. His *Best Word Book Ever* was done by making a black ink line drawing on an overlay and then doing three additional colors on blueboards. He loves to travel and during his service in the Army, he was an art director, moving from North Africa to Italy and then to France. His wife, Patricia, also writes children's books, some of which he has illustrated. The Scarrys, who have one son, Huck, live in Westport, Connecticut where Mr. Scarry's studio overlooks Long Island Sound.

SCHEELE, WILLIAM E.*

Born April 14, 1920 in Cleveland, Ohio where his childhood was spent. Attended Western Reserve University and Cleveland School of Art.

William E. Scheele's abilities were recognized when he was still very young and he was selected to attend junior and senior high schools that specialized in handling talented pupils. He won scholarships in art and biology to Western Reserve Uni-

versity from which he was graduated. In 1939 he won the first annual Bird Art Contest sponsored by the Cleveland Museum of Natural History, and the next day became a member of their staff. He writes, "I think that what most helped me to decide what I wanted to do was the fact that everybody in our family had a great interest in the out-of-doors. My father had it most strongly and he started his three children collecting everything we could. When I was in junior high school my uncle, who was a commercial artist, started to guide my activities. It was natural that during those years I should decide that if I had my choice I should like to be some sort of a natural history illustrator. My present job was an outgrowth of working with the Preparation Department of the Museum to help put myself through school." After his Army service, in 1946, Mr. Scheele was named head of the Department of Preparation and Exhibition; in April 1949, he was appointed director of the Cleveland Museum of Natural History, which position he has held ever since. He is married and has three sons. Their home is on their tree farm near Chardon, Ohio. For his children's books, Mr. Scheele works primarily in black-and-white using brush and ink as in *The Cave Hunters*; for museum related publications he works in color. His book *Prehistoric Man and The Primates* received the 1958 Gold Medal from the Boys' Club of America.

SCHICK, ELEANOR

Born April 15, 1942 in New York City where she spent her childhood.

Eleanor Schick began to study dance at the age of eight. She performed as a soloist with the Tamiris-Nagrin Dance Company while still in her teens, and trained to teach dance. Miss Schick writes, "However, I outgrew performing and dance altogether. I went into children's book writing and illustrating because it is comfortable to me and I enjoy it, and because it affords me a living. I always liked to draw for my own pleasure, and as a way of studying what I saw around me, I always considered drawing somewhat personal." Miss Schick usually writes her own text, but also illustrates for other authors. She works primarily in black-and-white using pen and ink and pencil. About her style Miss Schick writes, "I have tried more and more to be realistic. My earlier books are quite stylized. However, as I gain a greater facility, they are becoming more realistic, still, of course, conforming to my personal 'sense' of realism." Miss Schick works at home where she can be close to her daughter, Laura, and her husband, also an artist and her "severest critic."

SCHINDELMAN, JOSEPH

Born July 4, 1923 in New York where he spent his childhood. Attended WPA art classes; Art Students League; City College, New York.

When he was twelve, Joseph Schindelman enjoyed drawing caricatures and copying covers of the *Sunday Times Magazine*. His interest in art was renewed in high school, by the encouragement of his art teacher, and in his senior year he won several awards in the National Scholastic Art Competition. Also at that time the art program of the Works Progress Administration provided him with an opportunity to do life drawing and painting in the evenings and on weekends. World War II ended his formal training. After the war he worked for CBS for quite a few years, and is presently promotion art director for Papert, Koenig, Lois, Inc., an advertising agency. About his work as an illustrator Mr. Schindelman writes, "I can't really explain why I illustrate children's books. I don't think it's the money because my production rate per hour is extraordinarily slow. Every book is a struggle for me, and I am able to work only after my regular working hours. I like whimsy and the unexpected in illustrations and I've always felt that children enjoy detail. As a child I was mesmerized by those illustrations that were painstakingly done. They were always full of surprises." He works primarily in black-and-white, and for *The Great Picture Robbery* by Leon Harris used pen and ink drawings with color separations done in pencil. In his work he has used lettering for decoration in combination with the illustrations and sometimes to repeat a phrase or word in the story. He also designs his books. Joseph Schindelman lives with his wife and four children in Bayside, New York.

SCHOENHERR, JOHN CARL

Born July 5, 1935 in New York City where he spent his childhood. Attended Pratt Institute, New York.

John Schoenherr writes, "I illustrate because that way I can draw pictures without having to work at anything else. I have done illustrations for paperback book covers, science fiction magazines, *Reader's Digest* and adult books, but only recently have I become involved with children's books. From the time I was four years old I have liked drawing. When I was twelve, I saw some illustrations by N. C. Wyeth, which had a profound influence, and during high school I realized that I enjoyed drawing more than anything else. I went to Pratt Institute and got very poor grades (I always got poor grades in art, even in elementary school). After graduation I began free-lancing, and have never stopped." Mr. Schoenherr works primarily in black-and-white or three colors. For example, *Rascal* was done in black-and-white scratchboard. He has worked with ink on acetate and Bourges, and sometimes designs his books. He characterizes his work as "subjectively representational" and adds, "I work by myself, and with difficulty." In 1963 Schoenherr won first prize at the National Speleological Society Salon, and in 1965 was awarded the World Science Fiction Award as the best science fiction artist for that year. He has received several citations from the Society of Illustrators. At present, he lives on a 24-acre farm in Stockton, New Jersey with his wife and young daughter.

SCHRAMM, ULRIK

Born December 18, 1912 in Reichenbach, Vogtland, Germany. Childhood was spent at Pirna. Attended Gymnasium at Pirna; Art Academy at Dresden.

Ulrik Schramm began painting and drawing at an early age. While attending the Gymnasium, he commuted to evening classes at the Art Academy in Dresden. School vacations were spent at the Zoological Garden making animal studies. He took his degree in teaching art and, after graduation, worked in a graphic studio of Siemens, a large industrial concern. For several years during World War II, he was a war correspondent and did drawings of horses, especially in Russia. After the war he illustrated school primers which were successful and led to other commissions. Mr. Schramm works in a mixture of brush and pen. "The color application," he describes, "is often done with a refined reproduction method, but black-and-white is printed on material or paper in order to get more texture." He characterizes his style as realism which has gotten more lively over the years. Mr. Schramm writes, "I enjoy using many different techniques and materials and adjust my style and expression to the different tasks without always thinking of sales, and receive in this manner many ideas for my assignments. I believe that only unremitting work and constant willingness to learn and try new ways promises success in my field. Unfortunately, the situation in Germany today is such that the work of the book illustrators is not as well paid as the work of advertising illustrators in which I am also heavily engaged." Mr. Schramm lives in Feldafing, Germany.

SCHREITER, RICK

Born February 16, 1936 in Boston, Massachusetts where he spent his childhood. Attended Harvard College; Rhode Island School of Design.

"I believe my biggest asset," writes Mr. Schreiter, "is the fact that as a child I read voraciously, which, in turn, greatly expanded my imaginative powers. I was fortunate enough to have books to read that fearlessly showed both the good and the bad sides of life, and also books of a high literary quality, both in short supply today." Mr. Schreiter works primarily in black-and-white using pen and ink in all his books. He describes his work in color as being "very pale and just flat washes of ink, the delineation of form being entirely conveyed through a line drawing over the color." He designs as well as illustrates his books and enjoys putting calligraphy in his pictures. His real style, he feels, has developed since 1963 in such books as *How the Whale Became*. "I believe children are *not* frightened by the grotesque and fantastic and that further, they delight in such fare. I try to fill my pictures with detail which, more than anything, I think children enjoy." Rick Schreiter is also involved in doing adult satire. His home is in New York City.

SEIGNOBOSC, FRANÇOISE, see Françoise, pseud.

SENDAK, MAURICE*

Born June 10, 1928 in Brooklyn, New York where his childhood was spent. Attended Art Students League, New York.

Author-artist Maurice Sendak writes, "Born, the youngest of three, into an actively, if unprofessionally creative family, my earliest memories are of my father who, during my childhood, which was a long series of illnesses, invented beautiful, imaginative tales to tell me and my brother and sister. I feel now, that those stories, although I cannot remember a single one, are the first important root from which my work has developed. They brought back an old world — my parents' homeland — a rich deep past that added to my own personal sense of who and where I was. Probably most of my experiences have been colored with this 'old world feeling.' I drew as far back as I can remember. My brother, who is a writer, and I invented stories, wrote and illustrated, and had a generally marvelous time. There was no question after that as to my profession. Illustrating and writing books was a first dream and I worked for it." Maurice Sendak's professional experience has included working for a comic book syndicate, working in a display house and doing window displays for F. A. O. Schwarz. "This plus my training at the League certainly developed and strengthened my style: the hard, fast-paced demands of studio work force you (for the good) into many styles and techniques, which give a versatility and freedom that, I think, no strict school type training can ever do by itself." Among several books which Maurice Sendak illustrated for Ruth Krauss was *A Hole Is to Dig*. Like much of his early work this was in black-and-white. One of his early works in full color was *The Moon Jumpers*, runner-up for the Caldecott Medal. He had several runners-up for this award before receiving it for a book that he wrote and illustrated, *Where the Wild Things Are*. The first of the books that he wrote and illustrated was *Kenny's Window*. Along with his own books, he has continued to illustrate a great many for other authors, including *Zlateh the Goat and Other Stories* by Isaac Singer. Mr. Sendak, who lives in New York City, has written, "I find that the very thin line between what is real and unreal or fantastic keeps coming up in my work — this wonderful playfulness of moving from one world to another." Nat Hentoff in a *New Yorker* profile (January 22, 1966) describes Sendak's illustrations as "oddly compelling . . . intensely, almost palpably alive." Maurice Sendak sees his basic aim as an illustrator "to let the story speak for itself, with my pictures as a kind of background music — music in the right style and always in tune with the words." In addition to the *New Yorker* profile mentioned above, articles about Mr. Sendak have appeared in *American Artist*, September 1964; *Horn Book*, August 1964; *Library Journal*, March 15, 1964; and *Publishers' Weekly*, February 24, 1964. He is also the subject of a film,

"Maurice Sendak," produced in 1964 in which he discussed the evolution of his work to that date.

SEUSS, DR.,* pseud. (Theodor Seuss Geisel)

Born March 2, 1904 in Springfield, Massachusetts where childhood was spent. Attended Dartmouth College (1925); Oxford University.

Upon graduating from Dartmouth Theodor Geisel decided to become a professor of English Literature. After his year at Oxford, followed by a year in Europe, he returned to the United States intending to become an instructor in a college but, his publishers write, "He could not break himself of an old habit of putting on paper the unusual pictures conjured up in his dreams — this despite the fact that he had been warned by experts that he could never learn to be an artist." For fifteen years he did advertising for Standard Oil of New Jersey, originating the well-known slogan "Quick, Henry, the Flit." He has also done television animated commercials for the Ford Motor Company and during World War II, as a Lieutenant Colonel in the Signal Corps, he was awarded a Legion of Merit for educational and informational films. He has traveled extensively in thirty countries of Europe, the Near East and South America, has an amateur's interest in archaeology, and has done some mural painting and sculpture. For a while Mr. Geisel was a screen artist, working in Hollywood. He has also written several screen plays, including a classic animated cartoon *Gerald McBoing-Boing* which won an Academy Award in 1951; and another Academy Award winner, the documentary film *Design for Death* (on which his wife collaborated) in 1947. His wife, Helen Palmer Geisel, was a classmate at Oxford whom he married in 1927. Mr. Geisel who is now working exclusively in the children's field, has created twenty-seven highly successful picture books since 1937 when his first, *And to Think That I Saw It on Mulberry Street*, was published. He feels that in the last ten years his style has changed to the extent that he is now making "a greater and wider use of color." The original manuscripts and drawings of all his books are in the Special Collections Division of the Library at the University of California, Los Angeles. In 1955 Dartmouth College made Mr. Geisel an Honorary Doctor of Humane Letters. He makes his home in La Jolla, California.

SHAHN, BEN

Born September 12, 1898 in Kovno, Russia. Attended National Academy of Design, New York.

Ben Shahn came to this country when he was eight in 1906. Before taking courses at the National Academy of Design, he studied biology at New York University. In the late 1920's he traveled in Europe and North Africa and during World War II designed posters for various government departments. He has been highly acclaimed for both his graphic arts and his painting and has received numerous awards both here and abroad. Of a number of distinguished illustrated books Mr. Shahn has done in the last seventeen years, three have been books for children. Mr. Shahn and his wife, the artist Bernarda Bryson, make their home in Roosevelt, New Jersey.

SHECTER, BEN

Born April 28, 1935 in New York City where he spent his childhood. Attended Yale School of Drama.

Author-artist Ben Shecter, who lives in New York City, explains, "Probably the most important factor contributing to my becoming an artist was an understanding and encouraging father, who bought me my first paint set at the age of four. Sunday trips to museums and frequent library excursions have evidently laid the groundwork. While I was in the Army, I created a little girl. This child lived and grew with me until my discharge, after which I presented her to a literary agent. She, in turn, presented it to a publisher. As a result, a published author was inspired to write a book about this little girl. I had christened her Millicent and the book was published under the title of *Millicent's Ghost* by Joan Lexau. Within a year's time I wrote and illustrated my first book, *Emily, Girl Witch of New York*. Aside from writing and illustrating, I am a scenic and costume designer. I have designed for opera, ballet, television, and Broadway." *Partouche Plants a Seed*, for which he also wrote the text, was done in black ink line and two-color separation. Although he writes his own texts, he also illustrates and designs books for other authors.

SHEPARD, ERNEST HOWARD*

Born December 10, 1879 at St. John's Wood in London. Attended St. Paul's School, London, and studied at Heatherley School of Art and Royal Academy Schools, London.

Ernest Howard Shepard is the son of Henry Dunkin Shepard, an architect. His mother was the daughter of a well-known water color artist, William Lee. The autobiographical account of his seventh year, *Drawn from Memory*, gives a picture of the close, happy family life he and his older brother and sister shared before the death of their mother; and shows as well some of the roots out of which his work as an artist have grown: a clear recollection of the thoughts and feelings of childhood, and an acute memory for the details of his London boyhood. Among the many illustrations in this book are included a few of his drawings done when he was between seven and eight years old. A later autobiographical work, *Drawn From Life*, was published in 1963. Ernest Shepard, who has received medals for drawing and painting from life, was the Landseer Scholar in 1899, and exhibited his first picture at the Royal Academy in 1901. In 1915 he was commissioned in the Royal Artillery and served three years in France, Belgium and Italy. Mr. Shepard is a

member of the staff of *Punch*. He started drawing for that magazine in 1907 and was elected to the *Punch* table in 1921. He first came into prominence as an illustrator for children with his illustrations for *When We Were Very Young* and the three other books by A. A. Milne between 1924 and 1928. In the thirties he illustrated *Wind in the Willows* and other books by Kenneth Grahame. Since then he has illustrated more than thirty books, both for adults and children, in addition to his drawings for magazines. In 1964 he wrote and illustrated a book for children, *Ben and Brock*, about a boy and a badger published in the United States by Doubleday in 1966, and in 1965 he wrote another book for children, *Betsy and Joe*, about a tramp and a squirrel. Mr. Shepard, who works in black-and-white and full color, does many drawings in pen, as well as painting in water color and gouache. When illustrating books he makes suggestions on the design and does design the jackets; he generally makes special use of lettering. His daughter, Mary Eleanor, is also an artist. Mr. Shepard married his second wife, Norah Carroll, in 1944 and they live in Lodsworth in Sussex, England.

SHEPARD, MARY ELEANOR*

Born December 25, 1909 in England. Childhood spent in Surrey. Attended St. Monica's, Tadworth, Surrey; Villa Ste. Monique, Auteuil, Paris; Slade School of Fine Art, London, studying first under Professor Tonks and later Professor Schwabe.

Mary Shepard is the daughter of artists: her mother was Florence Eleanor Chaplin, and her father is Ernest H. Shepard. She writes that her earliest drawings were mostly on school arithmetic books. Her first published illustrations were for *Mary Poppins* by Pamela Travers, and were done at her Surrey home, Long Meadow, Guildford. She won a prize for a picture exhibited in a Summer Exhibition of Slade School, won a certificate for an etching exhibited in Paris, and has had two exhibitions in galleries in West End, London. In 1937 she married E. V. Knox, the editor of *Punch*, and has lived in London ever since.

SHERIN, RAY

Born June 26, 1926 in Elroy, Wisconsin. Childhood was spent in Winona, Minnesota. Attended Winona State Teachers College; University of Wisconsin, Madison.

Ray Sherin's great enthusiasm for the outdoors began early. He writes, "It's natural that a young man's life in the great northwest amidst the grandeur of the Mississippi valley would impress a curious mind. Observing and remembering much of nature's wild beauty was easy in such a stimulating environment. Later I found opportunities to share some of these experiences through illustration and art education." In high school he designed pages for the yearbook and found himself after college graduation designing yearbook covers for Stayles Press. Photography has been a big help in his work. Mr. Sherin explains, "A large collection of nature and sport slides provide research imagery for factual, representational illustrations. I have also used black-and-white photographs for a number of educational articles I have written for *Arts and Activity* magazine. A *Black Bear's Story* by Emil Liers, which received the Aurienne Award in 1964, had over 100 black-and-white illustrations reproduced by the direct positive method. The research material for these came partly from sketches afield, but mainly from photographs snapped during the spring of a growing bear family. The drawings were sketched on dinobase plastic with a wax base black pencil. I have also used pen and ink, water color and colored pencils for book jackets." Increasing his knowledge and breadth of experience involves a lot of travel for Mr. Sherin. His wife and three boys are often companions on these trips. His sons are also interested in art. The Sherins live in La Crosse, Wisconsin.

SHILLABEER, MARY ELEANOR

Born August 30, 1904 in Downton near Salisbury, England. Childhood spent in Downton and New Forest. Attended Central Schools of Arts and Crafts, London, England.

"I was brought up in the country in a New Forest village. As a child, the only indoor occupation we were allowed on Sunday was painting and reading, so from an early age I was interested in drawing and illustrations." At art school, she won two scholarships and in her last year, Mary Shillabeer recalls, "I met one of the directors of J. M. Dent & Sons and he offered me the job of illustrating a series of children's readers. For two years I illustrated under my maiden name, Mary Wright, and then when I married in 1926, I took on my married name for all my work. My husband, Paul Shillabeer, is a well-known photographer. We have two married daughters and six grandchildren." Mrs. Shillabeer has continued to paint in oil as well as doing illustration and has exhibited in various shows. About her material and techniques she writes, "In the past I have worked on zinc direct with the printer, but this presented considerable difficulties and the various forms of plastic are much simpler. The two methods I have used are 1) making a three-color drawing and then one overlay with the black line and 2) doing a black drawing with three separate overlays, one for each color. I still think that a perfectly free painting well reproduced is the most satisfactory." Mrs. Shillabeer's home is in Edinburgh, Scotland.

SHIMIN, SYMEON*

Born November 1, 1902 in Astrakhan on the Caspian Sea in Russia. Childhood spent in Russia until the age of ten, then the United States. Attended Cooper Union.

In Russia Symeon Shimin's father was a cabinet maker and later an antique dealer. In 1912 he brought his family of six to America. "For years," Mr. Shimin writes, "we lived in two tiny rooms at the rear of my parents' delicatessen store. After school and during the summer I worked in the store. Between customers my mother sewed buttons on sweaters — homework for which the sweat shop paid her three cents a sweater. It was my job to get the work and return it — mountains of sweaters!" He wanted to be a musician but because of his uncle's opposition he began to draw instead, becoming completely absorbed in this art, covering every scrap of paper, even the customers' paper bags, with his drawings. At fifteen he was apprenticed to a commercial artist and began to attend art classes at night. However, he is largely self-taught, finding his "real schooling" in museums and art galleries. At eighteen he began to paint in George Luk's studio and to do free-lance work at night. In 1929 he went to Europe, spending a year and a half in Spain and France. In 1939 he won an award for a mural painting in the Department of Justice Building in Washington, D. C. Recognition and many invitations to museum exhibitions followed. In 1961, he held his first and highly successful one-man exhibition. Among the first books for children that he illustrated are *How Big Is Big?* by Herman and Nina Schneider and Miriam Schlein's *Go With the Sun.* Mr. Shimin lives in New York City.

SHORE, ROBERT

Born February 27, 1924 in New York City where his childhood was spent. Attended Art Students League, New York City; Cranbrook Academy, Bloomfield Hills, Michigan; studied in England.

The three things that Robert Shore most liked to do as a child were to draw, to paint and to act. Though he was trained as a painter and sculptor, he has since also worked in all areas of illustration. It is book illustration that he says gives him the greatest sense of fulfillment. He has illustrated much of Melville, including the Macmillan edition of *Moby Dick*, the first book he illustrated. About his way of working he says, "I often use liquitex which is very versatile and prefer painting because you can run the whole scale of values. I paint whether it is for black-and-white or color. I try in illustrating to put myself into the incident and live it, combining drama and design and illustrating not just the action of the incident but the mood." In 1966, he received a Gold Medal from the Society of Illustrators. Mr. Shore makes his home in New York City.

SHORTALL, LEONARD*

Born in Seattle, Washington where his childhood was spent. Attended University of Washington.

Leonard Shortall has done advertising art and illustrations for many of the national magazines as well as for a large number of children's books. He works with a variety of materials in a style that is humorous and fairly realistic. In addition to writing and illustrating a regular feature for Scholastic Magazines, he also has written and illustrated several books of his own. He and his family live in Westport, Connecticut.

SHULEVITZ, URI

Born February 27, 1935 in Warsaw, Poland. Childhood was spent in Poland, France, and Israel. Attended Teacher's Seminary, Israel; Art Institute, Tel Aviv, Israel; Brooklyn Museum Art School, New York; Provincetown Summer Workshop, Massachusetts.

Mr. Shulevitz writes, "The encouragement of my parents, who were both artistically talented, probably contributed more than anything else to my early interest in drawing." In Paris, at the age of twelve, he won first prize in a competition in drawing held among all the grammar schools in his district. After traveling in Europe, he went to live in Israel, where at eighteen he was the youngest member of a drawing exhibition at the Museum of Tel Aviv. During his military service in Israel he was art director for a magazine for boys and girls, and while living in the kibbutz Ein Geddi, he designed a Passover Haggedah. "Although I had never studied graphic art (my formal studies had been concentrated in painting)," explains Mr. Shulevitz, "I found it to be a perfect medium for expressing my inclination for storytelling and fantasy. In the writing and illustrating of children's books, I have been able to incorporate all of my knowledge of literature and, especially, of painting. Having a visual approach, I sometimes conceive of a book like a movie, using words only when something cannot be said in pictures. Mostly (although not always, depending on the book's specific demand) I try to suggest and evoke rather than state rigidly, in order to encourage the child to participate actively, filling in with his own imagination. This approach is based on the belief that my audience is intelligent and active rather than passive." Mr. Shulevitz works mostly in pen and ink, sometimes with the addition of wash. His color work is separated, mostly on paper, either in aquarelle or tempera — a technique he feels has very rewarding results. He designs his books and frequently writes the text. For *Maximilian's World*, done with a Japanese reed pen, he incorporated lettering into the drawing. Uri Shulevitz has been cited by the Society of Illustrators and the American Institute of Graphic Arts. He and his wife, Helene, who is also an artist, live in New York City.

SIBLEY, DON

Born March 16, 1922 in Hornell, New York where he spent his childhood. Graduated from Pratt Institute, Brooklyn.

"I dreamed my way through childhood," writes Mr. Sibley, "and can't remember most of it. Two things stand out from that hazy time. One is sitting close to the radio in our living room and sketching pencilled figures depicting the actions of Jack Armstrong, Tom Mix, Green Hornet, and others. The other is a great love for the game of basketball. Entered Pratt Institute in September 1940 and went two years before World War II enveloped me. I flew B24's and B17's in that mess, then returned to marry, start a family, finish at Pratt, and start drawing for money. My approach to illustration is drawing with pencil outline. I had to proceed to work in ink for reproduction, but I still visualize in line rather than mass, and in black-and-white. When using color, I spot it throughout the illustration, giving service to local color fidelity only when it's convenient — my use of color being for design quality rather than being representational." Mr. Sibley does work primarily in black-and-white using pen and ink with occasional brush and lamp black to fill in large areas. Mr. Sibley describes his purpose as being "to quietly create an identification by the young reader with the time and place of a narrative." He continues, "He (the reader) must create his own excitement with his own imagination from the author's words. Any book which I work on must have a good author to be successful and I've been very lucky. Perhaps most lucky when I was assigned to illustrate for Robert Burch. With experience in advertising and institutional promotion work, as well as all types of publishing illustration, I most prefer children's book illustration because one is granted complete freedom to interpret and illustrate in the most individual and personal sense which is the nearest thing to free creative expression outside of fine arts." Don Sibley and his wife, Janet, have three grown children, Linda, Diane, and Mark. The Sibleys live in Roxbury, Connecticut.

SIDJAKOV, NICOLAS

Born December 16, 1924 in Riga, Latvia where he spent his childhood. Attended Ecole des Beaux Arts, Paris.

Besides illustrating children's books, Nicolas Sidjakov does graphic design and advertising illustration in a variety of colors and media. This desire for diversity began early in his career in Europe. With Paris as his home base, he traveled and worked in Italy, Switzerland, and Germany, learning to speak five languages and gaining wide experience in the graphic arts. About his approach to children's books, Mr. Sidjakov writes, "Each children's book poses a different visual problem that requires a different visual solution. This necessitates a perpetual exploration of techniques, typefaces and color schemes. Because of my previous work in Europe — mainly France — I am less inclined towards specialization, and welcome the challenge of an ever-changing subject matter." For *Baboushka and the Three Kings*, the book that won him the 1961 Caldecott Medal, he used a felt tip pen, dyes and liquitex on acetate. His style is decorative, changing as he experiments with different media. In addition to the Caldecott Medal, Sidjakov has received awards in the New York, Los Angeles, Chicago, Detroit, and San Francisco Art Directors' shows. The *New York Times* selected his illustrations for *Friendly Beasts*, 1957; *Baboushka and the Three Kings*, 1960; and *The Emperor and the Drummer Boy*, 1962, as among "The Ten Best Illustrated Children's Books" of the year. He has also been honored by the Society of Illustrators and the American Institute of Graphic Arts. Articles about Mr. Sidjakov have appeared in *CA*, June 1962; *Horn Book*, August 1961; and *Junior Libraries*, March 1961. He came to the United States in 1954 with his wife, Jean, whom he met and married in Paris. The Sidjakovs, who have one son, live in Sausalito, California.

SIEBEL, FRITZ (Frederick)

Born December 19, 1913 in Vienna, Austria. Childhood spent in Austria and Czechoslovakia. Attended Academy of Art, Vienna.

Mr. Siebel writes that he is primarily an industrial designer but loves to draw for his eight children and "others who might like it." Before coming to the United States, he lived in Czechoslovakia, where he served for two years in the Czech Army. He now lives in Rye, New York, and, as a commercial artist, has done many magazine illustrations as well as television animation. "Mr. Clean" was one of his creations. His books, most of which he designs, are illustrated in full color. *Who Took the Farmer's Hat* and *Amelia Bedelia* are examples of his work done in pen and ink with color separations.

SIEGL, HELEN

Born August 18, 1924 in Vienna, Austria, where she spent her childhood. Attended Academy for Applied Art, Vienna.

Helen Siegl writes, "I was born and raised in Vienna where art is important and much recognized, so I went to art school when it was thought that I had talent. After graduation, I worked as an assistant to a well-known architect, designed toys, illustrated books and decorated store windows. In 1952 I married and followed my husband to America. I made relief prints, usually from wood, linoleum or plaster blocks and offered them for sale in local art galleries. Eventually my work became better known, was handled by art galleries throughout the country and was represented in national shows. Then I was asked to illustrate specific manuscripts with woodblock prints. This is only a side line. My main work is in original prints." Mrs. Siegl's husband, Theodore, is Conservator of Paintings at the Philadelphia Museum of Art and she is the mother of five boys and one girl. An article concerning her work appears in *Artist's Proof*, No. 3, Spring 1962.

SILVERMAN, BURT (Burton Philip)

Born June 11, 1928 in Brooklyn, New York where he spent his childhood. Attended Art Students League, Columbia University, New York.

Mr. Silverman, painter and illustrator, writes, "As a child, I read rather 'omnivorously,' most of the romantic classics, and especially those illustrated by N. C. Wyeth and Howard Pyle. The contrast between the discordant shrieks of my contemporaries playing stick ball and the clash of pikes and 'claymores' in the book world of *The Scottish Chiefs* remains a vivid memory. But, for me, the illustrations brought this world more acutely into being. I think that it has affected some of my aesthetic sensibilities to the point where I feel the young reader of today ought to have a similar joy." Mr. Silverman has his studio in a large New York City apartment that overlooks the Hudson River. About his work he writes, "I generally use materials that are related to my more painterly techniques. As a rule, pen and ink are difficult for me since my drawing tends to be rapid and broadly conceived at the start; or I depend on strong chiaroscuro, which is inimical to the linear assumptions of pen and ink. I feel there are compensatory rewards due to the qualitative differences of illustration, as against painting. I enjoy taking a character through the story, and finding that he has somehow become more 'real' because of my little scratchings. On occasion, as in *Phantoms and Fantasies*, there are wonderful extremes of humor, and sobering bits of terror, that make illustration a joyous occupation, and even a noble one." Mr. Silverman works primarily in black-and-white using traditional materials such as pen, ink and charcoal in *The Caravan*. More about his work can be found in *American Artist*, October 1964.

SILVERMAN, MEL (Melvin Frank)

Born January 26, 1931 in Denver, Colorado. Graduated from Art Institute (B.F.A.), Chicago. Died September 16, 1966.

The first of several awards that Mr. Silverman received was a traveling fellowship from the Art Institute of Chicago. His work as a painter appeared in a number of exhibits and is owned by several museums and universities. He was instructor in graphics at Ein Harod, Israel and from 1956-1960 was a display designer in New York City. He illustrated seven children's books by other authors as well as writing and illustrating three of his own. These were *Ciri-Biri-Biri*, *The Good for Nothing Burro* and *Hymie's Fiddle*.

SIMON, HILDA RITA

Born November 22, 1921 in Santa Ana, California. Childhood was spent in California and Europe. Attended university in Germany.

"The talent for painting and drawing is inherent in my father's family," explains Miss Simon. "My grandfather, my father and my uncle all did some very beautiful drawings and paintings as a hobby. As a child in California, I was already busily engaged drawing animals, always a prime interest of mine. I did not study art, though, just did it on the side while studying languages, also one of my special interests. I thought at one time that I would make languages my career — but my love for painting and drawing, especially in color, took over, and I started to devote most of my time to art, where I developed my own techniques, especially in pastels. Later, my interest in animals, and the knowledge I had acquired both through observation and study, led to combining the two in first just illustrating, and later also writing nature books for young people. I constantly try to experiment with new techniques, always keeping in mind the difficulties of reproduction. I have perfected a way in which I can do full-color illustrations by making a set of four black line separations which will reproduce as half-tones. This is proving very effective for many types of illustrations." The separations are usually on dinobase or similar materials. In addition, she works with pencil, water color, and pen and ink. Much of her early work was done in black-and-white pen and ink drawings.

SIMON, HOWARD*

Born July 22, 1903 in New York City. His childhood was spent there and in its suburbs. Attended University of the State of New York; National Academy of Design; Académie Julien, Paris.

More at home in the backwoods of America than in its cities, Howard Simon, both as illustrator and painter, takes his subject matter wholly from his experiences with man and nature away from urban centers. He has lived for many years in the Ozark Mountains, in the Far West, and for long periods in France. His woodcuts, lithographs, paintings and drawings record these years of the artist's life. His illustrations, particularly, make full use of these background experiences. Mr. Simon has worked in a variety of media including full color water color as in *If You Were an Eel, How Would You Feel?* He has also worked with separations but prefers not to. Though the source of his work is nature, the interpretation is expressionistic. Mr. Simon finds his style has changed so that there is "less detail and more emphasis on movement and on the line itself." He frequently selects classics to illustrate and often designs his books. Howard Simon is Adjunct Associate Professor of Art at New York University and the author of *Techniques of Drawing, Art in Illustration,* and *Watercolor Painting* (Sterling). He is represented in the Metropolitan Museum of Art, New York City, in museums in California and elsewhere, as well as in many private collections. He is married to Mina Lewiton, the author, and has illustrated many of her books. They have a married daughter, Dr. Bettina S. Niederer, who is a pediatrician at Philadelphia General Hospital. Howard Simon lives and works at his studio at Stanfordville situated in the beginning rises of the Berkshire chain in New York State.

SIMONT, MARC*

Born November 23, 1915 in Paris, France. Childhood was spent in France, Spain, and the United States. Attended Académie Julien and Académie André Lhote, Paris.

"I spent my first twenty years shuttling back and forth between France, Spain, and the United States," writes Marc Simont, "seldom staying longer than five years at any one place. Like any other child I drew pictures, but unlike a lot of children, I never stopped. As I grew older my interest focused more and more on people. Friends, family, people I had seen on the street, or even animals became my subjects. The way my school teachers looked was more important to me than what they said — as my disastrous report cards testified. It is good for observation to come in contact with sharply contrasting types. Traveling as I did helped put an edge on whatever faculties of observation I had, and trying to jot down what it was that made one person different from another helped me to 'see,' which is the better half of drawing. I was also fortunate in having an artist right in the house, who taught me to handle the tools of the trade, and who has remained my most important teacher — my father, José Simont, who was for thirty years on the staff of *L'Illustration,* and is now working in Caracas, Venezuela. From 1932 to 1935 I studied in Paris where I attended several art schools. Then I came back to the United States and shortly after began working professionally." Mr. Simont describes his style as representational "with a humorous slant whenever I can." Although he feels it is tedious he sometimes uses separations because it produces better results for him. Marc Simont, who has written as well as illustrated several books, was Spanish before becoming a United States citizen. He received the 1957 Caldecott Medal for his illustrations, done in casein, for *A Tree Is Nice* by Janice May Udry. A short article about a different phase of Mr. Simont's career in the last ten years — sports illustrating which began with his drawings for Red Smith's *How to Get to First Base* — appeared in *Sports Illustrated,* October 11, 1965. Mr. Simont lives in New York City and has a summer home in Cornwall, Connecticut.

SLOANE, ERIC

Born February 27, 1910 in New York City. Attended Yale University, and the New York School of Fine and Applied Art.

When Eric Sloane first started his career, he wanted to paint clouds. Feeling it was best to research the subject first, he wrote a book about them called *Clouds, Air and Wind,* later used by the Air Force to teach meteorology to young flyers. Eventually he became an expert in the subject, writing more books, named to the Hall of Weather in the American Museum of Natural History, and acting as the first TV weatherman. He also painted his clouds. From the sky, he descended to paint

"Americana" subjects. The result was predictable — he is not only an author and painter, but also a historian of early Americana. He writes, designs, and illustrates his books in black-and-white and full color, and in them he makes extensive use of lettering. "My object," explains Eric Sloane, "is to make people aware of the good things of the past and not confuse nostalgia with history." He does this through his books and landscape paintings. He is married and lives in Warren, Connecticut. In *American Artist*, March 1965, Mr. Sloane writes about his work.

SLOBODKIN, LOUIS*

Born February 19, 1903 in Albany, New York, where his childhood was spent. Attended Beaux Arts Institute of Design, New York.

"My father and mother," Louis Slobodkin writes, "came from the province of Chernigov, Ukraine, and settled in Albany. Having somehow managed to reach my third year of high school at fifteen, and having read of the early development of the masters, I left school in 1918 and went down to New York to study sculpture, drawing, etc., at the Beaux Arts. From my fifteenth to my twentieth year I studied from life some nine to twelve hours a day. Was awarded twenty-two medals during this time and the Tiffany Foundation Scholarship. For the next ten years I worked as an assistant sculptor and did some travelling. In the middle of that period I married Florence Gersh. We have two sons, Larry and Michael. Since my thirtieth year, I have executed many large commissions on my own, exhibited in many museums, and in 1941, did my first drawings for a book, *The Moffats* by Eleanor Estes." In 1944, Mr. Slobodkin received the Caldecott Medal for his illustrations for James Thurber's *Many Moons*. In this year was also published *Magic Michael*, one of the first books he wrote as well as illustrated. Since then he has written and illustrated forty-four books of his own, collaborated on eighteen, and illustrated nineteen by other authors. Of one of his two adult books, *Sculpture, Principles and Practice* (1949) he writes, "I think I said all I wanted to say about sculpture in that book, and since then I have less and less interest in creating sculpture. I do a few pieces a year and devote the rest of my time to children's books." The Slobodkins now have three grandchildren, who continue to inspire their grandfather to do books.

SMITH, ALVIN

Born November 27, 1933 in Gary, Indiana where he spent his childhood. Graduated from State University of Iowa (B.A. 1955); University of Illinois (M.A. 1960); Teachers College, Columbia University, New York City (Doctoral Student in Art Education).

Trained as an illustrator and art teacher, Alvin Smith works at both professions, enjoying his work with and for children. "My

interest in drawing sprouted early," he writes, "and was encouraged both at home and at school. I would spend hours listening to my favorite radio programs. Afterwards, I would draw my own interpretations of these adventures, which my parents prominently displayed in our home. In school, as I recall, my teachers always encouraged students to read. In the lower grades, we would round out our reading activity by making imaginative illustrations. I forwarded my illustration of 'The Little Match Girl' to the editor of *Horn Book*. The editor's favorable response was very instrumental in the formation of my desire to become an illustrator." Mr. Smith works primarily in black-and-white, as in his illustrations for the 1965 Newbery Award winner, *Shadow of a Bull* by Maia Wojciechowska. He does, however, use separations often in designing multi-color book jackets as for *Fisherman's Choice* which was done on acetate. His style is realistic, seeking to heighten the drama by his visual interpretation of the events. The stories he illustrates usually have a lot of suspense and action. Alvin Smith lives in New York City with his wife, Pauline, an elementary school teacher. He is a winner of the *Chicago Tribune* Painting Award in 1954, and his art work hangs in the Atlanta University Permanent Collection of Contemporary American Art, and Dayton Art Institute.

SMITH, LAWRENCE BEALL

Born 1909 in Washington, D. C. Childhood spent in Vincennes, Indiana and Chicago, Illinois. Attended University of Chicago and Art Institute of Chicago.

Lawrence Beall Smith recalls that he always wanted to be an artist and though he went to the Art Institute in Chicago for a while part time, he has had little formal training. For the past twenty years he and his family have lived and worked in Cross River, New York. His wife is also an artist and they have two sons, one daughter and, now, one granddaughter. "Much of my activity," he writes, "is in fields outside book illustration, namely portrait painting, easel painting, lithography, and more recently sculpture. I suppose I have done book illustration because I enjoy it and because there is an element of illustration in all my work. During World War II, I was an artist war correspondent." Mr. Smith's illustrations have been in black-and-white or in full color for which he paints in oil. An example of this is *Jungle of Tonza Mara*.

SMITH, LEE, see Albion, Lee Smith

SNYDER, JEROME

Born April 20, 1916 in New York City, where his childhood was spent.

About his art training, Jerome Snyder writes, "I've had no formal training to speak of — some random courses but never any more than a semester at any one time." He has for a number of years been active in illustrating for magazines and advertising and has received various honors for his work from the Society of Illustrators and the Art Directors Club of New York. From 1954 to 1961 he was Art Director for *Sports Illustrated* and since then has been Art Director for *Scientific American*. His wife, Gertrude, is also an art director and designer and they have two sons, one in college and one in New York City's High School of Music and Art. Mr. Snyder is well-known for his black-and-white illustrations. Some of his more recent books have been in color such as *The Day the Sun Was Late* which was done in tempera and pencil crayon.

SOFIA, pseud. (Sophia Zeiger)*

Born August 29, 1926 in New York City. Childhood was spent in Greece and in the United States. Attended Washington Irving High School, New York, and Franklin School of Professional Arts.

"Born, reared and educated in New York City, I have punctuated my provincialism by periodic journeys — to the West, to Mexico and to Europe. Before striking out on my own I held only two jobs: first, in serving my apprenticeship, with Albert Staehle, a poster artist who introduced me to my profession, then, after graduating from art school, with Nieman-Marcus. The bright, spare landscapes of Greece and the lush vivid scenes of Mexico, in both of which almost antipodal countries I have lived for extended periods, have left their impress on my work. Though the canvases I finished there seem to have no commercial relevance, they have, I think, freshened and vivified my illustrations and advertising art. Two great teachers have helped me enormously: Clara Whitney, who taught me the elements of my profession; and Antonio Frasconi, who helped me realize my bent and refine my art. Influenced by Frasconi, I have been doing a variety of woodcuts." Sofia is married to Arthur Zeiger, a professor of English at City College, New York, and they have one daughter born in 1957, Melissa Fran, "who looks like my imagined children, only prettier." The Zeigers live in New York City. Sofia works primarily in black-and-white, using prismacolor crayon on acetate. For jackets, she uses two colors with crayons. Her style is both representational and decorative.

SOKOL, BILL

Born November 21, 1925 in Warsaw, Poland. Childhood was spent in New York City.

Bill Sokol, Associate Art Director of the *New York Times*, does the text, design, and illustrations for his children's books. Versatility with style, color and media mark his work. He has worked with separation, tusche, pen and ink, crayons, etc. *Profitt the Fox* was done with photostats. He sometimes uses type and lettering in special ways. He is keenly interested in graphics, and was chairman of the American Institute of Graphic Arts Children's Book Show for 1963-64. He has been cited many times by the Art Directors Club, the American Institute of Graphic Arts, and other graphic institutions. In 1956 he won the Art Directors' Medal for the best ad of that year. His work can be seen in many museums and his prints are found in the Library of Congress. More on his work can be found in *Graphis*, March 1958. He is married to Camille Sokol, who is both a writer and a weaver. They have two daughters.

SOLBERT, RONNI G.*

Born September 7, 1925 in Washington, D. C. Childhood was spent in Chicago and in Rochester, New York. Attended Vassar College, graduating with honors in 1946; Cranbrook Academy of Art, receiving an M.F.A. in painting in 1948.

Ronni Solbert writes, "The illustrators whose work I loved as a child were Boutet de Monvel, Rackham, Lear, Leech, Alken, Dulac and Nielsen. I would pore over the detail in a de Monvel or Rackham illustration for hours, and it was undoubtedly my fascination with them that prompted me to decorate, or desecrate, all unillustrated books that came my way — a habit that still persists. Illustrating books for children sometimes strikes me as presumptuous. The pictures children themselves make are often so much more imaginative, alive and expressive than those of the average adult illustrator. This is only to say that I feel children deserve the best perceptions of which an illustrator is capable. And I feel our standards in this regard are increasingly important when much of the world of visual communications, as well as our total environment, is so cluttered with slick sensationalism, superficiality, violence and ugliness. The best writing generates its own visual images. These can be of such intensity and so inescapable that the illustrator has his hands full living up to them. The illustrator's responsibilty, it seems to me, is to be true to the spirit of the writing, to do his best to illumine that spirit while bringing to it a fresh sense of wonder along with an imaginative awareness of the magic of everyday reality. I have been painting ever since art school, with some work in graphics (principally lithography and woodcuts) on the side. I taught (mostly learned from) children painting and sculpture in 1949 at the Memorial Art Gallery, Rochester, and this I think, plus my own recollected pleasure in children's books suggested that illustrating children's stories might be one of the pleasanter aspects of the illustrating field. As painting takes most of my time, illustration is something of an avocation for me — and a most rewarding one." Ronni Solbert received a Fulbright Fellowship to India in 1952-53, and while there served on a painting jury for Shankar's International Children's Art Competition. Her home is in New York City, but she has traveled widely, many times to Europe and also to Mexico, Central America, the Near East and the Orient. Ronni Solbert has used a variety of media for her illustrations in black-and-white or with color separations. *The Superlative Horse*, for example, was done with dry pigment and turpentine, tusche and sumi ink. She designs as well as illustrates her books.

SOREL, EDWARD

Born March 26, 1929 in New York City where he spent his childhood. Attended Cooper Union, New York.

Mr. Sorel writes, "As a child I was bedridden for almost two years with pneumonias of one sort or another, and during this period drew to pass the time. It is my belief that the decline in the quality of illustration is due to the discovery of penicillin some years later. I became an artist because my father was opposed to the idea." Mr. Sorel has been a staff artist for *Esquire*, CBS Television Promotion, and Push Pin Studios. He is now a free-lance illustrator and designer for advertising agencies and publishers. Children's books are a small part of his work that also includes political satire and caricature for magazines like *Ramparts* and *The Realist*, and in book form. *Moon Missing* (Simon and Schuster, 1962) is one of three books he has done of this kind. Mr. Sorel works in full color, occasionally making separations and always designing his books. *Gwendolyn, the Miracle Hen* was done in pen and ink drawing, colored with inks. He also uses pen and ink with color overlays. Articles about Edward Sorel have appeared in *Graphis*, January 1963 and *American Artist*, May 1960. He has received awards from the Art Directors Club of New York and the American Institute of Graphic Arts. His studio is in New York City and his home is in Carmel, New York. He is married and has one daughter. His wife, Elaine, is a noted interior designer.

SPANFELLER, JAMES JOHN

Born October 27, 1930 in Philadelphia, Pennsylvania where he spent his childhood. Attended Philadelphia Museum School of Art; Pennsylvania Academy of Fine Arts.

"Since there was no precedent for artists in my family," writes Mr. Spanfeller, "as a child, my interest in art was not looked upon very seriously. But, since about the fourth grade in school on, I was interested in drawing and also writing stories. I had no real formal art training until I was just eighteen and entered the Philadelphia Museum School of Art. The lack of art background was a big disadvantage at first, but now in retrospect I think it was most fortunate. When it comes to art, overtraining is worse than undertraining." After graduation, Mr. Spanfeller went into the Army for two years, returned for more study, and in 1957 moved to New York City where he began his career as a free-lance illustrator. One of his first jobs was illustrating Robert Paul Smith's best seller *Where Did You Go? Out! What Did You Do? Nothing*. Since then he has done illustrations for most of the major magazines including *Ladies Home Journal*, *Seventeen*, *Esquire*, as well as some twenty-six children's books. He

is currently working on his own children's book which he plans to convert into a movie. Although Mr. Spanfeller does more than half his work in black-and-white he has used most production methods, including five-color separation. He has used dyes, water colors, colored pencils, and designer's colors. Mr. Spanfeller describes his work as having "two directions from the same style — one semi-representational-decorative, the other satirical-fantasy." In 1964, he was named Artist of the Year by the Artists Guild of New York. In 1965, he held a one-man show at the Society of Illustrators. Articles on his work have appeared in *Art Direction*, February 1965; *Print*, March 1965; *A/D Assistant*, September 1966. James Spanfeller, his wife Patricia, and son James, Jr. live in Hastings-on-Hudson, New York.

SPENCE, GERALDINE

Born 1931 in Esher, Surrey, England. Attended Wimbledon School of Art; Royal College of Art, London.

After a year at art school, in 1949, Geraldine Spence took a job in the offices of the BBC. It proved to be a short period of work and then she returned to the Wimbledon School of Art and continued her studies with the intention of becoming an illustrator. She went on to study under Edward Bawden and John Nash at the Royal College of Art from 1953 to 1956. While there she experimented with typography and design at the Lion and Unicorn Press. Following her studies, Miss Spence began free-lancing and has been primarily illustrating children's books and book jackets.

SPIER, PETER*

Born June 6, 1927 in Amsterdam, Holland. Childhood was spent in Broek in Waterland, Holland. Attended Rijksakademie Voor Beeldende Kunsten, Amsterdam.

Peter Spier grew up in a small village in Holland, near Amsterdam. He served three years in the Royal Netherlands Navy, one year of which was spent in the West Indies and South America. After his experience in the Navy he lived for six months in Paris, returning to Holland to become Junior Editor of *Elsevier's Weekly*, the largest Dutch weekly. He came to the United States in 1951, going first to Houston, Texas, where Elsevier's Publishing Company had a branch. In 1952 he came to New York. *The Fox Went Out on a Chilly Night*, an old folk song in a new setting, designed and illustrated by Mr. Spier, was a runner-up for the Caldecott Medal in 1962. He has also received the Diploma di Triennale di Milano and two certificates from the American Institute of Graphic Arts. A United States citizen, he is now living in Port Washington, Long Island, New York.

SPILKA, ARNOLD

Born November 13, 1917 in New York City where he spent

his childhood. Attended Art Students League where he studied sculpture with John Hovannes and drawing with Rico Lebrun.

Arnold Spilka writes, "I can't remember ever wanting to be anything but an artist. An incident when I was two years old probably started it off. A photographer wandering the streets with his pony took my picture. According to my mother, when she hesitated accepting it because the pony's head had not photographed I drew it in to convince her to take it. Any child wanting a picture would have done the same. Obviously my mother's reaction to my effort, and occasional recall of the incident must have been a strong influence. After high school, I free-lanced as a gag cartoonist while painting and studying nights. Spent some years in the army and picked up afterwards where I had left off. Suddenly found my drawings of children in my cartoons developing in uncartoon ways. After years of false starts, I finally went all out for children's books some eight years ago. It is a soul-satisfying work." Mr. Spilka writes and designs his books as well as illustrating them. "All the children I have ever known have become models for my work. I frequently show my drawings to my nieces and nephew for whatever they may say." He generally uses dinobase and acetate for his separations, but finds heavy tracing paper best for soft gradations. He likes to work in oils thinned with turpentine. Oil painting was used for *Paint All Kinds of Pictures.* Arnold Spilka is still a New Yorker but enjoys traveling cross-country by car.

STAHL, BEN (Benjamin Albert)

Born September 7, 1910 in Chicago, Illinois where he spent his childhood.

Ben Stahl is best known as a painter and magazine illustrator. He entered the field of children's books with *Blackbeard's Ghost,* a book which he wrote and illustrated, now being filmed by Walt Disney Productions. His career began early. At the age of 12 he won a scholarship to the Chicago Art Institute and began his apprenticeship in commercial art at Young, Timmins and Smith art studio in Chicago. His career as a magazine illustrator began with a commission from the *Saturday Evening Post.* Since then he has done illustrations for most of the major magazines such as *McCall's, Good Housekeeping,* and *Coronet.* In 1944 Stahl and eleven other well-known artists founded the Famous Artists Schools in Westport, Connecticut. In 1950 he was commissioned by *Esquire* to travel in twelve European countries to paint the most beautiful woman found in each, and write her story. He has done a number of paintings with religious themes. In 1966 he completed a set of oil paintings of the Way of the Cross, now on permanent exhibit in the Sarasota Museum of the Cross, Florida. Ben Stahl paints in casein or oil. *Blackbeard's Ghost* was painted in full color casein and then reproduced in black-and-white. He and his wife, Ella, and their two children live in Sarasota, Florida.

Articles about his work have appeared in *American Artist,* March 1946 and September 1950.

STANDON, EDWARD CYRIL

Born May 31, 1929 in London, England where his childhood was spent. Attended St. Martin's School of Art, London.

Mr. Standon writes that he is a painter by profession. "My father is also an artist and even when I was very small he used to take me sketching with him so that I have been interested in painting ever since I can remember, although in my late teens I abandoned it for a short while to become a musician." He then became a cartoonist but always enjoyed drawing animals. "It was whilst doing this for my son's amusement that I found myself launched on my present career." His studio is at home "which is very useful as my nine-year-old son and the baby make excellent models and are highly critical — and my wife keeps me constantly supplied with coffee. My first book was *The Singing Rhinoceros* (1963) which I enjoyed doing tremendously. I work in India inks and like to experiment as much as possible with different textures." For many of his picture books his wife Anna writes the stories, although he has done other illustration work as well.

STEVENS, MARY E.*

Born September 9, 1920 in Bar Harbor, Maine, where her childhood was spent. Attended Vesper George School of Art, Boston; Art Students League, New York. Died October 1966.

Mary E. Stevens grew up in a Maine seacoast town. Her father and grandfather were artistic but turned it to practical use by restoring antiques. Her father's bedtime stories took the form of improvised yarns and pictures at a slate blackboard in the kitchen. Soon the children took up the blackboard too, combining lets-pretend and illustration in a strange game in which only bad people had eyebrows and the heroine always appeared in profile so the waves of her hair would show! (This early use of line rather than color was, Miss Stevens felt, the reason she preferred drawing to painting.) She had no training at all in art till out of high school, and even then was torn between art and chemistry as a career. In Boston she and her sister lived in one round room in an ormolu tower that shuddered on the edge of the railroad tracks. Later she lived and worked in Manhattan, and found that her best books were mostly about boys and old men! Between books she did carpentry, volunteer work at a cancer hospital, and explored the little-known back streets of every borough in New York. Miss Stevens died on October 18, 1966.

STOBBS, WILLIAM*

Born June 27, 1914 in South Shields, England. Childhood

was spent in County Durham. Attended King Edward VI School of Art; Durham University.

William Stobbs' childhood was spent in the North of England, almost always in sight of the sea and the River Tyne which is noted for its shipping, and his interest in boats has continued. At Durham University he obtained a First Class Honours Degree (B.A.) in History of Art, and subsequently obtained an M.A. degree in the same subject. He believes that the strong traditional influence on his work is due to this. He is especially influenced by Caravaggio. He was Head of the Design Department of the London School of Printing and Graphic Arts from 1950 to 1958 and is now Principal of the Maidstone College of Art. *Knight Crusader* by Ronald Welch which William Stobbs illustrated received in 1955 the Carnegie Medal for the best children's book of the year published in England.

STONE, HELEN*

Born October 31, 1904 in Englewood, New Jersey where childhood was spent. Attended New York School of Fine and Applied Art; Art Students League; and studied in Paris.

"When I was a child," Helen Stone writes, "seeing my mother at her easel stimulated me to experiment with brushes. So instead of selecting academic subjects to follow, I chose art." From study in New York Miss Stone went to Paris, and, after a few seasons of teaching, some designing, and commercial art, she became interested in painting. There followed years of studio life and work, travel — Europe, the American tropics, the Mediterranean islands, the West Indies — and marriage. Primarily interested in painting, it was more or less by chance that she "stumbled into the field of book illustration. It is, however, a rewarding field, giving full scope to the artist's feeling for design and color, enlivening the sense of humor and beauty." In 1944 Mrs. Stone began doing illustrations for children's stories, the first being *The Horse Who Lived Upstairs*, followed by *The Plain Princess*, both by Phyllis McGinley, and since then has illustrated over a score of children's books. Her home is in East Hampton, Long Island, New York. Miss Stone usually works in three colors and black. Although *Tell Me Mr. Owl* was illustrated with lithographs, most of her books are done in separations which she feels limit the artist but can be overcome by a freedom of style. Material about Miss Stone's work can be found in *Horn Book*, March, 1946. Autobiographical articles appeared in *Horn Book*, January 1946 and October 1953.

SUBA, SUSANNE*

Born in Budapest, Hungary. Childhood was spent in Europe and the United States. Attended Brooklyn Friends School, and Pratt Institute, Brooklyn.

At the age of three, crouched under a drawing board in her father's office in Budapest, Susanne Suba writes, she started her career as an artist. Her father, Miklos Suba, was an architect and painter; her mother, May Edwards, was a pianist. She was brought to the United States as a small child, settling in her mother's native Brooklyn. She is as much at home in the field of advertising as in that of book illustration. The Medal Award for newspaper advertising given by the Art Directors Club of Chicago has been presented to her, and several of her books have been included in the American Institute of Graphic Arts Fifty Books of the Year Exhibits. In addition, she has been honored by the Art Directors Club of New York, the Society of Typographic Arts in Chicago, Chicago Federated Advertising Club, and the Brooklyn Museum. She received a grant from the Michael Karolyi Memorial Foundation for painting. Her work hangs in the Brooklyn Museum, Art Institute of Chicago, and the Metropolitan Museum of Art in New York City. In 1964 the Art Center in Kalamazoo, Michigan gave a one-man show of her drawings, illustrations and paintings. Among her early children's book illustrations are those for Katherine Wigmore Eyre's *Lottie's Valentine*, 1941. More recently, there was *Sonny-Boy Sim* which was done in pen, ink and wash and *Rocket in My Pocket* which was done in pen line. *Spots by Suba*, a book of her *New Yorker* drawings was published in 1944. From 1951 to 1953 she spent three years living and traveling in Europe, and has returned several times since. Her home is now in New York City.

SWAIN, SU ZAN NOGUCHI

Born March 8, 1916 in Colorado. Childhood spent in northeastern Colorado. Attended University of Colorado (B.F.A. 1938), and studied at Penn State, Brooklyn Botanical Garden, American Museum of Natural History and Audubon Nature Camp.

"My parents are Japanese and came from homes where art was not only encouraged but the parents were artists. We lived on a large farm. When not in school, my four sisters and I were rather isolated. To keep us occupied, my parents provided us with many kinds of art materials. Our mother taught us all the basic steps in drawing and as we progressed my father helped us. They made us aware and appreciative of nature by taking us for rides, and to overcome the lack of a library or art gallery, they invested in basic books. One in particular was the *Famous Paintings* set. Often the whole family huddled around the book to discuss the merits of the paintings. We also had a set of encyclopedia and were encouraged to do our own digging for information." She is married to an entomologist, Ralph B. Swain, who in 1948 wrote the *Insect Guide*. Illustrating this book began her career, in the pursuit of which she has made many field trips to observe and collect material. She has excavated ant hills, been bitten by a leaf cutter in the tropics, gone into volcano craters, and kept many live specimens in her studio, including such spiders as black widows and tarantulas.

She usually works in black-and-white or full color using pen and ink, pencil or water color. She has written as well as illustrated three books, one of which, *Plants of Woodland and Wayside*, she dedicated to her parents, whom she feels were such a strong influence on her career. The Swains make their home in Chatham, New Jersey.

SWENEY, FRED (Frederic)

Born June 5, 1912 in Hollidaysburg, Pennsylvania. Childhood spent in Curwensville, Pennsylvania. Attended Cleveland Institute of Art.

Mr. Sweney was a recipient of the Frederick Augustus Kendall Scholarship at the Cleveland Institute of Art. After graduation he worked several years for advertising agencies and commercial studios, and spent nine years as a newspaper artist for the *Cleveland Press*. During World War II, he was a supervisor of technical illustration. Fred Sweney works in a variety of media. *Frightened Hare* was done in sumi ink with acetate color separations, and *Hawk in the Sky* with carbon pencil and terracotta chalk. The jackets were done as oil paintings. As an illustrator of nature, he considers that his subject matter requires realism. He is the author as well as illustrator of *Techniques of Drawing and Painting Wildlife* (Reinhold, 1959), *Course in Drawing and Painting Birds* (Reinhold, 1961), and *Painting the American Scene in Watercolor* (Reinhold, 1964). He lives in Sarasota, Florida where he has taught at the Ringling School of Art for fifteen years.

THOLLANDER, EARL GUSTAVE

Born April 13, 1922 in Kingsberg, California. Childhood was spent in the San Francisco area. Attended San Francisco City College; Art League of California and the Academy of Art, San Francisco; University of California at Berkeley; San Francisco Art Institute.

After serving in the Navy during World War II, Earl Thollander began his career as an illustrator working at basic advertising art techniques for two years at Patterson and Hall Art Service, San Francisco. His next job was for the *San Francisco Examiner* as a newspaper artist. Mr. Thollander writes, "While earning my living as an illustrator of books, advertising and editorial matter, I still devoted a great deal of time to painting. In 1955 I made a sketching trip to Mexico for three weeks. These drawings were used as a basis for many paintings as well as for illustrating the bilingual children's book *Ramon* published by Parnassus Press." This was the first of many drawing trips for various firms which have provided Mr. Thollander with the subject matter for his paintings and illustrations, as well as the particular project commissioned. His travels have sent him to Hawaii, Europe including Russia and Yugoslavia, the Orient, the Middle East, and the Caribbean. Free-lancing since 1959, he explains, "Through the years I have painted and exhibited my work in group, juried, invitational and one-man shows. I enjoy the hard work of painting and drawing. But I also enjoy commissioned work and the challenge that the solving of a particular visual problem brings." Mr. Thollander has used a variety of media including a speedball pen with a round tip, a bamboo pen, and grease pencil. *To Catch a Mongoose* was done with a bamboo pen of his own make and water color washes. The four-color separations for that book were done on water color paper, working on a light table, four halftones over one another. He adds, "Real guesswork which worked." Articles about his work have appeared in *American Artist*, April 1954 and March 1960 and in the *Journal of Commercial Art*, November 1959 and September 1962. Earl Thollander, his wife, Janet, and two children, Kristie and Wesley, live in San Francisco where he has his studio.

TOMES, MARGOT LADD

Born August 10, 1917 in Yonkers, New York. Childhood was spent in Rockville Center, Long Island, New York. Attended Pratt Institute, New York.

"Illustrating children's books is fairly new to me, although it is what I have always wanted to do," writes Margot Tomes. "But all these years I have been doing, and am still doing, fabric and wallpaper designs and occasional book jackets and illustrations for cook books. As to why I am an artist, I can only say that had I gone to college instead of art school I would probably be an English teacher. I say that, not irrelevantly, but because books seem to me to be the natural place for my kind of drawing. I don't think I would ever do a real painting even if I could. I loved books as a child. I've never enjoyed them as much since. My mother taught me to read at home, and I never went to school at all until the third grade. Guy Pène du Bois, the painter, William Pène du Bois, the illustrator, and Raoul Pène du Bois, the theatrical designer, are all my cousins and my mother drew delightful amateur pictures. It was, I suppose, inevitable that my sister, Jacqueline, and I should grow up to be artists of some kind." About her work, Margot Tomes adds, "I am old-fashioned about techniques and use pen and ink and poster paint. It makes me sound almost mid-Victorian." Miss Tomes works in her New York City apartment at a large drawing board in the kitchen "close to the stove and the icebox. As to *how* I work, it is always under great duress."

TREDEZ, ALAIN, see Trez, Alain

TRESILIAN, CECIL STUART*

Born July 12, 1891 in Bristol, England. There and in Liverpool and London childhood was spent. Attended Regent Street Polytechnic School, and Royal College of Art, London.

As a child, Cecil Stuart Tresilian was always interested in the ships and shipping at Liverpool, and used to draw what he saw. After studying at the Polytechnic for a few years, he taught as pupil teacher and then gained a Royal Exhibition Scholarship to the Royal College of Art. In 1914 when war broke out, he went into the service, was wounded and a prisoner of war. The drawings that he made during his imprisonment are now in The War Museum in London. In 1919, he married a fellow art student. They have a son and daughter and now five grandchildren. Until his retirement, he taught for many years at the Regent Street Polytechnic School. One of the first books he illustrated was Kipling's *All the Mowgli Stories* published in 1933. One of his most memorable commissions of the past ten years was collaborating with Sir Vivian Fuchs on a junior edition of his *Antarctic Adventure* (1959). Along with color photographs, this had Mr. Tresilian's line drawings done in brush and India ink on rough paper, about twice the actual size — "a method I enjoyed and felt suited the subject." An edition of *Kim* which he illustrated in 1958 was another book he particularly enjoyed. He writes, "I work very much on my own as I live in an old thatched house in Winslow near Bletchley Bucks (England) dated about 1560, renovated, of course, but delightful to live in. I was Master of the Art Workers' Guild for the year 1960 and was President of the Society of Graphic Artists from 1962 to 1965."

TREZ, ALAIN, pseud. (Tredez, Alain)

Born February 2, 1926 in Berck (Pas-de-Calais), France. Childhood was spent in Berck and Paris. Attended University of Paris and Ecole des Sciences Politiques.

As a student, Alain Tredez studied law and political science but always longed for a more active career. His military service was spent in the paratroops, a rugged section of the French armed forces. Some of his earliest works were decorations for various army recreation halls. Instead of returning to the law after his military service, he took a job as a cartoonist and was quite successful, drawing under the pen name "Trez." In 1950, he married a writer, Denise Laugier. Together they became editors of *Dominique*, a monthly magazine for children. This in turn led to the idea of doing books for children, the first of which was *Circus in the Jungle* in 1958. The ideas for their books may come from themselves or from their three children, Isabelle, Corinne and Florence. *The Royal Hiccups* was conceived, for example, during a family discussion of a dreamed-of trip to India which was interrupted when Florence got the hiccups. Along with the magazine and the books, Alain Tredez also spends a good deal of his time doing abstract painting. The Tredez family live in a duplex apartment on the Left Bank in Paris with a large workroom on the second floor for all the family projects.

TRNKA, JÍRÍ

Born in 1914 in Pilsen, Czechoslovakia.

Jírí Trnka is well-known in Czechoslovakia as a painter and film-maker as well as for the many children's books he has illustrated. His illustrations show the influence of the marionette theater with which he was involved from his youth. In his early years, he designed decorations for the dolls' stage at Pilsen and later had his own marionette theater in Prague. A number of his prize-winning films have been made with puppets. Three of his films were shown at the 1946 Cannes Film Festival and another was awarded a prize at the Brussels World's Fair. Mr. Trnka makes his home in Prague.

TROY, HUGH*

Born April 28, 1906 in Ithaca, New York where childhood was spent and Cornell University was attended. Died July 7, 1964.

After leaving college in 1927, Hugh Troy earned his living by painting mural decorations, augmenting this income by writing short articles and fiction. He has written that "through a desire to write and illustrate fanciful things, some children's books have been evolved." These included *Chippendale Dam* and *Five Golden Wrens*. During World War II Hugh Troy was a Captain in the 21st Bomber Command. After the war he lived for three years in Garrison, New York, and then moved to Washington, D. C.

TROYER, JOHANNES*

Born 1902 in the South Tirol which was then a part of Austria, but which became part of Italy after World War I. Studied in Austria and Germany.

Johannes Troyer lived for many years in Vienna and Innsbruck, working as illustrator and calligrapher for German, Swiss and American publishers. His posters won him numerous awards in both national and international competitions. From 1939 to 1949 he lived in Switzerland and in Liechtenstein, for which small principality he designed a number of postage stamps. He came to the United States in 1949. In addition to book illustration Mr. Troyer devoted much time to the creation of typographic ornaments and new designs for type faces. After his wife's death in 1961, he returned to Europe to live.

TUDOR, TASHA*

Born August 28, 1915 in Boston, Massachusetts. Attended Spring Hill School, Litchfield, Connecticut.

Tasha Tudor's father was W. Starling Burgess, designer of American Cup Defender yachts and a pioneer in airplane building. Her mother was Rosamond Tudor, a portrait painter who taught her the rudiments of water colors. As a child she loved the books of Beatrix Potter, Randolph Caldecott, and Walter Crane and feels she was probably influenced by them as well as by such artists as Edmund Dulac, Arthur Rackham, and Hugh Thomson. She wrote and illustrated her first book, *Pumpkin Moonshine*, published in 1938. Since then she has illustrated over thirty-six books, most of which she has also written. Two of the exceptions to this are the special editions she illustrated of *The Secret Garden* and *The Little Princess* by Frances Hodgson Burnett. Tasha Tudor works in water color and pencil, as in *Wings from the Wind* and usually designs as well as illustrates her books. With her husband, Allan John Woods, she lives in Webster, New Hampshire on a farm that appears often in her illustrations. Her "studio" is in her kitchen where she can be close to the hub of things, She writes, "We raise all our own food including our butter and cheese. I am a passionate gardener, one of the reasons why I never meet a deadline on time." She has four children by a previous marriage. The eldest, Bethany Tudor, has illustrated and written three picture books for small children. An article on Tasha Tudor appeared in the December 2, 1963 issue of *Publishers' Weekly*,

TUNIS, EDWIN*

Born December 8, 1897 at Cold Spring Harbor, New York. Childhood was spent on Long Island, and in North Carolina and Maryland. Attended Baltimore City College; Maryland Institute of Art and Design.

Edwin Tunis says that as a child he was not particularly good at schoolwork but, nevertheless, was an avid reader and developed an interest in Americana in his early teens. His art training was never formally completed because in 1917 he entered the war as a "fledgling flyer." After the war, he began work as a furniture designer and renderer of interiors and then switched to advertising illustration and layout. As free-lance artist after about 1925, he began doing murals. Research for a mural on the history of spices (for the McCormick Company in Baltimore) revealed that at the time there was no one book that covered the development of ships in a simple way. So *Oars, Sails and Steam* was written and illustrated and received several honors, including selection for the American Institute of Graphic Arts "Fifty Books of the Year" Show in 1953. His later books have also received various honors: *Wheels*, the Gold Medal of the Boys Clubs of America in 1955; *Colonial Living*, the Thomas A. Edison Foundation Award in 1957; *Frontier Living* was first Runner-up for the 1962 Newbery Medal; *Colonial Craftsmen* was an Honor Book in the 1965 New York *Herald Tribune* Children's Spring Book Festival. He is equally pleased that his books have been selected to be sold at historic sites such as Williamsburg and Old Sturbridge. "Time, age and mileage" have caused him to abandon all work other than book illustration. This he does primarily in black-and-white, the early books in pen and ink and the later ones, such as *Colonial Craftsmen*, in crayon. The larger drawings for *Shaw's Fortune* were made with carbon pencils over light grey washes to "hold them together." He characterizes his work as "didactic representation, as accurate and complete as I can make it."

More about his way of working is given in his article "Some Problems of a Writer-Illustrator" in the December 1966 *Horn Book*. Mr. Tunis and his wife live in Reisterstown, Maryland.

TURKLE, BRINTON CASSADAY

Born August 15, 1915 in Alliance, Ohio. Attended Carnegie Institute of Technology, Pittsburgh, Pennsylvania; School of the Museum of Fine Arts, Boston, Massachusetts; Institute of Design, Chicago, Illinois.

"The only artist in my home town," writes Mr. Turkle, "was Gertrude Alice Kay, a successful illustrator and writer of children's books. She was a family friend and gave me encouragement. I grew up with her books — and many others since my family knew that no gifts pleased me more than books. But I studied drama in college before going to Art School. This theatrical training included history of art, architecture, costume and stage design — where I learned about color. All of this has been of value to me as an illustrator. I esteem spontaneity and directness in illustration. In an effort to achieve this, I often work with a light box with charcoal, crayon, ink and water color in various combinations — but only after an enormous amount of sketching, planning, composing, and false starts." *Peter's Tent* was done in wash and crayon using two colors pre-separated. *Obadiah the Bold*, for which Mr. Turkle also wrote the text, was done in full color using wash and charcoal. He designs all the picture books he illustrates, but not the books for older children. He has also worked as an advertising illustrator and designer and has done theatrical caricatures "a la Hirschfeld" for various newspapers. He continued to use his theatrical training by acting in and directing various productions in Chicago and later Santa Fe, New Mexico, where he lived for ten years. Since moving to New York to be nearer the publishing industry, he has worked in two off-Broadway shows which, he writes, "demanded so much of me as actor and stagehand that I have not allowed myself the luxury of working in the theatre since." Brinton Turkle is married and has three children, Matilda, Haynes, and Jonathan.

UNGERER, TOMI

Born November 28, 1931 in Strasbourg, France where he spent his childhood.

Tomi Ungerer is a cartoonist, painter, writer, and illustrator. He feels that most of his education was gained walking and hitch-hiking throughout Europe — "the best way to travel, meet people and have adventure." Although born into a family of watchmakers, he soon followed another bent, making his living painting, drawing, and working in the graphic arts. He spent his military service in the Camel Caravan of the French Desert Police. After a visit to the United States, he returned in 1957 to settle in New York City. His work includes advertising; drawing for *Esquire*, *Fortune*, and *Harper's*; producing satirical cartoon collections — *The Underground Sketchbook* and *Horrible;* doing paintings and graphic art; and, of course, writing and illustrating books for children. He works in a variety of media including pen and ink, collage, oil and water color. As a means of providing variety, he likes sometimes to make special use of calligraphy or type. He usually designs as well as illustrates his books, and frequently writes the text also, adding, "writing the book is half the pleasure." About his work, Mr. Ungerer writes, "I enjoy trying different ways of expression to break the monotony. I hate to repeat myself in a formula." He adds that his style in all phases of his work is constantly changing. Articles about his work can be found in *Graphis,* March 1959 and #120, 1965; *Print,* July 1959 and January 1966; *Art in America,* December 1965; *Horizon,* January 1961, and *Esquire,* 1963. Tomi Ungerer lives with his wife and children in New York City.

UNWIN, NORA SPICER*

Born February 22, 1907 in Tolworth, Surrey, England. There and in Surbiton, near the Thames River, childhood was spent. Also studied in Leon Underwood's studio, Kingston School of Art, and Royal College of Art, London.

"My twin sister and I are the youngest of a family of five," writes Nora Unwin. "Our family has been closely connected with books, both through printing and publishing, for several generations, and I have often watched the whole process of book production in my father's printing works. I often used to watch the artist-father of a friend at work; many of his excellent tools and materials became mine in later years. After high school I had eight years of specialized training that were a continuing adventure for me — pottery, wood carving, embroidery, bookbinding, mural decoration, engraving, etching, architecture. All were explored, but wood engraving and book illustration became my greatest loves. Probably a strong influence on my work as an illustrator can be traced to the war years when my job placed me among a charming group of children from whom I learned a great deal. In April 1946, I came to America, at the invitation of my author-friend Elizabeth Yates McGreal. I have come to love New England greatly, and the way of life here. I think America encourages one to realize one's possibilities." Since 1961, she has greatly expanded her explorations in the field of water color. "Inspired by two summer sessions at the DeCordova Museum in Lincoln, Massachusetts I find transparent collage combined with water color an ideal medium for the ideas I want to express," writes Miss Unwin. Nora Unwin works primarily in black-and-white and two colors using pen and ink, brush-line and half-tone wash, wood engraving and, of course, water color. She generally does color separations on acetate. Now her paintings, as well as her prints, are widely exhibited in the East, and have received a number of awards. In the past ten years more time has been given to the writing of her own children's books. She adds, "It is a joyous

adventure to weave a story-idea and pictures together to make a satisfying whole. Articles about Miss Unwin can be found in *Horn Book,* March 1950 and *Yankee Magazine,* March 1949. Following three months of travel and study in Mexico, Miss Unwin moved to Wellesley, Massachusetts where she lived for four years, continuing her printmaking, illustrating and writing, as well as being in charge of the art department at Tenacre Country Day School. However, the beauties of New Hampshire and the possibilities of a charming little house in the McGreal's old orchard lured her back to Peterborough, New Hampshire, where she now lives.

VAN STOCKUM, HILDA*

Born February 9, 1908 in Rotterdam. Childhood was spent first in Holland, then in Ireland where she studied at the Dublin School of Art. Attended also Academy of Art, Amsterdam; and Corcoran School of Art, Washington, D. C.

Hilda Van Stockum has written, "My father was a captain in the Royal Netherlands Navy, and we were always traveling from one place to another. I loved drawing. Paper and pencils always headed the list of my birthday wishes. At twelve I was sent to a 'real artist' for lessons. Later when we went to Ireland, I was sent to a regular art school where I learned as much about human nature as about drawing. Back in Holland at nineteen I gained admission to the academy and there I was given a thorough grounding for four years. Returning to Dublin I studied lithography and started to get commissions to illustrate primers and paint portraits. This was interrupted by my meeting Ervin R. Marlin from New York. We married, and in 1934 I set foot in New York for the first time." In that same year her first book, *A Day on Skates,* was published. Since then she has written and illustrated stories laid in Holland, in Ireland, in the United States and Canada; has illustrated some books for other authors, and has had six children. Miss Van Stockum's illustrations have been either in black-and-white, using pen and ink or scratchboard, or in full color, using water color. She and her husband live in Washington, D. C. and now have four grandchildren.

VASILIU, MIRCEA*

Born July 16, 1920 in Bucharest, Rumania. His childhood was spent in Rumania where he was trained for a diplomatic career. Attended the University of Bucharest from which he received a law degree; later attended Corcoran School of Art, Washington, D. C., and Art Students League, New York.

At the age of thirteen Mircea Vasiliu was already a published author, and at sixteen his second book appeared. After military service as a cavalry lieutenant in the Royal Escort of the King, he became, at the age of twenty-three, an Attaché in the Rumanian Ministry for Foreign Affairs. In 1946 he came to the United States where he served as Third Secretary to the Rumanian Legation in Washington, at this same period studying art at the Corcoran School. In 1948, when Communism became master in Rumania, Mr. Vasiliu resigned his career in protest and received asylum in the United States. In his new life he tried many things before succeeding in his wish to become an artist: selling curtains in a department store, selling books at Brentano's, doing research for the National Committee for a Free Europe. Marriage to his Scottish-American wife and the decision to start his present career brought him to New York and the Art Students League. He has been free-lancing since 1951, illustrating, in addition to children's books, a number of adult books. Mircea Vasiliu works primarily in black-and-white, using a thin crisp line with pen and ink. He also combines this with a halftone overlay using pen and ink and wash. *The Year Goes Round* was done with a prismacolor pencil on dinobase, a technique that, he feels, "gives the drawing a halftone effect although it can be reproduced as a line drawing. The line is softened and the areas of color have a crayon-like effect." He uses color in a decorative manner. Mr. Vasiliu has designed those books for which he has also written the text. He characterizes his work as "representational — taking liberties for the sake of the decorative or the humorous." His own humorous autobiography, *The Pleasure Is Mine*, was published in 1955. He makes his home in Riverdale, New York.

VERNEY, JOHN

Born September 30, 1913 in London, England. Childhood was spent in India. Attended Eton College, Christ Church, Oxford.

John Verney, author, illustrator, and painter, attended the Architectural Association for two years before deciding to concentrate on painting and illustrating. He served for six years in World War II "with most weapons, starting with horses and ending with parachutes." After the war, he began his career doing humorous drawing, "and whenever possible, serious painting." He executed over 100 covers and many features for *Collins Magazine for Boys and Girls* (later called *The Elizabethan*) and eventually became its editor for the year 1961-62. About his technique Mr. Verney writes, "Mostly I work in pen and ink line, with a two or three color jacket. I have occasionally used lithography, silk-screen, and even copper engraving, but I became more and more interested simply in pen and ink which seems to me the most direct and honest means of expression for *me*." Mr. Verney, who designs his books whenever possible, works primarily in black-and-white and two colors. His most ambitious illustrations have been the four color ones for *The Mad King of Chickiboo*. His drawings have appeared in about six of his own books for children, as well as those of other authors. A sidelight to his career as a children's book author and illustrator that has found success in England is his invention and design of an elaborate diary-engagement-

doodle book called the "Dodo Pad." Mr. Verney concludes, "I do a great many straight watercolors, recording the everyday scene, and have an exhibition in London or the provinces about every two years."

VICTOR, JOAN BERG

Born July 11, 1937 in Chicago, Illinois. Childhood spent in Chicago and Michigan. Attended Newcomb College of Tulane University; Graduate School of Art and Architecture, Yale University (M.F.A.).

"From the time I was a very young child, I have always drawn and painted, sculpted and done ceramics. My father, my grandfather and I went for a while to a night sketch class, but until I was in college I had no formal art training. After college I spent a year in Chicago with my family — at that time I did free-lance graphic designing, painted and taught an adult life drawing class and art classes in a settlement house," writes Joan Victor. Her paintings have been shown in the Delgado Museum in New Orleans, Art Institute of Chicago and in exhibitions in New York City. Recently she has begun writing in addition to illustrating books, which before her marriage were done under her maiden name, Joan Berg. Mrs. Victor works in pencil and grey ink line; and for books she has done in color, she has used pencil and water color. Her home is now in New York City.

VON SCHMIDT, ERIC

Born May 28, 1931 in Bridgeport, Connecticut. Attended Jerry Farnsworth School of Art, Sarasota, Florida and Art Students League, New York City.

Mr. Von Schmidt writes, "My first training in illustration came very early because I grew up underfoot in my father's studio. That studio was a wonderful place. Horse skulls, Indian bonnets, flintlock rifles, books with pictures of naked ladies, good smells of turpentine and varnish. Everything a boy could ask for. When I wasn't drawing I would dress up in one of the costumes and fight imaginary battles. Chaplin, Disney, and Krazy Kat were my heroes. With the exception of Walt, they pretty much still are. I did my first professional work for *The American Magazine* and *True* when I was eighteen. Both art directors died shortly after. Work became hard to find after that, and I drifted into the streets. I got high with some companions by looking at a book of Piero reproductions and in a short time found I had become addicted to painting, a habit I haven't kicked to this day. I had some one-man shows and won some prizes. The nicest was a Fulbright Grant to study painting in Italy in 1955-56. When I came back, things were thin, so I started illustrating again. At night I played the guitar in coffee houses. At first, I illustrated other people's books and sang other people's songs. Then I got around to writing my own songs and books and even having my own children. I put my wife in my songs and my children in the books. That's the way we like it." Eric Von Schmidt works in a variety of media and techniques. He has used a simple black line as in *Chancy and the Grand Rascal*. *The Young Man Who Wouldn't Hoe Corn*, which he wrote and illustrated, was done with a duotone plate overlay, as well as a second color and old-fashioned type, Caslon Antique. Other techniques he has used are wet collage, four-color and two-color overlays, and plaster panels. He has used lettering on record and book jackets. His experiments with using two colors to give a third when overprinted were continued with good results on a series of jackets for children's records, put out by Pathways of Sound for whom Mr. Von Schmidt is Art Director. "At first," he writes, "I couldn't abide separations. Now I dig the whole crazy mess of effects and possibilities we have now that the old boys didn't." Eric Von Schmidt lives with his wife, Kay, and four children, Kittie, Gigi, Caitlin, and Megan in Sarasota, Florida, spending the summer in Henniker, New Hampshire.

WABER, BERNARD

Born September 27, 1924 in Philadelphia, Pennsylvania where he spent his childhood. Attended Philadelphia Museum College of Art; Pennsylvania Academy of Fine Arts.

"I don't remember possessing a strong inclination to art," explains Bernard Waber. "An older brother, now in electronics, was regarded as the family talent. My own most passionate interest was the movies. Fame and the famous preoccupied me. Hector P. Valenti, star of stage and screen in *The House on East 88th Street*, yearning for his break and Lyle the crocodile marching in a parade, having his picture taken and receiving loads of mail were manifestations of childhood fantasies. My first attempts at drawing were to copy photographs of movie stars. I would like to say that undeniable sparks of talent finally propelled me into a career in art. Truth was, I was simply better at it than I was at the likes of algebra and physics. I went through my first year or so of art school with the uncomfortable feeling I was committing a hoax — pretending to be an artist. After a time the art fever caught hold of me. I suppose my entrance into the children's book field had its origins in read-aloud sessions with my children. What impressed me most about children's books was the unlimited, unrestricted opportunity for creativity and originality. An illustrator could rise to the top of his talent or quickly come to grips with his own limitations. In one way or another, I seem to find myself thinking of children's books most of the time. And in one way or another I keep revising my attitude and philosophy toward them. I love the total involvement of putting a book together. Since I write the text for my book, many pictorial ideas seem to leap to life at the moment words are set to paper. I do not make a conscious effort to remember them. If they are at all worthwhile, they will remain with me, and, in fact, insist their way to realization. I try to avoid preparing an overly explicit dummy,

preferring instead to save myself for the final art. Then I leap in all at once, shoving, pushing, and changing things around. Almost all of my books have been illustrated with felt-tipped pens and Magic Markers. I have found their instant-dry characteristic most compatible with the quick and steady pace I like to keep under the stress and joy of 'creating.' Lately I have tried other media. For *You Look Ridiculous*, I experimented with inking various textures (cork, leaves, fabric, peeled corrugated board, etc.) pressing them against glass and transferring the impressions to paper. I make my own separations, using a medium weight vellum." *The House on East 88th Street* was an Honor Book in the 1962 *New York Herald Tribune* Spring Children's Book Festival. Bernard Waber has been layout artist for *Life* magazine since 1955. He lives with his wife and three children in Baldwin, New York.

WARD, LYND KENDALL*

Born June 26, 1905 in Chicago. Childhood was spent in Evanston, Illinois; Newton, Massachusetts; and Englewood, New Jersey. Was graduated from Teachers College, Columbia University, 1926; and attended State Academy of Graphic Arts, Leipzig, Germany.

Soon after Lynd Ward's return from Germany his first novel in woodcut was published: *Gods' Man*. This was followed by five others: *Madman's Drum, Wild Pilgrimage, Prelude to a Million Years, Song Without Words* and *Vertigo*. These were the first woodcut novels, without text, to be published in this country, and they established his reputation as a wood engraver. But he refuses to be typed in any one medium, and frequently works in water color, oil, lithography, in color as well as black-and-white, and mezzotint. Stimulated by the encouragement of Louise Seaman of Macmillan, in 1928 he illustrated his first book for children, *The Begging Deer*, by Dorothy Rowe, a collection of Japanese stories. The next year appeared *Prince Bantam*, the first book done in collaboration with his wife, May McNeer. Since that time he has worked continually on books. He has illustrated most of the books his wife has written, among them *America's Mark Twain* and *American Indian Story*, as well as ones he has written himself. Books he has illustrated by other authors include Elizabeth Coatsworth's *Cat Who Went to Heaven* and Esther Forbes' *Johnny Tremain*, both winners of the Newbery Medal. He has also done three books written by his oldest daughter, Nanda, who is now married and has a daughter of her own. These were *The Black Sombrero, The High Flying Hat* and *Hi, Tom*. He has illustrated many adult books for the Limited Editions Club and the Heritage Press, and in 1954 received the Limited Editions Silver Medal for twenty-five years of distinguished service in book illustration. Three years earlier he received the Carteret Book Club Award for Book Illustration; his books have been included often in the "Fifty Books" selections of the American Institute of Graphic Arts; and in 1953 he received the Caldecott Medal for *The Biggest Bear* which he wrote as well as illustrated. His interests are as varied in the books he illustrates as they are in the media he employs, and he gets as much pleasure from putting a children's book into pictures as he does the interpreting of adult ideas into form and color and visual life. About his work, he writes, "I try to give a feeling of the quality of the world and the people. If distortion or exaggeration will contribute to this — good." Although he sometimes does color separations he prefers to work directly in lithography whenever possible. An article about how he works in this medium appeared in the February 1964 issue of *Horn Book*. Other articles on Lynd Ward have appeared in *American Artist*, March 1955 and February 1959. One of the strongest influences in Lynd Ward's life has been the Canadian woods where he has a summer home and where he has spent a part of almost every year since early childhood. The Wards have two grown daughters and their home is in Cresskill, New Jersey.

WARNER, EDYTHE RECORDS

Born October 26, 1916 in St. Paul, Minnesota. Childhood was spent in Castle Rock and Walker, Minnesota. Attended St. Olaf College, Northfield, Minnesota; Minneapolis School of Art.

Edythe Warner's childhood spent in the Minnesota countryside provides the subject matter for her books, which she writes, designs, and illustrates. Her interest in animals, the outdoors, and drawing was kindled by her father. She writes, "He was interested in conservation — in fact, he was a state forester for years — and was a sportsman. I learned hunting and fishing instead of sewing or cooking. While I was still so small I had to be carried piggy back into trout streams, my father always took along pad and pencil for me. Then, when I got tired, I would sit under a bush or somewhere and draw the things I saw around me. And I learned to draw them as realistically as I could. I also developed the habit, which I still have, of taking sketch books wherever I go." When she was first married, Mrs. Warner did portraits, mostly of children, in oil and chalk. As her two boys grew up she began writing and illustrating children's books. About her work, she writes, "Because of my kind of writing I feel my illustrations should be realistic. In talking to children in schools and library groups I think that they, also, want realistic illustrations for true-to-life stories." She works primarily in black-and-white and full color, using thick lead pencils (prismacolor) on a heavy dinobase. *Tigers of Como Zoo* was in the American Institute of Graphic Arts Children's Book Show of 1961-62.

WARNER, PETER

Born March 1, 1939 in London, England. Childhood was spent in Mitcham, London and Surrey. Attended Catherham School; Wimbledon School of Art; Royal Academy of Painting, London.

After leaving school in 1963, Peter Warner began illustrating while continuing his painting. His special interest in drawing animals stems simply from loving them. "I have as pets three magnificent cats with devilish personalities, an enormous black Great Dane and a little white goat whose aim in life seems to be escaping and demolishing neighborhood gardens." About his work Mr. Warner writes, "My main inclination is toward the surrealistic. I find that even the most mundane event in a book has a touch of fantasy somewhere, and this I feel is the present day illustrator's unique function, which sets him apart from the recording illustrator of the days before photography, and, of course, from the photographer today." Peter Warner works with a variety of materials such as colored inks, water colors, "cryla" colors, brushes — and fingers, *Zomo the Rabbit* was done in black-and-white, using full color on the jacket. He designs and often writes the text for technical material, such as a British series for Pictorial Education on ships and musical instruments. His interest in musical instruments finds an outlet in playing the clarinet with two semi-professional orchestras in London. With what is left of his time, he restores vintage cars for daily transportation and traveling through Europe. Mr. Warner lives with his pets, clarinet, and antique cars in the Kent countryside near Westerham.

WATSON, ALDREN AULD*

Born May 10, 1917 in Brooklyn, New York. Attended Yale University, New Haven, Connecticut; Art Students League, New York City.

Aldren A. Watson is from a family of artists — Ernest W., Eva Auld, and Lyn A. Watson. Prior to his formal art education he carried on studies in drawing and painting, and color block printing, early developing an interest in type, lettering, and illustration. During this period he also began learning the art of hand bookbinding. Later, cartography was another area of interest and he did a series of maps for *Time* magazine, as well as many for textbooks. A mural commission won in competition gave him the opportunity to do an overmantel mural for the S. S. President Hayes. For four years during World War II, he and his wife, Nancy Dingman Watson, were field workers for the American Friends Service Committee. During this time he completed illustrations for an edition of Thoreau's *Walden*, working at night after cutting saw logs during the day. After the war, the Watsons moved to a farm in Putney, Vermont, where they now live with their eight children. Aldren Watson has illustrated well over 150 books for children and adults, and has also done illustrations for advertising and for promotional publications. He has served as design consultant for many private corporations. In 1963, he wrote and illustrated a manual on book binding, a subject that he has also taught in various schools. In 1954, with the publication of his wife's first children's book, *What Is One?*, a new family venture began. This book was followed by others, illustrated and frequently designed by Mr. Watson. For their fifth book, *What Does A Begin With?*, a new type face was used of Mr. Watson's own design, called Watson-Cameron after his daughter Cameron. Together the Watsons have completed twenty-five books for children. In his books, Aldren Watson relies heavily on the design of the line, underscoring these with two or sometimes three flat colors "which accent the light and shade as a means of delineating form." In making acetate separations, he frequently has one ink print over another to achieve effects which he believes are superior to process color reproduction. In recent years, his illustrations have been concerned with *how things work*, as a consequence of which an increased interest in precision and clarity have come to the fore. An article about Aldren Watson appeared in *American Artist*, March 1946.

WEBB, CLIFFORD CYRIL*

Born February 14, 1895 in London, England. Childhood was spent in Essex. Attended Westminster School of Art, London.

Clifford Webb writes, "I can remember drawing on the stone floor in the kitchen with colored chalks at the age of seven, emulating the pavement artists I so much admired. That I think was the beginning, and I have had a soft spot for the pavement artist ever since. At school I somehow managed to do a fair amount of drawing, though the school authority showed little interest in art in those days. Later as a soldier serving in Egypt, Iraq, and India, the color and movement and excitement of trying to transfer my impressions to canvas or paper decided my career. The children's books I have done, just one part of my art, were created for my own children, illustrated and written with them, and their instructions were carried out. The illustrations were completed first, the text being written around the illustrations. Books for children have always given me a great deal of pleasure to do. I hope I have succeeded in keeping a few thousand children quiet and interested and given poor parents like myself the chance to get on with their work." Among the early books written and illustrated by Mr. Webb for his children are *The Story of Noah* and *Butterwick Farm*. "My early books were done on scraper board but the later ones, such as *Animals From Everywhere*, are a mixture of poster colors, chalk and splatter work. I am mainly an engraver and do large color prints cut sometimes on oak or elm, a number of which are purchased for school decoration." Clifford Webb lives in Abinger Hammer, Surrey, England and has ten grandchildren. "It is up to them to keep me on the right path in my writing and illustrating."

WEIL, LISL*

Born in Vienna, Austria where her childhood was spent. Attended Wiener Kunstgewerbeschule.

Lisl Weil writes that she has always had an intense interest in drawing, dancing and music, and received a fine education in all three, concentrating more and more on drawing, and graduating with high honors from art school. While still in school she was illustrator and member of the staff of one of the most popular of Viennese magazines, and of a daily newspaper, drawing and writing about anything that appealed to her. She traveled extensively in Europe, and her drawings have been exhibited widely. She came to the United States in 1939 and worked in various fields of illustration until she found that "in doing art work for children I can do my best to my greatest contentment." She has illustrated many children's books since then, some of which she has written herself. Miss Weil has done books in two and three colors and also full color, but stresses that she is "primarily interested in drawing, expressing in a line mood, motion as well as details. I use colors only to accent important details or moods." She works with pen, crayon, or brush, using simple poster colors on any kind of paper. Miss Weil, who makes her own layouts, sometimes uses type or hand-lettering to make the book a harmonious unit. She adds, "I like to think of some of my work as reporting about the life and feelings of people or creatures I observe, wherever I happen to be." For one year Lisl Weil had a weekly television show called "Children's Sketch Book," and for eighteen years she has been performing with Thomas Scherman's Little Orchestra Society Concerts for Young People, illustrating on the stage in huge crayon drawings the story of the music and its rhythm, as it is being played by the orchestra. She has also performed with the Chicago Symphony Orchestra, the New Haven Symphony Orchestra, the Detroit Symphony Orchestra, and with Children's Concerts on nation-wide television. "It is like ballet with colored crayons. Best of all I like to draw happy and gay things and animals, to give pleasure to my audience whilst I have great joy in doing it. One of my books, *The Sorcerer's Apprentice*, has also been made into a motion picture by Weston Woods Studios, in which I am drawing the pictures to music, just as I do it on the concert stage." Miss Weil and her husband travel a good deal but make their home in New York City.

WEISGARD, LEONARD*

Born December 13, 1916 in New Haven, Connecticut. Childhood was spent in Connecticut, England, and in New York City and Brooklyn. Attended Pratt Institute, Brooklyn.

"A particular school teacher was responsible for provoking and developing my interest in drawing and painting," writes Mr. Weisgard. "Exposure to the dreary pictures and stories used in public school textbooks forced me to a resolve — someday I would perhaps try to change those books! The world could not be all that dreary and limited to only one color. As an only child, alone a great deal, books served as pathways to all the world outside my ken. And books for children which I devoured along with adult books at too early an age, greatly affected me. Illustration has always been influenced by all of man's art forms. The first primitive cave paintings, the earliest forms of design and depiction used before writing as a method of notation and communication, the remarkable Gothic and Renaissance transitions, the daring imaginative French children's book illustration of the 1920's, the textural approach of Russian books for children, and the wonderful joyous world of folk and primitive art, wherever it appeared, have all influenced my own viewpoint." Mr. Weisgard works in many media and colors. "I seem to use water color, gouache, poster paint, crayon, chalk, ink and whatever suggests itself for the story or text, or whatever is asked for by the production department." About color separations, he adds, "I work with and deeply resent acetate as a surface. I would rather work on sidewalk or wood or plaster." He often designs and sometimes writes the text for his books. He likes to work with type feeling it "is always an integral part of an illustration and its relationship to white space and the rest of the book's format is of great importance." In 1947 his illustrations for *The Little Island* by Golden MacDonald (Margaret Wise Brown) was awarded the Caldecott Medal. His books have also received awards from the American Institute of Graphic Arts and the Society of Illustrators. The costumes and sets he designed in 1953 for the first full length American *Nutcracker Suite* are still being used by the San Francisco Ballet. In addition, the art work for *Mr. Peaceable Paints* has been traveling through the Soviet Union and Middle Europe under the aegis of the United States Government. Leonard Weisgard lectures on art, creativity, and children's books at universities, colleges, and schools around the country, and "As a school board chairman in Roxbury, Connecticut and an officer of the Connecticut Association of Boards of Education, I stress wherever and whenever possible, the importance and need for libraries." Mr. Weisgard lives with his wife and children in Roxbury, Connecticut. Articles about his illustrating have appeared in the *Horn Book*, July 1947 and August 1964 and in *Library Journal*, July 1947.

WEISS, EMIL

Born August 14, 1896 in Olmutz, Moravia, Austria where he spent his childhood. Attended University of Vienna, Austria. Died January 6, 1965.

In 1919, Emil Weiss took a degree in architecture. Later while he worked at that profession, he also did illustrations and newspaper art. During World War I he was a war artist, and in the years after the war, he worked for the leading European newspapers, while living in Prague, Czechoslovakia. In 1939, he moved to London, England, and worked for the British Army, J. Arthur Rank, and the *Daily Telegraph*. At that time he was designing film sets and costumes as well as drawing. For the *Daily Telegraph* he covered many international conferences and developed a reputation for doing thumbnail sketches of leading political figures. Just after World War II he was commissioned to draw fifty famous Generals of the British Army for the Hall of Fame of the Royal Engineers. Also accredited to the United Nations as press artist from its inception, he wrote, "I have sketched royalties, presidents and leaders of nations from life, starting from the last days of the Emperor Francis-Joseph of Austria to President Eisenhower." In 1948 Emil Weiss moved to New York City where he lived until his death in 1965.

WEISS, HARVEY*

Born April 10, 1922 in New York City where his childhood was spent. Attended New York University; University of Missouri; Art Students League and National Academy School of Fine Arts, New York; and studied with Ossipe Zadkine in Paris.

Harvey Weiss writes, "I started my art career as a sculptor, and a large part of my time is still devoted to that medium." His work is in the permanent collections of several museums and three works were purchased by the Ford Foundation in 1964-65. "I've lived all my life in New York City, with the exception of a year at the University of Missouri studying journalism, three years in the army, and a year in Europe after the war, studying sculpture in Paris and roaming about the continent. At various times I've worked in the fields of advertising, printing and photography. It wasn't until I had met and married Miriam Schlein in 1954 that I first became aware of the fascination of children's books. I succumbed to the irrepressible urge to write one myself when I began to realize that there was an audience of perceptive, fresh, honest, unspoiled people — children. I had never realized this before. It seemed to me that this was an opportunity for direct and honest art — writing and illustrating — that is rarely found in the commercial world of today. And it had a very close relationship in spirit with the sculpture I had been doing most of my life." *Clay, Wood and Wire* is one of a series of simple arts and crafts books that Mr. Weiss has done in recent years. He writes as well as designs and illustrates these, usually with photographs. For his other illustrating he uses a variety of media. Mr. Weiss and his wife live in New York City and have one daughter.

WENNERSTROM, GENIA KATHERINE, see Genia, pseud.

WERTH, KURT*

Born September 21, 1896 in Germany where his childhood was spent. Attended Academy for Graphic Arts, Leipzig.

After studying for four years at the Academy for Graphic Arts, Kurt Werth went to Munich. There he began to illustrate books, mostly for limited editions, among them Shakespeare, Pushkin, Euripides, Wasserman, Kipling and Kleist. He writes, "The depression in Germany put an end to illustrated books, and I found work in the magazine field, contributing to *Simplicissimus* and *Querschnitt*. The Hitler regime did not allow me to work because of my Jewish wife and we had to leave Germany. So we came to the United States. Here I started from scratch, doing drawings for the *New York Times*, for a number of anti-Nazi magazines during the war and then back to the book — first textbooks and at last to children's books. The development of my work was profoundly inspired by Rembrandt, Daumier and Slevogt. In the past ten years my style has changed to a more expressive and modern approach." Mr. Werth works in full color, always doing the color separations. He, his wife and son, live in New York City but his favorite pastime is traveling in Europe.

WIBERG, HARALD ALBIN

Born March 1, 1908 in Ankarsrum, Sweden where he spent his childhood. Attended Konstfack and Edvin Ollers Malarskola, Stockholm, Sweden.

Mr. Wiberg writes, "As most children I was fond of drawing and did so very early. I do not think anyone gave it a second thought. That the family should breed an artist was something not even to be imagined. At an early stage, my interest in animals was awakened. In those times it was customary to keep pigs or hens, and these animals became my first models. I remember the first desperate attempts to draw the hens when they had settled for the night on their sticks, and how I was fascinated not only by the form of the birds, but also by the, in my opinion, supernatural air that seemed to encircle them. And then the pigs rooting in the sty. I even recollect my dismay at not being able to fix the odor of their enclosure on the paper. I had my favorites among the artists — Bruno Liljefors, Albert Engström and Ivar Arosenius, then already dead. But one who came to mean more than the others was Knut Stangenberg. Stangenberg was represented in almost every paper before 1920. In quirky poems — his own expression — and often with fine illustrations he gave an account of Sweden and its people with a mild critical touch." In 1930 Harald Wiberg went to Stockholm to study art, painting portraits in the summer to earn money. In 1939 he published a piece for the journal of the Swedish Hunting Association, *Svensk Jakt*. This was the beginning of his career writing about and painting the outdoors. In 1945 he held a successful exhibition in Stockholm. He was awarded a bronze plaque in 1954 for a watercolor painting at the international exhibition for animal painters at Düsseldorf. *The Tomten*, an adaptation of Viktor Rydberg's poem, was a favorite of his since he first read it in school. He adds, "After nearly 30 years of studying and planning, the series of pictures to Viktor Rydberg's 'Tomten' was completed. To begin with it was intended as a Christmas present to my two boys, Anders and Magnus, but became so popular with the publisher that it was given out in 'Klumpe-Dumpe,' one of their Christmas papers for children in 1954. In numerous letters they were asked to collect the pictures in a book and in

a larger scale." Mr. Wiberg works primarily in black-and-white or full color in practically any medium. He characterizes his work as "naturalistic and maybe a little romantic," and feels that in the last ten years his style has changed, becoming somewhat decorative and using less detail so that unessentials are excluded resulting in "a more strict construction of the picture. In 1964 he was honored by being asked to execute two Christmas cards for UNICEF, "Shepherds" and "Winter Night."

WIESE, KURT*

Born April 22, 1887 in Minden, Germany where his childhood was spent.

Kurt Wiese says that in Minden he lived for fifteen years under a remarkable collection of paintings of the Dusseldorf School. "However, to become an artist was something unheard of, so I was sent to Hamburg to learn the export trade to China. After being able to count the threads of a ten-shilling shirting just by feeling it with my hands, I was sent out to China. I arrived there at the time of a revolution, but I spent the next six years traveling and selling merchandise until the war with Japan broke out." Captured by the Japanese he was handed over to the British. Five years of captivity followed; one in Hongkong and four in Australia, including a trip through the South Sea Islands en route. In Australia, impressed by the animal life and natural scenery, he began to write and to draw for pleasure. When he returned to Germany in 1919 he sold his whole production to a publisher and continued for three years to make books for boys and girls — mostly animal stories. At the same time he designed settings for a film company, and when this firm closed its doors he left for a visit to Brazil. He was so delighted with the beauty of the country that he spent a year traveling "through another revolution, through jungles, meeting Indians," and two more years illustrating schoolbooks and children's books for a Brazilian publishing company, and doing newspaper cartoons and a children's page of a paper. At this time Mr. Wiese's work became widely known and he was offered a position in New York which he accepted. He has lived in the United States ever since. Well known among the many books he illustrated before 1946 are his own *Liang and Lo*, 1930, Marjorie Flack's *Story About Ping*, 1933, Phil Stong's *Honk the Moose*, 1935, Claire Huchet Bishop's *Five Chinese Brothers*, 1938, and Theodore Waldeck's *White Panther*, 1942. Mr. Wiese works primarily in color. *The Thief in the Attic*, which he also wrote, was done in four-color separations on acetate. Some of his early work was done directly on litho plates or on frosted glass. He and his wife live on a farm in Frenchtown, New Jersey, near the Delaware River. There is a schoolhouse next door and boys and girls drop in to visit at his studio to watch him work and bring him things they have found in the woods. Since 1928, when his first book was published in the United States, Mr. Wiese has illustrated well over three hundred books, fifteen of which he wrote as well as illustrated.

WIESNER, WILLIAM*

Born April 28, 1899 in Vienna, Austria where his childhood was spent. Attended Technische Hochschule, Vienna, where he received a degree in architecture and engineering.

After receiving his degree William Wiesner free-lanced as an architect, interior decorator and designer. As a hobby he created a shadow-puppet theater which became well known in Europe. At that time he began to write his own shows and to design them himself. Arriving in the United States in 1941 he tried to sell these puppet-shows to publishers, and to his surprise got his first commission — for an animated magic-book. That was the beginning. Now, in addition to book illustration, William Wiesner works with his wife in textile design. Their work was included in the Metropolitan Museum's "American Fabrics and Fashions" exhibit in 1945. Since 1960, William Wiesner has concentrated on writing and illustrating children's books and painting murals. *More Tongue Tanglers* by C. F. Potter, which he illustrated in four flat colors, was an Honor Book in the *New York Herald Tribune* Spring Children's Book Festival in 1964. He notes that he has, in his illustrating, moved from using naturalistic full color to black-and-white with two or three colors, made as separations. The Wiesners live in New York City.

WIKLAND, ILON

Born February 5, 1930 in Esthonia where she spent her childhood. Attended Skolan för Bok-Och Relkamkonst studying under Professor Akki Kumlien; Signe Barth's Painting School, Sweden.

Ilon Wikland spent most of her childhood with her grandparents in a small town by the Baltic Sea. In 1944 she came to Sweden as a refugee and began her art studies. After finishing school she went to work for two years at a decorating studio. In 1948 she was in England for a six months period of art studies. Back in Stockholm again, she started working for a big publishing company as a lay-out artist. In 1951 Ilon Wikland married a Swedish Naval officer and began working as a free-lance artist. 1954 was a year of great importance to her because she met Astrid Lindgren and did the illustrations for her book, *Mio, My Son*. Getting to know Astrid Lindgren meant much to Ilon Wikland personally, and doing the illustrations for her book finally convinced her that illustrating children's books was the kind of work she really wanted to do above all. In 1966, she received a working scholarship from the government. Miss Wikland works primarily in black-and-white or full color in a style that is "naturalistic" and about which she writes, "I have tried to pay special attention to the children's

way of moving and their expressions." Ilon Wikland now has three daughters, who are her ever-present models, helping her to draw and understand children. Traveling in Europe has been one of her favorite hobbies and sources of inspiration. She lived in Paris for half a year and has been to England several times to visit her mother. Italy is her family's favorite place for summer vacations. Their home is in Sundleyberg, Sweden.

WILDSMITH, BRIAN LAWRENCE

Born January 22, 1930 in Penistone, Yorkshire, England. Childhood was spent in Sheffield, Yorkshire, England. Attended Barnsley School of Art; Slade School of Fine Art, University College, London, England.

Brian Wildsmith writes, "I was born in 1930, amid the Yorkshire moors of England, where the people are bright, thrifty and industrious. I there and then decided that this was not the place for a chap like me. In 1940, age 10, I won a scholarship to De La Salle College in Sheffield, where I started reading chemistry for pleasure and decided to devote my life to test tubes. And then it happened, on October 25, 1946 at 1:30 P.M. — the moment of truth. I decided that what I wanted in life was to express myself, and I could fulfill it only in paint. Although I had shown no talent in painting, I left next day (amid stunned silence) for the Barnsley School of Art. In 1952 I found myself in the Army teaching math at the Royal Military School. From 1954 to 1957 I taught art full-time and then, taking courage, resigned my job to free-lance. My wife was marvellous about it and even withheld from me the news we were having a baby, until they had accepted my resignation. From that time on I have been illustrating children's books and painting large abstracts." Mr. Wildsmith works primarily in full color, painting in gouache, which, he explains, can be used thickly with impasto, or as thin and transparent as watercolor. He designs his books and frequently writes the text as well. His style is representational "with abstract tendencies." About his work, he adds, "It is necessary to get to the roots of the text — its essence — and then create a pictorial form that is at one with the text and yet is a thing unto itself — a true marriage between written word and pictorial form, each complementing the other yet able to exist without the other." More information about Brian Wildsmith can be found in the *Junior Bookshelf*, July 1963 and *Library Journal*, November 15, 1965. In 1963 he won the Kate Greenaway Award for his *ABC*, and was one of the few contemporary artists to be included in the Library of Congress Showcase Exhibit "Three Centuries of ABC Books."

WILKON, JOZEF

Born February 12, 1930 in Bogucice (near Cracow), Poland. Childhood spent in Wieliczka. Attended the Academy of Art; Jagiellonski University, Cracow, Poland.

The two things that contributed most to his becoming an artist, Jozef Wilkon feels, were his father, who was an artist, and going to the Secondary School of Fine Arts. He later studied painting and wood-carving at the Academy of Art, and the history of art at the University. After his studies he began to paint as well as work in the graphic arts, and has had several exhibitions of his work. He has illustrated for all of the Polish publishers as well as several French and German publishers, with to date more than fifty books to his credit. Among the awards that he has received for his illustrations are the Polish Editors' Award for the "Most Beautiful Book of the Year" in 1960 and 1962, and in 1965 for the "Most Beautiful" German book. Mr. Wilkon works in black-and-white and color, using such materials as designers' colors, inks, crayon, India ink, gouache, and a great deal of water color. His style is highly decorative but is modified to meet the needs of the text. His early work was "more similar to nature," changing as he looked for "poetic, synthetic signs to create a style more from the world of imagination. It changed as the technique was growing richer, starting from the classical (water color, black-and-white) toward the combination of different techniques in order to enrich the fabric." Jozef Wilkon lives and works in Warsaw, Poland.

WILLIAMS, GARTH MONTGOMERY*

Born April 16, 1912 in New York. Childhood was spent on a farm in New Jersey, then in Ontario, Canada, and at the age of ten he was taken to England for his schooling. In London he attended City of London School, Westminster Art School, and the Royal College of Art.

The parents of Garth Williams were both artists. In 1929 he was sent to the Westminster Art School and in 1931 he won a special talent scholarship for oil painting to the Royal College of Art, where he studied mural technique and the craft of painting. At this time he became interested in the theater and made sets for a small theater group. During the first four years at the College he did sculpture in the evenings at the Westminster Art School to improve his drawing, and soon became fully absorbed in sculpture. After finishing his studies at the Royal College of Art, he organized Luton Art School (1935-36), painted murals, including those for the Earl of Dudley's home in Belgrave Square. Garth Williams won the British Prix de Rome for sculpture in 1936. He returned from Rome in 1938, having studied art in Italy, France, Germany, Hungary, Yugoslavia, Albania, Greece, Turkey, Holland, and Czechoslovakia. In November 1941 he returned to the United States and in 1943 he began working for the New Yorker and was asked by E. B. White to illustrate his first children's book, Stuart Little. This started Mr. Williams on his present career. Since then, he has devoted much of his time to illustrating, his work including Charlotte's Web and a new edition of Laura Ingalls Wilder's eight "Little House" books. Illustrating the Wilder books was a task of many years. Before he felt he was ready to begin Mr. Williams visited Mrs. Wilder in Missouri, traveled over all the territory covered in the stories and explored every possible source for background material. In the Horn Book for December 1953, he wrote, "Illustrating books is not just making pictures of the houses, the people and the articles mentioned by the author: the artist has to see everything with the same eyes." About his way of working, Garth Williams says, "I have used what seemed to me the most sympathetic medium to accompany the mood of the text." The result is a great variety of techniques, beginning with Stuart Little, which was done in pen and ink. The Wilder books were done in pencil on tracing paper in their actual size so that the negative for reproduction could be made by direct contact with the drawing. The result was a litho-type drawing in which "whites remain white, drawing crisp, effect soft and warm." He has used this technique on several other books. He has also used gouache, oil, water color and litho crayon and has often done separations using acetate overlays. "The decision whether to use color, full or only one or two," he writes, "is made by the publisher, as it is a question of cost. We discuss the way the book would look best, then see if we can afford it; if not, I think of a cheaper way to reach the desired effect." Garth Williams designs the books he illustrates and has also written two of them, The Rabbits' Wedding and The Adventure of Benjamin Pink. He characterizes his work as "highly personalized representation," explaining, "I start with the real animal, working over and over until I can get the effect of human qualities and expressions and poses. I redesign animals as it were." He has four daughters and lives in Marfil, Guanajuato, Mexico. His spare time, when he is not traveling, is spent in continuing with his sculpture and painting.

WILLIAMS, JENNY

Born March 22, 1939 in London, England where her childhood was spent. Attended Wimbledon School of Art and London University Institute of Education.

Jenny Williams writes, "As a child drawing was my only hobby. During the war when paper was hard to come by, I used to tear all the fly leaves from my books to use as drawing paper! Luckily I married a graphic designer and together we managed to enter the world of free-lance commercial art. Our work covers almost every part of this field — book jackets, magazine illustrations, fashion drawing and all types of advertising. However, on the whole I find drawing for children more rewarding than anything else, and hope in the future to concentrate mainly on this aspect." For The Silver Wood she did alternating pages in color and black-and-white, "using colored inks, gouache, and acrylic paints, and a good deal of masking fluid." Her husband generally designs the typographical layout of the pages. They make their home in London.

WILSON, PEGGY

Born in Galveston, Texas where her childhood was spent. Attended Texas Woman's University, Denton, Texas; San Francisco State College.

"At an early age, drawing was an entertainment, a means of discovery, and an obsession," writes Peggy Wilson. "I learned to draw by drawing. I had no formal art training until college, at which time I also became interested in the dance." After Miss Wilson took training in the dance, she was with a ballet company from 1950 to 1952, when an injury caused her to return to her study of art. She has had one-man exhibitions of her paintings in galleries and museums throughout the Southwest. In 1966, the first book that she illustrated, *Ananse the Spider,* was chosen by the *New York Times* as one of the "Ten Best Illustrated Children's Books." The illustrations for this book were done in black-and-white with a felt pen. Since 1965, Peggy Wilson has been living and working in New York City.

WIMMER, HELMUT KARL

Born December 8, 1925 in Munich, Germany where he spent his childhood.

Helmut Wimmer served an apprenticeship from 1939-1943 as a sculptor and model maker working primarily in plaster. In 1943 he joined the German Army and served until 1945, when he was captured by Czech partisans six days after the end of the war. He was turned over to Russian troops as a prisoner of war and held in Russia until September 1949. During his captivity, he worked part of the time as a sculptor in the restoration of public buildings in the city of Maxim Gorky. Returned to Germany, he took up his work as a sculptor, principally restoring war-damaged buildings. He migrated to the United States in 1954, and was employed as an Assistant Artist at the Hayden Planetarium eight days after his arrival in this country. "The development of my ability to illustrate astronomy was not easy," writes Mr. Wimmer. "Since I had no knowledge of astronomy it took a lot of patience on the part of the Planetarium staff to explain their wishes to me. My experience as a model maker was a great help to me, since I had worked consistently in three dimensions. I could visualize anything as a finished model, if the astronomy was properly explained to me." Subsequently, Mr. Wimmer became Chief Artist and a skilled master of air-brush painting and illustration in astronomy and the physical sciences. About his work he writes, "My tools are very simple — a commercial air brush and an air compressor. Water colors are used exclusively, and they are sprayed on very lightly so that intensity can be accurately controlled. Drawings are made on heavy paper which I then cut out with razor blades to make templates. Panels in the template are removed and replaced to control application of pigments as the painting develops." In addition to his work for the Planetarium, Helmut Wimmer has done extensive illustration for both magazines and

a dozen books on science. He lives with his wife, Franzi, and two daughters in Bergenfield, New Jersey. In 1961, he and his wife became citizens of the United States.

WOHLBERG, MEG

Born February 6, 1905 in New York City. Childhood was spent in New York, Chicago, Illinois, and Rochester, New York. Attended Rochester Institute of Technology; National Academy of Design.

Designing and printing fabrics and then designing architectural glass were Meg Wolberg's first experiences after finishing art school. Since next to drawing she loved reading, she wanted to get into book illustrating. But the route was circuitous, involving first a job in an advertising art staff — "It seemed awful at the time but I have often been grateful for what I learned about basic problems of production, about working under direction, etc." She then went on to become an advertising illustrator specializing in babies and children and handled the Johnson and Johnson baby product account for fifteen years. She also began illustrating for a number of national magazines. "Somewhere along the line the urge to become a children's book illustrator could no longer be suppressed. For a while my careers as advertising and book illustrator overlapped." She now gives her full time to books, working in a studio in "a small elderly four-story New York City house with a garden. I live here with my husband, and always there is a pet or two. The house is one I remodelled myself."

WONDRISKA, WILLIAM

Born June 29, 1931 in Chicago, Illinois. Childhood spent in Oak Park, Illinois. Attended Art Institute of Chicago (B.A.E. 1953); Yale School of Art and Architecture (B.F.A. 1954; M.F.A. 1955).

William Wondriska says that he was "always visually oriented. A third grade teacher suggested that my parents encourage my art and they sent me to the Saturday school at the Chicago Art Institute." At the end of high school he won two scholarships for continuing his art training. After graduating from the Chicago Art Institute, he went on to Yale. "Albers had just been there three years, new people were coming to the Art School. It was a very exciting time to have been studying there." As one of the projects for his M.F.A. degree, Mr. Wondriska conceived and executed a children's book which he called *The Sound of Things.* It was accepted for the Children's Book Show of the American Institute of Graphic Arts and subsequently published in 1958 by Pantheon. After Yale, he served in the Korean War for over a year and then went to work for the designer Lester Beal. In 1958, he moved to West Hartford where he lives now, and combined teaching at the University of Hartford Art School and free-lancing in graphic arts. Since

1961, he has been free-lancing full time. His picture books, which he writes as well as illustrates, are now eight in number. One, *All By Myself*, was inspired by the oldest of his three daughters and photographs of her are combined in it with the illustrations. About his book work he comments, "The direction I am going in now is very different from the earlier books. It is looser, not so severe, not so heavily designed. 1 2 3, *A Book to See* was good in its design but very severe. *Tomato Patch* was perhaps the turning point. It is softer and more relaxed in its general style. I am very much involved in the printing processes in my graphic work and in some cases have made use of the technology, as in the repetition of the thirteen animal drawings in *Which Way to the Zoo?*" Articles on his work have appeared in *Graphic Design #1* and in the *Penrose Annual*.

WRONKER, LILI CASSEL*

Born May 5, 1924 in Berlin, Germany. Childhood spent in Germany and England. Attended Art Students League, New York City; Brooklyn Museum Art School.

"Mine was a lucky childhood," writes Lili Cassel Wronker, "in a Berlin home surrounded by a garden and the finest picture books my parents could find at the time. My father was a doctor who loved the theater and took my sister and myself to see plays of the books we had read, among them translations of American and English children's books. Very much influenced by Hedvig Collin's drawings for Karin Michaëlis' *Bibi*, I started sketching from life myself. During summer vacations I travelled to Denmark, Switzerland, Scotland and Czechoslovakia. In 1938 we had to flee from the Nazis to England. In 1940 we arrived in New York City. I attended Washington Irving High School, majoring in Art, and won a scholarship to the Art Students League. Later I studied lettering privately and learned a great deal from the designers whom I assisted on various jobs in the advertising, magazine and book fields. I designed book jackets and illustrated my first book, *Rainbow Mother Goose*, in 1947. Since 1948 I have been free-lancing for various book publishers, have studied and taught at the Brooklyn Museum Art School and have travelled to Israel." Mrs. Wronker works primarily in black-and-white using pen and ink, though *Tell Me About the Cowbarn, Daddy* was done in four-color separations. She characterizes her work as linear and realistic, adding that over the years it has become "a little less tight, more calligraphic, but never as free as my personal, private work." She designs her books, and since she is a recognized calligrapher, she has always had a particular interest in the use of lettering and type. This can be seen in her illustrations for *Happy New Year Round the World*. An article on her appears in *American Artist*, February 1958. Since her marriage in 1952 to Erich Wronker, she and her husband have enjoyed working together at various projects on their small handpress. Another of Mrs. Wronker's hobbies is an international collection of children's books, selected from an illustrator's point of view. The

Wronkers live in Jamaica, New York. Since Mr. Wronker is an Israeli working for the United Nations, their two children go to the United Nations International School and every two years the family takes a "home leave" trip to Israel.

WYNANTS, MICHE

Born March 12, 1934 in Louvain, Belgium where she spent her childhood. Attended Ecole Nationale Supérieure D'Architecture et Des Arts, Antwerp and Decoratifs de L'Abbaye de la Cambre, Brussels.

As a child growing up during World War II, Miche Wynants had few children's books. When she was older she preferred drawing to studying. After finishing school at eighteen, Miss Wynants writes, "I always remembered my mother saying that at that age she wanted to go to an academy, but her father refused. She was very sorry about it because she was very gifted. I thought maybe she would give me the chance, and she did." Miche Wynants studied decorative art and illustration, finishing with great distinction. She works primarily in full color, designing her books and also writing the texts. She uses lettering and type as part of the pictures. Her style has changed so that it is stronger with fewer unwanted details. She adds, "I'm always eager to know new techniques that can give me other dimensions for what I want to express." Miss Wynant is married to a potter, who helps her a great deal by judging and criticizing her work. "I know he is very often right," she adds. They live in Incourt (Brabant), Belgium.

YAMAGUCHI, MARIANNE ILLENBERGER

Born January 10, 1936 in Cuyahoga Falls, Ohio. Childhood was spent in Parma, Ohio near Cleveland. Attended Bowling Green State University, Bowling Green, Ohio; Rhode Island School of Design, Providence.

"My Ohio childhood was spent in an atmosphere where creative interests and activities were always supported and encouraged," explains Mrs. Yamaguchi. "Besides the study of music and art, there was also a deep love of fantasy and storytelling. An old Great Aunt from Sweden may be responsible for that. She charmed all the little ones of our family with stories about the animals and wildlife in the fields around us." While she was studying at Bowling Green State University, she took a course in Children's Literature that "opened a whole new direction." In 1960 she married Tohr Yamaguchi, and two years later, on the day their daughter Esme was born, she completed the illustrations for her husband's story, *The Golden Crane*. They completed *Two Crabs in the Moonlight* in 1965. Marianne Yamaguchi, who designs her books, works in black-and-white using charcoal pencil on white vellum. She adds, "To my own eyes, it is difficult to reproduce charcoal drawings so that they are as much a part of the paper as they were in the original. They seem so often to remain on the surface of the paper. The printer is confronted with the great problem of maintaining all the delicate changes in tones." Her style is representational and her goal is "a good black-and-white drawing where one doesn't sense an absence of color." In 1966, she and her husband went to study in Australia for three years.

YAROSLAVA, pseud. (Yaroslava Surmach Mills)

Born July 11, 1925 in New York City where she spent her childhood. Attended Cooper Union Art School, New York.

"I always wanted to be an artist," writes Yaroslava Mills, "My mother has saved scrapbooks of my scribbles from infanthood, and she probably encouraged me by her own example, decorating the kitchen walls, etc." After graduating from Cooper Union, she did book design and lettering, sold a few paintings and taught at Manhattanville College, where she became a full time instructor in art from 1951 to 1955. At the same time, she worked as Art Editor on *Humpty Dumpty's Magazine* (1951-1959) and did free-lance art work. She met the late C. Wright Mills during a vacation trip in Europe, and after their marriage continued doing free-lance work and painting. They traveled a good deal, and she became very interested in the hand crafts of the different countries, gathering material on it and collecting children's books of various countries. In Europe she found many examples of "reverse glass" painting, a folk art form she has successfully experimented with using colors that become glowing and luminous when painted on glass. About her work she writes, "Now my palette has acquired the bright 'folk art' colors and my illustrations have a 'sophisticated primitive' look to them. I feel so much at home with this style that I believe I'm really a 'folk artist' at heart. I came out of art school as a 'modern.' As art editor of a children's magazine I continued in this style, and it wasn't until later that the influence of European and some antique books I acquired, as well as having a child of my own, changed my view." Mrs. Mills works primarily in full color, designing the book and selecting the text. Although she has specialized in lettering, she has not yet used it in her children's books. *The Mitten*, an adaptation by Alvin Tresselt of a Ukrainian folk tale, was done in four-color separations. Her "Carol Singers" was a UNICEF Christmas card in 1965. Mrs. Mills and her son, Nikolas, live in West Nyack, New York.

YASHIMA, TARO*

Born September 21, 1908 in Kagoshima, Japan. Childhood was spent in the small village of Kyushu, Japan. Attended Provincial High School of Kagoshima City; Imperial Art Academy of Tokyo, 1927-1930; Art Students League, New York, 1939-1941.

In the years that Taro Yashima has been living in America he has received many honors, has had several one-man shows in New York, Los Angeles and Pasadena, and his paintings have been bought for permanent collections, including the Phillips Memorial Museum in Washington, D. C. He has done illustrations for magazines, notably *Vogue, Fortune* and *Harper's*, and has written a cartoon-autobiography of his early manhood in Japan. Mr. Yashima writes that from the time he was a little boy he was very fond of children younger than himself. "Even in the period of my early youth when I was suspicious and nihilistic toward everything and everybody, with no faith in the world at all, I could not be negative in my feeling toward the children." Later he put his understanding as well as talent into teaching an art class for children in a mission school. During the years of the Japanese invasion of China he felt the need to present deeper meanings in his painting, and though it meant leaving their five-year-old son, Mako, behind, the Yashimas came to the United States "to study the Western masters to see how they had painted what they understood. I am sure this decision in such a difficult period was also due largely to the inspiration that came from the fresh vision and imagination of the children in my art class." Mako was fifteen when he rejoined his parents, and at about this time their daughter, Momo, was born. During a long period of illness the tiny girl gave her father so much comfort, that he wanted to thank her with stories. "I thought that perhaps if I could recall the joyful experiences of my childhood and tell them to her just as they happened they might recreate the same joy in her." And so *The Village Tree*, and his later books as well, came into being. Momo, herself, figures in such books as *Umbrella* and *Momo's Kitten*. His wish is to give children in their books something to help them through the difficulties they must inevitably face. Mr. Yashima's wife, Mitsu, also an artist, is co-author of three of her husband's picture books. Their home is in Los Angeles, California. An article by Taro Yashima appeared in the December 1955 *Horn Book*.

ZABRANSKY, ADOLF

Born 1909 in Moravia, Czechoslovakia. Attended School of Industrial and Applied Art and Art Academy, Prague.

Adolf Zabransky's six years of studying art were followed by a short stay in Paris and then in 1939, he started work as an artist. At first he devoted himself to painting but shortly he turned his attention to book illustration. After the war, from 1945 on, he also widened his scope to include poster work, murals and grafittos. Though strongly influenced in the beginning of his artistic career — as indeed were all Czech painters of his generation — by the Paris school, he later consciously went over to the more or less realistic manner inherent in the native Czech tradition. In 1950 Zabransky was awarded the Prize of the City of Prague, in 1952 and 1956 he won the State Prize, and in 1959 was named Meritorious Artist of the Republic.

ZALLINGER, JEAN DAY

Born February 15, 1918 in Boston, Massachusetts. Childhood spent in Braintree, Massachusetts. Attended Massachusetts College of Art; Yale School of Art and Architecture.

Jean Zallinger writes, "As a child, I had a consuming interest in scrawling drawings on every bit of paper available. It was attention getting and I had a desire to succeed at something." She got scholarships for three of her four years at the Massachusetts College of Art and, on graduation, applied for a scholarship at Yale. There she met and married Rudolph Zallinger and they both graduated in 1942 with B.F.A. degrees. They now have three grown children all talented in art. "I started illustrating at Yale as a student to help support myself. These were technical illustrations for various professors." She still does some of this work as well as map-making and lettering certificates, since they have continued to live in New Haven. Mr. Zallinger, who is with the University, is well-known for his murals at the Peabody Museum. "In 1957 I helped a good friend complete illustrations for a book. His agent asked if she could represent me and she has been very successful, I would say." Besides her children's books, which are mostly in the field of natural history, she has illustrated for Time-Life books, Colliers Encyclopedia and the Wildlife Federation. "I use a water color rendering tight in technique." She has also used scratchboard and has worked on dinobase as in *The Valley of the Smallest*. She mainly uses this when separations are required.

ZEIGER, SOPHIA, see Sofia, pseud.

ZEMACH, MARGOT

Born November 30, 1931 in Los Angeles, California. Childhood was spent in New York City. Attended Los Angeles County Art Institute; Jepson Art Institute; Kann Art Institute.

"I have clear recollections from earliest childhood of looking and feeling my way into the pictures in books, and of living inside them for hours," writes Margot Zemach. "When I began to draw, it was with the same sort of obsessiveness. My desire to be a children's book illustrator dates from that time. My mother is an actress and my father, Benjamin Zemach, a dancer and director, whose energy and self-discipline have always made a very strong impression on me. My art school training was of the sort to build respect for draftsmanship, economy of expression, and the tradition of fine drawing. With this point of view, most of what I saw in contemporary children's book illustration, including some things which I realized would have

pleased me as a child, seemed mediocre, insipid, or too heavily influenced by the cold abstractness of the modern designer. There were exceptions, of course, but it was particularly Andre Francois' illustrations for *Travelers Three* and *The Magic Currant Bun* which reassured me that it was still possible to join the exacting standards of drawing with the wit and fantasy so necessary in children's books. Most of what I have done so far in illustration seems to me to be preparation and half-realized intentions, with the exception of occasional pages which manage to tell something true about the meaning of the text and how I think and feel about drawing. I begin to think that I can make whole books be 'true' in that sense. I prefer to work in ink line and wash, trying to use color in a way that will strengthen rather than negate the drawing, which is of primary importance to me. Frequently I draw the same page thirty or forty times before getting what seems absolutely right as to movement and expression, freedom and coherence. I do separations on thin water color paper over a light-box. I work at home in Newton Centre, Massachusetts, with the radio on, my three small children, Kaethe, Heidi and Rachel, and their friends in and out of the room, or after they go to bed, and usually with one cat on my lap and another cat drinking the paint water. My husband is a college history teacher, who also writes children's books, and has become very good at cutting illustration board, putting on register marks and getting me to stop after I've drawn the same page the fortieth time." In 1955-56 Miss Zemach had a Fulbright Scholarship in Vienna, Austria.

ZIMNIK, REINER*

Born December 30, 1930 in Beuthen, Upper Silesia, where his childhood was spent. Attended Academy of Fine Arts, Munich.

Reiner Zimnik's father was a city clerk in the finance department. He has four brothers and sisters. His childhood memories include a "nice house with a big green tile stove," and at the age of five, liking most to draw Indians and horses and knights. In January 1945 the family had to flee from their home and in March the father was killed in the war. For a while the boy worked in a carpentry shop in Bavaria, but soon went back to high school, finishing three years later. From there he went to the Academy of Fine Arts and during the summer vacations worked on farms. Reiner Zimnik has written as well as illustrated over thirteen books. He works in black-and-white with pen and ink in a style that he feels has, over the last ten years, "become more honest, clear and refined." His home is in Munich, Germany.

Part III:
BIBLIOGRAPHIES

52. ED EMBERLEY: *One Wide River to Cross*

FOREWORD

THE selection of illustrators and titles for both the biographies and bibliographies has been based largely on actual examination of the books themselves, after a thorough scrutiny on the part of the biographer and the bibliographer of publishers' catalogs, and an even closer consultation of selective lists such as *The Horn Book, The Booklist*, the *New York Public Library Annual Lists, Library Journal, Junior Booklist, Best Books for Children, The American Institute of Graphic Arts Catalogs*, and *The Children's Catalog*. The illustrations are of chief concern in the selection; however, it was felt that each book listed should have intrinsic merit as a children's book in order to be included. The bibliography is selective and representative in scope rather than all-inclusive, since lack of space in the volume prohibits the inclusion of all the titles illustrated by all the illustrators in the list.

In comparing the bibliography of illustrators of the 1957-1966 edition with that of the preceding 1946-1956 edition, one is impressed by the basic differences between the two bibliographies. There were approximately 500 illustrators listed in the former edition, whereas this edition contains 452 illustrators, or forty-eight illustrators less. However, the number of books (2,335) in this edition exceeds the number of books in the previous edition by about fifty. In the 1957-1966 period, twelve outstanding illustrators, such as Adrienne Adams, Edward Ardizzone, Roger Duvoisin, Leonard Everett Fisher, Paul Galdone, William Stobbs, Evaline Ness and Maurice Sendak, were represented by twenty or more books in the bibliography, and these books were selected from a much larger number of books illustrated by each of these artists. In the 1946-1956 edition, only three illustrators were represented by twenty or more books. In this edition, fifty illustrators were represented by ten or more books; only thirty-six were represented by ten or more books in the 1946-1956 edition. Throughout the two bibliographies, this difference occurs: the decrease in number of illustrators in the later edition is offset by the increase of books illustrated by each artist, as

compared with the 1946-1956 edition. One might also add that the earlier edition covered eleven years, while the later edition covers only ten years.

Children's book production has increased enormously in the past ten years. In 1956, 1,495 children's books were published; in 1966, 2,713 children's books were published — an increase of 1,218. However, many of these books, especially those in the non-fiction field, were illustrated with photographs and with reproductions of source materials rather than with original illustrations. Books such as those in the *American Heritage* series, profusely illustrated with paintings, diagrams and photographs of the periods covered, were widely published and in great demand.

It is not within the scope of this volume to include

a BIBLIOGRAPHY
of the ILLUSTRATORS
and their WORKS

COMPILED BY

Ruth Giles Lontoft

or evaluate photographically illustrated books for children, but recognition should be given to such books as Ross Hutchins' photographic nature books, and to *Chendru, Elsa, Beyond the High Hills,* and the Ylla books for the unusual contribution their photographs have made to book illustration for children.

There has been a wide exchange of books published in England and America, sometimes with surprising results. Often the English publisher used a different illustrator from that of the American edition, and vice versa. This variation in illustrator is revealed in the Bibliography of Authors, showing one book illustrated by two different artists. It was an illuminating experience for the bibliographer to visit the Library of Congress, where the English and American versions of each book could be seen together and differences noted.

Certain types of children's books published during this period gave the illustrator an opportunity to exercise his creative talents and abilities to the utmost. One was the single fairy or folk tale presented as a story picture book. A few books of this sort had been published before this period, but never in such numbers or of such fine quality in format and illustration. Aesop and La Fontaine fables were enlarged in text and given picture book format; single folk tales were retold and supplied with colorful pictures. However, the collections of Andersen and Grimm seemed to be the favored sources for the creation of this type of story picture book. The illustrations of Felix Hoffmann, Marcia Brown, Adrienne Adams, and Margot Zemach were preëminent in this field. No less than three versions of Andersen's *Nightingale* were illustrated respectively by Harold Berson, Nancy Burkert, and Bill Sokol. *Snow White and Rose Red* was illustrated by both Adrienne Adams and Barbara Cooney, while *The Twelve Dancing Princesses* was illustrated by Uri Shulevitz and Adrienne Adams.

Books of nonsense rhymes, American folk songs

and tall tales, and humorous poetry were very much in evidence, giving illustrators such as Glen Rounds, Beth and Joe Krush, Peter Spier, Bob McCloskey, and Tomi Ungerer, a free hand in creating amusing, vigorous drawings for characters and settings. Devotees of Edward Lear must have been delighted with the great variety of illustrations done for the Lear books of this period — from the facsimile edition of a Lear ABC, written in his own handwriting, to the

53. WALTER LORRAINE: *The Dog Who Thought He Was A Boy*

modern illustrations done in bold color by Lois Ehlert. In between these two extremes lay William Pène Du Bois' *The Owl and the Pussy Cat*, Barbara Cooney's *Le Hibou et la Poussiquette*, and Galdone's *Two Laughable Lyrics*.

Picture books with bi-lingual, tri-lingual and multi-lingual texts abounded. These served as introductory foreign books for the very young, and the illustrations clarified and extended the texts with lively, unusual pictures. Notable illustrators in this field were Antonio Frasconi, Leonard Weisgard, Earl Thollander and John Alcorn. And one must not forget Barbara Cooney's illustrations for *Mother Goose in French!*

The publication of Dr. Seuss's *The Cat in the Hat* in 1957 started a new trend for beginning readers with controlled vocabularies — certainly a happy antidote to the lamentable Dick and Jane series and their ilk. Illustrators such as Maurice Sendak, Syd Hoff, Eric Blegvad, Mary Chalmers, Garth Williams, and Clement Hurd soon entered the field and supplied genuinely appealing, amusing illustrations for these beguiling readers. *Little Bear's Visit*, illustrated by Sendak, was a runner-up for the Caldecott Award in 1962. The only criticism of these books has been that such labels on the covers as "Easy to Read," "I Can Read," are not only distracting artistically, but have been known to keep good readers away from this lively reading fare.

Illustrated nature books, quite prevalent in the last edition, continued to flourish in this period. Accurate, expressive drawings of Lois and Louis Darling, Olive Earle, Robert McClung, Su Zan Swain, and Winifred Lubel were among the illustrative interpreters of this genre.

Mother Goose may rest assured that "her melodies will never die" represented as she was by illustrators Brian Wildsmith, Philip Reed, Aldren Watson and Raymond Briggs.

In order to achieve a format uniform with that of adult fiction, many publishers have completely omitted illustrations from fiction books for older boys and girls. An illustrative device used in many books for pre-teen-agers has been the chapter heading illustration, somewhat enlarged, which effectively sets a mood for the chapter to come. This type of illustration was used by Janina Domanska in the new edition of *The Trumpeter of Krakow*, by Susan Einzig in *Tom's Midnight Garden*, and by Arnold Spilka in *You Better Come Home with Me*. Maurice Sendak was particularly successful with this kind of illustration in his full-page, sensitive drawings introducing each chapter of Randall Jarrell's *The Animal Family*.

A similar type of illustration has often been used in poetry books and anthologies for older boys and girls. Instead of having illustrations throughout the text, the illustrations, often full page, have appeared at the beginning of each subject section to set the mood for that section. Many of the illustrators of the distinguished books in the Crowell Poetry Series have used this type of illustration with impressive results.

Certainly one of the unique volumes published in the last ten years is *Flowers of Delight* (Pantheon 1965). It is a collection of over sixty little books published in England, 1765-1830, compiled by Leonard De Vries, from the Osborne Collection of Early Children's Books in the Toronto Public Library. An invaluable contribution, of special interest for the student of children's literature, it is hardly suitable for children today because of the obsolete ideas and moral tone of many of the stories and poems. The illustrations are superb — 700 beautiful woodcuts, 125 of which are in color.

Of particular interest to adults interested in children's book illustrations is *Arthur Rackham: His Life and Work* by Derek Hudson (Heinemann 1960/ Scribner 1961). A large, handsome volume, this sympathetic biography of Arthur Rackham contains a wide range of his illustrations, beautifully reproduced.

The following entries in the Bibliography have little significance without some explanation as to their nature and origin:

Aesop: Five Centuries of Illustrated Fables contains a wide variety of illustrations of Aesop's fables, ranging from the 15th Century German and Italian wood-cuts to the works of two contemporary artists, Antonio Frasconi and Joseph Low. Each illustration, selected by John J. McKendry of the Metropolitan Museum of Art, is matched with a contemporaneous translation of that fable.

Under *Bewick, Thomas:* Thomas Bewick's woodcuts from his *General History of Quadrupeds* and *History of Birds* were chosen to illustrate Pamela Travers' Christmas fable, *The Fox at the Manger.*

Under the heading *Fairy Tales of Hans Christian Andersen,* it should be noted that this collection contains twenty-five imaginative illustrations done by children of eighteen countries, selected from an exhibition of children's paintings illustrating Andersen's fairy tales, held in Denmark in 1955 to commemorate the 150th anniversary of Andersen's birth.

Grandville, J. J., pseud.: For his *Fables from Aesop* (in verse), Ennis Rees chose for the illustrations the wood engravings of Grandville which appeared in an edition of La Fontaine's *Fables* published in France in 1838.

Kittelsen, Theodor (with *Erik Werenskiold*): Special attention should be called to this notable edition, *Norwegian Folk Tales,* because it contains the illustrations done by the illustrators chosen by Asbjørnsen for the original Norwegian collections. Published in the United States for the first time in 1961.

Lear, Edward: Lear Alphabet: ABC: This is an exact reproduction of a manuscript, handwritten and illustrated by Lear, recently discovered and published for the first time.

Mother Goose in Hieroglyphics is a facsimile edition of a rebus Mother Goose first published by Frederick Brown in Boston in 1840.

Potter, Beatrix, Letters to Children: This is a small volume of nine letters written to the children of Beatrix Potter's governess. The letters are in Beatrix Potter's handwriting, and are illustrated with pen and ink sketches by her.

Under the heading *World Council of Christian Education* appear two titles, *Away in a Manger* and *In the Beginning.* The illustrations for these beautiful picture books, which give brief Biblical accounts of the Nativity and the Creation, were selected from over one thousand children's paintings submitted to the Children's Art Project of the Council through missionary stations and international art organizations throughout the world.

In the past ten years, illustrated children's books have been unsurpassed by those of any other period of similar duration in both quantity and quality. Never before have illustrators, as a rule, seemed more accomplished and gifted in their achievements. Children's book editors are responsible for a great deal of this excellence in children's book illustration. They have resurrected treasured books of the past, retaining the original illustrations of the books if they have present-day appeal; if not, having the books completely re-illustrated. These same editors have also forged ahead, trying out new techniques in illustration, or incorporating trends of contemporary modern art into book illustration for children.

It was necessary for the bibliographer to use the facilities of libraries and organizations to obtain books, both English and American, for evaluation. She is deeply grateful for the cooperation and assistance given to her at:

The Children's Book Council; The English Speaking Union; The Children's Book Section of the Library of Congress; The Children's Rooms of the Main Branch and the Sprain Brook Branch of the Yonkers Public Library; The Children's Rooms of the Donnell Branch and the Riverdale Branch of the New York Public Library; and The Central Children's Room of the New York Public Library.

She is also indebted to Grace Hogarth for valuable advice given in the selection of English children's books for the Bibliography.

54. NANCY BURKERT: *A Child's Calendar*

A BIBLIOGRAPHY OF ILLUSTRATORS
ACTIVE FROM 1957 THROUGH 1966

ABRAHAMS, HILARY RUTH
(1938-   ) English
  Abrahams, A.
    Polonius Penguin and the Flying Doctor.   Dobson 1966
    Polonius Penguin Comes to Town.   Dobson 1963
    Polonius Penguin Learns to Swim.   Dobson 1963/
      Watts 1964

ADAMS, ADRIENNE
(Ac. 1966)   American
  Andersen
    Thumbelina.   Scribner 1961
    The Ugly Duckling.   Scribner 1965
  Anderson,   *Ponies of Mypillengi.*   Scribner 1966
  Bring a Torch, Jeannette, Isabella.   Scribner 1963
  Carpenter,   *The Mouse Palace.*   McGraw 1964
  Field,   *The Rachel Field Story Book.*   Doubleday 1958
  Fisher
    Going Barefoot.   Crowell 1960
    In the Middle of the Night.   Crowell 1965
    Where Does Everyone Go?   Crowell 1961
  Godden
    Candy Floss.   Viking 1960
    Mouse House.   Viking 1957
    The Story of Holly and Ivy.   Viking 1958
  Goudey
    Butterfly Time.   Scribner 1964
    The Day We Saw the Sun Come Up.   Scribner 1961
    Houses from the Sea.   Scribner 1959
  Grimm
    The Shoemaker and the Elves.   Scribner 1960
    Snow White and Rose Red.   Scribner 1964
  Haviland,   *Favorite Fairy Tales Told in Scotland.*   Little
    1963
  Lang,   *The Twelve Dancing Princesses.*   Holt 1966
  Massey,   *The Littlest Witch.*   Knopf 1959
  Wahl,   *Cabbage Moon.*   Holt 1965

ADAMSON, GEORGE WORSLEY
(1913-   ) English
  Hall,   *The Royal Astrologer.*   Heinemann 1960/Coward
    1962
  Hughes,   *How the Whale Became.*   Faber 1963
  Ireson,   *The Barnes Book of Nursery Verse* (English
    title, *The Faber Book of Nursery Verse*).   Faber
    1958/Barnes 1960
  Lovett,   *Sir Halmanac and the Crimson Star.*   Faber 1965
  Widdecombe Fair.   Faber 1966

AESOP: FIVE CENTURIES OF ILLUSTRATED FABLES.
Metropolitan Museum 1964
(*See note in Foreword to this Bibliography*)

AKINO, FUKU
(1908-   ) Japanese
  Lifton
    The Cock and the Ghost Cat.   Atheneum 1965
    The Dwarf Pine Tree.   Atheneum 1963

ALAIN, pseud.
(DANIEL BRUSTLEIN)
(1904-   ) American
  Alain,   *One, Two, Three . . . Going to Sea.*   Scott 1964
  Fife
    A Dog Called Dunkel.   Coward 1966
    A Stork for the Bell Tower.   Coward 1964
  Janice,   *Minette.*   McGraw 1959

ALBION, LEE SMITH
(Ac. 1966)   American
  Prieto
    A Kite for Carlos.   Day 1966
    The Wise Rooster.   Day 1962

ALCORN, JOHN
(1935-   ) American
  Hine
    A Letter to Anywhere.   Harcourt 1965
    Money Round the World.   Harcourt 1963
    Where In the World Do You Live?   Harcourt 1962
  Joslin,   *La Petite Famille.*   Harcourt 1964
  McCain
    Books!   Simon 1962
    Writing!   Farrar 1964
  McGinley,   *Wonderful Time.*   Lippincott 1966
  Phelan,   *The Circus.*   Holt 1963
  Winn, (ed.)   *The Fireside Book of Children's Songs.*
    Simon 1966

ALIKI, pseud.
(ALIKI BRANDENBERG)
(1929-   ) American
  Aliki
    Keep Your Mouth Closed, Dear.   Dial 1966
    The Story of Johnny Appleseed.   Prentice 1963
    The Story of William Penn.   Prentice 1964
    The Wish Workers.   Dial 1962

Hawes,   *Bees and Beelines*.   Crowell 1964
Heilbroner,   *This Is the House Where Jack Lives*.
      Harper 1962
Hodges,   *What's for Lunch, Charlie?* Dial 1961
Kohn,   *One Day It Rained Cats and Dogs*. Coward 1965

AMBRUS, VICTOR G.
(1935-   )   English, b. in Hungary
Ambrus,   *The Three Poor Tailors*.   Oxford 1965/Harcourt 1966
Burton
   Castors Away.   Oxford 1962/World 1963
   Time of Trial.   Oxford 1963/World 1964
Farjeon and Mayne (eds.)
   A *Cavalcade of Kings* (English title, *The Hamish Hamilton Book of Kings*). Hamilton 1964/Walck 1965
   A *Cavalcade of Queens* (English title, *The Hamish Hamilton Book of Queens*). Hamilton 1965/Walck 1965
Griffiths,   *The Greyhound*. Hutchinson 1964/Doubleday 1966
Jenkins,   *White Horses and Black Bulls*.   Norton 1963
Kay,   *Hands for Pablo Picasso*.   Abelard 1965
Manning,   *Arripay*. Constable 1963/Farrar 1964
Manning-Sanders,   *The Red King and the Witch*.
      Oxford 1964/Roy 1965
Oliver,   *Watch for the Morning*. Macmillan 1964/St. Martin's 1964
Peyton,   *The Plan for Birdsmarsh*. Oxford 1965/World 1966
Picard,   *The Young Pretenders*. Criterion 1966
Pilkington,   *The Three Sorrowful Tales of Erin*.   Bodley 1965/Walck 1966
Sleigh (comp.),   *North of Nowhere*. Collins 1964/Coward 1966
Sutcliff,   *The Hound of Ulster*. Bodley 1963/Dutton 1964

AMES, LEE JUDAH
(Ac. 1966) American
Gallant
   Exploring Chemistry.   Doubleday 1958
   Exploring the Sun.   Doubleday 1958
Lancaster,   *The American Revolution*. Doubleday 1957
Meadowcroft,   *Land of the Free*. Crowell 1961

ANDERSON, CLARENCE WILLIAM
(1891-   )   American
Anderson
   Another Man o'War.   Macmillan 1966
   Blaze and the Mountain Lion.   Macmillan 1959

C. W. Anderson's Complete Book of Horses and Horsemanship.   Macmillan 1963
   A Filly for Joan.   Macmillan 1960
   Lonesome Little Colt.   Macmillan 1961
   Twenty Gallant Horses.   Macmillan 1965

ANGELO, VALENTI
(1897-   )   American, b. in Italy
Angelo
   The Acorn Tree.   Viking 1958
   Angelino and the Barefoot Saint.   Viking 1961
   The Honey Boat.   Viking 1959
   The Merry Marcos.   Viking 1963
   The Tale of a Donkey.   Viking 1966
Bulla,   *Benito*. Crowell 1961

ANGLUND, JOAN WALSH
(1926-   )   American
Anglund
   The Brave Cowboy.   Harcourt 1959
   Christmas Is a Time of Giving.   Harcourt 1961
   Cowboy and His Friend.   Harcourt 1961
   A Friend Is Someone Who Likes You.   Harcourt 1958
   Love Is a Special Way of Feeling.   Harcourt 1960
   Nibble, Nibble, Mousekin.   Harcourt 1962
Mother Goose, *In a Pumpkin Shell*.   Harcourt 1960
Untermeyer (comp.),   *The Golden Treasury of Poetry*.   Golden 1959

ARDIZZONE, EDWARD
(1900-   )   English
Ardizzone
   Johnny the Clockmaker.   Oxford 1960/Walck 1960
   The Little Girl and the Tiny Doll.   Constable 1966
   Peter the Wanderer.   Oxford 1963/Walck 1964
   Sarah and Simon and No Red Paint.   Constable 1965/Delacorte 1966
   Tim and Ginger.   Oxford 1965/Walck 1965
   Tim's Friend Towser.   Oxford 1962/Walck 1962
Brand,   *Nurse Matilda*. Brockhampton 1964/Dutton 1964
De La Mare,   *Stories from the Bible*.   Faber 1962/Knopf 1964
Estes
   The Alley.   Harcourt 1964
   Pinky Pye.   Harcourt 1958
   The Witch Family.   Harcourt 1961
Faralla,   *The Singing Cupboard*. Blackie, n.d./Lippincott 1963
Farjeon
   Italian Peepshow.   Oxford 1960/Walck 1961
   Jim at the Corner.   Blackwell 1958/Walck 1958
   Mrs. Malone.   Joseph 1961/Walck 1962
Graves

Ann at Highwood Hall. Cassell 1964/Doubleday 1966

The Penny Fiddle. Cassell 1961/Doubleday 1961

Marshall, *The Dragon.* Hamilton 1966

Reeves

Exploits of Don Quixote. Blackie 1959/Walck 1960

Prefabulous Animiles. Heinemann 1957/Dutton 1960

The Story of Jackie Thimble. Dutton 1964

Three Tall Tales. Abelard 1964

Titus in Trouble. Bodley 1959/Walck 1960

Symonds, *Elfrida and the Pig.* Harrap 1959/Watts 1960

Wahl, *Hello, Elephant.* Holt 1964

Williams, *Island MacKenzie.* Morrow 1960

Wuorio

The Island of Fish in the Trees. World 1962

The Land of Right Up and Down. World 1964

ARNO, ENRICO
(1913-) American, b. in Germany

Benary-Isbert, *Blue Mystery.* Harcourt 1957

Courlander

The King's Drum. Harcourt 1962

The Tiger's Whisker. Harcourt 1959

Courlander and Prempeh, *The Hat-Shaking Dance.* Harcourt 1957

Curry, *Down from the Lonely Mountain.* Harcourt 1965

De Treviño, *Nacar the White Deer.* Farrar 1963

Fillmore, *The Shepherd's Nosegay.* Harcourt 1961

Lin, *The Milky Way.* Harcourt 1961

Malcolmson, *A Taste of Chaucer.* Harcourt 1964

Ross (comp.)

The Blue Rose. Harcourt 1966

The Lost Half-Hour. Harcourt 1963

AUERBACH, MARJORIE
(1932-) American

Auerbach, *Seven Uncles Come to Dinner.* Knopf 1963

Coatsworth, *The Place.* Holt 1966

AVERILL, ESTHER
(1902-) American

Averill

The Fire Cat. Harper 1960

Jenny Goes to Sea. Harper 1957

Jenny's Bedside Book. Harper 1959

AYER, JACQUELINE
(1930-) American

Ayer

Nu Dang and His Kite. Harcourt 1959

The Paper-Flower Tree. Harcourt 1962

A Wish for Little Sister. Harcourt 1960

Yershov, *Humpy.* Harcourt 1966

BACON, PEGGY
(1895-) American

Bacon

The Good American Witch. Watts 1957

The Oddity. Pantheon 1962

Byars, *Rama, the Gypsy Cat.* Viking 1966

Cole (ed.), *Poems of Magic and Spells.* World 1960

Gates, *The Cat and Mrs. Cary.* Viking 1962

Govan, *Number 5 Hackberry Street.* World 1964

Koenig, *The Seven Special Cats.* World 1961

Smith

The Auction Pony. Little 1965

Miranda and the Cat. Little 1963

BALTZER, HANS
(1900-) German

Swift, *Gulliver's Travels.* Constable 1962/Duell 1963

BANNON, LAURA
(Ac. 1960-1963)

Bannon

Hop-High, the Goat. Bobbs 1960

Jo-Jo, The Talking Crow. Houghton 1958

Katy Comes Next. Whitman 1959

The Other Side of the World. Houghton 1960

BARKER, CAROL
(1938-) English

Bates, *Achilles the Donkey.* Dobson 1962/Watts 1963

Fisher, *I Wonder How, I Wonder Why.* Abelard 1962

Watts, *The Light Across Piney Valley.* Abelard 1965

BARRY, KATHARINA
(1936-) American, b. in Germany

Barry, *A Is for Anything.* Harcourt 1961

Joslin

Spaghetti for Breakfast. Harcourt 1965

There Is a Bull on My Balcony. Harcourt 1966

BARRY, ROBERT E.
(1931-) American

Barry

Faint George. Houghton 1957

Just Pepper. Houghton 1959

Mr. Willoughby's Christmas Tree. McGraw 1963

BARSS, WILLIAM
(1916-) American

Asimov

Words from the Myths. Houghton 1961

Words of Science. Houghton 1959

Walker, *Hilili and Dilili.* Follett 1965

BARTSCH, JOCHEN
(1906-   ) German
Krüss
My Great-Grandfather and I. Atheneum 1964
Pauline and the Prince in the Wind. Atheneum 1966

BAYNES, PAULINE
(1922-   ) English
Arabian Nights, Arabian Nights. Blackie, n.d./ Criterion 1958
Ensor, *The Adventures of Hatim Tai.* Harrap 1961/ Walck 1962
Malcolmson, *Miracle Plays.* Houghton 1959
Morris, *The Upstairs Donkey.* Faber 1962/Pantheon 1961
Opie (comp.), *A Family Book of Nursery Rhymes.* (Lond.) Oxford 1964
Pridham, *A Gift From the Heart.* Methuen 1966
Spenser, *Saint George and the Dragon.* Methuen 1961/ Houghton 1963
Tolkien, *The Adventures of Tom Bombadil.* Allen & Unwin 1962/Houghton 1963
Williams-Ellis (ed.), *Fairy Tales from the British Isles.* Warne 1964

BEATTY, HETTY BURLINGAME
(1906-   ) American
Beatty
Bryn. Houghton 1965
Bucking Horse. Houghton 1957
Moorland Pony. Houghton 1961
Voyage of the Sea Wind. Houghton 1959

BEER, RICHARD
(Ac. 1966) English
Green, *Tales from Shakespeare.* Gollancz 1964/ Atheneum 1965

BEHN, HARRY
(1898-   ) American
Behn
The Golden Hive. Harcourt 1966
Omen of the Birds. World 1964
The Painted Cave. Harcourt 1957

BELL, CORYDON
(1894-   ) American
Bell
A Dash of Pepper. Viking 1965
Thunderstorm. Viking 1960
The Two Worlds of Davy Blount. Viking 1962
Diggins, *String, Straightedge and Shadow.* Viking 1965
Gray, *I Will Adventure.* Viking 1962

BELTRÁN, ALBERTO
(1923-   ) Mexican
Von Hagen
The Incas, People of the Sun. World 1961
Maya, Land of the Turkey and the Deer. World 1960
The Sun Kingdom of the Aztecs. World 1958

BEMELMANS, LUDWIG
(1898-1962) American, b. in Austria
Bemelmans
Madeline and the Bad Hat. Viking 1957
Madeline and the Gypsies. Viking 1959
Madeline in London. Viking 1961
Welcome Home! Harper 1960

BENDICK, JEANNE
(1919-   ) American
Bendick
Lightning. Rand 1961
Sea So Big, Ship So Small. Rand 1963
The Wind. Rand 1964
Blough, *Who Lives in This House?* McGraw 1957

BENNETT, RAINEY
(1907-   ) American
Bennett
After the Sun Goes Down. World 1961
The Secret Hiding Place. World 1960
Cassedy, *Little Chameleon.* World 1966

BERG, JOAN
See Victor, Joan Berg

BERRILL, JACQUELINE
(1905-   ) American
Berrill
Wonders of Animal Migration. Dodd 1964
Wonders of the Antarctic. Dodd 1958
Wonders of the Fields and Ponds at Night. Dodd 1962

BERRY, WILLIAM D.
(1920-   ) American
Berry
Buffalo Land. Macmillan 1961
Deneki: An Alaskan Moose. Macmillan 1965
Brown, *How to Understand Animal Talk.* Little 1958

BERSON, HAROLD
(1926-   ) American
Andersen, *The Nightingale.* Lippincott 1962
Belloc, *The Bad Child's Book of Beasts, and More Beasts for Worse Children.* Grosset 1966.
Berson, *Raminogrobis and the Mice.* Seabury 1965

Burnett, *Racketty-Packetty House*. Scribner 1961

Byars, *The Dancing Camel*. Viking 1965

Chase, *Loretta Mason Potts*. Lippincott 1958

Farella, *The Wonderful Flying-Go-Round*. World 1965

Littlefield, *Seventh Son of a Seventh Son*. Lothrop 1959

McGinley, *Mince Pie and Mistletoe*. Lippincott 1961

Morrow, *A Pint of Judgment*. Knopf 1960

Walden, *The Nutcracker*. Lippincott 1959

BETTINA, pseud.
(BETTINA BAUER EHRLICH)
(1903-   ) English, b. in Austria
Bettina
   Angelo and Rosaline. Collins 1957
   For the Leg of a Chicken. Collins 1960/Watts 1960
   Pantaloni. Harper 1957
   Trovato. Ariel 1959
Haviland, *Favorite Fairy Tales Told in England*. Little 1959
Wuorio, *Tal and the Magic Barruget*. World 1965

BEWICK, THOMAS
(1753-1828) English
Travers, *The Fox at the Manger*. Norton 1962
   (See note in Foreword to this Bibliography)

BILECK, MARVIN
(1920-   ) American
Colver, *Nobody's Birthday*. Knopf 1961
De Regniers, *Penny*. Viking 1966
Scheer, *Rain Makes Applesauce*. Holiday 1964

BIRO, BALINT S.
See BIRO, VAL

BIRO, VAL
(1921-   ) English, b. in Hungary
Baum, *The Wonderful Wizard of Oz*. Dent 1965/ Dutton 1965
Biro, *Gumdrop*. Brockhampton 1966
Dawlish, *The Seas of Britain*. Benn 1963
Kamm, *The Story of Fanny Burney*. Methuen 1966
Stenhouse, *The Story of Scotland*. Benn 1961/Watts 1962

BJORKLUND, LORENCE F.
(Ac. 1966) American
Ives, *Steamboat Up the Colorado*. Little 1965
Grant
   American Forts: Yesterday and Today. Dutton 1965
   American Indians: Yesterday and Today. Dutton 1960
Heck

Cactus Kevin. World 1965
The Hopeful Years. World 1964
Lobdell, *The Fort in the Forest*. Houghton 1963
Vance, *Esther Wheelwright, Indian Captive*. Dutton 1964

BLAKE, QUENTIN
(1932-   ) English
Ezo, *My Son-in-Law the Hippopotamus*. Abelard 1962
Rees
   Pun Fun. Abelard 1965
   Riddles, Riddles Everywhere. Abelard 1964
Weir, *Albert the Dragon*. Abelard 1961

BLEGVAD, ERIK
(1923-   ) Danish
Allingham, *The Dirty Old Man*. Prentice 1965
Andersen
   The Emperor's New Clothes. Harcourt 1959
   The Swineherd. Harcourt 1958
Blegvad, L., *Mr. Jensen & Cat*. Harcourt 1965
Brenner, *The Five Pennies*. Knopf 1963
Holman
   Elizabeth the Bird Watcher. Macmillan 1963
   Elizabeth the Treasure Hunter. Macmillan 1964
Holt, *The Adventures of Rinaldo*. Atlantic-Little 1959
Kendall, *The Gammage Cup*. Harcourt 1959
Langton, *The Diamond in the Window*. Harper 1962
Livingston
   Happy Birthday! Harcourt 1964
   I'm Hiding. Harcourt 1961
   I'm Waiting. Harcourt 1966
   See What I Found. Harcourt 1962
Miles, *Having a Friend*. Knopf 1959
Norton, *Bed-Knob and Broomstick*. Harcourt 1957
Otto, *The Little Old Train*. Knopf 1960
Selsam, *Plenty of Fish*. Harper 1960
Smith, *Jack Mack*. Coward 1960
Stafford, *Elephi*. Farrar 1962
Winslow, *Mud Pies and Other Recipes*. Macmillan 1961

BOBRI, VLADIMIR
(1898-   ) American, b. in Russia
Branley, *What the Moon Is Like*. Crowell 1963
Gans, *Icebergs*. Crowell 1964
Gottlieb, *What Is Red?* Lothrop 1961
Littlefield, *The Whiskers of Ho Ho*. Lothrop 1958
Rice, *The March Wind*. Lothrop 1957
Slobodkina, *Boris and His Balalaika*. Abelard 1964
Zolotow, *Sleepy Book*. Lothrop 1958

BOCK, VERA
(Ac. 1966) American, b. in Russia

Brewton, *Birthday Candles Burning Bright.*   Macmillan 1960
Canty, *The Green Gate.*   McKay 1965
Newell, *His Own Good Daughter.*   McKay 1961
Savery, *The Reb and the Redcoats.*   McKay 1961

BODECKER, NILS MOGENS
(1922-   )   American, b. in Denmark
De Mille, *Book of the Dance.*   Golden 1963
Dickens, *David Copperfield.*   Macmillan 1962
Eager
    Magic by the Lake.   Harcourt 1957
    Magic or Not?   Harcourt 1959
    Seven-Day Magic.   Harcourt 1962
    The Time Garden.   Harcourt 1958
    The Well-Wishers.   Harcourt 1960
Hall, *Sylvester, the Mouse with the Musical Ear.*   Golden 1961
Schlein, *The Snake in the Carpool.*   Abelard 1963
Shura, *Shoe Full of Shamrock.*   Atheneum 1965

BOLOGNESE, DONALD
(1934-   )   American
Bishop, *Yesu, Called Jesus.*   Farrar 1966
Green, *Tales the Muses Told.*   Walck 1965
Lexau
    Benjie.   Dial 1964
    Josie's Christmas Secret.   Dial 1963
Palmer, *Dragons, Unicorns and Other Magical Beasts.*   Walck 1966
Ritchie, *Apple Seeds and Soda Straws.*   Walck 1965
Smith, M. B., *Plays and How to Put Them On.*   Walck 1961
Smith, W. J., *If I Had a Boat.*   Macmillan 1966
Walker, *Just Say Hic!*   Follett 1965

BONSALL, CROSBY NEWELL
(1921-   )   American
Bonsall
    The Case of the Cat's Meow.   Harper 1965
    The Case of the Hungry Stranger.   Harper 1963
    Who's a Pest?   Harper 1962
Nŏdset, *Go Away, Dog.*   Harper 1963
Ressner, *August Explains.*   Harper 1963

BOOTH, GRAHAM
(Ac. 1966)   American
Martin, *Sing, Sailor, Sing.*   Golden Gate 1966
Taylor, *Henry the Explorer.*   Atheneum 1966

BORTEN, HELEN
(1930-   )   American
Borten
    Do You Hear What I Hear?   Abelard 1960
    Do You Move As I Do?   Abelard 1963
    Do You See What I See?   Abelard 1959
    Hallowe'en.   Crowell 1965
    A Picture Has a Special Look.   Abelard 1961
Branley
    The Moon Seems to Change.   Crowell 1961
    What Makes Day and Night.   Crowell 1961

BOSWELL, JAMES
(Ac. 1966)   English
MacKenzie, *Little Cat Lost.*   Barrie 1965/Macmillan 1966

BRIGGS, RAYMOND
(1934-   )   English
Briggs
    Fee-Fi-Fo-Fum.   Hamilton 1964/Coward 1964
    Ring-A-Ring O'Roses.   Hamilton 1962/Coward 1962
    The White Land.   Hamilton 1963/Coward 1963
Duggan
    Arches and Spires.   Hamilton 1961/Pantheon 1962
    The Castle Book (English Title, *Look at Castles*) Hamilton 1960/Pantheon 1961
Hope-Simpson, *Hamish Hamilton Book of Myths and Legends.*   Hamilton 1964
Manning-Sanders
    Hamish Hamilton Book of Magical Beasts.   Hamilton 1965
    Peter and the Piskies.   Oxford 1958/Roy 1966
Mayne, *Whistling Rufus.*   Hamilton 1964/Dutton 1965
Mother Goose, *The Mother Goose Treasury.*   Hamilton 1966/Coward 1966

BRIGHT, ROBERT
(1902-   )   American
Bright
    The Friendly Bear.   Doubleday 1957
    Georgie and the Magician   Doubleday 1966
    Georgie's Hallowe'en.   Doubleday 1958
    My Hopping Bunny.   Doubleday 1960
    My Red Umbrella.   Morrow 1959

BROOMFIELD, ROBERT
(1930-   )   English
Broomfield (ed.), *The Twelve Days of Christmas.*   Bodley 1965/McGraw 1965
Dame Wiggins of Lee and Her Seven Wonderful Cats.   Bodley 1963/McGraw 1963
Hewett, *Mrs. Wopple's Washing Line.*   McGraw 1966

BROWN, JUDITH GWYN
(1933-   )   American
Brown, *Max and the Truffle Pig.*   Abingdon 1963

Colum, *The Stone of Victory.* McGraw 1966
Corbett, *Pippa Passes.* Holt 1966
Paradis, *Mr. De Luca's Horse.* Atheneum 1962

BROWN, MARCIA
(1918-   ) American
Andersen, *The Wild Swans.* Scribner 1963
Asbjørnsen and Moe, *The Three Billy Goats Gruff.*
    Harcourt 1957
Brown
    Backbone of the King. Scribner 1966
    Felice. Scribner 1958
    Peter Piper's Alphabet. Scribner 1959
    Tamarindo! Scribner 1960
Hitopadésa, *Once a Mouse . . .* Scribner 1961

BROWN, PALMER
(1919-   ) American
Brown
    Cheerful. Harper 1957
    Something for Christmas. Harper 1958

BRUNHOFF, LAURENT DE
(1925-   ) French
Brunhoff
    Babar's Fair. Random 1961
    Bonhomme. Pantheon 1965
    Captain Serafina. World 1963

BRUSTLEIN, DANIEL
See ALAIN, pseud.

BRYSON, BERNARDA
(1903-   ) American
Appel, *Shepherd of the Sun.* Obolensky 1961
Austen, *Pride and Prejudice.* Macmillan 1962
Belting
    Calendar Moon. Holt 1964
    The Sun Is a Golden Earring. Holt 1962
Best, *Bright Hunter of the Skies.* Macmillan 1961
Brontë, *Wuthering Heights.* Macmillan 1963
Bryson, *The Twenty Miracles of Saint Nicholas.*
    Atlantic-Little 1960
Clarke, *The Return of the Twelves.* Coward 1964

BUEHR, WALTER
(1897-   ) American
Buehr
    Chivalry and the Mailed Knight. Putnam 1963
    The French Explorers in America. Putnam 1961
    Knights and Castles and Feudal Life. Putnam 1957
    The Spanish Armada. Putnam 1962
    Strange Craft. Norton 1963
    Warrior's Weapons. Crowell 1963

BUFF, CONRAD
(1886-   ) American, b. in Switzerland
Buff
    Elf Owl. Viking 1958
    Forest Folk. Viking 1962
    Trix and Vix. Houghton 1960

BURCHARD, PETER
(1921-   ) American
Anderson, *Zeb.* Knopf 1966
Burchard
    The Carol Moran. Macmillan 1958
    Jed, the Story of a Yankee Soldier and a Southern Boy.
        Coward 1960
Corbin, *Pony for Keeps.* Coward 1958
Hays
    Easter Fires. Coward 1960
    The Fourth of July Raid. Coward 1959
Mann, *The Street of the Flower Boxes.* Coward 1966
Miers, *Pirate Chase.* Holt 1965
Shotwell, *Roosevelt Grady.* World 1963

BURGER, CARL
(1888-   ) American
Ackerman, *Tonk and Tonka.* Dutton 1962
Barker, *Winter-Sleeping Wildlife.* Harper 1958
Burnford, *The Incredible Journey.* Atlantic-Little 1961
North
    Hurry, Spring! Dutton 1966
    Little Rascal. Dutton 1965

BURKERT, NANCY EKHOLM
(1933-   ) American
Andersen, *The Nightingale.* Harper 1965
Carlson, *Jean-Claude's Island.* Harper 1963
Dahl, *James and the Giant Peach.* Knopf 1961
De Jong, *The Big Goose and the Little White Duck.*
    Harper 1963
Updike, *A Child's Calendar.* Knopf 1965

BURN, DORIS
(Ac. 1966) American
Burn, *Andrew Henry's Meadow.* Coward 1965

BURNINGHAM, JOHN
(1936-   ) English
Burningham
    Borka, Cape 1963/Random 1964
    Trubloff, Cape 1964/Random 1965
Fleming, *Chitty-Chitty-Bang-Bang.* Cape 1964/
    Random 1964

BURTON, VIRGINIA LEE
(1909-   ) American
Burton, *Life Story.* Houghton 1962

BUSONI, RAFAELLO
(1900-1962) American, b. in Germany
Busoni, *The Man Who Was Don Quixote.* Prentice 1958
Carmer, *The Hudson River.* Holt 1962
Rosen
  Doctor Paracelsus. Little 1959
  The Harmonious World of Johann Kepler. Little 1962
Tharp, *Louis Agassiz, Adventurous Scientist.* Little 1961

CAMERON, POLLY
(1928-   ) American
Cameron
  A Child's Book of Nonsense. Coward 1960
  "I Can't," Said the Ant. Coward 1961
  The 2 Ton Canary & Other Nonsense Riddles. Coward 1965

CARIGIET, ALOIS
(1902-   ) Swiss
Carigiet, *Anton the Goatherd.* Walck 1966
Chönz, *The Snowstorm.* Walck 1958

CARLONI, GIANCARLO
(Ac. 1966) Italian
Rocca, *Gaetano the Pheasant* (with GIULIO CINGOLI).
  Harper 1966

CARROLL, RUTH ROBINSON
(1899-   ) American
Carroll
  Danny and the Poi Pup. Walck 1965
  Runaway Pony, Runaway Dog. Walck 1963
  Tough Enough's Indians. Walck 1960
  Tough Enough's Pony. Walck 1957

CELLINI, JOSEPH
(1924-   ) American, b. in Hungary
Balch, *Keeping Horse.* Crowell 1966
Beaty, *Seeking of Seaways.* Pantheon 1966
Fall, *Canalboat to Freedom.* Dial 1966
Hunter, *The Kelpie's Pearls.* Funk 1966
Ross (comp.), *The Buried Treasure.* Lippincott 1958

CHALMERS, MARY EILEEN
(1927-   ) American
Boegehold, *Three to Get Ready.* Harper 1965
Chalmers
  The Cat Who Liked to Pretend. Harper 1959
  Kevin. Harper 1957
  Take a Nap, Harry. Harper 1964
Heilbroner, *The Happy Birthday Present.* Harper 1962

Lindquist, *The Crystal Tree.* Harper 1966
Nordstrom, *The Secret Language.* Harper 1960
Zolotow, *The Three Funny Friends.* Harper 1961

CHAMBERLAIN, CHRISTOPHER
(1918-   ) English
De Maré, *London's River* (with HEATHER COPLEY).
  Bodley 1964/McGraw 1965
Green, *Heroes of Greece and Troy* (with HEATHER COPLEY). Bodley 1960/Walck 1961

CHAPPELL, WARREN
(1904-   ) American
Chappell
  Coppelia. Knopf 1965
  The Magic Flute. Knopf 1962
  The Nutcracker. Knopf 1958
  The Sleeping Beauty. Knopf 1961
  They Say Stories. Knopf 1960
Fleischman, *The Ghost in the Noonday Sun.* Atlantic-Little 1965
Richter, *The Light in the Forest.* Knopf 1966
Updike, *The Ring.* Knopf 1964

CHARLIP, REMY
(1929-   ) American
Brown
  The Dead Bird. Scott 1958
  Four Fur Feet. Scott 1961
Charlip, *Where Is Everybody?* Scott 1957
Charlip and Supree, *Mother Mother I Feel Sick.*
  Parents' 1966
Miles
  A Day of Summer. Knopf 1960
  A Day of Winter. Knopf 1961

CHARLOT, JEAN
(1898-   ) American, b. in France
Brenner
  Dumb Juan & the Bandits. Scott 1957
  The Timid Ghost. Scott 1966

CHERMAYEFF, IVAN
(1932-   ) American, b. in England
Nash, *The New Nutcracker Suite.* Little 1962
Ott and Coley, *Peter Pumpkin.* Doubleday 1963
Smith, *Ho for a Hat!* Atlantic-Little 1964

CHWAST, JACQUELINE
(1932-   ) American
Dana, *Spencer and His Friends.* Atheneum 1966
Livingston
  Whispers. Harcourt 1958
  Wide Awake and Other Poems. Harcourt 1958

CINGOLI, GIULIO
(Ac. 1966) Italian
Rocca, *Gaetano the Pheasant* (with GIANCARLO
    CARLONI). Harper 1966

COBER, ALAN E.
(1935-) American
Cunningham, *Viollet.* Pantheon 1966
Polland, *The White Twilight.* Holt 1965
Sanderlin
    Eastward to India. Harper 1965
    First Around the World. Harper 1964
Withers (adapt.), *The Tale of the Black Cat.* Holt
    1966

CONNOLLY, JEROME P.
(1931-) American
Hutchins
    Lives of an Oak Tree. Rand 1962
    The Travels of Monarch X. Rand 1966

COOMBS, PATRICIA
(1926-) American
Coombs
    Dorrie and the Blue Witch. Lothrop 1964
    Dorrie and the Weather Box. Lothrop 1966
    Dorrie's Magic. Lothrop 1962

COONEY, BARBARA
(1917-) American
Cock Robin. Scribner 1965
Cooney
    The American Speller. Crowell 1961
    Chanticleer and the Fox. Crowell 1958
    The Little Juggler. Hastings 1961
De la Mare, *Peacock Pie.* Knopf 1961
Field, *Papillot, Clignot et Dodo.* Farrar 1964
Grimm, *Snow-White and Rose-Red.* Delacorte 1966
Haviland, *Favorite Fairy Tales Told in Spain.* Little
    1963
Jewett, *A White Heron.* Crowell 1963
Kay, *City Springtime.* Hastings 1957
Lear, *Le Hibou et la Poussiquette.* Little 1961
Molloy, *Shaun and the Boat.* Hastings 1965
Morse, *All in a Suitcase.* Little 1966
Mother Goose, *Mother Goose in French.* Crowell 1964

COPLEY, HEATHER
(1918-) English
Clark, *Drums and Trumpets.* Bodley 1962/Dufour
    1963
De Maré, *London's River* (with CHRISTOPHER CHAM-
    BERLAIN). Bodley 1964/McGraw 1965
Green, *Heroes of Greece and Troy* (with CHRISTOPHER
    CHAMBERLAIN). Bodley 1960/Walck 1961

CORCOS, LUCILLE
(1908-) American
Corcos, *From Ungskah 1 to Oyaylee 10.* Pantheon 1965

CORWIN, JUNE ATKIN
(1935-) American
Hodges, *Serendipity Tales.* Atheneum 1966

COSGRAVE, JOHN O'HARA, II
(1908-) American
Chase, *Sailing the Seven Seas.* Houghton 1962
Cosgrave
    America Sails the Seas. Houghton 1962
    Clipper Ship. Macmillan 1962
Frank, *Flashing Harpoons.* Crowell 1958
Meader, *The Voyage of the Javelin.* Harcourt 1959

COSGROVE, MARGARET
(1926-) American
Cosgrove, *The Strange World of Animal Senses.*
    Dodd 1961
Lavine
    Wonders of Animal Architecture. Dodd 1964
    Wonders of Animal Disguises. Dodd 1962
    Wonders of the Beetle World. Dodd 1962
Malkus, *Meadows in the Sea.* World 1960

CRICHLOW, ERNEST
(1914-) American
Lansdown, *Galumph.* Houghton 1963
Levy, *Corrie and the Yankee.* Viking 1959
Lexau, *Maria.* Dial 1964
Sterling, *Forever Free.* Doubleday 1963

DANSKA, HERBERT
(1926-) American
Haviland, *Favorite Fairy Tales Told in Russia.* Little
    1961
Orgel, *Story of Lohengrin.* Putnam 1966
Polland, *Queen Without a Crown.* Holt 1966

DARLING, LOIS MACINTYRE
(Ac. 1966) American
Darling
    Coral Reefs (with LOUIS DARLING). World 1963
    The Sea Serpents Around Us (with LOUIS DARLING),
        Little 1965
    Turtles (with LOUIS DARLING). Morrow 1962
Jones, *Wild Voyager.* Little 1966

DARLING, LOUIS
(1916-) American
Cleary

The Mouse and the Motorcycle.   Morrow 1965
Ribsy.   Morrow 1964
Darling
  Coral Reefs (with LOIS DARLING).   World 1963
  Kangaroos and Other Animals with Pockets.   Morrow
    1958
  The Sea Serpents Around Us (with LOIS DARLING).
    Little 1965
  Turtles (with LOIS DARLING).   Morrow 1962
Goetz
  Islands of the Ocean.   Morrow 1964
  Mountains.   Morrow 1962
  Swamps.   Morrow 1961

DAUGHERTY, JAMES
  (1889-   )   American
  Daugherty,   *The Picnic.*   Viking 1958
  Whitman,   *Walt Whitman's America.*   World 1964

D'AULAIRE, EDGAR PARIN
  (1898-   )   American, b. in Switzerland   and

D'AULAIRE, INGRI MORTENSEN PARIN
  (1904-   )   American, b. in Norway
    D'Aulaire
      D'Aulaires' Book of Greek Myths.   Doubleday 1962
      The Magic Meadow.   Doubleday 1958

DAVIS, DIMITRIS
  (1905-   )   Greek
  Bishop,   *A Present from Petros.*   Viking 1961
  Fenton,   *An Island for a Pelican.*   Doubleday 1963
  Graves,   *Greek Gods and Heroes.*   Doubleday 1961
  Snedeker,   *Theras and His Town.*   Doubleday 1961

DE ANGELI, MARGUERITE
  (1889-   )   American
  Bible,   *The Old Testament.*   Doubleday 1960
  De Angeli,   *The Empty Barn.*   Westminster 1966
  Grimm,   *The Goose Girl.*   Doubleday 1964
  Mother Goose,   *A Pocket Full of Posies.*   Doubleday
    1961

DE MISKEY, JULIAN
  (1908-   )   American, b. in Hungary
  Butterworth,   *The Trouble with Jenny's Ear.*   Atlantic-
    Little 1960
  Kalnay,   *Chúcaro, Wild Pony of the Pampa.*   Harcourt
    1960

DE PAOLA, TOMIE
  (Ac. 1966)   American
  Belpré,   *The Tiger and the Rabbit.*   Lippincott 1965
  De Paola,   *The Wonderful Dragon of Timlin.*   Bobbs
    1966
  Miller,   *Sound.*   Coward 1965

DENNIS, WESLEY
  (1903-   )   American
  Arundel
    Dugan and the Hobo.   McGraw 1960
    Jingo, Wild Horse of Abaco.   McGraw 1959
    Mighty Mo: The Story of an African Lion.   McGraw
      1961
    Simba of the White Mane.   McGraw 1958
    The Wildlife of Africa.   Hastings 1965
  Coates,   *That Colt, Fireplug.*   Scribner 1958
  Daly,   *The Ginger Horse.*   Dodd 1964
  Dennis,   *Tumble.*   Hastings 1966
  Hays,   *Little Lone Coyote.*   Little 1961
  Henry
    Black Gold.   Rand 1957
    Stormy: Misty's Foal.   Rand 1963
    White Stallion of Lipizza.   Rand 1964
  Reynolds,   *A Horse Called Mystery.*   Harper 1964
  Steinbeck,   *The Red Pony.*   Viking 1959

DIMSON, THEO AENEAS
  (1930-   )   Canadian
  McNeill
    The Double Knights.   Walck 1964
    The Sunken City.   Oxford 1959/Walck 1959

DINES, GLEN
  (1925-   )   American
  Berry,   *Mountain Men.*   Macmillan 1966
  Dines
    Bull Wagon.   Macmillan 1963
    Overland Stage.   Macmillan 1962

DOBRIN, ARNOLD JACK
  (1928-   )   American
  Dobrin
    Little Monk and the Tiger.   Coward 1965
    Taro and the Sea Turtles.   Coward 1966

DOMANSKA, JANINA
  (Ac. 1966)   American, b. in Poland
  Carlson,   *The Song of the Lop-Eared Mule.*   Harper
    1961
  Deutsch and Yarmolinsky (ed.),   *More Tales of Faraway
    Folk.*   Harper 1963
  Domanska (ed.),   *Why So Much Noise?*   Harper 1965
  Fisher,   *I Like Weather.*   Crowell 1963
  Fournier,   *The Coconut Thieves.*   Scribner 1964
  Hoge (adapt.),   *The Black Heart of Indri.*   Scribner
    1966
  Johnson,   *The Harper Book of Princes.*   Harper 1964
  Kelly,   *The Trumpeter of Krakow.*   Macmillan 1966
  Konopnicka,   *The Golden Seed.*   Scribner 1962
  Laskowski,   *Master of the Royal Cats.*   Seabury 1965

Leskov, *The Steel Flea.* Harper 1964
Lindgren, *Mischievous Meg.* Viking 1962

DRISCOLL, BARRY L.
(Ac. 1966) English
Guillot
  The King of the Cats. Collins 1962/Lothrop 1963
  Mountain with a Secret. Collins 1963/Van Nostrand 1965
Morris
  Apes and Monkeys. Bodley 1964/McGraw 1965
  The Big Cats. Bodley 1965/McGraw 1965
Swinton, *Digging for Dinosaurs.* Bodley 1962/Doubleday 1964

DRUMMOND, VIOLET H.
(1911-) English
Drummond
  The Flying Postman. Constable 1964/Walck 1964
  Little Laura on the River. Faber 1960
  Little Laura's Cat. Faber 1960
  Miss Anna Truly. Constable 1965
  Mrs. Easter and the Storks. Faber 1957/ Transatlantic Arts 1958

DU BOIS, WILLIAM PÈNE
(1916-) American
Caudill, *A Certain Small Shepherd.* Holt 1965
Child Study Association (ed.), *Castles and Dragons.* Crowell 1958
Dahl, *The Magic Finger.* Harper 1966
Du Bois
  The Alligator Case. Harper 1965
  Elizabeth the Cow Ghost. Viking 1964
  Lazy Tommy Pumpkinhead. Harper 1966
  Otto in Africa. Viking 1961
  Otto in Texas. Viking 1960
  The Three Policemen. Viking 1960
Fenton, *Fierce John.* Doubleday 1959
Lear, *The Owl and the Pussy Cat.* Doubleday 1962
MacDonald, *The Light Princess.* Crowell 1962
The Three Little Pigs. Viking 1962

DUCHESNE, JANET
(1930-) English
Duchesne, *Richard Goes Sailing.* Constable 1966
Mayne
  The Big Wheel and the Little Wheel. Hamilton 1965
  The Glass Ball. Hamilton 1961/Dutton 1962

DUVOISIN, ROGER ANTOINE
(1903-) American, b. in Switzerland
Aesop, *The Miller, His Son and Their Donkey.* McGraw 1962

Alarcón, *The Three-Cornered Hat.* Limited Editions Club 1959
Duvoisin
  Day and Night. Knopf 1960
  The Happy Hunter. Lothrop 1961
  Lonely Veronica. Knopf 1963
  Our Veronica Goes to Petunia's Farm. Knopf 1962
  Petunia, I Love You. Knopf 1963
  Petunia, Beware. Knopf 1968
  Spring Snow. Knopf 1963
  Veronica. Knopf 1961
Fatio
  The Happy Lion and the Bear. McGraw 1964
  The Happy Lion's Quest. McGraw 1961
  Red Bantam. McGraw 1963
  The Three Happy Lions. McGraw 1959
Frye
  Days of Sunshine — Days of Rain. McGraw 1965
  The Lamb and the Child. McGraw 1963
Haviland, *Favorite Fairy Tales Told in France.* Little 1959
Holl, *The Rain Puddle.* Lothrop 1965
Janice, *Angelique.* McGraw 1960
Lipkind, *Nubber Bear.* Harcourt 1966
Martin, *The Pointed Brush.* Lothrop 1959
Tresselt
  The Frog in the Well. Lothrop 1958
  Hide and Seek Fog. Lothrop 1965
  Wake Up, City! Lothrop 1957
Zolotow, *In My Garden.* Lothrop 1960

EARLE, OLIVE LYDIA
(Ac. 1966) American, b. in England
Earle
  Birds and Their Beaks. Morrow 1965
  Birds of the Crow Family. Morrow 1962
  Camels and Llamas. Morrow 1961
  Squirrels in the Garden. Morrow 1963
  Strange Companions in Nature. Morrow 1966
  Strange Lizards. Morrow 1964

EASTMAN, P(HILIP) D(AY)
(1909-) American
Eastman
  The Cat in the Hat Beginner Book Dictionary. Random 1964
  Go, Dog, Go. Random 1961
  Sam and the Firefly. Random 1958
Palmer, *A Fish Out of Water.* Random 1961

EHLERT, LOIS JANE
(1934-) American
Lear, *Limericks by Lear.* World 1965
O'Neill, *What Is That Sound!* Atheneum 1966

EHRLICH, BETTINA
See BETTINA, pseud.

EICHENBERG, FRITZ
(1901-   )   American, b. in Germany
Coatsworth,   *The Peaceable Kingdom and Other Poems.*
Pantheon 1958

EINZIG, SUSAN
(1922-   )   English, b. in Germany
Avery (ed.),   *In the Window Seat.*   Oxford 1960/Van
Nostrand 1965
Nesbit,   *The Bastables.*   Nonesuch 1965/Watts 1966
Pearce,   *Tom's Midnight Garden.*   Oxford 1958/Lip-
pincott 1959
Poston,   *Children's Song Book.*   Bodley 1961/Dufour
1963
Spence,   *Lillipilly Hill.*   Oxford 1960/Roy 1963

ELGIN, KATHLEEN
(1923-   )   American
Elgin,   *The First Book of Norse Legends.*   Ward 1965
Selsam
How Animals Live Together.   Morrow 1963
The Language of Animals.   Morrow 1962
Wood,   *The Golden Swan.*   Seabury 1965

EMBERLEY, ED   (Edward Randolph)
(1930-   )   American
Branley
The Big Dipper.   Crowell 1962
Flash, Crash, Rumble and Roll.   Crowell 1964
Emberley
One Wide River to Cross.   Prentice 1966
The Parade Book.   Little 1962
Punch & Judy.   Little 1965
The Story of Paul Bunyan.   Prentice 1963
The Wing on a Flea.   Little 1961
Schackburg,   *Yankee Doodle.*   Prentice 1965

ERDOES, RICHARD
(1912-   )   American, b. in Austria
Joyce,   *The Cat and the Devil.*   Dodd 1964
King,   *Memoirs of a Certain Mouse.*   McGraw 1966

ERHARD, WALTER
(1920-   )   American
Bloch,   *The Dollhouse Story.*   Walck 1961
Dow,   *My Time of Year.*   Walck 1961
McNeill
The Giant's Birthday.   Walck 1964
The Mouse and the Mirage.   Walck 1966

ETS, MARIE HALL
(1895-   )   American
Ets
Automobiles for Mice.   Viking 1964
Cow's Party.   Viking 1958
Gilberto and the Wind.   Viking 1963
Just Me.   Viking 1965
Mister Penny's Circus.   Viking 1961
Ets and Labastida,   *Nine Days to Christmas.*   Viking
1959

EVANS, KATHERINE
(1899-1964)   American
Elkin,   *Six Foolish Fishermen.*   Children's Press 1957
Evans
The Boy Who Cried Wolf.   A. Whitman 1960
A Donkey for Abou.   Abelard 1964
The Maid and Her Pail of Milk.   A. Whitman 1959
The Man, the Boy and the Donkey.   A. Whitman 1958

FAIRY TALES OF HANS CHRISTIAN ANDERSEN.
Orion 1958
(See note in Foreword to this Bibliography)

FALCONER, PEARL
(Ac. 1966)   Scottish
Carlson
The Happy Orpheline.   Blackie 1960
The Orphelines in the Enchanted Castle.   Blackie 1963
A Pet for the Orphelines.   Blackie 1963
Treadgold,   *Winter Princess.*   Brockhampton 1962

FAVA, RITA
See FEGIZ, RITA FAVA

FEASER, DANIEL DAVID
(1920-   )   American
Peterson
Forts in America.   Scribner 1964
A History of Firearms.   Scribner 1961
A History of Knives.   Scribner 1966

FEGIZ, RITA FAVA
(1932-   )   American, b. in Italy
Burgunder,   *From Summer to Summer.*   Viking 1965
Butler,   *Starlight in Tourrone.*   Little 1965
Cretan,   *A Gift from the Bride.*   Atlantic-Little 1964
Hallowell,   *The Long-Nosed Princess.*   Viking 1959
Priolo, *Piccolina and the Easter Bells.* Atlantic-Little 1962
Starbird,   *Speaking of Cows, and Other Poems.*
Lippincott 1960

FENNER, CAROL ELIZABETH
(1929-   )   American
  Fenner
    Christmas Tree on the Mountain.   Harcourt 1966
    Tigers in the Cellar.   Harcourt 1963

FERNS, RONALD GEORGE
(1925-   )   English
  Williams
    Fireworks for Semolina Silkpaws.   Methuen 1964
    Semolina Silkpaws Comes to Catstown.   Methuen 1962

FETZ, INGRID
(1915-   )   American
  Brewton (comp.), *Laughable Limericks.*   Crowell 1965
  Clymer
    The Adventure of Walter.   Atheneum 1965
    Chipmunk in the Forest.   Atheneum 1965
    The Tiny Little House.   Atheneum 1964
  Fox, *Maurice's Room.*   Macmillan 1966

FIAMMENGHI, GIOIA
(1929-   )   American
  Carleton, *Chester Jones.*   Holt 1963
  Corbett, *The Cave Above Delphi.*   Holt 1965
  Evans, *Rimbles.*   Doubleday 1961
  Fenton, *The Golden Doors.*   Doubleday 1957
  Gaeddert, *Noisy Nancy Norris.*   Doubleday 1965
  Hewett, *Dragon From the North.*   McGraw 1965
  Moore, *Papa Albert.*   Atheneum 1964

FISCHER, HANS ERICH
(1909-1958)   Swiss
  Grimm, *The Good-for-Nothings.*   Harcourt 1957
  Perrault, *Puss in Boots.*   Harcourt 1959

FISHER, LEONARD EVERETT
(1924-   )   American
  Ault, *This Is the Desert.*   Dodd 1959
  Bowman, *Mike Fink.*   Little 1957
  Bradford and Winslow (ed.), *Pilgrim Courage.*   Little 1962
  Columbus, *The Quest of Columbus.*   Little 1966
  Davis and Ashabranner, *Ten Thousand Desert Swords.*   Little 1960
  Ellis, *The Arabs.*   World 1958
  Engle, *Golden Child.*   Dutton 1962
  Felton
    A Horse Named Justin Morgan.   Dodd 1962
    Sergeant O'Keefe and His Mule, Balaam.   Dodd 1962
  Fisher, *The Silversmiths.*   Watts 1964
  Hale, *The Man Without a Country.*   Watts 1960
  Irving, *The Legend of Sleepy Hollow.*   Watts 1966
  Johnson

America Moves Forward.   Morrow 1960
    The Congress.   Morrow 1963
    The Supreme Court.   Morrow 1962
  Meredith and Smith
    The Coming of the Pilgrims.   Little 1964
    Riding with Coronado.   Little 1964
  Miller, *The Golden Spur.*   Holt 1964
  Surany
    The Burning Mountain.   Holiday 1965
    The Golden Frog.   Putnam 1963
    Ride the Cold Wind.   Putnam 1964
  Thayer, *Casey at the Bat.*   Watts 1964

FLEISHMAN, SEYMOUR
(1918-   )   American
  Thayer
    Gus Was a Friendly Ghost.   Morrow 1962
    Little Monkey.   Morrow 1959
    Part-Time Dog.   Morrow 1965

FLOETHE, RICHARD
(1901-   )   American, b. in Germany
  Floethe, L. L.
    The Cowboy on the Ranch.   Scribner 1959
    The Farmer and His Cows.   Scribner 1957
    The Fountain of the Friendly Lion.   Scribner 1966
    The Indian and His Pueblo.   Scribner 1964
    The Islands of Hawaii.   Scribner 1964
    Sara.   Farrar 1961
    Sea of Grass.   Scribner 1963
    Triangle X.   Harper 1960

FLORA, JAMES
(1914-   )   American
  Flora
    Charlie Yup and His Snip Snap Boys.   Harcourt 1959
    The Day the Cow Sneezed.   Harcourt 1957
    Grandpa's Farm.   Harcourt 1965
    Leopold, the See-Through Crumbpicker.   Harcourt 1961
    My Friend Charlie.   Harcourt 1964
    Sherwood Walks Home.   Harcourt 1966

FLOWERS OF DELIGHT. Pantheon 1966
(See note in Foreword to this Bibliography)

FORBERG, ATI
(1925-   )   American, b. in Germany
  Brontë, *Jane Eyre.*   Macmillan 1962
  Forberg (comp.), *On a Grass-Green Horn.*   Atheneum 1965
  Lund, *Attic of the Wind.*   Parents' 1966
  Orgel, *Cindy's Snowdrops.*   Knopf 1966
  Sanford and Mendoza, *The Puma and the Pearl.*   Walker 1962

FORTNUM, PEGGY
(1919-   ) English
Bond
   A Bear Called Paddington, Collins 1958/Houghton
      1960
   More About Paddington. Collins 1959/Houghton
      1962
   Paddington Helps Out. Collins 1960/Houghton 1961
Eastwick, A Camel for Saida. Collins 1961
Farjeon, The Children's Bells. Oxford 1957/Walck
   1960
Grahame, The Reluctant Dragon. Bodley 1959
McKay, Dolphin Boy. Harrap 1963
May, The Swan, the Story of Anna Pavlova. Lond.
   Nelson 1958/Nelson 1959
Storr
   The Freedom of the Seas. Faber 1962/Duell 1965
   Robin. Faber 1962

FOSTER, GENEVIEVE
(1898-   ) American
Foster
   Birthdays of Freedom II. Scribner 1957
   The World of Captain John Smith. Scribner 1959
   The World of Columbus and Sons. Scribner 1965

FOSTER, MARIAN CURTIS
See Mariana, pseud.

FRAME, PAUL
(1913-   ) American
Calhoun, Depend on Katie John. Harper 1961
Cavanah, Jenny Lind and Her Listening Cat. Van-
   guard 1961
Corbett, The Case of the Gone Goose. Little 1966
Parrish, Key to the Treasure. Macmillan 1966
Thayer, Casey at the Bat. Prentice 1964

FRANCÉS, ESTEBAN
(Ac. 1966) Spanish
Heathers
   A Handful of Surprises. Harcourt 1961
   The Thread Soldier. Harcourt 1960

FRANÇOIS, ANDRÉ
(1915-   ) French, b. in Russia
Le Marchand, The Adventures of Ulysses. Criterion 1959
Stéphane, Roland. Harcourt 1958
Symonds
   Grodge-Cat & the Window Cleaner. Pantheon 1965
   The Story George Told Me. Harrap 1963/Pantheon
      1964
   Tom and Tabby. Universe 1964

FRANÇOISE, pseud.
(Françoise Seignobosc)
(1897-1961) French
Françoise
   The Big Rain. Scribner 1961
   Chouchou. Scribner 1958
   Jeanne-Marie at the Fair. Scribner 1959
   Minou. Scribner 1962
   What Do You Want To Be? Scribner 1957
   What Time Is It, Jeanne-Marie? Scribner 1963

FRANKENBERG, ROBERT CLINTON
(1911-   ) American
Agle, Makon and the Dauphin. Scribner 1961
Grant, Zachary, the Governor's Pig. World 1960
Hamori, Adventures in Bangkok. Harcourt 1966
Heady, Jambo, Sungura: Tales from East Africa. Norton
   1965
Hill, Glooscap and His Magic. Dodd 1963
Jenkins, Wild Swans at Suvanto. Norton 1965
Mowat, Owls in the Family. Atlantic-Little 1962
Sawyer, Daddles. Little 1964

FRASCONI, ANTONIO
(1919-   ) American, b. in Uruguay
Frasconi
   The House That Jack Built. Harcourt 1958
   See Again, Say Again. Harcourt 1964
   The Snow and the Sun. Harcourt 1961

FRASER, BETTY (Elizabeth Marr)
(1928-   ) American
Alcott, Little Women. Macmillan 1962
Nesbit, The Enchanted Castle. Platt & Munk 1966
Polland, The Queen's Blessing. Holt 1964

FREEMAN, DON
(1908-   ) American
Freeman
   Come Again, Pelican. Viking 1961
   Dandelion. Viking 1964
   Fly High, Fly Low. Viking 1957
   The Night the Lights Went Out. Viking 1958
   Norman the Doorman. Viking 1959
   A Rainbow of My Own. Viking 1966
   The Turtle and the Dove. Viking 1964
White, The Uninvited Donkey. Viking 1957

FRY, ROSALIE KINGSMILL
(1911-   ) English
Fry
   The Echo Song. Dent 1962/Dutton 1962
   Lucinda and the Sailor Kitten. Dent 1959
   The Mountain Door. Dent 1960/Dutton 1961

The Secret of the Ron Mor Skerry (English title, *Child of the Western Isles*).   Dent 1957/Dutton 1959

FUJIKAWA, GYO
(Ac. 1966)   American
Stevenson,   *Child's Garden of Verses.*   Grosset 1957

FUNAI, MAMORU
(1932-   )   Japanese
Bryant,   *The Burning Ricefields.*   Holt 1963
Funai,   *The Tiger, the Brahman and the Jackal.*   Holt 1963
Ishii,   *The Dolls' Day for Yoshiko.*   Follett 1966
Newman,   *The Japanese.*   Atheneum 1964
Parker,   *The House That Guilda Drew.*   Bobbs 1964

GALDONE, PAUL
(Ac. 1966)   American, b. in Hungary
Aesop,   *The Hare and the Tortoise.*   McGraw 1962
Armour,   *Animals on the Ceiling.*   McGraw 1966
Bianki,   *Peek the Piper.*   Braziller 1964
Bible,   *Shadrach, Meshach and Abednego.*   McGraw 1965
Buckley,   *The Little Boy and the Birthdays.*   Lothrop 1965
Carryl,   *The Capital Ship, or The Walloping Window Blind.*   McGraw 1963
Gage
   The Ghost of Five Owl Farm.   World 1966
   Miss Osborne-the-Mop.   World 1963
Galdone
   The House That Jack Built.   McGraw 1961
   The Old Woman and Her Pig.   McGraw 1960
Hawthorne,   *The Golden Touch.*   McGraw 1959
The History of Simple Simon.   McGraw 1966
Holmes,   *The Deacon's Masterpiece.*   McGraw 1965
Hopkinson,   *The Battle of the Kegs.*   Crowell 1964
Jacobs,   *The Three Wishes.*   McGraw 1961
Kusan,   *Koko and the Ghosts.*   Harcourt 1966
Lear
   The Two Old Bachelors.   McGraw 1962
   Two Laughable Lyrics.   Putnam 1966
Longfellow,   *Paul Revere's Ride.*   Crowell 1963
Meeks,   *Jeff and Mr. James' Pond.*   Lothrop 1962
Merriam,   *A Gaggle of Geese.*   Knopf 1960
Mother Goose
   Old Mother Hubbard and Her Dog.   McGraw 1960
   Tom, Tom, the Piper's Son.   McGraw 1964
Saxe,   *The Blind Men and the Elephant.*   McGraw 1963
Titus
   Anatole and the Piano.   McGraw 1966
   Anatole and the Poodle.   McGraw 1965
   Anatole over Paris.   McGraw 1961
   Basil of Baker Street.   McGraw 1958

GALSTER, ROBERT MILLER
(1928-   )   American
Bulla,   *Stories of Favorite Operas.*   Crowell 1959
Goldin,   *Salt.*   Crowell 1966
Rinkoff,   *A Map Is a Picture.*   Crowell 1965

GEER, CHARLES
(1922-   )   American
Bowers,   *The Lost Dragon of Wessex.*   Walck 1957
Fenner,   *The Dark and Bloody Ground.*   Morrow 1963
Hicks,   *The Marvellous Inventions of Alvin Fernald.*   Holt 1960
Meigs,   *Wild Geese Flying.*   Macmillan 1957
Parker,   *M for Mischief.*   Duell 1966
White,   *Thunder in His Moccasins.*   Viking 1962

GEKIERE, MADELEINE
(1919-   )   American, b. in Switzerland
Ciardi
   John J. Plenty and Fiddler Dan.   Lippincott 1963
   The Reason for the Pelican.   Lippincott 1959
Grimm,   *The Fisherman and His Wife.*   Pantheon 1957

GENIA, pseud.
(GENIA KATERINE WENNERSTROM)
(1930-   )   American
Budd,   *Tekla's Easter.*   Rand 1962
Johnson,   *Happy Birthdays 'Round the World.*   Rand 1963

GERARD, JEAN IGNACE ISIDORE
See GRANDVILLE, J. J., pseud.

GILL, MARGERY JEAN
(1925-   )   English
Arthur
   A Candle in Her Room.   Atheneum 1966
   Dragon Summer.   Hutchinson 1962/Atheneum 1963
Bingley,   *The Story of Tit-Bé and His Friend.*   Abelard 1962
Boston,   *The Castle of Yew.*   Bodley 1965/Harcourt 1965
Cooper,   *Over Sea, Under Stone.*   Cape 1965/Harcourt 1966
Craig,   *What Did You Dream?*   Abelard 1964
Fry
   The Castle Family.   Dent 1965/Dutton 1966
   September Island.   Dent 1965/Dutton 1965
Guillot,   *The Blue Day.*   Bodley 1958/Abelard 1959
Hewett,   *The Tale of the Turnip.*   Bodley 1961/McGraw 1961
Lang (ed.),   *Fifty Favourite Fairy Tales.*   Nonesuch 1963/Watts 1964

Mayne, *A Day Without Wind.* Hamilton 1964/
Dutton 1964

Montgomerie (ed.), *This Little Pig Went to Market.*
Bodley 1966

Sanchez-Silva, *The Boy and the Whale.* Bodley 1963/
McGraw 1964

Thomas, *The Complete Fairy Tales of Edward Thomas*
(English title, *Four and Twenty Blackbirds*).
Bodley 1965/Watts 1966

GLANZMAN, LOUIS S.
(1922-   ) American
Lindgren
Pippi Goes on Board. Viking 1957
Pippi in the South Seas. Viking 1959
Stolz, *The Noonday Friends.* Harper 1965

GLASER, MILTON
(Ac. 1966) American
Aiken, *Cats and Bats and Things with Wings.*
Atheneum 1965
Tresselt, *The Smallest Elephant in the World.* Knopf
1959

GNOLI, DOMENICO
(1933-   ) Italian
Juster, *Alberic the Wise.* Pantheon 1965

GOBBATO, IMERO
(1923-   ) American
Kendall, *The Whisper of Glocken.* Harcourt 1965
Linde, *The White Stone.* Harcourt 1966
Merriam, *Catch a Little Rhyme.* Atheneum 1966

GORDON, MARGARET ANNA
(1939-   ) English
MacBeth, *Noah's Journey.* Macmillan 1966/Viking
1966
Smith, *Emily's Voyage.* Lond. Macmillan 1966

GOREY, EDWARD ST. JOHN
(1925-   ) American
Ciardi
The King Who Saved Himself from Being Saved.
Lippincott 1965
The Man Who Sang the Sillies. Lippincott 1961
The Monster Den. Lippincott 1966
You Know Who. Lippincott 1964
You Read to Me, I'll Read to You. Lippincott 1962
Wells, *War of the Worlds.* Random 1960

GORSLINE, DOUGLAS WARNER
(1913-   ) American
Bulla, *Viking Adventure.* Crowell 1963

Edmonds, *They Had a Horse.* Dodd 1962
Gardner, *Sky Pioneers.* Harcourt 1963
Wood
A Hound, a Bay Horse and a Turtle Dove. Pantheon
1963
Trust Thyself. Pantheon 1964

GRABIANSKI, JANUSZ
(1929-   ) Polish
Green (ed.)
The Big Book of Animal Fables. Dobson 1965/Watts
1965
The Big Book of Animal Stories. Dobson 1961/Watts
1962
The Big Book of Wild Animals. Dobson 1964/Watts
1964
Grimm, *Grimms' Fairy Tales.* Cape 1962

GRABOFF, ABNER
(1919-   ) American
Alexander, *Noise in the Night.* Rand 1960
Holl, *Mrs. McGarrity's Peppermint Sweater.* Lothrop
1966
Mills, *The Hungry Goat.* Rand 1964
Mills and Bonne, *I Know an Old Lady.* Rand 1961

GRAHAM, MARGARET BLOY
(1920-   ) American, b. in Canada
Zion
Harry and the Lady Next Door. Harper 1960
Harry by the Sea. Harper 1965
Jeffie's Party. Harper 1957
The Meanest Squirrel I Ever Met. Scribner 1962
No Roses for Harry! Harper 1958
The Plant Sitter. Harper 1959
The Sugar Mouse Cake. Scribner 1964

GRAMATKY, HARDIE
(1907-   ) American
Gramatky
Bolivar. Putnam 1961
Homer and the Circus Train. Putnam 1957
Little Toot on the Thames. Putnam 1964
Nikos and the Sea God. Putnam 1963

GRANDVILLE, J. J., pseud.
(JEAN IGNACE ISIDORE GERARD)
(1803-1847) French
Rees, *Fables from Aesop.* Oxford 1966
(See note in Foreword to this Bibliography.)

GREENWALD, SHEILA ELLEN
(1934-   ) American
Brink, *Pink Motel.* Macmillan 1959

Laughlin, *The Little Leftover Witch*.   Macmillan 1960
Worstell, *Jump the Rope Jingles*.   Macmillan 1961

GRIFALCONI, ANN
(1929-   )   American
Forbus, *Tawny's Trick*.   Viking 1965
Grifalconi, *City Rhythms*.   Bobbs 1966
Hoyt (ed.), *American Steamboat Stories*.   Abelard 1966
Weik, *The Jazz Man*.   Atheneum 1966

GROSSMAN, NANCY S.
(1940-   )   American
Caudill, *Did You Carry the Flag Today, Charley?* Holt 1966
De Jong, *Far Out the Long Canal*.   Harper 1964
Fisher, *You Were Princess Last Time*.   Holt 1965
Inyart, *Jenny*.   Watts 1966
Miller, *Ski the Mountain*.   Doubleday 1965

GROVES-RAINES, ANTONY (RALPH GORE)
(Ac. 1966)   Irish
Groves-Raines, *The Tidy Hen*.   Harcourt 1961
Langstaff, *On Christmas Day in the Morning*.   Harcourt 1959

GUGGENHEIM, HANS
(1924-   )   American, b. in Germany
Arora, *"What Then, Raman?"*   Follett 1960
Carpenter, *The Elephant's Bathtub*.   Doubleday 1962
Mirsky, *Balboa*.   Harper 1964

HAAS, IRENE
(1929-   )   American
De Regniers, *Something Special*.   Harcourt 1958
Enright
Tatsinda.   Harcourt 1963
Zeee.   Harcourt 1965
Joslin
Dear Dragon . . .   Harcourt 1962
There Is a Dragon in My Bed.   Harcourt 1961
Smith, *Emily's Voyage*.   Harcourt 1966

HADER, BERTA HOERNER
(Ac. 1966)   American and

HADER, ELMER STANLEY
(1889-   )   American
Hader
Little Chip.   Macmillan 1958
Quack Quack.   Macmillan 1961
Reindeer Trail.   Macmillan 1959
Two Is Company, Three's a Crowd.   Macmillan 1965

HALE, KATHLEEN
(1898-   )   English
Hale
Orlando and the Three Graces.   Murray 1965
Orlando (The Marmalade Cat) Buys a Cottage. Country Life 1963
Orlando's Magic Carpet.   Murray 1958

HALL, DOUGLAS
(1931-   )   English
Bell, *The Rebels of Journey's End*.   Hutchinson 1966
Green, *The Land Beyond the North*.   Bodley 1958/ Walck 1959
Huddy, *How Edward Saved St. George*.   Constable 1966
MacPherson, *The Rough Road*.   Harcourt 1966
Willard
Storm from the West (English title, *The Battle of Wednesday Week*).   Constable 1963/Harcourt 1964
Three and One to Carry.   Constable 1964/Harcourt 1964

HALL, NATALIE WATSON
(1923-   )   American
Hall
The Palace of Fun.   Viking 1965
A World in a City Block.   Viking 1960
Zig-Zag-Zeppo.   Viking 1961

HAMBERGER, JOHN F.
(1934-   )   American
Coatsworth, *The Fox Friend*.   Macmillan 1966
Hamberger, *The Day the Sun Disappeared*.   Norton 1964
Hill, *Badger, the Mischief Maker*.   Dodd 1965

HENDERSON, LE GRAND
See LE GRAND, pseud.

HIM, GEORGE
(1900-   )   English, b. in Poland
Herrmann
The Giant Alexander.   Methuen 1964/McGraw 1965
The Giant Alexander and the Circus.   McGraw 1966

HOBAN, LILLIAN
(1925-   )   American
Hoban, R.
Bread and Jam for Frances.   Harper 1964
Herman the Loser.   Harper 1961
Nothing To Do.   Harper 1964
The Sorely Trying Day.   Harper 1964
Holman, *Victoria's Castle*.   Norton 1966

HODGES, C. WALTER
(1909-   )   English
Baker
   Hannibal and the Bears.   Harrap 1965/Farrar 1966
   The Shoe Shop Bears.   Harrap 1963/Farrar 1965
Duggan
   Growing Up in 13th Century England (English title,
     Growing Up in the 13th Century).   Faber 1962/
     Pantheon 1962
   Growing Up with the Norman Conquest.   Faber 1965/
     Pantheon 1966
Dumas,   *The Three Musketeers.*   World 1957
Graves,   *The Siege and Fall of Troy.*   Cassell 1962/
   Doubleday 1962
Hodges
   Magna Carta.   Oxford n.d./Coward 1966
   The Namesake.   Bell 1964/Coward 1964
   The Norman Conquest.   Oxford 1966/Coward 1966
   Shakespeare's Theatre.   Oxford 1964/Coward 1964
Manning-Sanders,   *Red Indian Folk and Fairy Tales.*
   Oxford 1960/Roy 1962
Renault,   *The Lion in the Gateway.*   Longmans 1964/
   Harper 1964
Varble,   *Three Against London.*   Doubleday 1962

HOFF, SYD
(1912-   )   American
Hoff
   Danny and the Dinosaur.   Harper 1958
   Grizzwold.   Harper 1963
   Oliver.   Harper 1960
   Sammy the Seal.   Harper 1959

HOFFMANN, FELIX
(1911-   )   Swiss
Grimm
   Rapunzel.   Harcourt 1961
   The Seven Ravens.   Harcourt 1963
   The Sleeping Beauty.   Harcourt 1960
   The Wolf and the Seven Little Kids.   Harcourt 1959
Haller,   *He Served Two Masters.*   Pantheon 1962
Haviland,   *Favorite Fairy Tales Told in Poland.*   Little
   1963
Hoffmann,   *A Boy Went Out to Gather Pears.*   Har-
   court 1966
Voegli,   *Prince of Hindustan.*   Oxford 1961/Walck 1961

HOGNER, NILS
(1893-   )   American
Hogner, D. C.
   Butterflies.   Crowell 1962
   Grasshoppers and Crickets.   Crowell 1960
Hogner, N.
   Molly the Black Mare.   Walck 1962

Tanny.   Walck 1960
Jordan,   *Seeds by Wind and Water.*   Crowell 1962

HOGROGIAN, NONNY
(1932-   )   American
Burns,   *Hand in Hand We'll Go.*   Crowell 1965
Meredith,   *King of the Kerry Fair.*   Crowell 1961
Nic Leodhas
   Always Room for One More.   Holt 1965
   Gaelic Ghosts.   Holt 1964
   Ghosts Go Haunting.   Holt 1965
O'Neill,   *The White Palace.*   Crowell 1966
Schiller,   *The Kitchen Knight.*   Holt 1965
Schwartz,   *A Tale of Stolen Time.*   Prentice 1966
Tashjian,   *Once There Was and Was Not.*   Little 1966

HOLLAND, JANICE
(1913-   )   American
Holland
   Christopher Goes to the Castle.   Scribner 1957
   You Never Can Tell.   Scribner 1963
Quigley,   *The Blind Men and the Elephant.*   Scribner
   1959

HOLLING, HOLLING CLANCY
(1900-   )   American   and

HOLLING, LUCILLE WEBSTER
(1900-   )   American
Holling,   *Pagoo.*   Houghton 1957

HOUSER, ALLAN C.
(1914-   )   American
Clark,   *The Desert People.*   Viking 1962
Coatsworth,   *The Cave.*   Viking 1958

HOUSTON, JAMES ARCHIBALD
(1921-   )   Canadian
Houston
   Eagle Mask,   Harcourt 1965
   Tikta'liktak: An Eskimo Legend.   Harcourt 1966

HOWARD, ALAN
(1922-   )   English
Chukowsky,   *Crocodile.*   Faber 1964/Transatlantic Arts
   1966
De La Mare,   *Tales Told Again.*   Faber 1959/Knopf
   1959
Lines (ed.),   *The Faber Storybook.*   Faber 1961
Tomlinson,   *The Bus That Went to Church.*   Faber
   1965

HUGHES, SHIRLEY
(1929-   )   English
Andersen,   *Hans Andersen's Fairy Tales.*   Blackie 1961
Bull,   *Wayland's Keep.*   Collins 1966
Hughes.   *Lucy and Tom's Day.*   Gollancz 1960/Scott
      1960
Ireson (ed.),   *The Faber Book of Nursery Stories.*
      Faber 1966
McPherson,   *The Shinty Boys.*   Collins 1963/Harcourt
      1963
Morgan,   *Satchkin, Patchkin.*   Faber 1966
Sawyer,   *Roller Skates.*   Bodley 1964
Softly,   *Place Mill.*   Macmillan 1962/St. Martin's 1963
Storey
      Kate and the Family Tree.   Faber 1965
      The Smallest Doll.   Faber 1966

HURD, CLEMENT
(1908-   )   American
Hurd, E. T.
      Christmas Eve.   Harper 1962
      Come and Have Fun.   Harper 1962
      The Day the Sun Danced.   Harper 1965
      Follow Tomás.   Dial 1963
      Johnny Lion's Book.   Harper 1965
      No Funny Business.   Harper 1962
Stein,   *The World Is Round.*   Scott 1966
Valens
      Wildfire.   World 1963
      Wingfin and Topple.   World 1962

HUTCHINSON, WILLIAM M.
(1916-   )   American
Anckarsvärd
      Aunt Vinnie's Invasion.   Harcourt 1962
      Aunt Vinnie's Victorious Six.   Harcourt 1964
Barlow,   *Latin American Tales.*   Rand 1966
Uchida
      The Promised Year.   Harcourt 1959
      Takao and Grandfather's Sword.   Harcourt 1958
Winterfield
      Castaways in Lilliput.   Harcourt 1960
      Trouble at Timpetill.   Harcourt 1965
Young
      The Dollar Horse.   Harcourt 1961
      Secret of Stone House Farm.   Harcourt 1963

HUTTON, CLARKE
(1898-   )   English
Almedingen,   *A Picture History of Russia.*   Oxford 1964/
      Watts 1964
Clemens,   *The Prince and the Pauper.*   Heritage 1965
Commager,   *A Picture History of the United States.*
      Oxford 1958/Watts 1958

Crawford,   *A Picture History of Australia.*   Oxford 1962/
      Watts 1963
Hampden,   *A Picture History of India.*   Oxford 1965/
      Watts 1966
Jarman,   *A Picture History of Italy.*   Oxford 1961/
      Watts 1962

HYMAN, (TRINA) SCHART
(1939-   )   American
Haviland,   *Favorite Fairy Tales Told in Czechoslovakia.*
      Little 1966
O'Faolain,   *Children of the Salmon.*   Longmans 1965/
      Atlantic-Little 1965
Sawyer,   *Joy to the World!*   Little 1966
Warburg,   *Curl Up Small.*   Houghton 1964

IPCAR, DAHLOV
(1917-   )   American
Ipcar
      Bright Barnyard.   Knopf 1966
      Brown Cow Farm.   Doubleday 1959
      Deep Sea Farm.   Knopf 1961
      Horses of Long Ago.   Doubleday 1965
      I Like Animals.   Knopf 1960
      I Love My Anteater with an A.   Knopf 1964
      Lobsterman.   Knopf 1962
      Ten Big Farms.   Knopf 1958
      The Wonderful Egg.   Doubleday 1958

JACQUES, ROBIN
(1920-   )   English
Aiken
      Black Hearts in Battersea.   Doubleday 1964
      Nightbirds on Nantucket.   Doubleday 1966
Fry,   *Promise of the Rainbow.*   Farrar 1965
Manning-Sanders
      A Book of Dragons.   Methuen 1964/Dutton 1965
      A Book of Dwarfs.   Methuen 1962/Dutton 1964
      A Book of Giants.   Methuen 1962/Dutton 1963
      A Book of Witches.   Methuen 1965/Dutton 1966
Norton,   *Steel Magic.*   World 1965
Thwaite,   *The House in Turner Square.*   Constable
      1960/Harcourt 1961
Van Stockum,   *Mogo's Flute.*   Viking 1966
Verne,   *Around the World in Eighty Days.*   Doubleday
      1964

JANSSON, TOVE
(1914-   )   Finnish
Jansson
      Moominland Midwinter.   Benn 1958/Walck 1962
      Moominpappa at Sea.   Benn 1966
      Tales from Moominvalley   Benn 1963/Walck 1964
      Who Will Comfort Toffle?   Benn 1960

JAUSS, ANNE MARIE
(1907-   )   American, b. in Germany
Cathon and Schmidt (comps.), *Perhaps and Perchance.*
    Abingdon 1962
Jauss, *The River's Journey.* Lippincott 1957
Lauber, *Our Friend the Forest.* Doubleday 1959
Resnick
    Selections from Spanish Poetry. Harvey 1962
    Spanish-American Poetry. Harvey 1964
Spicer, *46 Days of Christmas.* Coward 1960
Toor, *The Golden Carnation.* Lothrop 1961
Wyatt
    The Golden Stag. McKay 1962
    King Beetle-Tamer. McKay 1963

JOHNSON, CROCKETT, pseud.
(DAVID JOHNSON LEISK)
(1906-   )   American
Johnson
    Ellen's Lion. Harper 1959
    Harold's ABC. Harper 1963
    A Picture for Harold's Room. Harper 1960
    *We Wonder What Will Walter Be? When He Grows
        Up.* Holt 1964

JOHNSON, EUGENE HARPER
(Ac. 1966)   American
Bontemps, *Frederick Douglass.* Knopf 1959
Booth, *Kalena.* McKay 1958
Bradley, *Meeting with a Stranger.* Lippincott 1964
Clair, *Bemba.* Harcourt 1962
Johnson, *Piankhy the Great.* Nelson 1962
Ladd, *A Fox Named Rufus.* Morrow 1960
Martin, *The Little Brown Hen.* Crowell 1960
Worcester, *War Pony.* Walck 1961

JOHNSON, JOHN E.
(1929-   )   American
Brenner, *Nicky's Sister.* Knopf 1966
Jacobs, *Just Around the Corner.* Holt 1964
Withers, *I Saw a Rocket Walk a Mile.* Holt 1965

JOHNSON, MILTON
(1932-   )   American
Colt, *Andrew Jackson.* Houghton 1965
Coolidge
    Lives of Famous Romans. Houghton 1965
    Men of Athens. Houghton 1962
Haugaard, *Orphans of the Wind.* Houghton 1966

JONES, CAROL ANN
(1942-   )   English
Boucher, *The Hornstranders.* Constable 1966

JONES, HAROLD
(1904-   )   English
Blake, *Songs of Innocence.* Faber 1958/Barnes 1961
Browning, *The Pied Piper of Hamelin.* Oxford 1962/
    Watts 1962
Hawthorne, *The Complete Greek Stories of Nathaniel
        Hawthorne.* Gollancz 1963/Watts 1963
Kingsley, *The Water Babies.* Gollancz 1961/Watts
    1961
Lines
    Noah and the Ark. Oxford 1961/Watts 1961
    Nursery Stories (English title, *Jack and the Beanstalk*).
        Oxford 1960/Watts 1961
    A Ring of Tales. Oxford 1958/Watts 1959
Shakespeare, *Songs from Shakespeare.* Faber 1961/
    Barnes 1961
Vipent, *Bless This Day.* Collins 1958/Harcourt 1958

KAHL, VIRGINIA CAROLINE
(1919-   )   American
Kahl
    The Baron's Booty. Scribner 1963
    The Perfect Pancake. Scribner 1960
Vacheron and Kahl
    Here Is Henri! Scribner 1959
    Voici Henri! Scribner 1959

KANE, HENRY BUGBEE
(1902-   )   American
Harris, *Flash: The Life Story of a Firefly.* Little 1966
McCord
    All Day Long. Little 1966
    Take Sky. Little 1962

KARLIN, EUGENE
(1918-   )   American
Church
    The Aeneid for Boys and Girls. Macmillan 1962
    The Iliad and The Odyssey of Homer. Macmillan 1964

KAUFMANN, JOHN
(1931-   )   American
Baker, *Killer-of-Death.* Harper 1963
Berry, *The Springing of the Rice.* Macmillan 1966
Carlson
    The Empty Schoolhouse. Harper 1965
    The Letter on the Tree. Harper 1964
Cottler, *Alfred Wallace, Explorer-Naturalist.* Little
    1966
Farmer, *The Magic Stone.* Chatto 1964/Harcourt 1964
Kendall, L., *Rain Boat.* Coward 1965
Murphy, *Wild Geese Calling.* Dutton 1966
Selsam
    Animals as Parents. Morrow 1965

The Courtship of Animals. Morrow 1964

Welty, *Birds with Bracelets.* Prentice 1965

KEATS, EZRA JACK
(1916-   ) American
Clark, *Tia Maria's Garden.* Viking 1963
Collins, *The Flying Cow.* Walck 1963
Fisher, *And Long Remember.* McGraw 1959
Keats, E. J.
    Jennie's Hat. Harper 1966
    John Henry. Pantheon 1965
    The Snowy Day. Viking 1962
    Whistle for Willy. Viking 1964
Keats, E. J. (ed.)
    God Is in the Mountain. Holt 1966
Keats, J., *The Naughty Boy.* Viking 1965
Lewis (ed.), *In a Spring Garden.* Dial 1964
McGovern, *Zoo, Where Are You?* Harper 1964
McKellar, *Wee Joseph.* McGraw 1957
Martin, *The Rice Bowl Pet.* Crowell 1962
Selsam, *How To Be a Nature Detective.* Harper 1966

KEEPING, CHARLES WILLIAM JAMES
(1924-   ) English
Almedingen
    The Knights of the Golden Table. Bodley 1963/
        Lippincott 1964
    The Treasure of Siegfried. Bodley 1964/Lippincott
        1965
Chandler, *Three Trumpets.* Abelard 1962
Crossley-Holland, *King Horn.* Macmillan 1965/
    Dutton 1966
Garner, *Elidor.* Collins 1965
Holding
    The King's Contest. Abelard 1964
    The Sky-Eater. Abelard 1966
Hunter, *The Smartest Man in Ireland* (English title,
    Patrick Kentigern Keenan). Blackie 1963/Funk
    1965
Keeping
    Black Dolly. Faber 1966
    Shaun and the Cart-Horse. Oxford 1966/Watts 1966
Macken, *Island of the Great Yellow Ox* (Lond.).
    Macmillan 1966
Picard, *Lost John.* Oxford 1962/Criterion 1963
Sutcliff
    Beowulf. Bodley 1961/Dutton 1962
    Heroes and History. Botsford 1965/Dutton 1965
    Knight's Fee. Oxford 1960/Walck 1961
    The Silver Branch. Oxford 1957/Walck 1958
Treece
    The Last Viking (English title, *The Last of the
        Vikings*). Brockhampton 1964/Pantheon 1966
    Splintered Sword. Brockhampton 1965/Duell 1966

KENNEDY, PAUL EDWARD
(1929-   ) American
De la Mare
    The Magic Jacket. Knopf 1962
    A Penny a Day. Knopf 1961
Erwin, *Aggie, Maggie and Tish.* Little 1965
Ferra-Mikura, *Twelve People Are Not a Dozen.* Bobbs
    1965
Longfellow, *The Skeleton in Armor.* Prentice 1964
MacManus, *Hibernian Nights.* Macmillan 1963
Mehdevi, *Persian Folk and Fairy Tales.* Knopf 1965
Rich, *Hannah Elizabeth.* Harper 1964
Robertson, *If Wishes Were Horses.* Harper 1958
Schroeder, *My Horse Says.* Coward 1965

KENNEDY, RICHARD
(1910-   ) English
Baker
    Castaway Christmas. Methuen 1963/Farrar 1964
    Cut Off from Crumpets. Methuen 1964
Berna, *The Horse Without a Head.* Pantheon 1958
Bosley, *Tales from the Long Lakes.* Gollancz 1966
Dillon
    A Family of Foxes. Faber 1964
    The Lion Cub. Hamilton 1966/Duell 1966
    The Road to Dunmore. Faber 1966
    The Sea Wall. Faber 1965
Guillot
    The Fantastic Brother. Methuen 1961/Rand 1963
    Riders of the Wind. Rand 1961
King, *The 22 Letters.* Hamilton 1966
Lindgren, *Pippi in the South Seas.* Hamilton 1966

KEPES, JULIET
(1919-   ) American, b. in England
Kepes
    Five Little Monkey Business. Houghton 1965
    Frogs, Merry. Pantheon 1961
    Lady Bird, Quickly. Atlantic-Little 1964
    Two Little Birds and Three. Houghton 1960
Miller, *Give a Guess.* Pantheon 1957
Smith
    Boy Blue's Book of Beasts. Atlantic-Little 1957
    Puptents and Pebbles. Atlantic-Little 1959

KESSLER, LEONARD P.
(1921-   ) American
Branley
    A Book of Astronauts for You. Crowell 1963
    A Book of Planets for You. Crowell 1961
Goldin, *Ducks Don't Get Wet.* Crowell 1965
Kessler, *All Aboard the Train.* Doubleday 1964
Wood, *The Elephant in the Barn.* Harper 1961

KETTELKAMP, LARRY DALE
(1933-   ) American
Kettelkamp
   Drums, Rattles and Bells.   Morrow 1960
   Singing Strings.   Morrow 1958
   Spinning Tops.   Morrow 1966
   Spirals.   Prentice 1964

KIDDELL-MONROE, JOAN
(1908-   ) English
   Aesop, *Aesop's Fables.*   Dent 1961/Dutton 1965
   Arnot, *African Myths and Legends.*   Oxford 1962/
      Walck 1963
   Birch, *Chinese Myths and Fantasies.*   Oxford 1961/
      Walck 1961
   Fenton, *Sher (Lord of the Jungle).*   Benn 1962
   Freeman, *The Owl and the Mirror.*   Blackwell 1960/
      Duell 1961
   Gray, *India's Tales and Legends.*   Oxford 1961/Walck
      1961
   Guillot, *Grishka and the Bear.*   Oxford 1959/Criterion
      1960
   Kingsley, *The Heroes.*   Dutton 1963
   Lang, *The Adventures of Odysseus.*   Dent 1962/Dutton
      1962
   Longfellow, *The Song of Hiawatha.*   Dent 1960/
      Dutton 1960
   McAlpine, *Japanese Tales and Legends.*   Oxford 1959/
      Walck 1959
   Müller-Guggenbühl, *Swiss-Alpine Folk Tales.*   Oxford
      1958/Walck 1958
   Picard
      German Hero-Sagas and Folk-Tales.   Oxford 1958/
         Walck 1958
      The Iliad of Homer.   Oxford 1959/Walck 1960
   Taylor, *The Aeneid of Virgil.*   Oxford 1961/Walck
      1961

KIMBALL, YEFFE
(1914-   ) American
   Leekley, *The World of Manabozho.*   Vanguard 1965

KIRN, ANN MINETTE
(1910-   ) American
   Kirn
      Full of Wonder.   World 1959
      I Spy.   Norton 1965
      Leopard on a String.   World 1959
      Two Pesos for Catalina.   Rand 1962

KITTELSEN, THEODOR
(1857-1914) Norwegian
   Asbjørnsen and Moe, *Norwegian Folk Tales* (with ERIK
      WERENSKIOLD).   Viking 1961
   (See note in Foreword to this Bibliography)

KNIGHT, HILARY
(1926-   ) American
   De Beaumont, *Beauty and the Beast.*   Macmillan 1963
   Dickens, *Captain Boldheart and The Magic Fishbone.*
      Macmillan 1964
   Henry, *Tiger's Chance.*   Harcourt 1957
   Knight, *Where's Wallace?*   Harper 1964

KOCSIS, J. C. (James Paul)
(1936-   ) American
   Armer, *Steve and the Guide Dogs.*   World 1965
   Huston and Yolen, *Trust a City Kid.*   Lothrop 1966
   Reeves, *The Strange Light.*   Rand 1966

KOMODA, KIYO (Kiyoaki)
(1937-   ) American, b. in Japan
   Goodwin, *Alonzo and the Army of Ants.*   Harper 1966
   Rosenbaum (ed.), *The Best Book of True Sea Stories.*
      Doubleday 1966

KRAUS, ROBERT
(1925-   ) American
   Kraus
      Amanda Remembers.   Harper 1965
      Ladybug, Ladybug.   Harper 1957
      The Littlest Rabbit.   Harper 1961
   Stevens, *Rabbit and Skunk and the Scary Rock.*   Scott
      1962

KREDEL, FRITZ
(1900-   ) American, b. in Germany
   Barker, *The Trojan Horse.*   Random 1959
   Bogan and Smith (comps.), *The Golden Journey.*
      Reilly 1965
   Brown and Crone, *The Silent Storm.*   Abingdon 1963
   Wibberley, *The Time of the Lamb.*   Washburn 1961

KRUSH, BETH
(1918-   ) American
   Cameron
      A Spell Is Cast (with JOE KRUSH).   Atlantic-Little
         1964
      The Terrible Churnadyne (with JOE KRUSH). Atlantic-
         Little 1959
      Crowell 1965
   Courlander, *The Piece of Fire* (with JOE KRUSH).
      Harcourt 1964
   Enright
      Gone Away Lake (with JOE KRUSH).   Harcourt 1957
      Return to Gone Away (with JOE KRUSH).   Harcourt
         1961
   Langstaff, *The Swapping Boy* (with JOE KRUSH).   Har-
      court 1960

Norton, *The Borrowers Afloat* (with JOE KRUSH).
Harcourt 1961

Ogburn, *Big Caesar* (with JOE KRUSH). Houghton 1958

Welty, *The Shoe Bird.* Harcourt 1964

KRUSH, JOE
(1918-   ) American
Cameron
A Spell Is Cast (with BETH KRUSH). Atlantic-Little
1964
The Terrible Churnadyne (with BETH KRUSH).
Atlantic-Little 1959
Constant, *Those Miller Girls!* (with BETH KRUSH).
Crowell 1965
Courlander, *The Piece of Fire* (with BETH KRUSH).
Harcourt 1964
Enright
Gone Away Lake (with BETH KRUSH). Harcourt 1957
Return to Gone Away (with BETH KRUSH). Harcourt
1961
Langstaff
Ol' Dan Tucker. Harcourt 1963
The Swapping Boy (with BETH KRUSH). Harcourt
1960
Norton, *The Borrowers Afloat* (with BETH KRUSH).
Harcourt 1961
Ogburn, *Big Caesar* (with BETH KRUSH). Houghton
1958

KUSKIN, KARLA SEIDMAN
(1932-   ) American
Kuskin
The Bear Who Saw the Spring. Harper 1961
In the Middle of the Trees. Harper 1958
The Rose on My Cake. Harper 1964
Square as a House. Harper 1960
Which Horse Is William? Harper 1959

LAITE, GORDON
(1925-   ) American
Belting, *Elves and Ellefolk.* Holt 1961
Hazeltine (ed.), *Hero Tales from Many Lands.*
Abingdon 1961
Luckhardt
Good King Wenceslas. Abingdon 1964
The Story of Saint Nicholas. Abingdon 1960
MacKay, *They Sang a New Song.* Abingdon 1959

LAMB, LYNTON
(1907-   ) English
Land, *Cats' Tales.* Faber 1959
Mayne, *The Grass Rope.* Oxford 1959/Dutton 1962
Reeves, *The Strange Light.* Heinemann 1964
Severn, *The Wild Valley* (English title, *Foxy-Boy*).
Bodley 1959/Dutton 1963

LANDAU, JACOB
(1917-   ) American
Appel, *Man and Magic.* Pantheon 1966
Latham, *This Dear-Bought Land.* Harper 1957

LANGNER, NOLA
(1930-   ) American
McGovern, *Little Wolf.* Abelard 1965
Olsen, *Bernadine and the Water Bucket.* Abelard
1966

LARSEN, SUZANNE KESTELOO
(1930-   ) American
Little, *Spook.* Atheneum 1965

LASELL, FEN H.
(1929-   ) American, b. in Germany
Kingman, *Peter's Pony.* Doubleday 1963
Lasell, *Fly Away, Goose.* Houghton 1965
Miles, *Teacher's Pet.* Atlantic-Little 1966

LASKER, JOE (Joseph Leon)
(1919-   ) American
Schlein
Snow Time. A. Whitman 1962
The Sun, the Wind, the Sea and the Rain. Abelard
1961
Simon, *Benjy's Bird.* A. Whitman 1965
Zolotow, *The Man with the Purple Eyes.* Abelard 1961

LATHROP, DOROTHY PULIS
(1891-   ) American
Lathrop
The Dog in the Tapestry Garden. Macmillan 1962
Follow the Brook. Macmillan 1960

LATTIMORE, ELEANOR FRANCES
(1904-   ) American
Lattimore
The Bus Trip. Morrow 1965
The Chinese Daughter. Morrow 1960
Laurie and Company. Morrow 1962
The Mexican Bird. Morrow 1965
The Wonderful Glass House. Morrow 1961

LAZARE, JERRY (Gerald John)
(1927-   ) Canadian
Burch, *Queenie Peavy.* Viking 1966
Little, *Home from Far.* Little 1965

LE GRAND, pseud.
(LE GRAND HENDERSON)
(1901-   ) American

Le Grand
> *How Baseball Began in Brooklyn.* Abingdon 1958
> *How Space Rockets Began.* Abingdon 1960

LEAR, EDWARD
(1812-1888) English
Lear, *Lear Alphabet: ABC.* McGraw 1965
(See note in Foreword to this Bibliography)

LEIGHTON, CLARE
(1899-) American, b. in England
Parker (comp.), *The Singing and the Gold.* Crowell 1962
Plotz (comp.)
> *The Earth Is the Lord's.* Crowell 1965
> *Untune the Sky.* Crowell 1957

LEISK, DAVID JOHNSON
See JOHNSON, CROCKETT, pseud.

LEMKE, HORST
(1922-) German
Denneborg
> *Grisella the Donkey.* McKay 1957
> *Jan and the Wild Horse.* McKay 1958
> *The Only Horse for Joan.* McKay 1961
Kastner, *When I Was a Boy* (English title, *When I Was a Little Boy*). Cape 1959/Watts 1961

LENSKI, LOIS
(1893-) American
Lenski
> *At Our House.* Walck 1959
> *Policeman Small.* Walck 1962
> *Shoo-Fly Girl.* Lippincott 1963

LENT, BLAIR
(1930-) American
Bartlett, *The Miracle of the Talking Jungle.* Van Nostrand 1965
Branley, *The Christmas Sky.* Crowell 1966
Economakis, *Oasis of the Stars.* Coward 1965
Hodges, *The Wave.* Houghton 1964
Lent
> *John Tabor's Ride.* Atlantic-Little 1966
> *Pistachio.* Atlantic-Little 1964
Small, *Baba Yaga.* Houghton 1966

LEVINE, DAVID
(1929-) American
Aesop, *Fables of Aesop.* Macmillan 1964
Hauff, *The Heart of Stone.* Macmillan 1964
Irving, *Rip Van Winkle and the Legend of Sleepy Hollow.* Macmillan 1963
Wood, *The Snark Was a Boojum.* Pantheon 1966

LEWIS, RICHARD WILLIAM
(1933-1966) American
Lewis, *A Summer Adventure.* Harper 1962
Scott, *Big Cowboy Western.* Lothrop 1965
Stapp, *Polliwog.* Harper 1962

LIONNI, LEO
(1910-) American, b. in Holland
Lionni
> *Inch by Inch.* Obolensky 1961
> *little blue and little yellow.* Obolensky 1959
> *Swimmy.* Pantheon 1963
> *Tico and the Golden Wings.* Pantheon 1964

LIPINSKY (de ORLOV), SIGISMONDO
(1908-) American, b. in Italy
Coolidge, *Roman People.* Houghton 1959
Jagendorf, *The Ghost of Peg-Leg Peter.* Vanguard 1965

LIPPMAN, PETER J.
(1936-) American
Selden
> *Oscar Lobster's Fair Exchange.* Harper 1966
> *Sparrow Socks.* Harper 1965

LOBEL, ANITA
(1934-) American, b. in Poland
De Jong, *Puppy Summer.* Harper 1966
Kapp, *Cock-A-Doodle-Doo! Cock-A-Doodle Dandy!* Harper 1966
Lobel
> *Sven's Bridge.* Harper 1965
> *The Troll Music.* Harper 1966

LOBEL, ARNOLD STARK
(Ac. 1966) American
Baker, *Little Runner of the Longhouse.* Harper 1962
Benchley, *Red Fox and His Canoe.* Harper 1964
Lobel
> *Giant John.* Harper 1964
> *A Holiday for Mister Muster.* Harper 1963
> *Martha, the Movie Mouse.* Harper 1966
Myrick, *The Secret Three.* Harper 1963
Ressner, *Dudley Pippin.* Harper 1965
Selsam
> *Greg's Microscope.* Harper 1963
> *Terry and the Caterpillars.* Harper 1962
Zolotow, *The Quarreling Book.* Harper 1963

LONETTE, REISIE DOMINEE
(1924-) American
Chase, *A Walk on an Iceberg.* Norton 1966
Holberg, *What Happened to Virgilia.* Doubleday 1963

Hoyt, *Aloha, Susan!* Doubleday 1961
Simon
  Best Friend. Lothrop 1964
  Cousins at Camm Corners. Lothrop 1963
Snedeker, *Lysis Goes to the Play.* Lothrop 1962

LORRAINE, WALTER HENRY
(1929-   ) American
Annett, *The Dog Who Thought He Was A Boy.*
       Houghton 1965
Holt, *David McCheever's 29 Dogs.* Houghton 1963
Love (comp.), *A Little Laughter.* Crowell 1957
McLeod, *One Snail and Me.* Atlantic-Little 1961
Nash, *The Adventures of Isabel.* Little 1963
Reid
  Allth. Houghton 1958
  Fairwater. Houghton 1957

LOW, JOSEPH
(1911-   ) American
Bro, *How the Mouse Deer Became King.* Doubleday
       1966
Bulla, *More Stories from Favorite Operas.* Crowell
       1965
De La Inglesia, *The Cat and the Mouse.* Pantheon
       1966
De La Mare, *Jack and the Beanstalk.* Knopf 1959
Goldin, *Spider Silk.* Crowell 1964
Low
  Adam's Book of odd Creatures. Atheneum 1962
  Smiling Duke. Houghton 1963
Mincieli, *Pulcinella.* Knopf 1960
Osborne, *Rudi and the Mayor of Naples.* Houghton
       1958
Schlein, *The Big Cheese.* Scott 1958

LUBELL, WINIFRED MILIUS
(1914-   ) American
Garthwaite, *The Twelfth Night Santons.* Doubleday
       1965
Lubell
  Green Is for Growing. Rand 1964
  Rosalie: the Bird Market Turtle. Rand 1962
  The Tall Grass Zoo. Rand 1960
Morrow, *See Up the Mountain.* Harper 1958
Selsam
  Birth of an Island. Harper 1959
  See Through the Jungle. Harper 1957
Sterling
  Caterpillars. Doubleday 1961
  Fall Is Here. Doubleday 1966
  Spring Is Here. Doubleday 1964

LUZZATI, EMANUELE
(1921-   ) Italian
Rugoff, *Hurly Burly and the Knights.* Platt & Munk
       1963

MC CLOSKEY, ROBERT JOHN
(1914-   ) American
McCloskey
  Burt Dow: Deep Water Man. Viking 1963
  Time of Wonder. Viking 1957
Robertson
  Henry Reid, Inc. Viking 1958
  Henry Reid's Baby-Sitting Service. Viking 1966
  Henry Reid's Journey. Viking 1963

MC CLUNG, ROBERT MARSHALL
(1916-   ) American
McClung
  Buzztail. Morrow 1958
  Ladybug. Morrow 1966
  Possum. Morrow 1963
  Spotted Salamander. Morrow 1964

MC CREA, JAMES
(1920-   ) American   and

MC CREA, RUTH
(1921-   ) American
McCrea
  The Birds. Atheneum 1966
  The King's Procession. Atheneum 1963
  The Magic Tree. Atheneum 1965
  The Story of Olaf. Atheneum 1964

MC CULLY, EMILY ARNOLD
(1939-   ) American
Neville, *The Seventeenth-Street Gang.* Harper 1966
Panetta, *Sea Beach Express.* Harper 1966

MC GAW, JESSIE BREWER
(1913-   ) American
McGaw
  Little Elk Hunts Big Buffalo. Nelson 1961
  Painted Pony Runs Away. Nelson 1958

MAC KENZIE, GARRY
(1921-   ) American, b. in Canada
Bailey, *Flickertail!* Walck 1962
Goudey
  Here Come the Beavers! Scribner 1957
  Here Come the Dolphins! Scribner 1961
  Here Come the Raccoons! Scribner 1959
  Here Come the Squirrels! Scribner 1962

MC MULLAN, JIM (James)
(1934-   )   American, b. in China
Braun,   *Kangaroo & Kangaroo*.   Doubleday 1965
De Jong,   *The Last Little Cat*.   Harper 1961

MAITLAND, ANTONY JASPER
(1935-   )   English
Garfield
Devil-in-the-Fog.   Pantheon 1966
Jack Holborn.   Constable 1964/Pantheon 1966
Locke,   *The Runaway Settlers*.   Cape 1966/Dutton
1966
Maitland
James and the Roman Silver.   Constable 1965
The Secret of the Shed.   Constable 1962/Duell 1963
Molloy,   *A Proper Place for Chip*.   Constable 1963/
Hastings 1963
Pearce
A Dog So Small.   Constable 1962/Lippincott 1963
Mrs. Cockle's Cat.   Constable 1961/Lippincott 1962
Wier,   *The Loner*.   Constable 1966

MARIANA, pseud.
(MARIAN CURTIS FOSTER)
(Ac. 1966)   American
Janice,   *Little Bear's Christmas*.   Lothrop 1964
Mariana
The Journey of Bangwell Putt.   Lothrop 1965
Miss Flora McFlimsey's Valentine.   Lothrop n.d.

MARINO, DOROTHY BRONSON
(1912-   )   American
Marino
Buzzy Bear and the Rainbow.   Watts 1962
Buzzy Bear Goes South.   Watts 1961
Buzzy Bear in the Garden.   Watts 1963

MAROKVIA, ARTUR
(1909-   )   American, b. in Germany
Conklin
If I Were a Bird.   Holiday 1965
We Like Bugs.   Holiday 1962
Haviland,   *Favorite Fairy Tales Told in Ireland*.   Little
1961
Kim
Blue in the Seed.   Little 1964
The Happy Days.   Little 1960
Marokvia
A French School for Paul.   Lippincott 1963
Jannot.   Lippincott 1959
Nanette, a French Goat.   Lippincott 1960
Molloy,   *The Christmas Rocket*.   Hastings 1958

MARRIOTT, PAT (Patricia)
(1920-   )   English
Aiken
Black Hearts in Battersea.   Cape 1963
The Wolves of Willoughby Chase.   Cape 1962/
Doubleday 1963
Colson,   *Rinkin of Dragon's Wood*.   Cape 1965/Dutton
1965

MARS, WITOLD T.
(1908-   )   American, b. in Poland
Arnold,   *Kings, Bishops, Knights and Pawns*.   Norton
1964
Black,   *Castle, Abbey and Town*.   Holiday 1963
Brink,   *Andy Buckram's Tin Men*.   Viking 1966
Calhoun,   *High Wind for Kansas*.   Morrow 1965
Dillon,   *The Sea Wall*.   Farrar 1965
Duncombe,   *Cassie's Village*.   Lothrop 1965
Johnston
Joan of Arc.   Doubleday 1961
The Story of Hannibal.   Doubleday 1960
Kjelgaard,   *Boomerang Hunter*.   Holiday 1960
Krasilovsky,   *Benny's Flag*.   World 1960
McLean and Wiseman,   *Adventures of the Greek Heroes*.
Houghton 1961
Mehta,   *Ramu: A Story of India*.   McGraw 1966
Mirsky,   *Nomusa and the New Magic*.   Follett 1962
Morgan,   *Journey for Tobiijab*.   Random 1966
Newton,   *Seafarers of the Pacific*.   World 1964
Rumsey,   *Devil's Doorstep*.   Morrow 1966

MARTIN, STEFAN
(1936-   )   American
Coatsworth
Ronnie and the Chief's Son.   Macmillan 1962
The Sparrow Bush.   Norton 1966

MASON, GEORGE FREDERICK
(1904-   )   American
Mason
Animal Baggage.   Morrow 1961
Animal Habits.   Morrow 1959
The Deer Family.   Morrow 1962
The Wildlife of North America.   Hastings 1966
The Wildlife of South America.   Hastings 1966

MASSIE, DIANE REDFIELD
(1930-   )   American
Massie
A Birthday for Bird.   Parents' 1966
A Turtle and a Loon.   Atheneum 1965

MATHIESEN, EGON
(1907-   )   Danish
  Mathiesen
    A Jungle in the Wheat Field.   Obolensky 1960
    Oswald the Monkey.   Obolensky 1959

MAXEY, DALE
(1927-   )   American
  Maxey
    Fidgit.   Collins 1965/Dodd 1965
    Seeing London.   Collins 1966
  Shulman, *Preep.*   Random 1964

MAYS, LEWIS VICTOR, JR.
(1927-   )   American
  Asimov, *The Kite That Won the Revolution.*
      Houghton 1963
  Campion, *Patrick Henry: Firebrand of the Revolution.*
      Little 1961
  Corbett, *One by Sea.*   Atlantic-Little 1965
  Hyde, *Under the Pirate Flag.*   Houghton 1965
  Martin, *Yankee Doodle Boy.*   Scott 1964
  Mason, *The Battle for Quebec.*   Houghton 1965

MILHOUS, KATHERINE
(1894-   )   American
  Milhous, *Through These Arches.*   Lippincott 1964

MILLER, EDNA ANITA
(1920-   )   American
  Miller
    Mousekin's Christmas Eve.   Prentice 1965
    Mousekin's Golden House.   Prentice 1964

MILLER, MARILYN JEAN
(1925-   )   American
  Allen, *Up from the Sea Came an Island.*   Scribner 1962
  Byrd, *Ice King.*   Scribner 1965
  Fife, *The Fish in the Castle.*   Coward 1965

MILLER, SHANE
(1907-   )   American
  Jagendorf, *Noodlehead Stories from Around the World.*
      Vanguard 1957
  Ochsenshlager, *The Egyptians in the Middle Kingdom.*
      Coward 1963
  Sutton, *Queen's Champion.*   St. Martin's 1961

MILLS, YAROSLAVA SURMACH
  See Yaroslava, pseud.

MINALE, MARCELLO
(1938-   )   English, b. in Libya
  Flanders, *Creatures Great and Small.*   Dobson 1964/
      Holt 1965

MITSUI, EIICHI
(Ac. 1966)   Japanese
  Lifton
    Joji and the Amanojaku.   Norton 1965
    Joji and the Dragon.   Morrow 1957
    Kap the Kappa.   Morrow 1960
    The Rice-Cake Rabbit.   Norton 1966

MIZUMURA, KAZUE
(Ac. 1966)   American, b. in Japan
  Gans, *It's Nesting Time.*   Crowell 1964
  Gray, *The Cheerful Heart.*   Viking 1959
  Lewis, *Keiko's Bubble.*   Doubleday 1961
  Martin
    The Greedy One.   Rand 1964
    Suzu and the Bride Doll.   Rand 1960
  Matsuno
    Chie and the Sports Day.   World 1965
    A Pair of Red Clogs.   World 1960
    Taro and the Tōfu.   World 1962
  Mizumura, *I See the Winds.*   Crowell 1966
  Serage, *The Prince Who Gave Up a Throne.*   Crowell
      1966
  Stamm
    The Dumplings and the Demons.   Viking 1964
    Three Strong Women.   Viking 1962
    The Very Special Badgers.   Viking 1960
  Uchida
    The Forever Christmas Tree.   Scribner 1963
    Rokubei and the Thousand Rice Bowls.   Scribner 1962
    Sumi's Prize.   Scribner 1964
    Sumi's Special Happening.   Scribner 1966

MONTGOMERIE, NORAH MARY
(1913-   )   Scottish
  Lines and Montgomerie, *Poems and Pictures.*   Abelard
      1959
  Montgomerie, *Twenty-Five Fables.*   Abelard 1961
  Montgomerie, N. M. and W. Montgomerie (eds.),
      A Book of Scottish Nursery Rhymes (with R.
      Richie).   Oxford 1965

MONTRESOR, BENI
(1926-   )   American, b. in Italy
  Brown, *On Christmas Eve.*   Scott 1961
  De Regniers, *May I Bring a Friend?*   Atheneum 1964
  Garelick, *Sounds of a Summer Night.*   Scott 1963
  Johnson, *The Princesses.*   Harper 1962
  Mincieli, *Old Neapolitan Fairy Tales.*   Knopf 1963
  Montresor
    Cinderella.   Knopf 1965
    House of Flowers, House of Stars.   Knopf 1962
    The Witches of Venice.   Knopf 1963

Spender, *The Magic Flute*. Putnam 1966
Stolz
    Belling the Tiger. Harper 1961
    The Great Rebellion. Harper 1961
    Siri the Conquistador. Harper 1963

MORDVINOFF, NICOLAS
See NICOLAS, pseud.

MOTHER GOOSE IN HIEROGLYPHICS. Houghton 1962
(See note in Foreword to this Bibliography)

MOY, SEONG
(1921-   ) American, b. in China
Bro, *The Animal Friends of Peng-U*. Doubleday 1965
Harris, *Uncle Remus, His Songs and Sayings*. Geo. Macy 1957

MOZLEY, CHARLES
(1915-   ) English
Guillot, *Nicolette and the Mill*. Abelard 1960
Kyle
    Girl with a Destiny. Watts 1964
    Girl with a Pen. Evans 1964
MacDonald, *At the Back of the North Wind*. Nonesuch 1963/Watts 1964
Mozley, *The First Book of Tales of Ancient Egypt*. Watts 1960
Streatfeild, *A Vicarage Family*. Collins 1963/Watts 1963
Ure, *Rumanian Folk Tales* (English title, *Pacala and Tandala*). Watts 1961
Wilde, *Fairy Tales* (English title, *Complete Fairy Tales of Oscar Wilde*). Bodley 1960/Watts 1960

MUNARI, BRUNO
(1907-   ) Italian
Munari
    Animals for Sale. World 1957
    The Birthday Present. World 1959
    Bruno Munari's ABC. World 1960
    Bruno Munari's Zoo. World 1963
    The Elephant's Wish. World 1959
    Jimmy Has Lost His Cap. World 1959
    Tic, Tac and Toc. World 1957
    Who's There? Open the Door. World 1957

NESBITT, ESTA
(1918-   ) American
Belting
    The Earth Is on a Fish's Back. Holt 1965
    The Stars Are Silver Reindeer. Holt 1966
Coatsworth, *Jon the Unlucky*. Holt 1964
Polland, *The Town Across the Water*. Holt 1963

NESS, EVALINE
(1911-   ) American
Alexander, *Coll and His White Pig*. Holt 1965
Buckley, *Josie and the Snow*. Lothrop 1964
Cassedy, *Pierino and the Bell*. Doubleday 1966
Caudill, *A Pocketful of Cricket*. Holt 1964
Coatsworth
    Lonely Maria. Pantheon 1960
    The Princess and the Lion. Pantheon 1963
Cunningham
    Candle Tales. Pantheon 1964
    Macaroon. Pantheon 1962
    Haviland, *Favorite Fairy Tales Told in Italy*. Little 1965
Jacobs, *Tom Tit Tot*. Scribner 1965
Ness
    Exactly Alike. Scribner 1964
    A Gift for Sula Sula. Scribner 1963
    Josefina February. Scribner 1963
    Pavo and the Princess. Scribner 1964
    Sam, Bangs and Moonshine. Holt 1966
Nic Leodhas
    All in the Morning Early. Holt 1963
    Thistle and Thyme. Holt 1962
Ogburn, *The Bridge*. Houghton 1957
Osborne, *Ondine*. Houghton 1960
Pope, *The Sherwood Ring*. Houghton 1958
Robinson, *Across from Indian Shore*. Lothrop 1962

NETHERWOOD, ANNE
(1940-   ) English
Causley (comp.), *Modern Ballads and Story Poems* (English title, *Rising Early*). Brockhampton 1964/ Watts 1965

NICKLESS, WILL
(1901-   ) English
Knight, *Stories of Famous Adventurers*. Oliver & Boyd 1966
Nickless, *Owlglass*. Day 1966
Nickless (comp.), *Book of Fables*. Warne 1963

NICOLAS, pseud.
(NICOLAS MORDVINOFF)
(1911-   ) American, b. in Russia
Carlson
    Evangeline, Pigeon of Paris. Harcourt 1960
    Hortense, the Cow for a Queen. Harcourt 1957
Lipkind
    Billy the Kid. Harcourt 1961
    The Boy and the Forest. Harcourt 1964
    Four-Leaf Clover. Harcourt 1959
    The Little Tiny Rooster. Harcourt 1960

The Magic Feather Duster.   Harcourt 1958
Russet and the Two Reds.   Harcourt 1962
Sleepyhead.   Harcourt 1957
Steele,   *Daniel Boone's Echo.*   Harcourt 1957

NONNAST, MARIE
(1924-   )   American
Goudey
Graywings.   Scribner 1964
Red Legs.   Scribner 1966
Montgomery,   *Whitetail.*   World 1958

NORDENSKÖLD, BIRGITTA
(1919-   )   Swedish
Oterdahl
April Adventure.   Harcourt 1962
Island Summer.   Harcourt 1964
Tina and the Latchkey Child.   Harcourt 1963

NUSSBAUMER, PAUL EDMUND
(1934-   )   Swiss
Nussbaumer,   *Away in a Manger.*   Constable 1965/ Harcourt 1965

OBLIGADO, LILIAN
(1931-   )   American, b. in Argentina
Coatsworth,   *Jock's Island.*   Viking 1963
Eiseman,   *Candido.*   Macmillan 1965
Jackson,   *The Taste of Spruce Gum.*   Little 1966
Kendall, C.,   *The Big Splash.*   Viking 1960
Thompson,   *Sad Day, Glad Day.*   Holiday 1962
White,   *A Dog Called Scholar.*   Viking 1963
Zolotow,   *The White Marble.*   Abelard 1963

OECHSLI, KELLY
(1918-   )   American
Carroll,   *The Hunting of the Snark.*   Pantheon 1966
Craig,   *The Dragon in the Clock Box.*   Norton 1962
Larrick (ed.)
Piper, Pipe That Song Again!   Random 1965
Poetry for Holidays.   Garrard 1966
Shakespeare,   *Seeds of Time.*   Atheneum 1963

OHLSSON, IB
(1935-   )   Danish
Craig,   *The Long and Dangerous Journey.*   Norton 1965
Holman,   *Professor Diggins' Dragons.*   Macmillan 1966
Williams,   *Philbert the Fearful.*   Norton 1966

OLDS, ELIZABETH
(1897-   )   American
Olds
Deep Treasure.   Houghton 1958
Little Una.   Scribner 1963
Plop Plop Ploppie.   Scribner 1962

OLSEN, IB SPANG
(1921-   )   American, b. in Denmark
Jensen,   *Lars-Peter's Birthday.*   Abingdon 1959
Olsen
The Boy in the Moon.   Abingdon 1963
The Marsh Crone's Brew.   Abingdon 1960

OSBORN, ROBERT CHESLEY
(1904-   )   American
Ciardi,   *I Met a Man.*   Houghton 1961
Rees,   *The Song of Paul Bunyan & Tony Beaver.*   Pantheon 1964

PALAZZO, TONY
(1905-   )   American
Colver,   *Old Bet.*   Knopf 1957
Palazzo
Bianca and the New World.   Viking 1957
Jan and the Reindeer.   Garrard 1963

PAPAS, WILLIAM
(1927-   )   English, b. in South Africa
Downing,   *Tales of the Hodja.*   Oxford 1965/Walck 1965
Guillot,   *Guillot's African Folk Tales.*   Watts 1965
Manning-Sanders,   *Damien and the Dragon.*   Oxford 1965/Roy 1965
Papas, T.,   *The Story of Mr. Nero.*   Oxford 1965/ Coward 1966
Turner,   *The Grange at High Force.*   Oxford 1965

PARKER, EDGAR
(1925-   )   American
Parker
The Dream of the Dormouse.   Houghton 1960
The Duke of Sycamore.   Houghton 1959
The Enchantress.   Pantheon 1960
The Flower of the Realm.   Houghton 1966
The Question of a Dragon.   Pantheon 1964
Stuff and Nonsense.   Pantheon 1961

PARNALL, PETER
(1936-   )   American
Shura,   *A Tale of Middle Length.*   Atheneum 1966

PASCAL, DAVID
(1918-   )   American
Krylov,   *15 Fables of Krylov.*   Macmillan 1965

PATON, JANE
(1934-   )   English
Cenac,   *Four Paws into Adventure.*   Harrap 1965
Farjeon,   *Mr. Garden.*   Hamilton 1966/Walck 1966

Guillot, *Three Girls and a Secret*.   Harrap 1963/Watts
  1963
MacDonald, *The Princess and the Goblin*.   Blackie
  1960
Reeves, *Ragged Robin*.   Heinemann 1961/Dutton 1961
Willard, *Surprise Island*.   Hamilton 1966
Williams, *Beware of This Animal*.   Hamilton 1963/
  Dial 1965

PAYNE, JOAN BALFOUR
 (1923-   )   American
  Lloyd, *The Desperate Dragons*.   Hastings 1960
  Payne
    Charlie From Yonder.   Hastings 1962
    General Billycock's Pigs.   Hastings 1961
    The Leprechaun of Bayou Luce.   Hastings 1957
    Pangur Ban.   Hastings 1966

PEET, BILL
 (1915-   )   American
  Peet
    Chester the Worldly Pig.   Houghton 1965
    Farewell to Shady Grove.   Houghton 1966
    Hubert's Hair-Raising Adventure.   Houghton 1959
    Kermit the Hermit.   Houghton 1965
    Randy's Dandy Lions.   Houghton 1964
    Smokey.   Houghton 1962

PERL, SUSAN
 (1922-   )   American, b. in Austria
  Conger, *Who Has Seen the Wind?*   Abingdon 1959
  Kravetz
    A Horse of Another Color.   Little 1962
    A Monkey's Tale.   Little 1964
  Milne, *Once On a Time*.   N. Y. Graphic 1962

PETERSHAM, MAUD FULLER
 (1889-   )   American
  Petersham, *The Shepherd Psalm*.   Macmillan 1962

PETERSON, BETTY F.
 (1917-   )   American, b. in England
  Aldridge, *The Best of Friends*.   Parnassus 1963
  Priolo, *Bravo, Marco!*   Parnassus 1963
  Zolotow, *The Bunny Who Found Easter*.   Parnassus
  1959

PETERSON, RUSSELL FRANCIS
 (Ac. 1966)   American
  Geis, *Dinosaurs and Other Prehistoric Animals*.
    Grosset 1959
  Peterson, *Whitefoot Mouse*.   Holiday 1959
  Sanger, *Mangrove Island*.   World 1963
  Von Humboldt, *Stars, Mosquitos and Crocodiles*.
    Harper 1962

PETRIDES, HEIDRUM
 (1944-   )   German, b. in Poland
  Petrides, *Hans and Peter*.   Oxford 1962/Harcourt 1963

PIATTI, CELESTINO
 (1922-   )   Swiss
  Piatti
    Celestino Piatti's Animal ABC.   Benn 1965/Atheneum
      1966
    The Happy Owls.   Atheneum 1964

PINKNEY, JERRY
 (1939-   )   American
  Arkhurst, *The Adventures of Spider*.   Little 1964
  Gershin, *The Traveling Frog*.   McGraw 1966

PITZ, HENRY C.
 (1895-   )   American
  Cooper, *The Spy*.   Limited Editions Club 1963
  Fall
    Edge of Manhood.   Dial 1964
    Wild Boy.   Dial 1965
  Peare, *William Penn*.   1958

POLITI, LEO
 (1908-   )   American
  Coatsworth, *The Noble Doll*.   Viking 1961
  Politi
    The Butterflies Come.   Scribner 1957
    Lito and the Clown.   Scribner 1964
    Moy, Moy.   Scribner 1961
    Piccolo's Prank.   Scribner 1965
    Rosa.   Scribner 1963
    Saint Francis and the Animals.   Scribner 1959

POLLACK, REGINALD MURRAY
 (1924-   )   American
  Hollander, *The Quest of the Gole*.   Atheneum 1966

PORTAL, COLETTE
 (1936-   )   French
  Portal, *The Life of a Queen*.   Braziller 1964

POTTER, BEATRIX
 (1866-1943)   English
  Potter, *Letters to Children*.   Walker 1966
  (*See note in Foreword to this Bibliography*)

POWERS, RICHARD M.
 (1921-   )   American
  Chubb
    The Byzantines.   World 1959
    The Northmen.   World 1964
  Cottrell, *Land of the Pharaohs*.   World 1960

De Regniers, *David and Goliath*. Viking 1965
Fairservis
    Horsemen of the Steppes. World 1962
    India. World 1961
Jordan, *The Burro Benedicto*. Coward 1960
Lamb, *Tales from Shakespeare*. Macmillan 1963
Powers, *The Cave Dwellers in the Old Stone Age*.
    Coward 1963
Stoutenberg, *American Tall Tales*. Viking 1966

PRICE, CHRISTINE
(1928-   ) American, b. in England
Belpré, *Juan Bobo and the Queen's Necklace*. Warne
    1962
Price, C.
    Made in the Middle Ages. Dutton 1961
    Made in the Renaissance. Dutton 1963
    The Valiant Chattee Maker. Warne 1961
Price, H. C., *The Song of Roland*. Warne 1961
Sanger, *Cypress Country*. World 1965
Savery, *Magic in My Shoes*. McKay 1958
Treece
    Ride Into Danger. Criterion 1959
    Viking's Sunset. Criterion 1961
Uttley, *A Traveler in Time*. Viking 1964
Waltrip, *White Harvest*. McKay 1960
Wier, *The Loner*. McKay 1963

PRICE, GARRETT
(1896-   ) American
Johnson, *No Magic, Thank You*. Little 1964
Nash
    Mrs. Coverlet's Detectives. Little 1965
    Mrs. Coverlet's Magicians. Little 1961
    While Mrs. Coverlet Was Away. Little 1958

PRIMROSE, JEAN
(1917-   ) English
De Gasztold
    The Creatures' Choir. Viking 1965
    Prayers from the Ark. Viking 1962
Godden
    Home Is the Sailor. Macmillan 1964/Viking 1964
    Little Plum. Macmillan 1963/Viking 1963
    Miss Happiness and Miss Flower. Macmillan 1961/
        Viking 1961
    St. Jerome and the Lion. Macmillan 1961/Viking
        1961

PROVENSON, ALICE
(1918-   ) American and

PROVENSON, MARTIN
(1918-   ) American

Aesop, *Aesop's Fables*. Golden 1965
Shakespeare, *Ten Great Plays*. Golden 1962
Tennyson, *The Charge of the Light Brigade*. Golden
    1964
White, *The Golden Treasury of Myths and Legends*.
    Golden 1959

PURDY, SUSAN GOLD
(1939-   ) American
Purdy
    If You Have a Yellow Lion. Lippincott 1966
    My Little Cabbage. Lippincott 1965

QUACKENBUSH, ROBERT
(1929-   ) American
Bloch, *The Two Worlds of Damyan*. Atheneum 1966
McKown, *Rakoto and the Drongo Bird*. Lothrop 1966
Rice, *A Long, Long Time*. Lothrop 1964

RACKHAM, ARTHUR
(1867-1939) English
Hudson, *Arthur Rackham: His Life and Work*. Heine-
    mann 1960/Scribner 1961
(See note in Foreword to this Bibliography)

RAIBLE, ALTON
(1918-   ) American
Green, *Good-by, Gray Lady*. Atheneum 1964
Martin, *Rolling the Cheese*. Atheneum 1966
Snyder
    Season of Ponies. Atheneum 1964
    The Velvet Room. Atheneum 1965

RAND, PAUL
(1914-   ) American
Rand, A.
    Little One. Harcourt 1962
    Sparkle and Spin. Harcourt 1957

RASKIN, ELLEN
(1928-   ) American
Blake
    Songs of Innocence, v. 1, Poetry. Doubleday 1966
    Songs of Innocence, v. 2, Songs. Doubleday 1966
Poe
    Poems of Edgar Allan Poe. Crowell 1965
Raskin, *Nothing Ever Happens on My Block*.
    Atheneum 1966
Thomas, *A Child's Christmas in Wales*. New
    Directions 1959

RAVIELLI, ANTHONY
(1916-   ) American
Darwin, *The Voyage of the Beagle*. Harper 1959

Hirsch, *This Is Automation.* Viking 1964
Irwin, *The Romance of Chemistry.* Viking 1959
Ravielli
    An Adventure in Geometry. Viking 1957
    The World Is Round. Viking 1963
Weyl, *Men, Ants and Elephants.* Viking 1959

REED, PHILIP
(1908-) American
    Arabian Nights, *The Seven Voyages of Sindbad the Sailor.* Atheneum 1962
    Mother Goose, *Mother Goose and Nursery Rhymes.* Atheneum 1963

REY, HANS AUGUSTO
(1898-) American, b. in Germany
    Rey, H. A.
        Curious George Gets a Medal. Houghton 1957
        Curious George Learns the Alphabet. Houghton 1963
    Rey, M.
        Curious George Flies a Kite. Houghton 1958
        Curious George Goes to the Hospital. Houghton 1966

RIBBONS, IAN
(1924-) English
    Farmer, *Sea Gull.* Brockhampton 1964/Harcourt 1966
    Goudge, *Linnets and Valerians.* Brockhampton 1964/Coward 1964
    Turner, *Sea Peril.* Oxford 1966
    Welch, *Bowman of Crecy.* Oxford 1966

RIPPER, CHARLES L.
(1929-) American
    Ripper
        Foxes and Wolves. Morrow 1961
        Ground Birds. Morrow 1960
        Swallows. Morrow 1964
        The Weasel Family. Morrow 1959

RISWOLD, GILBERT
(Ac. 1966) American
    Carlson, *School Bell in the Valley.* Harcourt 1963
    Johnson, *The Grizzly.* Harper 1964
    Wilde, *The Happy Prince.* Prentice 1965
    Wordsworth, *Lucy Gray.* Prentice 1964

RIVOLI, MARIO
(1943-) American
    Wersba
        Do Tigers Ever Bite Kings? Atheneum 1966
        A Song for Clowns. Atheneum 1965

ROBBINS, RUTH
(1918-) American
    Aldridge
        Fisherman's Luck. Parnassus 1966
        A Penny and a Periwinkle. Parnassus 1961
    Byrd, *The Black Wolf of Savage River.* Parnassus 1959
    Fisher, *Stories California Indians Told.* Parnassus 1957
    Stoutenberg, *Wild Animals of the Far West.* Parnassus 1958

ROBERTS, DOREEN
(1922-) English
    Moss, *The Story of Saul the King.* Constable 1966/David White 1966

ROCKER, FERMIN
(1907-) American, b. in England
    Anckarsvärd, *Doctor's Boy.* Harcourt 1965
    Arthur, *My Daughter, Nicola.* Atheneum 1965
    Carlson
        Carnival in Paris. Harper 1962
        A Pet for the Orphelines. Harper 1962
    Harper (comp.), *Merry Christmas to You.* Dutton 1965
    Sorensen, *Lotte's Locket.* Harcourt 1964
    Stevens, *The Piper.* Atheneum 1964

ROJANKOVSKY, FEODOR
(1891-) Russian
    Fisher, *A Cricket in a Thicket.* Scribner 1963
    Fritz, *The Cabin Faced West.* Coward 1958
    Langstaff, *Over in the Meadow.* Harcourt 1957
    Rand, *So Small.* Harcourt 1962
    Rojankovsky, *Animals in the Zoo.* Knopf 1962
    Thayer, *The Outside Cat.* Morrow 1957
    Varley, *The Whirly Bird.* Knopf 1961

ROSE, GERALD
(1935-) English, b. in Hong Kong
    Bourliaguet, *The Giant Who Drank from His Shoe.* Abelard 1966
    Hughes
        The Emperor's Oblong Pancake. Abelard 1962
        The King Who Loved Candy. Abelard 1964
    Ireson
        Seven Thieves and Seven Stars. Faber 1960/Barnes 1961
        The Story of the Pied Piper. Faber 1961/Barnes 1961
    Joyce, *The Cat and the Devil.* Faber 1965
    Rose, E.
        The Big River. Faber 1962/Norton 1964
        How St. Francis Tamed the Wolf. Faber 1958/Harcourt 1959

Old Winkle and the Sea Gulls.   Faber 1960/Barnes 1960

St. George and the Fiery Dragon.   Faber 1963/Norton 1964

Wuffles Goes to Town.   Faber 1959/Barnes 1960

ROSS, CLARE ROMANO
(1922-   )   American   and

ROSS, JOHN
(1921-   )   American
Bulla, *The Ring and the Fire.*   Crowell 1962
McDonald (comp.), *A Way of Knowing.*   Crowell 1959
Morrison (comp.), *Sprints and Distances.*   Crowell 1965
Whitman, *Poems of Walt Whitman.*   Crowell 1964

ROSSELLI, COLETTE
(1916-   )   Italian, b. in Switzerland
Cole (ed.), *I Went to the Animal Fair.*   World 1958

ROUNDS, GLEN
(1906-   )   American
Adams, *Trail Drive.*   Holiday 1965
Chase (ed.), *Billy Boy.*   Golden Gate 1966
Gage
    Dan and the Miranda.   World 1962
    A Wild Goose Tale.   World 1961
Rounds
    Beaver Business.   Prentice 1960
    The Snake Tree.   World 1966
    Whitey and the Wild Horse.   Holiday 1958
    Wild Orphan.   Holiday 1961
    Wildlife at Your Doorstep.   Prentice 1958
Stoutenberg, *The Crocodile's Mouth.*   Viking 1966

RUBIN, EVA JOHNSON
(1926-   )   German
Krüss, *3 x 3: Three by Three.*   Methuen 1965/Macmillan 1965

RUSSON, MARY GEORGINA
(1937-   )   English
Lowe, *Tales of the Black and White Pig.*   Faber 1965
Mayne
    Pig in the Middle.   Hamilton 1965/Dutton 1966
    Rooftops.   Hamilton 1966

SANDBERG, LASSE E. M.
(1924-   )   Swedish
Sandberg, I.
    Little Anna and the Magic Hat.   Lothrop 1965
    Little Anna's Mamma Has a Birthday.   Lothrop 1966
    What Anna Saw.   Lothrop 1964

SARGENT, ROBERT EDWARD
(1933-   )   American
Sargent
    The Alligator's Problem.   Scribner 1966
    The Restless Rabbit.   McGraw 1966
    A Trick on a Lion.   McGraw 1966

SASEK, MIROSLAV
(1916-   )   German Resident, b. in Czechoslovakia
Sasek
    This Is Edinburgh.   Macmillan 1961
    This Is Greece.   Macmillan 1966
    This Is Hong Kong.   Macmillan 1965
    This Is Ireland.   Macmillan 1965
    This Is Israel.   Macmillan 1962
    This Is London.   Macmillan 1959
    This Is Munich.   Macmillan 1961
    This Is New York.   Macmillan 1960
    This Is Paris.   Macmillan 1959
    This Is Rome.   Macmillan 1960
    This Is San Francisco.   Macmillan 1961

SAVIOZZI, ADRIANA
(1928-   )   American, b. in Italy
Carlson, *The Orphelines in the Enchanted Castle.*   Harper 1964
Saviozzi, *Somebody Saw.*   World 1962

SCARRY, RICHARD MC CLURE
(1919-   )   American
Scarry
    Richard Scarry's Best Word Book Ever.   Golden 1963
    Richard Scarry's Busy, Busy World.   Golden 1965

SCHEELE, WILLIAM EARL
(1920-   )   American
Scheele
    The Earliest Americans.   World 1963
    The Mound Builders.   World 1960

SCHICK, ELEANOR
(1942-   )   American
Schick
    I'm Going to the Ocean.   Macmillan 1966
    The Little School at Cottonwood Corners.   Harper 1965
    A Surprise in the Forest.   Harper 1964

SCHINDELMAN, JOSEPH
(1923-   )   American
Dahl, *Charlie and the Chocolate Factory.*   Knopf 1964
Harris, *The Great Picture Robbery.*   Atheneum 1963
Merriam, *There Is No Rhyme for Silver.*   Atheneum 1962

SCHOENHERR, JOHN CARL
(1935-   ) American
Freschet,   *Kangaroo Red.*   Scribner 1966
Miles
    Fox and Fire.   Atlantic-Little 1966
    Mississippi Possum.   Atlantic-Little 1965
Morey,   *Gentle Ben.*   Dutton 1965
Murphy,   *The Golden Eagle.*   Dutton 1965
North,   *Rascal.*   Dutton 1963

SCHRAMM, ULRIK
(1921-   ) German
Baumann
    The Barque of the Brothers.   Oxford 1958/Walck
      1958
    I Marched with Hannibal.   Oxford 1961/Walck 1962
Grimm,   *Grimm's Fairy Tales.*   Oxford 1962/Walck
    1962
Thomas,   *Alexander von Humboldt.*   Pantheon 1960

SCHREITER, RICK
(1936-   ) American
Hughes, R.   *Gertrude's Child.*   Harlan Quist 1966
Hughes, T.   *How the Whale Became.*   Atheneum 1964
Kastner,   *The Little Man.*   Knopf 1966
Poe,   *The Purloined Letter, and The Murders in the
    Rue Morgue.*   Watts 1966

SEIGNOBOSC, FRANÇOISE
See Françoise, pseud.

SENDAK, MAURICE
(1928-   ) American
Andersen,   *Seven Tales.*   Harper 1959
Brentano
    Schoolmaster Whackwell's Wonderful Sons.   Random
      1962
    The Tale of Gockel, Hinkel and Gackeliah.   Random
      1961
Engvick (ed.),   *Lullabies and Night Songs.*   Harper
    1965
Hauff,   *Dwarf Long-Nose.*   Random 1960
Jarrell
    The Animal Family.   Pantheon 1965
    The Bat Poet.   Macmillan 1964
Joslin
    What Do You Do, Dear?   Scott 1961
    What Do You Say, Dear?   Scott 1958
Krauss,   *Open House for Butterflies.*   Harper 1960
Minarik
    Father Bear Comes Home.   Harper 1959
    Little Bear.   Harper 1957
    Little Bear's Friend.   Harper 1960

    Little Bear's Visit.   Harper 1961
Orgel,   *Sarah's Room.*   Harper 1963
Sendak, J.,   *Circus Girl.*   Harper 1957
Sendak, M.
    Hector Protector, and As I Went Over the Water.
      Harper 1965
    *Nutshell Library: Alligators All Around; Chicken Soup
      with Rice; One Was Johnny; Pierre.*   Harper
      1962
    Where the Wild Things Are.   Harper 1963
Singer,   *Zlateh the Goat.*   Harper 1966
Stockton
    The Bee-Man of Orn.   Holt 1964
    The Griffin and the Minor Canon.   Holt 1963
Udry
    Let's Be Enemies.   Harper 1961
    The Moon Jumpers.   Harper 1959
Wahl,   *Pleasant Fieldmouse.*   Harper 1964
Zolotow,   *Mr. Rabbit and the Lovely Present.*   Harper
    1962

SEUSS, DR., pseud.
(THEODOR SEUSS GEISEL)
(1904-   )   American
Seuss
    The Cat in the Hat.   Random 1957
    The Cat in the Hat Comes Back.   Random 1958
    Dr. Seuss's ABC.   Random 1963
    Dr. Seuss's Sleep Book.   Random 1962
    How the Grinch Stole Christmas.   Random 1957
    I Had Trouble in Getting to Solla Sollew.   Random
      1965
    Yertle the Turtle.   Random 1958

SHAHN, BEN
(1898-   )   American, b. in Lithuania
Ish-Kishor,   *A Boy of Old Prague.*   Pantheon 1963
Reid,   *Ounce, Dice, Trice.*   Atlantic-Little 1958
Samstag,   *Kay-Kay Comes Home.*   Obolensky 1962

SHECTER, BEN
(1935-   )   American
Brelis,   *The Mummy Market.*   Harper 1966
Lexau,   *Millicent's Ghost.*   Dial 1963
Shecter,   *Partouche Plants a Seed.*   Harper 1966

SHEPARD, ERNEST HOWARD
(1879-   )   English
Andersen,   *Hans Andersen's Fairy Tales.*   Oxford 1961/
    Walck 1962
Grahame,   *The Wind in the Willows* (Golden Anni-
    versary Edition).   Scribner 1960
Green,   *Old Greek Fairy Tales.*   Bell 1958

Milne

 The Pooh Story Book. Dutton 1965

 The World of Christopher Robin. Dutton 1958

 The World of Pooh. Dutton 1957

Rieu, *The Flattered Flying Fish.* Dutton 1962

Shepard, *Ben and Brock.* Doubleday 1966

SHEPARD, MARY ELEANOR
(1909-) English

Milne, *Prince Rabbit, and The Princess Who Could Not Laugh.* Dutton 1966

Travers, *Mary Poppins from A to Z.* Harcourt 1962

SHERIN, RAY
(1926-) American

Liers

 A Beaver's Story. Viking 1958

 A Black Bear's Story. Viking 1962

SHILLABEER, MARY
(1904-) English

Lynch, *Mona of the Isle.* Dent 1965

Stevenson, *A Child's Garden of Verses.* Dent 1960/ Dutton 1960

SHIMIN, SYMEON
(1902-) American, b. in Russia

Cretan, *All Except Sammy.* Atlantic-Little 1966

Fisher, *Listen, Rabbit.* Crowell 1964

Hoover, *Animals at My Doorstep.* Parents' 1966

Krumgold, *Onion John.* Crowell 1959

Schweitzer, *One Small Blue Bead.* Macmillan 1965

SHORE, ROBERT
(Ac. 1966) American

Kipling, *The Jungle Books.* Macmillan 1964

Melville, *Moby Dick.* Macmillan 1962

Simeons, *Ramlal.* Atheneum 1965

SHORTALL, LEONARD
(Ac. 1966) American

Clymer, *Harry the Wild West Horse.* Atheneum 1963

Felton, *Pecos Bill and the Mustang.* Prentice 1965

Fritz

 How to Read a Rabbit. Coward 1959

 Tap, Tap, Lion — 1, 2, 3. Coward 1962

Mannix, *The Outcasts.* Dutton 1965

Sobol, *Encyclopedia Brown, Boy Detective.* Nelson 1963

Stolz

 The Bully of Barkham Street. Harper 1963

 A Dog on Barkham Street. Harper 1960

SHULEVITZ, URI
(1935-) American, b. in Poland

Grimm, *The Twelve Dancing Princesses.* Scribner 1966

Ish-Kishor, *The Carpet of Solomon.* Pantheon 1966

Sendak, J., *The Second Witch.* Harper 1965

Stolz

 Maximilian's World. Harper 1966

 The Mystery of the Woods. Harper 1964

SIBLEY, DON
(1922-) American

Burch

 Skinny. Viking 1964

 Tyler, Wilkin and Skee. Viking 1963

Meader

 The Commodore's Cup. Harcourt 1958

 Snow on Blueberry Mountain. Harcourt 1961

SIDJAKOV, NICOLAS
(1924-) American, b. in Russia

Baker, *The Friendly Beasts.* Parnassus 1957

Robbins

 Baboushka and the Three Kings. Parnassus 1961

 The Emperor and the Drummer Boy. Parnassus 1962

 Harlequin & Mother Goose. Parnassus 1965

SIEBEL, FRITZ (Frederick)
(1913-) American, b. in Austria

Bonsall, *Tell Me Some More.* Harper 1961

Minarik, *Cat and Dog.* Harper 1960

Nödset, *Who Took the Farmer's Hat?* Harper 1963

Parish

 Amelia Bedelia. Harper 1963

 Amelia Bedelia and the Surprise Shower. Harper 1966

SIEGL, HELEN
(1924-) American, b. in Austria

Aesop, *Aesop's Fables.* Random 1964

Cole (comp.), *The Birds and the Beasts Were There.* World 1963

Grace, *Earrings for Celia.* Pantheon 1963

SILVERMAN, BURT (BURTON PHILIP)
(1928-) American

Bentley, *The Adventures of Tom Leigh.* Doubleday 1966

Hauff, *The Caravan.* Crowell 1964

Hirsch, *The Globe for the Space Age.* Viking 1963

Kingman

 Private Eyes. Doubleday 1964

 The Saturday Gang. Doubleday 1961

SILVERMAN, MEL (MELVIN FRANK)
(1931-1966) American
Allstrom, *Songs Along the Way*.   Abingdon 1961
Behn
    Roderick.   Harcourt 1961
    The Two Uncles of Pablo.   Harcourt 1959
Fox, *Apprentice to Liberty*.   Abingdon 1960
Hámori, *Flight to the Promised Land*.   Harcourt 1963
Silverman, *Hymie's Fiddle*.   World 1960

SIMON, HILDA RITA
(Ac. 1966) American
Brindze, *The Story of the Trade Winds*.   Vanguard
    1960
Simon
    Exploring the World of Social Insects.   Vanguard 1962
    Wonders of Hummingbirds.   Dodd 1964
    Wonders of the Butterfly World.   Dodd 1963

SIMON, HOWARD
(1903-) American
Coleridge, *The Rime of the Ancient Mariner*.   Duell
    1966
Longfellow
    Evangeline.   Duell 1966
    The Song of Hiawatha,   Duell 1966
Maizel, *Son of Condor*.   Criterion 1964
Simon, M. L.
    Candita's Choice.   Harper 1959
    If You Were an Eel, How Would You Feel?   Follett
    1963
    That Bad Carlos.   Harper 1964

SIMONT, MARC
(1915-) American, b. in France
Ladas, *The Seal That Couldn't Swim*.   Little 1959
Leach, *The Rainbow Book of American Folk Tales and
    Legends*.   World 1958
Simont, *The Contest at Paca*.   Harper 1959
Thurber, *The Wonderful O*.   Simon 1957

SLOANE, ERIC
(1910-) American
Sloane
    ABC of Early Americana.   Doubleday 1963
    The Sound of Bells.   Doubleday 1966

SLOBODKIN, LOUIS
(1903-) American
Davis, *Martin's Dinosaur*.   Crowell 1959
Friedrich, *The Marshmallow Ghosts*.   Lothrop 1960
Slobodkin
    Colette And the Princess.   Dutton 1965

The Late Cuckoo.   Vanguard 1962
Moon Blossom and the Golden Penny.   Vanguard 1963
Thank You — You're Welcome.   Vanguard 1957
Unnerstad, *Little O*.   Macmillan 1957
Upington, *The Beautiful Culpeppers*.   Watts 1963

SMITH, ALVIN
(1933-) American
Felton, *William Phips and the Treasure Ship*.   Dodd
    1965
Pedersen, *Fisherman's Choice*.   Atheneum 1965
Wojciechowska, *Shadow of a Bull*.   Atheneum 1964

SMITH, LAWRENCE BEALL
(1909-) American
Andersen, *Andersen's Fairy Tales*.   Macmillan 1963
Stucley, *Family Walkup (English title, Magnolia Build-
    ings)*.   Bodley 1960/Watts 1961
Wiggin, *Rebecca of Sunnybrook Farm*.   Macmillan
    1962

SMITH, LEE
See Albion, Lee Smith

SNYDER, JEROME
(1916-) American
Elkin, *Why the Sun Was Late*.   Parents 1966
Gurko, *The Lives and Times of Peter Cooper*.   Crowell
    1959
Kirtland
    One Day in Ancient Rome.   Harcourt 1961
    One Day in Aztec Mexico.   Harcourt 1963
    One Day in Elizabethan England.   Harcourt 1962
Lipkind, *Days to Remember*.   Obolensky 1961
Rand, *Umbrellas, Hats and Wheels*.   Harcourt 1961

SOFIA, pseud.
(Sofia Zeiger)
(1926-) American
Clewes
    All the Fun of the Fair.   Coward 1962
    The Branch Line.   Coward 1963
    The Holiday.   Coward 1964
Spicer
    13 Ghosts.   Coward 1965
    13 Giants   Coward 1966

SOKOL, BILL
(1925-) American, b. in Poland
Andersen, *The Emperor and the Nightingale*.
    Pantheon 1959
De Regniers
    Cats, Cats, Cats, Cats, Cats.   Pantheon 1958

A Child's Book of Dreams.   Harcourt 1957
Miller, *All Aboard.*   Pantheon 1958
Sokol, C.
  Dis-Moi.   Holt 1963
  La Pluche.   Holt 1963

SOLBERT, RONNI G.
(1925-   ) American
Chafetz
  The Legend of Befana.   Houghton 1958
  Thunderbird, and Other Stories.   Pantheon 1964
De Leeuw, *Indonesian Legends and Folk Tales.*
  Nelson 1961
Haviland, *Favorite Fairy Tales Told in Sweden.*   Little
  1966
Johnson
  The Little Knight.   Little 1957
  The Three-in-One Prince.   Little 1961
Low, *Snug in the Snow.*   Little 1963
Merrill
  Emily Emerson's Moon.   Little 1960
  High, Wide and Handsome and Their Three Tall Tales.
    Scott 1964
  The Pushcart War.   Scott 1964
  Shan's Luck Knife.   Scott 1960
  The Superlative Horse.   Scott 1961
Neville, *Woody and Me.*   Pantheon 1966
Thampi, *Geeta and the Village School.*   Doubleday
  1960

SOREL, EDWARD
(1928-   ) American
Miller
  The Goings-On at Little Wishful.   Little 1959
  King Carlo of Capri.   Harcourt 1958
  Pablo Paints a Picture.   Little 1959
Sherman
  Gwendolyn and the Weather Cock.   Golden 1963
  Gwendolyn the Miracle Hen.   Golden 1961

SPANFELLER, JAMES JOHN
(1930-   ) American
Bulla, *Indian Hill.*   Crowell 1963
Farmer
  Emma in Winter.   Harcourt 1966
  The Summer Birds.   Chatto 1962/Harcourt 1962
Parker, *The Boy Who Wasn't Lonely.*   Bobbs 1965
Shura, *Run Away Home.*   Knopf 1965

SPENCE, GERALDINE
(1931-   ) English
Berna, *Threshold of the Stars.*   Bodley 1958/Abelard
  1961

Chauncy, *Devils' Hill.*   Oxford 1958/Watts 1960
Mayne, *The Blue Boat.*   Oxford 1957/Dutton 1960
Roland, *The Forbidden Bridge.*   Bodley 1961/McGraw
  1965
Spence, E., *The Green Laurel.*   Oxford 1963/Roy 1965

SPIER, PETER
(1927-   ) American, b. in the Netherlands
Davis, *Island City.*   Doubleday 1961
De Jong, *The Level Land.*   Scribner 1961
Dodge, *Hans Brinker.*   Scribner 1958
The Fox Went Out on a Chilly Night.   Doubleday 1961
Krasilovsky, *The Cow Who Fell in the Canal.*
  Doubleday 1957
Parker (ed.), *100 More Story Poems.*   Crowell 1960
Shemin, *The Little Riders.*   Coward 1963

SPILKA, ARNOLD
(1917-   ) American
Fisher, *Best Little House.*   Crowell 1966
Lawson, *You Better Come Home with Me.*   Crowell
  1966
Russell, *Lines and Shapes.*   Walck 1965
Spilka
  A Lion I Can Do Without.   Walck 1964
  Little Birds Don't Cry.   Viking 1965
  Paint All Kinds of Pictures.   Walck 1963

STAHL, BEN (BENJAMIN ALBERT)
(1910-   ) American
Stahl, *Blackbeard's Ghost.*   Houghton 1965

STANDON, EDWARD CYRIL
(1929-   ) English
Standon, A.
  The Hippo Had Hiccoughs.   Constable 1964/Coward
    1965
  Little Duck Lost.   Constable 1965/Delacorte 1966
  The Singing Rhinoceros.   Constable 1963/Coward
    1963

STEVENS, MARY E.
(1920-   ) American
Cleary, *The Real Hole.*   Morrow 1960
Gage, *The Secret of Fiery Gorge.*   World 1960
Guilfoile, *Nobody Listens to Andrew.*   Follett 1957
Moore, *The Snake That Went to School.*   Random
  1957
Parkinson, *Good Old Archibald.*   Abingdon 1960

STOBBS, WILLIAM
(1914-   ) English
Cass, *The Cat Thief.*   Abelard 1962
Chekhov, *Kashtanka.*   Oxford 1959/Walck 1961

Hewett, *The Little White Hen.* Oxford 1962/
McGraw 1963

Lewis, *Here Comes Harry.* Oxford 1960/Criterion
1961

Manning-Sanders (comp.), *A Bundle of Ballads.*
Oxford 1959/Lippincott 1961

Polland
Beorn the Proud. Constable 1961/Holt 1962
The White Twilight. Constable 1962

Serraillier
The Clashing Rocks. Oxford 1963/Walck 1964
The Gorgon's Head. Oxford 1961/Walck 1962
The Way of Danger. Oxford 1962/Walck 1963

Stobbs
Jack and the Beanstalk. Constable 1965/Delacorte
1966
The Story of the Three Bears. Bodley 1964/McGraw
1965

Syme
Captain Cook, Pacific Explorer. Morrow 1960
De Soto: Finder of the Mississippi. Morrow 1957
Francisco Pizarro, Finder of Peru. Morrow 1963
Sir Henry Morgan, Buccaneer. Morrow 1965

Treece, *The Golden One.* Bodley 1961/Criterion
1962

Welch, *Escape from France.* Oxford 1960/Criterion
1961

Williams-Ellis (comp.), *Round the World Fairy Tales.*
Warne 1966

STONE, HELEN
(1904-   )   American
Branley, *Snow Is Falling.* Crowell 1963
Foster, *Tell Me, Mr. Owl.* Lothrop 1957
Hawes, *Watch Honeybees with Me.* Crowell 1964
Koch, *Let It Rain!* Holiday 1959
McGinley, *Lucy McLockett.* Lippincott 1959

SUBA, SUSANNE
(1913-   )   American, b. in Hungary
Burch, *The Travelling Bird.* Obolensky 1959
Cumming, *A Valentine for Candy.* Harcourt 1959
Haviland, *Favorite Fairy Tales Told in Germany.*
Little 1959
Vance, *A Flower from Dinah.* Dutton 1962

SWAIN, SU ZAN NOGUCHI
(1916-   )   American
Shuttlesworth
The Story of Ants. Doubleday 1964
The Story of Spiders. Doubleday 1959
Swain
The Doubleday First Guide to Insects. Doubleday
1964
Plants of Woodland and Wayside. Doubleday 1958

SWENEY, FREDERIC
(1912-   )   American
Russell
The Frightened Hare. Holt 1966
Hawk in the Sky. Holt 1965

THOLLANDER, EARL GUSTAVE
(1922-   )   American
Ritchie
Ramon Makes a Trade. Parnassus 1959
To Catch a Mongoose. Parnassus 1964

TOMES, MARGOT LADD
(1917-   )   American
Day, *Landslide!* Bodley 1961/Coward 1964
Fisher, *In the Woods, in the Meadow, in the Sky.*
Scribner 1965
Reggiani, *Five Children and a Dog.* Collins 1963/
Coward 1965
Wersba
The Brave Balloon of Benjamin Buckley. Atheneum
1963
The Land of Forgotten Beasts. Atheneum 1964

TREDEZ, ALAIN
See TREZ, ALAIN, pseud.

TRESILIAN, CECIL STUART
(1891-   )   English
Gaunt
Brim Sails Out. Cape 1966
Brim's Boat. Cape 1965/Coward 1966

TREZ, ALAIN, pseud.
(ALAIN TREDEZ)
(Ac. 1966)   French
Trez
Circus in the Jungle. World 1958
Fifi. World 1959
The Little Knight's Dream. World 1963
Le Petit Chien. World 1961
Le Vilain Chat. World 1965
The Royal Hiccups. Viking 1965

TRNKA, JIŘÍ
(1914-   )   Czechoslovakian
Andersen, *Fairy Tales.* Hamlyn 1961
Grimm, *Fairy Tales.* Hamlyn 1961
Hauff, *Fairy Tales.* Hamlyn 1961

TROY, HUGH
(1906-1964)   American
Sawyer, *The Year of the Christmas Dragon.* Viking
1960

TROYER, JOHANNES
(1902-   )   Austrian
Baker (comp.),   *The Golden Lynx and Other Tales.*
Lippincott 1960
Baudouy,   *Bruno, King of the Mountain.*   Harcourt 1961
Cole (ed.),   *Poems for Seasons and Celebrations.*
World 1961
Leekley,   *The Riddle of the Black Knight.*   Vanguard
1957

TUDOR, TASHA
(1915-   )   American
Alcott,   *A Round Dozen.*   Viking 1963
Bruce (ed.),   *Tasha Tudor Book of Fairy Tales.*   Platt
1961
Burnett
A Little Princess.   Lippincott 1963
The Secret Garden.   Lippincott 1962
Godden,   *The Doll's House.*   Viking 1962
Grahame,   *The Wind in the Willows.*   World 1966
Tudor
Around the Year.   Walck 1957
Becky's Christmas.   Viking 1961
Tudor (comp.)
Take Joy!   World 1966
Wings from the Winds.   Lippincott 1964

TUNIS, EDWIN
(1897-   )   American
Tunis
Colonial Craftsmen.   World 1965
Colonial Living.   World 1957
Frontier Living.   World 1961
Indians.   World 1959
Shaw's Fortune.   World 1966

TURKLE, BRINTON CASSADAY
(1915-   )   American
Burt,   *War Cry of the West.*   Holt 1964
Cenac,   *Four Paws into Adventure.*   Watts 1965
Turkle,   *Obadiah the Bold.*   Viking 1965
York,   *The Doll in the Bakeshop.*   Watts 1965

UNGERER, TOMI
(1931-   )   American, b. in France
Brenner,   *Mr. Tall and Mr. Small.*   Scott 1966
Brown,   *Flat Stanley.*   Harper 1964
Cole (ed.)
Beastly Boys and Ghastly Girls.   World 1964
Oh, What Nonsense!   Viking 1966
Stolz,   *Frédou.*   Harper 1962
Ungerer
Crictor.   Harper 1958
Emile.   Harper 1960

The Mellops Go Flying.   Harper 1957
The Mellops Go Spelunking.   Harper 1963
One, Two, Where's My Shoe?   Harper 1964
Orlando the Brave Vulture.   Harper 1966
Rufus.   Harper 1961
Snail, Where Are You?   Harper 1962
The Three Robbers,   Atheneum 1962

UNWIN, NORA SPICER
(1907-   )   English
De Banke
More Tabby Magic.   Hutchinson 1961
Tabby Magic.   Hutchinson 1959
Hunt,   *Cupola House.*   Lippincott 1961
McKellar
A Dog Like No Other.   McKay 1965
Two for the Fair.   McGraw 1958
Unwin
Joyful the Morning.   McKay 1963
Poquito, the Little Mexican Duck.   McKay 1959
Two Too Many.   McKay 1962
Yates,   *Carolina's Courage.*   Dutton 1964
Young,   *How the Manx Cat Lost Its Tail.*   McKay 1959

VAN STOCKUM, HILDA
(1908-   )   American, b. in the Netherlands
Van Stockum
Friendly Gables.   Viking 1958
Little Old Bear.   Viking 1962
The Winged Watchman.   Farrar 1962

VASILIU, MIRCEA
(1920-   )   American, b. in Rumania
Montrose,   *The Winter Flower, and Other Fairy Stories.*
Viking 1964
Vasiliu,   *The Year Goes Round.*   Day 1964

VERNEY, JOHN
(1913-   )   English
Avery,   *To Tame a Sister.*   Collins 1961/Van Nostrand
1964
Avery (ed.),   *Unforgettable Journeys.*   Watts 1965
Verney
February's Road.   Collins 1961/Holt 1966
Friday's Tunnel.   Collins 1959/Holt 1966

VICTOR, JOAN BERG
(1937-   )   American
Beaty,   *Plants in His Pack.*   Pantheon 1964
Benedict,   *Oh . . . Brother Juniper!*   Pantheon 1963
Bloch,   *Aunt America.*   Atheneum 1963
Clymer,   *Search for a Living Fossil.*   Holt 1963
Hodges,   *The Three Princes of Serendip.*   Atheneum
1964

Martin, *Little Two and the Peach Tree*. Atheneum
1963
Piper, *Little Red*. Scribner 1963
Zolotow, *Flocks of Birds*. Abelard 1965

VON SCHMIDT, ERIC
(1931-   )   American
Fleischman
By the Great Horn Spoon. Atlantic-Little 1963
Chancy and the Grand Rascal. Atlantic-Little 1966
Mr. Mysterious & Company. Atlantic-Little 1962
Von Schmidt (comp.), *Come for to Sing*. Houghton
1963
Weeks, *Tales of a Common Pigeon*. Houghton 1960

WABER, BERNARD
(1924-   )   American
Waber
The House on East 88th Street. Houghton 1962
Just Like Abraham Lincoln. Houghton 1964
Lyle and the Birthday Party. Houghton 1966
Lyle, Lyle, Crocodile. Houghton 1965
Rich Cat, Poor Cat. Houghton 1963
You Look Ridiculous, Said the Rhinoceros to the
Hippopotamus. Houghton 1966

WARD, LYND KENDALL
(1905-   )   American
Fritz, *Brady*. Coward 1961
Henry, *Gaudenzia*. Rand 1960
McNeer
The American Indian Story. Farrar 1963
America's Abraham Lincoln. Houghton 1957
America's Mark Twain. Houghton 1962
Armed with Courage. Abingdon 1957
The Canadian Story. Farrar 1958
My Friend Mac. Houghton 1960
Give Me Freedom. Abingdon 1964
Swift
The Edge of April. Morrow 1957
From the Eagle's Wing. Morrow 1962
Shakespeare, *Five Plays from Shakespeare*. Houghton
1964
Ward, *Nic of the Woods*. Houghton 1965

WARNER, EDYTHE RECORDS
(1916-   )   American
Warner
The Little Dark Horse. Viking 1960
Siamese Summer. Viking 1964
The Tigers of Como Zoo. Viking 1961

WARNER, PETER
(1939-   )   English

George, *The Happy Fisherman*. Hamilton 1965
Hope-Simpson, *The Edge of the World*. Coward 1966
Jackson, *The Witch of Castle Kerry*. Chatto 1966
Mayne, *No More School*. Hamilton 1965
Sturton, *Zomo: The Rabbit*. Atheneum 1966

WATSON, ALDREN AULD
(1917-   )   American
Bartlett, *The Clean Brook*. Crowell 1961
Constant, *Willie and the Wildcat Well*. Crowell 1962
Evans, *The Snow Book*. Little 1965
Felton, *Mike Fink, Best of the Keelboatmen*. Dodd
1960
Mother Goose, *Nursery Rhymes*. Dutton 1958
Muehl, *My Name Is - - -*. Holiday 1959
Watson, A. A., *My Garden Grows*. Viking 1962
Watson, N. D.
Annie's Spending Spree. Viking 1957
Katie's Chickens. Knopf 1965
Sugar on Snow. Viking 1964

WEBB, CLIFFORD CYRIL
(1895-   )   English
Monckton, *The Boy and the Mountain*. Warne 1961
Webb, *The Thirteenth Pig*. Warne 1966

WEIL, LISL
(Ac. 1966)   American, b. in Austria
McLeod, *Clancy's Witch*. Atlantic-Little 1959
Weil
Bitzli and the Big Bad Wolf. Houghton 1960
The Busiest Boy in Holland. Houghton 1959
Eyes So-o Big. Houghton 1964
Happy Ski ABC. Putnam 1964
Mimi. Houghton 1961
Weil (adapt.), *The Sorcerer's Apprentice*. Little 1962

WEISGARD, LEONARD
(1916-   )   American
Ames and Wyler, *First Days of the World*. Harper
1958
Brown, *Nibble, Nibble*. Scott 1959
Bulla
The Valentine Cat. Crowell 1959
White Bird. Crowell 1966
Colman, *Peter's Brownstone House*. Morrow 1963
Dalgliesh, *Adam and the Golden Cock*. Scribner 1959
Fisher, *Like Nothing at All*. Crowell 1962
Franchere, *Willa*. Crowell 1958
Fry, *The Boat That Mooed*. Macmillan 1965
Garelick, *Where Does the Butterfly Go When It Rains?*
Scott 1961
Haviland, *Favorite Fairy Tales Told in Norway*. Little
1961

Holl, *Sir Kevin of Devon*. Lothrop 1963

Johnston, *Penguin's Way*. Doubleday 1962

Joslin

    Baby Elephant and the Secret Wishes. Harcourt 1962

    Baby Elephant Goes to China. Harcourt 1963

    Baby Elephant's Trunk. Harcourt 1961

    Brave Baby Elephant. Harcourt 1960

    Señor Baby Elephant, the Pirate. Harcourt 1962

Kumin, *The Beach Before Breakfast*. Putnam 1964

Nathan, *The Snowflake and the Starfish*. Knopf 1959

O'Neill, *Hailstones and Halibut Bones*. Doubleday 1961

Selsam, *See Along the Shore*. Harper 1961

Thompson (comp.), *Hawaiian Myths of Earth, Sea and Sky*. Holiday 1966

WEISS, EMIL

(1896-1965) American, b. in Austria

Byron, *Chesapeake Duke*. Rand 1965

Fritz, *San Francisco*. Rand 1962

Hall, E. J., *The Volga*. Rand 1965

Hall, R. *The Dog's Boy*. Lothrop 1962

Neville, *It's Like This, Cat*. Harper 1963

Polk, *Delhi — Old and New*. Rand 1963

Samachson, *Rome*. Rand 1964

Smith

    Paris. Rand 1961

    Washington, D. C. Rand 1964

WEISS, HARVEY

(1922-   ) American

De Jong, *Looking for Alexander*. Atlantic-Little 1963

Schlein

    Amazing Mr. Pelgrew. Abelard 1957

    The Raggle-Taggle Fellow. Abelard 1959

Weiss

    The Expeditions of Willis Partridge. Abelard 1960

    A Gondola for Fun. Putnam 1957

    Horse in No Hurry. Putnam 1961

    The Very Private Tree House. Abelard 1964

WENNERSTROM, GENIA KATERINE

See GENIA, pseud.

WERENSKIOLD, ERIK

(1855-1938) Norwegian

Asbjørnsen and Moe, *Norwegian Folk Tales* (with THEODOR KITTELSEN). Viking 1961

(*See note in Foreword to this Bibliography*)

WERTH, KURT

(1896-   ) American

Adams, *Mr. Picklepaw's Popcorn*. Lothrop 1965

Curren, *Hear Ye of Boston*. Lothrop 1964

Feuerlicht, *The Legends of Paul Bunyan*. Macmillan 1965

Fleischman, *McBroom Tells the Truth*. Norton 1966

Foster, *Honker Visits the Island*. Lothrop 1962

Johnston, *Great Gravity the Cat*. Knopf 1958

Leach (ed.)

    The Luck Book. World 1964

    Noodles, Nitwits and Numskulls. World 1961

McGinley, *The Year Without a Santa Claus*. Lippincott 1957

Mincieli, *Tales Merry and Wise*. Holt 1958

WIBERG, HARALD ALBIN

(1908-   ) Swedish

Burman, *Three Wolverines of Rushing Valley*. Dutton 1966

Lindgren

    Christmas in the Stable. Coward 1962

    The Tomten. Coward 1961

    The Tomten and the Fox. Coward 1965

WIESE, KURT

(1887-   ) American, b. in Germany

Bishop, *Twenty-Two Bears*. Viking 1964

Clymer, *Mr. Piper's Bus*. Dodd 1961

Coatsworth, *Pika and the Roses*. Pantheon 1959

Gallant, *The Flute Player of Beppu*. Coward 1960

Wiese

    The Groundhog and His Shadow. Viking 1959

    Rabbit Bros. Circus, One Night Only. Viking 1963

    The Thief in the Attic. Viking 1965

WIESNER, WILLIAM

(1899-   ) American, b. in Austria

Elkin, *Al and the Magic Lamp*. Harper 1963

Harper (comp.), *Ghosts and Goblins*. Dutton 1965

Potter (comp.)

    More Tongue Tanglers and a Rigamarole. World 1964

    Tongue Tanglers. World 1962

Wiesner, *Joco and the Fishbone*. Viking 1966

Wiesner (comp.)

    A Pocketful of Riddles. Dutton 1966

    Too Many Cooks . . . Lippincott 1961

WIKLAND, ILON

(1930-   ) Swedish

Linde, *Chimney-Top Lane*. Harcourt 1965

Lindgren

    The Children of Noisy Village. Viking 1962

    Christmas in Noisy Village. Viking 1964

    Happy Times in Noisy Village. Viking 1963

    Springtime in Noisy Village. Viking 1966

Unnerstad
  Little O. Joseph 1965
  The Peep-Larssons Go Sailing. Macmillan 1966

WILDSMITH, BRIAN
  (1930-   )   English
  Arabian Nights, Tales from the Arabian Nights. Oxford
    1961/Watts 1962
  Blishen (comp.), *Oxford Book of Poetry for Children.*
    Oxford 1960/Watts 1962
  Chauncy, *The Secret Friends.* Oxford 1960/Watts
    1962
  Crossley-Holland, *Havelok the Dane.* Macmillan 1964/
    Dutton 1965
  Green, *Myths of the Norsemen.* Bodley 1962
  Grice, *Out of the Mines.* (English title, *The Bonny Pit
    Laddy.*) Oxford 1960/Watts 1961
  La Fontaine
    The Hare and the Tortoise. Oxford 1966
    The Lion and the Rat. Oxford 1963/Watts 1964
    The North Wind and the Sun. Oxford 1964/Watts
      1964
    The Rich Man and the Shoemaker. Oxford 1965/
      Watts 1965
  Mother Goose, *Brian Wildsmith's Mother Goose.*
    Oxford 1964/Watts 1965
  Polland, *The Town Across the Water.* Constable 1961
  Stevenson, *A Child's Garden of Verses.* Oxford 1966/
    Watts 1966
  Wildsmith
    Brian Wildsmith's ABC. Oxford 1962/Watts 1963
    Brian Wildsmith's 1, 2, 3's. Oxford 1965/Watts 1965

WILKON, JOZEF
  (1930-   )   Polish
  Schaaf, *The Crane with One Leg.* Warne 1965
  Valentin, *Herr Minkepatt and His Friends.* Dobson
    1965/Braziller 1965

WILLIAMS, GARTH MONTGOMERY
  (1912-   )   American
  Carlson
    A Brother for the Orphelines. Harper 1959
    The Family Under the Bridge. Harper 1958
    The Happy Orpheline. Harper 1957
  Colver, *Bread-and-Butter Indian.* Holt 1964
  Hoban, *Bedtime for Frances.* Harper 1960
  Lindquist, *The Little Silver House.* Harper 1959
  Schweitzer. *Amigo.* Macmillan 1963
  Selden, *The Cricket in Times Square.* Farrar 1960
  Sharp
    Miss Bianca. Collins 1962/Little 1962
    Miss Bianca in the Salt Mines. Heinemann 1966/
      Little 1966

The Rescuers.   Collins 1959/Little 1959
The Turret.   Little 1963
Stolz,   *Emmett's Pig.*   Harper 1959
Zolotow
  Do You Know What I'll Do?   Harper 1958
  Over and Over.   Harper 1957
  The Sky Was Blue.   Harper 1963

WILLIAMS, JENNY
  (1939-   )   English
  Kirby,   *The Silver Wood.*   Constable 1966

WILSON, PEGGY
  (Ac. 1966)   American
  Appiah,   *Ananse and the Spider.*   Pantheon 1966

WIMMER, HELMUT KARL
  (1925-   )   American, b. in Germany
  Branley
    Mars: Planet Number Four.   Crowell 1962
    The Moon: Earth's Natural Satellite.   Crowell 1960
    The Nine Planets.   Crowell 1958
    The Sun: Star Number One.   Crowell 1964

WOHLBERG, MEG
  (1905-   )   American
  De Leeuw,   *Donny, the Boy Who Made a Home for
    Animals.*   Little 1957
  Thayer,   *Andy and the Runaway Horse.*   Morrow 1963

WONDRISKA, WILLIAM
  (1931-   )   American
  Budnay,   *A Cat Can't Count.*   Lothrop 1962
  Wondriska
    The Tomato Patch.   Holt 1964
    Which Way to the Zoo?   Holt 1962

**WORLD COUNCIL OF CHRISTIAN EDUCATION
(Sponsors)**
  Bible
    Away in a Manger.   Nelson 1963
    In the Beginning.   Nelson 1965
  (*See note in Foreword to this Bibliography*)

WRONKER, LILI CASSEL
  (1924-   )   American, b. in Germany
  Crandall,   *Santa Fé.*   Rand 1965
  Fenisong,   *Boy Wanted.*   Harper 1964
  Johnson,   *Happy New Year 'Round the World.*   Rand
    1966

WYNANTS, MICHE
  (1934-   )   Belgian
  Wynants,   *Noah's Ark.*   Faber 1965/Harcourt 1965

YAMAGUCHI, MARIANNE ILLENBERGER

(1939-   )   American
Larson,   *Palace in Bagdad*.   Scribner 1966
Uchida,   *The Sea of Gold*.   Scribner 1965
Yamaguchi, T.
    The Golden Crane.   Holt 1963
    Two Crabs and the Moonlight.   Holt 1965

YAROSLAVA, pseud.

(YAROSLAVA SURMACH MILLS)
(Ac. 1966)   American
Kay
    An Egg Is for Wishing.   Abelard 1966
    A Stocking for a Kitten.   Abelard 1965
Tresselt (adapt.),   *The Mitten*.   Lothrop 1964

YASHIMA, TARO

(1908-   )   American, b. in Japan
Behrens,   *Soo Ling Finds a Way*.   Golden Gate 1965
Yashima
    Momo's Kitten.   Viking 1961
    Umbrella.   Viking 1958
    Youngest One.   Viking 1962
Yashima and Muku,   *The Golden Footprints*.   World
    1960

ZÁBRANSKÝ, ADOLF

(1909-   )   Czechoslovakian
Stearns
    Ring-A-Ling.   Lippincott 1959
    Underneath My Apple Tree.   Lippincott 1960

ZALLINGER, JEAN DAY

(1918-   )   American
Andrews,   *In the Days of Dinosaurs*.   Random 1959
Fisher,   *Valley of the Smallest*.   Crowell 1966
May,   *They Turned to Stone*.   Holiday 1965

ZEIGER, SOFIA

See SOFIA, pseud.

ZEMACH, MARGOT

(1931-   )   American
Grimm,   *The Fisherman and His Wife*.   Norton 1966
Hahn,   *Take a Giant Step*.   Little 1960
Sendak, J.   *The King of the Hermits*.   Farrar 1966
Williams,   *The Question Box*.   Norton 1965
Zemach, H. (adapt.)
    Mommy, Buy Me a China Doll.   Follett 1966
    Nail Soup.   Follett 1964
    Salt.   Follett 1965
    The Speckled Hen.   Holt 1966
Zemach, M. (adapt.)
    The Little Tiny Woman.   Bobbs 1965
    The Three Sillies.   Holt 1963
    The Tricks of Master Dabble.   Holt 1965

ZIMNIK, REINER

(1930-   )   German
De Regniers,   *The Snow Party*.   Pantheon 1959
Zimnik
    The Bear on the Motorcycle.   Atheneum 1963
    The Little Roaring Tiger.   Pantheon 1961
    The Proud Circus Horse.   Pantheon 1957

NOTE: THE BIBLIOGRAPHY WHICH FOLLOWS IS OF THE AUTHORS OF
ILLUSTRATED BOOKS LISTED ABOVE.

A BIBLIOGRAPHY OF THE AUTHORS

ABRAHAMS, ANTHONY
Polonius and the Flying Doctor.   *H. Abrahams*
Polonius Penguin Comes to Town.   *H. Abrahams*
Polonius Penguin Learns to Swim.   *H. Abrahams*

ACKERMAN, EUGENE
Tonk and Tonka.   *Burger*

ADAMS, ANDY
Trail Drive.   *Rounds*

ADAMS, RUTH
Mr. Picklepaw's Popcorn.   *Werth*

AESOP
Aesop: Five Centuries of Illustrated Fables.
Aesop's Fables.   *Kiddell-Monroe*
Aesop's Fables.   *Provenson*
Aesop's Fables.   *Siegl*
Fables of Aesop.   *Levine*
The Hare and the Tortoise.   *Galdone*
The Miller, His Son and Their Donkey.   *Duvoisin*

AGLE, NAN HAYDEN
Makon and the Dauphin. *Frankenberg*

AIKEN, CONRAD
Cats and Bats and Things with Wings.   *Glaser*

AIKEN, JOAN
Black Hearts in Battersea.   *Jacques*
Black Hearts in Battersea.   *Marriott*
Nightbirds on Nantucket.   *Jacques*
The Wolves of Willoughby Chase.   *Marriott*

ALAIN, pseud.
(DANIEL BRUSTLEIN)
One, Two, Three . . . Going to Sea.   *Alain*

ALARCÓN, PEDRO ANTONIO DE
The Three-Cornered Hat.   *Duvoisin*

ALCOTT, LOUISA MAY
Little Women.   *Fraser*
A Round Dozen.   *Tudor*

ALDRIDGE, JOSEPHINE HASKELL
The Best of Friends.   *Peterson*
Fisherman's Luck.   *Robbins*
A Penny and a Periwinkle.   *Robbins*

ALEXANDER, ANNE
Noise in the Night.   *Graboff*

ALEXANDER, LLOYD
Coll and His White Pig.   *Ness*

ALGER, LECLAIRE
See NIC LEODHAS, SORCHE, pseud.

ALIKI, pseud.
(ALIKI BRANDENBERG)
Keep Your Mouth Closed, Dear.   *Aliki*
The Story of Johnny Appleseed.   *Aliki*
The Story of William Penn.   *Aliki*
The Wish Workers.   *Aliki*

ALLEN, HAZEL
Up from the Sea Came an Island.   *M. Miller*

ALLINGHAM, WILLIAM
The Dirty Old Man.   *Blegvad*

ALLSTROM, ELIZABETH
Songs Along the Way.   *M. Silverman*

ALMEDINGEN, MARTHA EDITH
The Knights of the Golden Table.   *Keeping*
A Picture History of Russia.   *Hutton*
The Treasure of Siegfried.   *Keeping*

AMBRUS, VICTOR G.
The Three Poor Tailors.   *Ambrus*

AMES, GERALD and ROSE WYLER
First Days of the World.   *Weisgard*

ANCKARSVÄRD, KARIN
Aunt Vinnie's Invasion.   *Hutchinson*
Aunt Vinnie's Victorious Six.   *Hutchinson*
Doctor's Boy.   *Rocker*

ANDERSEN, HANS CHRISTIAN
Andersen's Fairy Tales.   *L. B. Smith*
The Emperor and the Nightingale.   *Sokol*
The Emperor's New Clothes.   *Blegvad*
Fairy Tales.   *Trnka*
Fairy Tales of Hans Christian Andersen
Hans Andersen's Fairy Tales.   *Hughes*
Hans Andersen's Fairy Tales.   *E. H. Shepard*
The Nightingale.   *Berson*
The Nightingale.   *Burkert*
Seven Tales.   *Sendak*
The Swineherd.   *Blegvad*
Thumbelina.   *Adams*
The Ugly Duckling.   *Adams*
The Wild Swans.   *M. Brown*

ANDERSON, CLARENCE WILLIAM
Another Man o' War. *Anderson*
Blaze and the Mountain Man.   *Anderson*
C. W. Anderson's Complete Book of Horses and

Horsemanship. *Anderson*
A Filly for Joan. *Anderson*
Lonesome Little Colt. *Anderson*
Twenty Gallant Horses. *Anderson*

ANDERSON, LONZO
Ponies of Mypillengi. *Adams*
Zeb. *Burchard*

ANDREWS, ROY CHAPMAN
In the Days of Dinosaurs. *Zallinger*

ANGELO, VALENTI
The Acorn Tree. *Angelo*
Angelino and the Barefoot Saint. *Angelo*
The Honey Boat. *Angelo*
The Merry Marcos. *Angelo*
The Tale of a Donkey. *Angelo*

ANGLUND, JOAN WALSH
The Brave Cowboy. *Anglund*
Christmas Is a Time of Giving. *Anglund*
Cowboy and His Friend. *Anglund*
A Friend Is Someone Who Likes You. *Anglund*
Love Is a Special Way of Feeling. *Anglund*
Nibble, Nibble, Mousekin. *Anglund*

ANNETT, CORA
The Dog Who Thought He Was A Boy. *Lorraine*

APPEL, BENJAMIN
Man and Magic. *Landau*
Shepherd of the Sun. *Bryson*

APPIAH, PEGGY
Ananse and the Spider. *Wilson*

ARABIAN NIGHTS ENTERTAINMENTS
The Arabian Nights. *Baynes*
The Seven Voyages of Sinbad the Sailor. *Reed*
Tales from the Arabian Nights. *Wildsmith*

ARDIZZONE, EDWARD
Johnny the Clockmaker. *Ardizzone*
The Little Girl and the Tiny Doll. *Ardizzone*
Peter the Wanderer. *Ardizzone*
Sarah and Simon and No Red Paint. *Ardizzone*
Tim and Ginger. *Ardizzone*
Tim's Friend Towser. *Ardizzone*

ARKHURST, JOYCE COOPER
The Adventures of Spider. *Pinkney*

ARMER, ALBERTA
Steve and the Guide Dogs. *Kocsis*

ARMOUR, RICHARD
Animals on the Ceiling. *Galdone*

ARNOLD, RALPH
Kings, Bishops, Knights and Pawns. *Mars*

ARNOTT, KATHLEEN (comp.)
African Myths and Legends. *Kiddell-Monroe*

ARORA, SHIRLEY LEASE
"What Then, Raman?" *Guggenheim*

ARTHUR, RUTH M.
A Candle in Her Room. *Gill*
Dragon Summer. *Gill*
My Daughter, Nicola. *Rocker*

ARUNDEL, JOCELYN
Dugan and the Hobo. *Dennis*
Jingo, Wild Horse of Abaco. *Dennis*
Mighty Mo. *Dennis*
Simba of the White Mane. *Dennis*
The Wildlife of Africa. *Dennis*

ASBJØRNSEN, PETER CHRISTEN and
JØRGEN ENGEBRETSEN MOE
Norwegian Folk Tales. *Werenskiold and Kittelsen*
The Three Billy Goats Gruff. *M. Brown*

ASHABRANNER, BRENT (jt. author)
See DAVIS, RUSSELL

ASIMOV, ISAAC
The Kite That Won the Revolution. *Mays*
Words from the Myths. *Barss*
Words of Science. *Barss*

AUERBACH, MARJORIE
Seven Uncles Come to Dinner. *Auerbach*

AULT, PHILIP H.
This Is the Desert. *Fisher*

AUSTEN, JANE
Pride and Prejudice. *Bryson*

AVERILL, ESTHER
The Fire Cat. *Averill*
Jenny Goes to Sea. *Averill*
Jenny's Bedside Book. *Averill*

AVERY, GILLIAN (ed.)
In the Window Seat. *Einzig*
Unforgettable Journeys. *Verney*

AYER, JACQUELINE
Nu Dang and His Kite. *Ayer*
The Paper-Flower Tree. *Ayer*
A Wish for Little Sister. *Ayer*

BACON, PEGGY
The Good American Witch. *Bacon*
The Oddity. *Bacon*

BAILEY, CAROLYN SHERWIN
Flickertail. *MacKenzie*

BAKER, AUGUSTA (comp.)
The Golden Lynx. *Troyer*

BAKER, BETTY
Killer-of-Death. *Kaufmann*
Little Runner of the Longhouse. *Arnold Lobel*

BAKER, LAURA NELSON
The Friendly Beasts. *Sidjakov*

BAKER, MARGARET JOYCE
Castaway Christmas. *R. Kennedy*
Cut Off from Crumpets. *R. Kennedy*
Hannibal and the Bears. *Hodges*
The Shoeshop Bears. *Hodges*

BALCH, GLENN
Keeping Horse. *Cellini*

BANNON, LAURA
Hop-High, the Goat. *Bannon*
Jo-Jo, the Talking Crow. *Bannon*
Katy Comes Next. *Bannon*
The Other Side of the World. *Bannon*

BARKER, SHIRLEY
The Trojan Horse. *Kredel*

BARKER, WILL
Winter-Sleeping Wildlife. *Burger*

BARLOW, GENEVIEVE (comp.)
Latin American Tales. *Hutchinson*

BARRY, KATHARINA
A Is for Anything. *K. Barry*

BARRY, ROBERT E.
Faint George. *R. E. Barry*
Just Pepper. *R. E. Barry*
Mr. Willoughby's Christmas Tree. *R. E. Barry*

BARTLETT, MARGARET FARRINGTON
The Clean Brook. *Watson*

BARTLETT, RUTH
The Miracle of the Talking Jungle. *Lent*

BATES, HERBERT ERNEST
Achilles the Donkey. *Barker*

BAUDOUY, MICHEL-AIMÉ
Bruno, King of the Mountain. *Troyer*

BAUM, FRANK
The Wonderful Wizard of Oz. *Biro*

BAUMANN, HANS
The Barque of the Brothers. *Schramm*
I Marched with Hannibal. *Schramm*

BEATTY, HETTY BURLINGAME
Bryn. *Beatty*
Bucking Horse. *Beatty*
Moorland Pony. *Beatty*
Voyage of the Sea Wind. *Beatty*

BEATY, JANICE J.
Plants in His Pack. *Victor*
Seeker of Seaways. *Cellini*

BEHN, HARRY
The Golden Hive. *Behn*
Omen of the Birds. *Behn*
The Painted Cave. *Behn*
Roderick. *M. Silverman*
The Two Uncles of Pablo. *M. Silverman*

BEHRENS, JUNE
Soo Ling Finds a Way. *Yashima*

BELL, DIANA FRANCES
The Rebels of Journey's End. *D. Hall*

BELL, THELMA HARRINGTON
A Dash of Pepper. *C. Bell*
Thunderstorm. *C. Bell*
The Two Worlds of Davy Blount. *C. Bell*

BELLOC, HILAIRE
The Bad Child's Book of Beasts, and More Beasts for Worse
    Children. *Berson*

BELPRÉ, PURA
Juan Bobo and the Queen's Necklace. *C. Price*
The Tiger and the Rabbit. *De Paola*

BELTING, NATALIA MAREE
Calendar Moon. *Bryson*
The Earth Is on a Fish's Back. *Nesbitt*
Elves and Ellefolk. *Laite*
The Stars Are Silver Reindeer. *Nesbitt*
The Sun Is a Golden Earring. *Bryson*

BEMELMANS, LUDWIG
Madeline and the Bad Hat. *Bemelmans*
Madeline and the Gypsies. *Bemelmans*
Madeline in London. *Bemelmans*
Welcome Home! *Bemelmans*

BENARY-ISBERT, MARGOT
Blue Mystery. *Arno*

BENCHLEY, NATHANIEL
Red Fox and His Canoe. *Arnold S. Lobel*

BENDICK, JEANNE
  Lightning. *Bendick*
  Sea So Big, Ship So Small. *Bendick*
  The Wind. *Bendick*

BENEDICT, REX
  Oh . . . Brother Juniper! *Victor*

BENNETT, RAINEY
  After the Sun Goes Down. *Bennett*
  The Secret Hiding Place. *Bennett*

BENTLEY, PHYLLIS
  The Adventures of Tom Leigh. *B. Silverman*

BERNA, PAUL
  The Horse Without a Head. *R. Kennedy*
  Threshold of the Stars. *Spence*

BERRILL, JACQUELINE
  Wonders of Animal Migration. *Berrill*
  Wonders of the Antarctic. *Berrill*
  Wonders of the Fields and Ponds at Night. *Berrill*

BERRY, ERICK, pseud.
  (ALLENA CHAMPLIN BEST)
  The Springing of the Rice. *Kaufmann*

BERRY, DON
  Mountain Men. *Dines*

BERRY, WILLIAM D.
  Buffalo Land. *Berry*
  Deneki: An Alaskan Moose. *Berry*

BERSON, HAROLD
  Raminogrobis and the Mice. *Berson*

BEST, ALLENA CHAMPLIN
  See BERRY, ERICK, pseud.

BEST, HERBERT
  Bright Hunter of the Skies. *Bryson*

BETTINA, pseud.
  (BETTINA BAUER EHRLICH)
  Angelo and Rosaline. *Bettina*
  For the Leg of a Chicken. *Bettina*
  Pantaloni. *Bettina*
  Trovato. *Bettina*

BIANKI, VITALI
  Peek the Piper. *Galdone*

BIBLE
  Away in a Manger. *World Council of Christian Ed.*
    (Sponsor)
  The First Nowell. *Provenson*
  In the Beginning. *World Council of Christian Ed.*
    (Sponsor)
  The Old Testament. *De Angeli*
  Shadrach, Meshach and Abednego. *Galdone*

BINGLEY, BARBARA
  The Story of Tit-Bé and His Friend. *Gill*

BIRCH, CYRIL
  Chinese Myths and Fantasies. *Kiddell-Monroe*

BIRO, VAL
  Gumdrop. *Biro*

BISHOP, CLAIRE HUCHET
  A Present from Petros. *Davis*
  Twenty-Two Bears. *Wiese*
  Yeshu, Called Jesus. *Bolognese*

BLACK, IRMA SIMONTON
  Castle, Abbey and Town. *Mars*

BLAKE, WILLIAM
  Songs of Innocence. *Jones*
  Songs of Innocence, v.1, Poetry. *Raskin*
  Songs of Innocence, v.2, Songs for Voice, Piano and Guitar.
    Raskin

BLAND, EDITH NESBIT
  See NESBIT, E., pseud.

BLEGVAD, LENORE
  Mr. Jensen and Cat. *E. Blegvad*

BLISHEN, EDWARD (comp.)
  The Oxford Book of Poetry for Children. *Wildsmith*

BLOCH, MARIE HALUN
  Aunt America. *Victor*
  The Dollhouse Story. *Erhard*
  The Two Worlds of Damyan. *Quackenbush*

BLOUGH, GLENN ORLANDO
  Who Lives in This House? *Bendick*

BOEGEHOLD, BETTY
  Three to Get Ready. *Chalmers*

BOGAN, LOUISE and WILLIAM JAY SMITH (comp.)
  The Golden Journey. *Kredel*

BOND, MICHAEL
  A Bear Called Paddington. *Fortnum*
  More about Paddington. *Fortnum*
  Paddington Helps Out. *Fortnum*

BONNE, ROSE (jt. author)
  See MILLS, ALAN, pseud.

BONSALL, CROSBY NEWELL
  The Case of the Cat's Meow. *Bonsall*
  The Case of the Hungry Stranger. *Bonsall*
  Tell Me Some More. *Siebel*
  Who's a Pest? *Bonsall*

BONTEMPS, ARNA
Frederick Douglass. *E. H. Johnson*

BOOTH, ESME RIDEOUT
Kalena. *E. H. Johnson*

BORTEN, HELEN
Do You Hear What I Hear? *Borten*
Do You Move As I Do? *Borten*
Do You See What I See? *Borten*
Hallowe'en. *Borten*
A Picture Has a Special Look. *Borten*

BOSLEY, KEITH
Tales from the Long Lakes. *R. Kennedy*

BOSTON, LUCY MARIA
The Castle of Yew. *Gill*

BOUCHER, ALAN
The Hornstranders. *C. A. Jones*

BOURLIAGUET, LÉONCE
The Giant Who Drank from His Shoe. *Rose*

BOWERS, GWENDOLYN
The Lost Dragon of Wessex. *Geer*

BOWMAN, JAMES CLOYD
Mike Fink. *Fisher*

BRADFORD, WILLIAM
Pilgrim Courage. *Fisher*

BRAND, CHRISTIANNA
Nurse Matilda. *Ardizzone*

BRADLEY, DUANE
Meeting with a Stranger. *E. H. Johnson*

BRANLEY, FRANKLYN MANSFIELD
The Big Dipper. *Emberley*
A Book of Astronauts for You. *Kessler*
A Book of Planets for You. *Kessler*
The Christmas Sky. *Lent*
Flash, Crash, Rumble and Roll. *Emberley*
Mars: Planet Number Four. *Wimmer*
The Moon: Earth's Natural Satellite. *Wimmer*
The Moon Seems to Change. *Borten*
The Nine Planets. *Wimmer*
Snow Is Falling. *Stone*
The Sun: Star Number One. *Wimmer*
What Makes Day and Night. *Borten*
What the Moon Is Like. *Bobri*

BRAUN, KATHY
Kangaroo & Kangaroo. *McMullan*

BRELIS, NANCY
The Mummy Market. *Shecter*

BRENNER, ANITA
Dumb Juan and the Bandits. *Charlot*
The Timid Ghost. *Charlot*

BRENNER, BARBARA
The Five Pennies. *Blegvad*
Mr. Tall and Mr. Small. *Ungerer*
Nicky's Sister. *J. E. Johnson*

BRENTANO, CLEMENS MARIA
Schoolmaster Whackwell's Wonderful Sons. *Sendak*
The Tale of Gockel, Hinkel & Gackeliah. *Sendak*

BREWTON, SARAH and JOHN E. BREWTON (comps.)
Birthday Candles Burning Bright. *Bock*
Laughable Limericks. *Fetz*

BRIGGS, RAYMOND (comp.)
Fee-Fi-Fo-Fum. *Briggs*
Ring-A-Ring O'Roses. *Briggs*
The White Land. *Briggs*

BRIGHT, ROBERT
The Friendly Bear. *Bright*
Georgie and the Magician. *Bright*
Georgie's Hallowe'en. *Bright*
My Hopping Bunny. *Bright*
My Red Umbrella. *Bright*

BRINDZE, RUTH
The Story of the Trade Winds. *H. R. Simon*

BRING A TORCH, JEANNETTE, ISABELLA. *Adams*

BRINK, CAROL RYRIE
Andy Buckram's Tin Men. *Mars*
Pink Motel. *Greenwald*

BRO, MARGUERITTE HARMON
How the Mouse Deer Became King. *Low*
The Animal Friends of Peng-U. *Moy*

BRONTË, CHARLOTTE
Jane Eyre. *Forberg*

BRONTË, EMILY
Wuthering Heights. *Bryson*

BROOMFIELD, ROBERT (ed.)
The Twelve Days of Christmas. *Broomfield*

BROWN, JEFF
Flat Stanley. *Ungerer*

BROWN, JUDITH GWYN
Max and the Truffle Pig. *Brown*

BROWN, MARCIA
Backbone of the King. *Brown*
Felice. *Brown*

Peter Piper's Alphabet.　*Brown*
Tamarindo!　*Brown*

BROWN, MARGARET WISE
The Dead Bird.　*Charlip*
Four Fur Feet.　*Charlip*
Nibble, Nibble.　*Weisgard*
On Christmas Eve.　*Montresor*

BROWN, MARION MARSH, and RUTH CRONE
The Silent Storm.　*Kredel*

BROWN, PALMER
Cheerful.　*Brown*
Something for Christmas.　*Brown*

BROWN, VINSON
How to Understand Animal Talk.　*Berry*

BROWNING, ROBERT
The Pied Piper of Hamelin.　*H. Jones*

BRUCE, DANA (ed.)
Tasha Tudor Book of Fairy Tales.　*Tudor*

BRUNHOFF, LAURENT DE
Babar's Fair.　*Brunhoff*
Bonhomme.　*Brunhoff*
Captain Serafina.　*Brunhoff*

BRUSTLEIN, DANIEL
See ALAIN, pseud.

BRUSTLEIN, JANICE
See JANICE, pseud.

BRYANT, SARA CONE
The Burning Ricefields.　*Funai*

BRYSON, BERNADA
The Twenty Miracles of Saint Nicholas.　*Bryson*

BUCKLEY, HELEN ELIZABETH
Josie and the Snow.　*Ness*
The Little Boy and the Birthdays.　*Galdone*

BUDD, LILLIAN
Tekla's Easter.　*Genia*

BUDNEY, BLOSSOM
A Cat Can't Count.　*Wondriska*

BUEHR, WALTER
Chivalry and the Mailed Knight.　*Buehr*
The French Explorers in America.　*Buehr*
Knights and Castles and Feudal Life.　*Buehr*
The Spanish Armada.　*Buehr*
Strange Craft.　*Buehr*
Warriors' Weapons.　*Buehr*

BUFF, CONRAD and MARY MARSH BUFF
Elf Owl.　*C. Buff*
Forest Folk.　*C. Buff*
Trix and Vix.　*C. Buff*

BUFF, MARY MARSH (jt. author)
See BUFF, CONRAD

BULL, ANGELA
Wayland's Keep.　*Hughes*

BULLA, CLYDE ROBERT
Benito.　*Angelo*
Indian Hill.　*Spanfeller*
More Stories of Favorite Operas.　*Low*
The Ring and the Fire.　*C. and J. Ross*
Stories of Favorite Operas.　*Galster*
The Valentine Cat.　*Weisgard*
Viking Adventure.　*Gorsline*
White Bird.　*Weisgard*

BURCH, ROBERT
Queenie Peavy.　*Lazare*
Skinny.　*Sibley*
The Travelling Bird.　*Suba*
Tyler, Wilkin and Skee.　*Sibley*

BURCHARD, PETER
The Carol Moran.　*Burchard*
Jed.　*Burchard*

BURGUNDER, ROSE
From Summer to Summer.　*Fegiz*

BURMAN, EDOR
Three Wolverines of Rushing Valley.　*Wiberg*

BURN, DORIS
Andrew Henry's Meadow.　*Burn*

BURNETT, FRANCES HODGSON
A Little Princess.　*Tudor*
Racketty-Packetty House.　*Berson*
The Secret Garden.　*Tudor*

BURNFORD, SHEILA
The Incredible Journey.　*Burger*

BURNINGHAM, JOHN
Borka: The Adventures of a Goose with No Feathers.
　Burningham
Trubloff.　*Burningham*

BURNS, ROBERT
Hand in Hand We'll Go.　*Hogrogian*

BURT, NATHANIEL
War Cry of the West.　*Turkle*

BURTON, HESTER
Castors Away. *Ambrus*
Time of Trial. *Ambrus*

BURTON, VIRGINIA LEE
Life Story. *Burton*

BUSONI, RAFAELLO
The Man Who Was Don Quixote. *Busoni*

BUTLER, SUZANNE
Starlight in Tourrone. *Fegiz*

BUTTERWORTH, OLIVER
The Trouble with Jenny's Ear. *De Miskey*

BYARS, BETSY C.
The Dancing Camel. *Berson*
Rama, the Gypsy Cat. *Bacon*

BYRD, ERNESTINE N.
The Black Wolf of Savage River. *Robbins*
Ice King. *M. J. Miller*

BYRON, GILBERT
Chesapeake Duke. *E. Weiss*

CALHOUN, MARY
Depend on Katie John. *Frame*
High Wind for Kansas. *Mars*

CAMERON, ELEANOR
A Spell Is Cast. *B. and J. Krush*
The Terrible Churnadyne. *B. and J. Krush*

CAMERON, POLLY
A Child's Book of Nonsense. *Cameron*
"I Can't," Said the Ant. *Cameron*
The 2 Ton Canary & Other Nonsense Riddles. *Cameron*

CAMPION, NARDI REEDER
Patrick Henry: Firebrand of the Revolution. *Mays*

CANTY, MARY
The Green Gate. *Bock*

CARIGIET, ALOIS
Anton the Goatherd. *Carigiet*

CARLETON, BARBEE OLIVER
Chester Jones. *Fiammenghi*

CARLSON, NATALIE SAVAGE
A Brother for the Orphelines. *G. M. Williams*
Carnival in Paris. *Rocker*
The Empty Schoolhouse. *Kaufmann*
Evangeline, Pigeon of Paris. *Nicolas*
The Family Under the Bridge. *G. M. Williams*
The Happy Orpheline. *Falconer*
The Happy Orpheline. *G. M. Williams*
Hortense, the Cow for a Queen. *Nicolas*

Jean-Claude's Island. *Burkert*
The Letter on the Tree. *Kaufmann*
The Orphelines in the Enchanted Castle. *Falconer*
The Orphelines in the Enchanted Castle. *Saviozzi*
A Pet for the Orphelines. *Falconer*
A Pet for the Orphelines. *Rocker*
School Bell in the Valley. *Riswold*
The Song of the Lop-Eared Mule. *Domanska*

CARMER, CARL
The Hudson River. *Busoni*

CARPENTER, FRANCES
The Mouse Palace. *Adams*
The Elephant's Bathtub. *Guggenheim*

CARROLL, LATROBE (jt. author)
See CARROLL, RUTH ROBINSON

CARROLL, LEWIS, pseud.
(CHARLES LUTWIDGE DODGSON)
The Hunting of the Snark. *Oechsli*

CARROLL, RUTH ROBINSON and
LATROBE CARROLL
Danny and the Poi Pup. *R. R. Carroll*
Runaway Pony, Runaway Dog. *R. R. Carroll*
Tough Enough's Indians. *R. R. Carroll*
Tough Enough's Pony. *R. R. Carroll*

CARRYL, CHARLES
The Capital Ship, or The Walloping Window Blind.
Galdone

CASS, JOAN
The Cat Thief. *Stobbs*

CASSEDY, SYLVIA
Little Chameleon. *Bennett*
Pierino and the Bell. *Ness*

CATHON, LAURA E. and THUSNELDA SCHMIDT
(comps.)
Perhaps and Perchance. *Jauss*

CAUDILL, REBECCA
A Certain Small Shepherd. *Du Bois*
Did You Carry the Flag Today, Charley? *Grossman*
A Pocketful of Cricket. *Ness*

CAUSLEY, CHARLES (comp.)
Modern Ballads and Story Poems (English title, Rising Early).
Netherwood

CAVANAH, FRANCES
Jenny Lind and Her Listening Cat. *Frame*

CENAC, CLAUDE
Four Paws into Adventure. *Paton*
Four Paws into Adventure. *Turkle*

CHAFETZ, HENRY
  The Legend of Befana. *Solbert*
  Thunderbird, and Other Stories. *Solbert*

CHALMERS, MARY
  The Cat Who Liked to Pretend. *Chalmers*
  Kevin. *Chalmers*
  Take a Nap, Harry. *Chalmers*

CHANDLER, RUTH
  Three Trumpets. *Keeping*

CHAPPELL, WARREN
  Coppelia. *Chappell*
  The Magic Flute. *Chappell*
  The Sleeping Beauty. *Chappell*
  They Say Stories. *Chappell*

CHARLIP, REMY
  Where Is Everybody? *Charlip*

CHARLIP, REMY and BURTON SUPREE (comps.)
  Mother, Mother, I Feel Sick . . . *Charlip*

CHASE, MARY
  Loretta Mason Potts. *Berson*

CHASE, MARY ELLEN
  Sailing the Seven Seas. *Cosgrave*
  A Walk on an Iceberg. *Lonette*

CHASE, RICHARD (ed.)
  Billy Boy. *Rounds*

CHAUNCY, NAN
  Devils' Hill. *Spence*
  The Secret Friends. *Wildsmith*

CHEKHOV, ANTON PAVLOVICH
  Kashtanka. *Stobbs*

CHILD STUDY ASSOCIATION (comp.)
  Castles and Dragons. *Du Bois*

CHÖNZ, SELINA
  The Snowstorm. *Carigiet*

CHUBB, THOMAS CALDECOT
  The Byzantines. *Powers*
  The Northmen. *Powers*

CHUKOWSKY, KORNEI IVANOVICH
  Crocodile. *Howard*

CHURCH, ALFRED JOHN
  The Aeneid for Boys and Girls. *Karlin*
  The Iliad for Boys and Girls. *Karlin*

CIARDI, JOHN
  I Met a Man. *Osborn*
  John J. Plenty and Fiddler Dan. *Gekiere*

  The King Who Saved Himself from Being Saved. *Gorey*
  The Man Who Sang the Sillies. *Gorey*
  The Monster Den. *Gorey*
  The Reason for the Pelican. *Gekiere*
  You Know Who. *Gorey*
  You Read to Me, I'll Read to You. *Gorey*

CLAIR, ANDRÉE
  Bemba. *E. H. Johnson*

CLARK, ANN NOLAN
  The Desert People. *Houser*
  Tia Maria's Garden. *Keats*

CLARK, LEONARD (comp.)
  Drums and Trumpets. *Copley*

CLARKE, PAULINE
  The Return of the Twelves. *Bryson*

CLEARY, BEVERLY
  The Mouse and the Motorcycle. *Louis Darling*
  The Real Hole. *Stevens*
  Ribsy. *Louis Darling*

CLEMENS, SAMUEL LANGHORNE
  See TWAIN, MARK, pseud.

CLEWES, DOROTHY
  All the Fun of the Fair. *Sofia*
  The Branch Line. *Sofia*
  The Holiday. *Sofia*

CLYMER, ELEANOR
  The Adventure of Walter. *Fetz*
  Chipmunk in the Forest. *Fetz*
  Harry, the Wild West Horse. *Shortall*
  Mr. Piper's Bus. *Wiese*
  Search for a Living Fossil. *Victor*
  The Tiny Little House. *Fetz*

COATES, BELLE
  That Colt, Fireplug. *Dennis*

COATSWORTH, ELIZABETH
  The Cave. *Houser*
  The Fox Friend. *Hamberger*
  Jock's Island. *Obligado*
  Jon the Unlucky. *Nesbitt*
  Lonely Maria. *Ness*
  The Noble Doll. *Politi*
  The Peaceable Kingdom, and Other Poems. *Eichenberg*
  Pika and the Roses. *Wiese*
  The Place. *Auerbach*
  The Princess and the Lion. *Ness*
  Ronnie and the Chief's Son. *Martin*
  The Sparrow Bush. *Martin*

COCK ROBIN. *Cooney*

COIT, MARGARET L.
Andrew Jackson. *M. Johnson*

COLE, WILLIAM (comp.)
Beastly Boys and Ghastly Girls. *Ungerer*
The Birds and the Beasts Were There. *Siegl*
I Went to the Animal Fair. *Rosselli*
Oh What Nonsense! *Ungerer*
Poems for Seasons and Celebrations. *Troyer*
Poems of Magic and Spells. *Bacon*

COLERIDGE, SAMUEL TAYLOR
The Rime of the Ancient Mariner. *H. Simon*

COLLINS, RUTH PHILPOTT
The Flying Cow. *Keats*

COLSON, THORA
Rinkin of Dragon's Wood. *Marriott*

COLUM, PADRAIC
The Stone of Victory. *J. G. Brown*

COLUMBUS, FERDINAND
The Quest of Columbus. *Fisher*

COLVER, ANNE
Bread-and-Butter Indian. *G. M. Williams*
Nobody's Birthday. *Bileck*
Old Bet. *Palazzo*

COMMAGER, HENRY STEELE
A Picture History of the United States. *Hutton*

CONGER, MARION
Who Has Seen the Wind? *Perl*

CONKLIN, GLADYS PLEMON
If I Were a Bird. *Marokvia*
We Like Bugs. *Marokvia*

CONSTANT, ALBERTA WILSON
Those Miller Girls! *B. and J. Krush*
Willie and the Wildcat Well. *Watson*

COOLIDGE, OLIVIA
Lives of Famous Romans. *M. Johnson*
Men of Athens. *M. Johnson*
Roman People. *Lipinsky*

COOMBS, PATRICIA
Dorrie and the Blue Witch. *Coombs*
Dorrie and the Weather Box. *Coombs*
Dorrie's Magic. *Coombs*

COONEY, BARBARA
The American Speller. *Cooney*
Chanticleer and the Fox. *Cooney*
The Little Juggler. *Cooney*

COOPER, JAMES FENIMORE
The Sky. *Pitz*

COOPER, SUSAN
Over Sea, Under Stone. *Gill*

CORBETT, SCOTT
The Case of the Gone Goose. *Frame*
The Cave Above Delphi. *Fiammenghi*
One by Sea. *Mays*
Pippa Passes. *J. G. Brown*

CORBIN, WILLIAM
Pony for Keeps. *Burchard*

CORCOS, LUCILLE
From Ungskah 1 to Oyaylee 10. *Corcos*

COSGRAVE, JOHN O'HARA, II
America Sails the Seas. *Cosgrave*
Clipper Ship. *Cosgrave*

COSGROVE, MARGARET
The Strange World of Animal Senses. *Cosgrove*

COTTLER, JOSEPH
Alfred Wallace, Explorer-Naturalist. *Kaufmann*

COTTRELL, LEONARD
Land of the Pharaohs. *Powers*

COURLANDER, HAROLD
The King's Drum. *Arno*
The Tiger's Whisker. *Arno*
The Piece of Fire. *B. and J. Krush*

COURLANDER, HAROLD and
ALBERT KOFE PREMPEH
The Hat-Shaking Dance. *Arno*

CRAIG, JEAN
The Dragon in the Clock Box. *Oechsli*
The Long and Dangerous Journey. *Ohlsson*
What Did You Dream? *Gill*

CRANDALL, ELIZABETH L.
Santa Fé. *Wronker*

CRAWFORD, RAYMOND MAXWELL
A Picture History of Australia. *Hutton*

CRETAN, GLADYS YESSAYON
All Except Sammy. *Shimin*
A Gift from the Bride. *Fegiz*

CRONE, RUTH (jt. author)
See Brown, Marion

CROSSLEY-HOLLAND, KEVIN
Havelok the Dane. *Wildsmith*
King Horn. *Keeping*

CUMMING, MARIAN
  A Valentine for Candy.   *Suba*

CUNNINGHAM, JULIA
  Candle Tales.   *Ness*
  Macaroon.   *Ness*
  Viollet.   *Cober*

CURREN, POLLY
  Hear Ye of Boston.   *Werth*

CURRY, JANE LOUISE
  Down from the Lonely Mountain.   *Arno*

DAHL, RAOLD
  Charlie and the Chocolate Factory.   *Schindelman*
  James and the Giant Peach.   *Burkert*
  The Magic Finger.   *Du Bois*

DALGLIESH, ALICE
  Adam and the Golden Cock.   *Weisgard*

DALY, MAUREEN
  The Ginger Horse.   *Dennis*

DAME WIGGINS OF LEE AND HER
  SEVEN WONDERFUL CATS.   *Broomfield*

DANA, BARBARA
  Spencer and His Friends.   *Chwast*

DARLING, LOIS and LOUIS DARLING
  Coral Reefs.   *L. and L. Darling*
  Turtles.   *L. and L. Darling*
  The Sea Serpents Around Us.   *L. and L. Darling*

DARLING, LOUIS
  Kangaroos, and Other Animals with Pockets.
    Louis Darling

DARLING, LOUIS (jt. author)
  See DARLING, LOIS

DARWIN, CHARLES
  The Voyage of the Beagle.   *Ravielli*

DAUGHERTY, JAMES
  The Picnic.   *Daugherty*

D'AULAIRE, EDGAR PARIN and
  INGRI MORTENSEN PARIN D'AULAIRE
  D'Aulaires' Book of Greek Myths.   *D'Aulaire*
  The Magic Meadow.   *D'Aulaire*

D'AULAIRE, INGRI MORTENSEN PARIN (jt. author)
  See D'AULAIRE, EDGAR PARIN

DAVIS, LAVINIA
  Island City.   *Spier*

DAVIS, REDA
  Martin's Dinosaur.   *Slobodkin*

DAVIS, RUSSELL and BRENT ASHABRANNER
  Ten Thousand Desert Swords.   *Fisher*

DAWLISH, PETER
  The Seas of Britain.   *Biro*

DAY, VÉRONIQUE
  Landslide.   *Tomes*

DE ANGELI, ARTHUR C. and
  MARGUERITE DE ANGELI
  The Empty Barn.   *M. De Angeli*

DE ANGELI, MARGUERITE (jt. author)
  See DE ANGELI, ARTHUR C.

DE BANKE, CECILE
  More Tabby Magic.   *Unwin*
  Tabby Magic.   *Unwin*

DE BEAUMONT, MARIE LE PRINCE
  Beauty and the Beast.   *Knight*

DE GASZTOLD, CARMEN BERNOS
  The Creatures' Choir.   *Primrose*
  Prayers from the Ark.   *Primrose*

DE JONG, DAVID CORNEL
  Looking for Alexander.   *H. Weiss*

DE JONG, DOLA
  The Level Land.   *Spier*

DE JONG, MEINDERT
  The Big Goose and the Little White Duck.   *Burkert*
  Puppy Summer.   *Anita Lobel*
  The Last Little Cat.   *McMullan*
  Far Out the Long Canal.   *Grossman*

DE LA IGLESIA, MARIA ELENA
  The Cat and the Mouse.   *Low*

DE LA MARE, WALTER JOHN
  Jack and the Beanstalk.   *Low*
  The Magic Jacket.   *P. Kennedy*
  Peacock Pie.   *Cooney*
  A Penny a Day.   *P. Kennedy*
  Stories from the Bible.   *Ardizzone*
  Tales Told Again.   *Howard*

DE LEEUW, ADELE
  Donny, the Boy Who Made a Home for Animals.
    Wohlberg
  Indonesian Legends and Folk Tales.   *Solbert*

DE MARÉ, ERIC
  London's River.   *Copley and Chamberlain*

DE MILLE, AGNES
  Book of the Dance.   *Bodecker*

DE PAOLA, TOMIE
  The Wonderful Dragon of Timlin.   *De Paola*

DE REGNIERS, BEATRICE SCHENK
  Cats Cats Cats Cats Cats.   *Sokol*
  A Child's Book of Dreams.   *Sokol*
  David and Goliath.   *Powers*
  May I Bring a Friend?   *Montresor*
  Penny.   *Bileck*
  The Snow Party.   *Zimnik*
  Something Special.   *Haas*

DE TREVIÑO, ELIZABETH BORTON
  Nacar the White Deer.   *Arno*

DENNEBORG, HEINRICH MARIE
  Grisella the Donkey.   *Lemke*
  Jan and the Wild Horse.   *Lemke*
  The Only Horse for Joan.   *Lemke*

DENNIS, WESLEY
  Tumble.   *Dennis*

DEUTSCH, BABETTE and
AVRAHM YARMOLINSKY (eds.)
  More Tales of Faraway Folk.   *Domanska*

DICKENS, CHARLES
  Captain Boldheart and The Magic Fishbone.   *Knight*
  David Copperfield.   *Bodecker*

DIGGINS, JULIA E.
  String, Straightedge and Shadow.   *Bell*

DILLON, EILÍS
  A Family of Foxes.   *R. Kennedy*
  The Lion Cub.   *R. Kennedy*
  The Road to Dunmore.   *R. Kennedy*
  The Sea Wall.   *R. Kennedy*
  The Sea Wall.   *Mars*

DINES, GLEN
  Bull Wagon.   *Dines*
  Overland Stage.   *Dines*

DOBRIN, ARNOLD
  Little Monk and the Tiger.   *Dobrin*
  Taro and the Sea Turtles.   *Dobrin*

DODGE, MARY MAPES
  Hans Brinker.   *Spier*

DODGSON, CHARLES LUTWIDGE
  See CARROLL, LEWIS, pseud.

DOMANSKA, JANINA (ed.)
  Why So Much Noise?   *Domanska*

DOW, KATHARINE
  My Time of Year.   *Erhard*

DOWNING, CHARLES
  Tales of the Hodja.   *Papas*

DRUMMOND, VIOLET H.
  The Flying Postman.   *Drummond*
  Little Laura on the River.   *Drummond*
  Little Laura's Cat.   *Drummond*
  Miss Anna Truly.   *Drummond*
  Mrs. Easter and the Storks.   *Drummond*
  Phewtus the Squirrel.   *Drummond*

DU BOIS, WILLIAM PÈNE
  The Alligator Case.   *Du Bois*
  Elizabeth the Cow Ghost.   *Du Bois*
  Lazy Tommy Pumpkinhead.   *Du Bois*
  Otto in Africa.   *Du Bois*
  Otto in Texas.   *Du Bois*
  The Three Policemen.   *Du Bois*

DUCHESNE, JANET
  Richard Goes Sailing.   *Duchesne*

DUGGAN, ALFRED
  Arches and Spires.   *Briggs*
  The Castle Book (English title, Look at Castles).   *Briggs*
  Growing up in 13th Century England (English title,
    Growing up in the 13th Century).   *Hodges*
  Growing up with the Norman Conquest.   *Hodges*

DUMAS, ALEXANDRE
  The Three Musketeers.   *Hodges*

DUNCOMBE, FRANCES RIKER
  Cassie's Village.   *Mars*

DUVOISIN, ROGER
  Day and Night.   *Duvoisin*
  The Happy Hunter.   *Duvoisin*
  Lonely Veronica.   *Duvoisin*
  Our Veronica Goes to Petunia's Farm.   *Duvoisin*
  Petunia, Beware.   *Duvoisin*
  Petunia, I Love You.   *Duvoisin*
  Spring Snow.   *Duvoisin*
  Veronica.   *Duvoisin*

EAGER, EDWARD
  Magic by the Lake.   *Bodecker*
  Magic Or Not?   *Bodecker*
  Seven-Day Magic.   *Bodecker*
  The Time Garden.   *Bodecker*
  The Well Wishers.   *Bodecker*

EARLE, OLIVE LYDIA
  Birds and Their Beaks.   *Earle*
  Birds of the Crow Family.   *Earle*
  Camels and Llamas.   *Earle*
  Squirrels in the Garden.   *Earle*

Strange Companions in Nature.   *Earle*
Strange Lizards.   *Earle*

EASTMAN, PHILIP D.
The Cat in the Hat Beginner Book Dictionary.   *Eastman*
Go, Dog, Go.   *Eastman*
Sam and the Firefly.   *Eastman*

EASTWICK, IVY
A Camel for Saida.   *Fortnum*

ECONOMAKIS, OLGA
Oasis of the Stars.   *Lent*

EDMONDS, WALTER DUMAUX
They Had a Horse.   *Gorsline*

EHRLICH, BETTINA BAUER
See BETTINA, pseud.

EISEMAN, ALBERTA
Candido.   *Obligado*

ELGIN, KATHLEEN
The First Book of Norse Legends.   *Elgin*

ELKIN, BENJAMIN
Al and the Magic Lamp.   *Wiesner*
Six Foolish Fishermen.   *Evans*
Why the Sun Was Late.   *Snyder*

ELLIS, HARRY B.
The Arabs.   *Fisher*

EMBERLEY, ED
One Wide River to Cross.   *Emberley*
The Parade Book.   *Emberley*
Punch and Judy.   *Emberley*
The Story of Paul Bunyan.   *Emberley*
The Wing on a Flea.   *Emberley*

ENGLE, PAUL
Golden Child.   *Fisher*

ENGVICK, WILLIAM (ed.)
Lullabies and Night Songs.   *Sendak*

ENRIGHT, ELIZABETH
Gone Away Lake.   *B. and J. Krush*
Return to Gone Away.   *B. and J. Krush*
Tatsinda.   *Haas*
Zeee.   *Haas*

ENSOR, DOROTHY
The Adventures of Hatim Tai.   *Baynes*

ERWIN, BETTY K.
Aggie, Maggie and Tish.   *P. Kennedy*

ESTES, ELEANOR
The Alley.   *Ardizzone*

Pinky Pye.   *Ardizzone*
The Witch Family.   *Ardizzone*

ETS, MARIE HALL
Automobiles for Mice.   *Ets*
Cow's Party.   *Ets*
Gilberto and the Wind.   *Ets*
Just Me.   *Ets*
Mister Penny's Circus.   *Ets*

ETS, MARIE HALL, and AURORA LABASTIDA
Nine Days to Christmas.   *Ets*

EVANS, EVA KNOX
The Snow Book.   *Watson*

EVANS, KATHERINE
The Boy Who Cried Wolf.   *Evans*
A Donkey for Abou.   *Evans*
The Maid and Her Pail of Milk.   *Evans*
The Man, the Boy and the Donkey.   *Evans*

EVANS, PATRICIA
Rimbles.   *Fiammenghi*

EZO, pseud.
My Son-in-Law the Hippopotamus.   *Q. Blake*

FAIRSERVIS, WALTER ASHLIN
Horsemen of the Steppes.   *Powers*
India.   *Powers*

FALL, THOMAS
Canalboat to Freedom.   *Cellini*
Edge of Manhood.   *Pitz*
Wild Boy.   *Pitz*

FARALLA, DANA
The Singing Cupboard.   *Ardizzone*
The Wonderful Flying-Go-Round.   *Berson*

FARJEON, ELEANOR
The Children's Bells.   *Fortnum*
Italian Peepshow.   *Ardizzone*
Jim at the Corner.   *Ardizzone*
Mr. Garden.   *Paton*
Mrs. Malone.   *Ardizzone*

FARJEON, ELEANOR and WILLIAM MAYNE (eds.)
A Cavalcade of Kings.   *Ambrus*
A Cavalcade of Queens.   *Ambrus*

FARMER, PENELOPE
Emma in Winter.   *Spanfeller*
The Magic Stone.   *Kaufmann*
Sea Gull.   *Ribbons*
The Summer Birds.   *Spanfeller*

FATIO, LOUISE
The Happy Lion and the Bear.   *Duvoisin*

The Happy Lion's Quest. *Duvoisin*
Red Bantam. *Duvoisin*
The Three Happy Lions. *Duvoisin*

FELTON, HAROLD W.
A Horse Named Justin Morgan. *Fisher*
Mike Fink, Best of the Keelboatmen. *Watson*
Pecos Bill and the Mustang. *Shortall*
Sergeant O'Keefe and His Mule, Balaam. *Fisher*
William Phips and the Treasure Ship. *A. Smith*

FENISONG, RUTH
Boy Wanted. *Wronker*

FENNER, CAROL
Christmas Tree on the Mountain. *Fenner*
Tigers in the Cellar. *Fenner*

FENNER, PHYLLIS
The Dark and Bloody Ground. *Geer*

FENTON, EDWARD
Fierce John. *Du Bois*
The Golden Doors. *Fiammenghi*
An Island for a Pelican. *Davis*

FENTON, EUGÉNIE
Sher (Lord of the Jungle). *Kiddell-Monroe*

FERRA-MIKURA, VERA
Twelve People Are Not a Dozen. *P. Kennedy*

FEUERLICHT, ROBERTA STRAUSS
The Legends of Paul Bunyan. *Werth*

FIELD, EUGENE
Papillot, Clignot et Dodo. *Cooney*

FIELD, RACHEL
The Rachel Field Story Book. *Adams*

FIFE, DALE
A Dog Called Dunkel. *Alain*
The Fish in the Castle. *M. J. Miller*
A Stork for the Bell Tower. *Alain*

FILLMORE, PARKER
Shepherd's Nosegay. *Arno*

FISHER, AILEEN
Best Little House. *Spilka*
A Cricket in a Thicket. *Rojankovsky*
Going Barefoot. *Adams*
I Like Weather. *Domanska*
I Wonder How, I Wonder Why. *Barker*
In the Middle of the Night. *Adams*
Like Nothing at All. *Weisgard*
Listen, Rabbit. *Shimin*
Valley of the Smallest. *Zallinger*
Where Does Everyone Go? *Adams*

FISHER, ANNE B.
Stories California Indians Told. *Robbins*

FISHER, DOROTHY CANFIELD
And Long Remember. *Keats*

FISHER, LAURA
You Were Princess Last Time. *Grossman*

FISHER, LEONARD EVERETT
The Silversmiths. *Fisher*

FLANDERS, MICHAEL
Creatures Great and Small. *Minale*

FLEISCHMAN, ALBERT SIDNEY
By the Great Horn Spoon. *Von Schmidt*
Chancy and the Grand Rascal. *Von Schmidt*
The Ghost in the Noonday Sun. *Chappell*
McBroom Tells the Truth. *Werth*
Mr. Mysterious & Company. *Von Schmidt*

FLEMING, IAN
Chitty-Chitty-Bang-Bang. *Burningham*

FLOETHE, LOUISE LEE
The Cowboy on the Ranch. *R. Floethe*
The Farmer and His Cows. *R. Floethe*
The Fountain of the Friendly Lion. *R. Floethe*
The Indian and His Pueblo. *R. Floethe*
The Islands of Hawaii. *R. Floethe*
Sara. *R. Floethe*
Sea of Grass. *R. Floethe*
Triangle X. *R. Floethe*

FLORA, JAMES
Charlie Yup and His Snip Snap Boys. *Flora*
The Day the Cow Sneezed. *Flora*
Grandpa's Farm. *Flora*
Leopold, the See-Through Crumbpicker. *Flora*
My Friend Charlie. *Flora*
Sherwood Walks Home. *Flora*

FORBERG, ATI (comp.)
On a Grass-Green Horn. *Forberg*

FORBUS, INA B.
Tawny's Trick. *Grifalconi*

FOSTER, DORIS VAN LIEW
Honker Visits the Island. *Werth*
Tell Me, Mr. Owl. *Stone*

FOSTER, GENEVIEVE
Birthdays of Freedom, v.2. *Foster*
The World of Captain John Smith. *Foster*
The World of Columbus and Sons. *Foster*

FOURNIER, CATHARINE
The Coconut Thieves. *Domanska*

FOX, MARY VIRGINIA
  Apprentice to Liberty.   *M. Silverman*

FOX, PAULA
  Maurice's Room.   *Fetz*

THE FOX WENT OUT ON A CHILLY NIGHT.
  Spier

FRANCHERE, RUTH
  Willa.   *Weisgard*

FRANÇOISE, pseud.
  (FRANCOISE SEIGNOBOSC)
  The Big Rain.   *Françoise*
  Chouchou.   *Françoise*
  Jeanne-Marie at the Fair.   *Françoise*
  Minou.   *Françoise*
  What Do You Want To Be?   *Françoise*
  What Time Is it, Jeanne-Marie?   *Françoise*

FRANK, R., JR.
  Flashing Harpoons.   *Cosgrave*

FRASCONI, ANTONIO
  The House That Jack Built.   *Frasconi*
  See Again, Say Again.   *Frasconi*
  The Snow and the Sun.   *Frasconi*

FREEMAN, DON
  Come Again, Pelican.   *Freeman*
  Dandelion.   *Freeman*
  Fly High, Fly Low.   *Freeman*
  The Night the Lights Went Out.   *Freeman*
  Norman, the Doorman.   *Freeman*
  A Rainbow of My Own.   *Freeman*
  The Turtle and the Dove.   *Freeman*

FREEMAN, GODFREY
  The Owl and the Mirror.   *Kiddell-Monroe*

FRESCHET, BERNIECE
  Kangaroo Red.   *Schoenherr*

FRIEDRICH, OTTO (jt. author)
  See FRIEDRICH, PRISCILLA

FRIEDRICH, PRISCILLA and OTTO FRIEDRICH
  The Marshmallow Ghosts.   *Slobodkin*

FRITZ, JEAN
  Brady.   *Ward*
  The Cabin Faced West.   *Rojankovsky*
  How to Read a Rabbit.   *Shortall*
  San Francisco.   *E. Weiss*
  Tap, Tap, Lion — 1, 2, 3.   *Shortall*

FRY, CHRISTOPHER
  The Boat That Mooed.   *Weisgard*

FRY, ROSALIE K.
  The Echo Song.   *Fry*
  Lucinda and the Sailor Kitten.   *Fry*
  The Mountain Door.   *Fry*
  The Secret of the Ron Mor Skerry.   *Fry*
  The Castle Family.   *Gill*
  September Island.   *Gill*
  Promise of the Rainbow.   *Jacques*

FRYE, DEAN
  The Lamb and the Child.   *Duvoisin*
  Days of Sunshine — Days of Rain.   *Duvoisin*

FUNAI, MAMORU
  The Tiger, the Brâhman and the Jackal.   *Funai*

GAEDDERT, LOU ANN BIGGE
  Noisy Nancy Norris.   *Fiammenghi*

GAGE, WILSON, pseud.
  (MARY Q. STEELE)
  Dan and the Miranda.   *Rounds*
  The Ghost of Five Owl Farm.   *Galdone*
  Miss Osborne-the-Mop.   *Galdone*
  The Secret of Fiery Gorge.   *Stevens*
  A Wild Goose Tale.   *Rounds*

GALDONE, PAUL
  The House That Jack Built.   *Galdone*
  The Old Woman and Her Pig.   *Galdone*

GALLANT, KATHRYN
  The Flute Player of Beppu.   *Wiese*

GALLANT, ROY A.
  Exploring Chemistry.   *Ames*
  Exploring the Sun.   *Ames*

GANS, ROMA
  Icebergs.   *Bobri*
  It's Nesting Time.   *Mizumura*

GARDNER, JEANNE LE MONNIER
  Sky Pioneers.   *Gorsline*

GARELICK, MAY
  Sounds of a Summer Night.   *Montresor*
  Where Does the Butterfly Go When It Rains?   *Weisgard*
  Winter Birds.   *Hurd*

GARFIELD, LEON
  Jack Holborn.   *Maitland*
  Devil-in-the-Fog.   *Maitland*

GARNER, ALAN
  Elidor.   *Keeping*

GARSHIN, VSEVOLOD MIKHAILOVICH
  The Traveling Frog.   *Pinkney*

GARTHWAITE, MARION
    The Twelfth Night Santons. *Lubell*

GATES, DORIS
    The Cat and Mrs. Cary. *Bacon*

GAUNT, MICHAEL
    Brim Sails Out. *Tresilian*
    Brim's Boat. *Tresilian*

GEIS, DARLENE
    Dinosaurs and Other Prehistoric Animals. *R. F. Peterson*

GEISEL, THEODOR SEUSS
    See SEUSS, DR., pseud.

GEORGE, SIDNEY CHARLES
    The Happy Fisherman. *P. Warner*

GODDEN, RUMER
    Candy Floss. *Adams*
    The Dolls' House. *Tudor*
    Home Is the Sailor. *Primrose*
    Little Plum. *Primrose*
    Miss Happiness and Miss Flower. *Primrose*
    Mouse House. *Adams*
    St. Jerome and the Lion. *Primrose*
    The Story of Holly and Ivy. *Adams*

GOETZ, DELIA
    Islands of the Ocean. *Louis Darling*
    Mountains. *Louis Darling*
    Swamps. *Louis Darling*

GOLDIN, AUGUSTA
    Ducks Don't Get Wet. *Kessler*
    Salt. *Galster*
    Spider Silk. *Low*

GOODWIN, MURRAY
    Alonzo and the Army of Ants. *Komoda*

GOTTLIEB, SUZANNE
    What Is Red? *Bobri*

GOUDEY, ALICE E.
    Butterfly Time. *Adams*
    The Day We Saw the Sun Come Up. *Adams*
    Graywings. *Nonnast*
    Here Come the Beavers! *MacKenzie*
    Here Come the Dolphins! *MacKenzie*
    Here Come the Raccoons! *MacKenzie*
    Here Come the Squirrels! *MacKenzie*
    Houses from the Sea. *Adams*
    Red Legs. *Nonnast*

GOUDGE, ELIZABETH
    Linnets and Valerians. *Ribbons*

GOVAN, CHRISTINE
    Number 5 Hackberry Street. *Bacon*

GRAHAME, KENNETH
    The Reluctant Dragon. *Fortnum*
    The Wind in the Willows (Golden Anniversary Edition).
        E. H. Shepard
    The Wind in the Willows. *Tudor*

GRAMATKY, HARDIE
    Bolivar. *Gramatky*
    Homer and the Circus Train. *Gramatky*
    Little Toot on the Thames. *Gramatky*
    Nikos and the Sea God. *Gramatky*

GRANT, BRUCE
    American Forts, Yesterday and Today. *Bjorklund*
    American Indians, Yesterday and Today. *Bjorklund*
    Zachary, the Governor's Pig. *Frankenberg*

GRAVES, ROBERT
    Anne at Highwood Hall. *Ardizzone*
    Greek Gods and Heroes. *Davis*
    The Penny Fiddle. *Ardizzone*
    The Siege and Fall of Troy. *Hodges*

GRAY, JOHN E. B.
    India's Tales and Legends. *Kiddell-Monroe*

GRAY, ELIZABETH JANET
    The Cheerful Heart. *Mizumura*
    I Will Adventure. *Bell*

GREEN, ANNE M.
    Good-By, Gray Lady. *Raible*

GREEN, MARGARET (ed.)
    The Big Book of Animal Fables. *Grabianski*
    The Big Book of Animal Stories. *Grabianski*
    The Big Book of Wild Animals. *Grabianski*

GREEN, ROGER LANCELYN
    A Book of Myths. *Kiddell-Monroe*
    Heroes of Greece and Troy. *Copley and Chamberlain*
    The Land Beyond the North. *D. Hall*
    Myths of the Norsemen. *Wildsmith*
    Old Greek Fairy Tales. *E. H. Shepard*
    Tales from Shakespeare. *Beer*
    Tales the Muses Told. *Bolognese*

GRICE, FRED
    Out of the Mines (English title, The Bonny Pit Laddie).
        Wildsmith

GRIFALCONI, ANN
    City Rhythms. *Grifalconi*

GRIFFITHS, HELEN
    The Greyhound. *Ambrus*

GRIMM, JAKOB LUDWIG and
    WILHELM KARL GRIMM
    Fairy Tales. *Trnka*
    The Fisherman and His Wife. *Gekiere*
    The Fisherman and His Wife. *Zemach*
    The Good-for-Nothings. *Fischer*
    The Goose Girl. *De Angeli*
    Grimms' Fairy Tales. *Grabianski*
    Grimms' Fairy Tales. *Schramm*
    Rapunzel. *Hoffmann*
    The Seven Ravens. *Hoffmann*
    The Shoemaker and the Elves. *Adams*
    The Sleeping Beauty. *Hoffmann*
    Snow White and Rose Red. *Adams*
    Snow White and Rose Red. *Cooney*
    The Twelve Dancing Princesses. *Shulevitz*
    The Wolf and the Seven Little Kids. *Hoffmann*

GRIMM, WILHELM KARL (jt. author)
    See GRIMM, JAKOB LUDWIG

GROVES-RAINES, ANTONY
    The Tidy Hen. *Groves-Raines*

GUILFOILE, ELIZABETH
    Nobody Listens to Andrew. *Stevens*

GUILLOT, RENÉ
    The Blue Day. *Gill*
    The Fantastic Brother. *R. Kennedy*
    Grishka and the Bear. *Kiddell-Monroe*
    Guillot's African Folk Tales. *Papas*
    The King of the Cats. *Driscoll*
    Mountain with a Secret. *Driscoll*
    Nicolette and the Mill. *Mozley*
    Riders of the Wind. *R. Kennedy*
    Three Girls and a Secret. *Paton*

GURKO, MIRIAM
    The Lives and Times of Peter Cooper. *Snyder*

HADER, BERTA HOERNER and
    ELMER STANLEY HADER
    Little Chip. *Hader*
    Quack Quack. *Hader*
    Reindeer Trail. *Hader*
    Two Is Company, Three's a Crowd. *Hader*

HADER, ELMER STANLEY (jt. author)
    See HADER, BERTA HOERNER

HAHN, HANNELORE
    Take a Giant Step. *Zemach*

HALE, EDWARD EVERETT
    The Man without a Country. *Fisher*

HALE, KATHLEEN
    Orlando and the Three Graces. *Hale*
    Orlando (The Marmalade Cat) Buys a Cottage. *Hale*
    Orlando's Magic Carpet. *Hale*

HALL, ADELAIDE
    Sylvester, the Mouse with the Musical Ear. *Bodecker*

HALL, ELVA JEAN
    The Volga. *E. Weiss*

HALL, NATALIE
    The Palace of Fun. *Hall*
    The World in a City Block. *Hall*
    Zig-Zag-Zeppo. *Hall*

HALL, ROSALYS
    The Dog's Boy. *E. Weiss*

HALL, WILLIS
    The Royal Astrologer. *Adamson*

HALLER, ADOLF
    He Served Two Masters. *Hoffmann*

HALLOWELL, PRISCILLA
    The Long-Nosed Princess. *Fegiz*

HAMBERGER, JOHN
    The Day the Sun Disappeared. *Hamberger*

HÁMORI, LÁSZLÓ
    Adventures in Bangkok. *Frankenberg*
    Flight to the Promised Land. *M. Silverman*

HAMPDEN, JOHN
    A Picture History of India. *Hutton*

HARPER, WILHELMINA (comp.)
    Ghosts and Goblins. *Wiesner*
    Merry Christmas to You. *Rocker*

HARRIS, JOEL CHANDLER
    Uncle Remus, His Songs and Sayings. *Moy*

HARRIS, LEON
    The Great Picture Robbery. *Schindelman*

HARRIS, LOUISE DYER and
    NORMAN DYER HARRIS
    Flash: the Life Story of a Firefly. *Kane*

HARRIS, NORMAN DYER (jt. author)
    See HARRIS, LOUISE DYER

HAUFF, WILHELM
    The Caravan. *B. Silverman*
    Dwarf Long-Nose. *Sendak*
    Fairy Tales. *Trnka*
    The Heart of Stone. *Levine*

HAUGAARD, ERIK CHRISTIAN
    Orphans of the Wind.   *M. Johnson*

HAVILAND, VIRGINIA
    Favorite Fairy Tales Told in Czechoslovakia.   *Hyman*
    Favorite Fairy Tales Told in England.   *Bettina*
    Favorite Fairy Tales Told in France.   *Duvoisin*
    Favorite Fairy Tales Told in Ireland.   *Marokvia*
    Favorite Fairy Tales Told in Italy.   *Ness*
    Favorite Fairy Tales Told in Norway.   *Weisgard*
    Favorite Fairy Tales Told in Poland.   *Hoffmann*
    Favorite Fairy Tales Told in Russia.   *Danska*
    Favorite Fairy Tales Told in Scotland.   *Adams*
    Favorite Fairy Tales Told in Spain.   *Cooney*
    Favorite Fairy Tales Told in Sweden.   *Solbert*

HAWES, JUDY
    Bees and Beelines.   *Aliki*
    Watch Honeybees with Me.   *Stone*

HAWTHORNE, NATHANIEL
    The Complete Greek Stories of Nathaniel Hawthorne.
        H. Jones
    The Golden Touch.   *Galdone*

HAYS, WILMA PITCHFORD
    Easter Fires.   *Burchard*
    The Fourth of July Raid.   *Burchard*
    Little Lone Coyote.   *Dennis*

HAZELTINE, ALICE ISABEL (comp.)
    Hero Tales from Many Lands.   *Laite*

HEADY, ELEANOR B.
    Jambo, Sungura.   *Frankenberg*

HEATHERS, ANNE
    A Handful of Surprises.   *Francés*
    The Thread Soldier.   *Francés*

HECK, BESSIE HOLLAND
    Cactus Kevin.   *Bjorklund*
    The Hopeful Years.   *Bjorklund*

HEILBRONER, JOAN
    The Happy Birthday Present.   *Chalmers*
    This Is the House Where Jack Lives.   *Aliki*

HENRY, JAN
    Tiger's Chance.   *Knight*

HENRY, MARGUERITE
    Black Gold.   *Dennis*
    Gaudenzia.   *Ward*
    Stormy, Misty's Foal.   *Dennis*
    White Stallion of Lipizza.   *Dennis*

HERRMANN, FRANK
    The Giant Alexander.   *Him*
    The Giant Alexander and the Circus.   *Him*

HEWETT, ANITA
    Dragon from the North.   *Fiammenghi*
    The Little White Hen.   *Stobbs*
    Mrs. Mopple's Washing Line.   *Broomfield*
    The Tale of the Turnip.   *Gill*

HICKS, CLIFFORD B.
    The Marvellous Inventions of Alvin Fernald.   *Geer*

HILL, KAY
    Glooscap and His Magic.   *Frankenberg*
    Badger the Mischief Maker.   *Hamberger*

HINE, AL
    A Letter to Anywhere.   *Alcorn*
    Money Round the World.   *Alcorn*
    Where in the World Do You Live?   *Alcorn*

HIRSCH, S. CARL
    The Globe for the Space Age.   *B. Silverman*
    This Is Automation.   *Ravielli*

THE HISTORY OF SIMPLE SIMON.   *Galdone*

HITOPADÉSA
    Once a Mouse . . .   *M. Brown*

HOBAN, RUSSELL
    Bedtime for Frances.   *G. M. Williams*
    Bread and Jam for Frances.   *L. Hoban*
    Herman the Loser.   *L. Hoban*
    Nothing To Do.   *L. Hoban*
    The Sorely Trying Day.   *L. Hoban*

HODGES, CYRIL WALTER
    Magna Carta.   *Hodges*
    The Namesake.   *Hodges*
    The Norman Conquest.   *Hodges*
    Shakespeare's Theatre.   *Hodges*

HODGES, ELIZABETH JAMISON
    Serendipity Tales.   *Corwin*
    The Three Princes of Serendip.   *Victor*

HODGES, MARGARET
    The Wave.   *Lent*
    What's for Lunch, Charlie?   *Aliki*

HOFF, SYD
    Danny and the Dinosaur.   *Hoff*
    Grizzwold.   *Hoff*
    Oliver.   *Hoff*
    Sammy the Seal.   *Hoff*

HOFFMANN, FELIX
    A Boy Went Out to Gather Pears.   *Hoffmann*

HOGE, DOROTHY
    The Black Heart of Indri.   *Domanska*

HOGNER, DOROTHY CHILDS
  Butterflies. *N. Hogner*
  Grasshoppers and Crickets. *N. Hogner*

HOGNER, NILS
  Molly the Black Mare. *Hogner*
  Tanny. *Hogner*

HOLBERG, RUTH LANGLAND
  What Happened to Virgilia. *Lonette*

HOLDING, JAMES
  The King's Contest. *Keeping*
  The Sky-Eater. *Keeping*

HOLL, ADELAIDE
  Mrs. McGarrity's Peppermint Sweater. *Graboff*
  The Rain Puddle. *Duvoisin*
  Sir Kevin of Devon. *Weisgard*

HOLLAND, JANICE
  Christopher Goes to the Castle. *Holland*
  You Never Can Tell. *Holland*

HOLLANDER, JOHN
  The Quest of the Gole. *Pollack*

HOLLING, HOLLING CLANCY and
  LUCILLE WEBSTER HOLLING
  Pagoo. *Holling*

HOLLING, LUCILLE WEBSTER (jt. author)
  See HOLLING, HOLLING CLANCY

HOLMAN, FELICE
  Elizabeth the Bird Watcher. *Blegvad*
  Elizabeth the Treasure Hunter. *Blegvad*
  Professor Diggins' Dragons. *Ohlsson*
  Victoria's Castle. *Hoban*

HOLMES, OLIVER WENDELL
  The Deacon's Masterpiece. *Galdone*

HOLT, ISABELLA
  The Adventures of Rinaldo. *Blegvad*

HOLT, MARGARET
  David McCheever's 29 Dogs. *Lorraine*

HOOVER, HELEN
  Animals at My Doorstep. *Shimin*

HOPE-SIMPSON, JACYNTH
  The Edge of the World. *P. Warner*
  The Hamish Hamilton Book of Myths and Legends. *Briggs*

HOPKINSON, FRANCIS
  The Battle of the Kegs. *Galdone*

HOUSTON, JAMES
  Eagle Mask. *Houston*
  Tikta'liktak. *Houston*

HOYT, EDWIN P. (ed.)
  American Steamboat Stories. *Grifalconi*

HOYT, HELEN
  Aloha, Susan. *Lonette*

HUDDY, DELIA
  How Edward Saved St. George. *D. Hall*

HUDSON, DEREK
  Arthur Rackham: His Life and Work. *Rackham*

HUGHES, PETER
  The Emperor's Oblong Pancake. *Rose*
  The King Who Loved Candy. *Rose*

HUGHES, RICHARD
  Gertrude's Child. *Schreiter*

HUGHES, SHIRLEY
  Lucy and Tom's Day. *Hughes*

HUGHES, TED
  How the Whale Became. *Adamson*
  How the Whale Became. *Schreiter*

HUNT, MABEL LEIGH
  Cupola House. *Unwin*

HUNTER, MOLLIE
  The Smartest Man in Ireland (English title,
    Patrick Kentigern Keenan). *Keeping*
  The Kelpie's Pearls. *Cellini*

HURD, EDITH THACHER
  Christmas Eve. *C. Hurd*
  Come and Have Fun. *C. Hurd*
  The Day the Sun Danced. *C. Hurd*
  Follow Tomás. *C. Hurd*
  Johnny Lion's Book. *C. Hurd*
  No Funny Business. *C. Hurd*

HUSTON, ANNE and JANE YOLEN
  Trust a City Kid. *Kocsis*

HUTCHINS, ROSS E.
  Lives of an Oak Tree. *Connolly*
  The Travels of Monarch X. *Connolly*

HYDE, LAWRENCE
  Under the Pirate Flag. *Mays*

INYART, GENE
  Jenny. *Grossman*

IPCAR, DAHLOV
  Bright Barnyard. *Ipcar*
  Brown Cow Farm. *Ipcar*
  Deep Sea Farm. *Ipcar*
  Horses of Long Ago. *Ipcar*

I Like Animals. *Ipcar*
I Love My Anteater with an A. *Ipcar*
Lobsterman. *Ipcar*
Ten Big Farms. *Ipcar*
The Wonderful Egg. *Ipcar*

IRESON, BARBARA
Seven Thieves and Seven Stars. *Rose*
The Story of the Pied Piper. *Rose*

IRESON, BARBARA (ed.)
The Barnes Book of Nursery Verse (English title,
    The Faber Book of Nursery Verse). *Adamson*
The Faber Book of Nursery Stories. *Hughes*

IRVING, WASHINGTON
The Legend of Sleepy Hollow. *Fisher*
Rip Van Winkle and The Legend of Sleepy Hollow.
    Levine

IRWIN, KEITH GORDON
The Romance of Chemistry. *Ravielli*

ISH-KISHOR, SULAMITH
A Boy of Old Prague. *Shahn*
The Carpet of Solomon. *Shulevitz*

ISHII, MOMOKO
The Dolls' Day for Yoshiko. *Funai*

IVES, JOSEPH CHRISTMAS
Steamboat up the Colorado. *Bjorklund*

JACKSON, JACQUELINE
The Taste of Spruce Gum. *Obligado*

JACKSON, R E.
The Witch of Castle Kerry. *P. Warner*

JACOBS, JOSEPH
The Three Wishes. *Galdone*
Tom Tit Tot. *Ness*

JACOBS, LELAND BLAIR
Just Around the Corner. *J. E. Johnson*

JAGENDORF, MORITZ ADOLF
The Ghost of Peg-Leg Peter. *Lipinsky*
Noodlehead Stories from Around the World. *S. Miller*

JANICE (pseud.)
(JANICE BRUSTLEIN)
Angélique. *Duvoisin*
Little Bear's Christmas. *Mariana*
Minette. *Alain*

JANSSON, TOVE
Moominland Midwinter. *Jansson*
Moominpappa at Sea. *Jansson*
Tales from Moominvalley. *Jansson*
Who Will Comfort Toffle? *Jansson*

JARMAN, THOMAS LECKIE
A Picture History of Italy. *Hutton*

JARRELL, RANDALL
The Animal Family. *Sendak*
The Bat-Poet. *Sendak*

JAUSS, ANNE MARIE
The River's Journey. *Jauss*

JENKINS, ALAN C.
White Horses and Black Bulls. *Ambrus*
Wild Swans at Suvanto. *Frankenberg*

JENSEN, VIRGINIA ALLEN
Lars-Peter's Birthday. *Olsen*

JEWETT, SARAH ORNE
A White Heron. *Cooney*

JOHNSON, ANNABEL and EDGAR JOHNSON
The Grizzly. *Riswold*

JOHNSON, CROCKETT (pseud.)
(DAVID JOHNSON LEISK)
Ellen's Lion. *Johnson*
Harold's ABC. *Johnson*
A Picture for Harold's Room. *Johnson*
We Wonder What Will Walter Be? When He Grows Up.
    Johnson

JOHNSON, EDGAR (jt. author)
See JOHNSON, ANNABEL

JOHNSON, ELIZABETH
The Little Knight. *Solbert*
No Magic, Thank You. *Price*
The Three-in-One Prince. *Solbert*

JOHNSON, EUGENE HARPER
Piankhy the Great. *Johnson*

JOHNSON, GERALD WHITE
America Moves Forward. *Fisher*
The Congress. *Fisher*
The Supreme Court. *Fisher*

JOHNSON, LOIS
Happy Birthdays 'Round the World. *Genia*
Happy New Year 'Round the World. *Wronker*

JOHNSON, SALLY PATRICK
The Harper Book of Princes. *Domanska*
The Princesses. *Montresor*

JOHNSTON, JOANNA
Great Gravity the Cat. *Werth*
Joan of Arc. *Mars*
Penguin's Way. *Weisgard*
The Story of Hannibal. *Mars*

JONES, ADRIENNE
    Wild Voyager. *Lois Darling*

JORDAN, HELENE JAMIESON
    Seeds by Wind and Water. *Hogner*

JORDAN, PHILIP DILLON
    The Burro Benedicto. *Powers*

JOSLIN, SESYLE
    Baby Elephant and the Secret Wishes. *Weisgard*
    Baby Elephant Goes to China. *Weisgard*
    Baby Elephant's Trunk. *Weisgard*
    Brave Baby Elephant. *Weisgard*
    Dear Dragon . . . *Haas*
    La Petite Famille. *Alcorn*
    Señor Baby Elephant, the Pirate. *Weisgard*
    Spaghetti for Breakfast. *Barry*
    There Is a Bull on My Balcony. *Barry*
    There Is a Dragon in My Bed. *Haas*
    What Do You Do, Dear? *Sendak*
    What Do You Say, Dear? *Sendak*

JOYCE, JAMES
    The Cat and the Devil. *Erdoes*
    The Cat and the Devil. *Rose*

JUSTER, NORTON
    Alberic the Wise. *Gnoli*

KAHL, VIRGINIA
    The Baron's Booty. *Kahl*
    The Perfect Pancake. *Kahl*

KALNAY, FRANCIS
    Chúcaro. *De Miskey*

KAMM, JOSEPHINE
    The Story of Fanny Burney. *Biro*

KAPP, PAUL
    Cock-A-Doodle-Doo! Cock-A-Doodle-Dandy! *Anita Lobel*

KASTNER, ERICH
    The Little Man. *Schreiter*
    When I Was a Boy
    (English title, When I Was a Little Boy). *Schreiter*

KAY, HELEN
    City Springtime. *Cooney*
    An Egg Is for Wishing. *Yaroslava*
    Henri's Hands for Pablo Picasso. *Ambrus*
    A Stocking for a Kitten. *Yaroslava*

KEATS, EZRA JACK
    Jennie's Hat. *Keats*
    John Henry. *Keats*
    The Snowy Day. *Keats*
    Whistle for Willy. *Keats*

KEATS, EZRA JACK (ed.)
    God Is in the Mountain. *Keats*

KEATS, JOHN
    The Naughty Boy. *Keats*

KEEPING, CHARLES
    Black Dolly. *Keeping*
    Shaun and the Cart-Horse. *Keeping*

KELLY, ERIC
    The Trumpeter of Krakow. *Domanska*

KENDALL, CAROL
    The Big Splash. *Obligado*
    The Gammage Cup. *Blegvad*
    The Whisper of Glocken. *Gobbato*

KENDALL, LACE (pseud.)
    See STOUTENBERG, ADRIAN

KEPES, JULIET
    Five Little Monkey Business. *Kepes*
    Frogs Merry. *Kepes*
    Lady Bird, Quickly. *Kepes*
    Two Little Birds and Three. *Kepes*

KESSLER, ETHEL (jt. author)
    See KESSLER, LEONARD P.

KESSLER, LEONARD P. and ETHEL KESSLER
    All Aboard the Train. *Kessler*

KETTELKAMP, LARRY
    Drums, Rattles, and Bells. *Kettelkamp*
    Singing Strings. *Kettelkamp*
    Spirals. *Kettelkamp*
    Spinning Tops. *Kettelkamp*

KIM, YONG-IK
    Blue in the Seed. *Marokvia*
    The Happy Days. *Marokvia*

KING, ALEXANDER
    Memoirs of a Certain Mouse. *Erdoes*

KINGMAN, LEE
    Peter's Pony. *Lasell*
    Private Eyes. *B. Silverman*
    The Saturday Gang. *B. Silverman*

KINGSLEY, CHARLES
    The Heroes. *Kiddell-Monroe*
    The Water Babies. *H. Jones*

KIPLING, RUDYARD
    The Jungle Books. *Shore*

KIRBY, DOUGLAS
    The Silver Wood. *J. Williams*

KIRN, ANN
Full of Wonder. *Kirn*
I Spy. *Kirn*
Leopard on a String. *Kirn*
Nine in a Line. *Kirn*
Two Pesos for Catalina. *Kirn*

KIRTLAND, G. B.
One Day in Ancient Rome. *Snyder*
One Day in Aztec Mexico. *Snyder*
One Day in Elizabethan England. *Snyder*

KJELGAARD, JAMES ARTHUR
Boomerang Hunter. *Mars*

KNIGHT, FRANK (ed.)
Stories of Famous Adventurers. *Nickless*

KNIGHT, HILARY
Where's Wallace? *Knight*

KOCH, DOROTHY
Let It Rain! *Stone*

KOENIG, RICHARD
The Seven Special Cats. *Bacon*

KOHN, BERNICE
One Day It Rained Cats and Dogs. *Aliki*

KONOPNICKA, MARIA
The Golden Seed. *Domanska*

KRASILOVSKY, PHYLLIS
Benny's Flag. *Mars*
The Cow Who Fell in the Canal. *Spier*

KRAUS, ROBERT
Amanda Remembers. *Kraus*
Ladybug, Ladybug. *Kraus*
The Littlest Rabbit. *Kraus*

KRAUSS, RUTH
Open House for Butterflies. *Sendak*

KRAVETZ, NATHAN
A Horse of Another Color. *Perl*
A Monkey's Tale. *Perl*

KRUMGOLD, JOSEPH
Onion John. *Shimin*

KRÜSS, JAMES
My Great-Grandfather and I. *Bartsch*
Pauline and the Prince in the Wind. *Bartsch*
3 x 3: Three by Three. *Rubin*

KRYLOV, IVAN ANDREEVICH
15 Fables of Krylov. *Pascal*

KUMIN, MAXINE W.
The Beach Before Breakfast. *Weisgard*

KUSAN, IVAN
Koko and the Ghosts. *Galdone*

KUSKIN, KARLA
The Bear Who Saw the Spring. *Kuskin*
In the Middle of the Trees. *Kuskin*
The Rose on My Cake. *Kuskin*
Square as a House. *Kuskin*
Which Horse Is William? *Kuskin*

KYLE, ELIZABETH, pseud.
(AGNES MARY DUNLOP)
Girl with a Destiny. *Mozley*
Girl with a Pen. *Mozley*

LA FONTAINE, JEAN DE
The Hare and the Tortoise. *Wildsmith*
The Lion and the Rat. *Wildsmith*
The North Wind and the Sun. *Wildsmith*
The Rich Man and the Shoemaker. *Wildsmith*

LABASTIDA, AURORA (jt. author)
See ETS, MARIE HALL

LADAS, ALEXIS
The Seal That Couldn't Swim. *Simont*

LADD, ELIZABETH
A Fox Named Rufus. *E. H. Johnson*

LAMB, CHARLES and MARY LAMB
Tales from Shakespeare. *Powers*

LAMB, LYNTON
Cats' Tales. *Lamb*

LAMB, MARY (jt. author)
See LAMB, CHARLES

LANCASTER, BRUCE
The American Revolution. *Ames*

LANG, ANDREW
The Adventures of Odysseus. *Kiddell-Monroe*
Fifty Favourite Fairy Tales. *Gill*
The Twelve Dancing Princesses. *Adams*

LANGSTAFF, JOHN
Ol' Dan Tucker. *J. Krush*
On Christmas Day in the Morning. *Groves-Raines*
Over in the Meadow. *Rojankovsky*
The Swapping Boy. *B. and J. Krush*

LANGTON, JANE
The Diamond in the Window. *Blegvad*

LANSDOWN, BRENDA
Galumph *Crichlow*

LARRICK, NANCY (ed.)
Piper, Pipe That Song Again!   *Oechsli*
Poetry for Holidays.   *Oechsli*

LARSON, JEAN RUSSELL
Palace in Bagdad.   *Yamaguchi*

LASELL, FEN H.
Fly Away, Goose.   *Lasell*

LASKOWSKI, JERZY
Master of the Royal Cats.   *Domanska*

LATHAM, JEAN LEE
This Dear-Bought Land.   *Landau*

LATHROP, DOROTHY PULIS
The Dog in the Tapestry Garden.   *Lathrop*
Follow the Brook.   *Lathrop*

LATTIMORE, ELEANOR FRANCES
The Bus Trip.   *Lattimore*
The Chinese Daughter.   *Lattimore*
Laurie and Company.   *Lattimore*
The Mexican Bird.   *Lattimore*
The Wonderful Glass House.   *Lattimore*

LAUBER, PATRICIA
Our Friend the Forest.   *Jauss*

LAUGHLIN, FLORENCE
The Little Leftover Witch.   *Greenwald*

LAVINE, SIGMUND A.
Wonders of Animal Architecture.   *Cosgrove*
Wonders of Animal Disguises.   *Cosgrove*
Wonders of the Beetle World.   *Cosgrove*

LAWSON, JOHN
You Better Come Home with Me.   *Spilka*

LE GRAND, pseud.
(LE GRAND HENDERSON)
How Baseball Began in Brooklyn.   *Le Grand*
How Space Rockets Began.   *Le Grand*

LE MARCHAND, JACQUES
The Adventures of Ulysses.   *François*

LEACH, MARIA (ed.)
The Luck Book.   *Werth*
Noodles, Nitwits and Numskulls.   *Werth*
The Rainbow Book of American Folk Tales and Legends.
Simont

LEAR, EDWARD
Lear Alphabet: ABC.   *Lear*
Le Hibou et la Poussiquette.   *Cooney*
Limericks by Lear.   *Ehlert*
The Owl and the Pussy Cat.   *Du Bois*
Two Laughable Lyrics.   *Galdone*
The Two Old Bachelors.   *Galdone*

LEEKLEY, THOMAS B.
The Riddle of the Black Knight.   *Troyer*
The World of Manabozho.   *Kimball*

LEISK, DAVID JOHNSON
See JOHNSON, CROCKETT, pseud.

LENSKI, LOIS
At Our House.   *Lenski*
Policeman Small.   *Lenski*
Shoo-Fly Girl.   *Lenski*

LENT, BLAIR
John Tabor's Ride.   *Lent*
Pistachio.   *Lent*

LESKOV, NICHOLAS
The Steel Flea.   *Domanska*

LEVY, MIMI C.
Corrie and the Yankee.   *Crichlow*

LEWIS, HILDA
Here Comes Harry.   *Stobbs*

LEWIS, JANET
Keiko's Bubble.   *Mizumura*

LEWIS, RICHARD (ed.)
In a Spring Garden.   *Keats*

LEWIS, RICHARD WILLIAM
A Summer Adventure.   *Lewis*

LEWITON, MINA
See SIMON, MINA LEWITON

LEXAU, JOAN M.
Benjie.   *Bolognese*
Josie's Christmas Secret.   *Bolognese*
Maria.   *Crichlow*
Millicent's Ghost.   *Shecter*

LIERS, EMIL E.
A Beaver's Story.   *Sherin*
A Black Bear's Story.   *Sherin*

LIFTON, BETTY JEAN
The Cock and the Ghost Cat.   *Akino*
The Dwarf Pine Tree.   *Akino*
Joji and the Amanojaku.   *Mitsui*
Joji and the Dragon.   *Mitsui*
Kap the Kappa.   *Mitsui*
The Rice-Cake Rabbit.   *Mitsui*

LIN, ADET
The Milky Way.   *Arno*

LINDE, GUNNEL
Chimney-Top Lane.   *Wikland*
The White Stone.   *Gobbato*

LINDGREN, ASTRID
    The Children of Noisy Village. *Wikland*
    Christmas in Noisy Village. *Wikland*
    Christmas in the Stable. *Wiberg*
    Happy Times in Noisy Village. *Wikland*
    Mischievous Meg. *Domanska*
    Pippi Goes on Board. *Glanzman*
    Pippi in the South Seas. *Glanzman*
    Pippi in the South Seas. *R. Kennedy*
    Springtime in Noisy Village. *Wikland*
    The Tomten. *Wiberg*
    The Tomten and the Fox. *Wiberg*

LINDQUIST, JENNIE DOROTHEA
    The Crystal Tree. *Chalmers*
    The Little Silver House. *G. M. Williams*

LINES, KATHLEEN
    Noah and the Ark. *H. Jones*

LINES, KATHLEEN (ed.)
    The Faber Storybook. *Howard*
    Nursery Stories (English title, Jack and the Beanstalk).
      H. Jones
    A Ring of Tales. *H. Jones*

LINES, KATHLEEN, and
    NORAH MARY MONTGOMERIE (eds.)
    Poems and Pictures. *Montgomerie*

LIONNI, LEO
    Inch by Inch. *Lionni*
    little blue and little yellow. *Lionni*
    Swimmy. *Lionni*
    Tico and the Golden Wings. *Lionni*

LIPKIND, WILLIAM
    Billy the Kid. *Nicolas*
    The Boy and the Forest. *Nicolas*
    Days to Remember. *Snyder*
    Four-Leaf Clover. *Nicolas*
    The Little Tiny Rooster. *Nicolas*
    The Magic Feather Duster. *Nicolas*
    Nubber Bear. *Duvoisin*
    Russet and the Two Reds. *Nicolas*
    Sleepyhead. *Nicolas*

LITTLE, JANE
    Spook. *Larsen*

LITTLE, JEAN
    Home from Far. *Lazare*

LITTLEFIELD. WILLIAM
    Seventh Son of a Seventh Son. *Berson*
    The Whiskers of Ho Ho. *Bobri*

LIVINGSTON, MYRA COHN
    Happy Birthday! *Blegvad*

    I'm Hiding. *Blegvad*
    I'm Waiting. *Blegvad*
    See What I Found. *Blegvad*
    Whispers. *Chwast*
    Wide Awake, and Other Poems. *Chwast*

LLOYD, NORRIS
    The Desperate Dragons. *Payne*

LOBDELL, HELEN
    The Fort in the Forest. *Bjorklund*

LOBEL, ANITA
    Sven's Bridge. *Lobel*
    Troll Music. *Lobel*

LOBEL, ARNOLD
    Giant John. *Lobel*
    A Holiday for Mister Muster. *Lobel*
    Martha the Movie Mouse. *Lobel*

LOCKE, ELSIE
    The Runaway Settlers. *Maitland*

LONGFELLOW, HENRY WADSWORTH
    Evangeline. *H. Simon*
    Paul Revere's Ride. *Galdone*
    The Skeleton in Armor. *P. Kennedy*
    The Song of Hiawatha. *Kiddell-Monroe*
    The Song of Hiawatha. *H. Simon*

LOVE, KATHERINE (comp.)
    A Little Laughter. *Lorraine*

LOVETT, MARGARET
    Sir Halmanac and the Crimson Star. *Adamson*

LOW, ELIZABETH
    Snug in the Snow. *Solbert*

LOW, JOSEPH
    Adam's Book of odd Creatures. *Low*
    Smiling Duke. *Low*

LOWE, MARGARET
    Tales of the Black and White Pig. *Russon*

LUBELL, CECIL
    Green Is for Growing. *Lubell*

LUBELL, CECIL and WINIFRED MILIUS LUBELL
    Rosalie: The Bird Market Turtle. *Lubell*

LUBELL, WINIFRED
    The Tall Grass Zoo. *Lubell*

LUBELL, WINIFRED MILIUS (jt. author)
    See LUBELL, CECIL

LUCKHARDT, MILDRED
Good King Wenceslas. *Laite*
The Story of Saint Nicolas. *Laite*

LUND, DORIS HEROLD
Attic of the Wind. *Forberg*

LYNCH, PATRICIA
Mona of the Isle. *Shillabeer*

MC ALPINE, HELEN and WILLIAM MC ALPINE
Japanese Tales and Legends. *Kiddell-Monroe*

MC ALPINE, WILLIAM (jt. author)
See McAlpine, Helen

MAC BETH, GEORGE
Noah's Journey. *Gordon*

MC CAIN, MURRAY
Books! *Alcorn*
Writing! *Alcorn*

MC CLOSKEY, ROBERT
Burt Dow: Deep Water Man. *McCloskey*
Time of Wonder. *McCloskey*

MC CLUNG, ROBERT MARSHALL
Buzztail. *McClung*
Ladybug. *McClung*
Possum. *McClung*
Spotted Salamander. *McClung*

MC CORD, DAVID
All Day Long. *Kane*
Take Sky. *Kane*

MC CREA, JAMES and RUTH MC CREA
The Birds. *McCrea*
The King's Procession. *McCrea*
The Magic Tree. *McCrea*
The Story of Olaf. *McCrea*

MC CREA, RUTH (jt. author)
See McCrea, James

MACDONALD, GEORGE
At the Back of the North Wind. *Mozley*
The Light Princess. *Du Bois*
The Princess and the Goblin. *Paton*

MC DONALD, GERALD (comp.)
A Way of Knowing. *C. and J. Ross*

MC GAW, JESSIE BREWER
Little Elk Hunts Big Buffalo. *McGaw*
Painted Pony Runs Away. *McGaw*

MC GINLEY, PHYLLIS
Lucy McLockett. *Stone*

Mince Pie and Mistletoe. *Berson*
Wonderful Time. *Alcorn*
The Year Without a Santa Claus. *Werth*

MC GOVERN, ANN
Zoo, Where Are You? *Keats*
Little Wolf. *Langner*

MC KAY, MARGARET
Dolphin. *Fortnum*

MC KAY, RUTH
They Sang a New Song. *Laite*

MC KELLAR, WILLIAM
A Dog Like No Other. *Unwin*
Two for the Fair. *Unwin*
Wee Joseph. *Keats*

MACKEN, WALTER
Island of the Great Yellow Ox. *Keeping*

MAC KENZIE, COMPTON
Little Cat Lost. *Boswell*

MC KOWN, ROBIN
Rakoto and the Drongo Bird. *Quackenbush*

MC LEAN, MOLLIE and ANN WISEMAN
Adventures of the Greek Heroes. *Mars*

MC LEOD, EMILIE WARREN
Clancy's Witch. *Weil*
One Snail and Me. *Lorraine*

MAC MANUS, SEUMAS
Hibernian Nights. *P. Kennedy*

MC NEER, MAY
The American Indian Story. *Ward*
America's Abraham Lincoln. *Ward*
America's Mark Twain. *Ward*
Armed with Courage. *Ward*
The Canadian Story. *Ward*
Give Me Freedom. *Ward*
My Friend Mac. *Ward*

MC NEILL, JAMES
The Double Knights. *Dimson*
The Sunken City. *Dimson*

MC NEILL, JANET
The Giant's Birthday. *Erhard*
The Mouse and the Mirage. *Erhard*

MC PHERSON, MARGARET
The Rough Road. *D. Hall*
The Shinty Boys. *Hughes*

MAITLAND, ANTONY
    James and the Roman Silver. *Maitland*
    The Secret of the Shed. *Maitland*

MAIZEL, CLARICE
    Son of Condor. *H. Simon*

MALCOLMSON, ANNE
    A Taste of Chaucer. *Arno*
    Miracle Plays. *Baynes*

MALKUS, ALIDA SIMS
    Meadows in the Sea. *Cosgrove*

MANN, PEGGY
    The Street of the Flower Boxes. *Burchard*

MANNING, ROSEMARY JOY
    Arripay. *Ambrus*

MANNING-SANDERS, RUTH (comp.)
    A Book of Dragons. *Jacques*
    A Book of Dwarfs. *Jacques*
    A Book of Giants. *Jacques*
    A Book of Witches. *Jacques*
    A Bundle of Ballads. *Stobbs*
    Damien and the Dragon. *Papas*
    The Hamish Hamilton Book of Magical Beasts. *Briggs*
    Peter and the Piskies. *Briggs*
    Red Indian Folk and Fairy Tales. *Hodges*
    The Red King and the Witch. *Ambrus*

MANNIX, DANIEL
    The Outcasts. *Shortall*

MARIANA, pseud.
    (MARIAN CURTIS FOSTER)
    The Journey of Bangwell Putt. *Mariana*
    Miss Flora McFlimsey's Valentine. *Mariana*

MARINO, DOROTHY
    Buzzy Bear and the Rainbow. *Marino*
    Buzzy Bear Goes South. *Marino*
    Buzzy Bear in the Garden. *Marino*

MAROKVIA, ARTUR
    A French School for Paul. *Marokvia*
    Jannot. *Marokvia*
    Nanette, a French Goat. *Marokvia*

MARSHALL, ARCHIBALD
    The Dragon. *Ardizzone*

MARTIN, JOSEPH PLUMB
    Yankee Doodle Boy. *Mays*

MARTIN, PATRICIA MILES
    The Greedy One. *Mizumura*
    The Little Brown Hen. *E. H. Johnson*
    Little Two and the Peach Tree. *Victor*

The Pointed Brush. *Duvoisin*
The Rice Bowl Pet. *Keats*
Rolling the Cheese. *Raible*
Sing, Sailor, Sing. *Booth*
Suzu and the Bride Doll. *Mizumura*

MASON, FRANCIS VAN WYCK
    The Battle for Quebec. *Mays*

MASON, GEORGE FREDERICK
    Animal Baggage. *Mason*
    Animal Habits. *Mason*
    The Deer Family. *Mason*
    The Wildlife of North America. *Mason*
    The Wildlife of South America. *Mason*

MASSEY, JEANNE
    The Littlest Witch. *Adams*

MASSIE, DIANE REDFIELD
    A Birthday for Bird. *Massie*
    A Turtle and a Loon. *Massie*

MATHIESEN, EGON
    A Jungle in the Wheat Field. *Mathiesen*
    Oswald the Monkey. *Mathiesen*

MATSUNO, MASAKO
    Chie and the Sports Day. *Mizumura*
    A Pair of Red Clogs. *Mizumura*
    Taro and the Tōfu. *Mizumura*

MAXEY, DALE
    Fidgit. *Maxey*
    Seeing London. *Maxey*

MAY, HELEN
    The Swan, the Story of Anna Pavlova. *Fortnum*

MAY, JULIAN
    They Turned to Stone. *Zallinger*

MAYNE, WILLIAM
    The Big Wheel and the Little Wheel. *Duchesne*
    The Blue Boat. *Spence*
    A Day Without Wind. *Gill*
    The Glass Ball. *Duchesne*
    The Grass Rope. *Lamb*
    No More School. *P. Warner*
    Pig in the Middle. *Russon*
    Rooftops. *Russon*
    Whistling Rufus. *Briggs*

MAYNE, WILLIAM (jt. editor)
    See FARJEON, ELEANOR

MEADER, STEPHEN WARREN
    The Commodore's Cup. *Sibley*
    Snow on Blueberry Mountain. *Sibley*
    The Voyage of the Javelin. *Cosgrave*

MEADOWCROFT, ENID LA MONTE
Land of the Free.   *Ames*

MEEKS, ESTHER MC BAIN
Jeff and Mr. James' Pond.   *Galdone*

MEHDEVI, ANNE SINCLAIR
Persian Folk and Fairy Tales.   *P. Kennedy*

MEHTA, RAMA
Ramu: A Story of India.   *Mars*

MEIGS, CORNELIA
Wild Geese Flying.   *Geer*

MELVILLE, HERMAN
Moby Dick.   *Shore*

MENDOZA, GEORGE (jt. author)
See SANFORD, WENDY

MEREDITH, NICOLETE
King of the Kerry Fair.   *Hogrogian*

MEREDITH, ROBERT K. and
EDRIC BROOKS SMITH (eds.)
The Coming of the Pilgrims.   *Fisher*
Riding with Coronado.   *Fisher*

MERRIAM, EVE
Catch a Little Rhyme.   *Gobbato*
A Gaggle of Geese.   *Galdone*
There Is No Rhyme for Silver.   *Schindelman*

MERRILL, JEAN
Emily Emerson's Moon.   *Solbert*
High, Wide, and Handsome and Their Three Tall Tales.
  Solbert
The Pushcart War.   *Solbert*
Shan's Luck Knife.   *Solbert*
The Superlative Horse.   *Solbert*

MIAN, MARY
The Nip and Tuck War.   *B. and J. Krush*

MIERS, EARL SCHENK
Pirate Chase.   *Burchard*

MILES, BETTY
Having a Friend.   *Blegvad*
A Day of Summer.   *Charlip*
A Day of Winter.   *Charlip*

MILES, MISKA
Fox and Fire.   *Schoenherr*
Kickapoo.   *Dennis*
Mississippi Possum.   *Schoenherr*
Teacher's Pet.   *Lasell*

MILHOUS, KATHERINE
Through These Arches.   *Milhous*

MILLER, ALBERT
See MILLS, ALAN, pseud.

MILLER, EDNA ANITA
Mousekin's Christmas Eve.   *Miller*
Mousekin's Golden House.   *Miller*

MILLER, EUGENIA
The Golden Spur.   *Fisher*

MILLER, HELEN MARKLEY
Ski the Mountain.   *Grossman*

MILLER, LISA
Sound.   *De Paola*

MILLER, MARY BRITTON
All Aboard.   *Sokol*
Give a Guess.   *Kepes*

MILLER, WARREN
The Goings-On at Little Wishful.   *Sorel*
King Carlo of Capri.   *Sorel*
Pablo Paints a Picture.   *Sorel*

MILLS, ALAN, pseud.
(ALBERT MILLER)
The Hungry Goat.   *Graboff*

MILLS, ALAN, pseud., and ROSE BONNE
I Know an Old Lady.   *Graboff*

MILNE, ALAN ALEXANDER
Once on a Time.   *Perl*
The Pooh Story Book.   *E. H. Shepard*
Prince Rabbit and The Princess Who Could Not Laugh.
  M. E. Shepard
The World of Christopher Robin.   *E. H. Shepard*
The World of Pooh.   *E. H. Shepard*

MINARIK, ELSE HOLMLUND
Cat and Dog.   *Siebel*
Father Bear Comes Home.   *Sendak*
Little Bear.   *Sendak*
Little Bear's Friend.   *Sendak*
Little Bear's Visit.   *Sendak*

MINCIELI, ROSE LAURA
Old Neapolitan Fairy Tales.   *Montresor*
Pulcinella.   *Low*
Tales Wise and Merry.   *Werth*

MIRSKY, JEANNETTE
Balboa: Discoverer of the Pacific.   *Guggenheim*

MIRSKY, REBA PAEFF
Nomusa and the New Magic.   *Mars*

MIZUMURA, KAZUE
I See the Winds.   *Mizumura*

MOE, JØRGEN ENGEBRETSEN (jt. author)
See ASBJORNSEN, PETER CHRISTEN

MOLLOY, ANNE
A Proper Place for Chip. *Maitland*
Shaun and the Boat. *Cooney*

MONCKTON, ELLA
The Boy and the Mountain. *Webb*

MONTGOMERIE, NORAH MARY (ed.)
This Little Pig Went to Market. *Gill*
Twenty-Five Fables. *Montgomerie*

MONTGOMERIE, NORAH MARY (jt. editor)
See LINES, KATHLEEN

MONTGOMERIE, NORAH MARY and
WILLIAM MONTGOMERIE (eds.)
A Book of Scottish Nursery Rhymes.
  Montgomerie and Ritchie

MONTGOMERIE, WILLIAM (jt. editor)
See MONTGOMERIE, NORAH MARY

MONTGOMERY, RUTHERFORD G.
Whitetail. *Nonnast*

MONTRESOR, BENI
Cinderella. *Montresor*
House of Flowers, House of Stars. *Montresor*
The Witches of Venice. *Montresor*

MONTROSE, ANNE
The Winter Flower, and Other Fairy Stories. *Vasiliu*

MOORE, LILIAN
Papa Albert. *Fiammenghi*
The Snake That Went to School. *Stevens*

MOREY, WALT
Gentle Ben. *Schoenherr*

MORGAN, BARBARA E.
Journey for Tobiijab. *Mars*

MORRIS, DESMOND
Apes and Monkeys. *Driscoll*
The Big Cats. *Driscoll*

MORRIS, JAMES
The Upstairs Donkey. *Baynes*

MORRISON, LILLIAN (comp.)
Sprints and Distances. *C. and J. Ross*

MORROW, BETTY and MILLICENT SELSAM
See Up the Mountain. *Lubell*

MORROW, ELIZABETH
A Pint of Judgment. *Berson*

MORSE, SAMUEL FRENCH
All in a Suitcase. *Cooney*

MOSS, ELAINE
The Story of Saul the King. *Roberts*

MOTHER GOOSE
Brian Wildsmith's Mother Goose. *Wildsmith*
In a Pumpkin Shell. *Anglund*
Mother Goose and Nursery Rhymes. *Reed*
Mother Goose in French. *Cooney*
Mother Goose in Hieroglyphics
Mother Goose Treasury. *Briggs*
Nursery Rhymes. *Watson*
Old Mother Hubbard and Her Dog. *Galdone*
A Pocket Full of Posies. *De Angeli*
Tom, Tom, the Piper's Son. *Galdone*

MOWAT, FARLEY
Owls in the Family. *Frankenberg*

MOZLEY, CHARLES
The First Book of Tales of Ancient Egypt. *Mozley*

MUEHL, LOIS BAKER
My Name Is - - -. *Watson*

MUKU, HATOJU (jt. author)
See YASHIMA, TARO

MÜLLER-GUGGENBÜHL, FRITZ
Swiss-Alpine Folk Tales. *Kiddell-Monroe*

MUNARI, BRUNO
Animals for Sale. *Munari*
The Birthday Present. *Munari*
Bruno Munari's ABC. *Munari*
Bruno Munari's Zoo. *Munari*
The Elephant's Wish. *Munari*
Jimmy Has Lost His Cap. *Munari*
Tic, Tac, and Toc. *Munari*
Who's There? Open the Door. *Munari*

MURPHY, ROBERT
The Golden Eagle. *Schoenherr*
Wild Geese Calling. *Kaufmann*

MYRICK, MILDRED
The Secret Three. *Arnold Lobel*

NASH, MARY
Mrs. Coverlet's Detectives. *Price*
Mrs. Coverlet's Magicians. *Price*
While Mrs. Coverlet Was Away. *Price*

NASH, OGDEN
The Adventures of Isabel. *Lorraine*
The New Nutcracker Suite. *Chermayeff*

NATHAN, ROBERT
The Snowflake and the Starfish. *Weisgard*

NESBIT, E., pseud.
(EDITH NESBIT BLAND)
The Bastables. *Einzig*
The Enchanted Castle. *Fraser*

NESS, EVALINE
Exactly Alike. *Ness*
A Gift for Sula Sula. *Ness*
Josefina February. *Ness*
Pavo and the Princess. *Ness*
Sam, Bangs and Moonshine. *Ness*

NEVILLE, EMILY CHENEY
It's Like This, Cat. *E. Weiss*
The Seventeenth-Street Gang. *McCully*
Woody and Me. *Solbert*

NEWELL, VIRGINIA
His Own Good Daughter. *Bock*

NEWMAN, ROBERT
The Japanese. *Funai*

NEWTON, DOUGLAS
Seafarers of the Pacific. *Mars*

NIC LEODHAS, SORCHE, pseud.
(LE CLAIRE ALGER)
All in the Morning Early. *Ness*
Always Room for One More. *Hogrogian*
Gaelic Ghosts. *Hogrogian*
Ghosts Go Haunting. *Hogrogian*
Thistle and Thyme. *Ness*

NICKLESS, WILL
Owlglass. *Nickless*

NICKLESS, WILL (comp.)
Book of Fables. *Nickless*

NÖDSET, JOAN L.
Go Away, Dog. *Bonsall*
Who Took the Farmer's Hat? *Siebel*

NORDSTROM, URSULA
The Secret Language. *Chalmers*

NORTH, STERLING
Hurry, Spring. *Burger*
Little Rascal. *Burger*
Rascal. *Schoenherr*

NORTON, ALICE MARY
See NORTON, ANDRÉ, pseud.

NORTON, ANDRÉ
Steel Magic. *Jacques*

NORTON, MARY
Bed-Knob and Broomstick. *Blegvad*
The Borrowers Afloat. *B. and J. Krush*

NUSSBAUMER, MARES (jt. author)
See NUSSBAUMER, PAUL

NUSSBAUMER, PAUL and MARES NUSSBAUMER
Away in a Manger. *Nussbaumer*

OCHSENSCHLAGER, EDWARD
The Egyptians in the Middle Kingdom. *S. Miller*

O'FAOLAIN, EILEEN
Children of the Salmon. *Hyman*

OGBURN, CHARLTON, JR.
Big Caesar. *B. and J. Krush*
The Bridge. *Ness*

OLDS, ELIZABETH
Deep Treasure. *Olds*
Little Una. *Olds*
Plop, Plop, Ploppie. *Olds*

OLIVER, JANE
Watch for the Morning. *Ambrus*

OLSEN, AILEEN
Bernadine and the Water Bucket. *Langner*

OLSEN, IB SPANG
The Boy in the Moon. *Olsen*
The Marsh Crone's Brew. *Olsen*

O'NEILL, MARY
Hailstones and Halibut Bones. *Weisgard*
What Is That Sound! *Ehlert*
The White Palace. *Hogrogian*

OPIE, IONA (comp.)
A Family Book of Nursery Rhymes. *Baynes*

ORGEL, DORIS
Cindy's Snowdrops. *Forberg*

OSBORNE, MAURICE M., JR.
Ondine. *Ness*
Rudi and the Mayor of Naples. *Low*

OTERDAHL, JEANNA
April Adventure. *Nordenskjöld*
Island Summer. *Nordenskjöld*
Tina and the Latchkey Child. *Nordenskjöld*

OTT, JOHN and PETE COLEY
Peter Pumpkin. *Chermayeff*

OTTO, MARGARET G.
The Little Old Train. *Blegvad*

PALAZZO, TONY
  Bianca and the New World.   *Palazzo*
  Jan and the Reindeer.   *Palazzo*

PALMER, HELEN MARION
  A Fish Out of Water.   *Eastman*

PALMER, ROBIN
  Dragons, Unicorns and Other Magical Beasts.   *Bolognese*

PANETTA, GEORGE
  The Sea Beach Express.   *McCully*

PAPAS, THEODORE
  The Story of Mr. Nero.   *Papas*

PARADIS, MARJORIE
  Mr. De Luca's Horse.   *J. G. Brown*

PARISH, PEGGY
  Amelia Bedelia.   *Siebel*
  Amelia Bedelia and the Surprise Shower.   *Siebel*

PARKER, EDGAR
  The Dream of the Dormouse.   *Parker*
  The Duke of Sycamore.   *Parker*
  The Enchantress.   *Parker*
  The Flower of the Realm.   *Parker*
  The Question of the Dragon.   *Parker*
  Stuff and Nonsense.   *Parker*

PARKER, ELINOR MILNOR (comp.)
  100 More Story Poems.   *Spier*
  The Singing and the Gold.   *Leighton*

PARKER, RICHARD
  The Boy Who Wasn't Lonely.   *Spanfeller*
  The House That Guilda Drew.   *Funai*
  M for Mischief.   *Geer*

PARKINSON, ETHELYN
  Good Old Archibald.   *Stevens*

PARRISH, PEGGY
  Key to the Treasure.   *Frame*

PAYNE, JOAN BALFOUR
  Charlie from Yonder.   *Payne*
  General Billycock's Pigs.   *Payne*
  The Leprechaun of Bayou Luce.   *Payne*
  Pangur Ban.   *Payne*

PEARCE, PHILIPPA
  A Dog So Small.   *Maitland*
  Mrs. Cockle's Cat.   *Maitland*
  Tom's Midnight Garden.   *Einzig*

PEARE, CATHERINE OWENS
  William Penn.   *Pitz*

PEDERSEN, ELSA
  Fisherman's Choice.   *A. Smith*

PEET, BILL
  Chester the Worldly Pig.   *Peet*
  Farewell to Shady Grove.   *Peet*
  Hubert's Hair-Raising Adventure.   *Peet*
  Kermit the Hermit.   *Peet*
  Randy's Dandy Lions.   *Peet*
  Smokey.   *Peet*

PERRAULT, CHARLES
  Puss in Boots.   *Fischer*

PETERSHAM, MAUD FULLER
  The Shepherd Psalm.   *Petersham*

PETERSON, BARBARA and RUSSELL PETERSON
  Whitefoot Mouse.   *R. F. Peterson*

PETERSON, HAROLD LESLIE
  Forts in America.   *Feaser*
  A History of Firearms.   *Feaser*
  A History of Knives.   *Feaser*

PETERSON, RUSSELL (jt. author)
  See PETERSON, BARBARA

PETRIDES, HEIDRUN
  Hans and Peter.   *Petrides*

PEYTON, K. M.
  The Plan for Birdsmarsh.   *Ambrus*

PHELAN, MARY KAY
  The Circus.   *Alcorn*

PIATTI, CELESTINO
  Celestino Piatti's Animal ABC.   *Piatti*
  The Happy Owls.   *Piatti*

PICARD, BARBARA LEONIE
  German Hero-Sagas and Folk-Tales.   *Kiddell-Monroe*
  The Iliad of Homer.   *Kiddell-Monroe*
  Lost John.   *Keeping*
  The Young Pretenders.   *Ambrus*

PILKINGTON, FRANCIS MEREDITH
  The Three Sorrowful Tales of Erin.   *Ambrus*

PIPER, ROBERTA
  Little Red.   *Victor*

PLOTZ, HELEN (comp.)
  The Earth Is the Lord's.   *Leighton*
  Untune the Sky.   *Leighton*

POE, EDGAR ALLAN
  Poems of Edgar Allan Poe.   *Raskin*
  The Purloined Letter, and The Murders in the Rue Morgue.
    Schreiter

POLITI, LEO
    The Butterflies Come. *Politi*
    Lito and the Clown. *Politi*
    Moy Moy. *Politi*
    Piccolo's Prank. *Politi*
    Rosa. *Politi*
    Saint Francis and the Animals. *Politi*

POLK, EMILY
    Delhi — Old and New. *E. Weiss*

POLLAND, MADELEINE
    Beorn the Proud. *Stobbs*
    Queen Without a Crown. *Danska*
    The Queen's Blessing. *Fraser*
    The Town Across the Water. *Nesbitt*
    The Town Across the Water. *Wildsmith*
    The White Twilight. *Cober*
    The White Twilight. *Stobbs*

POPE, ELIZABETH MARIE
    The Sherwood Ring. *Ness*

PORTAL, COLETTE
    The Life of a Queen. *Portal*

POSTON, ELIZABETH
    Children's Song Book. *Einzig*

POTTER, BEATRIX
    Letters to Children. *Potter*

POTTER, CHARLES FRANCIS (comp.)
    More Tongue Tanglers and a Rigamarole. *Wiesner*
    Tongue Tanglers. *Wiesner*

POWERS, RICHARD M.
    The Cave Dwellers in the Old Stone Age. *Powers*

PREMPEH, ALBERT KOFE (jt. author)
    See COURLANDER, HAROLD

PRICE, CHRISTINE
    Made in the Middle Ages. *C. Price*
    Made in the Renaissance. *C. Price*
    The Valiant Chattee-Maker. *C. Price*

PRICE, HILDA CUMMINGS
    The Song of Roland. *C. Price*

PRIDHAM, RADOST
    A Gift from the Heart. *Baynes*

PRIETO, MARIANA
    A Kite for Carlos. *Albion*
    The Wise Rooster. *Albion*

PRIOLO, PAULINE
    Bravo, Marco. *B. F. Peterson*
    Piccolina and the Easter Bells. *Fegiz*

PURDY, SUSAN
    If You Have a Yellow Lion. *Purdy*
    My Little Cabbage. *Purdy*

QUIGLEY, LILLIAN
    The Blind Man and the Elephant. *Holland*

RAND, ANN
    Little One. *Rand*
    Sparkle and Spin. *Rand*
    Umbrellas, Hats and Wheels. *Snyder*

RASKIN, ELLEN
    Nothing Ever Happens on My Block. *Raskin*

RAVIELLI, ANTHONY
    An Adventure in Geometry. *Ravielli*
    The World Is Round. *Ravielli*

REES, ENNIS
    Fables from Aesop. *Grandville*
    Pun Fun. *Q. Blake*
    Riddles, Riddles Everywhere. *Q. Blake*
    The Song of Paul Bunyan & Tony Beaver. *Osborn*

REEVES, JAMES
    Exploits of Don Quixote. *Ardizzone*
    Prefabulous Animiles. *Ardizzone*
    Ragged Robin. *Paton*
    The Story of Jackie Thimble. *Ardizzone*
    The Strange Light. *Kocsis*
    The Strange Light. *Lamb*
    Three Tall Tales. *Ardizzone*
    Titus in Trouble. *Ardizzone*

REGGIANI, RENÉE
    Five Children and a Dog. *Tomes*

REID, ALASTAIR
    Allth. *Lorraine*
    Fairwater. *Lorraine*
    Ounce, Dice, Trice. *Shahn*

RENAULT, MARY
    The Lion in the Gateway. *Hodges*

RESNICK, SEYMOUR
    Selections from Spanish Poetry. *Jauss*
    Spanish-American Poetry. *Jauss*

RESSNER, PHIL
    August Explains. *Bonsall*
    Dudley Pippin. *Arnold Lobell*

REY, HANS AUGUSTO
    Curious George Gets a Medal. *Rey*
    Curious George Learns the Alphabet. *Rey*

REY, MARGARET
  Curious George Flies a Kite.   *Rey*
  Curious George Goes to the Hospital.   *Rey*

REYNOLDS, MARJORIE
  A Horse Called Mystery.   *Dennis*

RICE, INEZ
  A Long, Long Time.   *Quackenbush*
  The March Wind.   *Bobri*

RICH, ELAINE SOMMERS
  Hannah Elizabeth.   *P. Kennedy*

RICHTER, CONRAD
  The Light in the Forest.   *Chappell*

RIEU, EMILE VICTOR
  The Flattered Flying Fish.   *E. H. Shepard*

RINKOFF, BARBARA
  A Map Is a Picture.   *Galster*

RIPPER, CHARLES L.
  Foxes and Wolves.   *Ripper*
  Ground Birds.   *Ripper*
  Swallows.   *Ripper*
  The Weasel Family.   *Ripper*

RITCHIE, BARBARA
  Ramon Makes a Trade.   *Thollander*
  To Catch a Mongoose.   *Thollander*

RITCHIE, JEAN
  Apple Seeds and Soda Straws.   *Bolognese*

ROBBINS, RUTH
  Baboushka and the Three Kings.   *Sidjakov*
  The Emperor and the Drummer Boy.   *Sidjakov*
  Harlequin and Mother Goose.   *Sidjakov*

ROBERTSON, KEITH
  Henry Reed, Inc.   *McCloskey*
  Henry Reed's Baby-Sitting Service.   *McCloskey*
  Henry Reed's Journey.   *McCloskey*
  If Wishes Were Horses.   *P. Kennedy*

ROBINSON, BARBARA
  Across from Indian Shore.   *Ness*

ROCCA, GUIDO
  Gaetano the Pheasant.   *Cingoli and Carloni*

ROLAND, BETTY
  The Forbidden Bridge.   *Spence*

ROSE, ELIZABETH
  The Big River.   *Rose*
  How St. Francis Tamed the Wolf.   *Rose*
  Old Winkle and the Sea Gulls.   *Rose*

St. George and the Fiery Dragon.   *Rose*
  Wuffles Goes to Town.   *Rose*

ROSEN, SIDNEY
  Doctor Paracelsus.   *Busoni*
  The Harmonious World of Johann Kepler.   *Busoni*

ROSENBAUM, ROBERT A. (ed.)
  The Best Book of True Sea Stories.   *Komoda*

ROSS, EULALIE STEINMETZ (comp.)
  The Blue Rose.   *Arno*
  The Buried Treasure.   *Cellini*
  The Lost Half-Hour.   *Arno*

ROUNDS, GLEN
  Beaver Business.   *Rounds*
  The Snake Tree.   *Rounds*
  Whitey and the Wild Horse.   *Rounds*
  Wild Orphan.   *Rounds*
  Wildlife at Your Doorstep.   *Rounds*

RUGOFF, MILTON
  Hurly Burly and the Knights.   *Luzzati*

RUMSEY, MARIAN
  Devil's Doorstep.   *Mars*

RUSSELL, FRANKLIN
  The Frightened Hare.   *Sweney*
  Hawk in the Sky.   *Sweney*

RUSSELL, SOLVEIG PAULSON
  Lines and Shapes.   *Spilka*

SAMACHSON, DOROTHY and JOSEPH SAMACHSON
  Rome.   *E. Weiss*

SAMACHSON, JOSEPH (jt. author)
  See SAMACHSON, DOROTHY

SAMSTAG, NICHOLAS
  Kay-Kay Comes Home.   *Shahn*

SANCHEZ-SILVA, JOSÉ MARIA
  The Boy and the Whale.   *Gill*

SANDBERG, INGER
  Little Anna and the Magic Hat.   *Sandberg*
  Little Anna's Mamma Has a Birthday.   *Sandberg*
  What Little Anna Saw.   *Sandberg*

SANDERLIN, GEORGE
  Eastward to India.   *Cober*
  First Around the World.   *Cober*

SANFORD, WENDY and GEORGE MENDOZA
  The Puma and the Pearl.   *Forberg*

SANGER, MARJORIE BARTLETT
  Cypress Country.   *C. Price*
  Mangrove Island.   *R. F. Peterson*

SARGENT, ROBERT EDWARD
 The Alligator's Problem. *Sargent*
 The Restless Rabbit. *Sargent*
 A Trick on a Lion. *Sargent*

SASEK, MIROSLAV
 This Is Edinburgh. *Sasek*
 This Is Greece. *Sasek*
 This Is Hong Kong. *Sasek*
 This Is Ireland. *Sasek*
 This Is Israel. *Sasek*
 This Is London. *Sasek*
 This Is Munich. *Sasek*
 This Is New York. *Sasek*
 This Is Paris. *Sasek*
 This Is Rome. *Sasek*
 This Is San Francisco. *Sasek*

SAVERY, CONSTANCE
 Magic in My Shoes. *C. Price*
 The Reb and the Redcoats. *Bock*

SAVIOZZI, ADRIANA
 Somebody Saw . . . *Saviozzi*

SAWYER, RUTH
 Daddles. *Frankenberg*
 Joy to the World. *Hyman*
 Roller Skates. *Hughes*
 The Year of the Christmas Dragon. *Troy*

SAXE, JOHN GODFREY
 The Blind Men and the Elephant. *Galdone*

SCARRY, RICHARD MC CLURE
 Richard Scarry's Best Word Book Ever. *Scarry*
 Richard Scarry's Busy, Busy World. *Scarry*

SCHAAF, PAUL
 The Crane with One Leg. *Wilkon*

SCHACKBURG, RICHARD
 Yankee Doodle. *Emberley*

SCHEELE, WILLIAM EARL
 The Earliest Americans. *Scheele*
 The Mound Builders. *Scheele*

SCHEER, JULIAN
 Rain Makes Applesauce. *Bileck*

SCHICK, ELEANOR
 I'm Going to the Ocean. *Schick*
 The Little School at Cottonwood Corners. *Schick*
 A Surprise in the Forest. *Schick*

SCHILLER, BARBARA
 The Kitchen Knight. *Hogrogian*

SCHLEIN, MIRIAM
 Amazing Mr. Pelgrew. *H. Weiss*
 The Big Cheese. *Low*
 The Raggle-Taggle Fellow. *H. Weiss*
 The Snake in the Carpool. *Bodecker*
 Snow Time. *Lasker*
 The Sun, the Wind, the Sea and the Rain. *Lasker*

SCHMIDT, THUSNELDA (jt. author)
 See CATHON, LAURA E.

SCHROEDER, MARY
 My Horse Says. *P. Kennedy*

SCHWARTZ, EVGENY
 A Tale of Stolen Time. *Hogrogian*

SCHWEITZER, BYRD BAYLOR
 Amigo. *G. M. Williams*
 One Small Blue Bead. *Shimin*

SCOTT, ANN HERBERT
 Big Cowboy Western. *Lewis*

SELDEN, GEORGE, pseud.
 (GEORGE SELDEN THOMPSON)
 The Cricket in Times Square. *G. M. Williams*
 Oscar Lobster's Fair Exchange. *Lippman*
 Sparrow Socks. *Lippman*

SELSAM, MILLICENT
 Animals as Parents. *Kaufmann*
 Birth of an Island. *Lubell*
 The Courtship of Animals. *Kaufmann*
 Greg's Microscope. *Arnold Lobel*
 How Animals Live Together. *Elgin*
 How To Be a Nature Detective. *Keats*
 The Language of Animals. *Elgin*
 Plenty of Fish. *Blegvad*
 See Along the Shore. *Weisgard*
 See Through the Jungle. *Lubell*
 Terry and the Caterpillars. *Arnold Lobel*

SELSAM, MILLICENT (jt. author)
 See MORROW, BETTY

SENDAK, JACK
 Circus Girl. *Sendak*
 The Second Witch. *Shulevitz*

SENDAK, MAURICE
 Hector Protector, and As I Went Over the Water. *Sendak*
 Nutshell Library: Alligators All Around; Chicken Soup with Rice; One Was Johnny; Pierre. *Sendak*
 Where the Wild Things Are. *Sendak*

SERAGE, NANCY
 The Prince Who Gave Up a Throne. *Mizumura*

SERRAILLIER, IAN
  The Clashing Rocks. *Stobbs*
  The Gorgon's Head. *Stobbs*
  The Way of Danger. *Stobbs*

SEUSS, DR., pseud.
  (THEODOR SEUSS GEISEL)
  The Cat in the Hat. *Seuss*
  The Cat in the Hat Comes Back. *Seuss*
  Dr. Seuss's ABC. *Seuss*
  Dr. Seuss's Sleep Book. *Seuss*
  How the Grinch Stole Christmas. *Seuss*
  I Had Trouble in Getting to Solla Sollew. *Seuss*
  Yertle the Turtle. *Seuss*

SEVERN, DAVID
  The Wild Valley (English title, Foxy-Boy). *Lamb*

SHAKESPEARE, WILLIAM
  Five Plays from Shakespeare. *Ward*
  Seeds of Time. *Oechsli*
  Songs from Shakespeare. *H. Jones*
  Ten Great Plays. *Provenson*

SHARP, MARGERY
  Miss Bianca. *G. M. Williams*
  Miss Bianca in the Salt Mines. *G. M. Williams*
  The Rescuers. *G. M. Williams*
  The Turret. *G. M. Williams*

SHECTER, BEN
  Partouche Plants a Seed. *Shecter*

SHEMIN, MARGARETHE
  The Little Riders. *Spier*

SHEPARD, ERNEST HOWARD
  Ben and Brock. *Shepard*

SHERLOCK, PHILIP (comp.)
  West Indian Folk Tales. *Kiddell-Monroe*

SHERMAN, NANCY
  Gwendolyn and the Weather Cock. *Sorel*
  Gwendolyn the Miracle Hen. *Sorel*

SHOTWELL, LOUISA R.
  Roosevelt Grady. *Burchard*

SHULMAN, MILTON
  Preep. *Maxey*

SHURA, MARY FRANCES
  Run Away Home. *Spanfeller*
  Shoe Full of Shamrock. *Bodecker*
  A Tale of Middle Length. *Parnall*

SHUTTLESWORTH, DOROTHY
  The Story of Ants. *Swain*
  The Story of Spiders. *Swain*

SILVERMAN, MEL (MELVIN FRANK)
  Hymie's Fiddle. *Silverman*

SIMEONS, A. T. W.
  Ramlal. *Shore*

SIMON, HILDA RITA
  Exploring the World of Social Insects. *Simon*
  Wonders of Hummingbirds. *Simon*
  Wonders of the Butterfly World. *Simon*

SIMON, MINA LEWITON
  Candita's Choice. *H. Simon*
  If You Were an Eel, How Would You Feel? *H. Simon*
  That Bad Carlos. *H. Simon*

SIMON, NORA
  Benjy's Bird. *Lasker*

SIMONT, MARC
  The Contest at Paca. *Simont*

SINGER, ISAAC BASHEVIS
  Zlateh the Goat. *Sendak*

SLEIGH, BARBARA (comp.)
  North of Nowhere. *Ambrus*

SLOANE, ERIC
  ABC of Early Americana. *Sloane*
  The Sound of Bells. *Sloane*

SLOBODKIN, LOUIS
  Colette and the Princess. *Slobodkin*
  The Late Cuckoo. *Slobodkin*
  Moon Blossom and the Golden Penny. *Slobodkin*
  Thank You — You're Welcome. *Slobodkin*

SLOBODKINA, ESPHYR
  Boris and His Balalaika. *Bobri*

SMALL, ERNEST
  Baba Yaga. *Lent*

SMITH, EDRIC BROOKS (jt. author)
  See MEREDITH, ROBERT K.

SMITH, EMMA
  Emily's Voyage. *Gordon*
  Emily's Voyage. *Haas*

SMITH, IRENE
  Paris. *E. Weiss*
  Washington, D. C. *E. Weiss*

SMITH, LINELL (NASH)
  The Auction Pony. *Bacon*
  Miranda and the Cat. *Bacon*

SMITH, MOYNE RICE
  Plays and How to Put Them On. *Bolognese*

SMITH, ROBERT PAUL
Jack Mack. *Blegvad*

SMITH, WILLIAM JAY
Boy Blue's Book of Beasts. *Kepes*
Ho for a Hat! *Chermayeff*
If I Had a Boat. *Bolognese*
Puptents and Pebbles. *Kepes*

SMITH, WILLIAM JAY (jt. author)
See BOGAN, LOUISE

SNEDEKER, CAROLINE DALE
Lysis Goes to the Play. *Lonette*
Theras and His Town. *Davis*

SNYDER, ZILPHA KEATLEY
Season of Ponies. *Raible*
The Velvet Room. *Raible*

SOBOL, DONALD J.
Encyclopedia Brown, Boy Detective. *Shortall*

SOFTLY, BARBARA
Place Mill. *Hughes*

SOKOL, CAMILLE
Dis-Moi. *Sokol*
La Pluche. *Sokol*

SORENSEN, VIRGINIA
Lotte's Locket. *Rocker*

SPENCE, ELEANOR
The Green Laurel. *Spence*
Lillipilly Hill. *Einzig*

SPENDER, STEPHEN
The Magic Flute. *Montresor*

SPENSER, EDMUND
Saint George and the Dragon. *Baynes*

SPICER, DOROTHY GLADYS
46 Days of Christmas. *Jauss*
13 Ghosts. *Sofia*
13 Giants. *Sofia*

SPILKA, ARNOLD
A Lion I Can Do Without. *Spilka*
Little Birds Don't Cry. *Spilka*
Paint All Kinds of Pictures. *Spilka*

STAFFORD, JEAN
Elephi. *Blegvad*

STAHL, BEN (BENJAMIN ALBERT)
Blackbeard's Ghost. *Stahl*

STAMM, CLAUS
The Dumplings and the Demons. *Mizumura*
Three Strong Women. *Mizumura*
The Very Special Badgers. *Mizumura*

STANDON, ANNA
The Hippo Had Hiccups. *Standon*
Little Duck Lost. *Standon*
The Singing Rhinoceros. *Standon*

STAPP, ARTHUR D.
Polliwog. *Lewis*

STARBIRD, KAYE
Speaking of Cows, and Other Poems. *Fegiz*

STEARNS, MONROE
Ring-A-Ling. *Zábransky*
Underneath My Apple Tree. *Zábransky*

STEELE, MARY Q.
See GAGE, WILSON, pseud.

STEELE, WILLIAM OWEN
Daniel Boone's Echo. *Nicolas*

STEIN, GERTRUDE
The World Is Round. *Hurd*

STEINBECK, JOHN
The Red Pony. *Dennis*

STENHOUSE, LAWRENCE
The Story of Scotland. *Biro*

STÉPHANE, NELLY
Roland. *François*

STERLING, DOROTHY
Caterpillars. *Lubell*
Fall Is Here. *Lubell*
Forever Free. *Crichlow*
Spring Is Here. *Lubell*

STEVENS, CARLA
Rabbit and Skunk and the Scary Rock. *Kraus*

STEVENS, EDEN VALE
The Piper. *Rocker*

STEVENSON, ROBERT LOUIS
A Child's Garden of Verses. *Fujikawa*
A Child's Garden of Verses. *Shillabeer*
A Child's Garden of Verses. *Wildsmith*

STOBBS, WILLIAM
Jack and the Beanstalk. *Stobbs*
The Story of the Three Bears. *Stobbs*

STOCKTON, FRANK RICHARD
The Bee-Man of Orn. *Sendak*
The Griffin and the Minor Canon. *Sendak*

STOLZ, MARY
  Belling the Tiger.   *Montresor*
  The Bully of Barkham Street.   *Shortall*
  A Dog on Barkham Street.   *Shortall*
  Emmett's Pig.   *G. M. Williams*
  Frédou.   *Ungerer*
  The Great Rebellion.   *Montresor*
  Maximilian's World.   *Shulevitz*
  The Mystery of the Woods.   *Shulevitz*
  The Noonday Friends.   *Glanzman*
  Siri the Conquistador.   *Montresor*

STOREY, MARGARET
  Kate and the Family Tree.   *Hughes*
  The Smallest Doll.   *Hughes*

STORR, CATHERINE
  The Freedom of the Seas.   *Fortnum*
  Robin.   *Fortnum*

STOUTENBERG, ADRIAN
  Rain Boat.   *Kaufmann*
  Wild Animals of the Far West.   *Robbins*

STOUTENBERG, ADRIAN (comp.)
  American Tall Tales.   *Powers*
  The Crocodile's Mouth.   *Rounds*

STREATFEILD, NOEL
  A Vicarage Family.   *Mozley*

STUCLEY, ELIZABETH FLORENCE
  Family Walkup (English title, Magnolia Buildings).
    L. B. Smith

STURTON, HUGH
  Zomo: The Rabbit.   *P. Warner*

SUPREE, BURTON (jt. author)
  See CHARLIP, REMY

SURANY, ANICO
  The Burning Mountain.   *Fisher*
  The Golden Frog.   *Fisher*
  Ride the Cold Wind.   *Fisher*

SUTCLIFF, ROSEMARY
  Beowulf.   *Keeping*
  Heroes and History.   *Keeping*
  The Hound of Ulster.   *Ambrus*
  Knight's Fee.   *Keeping*
  The Shield Ring.   *Hodges*
  The Silver Branch.   *Keeping*

SUTTON, SHAUN
  Queen's Champion.   *S. Miller*

SWAIN, SU ZAN NOGUCHI
  The Doubleday First Guide to Insects.   *Swain*
  Plants of Woodland and Wayside.   *Swain*

SWIFT, HILDEGARDE HOYT
  The Edge of April.   *Ward*
  From the Eagle's Wing.   *Ward*

SWIFT, JONATHAN
  Gulliver's Travels.   *Baltzer*

SWINTON, WILLIAM ELGIN
  Digging for Dinosaurs.   *Driscoll*

SYME, RONALD
  Captain Cook, Pacific Explorer.   *Stobbs*
  De Soto: Finder of the Mississippi.   *Stobbs*
  Francisco Pizarro, Finder of Peru.   *Stobbs*
  Sir Henry Morgan, Buccaneer.   *Stobbs*

SYMONDS, JOHN
  Elfrida and the Pig.   *Ardizzone*
  Grodge-Cat and the Window Cleaner.   *François*
  The Story George Told Me.   *François*
  Tom and Tabby.   *François*

TASHJIAN, VIRGINIA A.
  Once There Was and Was Not.   *Hogrogian*

TAYLOR, MARK
  Henry the Explorer.   *Booth*

TAYLOR, N. B.
  The Aeneid of Virgil.   *Kiddell-Monroe*

TENNYSON, ALFRED TENNYSON, baron
  The Charge of the Light Brigade.   *Provenson*

THAMPI, PARVATHI
  Geeta and the Village School.   *Solbert*

THARP, LOUISE HALL
  Louis Agassiz, Adventurous Scientist.   *Busoni*

THAYER, ERNEST LAWRENCE
  Casey at the Bat.   *Fisher*
  Casey at the Bat.   *Frame*

THAYER, JANE
  Andy and the Runaway Horse.   *Wohlberg*
  Gus Was a Friendly Ghost.   *Fleishman*
  Little Monkey.   *Fleishman*
  The Outside Cat.   *Rojankovsky*
  Part-Time Dog.   *Fleishman*

THOMAS, DYLAN
  A Child's Christmas in Wales.   *Raskin*

THOMAS, EDWARD
  The Complete Fairy Tales of Edward Thomas
  (English title, Four and Twenty Blackbirds).   *Gill*

THOMAS, M. Z., pseud.
  (THOMAS MICHAEL ZOTTMANN)
  Alexander von Humboldt.   *Schramm*

THOMPSON, GEORGE SELDEN
    See SELDEN, GEORGE, pseud.

THOMPSON, VIVIAN LAUBACH
    Sad Day, Glad Day. *Obligado*

THOMPSON, VIVIAN LAUBACH (comp.)
    Hawaiian Myths of Earth, Sea and Sky. *Weisgard*

THE THREE LITTLE PIGS. *Du Bois*

THURBER, JAMES
    The Wonderful O. *Simont*

THWAITE, ANN
    The House in Turner Square. *Jacques*

TITUS, EVE
    Anatole and the Piano. *Galdone*
    Anatole and the Poodle. *Galdone*
    Anatole over Paris. *Galdone*
    Basil of Baker Street. *Galdone*

TOLKIEN, JOHN RONALD R.
    The Adventures of Tom Bombadil. *Baynes*

TOMLINSON, JILL
    The Bus That Went to Church. *Howard*

TOOR, FRANCES
    The Golden Carnation. *Jauss*

TRAVERS, PAMELA L.
    The Fox at the Manger. *Bewick*
    Mary Poppins from A to Z. *M. E. Shepard*

TREADGOLD, MARY
    Winter Princess. *Falconer*

TREDEZ, ALAIN
    See TREZ, ALAIN, pseud.

TREDEZ, DENISE
    See TREZ, ALAIN and DENISE TREZ (pseuds.)

TREECE, HENRY
    The Golden One. *Stobbs*
    The Last Viking (English title, The Last of the Vikings).
        Keeping
    Ride into Danger. *C. Price*
    Splintered Sword. *Keeping*
    Viking's Sunset. *C. Price*

TRESSELT, ALVIN
    The Frog in the Well. *Duvoisin*
    Hide and Seek Fog. *Duvoisin*
    The Mitten. *Yaroslava*
    The Smallest Elephant in the World. *Glaser*
    Wake Up, City. *Duvoisin*

TREZ, ALAIN and DENISE TREZ, pseuds.
    (ALAIN and DENISE TREDEZ)
    Circus in the Jungle. *Trez*
    Fifi. *Trez*
    The Little Knight's Dragon. *Trez*
    Le Petit Chien. *Trez*
    Le Vilain Chat. *Trez*
    The Royal Hiccups. *Trez*

TREZ, DENISE, pseud. (jt. author)
    See TREZ, ALAIN

TUDOR, TASHA
    Around the Year. *Tudor*
    Becky's Christmas. *Tudor*

TUDOR, TASHA (comp.)
    Take Joy! *Tudor*
    Wings from the Winds. *Tudor*

TUNIS, EDWIN
    Colonial Craftsmen. *Tunis*
    Colonial Living. *Tunis*
    Frontier Living. *Tunis*
    Indians. *Tunis*
    Shaw's Fortune. *Tunis*

TURKLE, BRINTON CASSADAY
    Obadiah the Bold. *Turkle*

TURNBULL, AGNES SLIGH
    George. *Hyman*

TURNER, PHILIP
    The Grange at High Force. *Papas*
    Sea Peril. *Ribbons*

TWAIN, MARK, pseud.
    (SAMUEL LANGHORNE CLEMENS)
    The Prince and the Pauper. *Hutton*

UCHIDA, YOSHIKO
    The Forever Christmas Tree. *Mizumura*
    The Promised Year. *Hutchinson*
    Rokubei and the Thousand Rice Bowls. *Mizumura*
    The Sea of Gold. *Yamaguchi*
    Sumi's Prize. *Mizumura*
    Sumi's Special Happening. *Mizumura*
    Takao and Grandfather's Sword. *Hutchinson*

UDRY, JANICE MAY
    Let's Be Enemies. *Sendak*
    The Moon Jumpers. *Sendak*

UNGERER, TOMI
    Crictor. *Ungerer*
    Emile. *Ungerer*
    The Mellops Go Flying. *Ungerer*
    The Mellops Go Spelunking. *Ungerer*

One, Two, Where's My Shoe? *Ungerer*
Orlando the Brave Vulture. *Ungerer*
Rufus. *Ungerer*
Snail, Where Are You? *Ungerer*
The Three Robbers. *Ungerer*

UNNERSTAD, EDITH
Little O. *Slobodkin*
Little O. *Wikland*
The Peep-Larssons Go Sailing. *Wikland*

UNTERMEYER, LOUIS (comp.)
The Golden Treasury of Poetry. *Anglund*

UNWIN, NORA SPICER
Joyful the Morning. *Unwin*
Poquita, the Little Mexican Duck. *Unwin*
Two Too Many. *Unwin*

UPDIKE, JOHN
A Child's Calendar. *Burkert*
The Ring. *Chappell*

UPINGTON, MARION
The Beautiful Culpeppers. *Slobodkin*

URE, JEAN
Rumanian Folk Tales (English title, Pacala and Tandala).
Mozley

UTTLEY, ALISON
A Traveler in Time. *C. Price*

VACHERON, EDITH
Here Is Henri! *Kahl*
Voici Henri! *Kahl*

VALENS, EVAN G., Jr.
Wildfire. *Hurd*
Wingfin and Topple. *Hurd*

VALENTIN, URSULA
Herr Minkepatt and His Friends (English title,
Mr. Minkepatt and His Friends). *Wilkon*

VAN STOCKUM, HILDA
Friendly Gables. *Van Stockum*
Little Old Bear. *Van Stockum*
Mogo's Flute. *Jacques*
The Winged Watchman. *Van Stockum*

VANCE, MARGUERITE
Esther Wheelwright, Indian Captive. *Bjorklund*
A Flower from Dinah. *Suba*

VARBLE, RACHEL
Three Against London. *Hodges*

VARLEY, DIMITRY
The Whirly Bird. *Rojankovsky*

VASILIU, MIRCEA
The Year Goes Round. *Vasiliu*

VERNE, JULES
Around the World in Eighty Days. *Jacques*

VERNEY, JOHN
February's Road. *Verney*
Friday's Tunnel. *Verney*

VIPONT, ELFRIDA
Bless This Day. *H. Jones*

VOEGLI, MAX
Prince of Hindustan. *Hoffmann*

VON HAGEN, VICTOR WOLFGANG
The Incas, People of the Sun. *Beltrán*
Maya, Land of the Turkey and the Deer. *Beltrán*
The Sun Kingdom of the Aztecs. *Beltrán*

VON HUMBOLDT, ALEXANDER
Stars, Mosquitos and Crocodiles. *R. F. Peterson*

VON SCHMIDT, ERIC (comp.)
Come for to Sing. *Von Schmidt*

WABER, BERNARD
The House on East 88th Street. *Waber*
Just Like Abraham Lincoln. *Waber*
Lyle and the Birthday Party. *Waber*
Lyle Lyle Crocodile. *Waber*
Rich Cat, Poor Cat. *Waber*
You Look Ridiculous, Said the Rhinoceros to the
Hippopotamus. *Waber*

WAHL, JAN
Cabbage Moon. *Adams*
Hello Elephant. *Ardizzone*
Pleasant Fieldmouse. *Sendak*

WALDEN, DANIEL
The Nutcracker. *Berson*

WALKER, BARBARA K.
Hilili and Dilili. *Barss*
Just Say Hic! *Bolognese*

WALTRIP, LELA and RUFUS WALTRIP
White Harvest. *C. Price*

WALTRIP, RUFUS (jt. author)
See WALTRIP, LELA

WARD, LYND KENDALL
Nic of the Woods. *Ward*

WARNER, EDYTH RECORDS
The Little Dark Horse. *Warner*
Siamese Summer. *Warner*
The Tigers of Como Zoo. *Warner*

WATSON, ALDREN AULD
My Garden Grows. *Watson*

WATSON, NANCY DINGMAN
Annie's Spending Spree.   *Watson*
Katie's Chickens.   *Watson*
Sugar on Snow.   *Watson*

WATTS, MABEL
The Light Across Piney Valley.   *Barker*

WEBB, CLIFFORD CYRIL
The Thirteenth Pig.   *Webb*

WEEKS, SARA
Tales of a Common Pigeon.   *Von Schmidt*

WEIK, MARY HAYS
The Jazz Man.   *Grifalconi*

WEIL, LISL
Bitzli and the Big Bad Wolf.   *Weil*
The Busiest Boy in Holland.   *Weil*
Eyes So-o Big.   *Weil*
Happy Ski ABC.   *Weil*
Mimi.   *Weil*
The Sorcerer's Apprentice.   *Weil*

WEIR, ROSEMARY
Albert the Dragon.   *Q. Blake*

WEISS, HARVEY
The Expeditions of Willis Partridge.   *Weiss*
A Gondola for Fun.   *Weiss*
Horse in No Hurry.   *Weiss*
The Very Private Tree House.   *Weiss*

WELCH, RONALD
Bowman of Crécy.   *Ribbons*
Escape from France.   *Stobbs*

WELLS, HERBERT GEORGE
War of the Worlds.   *Gorey*

WELTY, EUDORA
The Shoe Bird.   *B. Krush*

WELTY, SUSAN F.
Birds with Bracelets.   *Kaufmann*

WERSBA, BARBARA
The Brave Balloon of Benjamin Buckley.   *Tomes*
Do Tigers Ever Bite Kings?   *Rivoli*
The Land of Forgotten Beasts.   *Tomes*
A Song for Clowns.   *Rivoli*

WEYL, PETER K.
Men, Ants and Elephants.   *Ravielli*

WHITE, ANN TERRY
The Golden Treasury of Myths and Legends.   *Provenson*

WHITE, ANNE HITCHCOCK
A Dog Called Scholar.   *Obligado*
The Uninvited Donkey.   *Freeman*

WHITE, DALE
Thunder in His Moccasins.   *Geer*

WHITMAN, WALT
Poems of Walt Whitman.   *C. and J. Ross*
Walt Whitman's America.   *Daugherty*

WIBBERLEY, LEONARD
The Time of the Lamb.   *Kredel*

WIDDECOMBE FAIR.   *Adamson*

WIER, ESTER
The Loner.   *Maitland*
The Loner.   *C. Price*

WIESE, KURT
The Groundhog and His Shadow.   *Wiese*
Rabbit Bros. Circus, One Night Only.   *Wiese*
The Thief in the Attic.   *Wiese*

WIESNER, WILLIAM
Joco and the Wishbone.   *Wiesner*

WIESNER, WILLIAM (comp.)
A Pocketful of Riddles.   *Wiesner*
Too Many Cooks . . .   *Wiesner*

WIGGIN, KATE DOUGLAS
Rebecca of Sunnybrook Farm.   *L. B. Smith*

WILDE, OSCAR
Fairy Tales (English title, Complete Fairy Tales of
   Oscar Wilde).   *Mozley*
The Happy Prince.   *Riswold*

WILDSMITH, BRIAN
Brian Wildsmith's ABC.   *Wildsmith*
Brian Wildsmith's 1, 2, 3's.   *Wildsmith*

WILLARD, BARBARA
Storm from the West.   *D. Hall*
Surprise Island.   *Paton*
Three and One to Carry.   *D. Hall*

WILLIAMS, JAY
Philbert the Fearful.   *Ohlsson*
The Question Box.   *Zemach*

WILLIAMS, GLADYS
Fireworks for Semolina Silkpaws.   *Ferns*
Semolina Silkpaws Comes to Catstown.   *Ferns*

WILLIAMS, URSULA MORAY
Beware of This Animal.   *Paton*
Island MacKenzie.   *Ardizzone*

WILLIAMS-ELLIS, AMABEL
Fairy Tales from the British Isles.   *Baynes*
Round the World Fairy Tales.   *Stobbs*

WINN, MARIE (ed.)
The Fireside Book of Children's Songs.   *Alcorn*

WINSLOW, MARJORIE
  Mud Pies, and Other Recipes.   *Blegvad*

WINTERFIELD, HENRY
  Castaways in Lilliput.   *Hutchinson*
  Trouble at Timpetill.   *Hutchinson*

WISEMAN, ANN (jt. author)
  See McLean, Mollie

WITHERS, CARL (adapt.)
  I Saw a Rocket Walk a Mile.   *J. E. Johnson*
  The Tale of the Black Cat.   *Cober*

WOJCIECHOWSKA, MAIA
  Shadow of a Bull.   *A. Smith*

WONDRISKA, WILLIAM
  The Tomato Patch.   *Wondriska*
  Which Way to the Zoo?   *Wondriska*

WOOD, JAMES PLAYSTED
  The Elephant in the Barn.   *Kessler*
  The Golden Swan.   *Elgin*
  A Hound, a Bay Horse and a Turtle.   *Gorsline*
  The Snark Was a Boojum.   *Levine*
  Trust Thyself.   *Gorsline*

WORCESTER, DONALD
  War Pony.   *E. H. Johnson*

WORDSWORTH, WILLIAM
  Lucy Gray.   *Riswold*

WORSTELL, EMMA VIETOR (comp.)
  Jump the Rope Jingles.   *Greenwald*

WUORIO, EVA-LIS
  The Island of Fish in the Trees.   *Ardizzone*
  The Land of Right Up and Down.   *Ardizzone*
  Tal and the Magic Barruget.   *Bettina*

WYATT, ISABEL
  The Golden Stag.   *Jauss*
  King Beetle-Tamer.   *Jauss*

WYNANTS, MICHE
  Noah's Ark.   *Wynants*

WYLER, ROSE (jt. author)
  See Ames, Gerald

YAMAGUCHI, TOHR
  The Golden Crane.   *Yamaguchi*
  Two Crabs and the Moonlight.   *Yamaguchi*

YASHIMA, TARO
  Umbrella.   *Yashima*
  The Youngest One.   *Yashima*

YASHIMA, TARO and HATOJU MUKU
  The Golden Footprints.   *Yashima*
  Momo's Kitten.   *Yashima*

YATES, ELIZABETH
  Carolina's Courage.   *Unwin*

YERSHOV, PETER
  Humpy.   *Ayer*

YOLEN, JANE (jt. author)
  See Huston, Anne

YORK, CAROL BEACH
  The Doll in the Bakeshop.   *Turkle*

YOUNG, BLANCHE COWLEY
  How the Manx Cat Lost Its Tail.   *Unwin*

YOUNG, MIRIAM
  The Dollar Horse.   *Hutchinson*
  The Secret of Stone House Farm.   *Hutchinson*

ZEMACH, HARVÉ (adapt.)
  Mommy, Buy Me a China Doll.   *Zemach*
  Nail Soup.   *Zemach*
  Salt.   *Zemach*
  The Speckled Hen.   *Zemach*

ZEMACH, MARGOT (adapt.)
  The Little Tiny Woman.   *Zemach*
  The Three Sillies.   *Zemach*
  The Tricks of Master Dabble.   *Zemach*

ZIMNIK, REINER
  The Bear on the Motorcycle.   *Zimnik*
  The Little Roaring Tiger.   *Zimnik*
  The Proud Circus Horse.   *Zimnik*

ZION, GENE
  Harry and the Lady Next Door.   *Graham*
  Harry by the Sea.   *Graham*
  Jeffie's Party.   *Graham*
  The Meanest Squirrel I Ever Met.   *Graham*
  No Roses for Harry!   *Graham*
  The Plant Sitter.   *Graham*
  The Sugar Mouse Cake.   *Graham*

ZOLOTOW, CHARLOTTE
  The Bunny Who Found Easter.   *B. F. Peterson*
  Do You Know What I'll Do?   *G. M. Williams*
  Flocks of Birds.   *Victor*
  In My Garden.   *Duvoisin*
  The Man with the Purple Eyes.   *Lasker*
  Mr. Rabbit and the Lovely Present.   *Sendak*
  Over and Over.   *G. M. Williams*
  Sleepy Book.   *Bobri*
  The Three Funny Friends.   *Chalmers*
  The Quarreling Book.   *Arnold Lobel*
  The Sky Was Blue.   *G. M. Williams*
  The White Marble.   *Obligado*

ZOTTMANN, THOMAS MICHAEL
  See Thomas, M. Z., pseud.

Part IV:
APPENDIX

THE KATE GREENAWAY MEDAL
in the United Kingdom

The Library Association Kate Greenaway Medal is intended to recognize the importance of illustrations in children's books. It is awarded to the artist who, in the opinion of the Library Association, has produced the most distinguished work in the illustration of children's books during the preceding year. The artist must be a British subject and the work published in the United Kingdom. Books intended for older as well as younger children are included, and reproduction is taken into account. Recommendations for the award are invited from members of the Library Association who are asked to submit a preliminary list of not more than three titles.

KATE GREENAWAY MEDAL WINNERS

1955 Prize withheld as no book considered suitable.

1956 EDWARD ARDIZZONE. *Tim All Alone.* Oxford.

1957 V. H. DRUMMOND. *Mrs. Easter and the Storks.* Faber.

1958 Prize withheld as no book considered suitable.

1959 WILLIAM STOBBS. *Kashtanka.* Oxford.
A Bundle of Ballads. Oxford.

1960 GERALD ROSE. *Old Wrinkle and the Seagulls.* Faber.

1961 ANTONY MAITLAND. *Mrs. Cockle's Cat.* Constable.

1962 BRIAN WILDSMITH. *Brian Wildsmith's A B C.* Oxford.

1963 JOHN BURNINGHAM. *Borka.* Cape.

1964 C. WALTER HODGES. *Shakespeare's Theatre.* Oxford.

1965 VICTOR AMBRUS. *For his work in general.* Oxford.

1966 RAYMOND BRIGGS. *Mother Goose.* Hamish Hamilton.

Commended

1959 EDWARD ARDIZZONE. *Titus in Trouble.* Bodley Head.
GERALD ROSE. *Wuffles Goes to Town.* Faber.

1962 CAROL BARKER. *Achilles the Donkey.* Dobson.

1963 VICTOR AMBRUS. *Royal Navy.* Oxford.
Time of Trial. Oxford.
BRIAN WILDSMITH. *The Lion and the Rat.* Oxford.
Oxford Book of Poetry. Oxford.

1964 VICTOR AMBRUS. *For his work in general.*
WILLIAM PAPAS. *For his work in general.*
RAYMOND BRIGGS. *Fee Fi Fo Fum.* Hamish Hamilton.

1965 VICTOR AMBRUS. *The Three Poor Tailors.*

1966 CHARLES KEEPING. *Shaun and the Cart Horse.* Oxford.
DOREEN ROBERTS. *The Story of Saul the King* (by Helen Waddell). Constable.

LIST OF ARTISTS REPRESENTED BY ILLUSTRATIONS

Adams, Adrienne   24, 31-34

Ambrus, Victor   51

Ardizzone, Edward   38

Blegvad, Erik   25

Brown, Marcia   1, 27

Burkert, Nancy   205

Burningham, John   51

Chermayeff, Ivan   11

Cooney, Barbara   41, 42

Domanska, Janina   8

Duvoisin, Roger   6

Emberley, Ed   199

Frasconi, Antonio   14

Gobbato, Imero   68

Hoffmann, Felix   18

Hogrogian, Nonny   10

Hutton, Clarke   48

Keats, Ezra Jack   52

Kepes, Juliet   17

Lent, Blair   15

Lionni, Leo   16

Lorraine, Walter   202

Low, Joseph   14

McCloskey, Robert   53

Maitland, Antony   39, 40

Montresor, Beni   9

Mordvinoff, Nicolas (see Nicolas)   4

Munari, Bruno   12

Ness, Evaline   5

Nicolas   4

Piatti, Celestino   21

Potter, Beatrix   57, 58, 60, 61, 64

Rand, Paul   12

Raskin, Ellen   65

Sendak, Maurice   20

Shahn, Ben   7

Standon, Edward   47

Stobbs, William   45

Ungerer, Tomi   26

Waber, Bernard   69

Ward, Lynd   49

Watteau, Monique-Alika   43

Werenskiold, Erik   19

Wildsmith, Brian   53

Williams, Jenny   50

Zemach, Margot   23

Zimnik, Reiner   22

292

INDEX TO PART I AND FOREWORDS OF PART II AND PART III

Illustrations are indicated by boldface type.

Adam's Book of odd Creatures **14**
Adams, Adrienne xvi, 5, 23, **24**, 30, 31-34, 54, 200, 202
Aesop 201, 203
Alcorn, John 203
Alice in Wonderland 63
Alice's Adventures in Wonderland 44
Ambrus, Victor 50, **51**
American Heritage 200
American Institute of Graphic Arts 9
American Institute of Graphic Arts Catalogs 200
Andersen, Hans Christian 23, 201, 202
Andersen, Hans Christian, Award xvii
Animal Family, The 203
Anton the Goatherd xvii
Appley Dapply's Nursery Rhymes 63
Ardizzone, Edward 5, 37, 38, **38**, 39, 45, 48, 49, 66, 200
Arno, Enrico 25
Art of Beatrix Potter, The 54
Asbjørnsen 204
Away in a Manger 204

Backbone of the King 1
Barker, Carol 54
Baynes, Pauline 49
Becker, May Lamberton 43
Bee-Man of Orn, The **20**
Bemelmans, Ludwig 49, 66
Berson, Harold 202
Best Books for Children 200
Bewick, Thomas 204
Beyond the High Hills 201
Bienniale of Illustrations Bratislava xvii
Bileck, Marvin 3, 21
Birnbaum, A. 4
Blake 11
Blegvad, Erik 5, 23, **25**, 203
Booklist, The 200
Boy Who Went Out to Gather Pears, A 18
Brian Wildsmith's ABC **53**
Briggs, Raymond 203
Brooke, Leslie 45, 46
Brown, Marcia xiv, xv, xvi, **1**, **27**, 48, 52, 202
Bruno Munari's Zoo **12**
Bryson, Bernarda 3
Bunyan 39
Burkert, Nancy 23, 202, **205**
Burningham, John 50, **51**
Burt Dow, Deep-Water-Man **53**
Burton, Virginia Lee 49
Butterfly Time 30

Caldecott Medal awards xv, xvi, 36, 37, 44, 203

Caldecott, Randolph 36, 38, 45, 48
Cameron, Miss 57, 58
Carigiet, Alois xvii, 21
Carnegie Award 36
Cat in the Hat, The 203
Cecily Parsley's Nursery Rhymes 63
Cellini, Joseph xiv
Chalmers, Mary 203
Chanticleer and the Fox xvi, 47
Charlip, Remy 11
Chendru 201
Chermayeff, Ivan 11, **11**
Children's Catalog, The 200
Child's Christmas in Wales, A 11
Chitty-Chitty-Bang-Bang 51
Cole, Joan C. 69
Cole, William 21
Comenius 36
Constable 56
Constable Young Books, Ltd. 49
Cooney, Barbara xvi, 21, 40, **41**, 42, **42**, 47, 48, 52, 66, 202, 203
Cowell, W. S. 50
Crane, Walter 36, 45, 48
Crowell Poetry Series 203
Crowell, Thomas Y. 41, 49
Cruikshank 20, 38

Dalphin, Marcia xiv
Darling, Lois and Louis 203
d'Aulaires, the xvi
de la Mare, Walter 39
De Vries, Leonard 203
Dickens 38
Dictionary of Chivalry, A 49
Dog Who Thought He Was A Boy, The **202**
Domanska, Janina 3, **8**, 203
Doyle, Richard 20
Dress Up 11
Drummond, V. H. 48
du Bois, William Pène xiv, 5, 54, 203
Duvoisin, Roger xvi, 5, 6, **6**, 67, 200

Earle, Olive 203
Ehlert, Lois 203
Einzig, Susan 203
Elsa 201
Emberley, Ed **199**
Evans, Edmund 36, 46, 63

Fables from Aesop 204
Fables [La Fontaine] 204

Fairy Tales of Hans Christian Andersen   204
Farjeon, Eleanor   39
Fischer, Hans   4
Fisher, Leonard Everett   5, 15, 200
Fisher, Margery   40
Five Centuries of Illustrated Fables   203-204
Fletcher, David   44
Flowers of Delight   203
Folmsbee, Beulah   xiii
Fortunately   11
Fortune   46
Foster, Joanna   xiv
Four Fur Feet   11
Four Winds Press   50
Fox at the Manger, The   204
Frasconi, Antonio   13, **14**, 203, 204
Françoise   4, 66

Galdone, Paul   200, 203
Gekiere, Madeline   xv, 25
General History of Quadrupeds   204
George, Mabel   36
Ginger and Pickles   62
Gobbato, Imero   68, **68**
Godden, Rumer   xvii
Grandville, J. J.   204
Greenaway, Kate   36, 48
Greenaway, Kate, Medal Award   xvii, 36, 39, 44, 50
Grifalconi, Ann   3
Grimm   18, 38, 201
Growing Point   40

Hammond, Miss   57
Happy Owls, The   **21**
Hauff, Wilhelm   19
Hibou et la Poussiquette, Le   42, **42**, **43**, 203
History of Birds   204
Hoff, Syd   203
Hoffmann, Felix   18, **18**, 201
Hogarth, Grace Allen   xvi, 204
Hogrogian, Nonny   3, **10**, 11, 44, 52
Holland, Janice   xv
Horn Book Magazine, The   44, 200
Houses from the Sea   29
Hudson, Derek   203
Hurd, Clement   203
Hutchins, Ross   201
Hutton, Clarke   48, **48**

Illustrators of Children's Books: 1744-1945   xiii, 66
Illustrators of Children's Books: 1946-1956   xiii, xiv, xvi, xvii, 36
Illustrators of Children's Books: 1957-1966   xiv, 68
Inch by Inch   16, **16**
In the Beginning   204

Jack and the Beanstalk   45
Jarrell, Randall   19, 203

Jennie's Hat   **52**
Jewett, Sarah Orne   40
Journal of Beatrix Potter from 1881 to 1897, The   54, 55, 58, 59, 60, 62
Junior Booklist   200

Kauffman, Angelica   60
Keats, Ezra Jack   xvi, 15, 52, **52**
Keeping, Charles   xiv
Kellmann, Amy   69
Kepes, Juliet   **17**, 25
Kirby, Douglas J.   50
Kittelson, Theodor   204
Krauss, Ruth   11
Krush, Beth and Joe   202

La Fontaine   201, 204
Lane, Margaret   54, 56, 62
Latimer, Louise P.   xiii
Lear Alphabet: ABC   202, 204
Lear, Edward   21, 22, 42, 202, 204
LeGrand   66
Lenski, Lois   xvi
Lent, Blair   15, **15**
Letters to Children [Beatrix Potter]   204
Library Journal   200
Library of Congress   201
Light in the Tower, The   29
Lion and the Rat, The   38
Lionni, Leo   3, 16, **16**
Linder, Leslie   54, 55, 63
Little Bear's Visit   203
little blue and little yellow   16
Little House, The   49
Little Juggler, The   47
Little 1   13
Little Tim and the Brave Sea Captain   45, 46, 48
Lobel, Anita   3
Lobel, Arnold   xvi
Lontoft, Ruth Giles   xiv
Lorraine, Walter   25, **202**
Low, Joseph   3, **14**, 15, 66, 204
Lubel, Winifred   203
Lyle, Lyle Crocodile   **69**

McCloskey, Robert   37, 52, **53**, 202
McClung, Robert   203
McKendry, John J.   204
McLuhan, Marshall   xv
Madeline   49
Magic Feather Duster, The   **4**
Mahony, Bertha E.   (see Miller, Bertha Mahony)   xiii
Maitland, Antony   39, **39**, **40**
Make Way for Ducklings   37
Malcolmson, Anne   37
Mama, I Wish I Was Snow: Child, You'd Be Very Cold   11
Massee, May   37
Matsuoka, Kyoko   xvii

Miller, Bertha Mahony   xiii, xiv, xvi, xvii
Mrs. Cockle's Cat   39, **39, 40**
Mr. Jensen & Cat   **25**
Millais, Sir John Everett   54, 58, 59, 60
Milne, A. A.   56
Montresor, Beni   3, **9**
Mordvinoff, Nicolas   (see Nicolas)   **4,** 6
Mother Goose   203, 204
Mother Goose in French   203
Mother Goose in Hieroglyphics   204
*Mother Mother I Feel Sick Send for the Doctor Quick Quick
   Quick*   11
Munari, Bruno   **12,** 13
My Friend Mac   **49**

Nail Soup   22
Nash, Ogden   11
National Book League   55
nella notte buia   13
Ness, Evaline   5, **5,** 52, 200
Newbery Medal Award   36
New Nutcracker Suite and Other Innocent Verses, The   11, **11**
New York Public Library Annual Lists   200
Nicolas   4, **4,** 6
Nightingale, The   202
Norwegian Folk Tales   **19,** 204
Nubber Bear   **6**

Oh What Nonsense!   21, **26**
Once There Was and Was Not   **10,** 11
One Wide River to Cross   **199**
Ounce Dice Trice   6, **7**
Owl and the Pussycat, The   42, 203
Oxford University Press   36, 45

Palmer, Samuel   56
Paul, The Hero of the Fire   **38**
Peacock Pie   39
Pearce, Philippa   39
Phizz   38
Piatti, Celestino   3, 21, **21**
Picture History of Britain, A   **48**
Pilgrim's Progress, The   39
Potter, Beatrix   xvi, xvii, 46, 54-64, **57, 58,** 60, **61, 64,** 204
Potter, Bertram   56, 62
Potter, Mr. and Mrs. Rupert   54, 59, 61
Pratt Institute   xv
Primrose, Jean   54

Rackham, Arthur   38, 203
Arthur Rackham: His Life and Work   203
Rand, Ann   13
Rand, Paul   **12,** 13
Raskin, Ellen   11, **65**
Ravielli, Anthony   5
Reed, Philip   15, 203
Rees, Ennis   204
Reeves, James   39

Reid, Alastair   6
Rey, H. A.   48
Richards, Laura E.   43
Riley, Elizabeth   41
Ross, John and Clare   15
Rounds, Glen   202

St. Nicholas Magazine   43
Sam, Bangs & Moonshine   5, **5**
Sendak, Maurice   19, 20, **20,** 23, 48, 52, 200, 203
Senefelder   46
Seuss, Dr.   203
Shahn, Ben   6, **7**
Shepard, Ernest   5
Shimin, Symeon   5
Shire, Ruth   69
Shoemaker and the Elves, The   **24**
Shulevitz, Uri   xiv, 202
Sidjakov, Nicolas   3
Siegl, Helen   25
Silver Wood, The   50, **50**
Singing Rhinoceros, The   **47**
Sleeping Beuty, The,   **18**
Snow and the Sun, The   **14**
Snow Party, The   22
Snow White and Rose Red   202
Sokol, Bill   23, 25, 202
Songs of Innocence   11, **65**
Sorel, Edward   3
Sparkle and Spin   **12**
Speckled Hen, The   22, **23**
Spenser   44
Spier, Peter   202
Spilka, Arnold   203
Standon, Anna   50
Standon, Edward   **47,** 50
Steegmuller, Francis   42
Stobbs, William   44, **45,** 48, 200
Stockton, Frank   19
Supree, Burton   11
Swain, Su Zan   203
Swimmy   16

Tailor of Gloucester, The   62, 63
Tale of Beatrix Potter, The   56, 62
Tale of Benjamin Bunny, The   63
Tale of Johnny Town Mouse, The   63
Tale of Peter Rabbit, The   63
Tale of Two Bad Mice, The   64
Tashjian, Virginia   11
Tenniel   20
Thinking Book, The   11
Thollander, Earl   203
Thomas, Dylan   11
Three Poor Tailors, The   50, **51**
Three Sillies, The   22
Time of Wonder   37
Tirra Lirra   43

Tom's Midnight Garden 203
Travers, Pamela 204
Trumpeter of Krakow, The 203
Twelve Dancing Princesses, The 202
Two Laughable Lyrics 203
Two Little Birds and Three 17

Uden, Grant 49
Ungerer, Tomi 3, 21, **26**, 202

Vario-Klischograph 49, 50
Viguers, Ruth Hill xiv
Viking Press 37
von Schmidt, Eric xvi, 67

Waber, Bernard 68, **69**
Ward, Lynd xiv, 48, **49**
Warne, Frederick, and Company 54, 55, 63
Watson, Aldren 203
Watteau, Monique-Alika 42, **43**
Watts, Franklin 37
Watts, Helen Hoke 37
Wave, The **15**

Weisgard, Leonard xvi, 66, 203
Werenskiold, Erik **19**, 204
Whitman 15
Why So Much Noise? **8**
Wildsmith, Brian 36, 37, 50, **53**, 203
Wild Swans, The **27**
Williams, Garth 203
Williams, Jenny 50, **50**
Winnie the Pooh 56
Witches of Venice, The **9**
Wittenborn 13
Wondriska, William 11
What Makes a Shadow? 29
White Heron, A 40, **41**, 47
White Stone, The 68
World Council of Christian Education 204

Yankee Doodle's Cousins 37
Ylla 201
You Better Come Home With Me 203

Zemach, Margot xvi, 3, 22, **23**, 202
Zimnik, Reiner 21, **22**